always up to date

The law changes, but Nolo is on top of it! We offer several ways to make sure you and your Nolo products are up to date:

1 **Nolo's Legal Updater**
We'll send you an email whenever a new edition of this book is published! Sign up at **www.nolo.com/legalupdater**.

2 **Updates @ Nolo.com**
Check **www.nolo.com/update** to find recent changes in the law that affect the current edition of your book.

3 **Nolo Customer Service**
To make sure that this edition of the book is the most recent one, call us at **800-728-3555** and ask one of our friendly customer service representatives. Or find out at **www.nolo.com**.

please note

We believe accurate, plain-English legal information should help you solve many of your own legal problems. But this text is not a substitute for personalized advice from a knowledgeable lawyer. If you want the help of a trained professional—and we'll always point out situations in which we think that's a good idea—consult an attorney licensed to practice in your state.

13th edition

U.S. Immigration Made Easy

Willow International Center Library

by Attorney Ilona Bray
updated by Attorney Carl Falstrom

Thirteenth Edition	AUGUST 2007
Editor	ILONA BRAY
Book Design	TERRI HEARSH
Cover Design	SUSAN PUTNEY
Index	BAYSIDE INDEXING SERVICE
Production	SARAH HINMAN
Proofreading	ROBERT WELLS
Printing	CONSOLIDATED PRINTERS, INC.

International Standard Serial Number (ISSN) 1055-9647
ISBN 1-4133-0652-7

Quantity sales: For information on bulk purchases or corporate premium sales, please contact the Special Sales department. For academic sales or textbook adoptions, ask for Academic Sales, 800-955-4775. Nolo, 950 Parker St., Berkeley, CA, 94710.

Acknowledgments

This book was originally authored by Laurence A. Canter and Martha S. Siegel. For help in updating and revising it for recent editions, special thanks are owed to:

Emily Doskow, an attorney in private practice and Nolo author/editor (based in Berkeley, California), for her contribution regarding international adoptions by same-sex couples.

Jimmy Go, of the law firm Go & Laster (Portland, Oregon), for his contribution regarding investor visas.

Julia Day Marquez, of the law firm Fallon, Bixby, Cheng & Lee (San Francisco, California, www.fbcl-visa.com), for her contribution regarding labor certification.

Under Nolo's roof, thanks go to Betsy Simmons for inspired last-minute editing of the 12th edition, and Nolo's Production Department for doing the layout.

Table of Contents

Introduction
Your Immigration Companion

Part I
Getting Started: U.S. Immigration Eligibility and Procedures

5 Special Rules for Canadians and Mexicans

6 How and When to Find a Lawyer

Part II

Introduction to Permanent U.S. Residence (Green Cards)

7 Getting a Green Card Through Family Members in the U.S.

Part III

Nonimmigrant (Temporary) Visas

15 Getting a Business or Tourist (B-1 or B-2) Visa

16 Getting a Temporary Specialty Worker (H-1B) Visa

24 Getting a Visa as a Temporary Worker in a Selected Occupation (O, P, or R Visa)

Glossary

Index

Your Immigration Companion

If you're considering emigrating to the United States, or are helping someone who is, then this book was written for you. Unlike many books about immigration law, this one was written for real people, not for lawyers. We try to give you a realistic view of your immigration possibilities and how to succeed in reaching your goals.

But why is this book so thick—especially considering that the title promises it will be "easy"? Don't worry, you won't have to read the whole book. It's just that we cover a lot of ground, including some categories of visas and green cards that other books don't discuss—useful if you're having trouble finding a category that fits you. Also, the original law that we're trying to describe for you is not easy at all—it contains many categories of potential visas and green cards, complex criteria for who qualifies, and paperwork-intensive application procedures. And all of that takes space to explain! So what we've done is to start the book with an overview of your possibilities, then direct you toward one or two particular chapters that will lay out all you need to know.

Some people will find that they don't qualify for U.S. immigration at all, or at least not yet—as we said, it's a complicated and narrow system. But the good news is that huge numbers of people successfully come from other countries to the U.S. every year—approximately one million receive green cards, and 30 million receive temporary visas (such as tourist, work, and student visas). With the right information and preparation you can be one of them. This book will help you:

- learn whether you match the criteria to receive either a green card (permanent residence) or a temporary (nonimmigrant) visa
- learn what difficulties you'll have to overcome
- strategize the fastest and safest way through the application process
- deal with bureaucrats and delays, and
- know when it's time to consult a lawyer.

You may feel lost and confused as you begin the process of applying for U.S. immigration. This book is intended to be your legal companion, providing practical and supportive advice and information along the way, and helping you find a warm welcome in the United States.

 We'll tell you if the immigration laws change. Immigration laws and application procedures change regularly. In fact, at the time this book went to print, the U.S. Congress had recently considered and then failed to pass a comprehensive immigration reform bill. Fortunately, Nolo's website provides a way for you to get authoritative advice on how these changes affect what's discussed in this book. (Don't rely solely on rumors and newspaper articles!) Simply go to www.nolo.com, locate the page where the book is being sold, and click the "Updates" tab. ■

Part I

Getting Started:
U.S. Immigration Eligibility and Procedures

Chapter 1

Where to Begin on Your Path Toward Immigration

If you've already tried to research how to immigrate to the United States, you may have come away more confused than enlightened. We've heard immigrants ask frustrated questions like, "Are they trying to punish me for doing things legally?" or "I can't tell whether they want to let me in, or keep me out!"

The trouble is, the U.S. immigration system is a little like a mythical creature with two heads. One head is smiling, and granting people the right to live or work in the United States, temporarily or permanently—especially people who:

- will pump money into the U.S. economy (such as tourists, students, and investors)
- can fill gaps in the U.S. workforce (mostly skilled workers)
- are joining up with close family members who are already U.S. citizens or permanent residents, or
- need protection from persecution or other humanitarian crises.

This creature's other head wears a frown. It is afraid of the United States being overrun by huge numbers of immigrants, and so it tries to keep out anyone who:

- doesn't fit the narrow eligibility categories set forth in the U.S. immigration laws
- has a criminal record
- is a threat to U.S. ideology or national security
- has spent a long time in the U.S. illegally or committed other immigration violations
- is attempting fraud in order to immigrate, or
- will not earn enough money to stay off government assistance.

Not surprisingly, these two heads don't always work together very well. You may find that, even when you know you have a right to visit, live, or work in the United States, and you're trying your best to fill out the applications and complete your case properly, you feel as if you're being treated like a criminal. The frowning head doesn't care. It views you as just another number, and as no great loss if your application fails—or is, literally, lost in the files of thousands of other applications.

⚠ Have you heard people say that a U.S. citizen could simply invite a friend from overseas to live here? Those days are gone. Now, every immigrant has to find a legal category that he or she fits within, deal with demanding application forms and procedures, and pass security and other checks.

⚠ **Almost everyone should at least attend a consultation with an experienced immigration attorney before submitting an application.** Unless your case presents no complications whatsoever, it's best to have an attorney confirm that you haven't overlooked anything. However, by preparing yourself with the information in this book, you can save money and make sure you're using a good attorney for the right services.

> **EXAMPLE:** An American woman was engaged to a man from Mexico, and figured, since she herself had been to law school, that she didn't need an attorney's help. She read that a foreign-born person who was in the U.S. on a tourist visa could get married and then apply for a green card within the United States. Unfortunately, what she didn't realize was that this possibility only works for people who decide to get married *after* entering the United States. *Applying* for a tourist visa with the idea of getting married and getting a green card amounts to visa fraud, and can ruin a person's chances of immigrating. Are you already confused by this story? That's all right, the U.S. immigration system doesn't always make a lot of sense. This is why an attorney's help is often needed —to get you through legal hoops that you'd never imagined existed.

A. Roadmap to U.S. Immigration

This book will cover a lot of territory —almost all of U.S. immigration law, including your basic rights, strategies, and the procedures for getting where you need to go. Any time you cover this much ground, it helps to have a road map—particularly so you'll know which subjects or chapters you can skip entirely.

Take a look at the imaginary map below, then read the following subsections to orient you to the main topics on the map.

As you can see, the first stop along the way is **The Inadmissibility Gate.** This gate represents a legal problem that can stop your path to a visa or green card before you've even started. If you have, for example, committed certain crimes, been infected with certain contagious diseases, appear likely to need welfare or government assistance, violated U.S. immigration laws, or you match another description on the U.S. government's list of concerns, you are considered "inadmissible." That means you won't be allowed any type of U.S. visa or green card, except under special circumstances or with legal forgiveness called a waiver. This gate gets closed on a lot of people who lived in the U.S. illegally for more than six months, which creates either a three-year or ten-year bar to immigrating. Even if you think you haven't done anything

Roadmap to U.S. Immigration

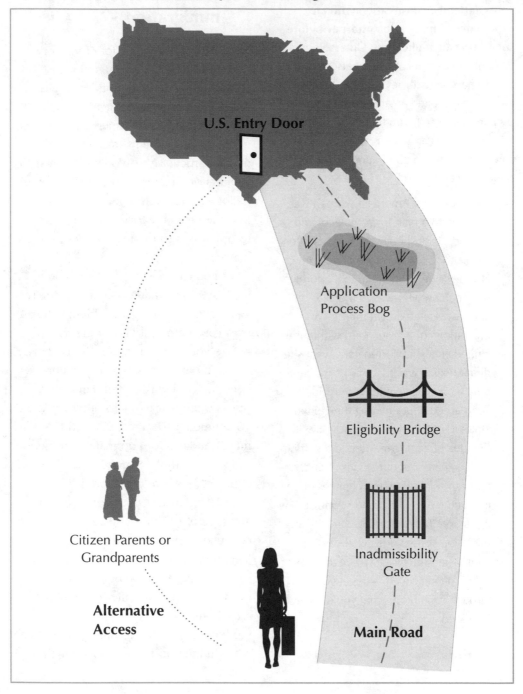

Words You'll Need to Know

We try not to use confusing legal language in this book. However, there are a few words that will be helpful for you to know, especially if you look at other books or websites. For further definitions, see "Words Commonly Used in Immigration Law," at the back of this book.

Citizen (U.S.). A person who owes allegiance to the U.S. government, is entitled to its protection, and enjoys the highest level of rights due to members of U.S. society. A person can become a U.S. citizen through birth in the United States or its territories; through parents or grandparents who are citizens; or through naturalization (after applying for citizenship and passing the citizenship exam). Citizens cannot have their status taken away except for certain extraordinary reasons.

Immigrant. Though the general public usually calls any foreign-born newcomer to the United States an immigrant, the U.S. government prefers to think of immigrants as only including those people who have attained permanent residence or a green card.

Nonimmigrant. Everyone who comes to the United States legally but with only a short-term intent to stay is considered a nonimmigrant. For instance, students and tourists are nonimmigrants.

Green card. No longer green, this slang term refers to the identification card carried by lawful permanent residents of the United States. The government name for the green card is an I-551, or Alien Registration Receipt Card (ARC).

Lawful permanent resident. See Permanent resident, below.

Permanent resident. A green card holder. This is a person who has been approved to live in the United States for an unlimited amount of time. However, the status can be taken away for certain reasons, such as having committed a crime or made one's home outside the United States. Usually after five years, a permanent resident can apply for U.S. citizenship.

Visa. A right to enter the United States. An immigrant visa gives someone the right to enter the United States permanently; a nonimmigrant visa gives them the right to enter for a short-term, temporary stay. Physically, the visa usually appears as a stamp in the applicant's passport, given by a U.S. consulate overseas.

If you forget these words, or encounter other words that you don't understand, check the list at the back of this book.

wrong, please read Chapter 3 for more on the problem of inadmissibility.

If you get past the inadmissibility gate, the next stop along your theoretical journey is **The Eligibility Bridge.** This is where you must answer the question, "What type of visa or green card are you eligible for?" Answering this question will involve some research on your part. You might already know the answer—for example, if you've just married a U.S. citizen, it's pretty obvious that you want to apply for a green card on this basis, and should read the appropriate chapter of this book (Chapter 7). Or, if your main goal is to attend college in the United States, then you probably know that you need a student visa, and can proceed straight to the chapter covering that topic (Chapter 22).

If you don't already know you're eligible for a certain type of visa or green card, however, then start by reading Section B, below, which reviews the possibilities for spending time in the U.S. and directs you to the appropriate chapters for follow-up. You'll see that this book covers more than just permanent green cards—we know that not everyone will either want, or be eligible to receive, the right to live in the United States their whole life. However, there are many useful ways to stay in the United States temporarily, for example on a student or employment-based visa. And even if you don't fit into one of the usual categories,

there may be an emergency or other special category that helps you.

Not many people will travel down the **Citizen Parents or Grandparents Side Road.** It's for the lucky few who, after doing a little research, realize that they are already U.S. citizens because their parents or grandparents had U.S. citizenship. Okay, we admit that this is rare. Most people would not be picking up a book on immigration if they were already U.S. citizens. Nevertheless, a few people are surprised to find that, because their parents or grandparents were either born in the U.S. or became U.S. citizens later, they are already U.S. citizens themselves—in which case they can put this book back down and go get a U.S. passport. See Chapter 2 for a full discussion of who can claim U.S. citizenship through parents or grandparents.

The next stop along your journey is the **Application Process Bog.** We added this because, even after you realize that you match the eligibility requirements for a U.S. visa or green card, you can't just march into a U.S. immigration office and claim your rights on the spot. The application process involves intensive document collection, form preparation, and generally molding your life around monitoring the handling of your case until you've gotten what you want. Even if you do your part correctly, most visas and green cards take a much longer time to obtain that you would ever imagine—anywhere from a few months to several years.

Some people never make it through the bog, simply because they failed to adequately prepare their applications or to respond to government follow-up requests on time. Others get bogged down through no fault of their own because the U.S. government loses track of their application. Dealing with bureaucracy and delays is such a large concern that we've devoted a whole chapter of this book to it: Chapter 4. And you should also read Chapter 6, on how to find and work with a high-quality immigration attorney. Attorneys are familiar with the difficulties of the application process, and the good ones will have access to inside phone numbers or email addresses to use when there's a problem.

If you make it this far, then the door to U.S. immigration will be opened to you.

B. Immigration Eligibility Self-Quiz

Since we don't know who you are, we're going to start with a very broad assumption: that you're looking for any possible way to spend time in the United States, preferably permanently. With that idea in mind, we offer the following quiz to help you find out what type of visa or green card you might be eligible for, and which chapter of this book to read for more information. This quiz will also help introduce you to U.S. immigration law—it covers almost all the categories for entering or staying legally.

Immigration Eligibility Self-Quiz

Question	Possible rights to a visa or green card	For more information
Are you from Canada or Mexico?	You have rights and visa possibilities that others don't.	See Chapter 5 for more on immigration possibilities for Canadians and Mexicans.
Are you engaged to marry a U.S. citizen?	You may be eligible for a fiancé visa, allowing you to enter the United States in order to get married.	See Chapter 8 more on obtaining a fiancé visa.
Do you have any close family members (parents, husband or wife, children over 21, or brothers and sisters) who are U.S. citizens?	You may qualify for a green card if one of them is willing to petition for you.	See Chapter 7 for more information on obtaining a green card through family.
Do you have any close family members (parents, husband or wife) who are U.S. permanent residents (green card holders)?	You may qualify for a green card if one of them is willing to petition for you.	See Chapter 7 for more information on obtaining a green card through family.
Are you a U.S. citizen who wishes to adopt a child from overseas?	You may be able to adopt an orphan or a child under age 16.	See Chapter 7 for more information on obtaining green cards for adopted children.
Do you have a job offer from a U.S. employer?	You may be able to obtain a green card, if you have the right background and qualifications, if the employer is willing to sponsor you, and in most cases, if no U.S. workers are willing or able to take the job.	See Chapter 9 for more information on getting a green card through employment.
NOTE: Some job offers may qualify you for temporary work visas; keep a lookout for these farther on in this quiz.		
Do you come from a country on the State Department's list of countries eligible to participate in the visa lottery?	You and other family members who meet the educational and other qualifying criteria can enter the visa lottery once a year. Winners can apply for a green card.	See Chapter 10 for more on how the visa lottery works.
Do you have $500,000 or more to invest in the creation or expansion of a U.S. business?	You may be eligible for an investment-based green card.	See Chapter 11 for more information on obtaining an investment-based green card.
Are you a member of the clergy or a religious worker wishing to come to the U.S. to work for the same religious organization that you've already been working for over the last two years?	You may qualify for a green card as a special immigrant.	See Chapter 12 for more information on obtaining a green card as a special immigrant.

PERMANENT GREEN CARDS

Immigration Eligibility Self-Quiz (cont'd)

Question	Possible rights to a visa or green card	For more information
Are you a graduate of a foreign medical school who came to the United States before January 10, 1978, and are you still living in the United States?	You may qualify for a green card as a special immigrant.	See Chapter 12 for more information on obtaining a green card as a special immigrant.
Are you a former overseas U.S. government worker, or a retired employee of an international organization, and have you worked half of the last seven years in the United States?	You may qualify for a green card as a special immigrant.	See Chapter 12 for more information on obtaining a green card as a special immigrant.
Are you a child (or are you helping a child) who is living in the U.S. and has been declared dependent on a juvenile court and eligible for a long-term foster or state agency care?	The child may qualify for a green card as a special immigrant.	See Chapter 12 for more information on obtaining a green card as a special immigrant.
Have you served in the U.S. armed services for a total of 12 years or more after October 15, 1978?	You may qualify for a green card as a special immigrant.	See Chapter 12 for more information on obtaining a green card as a special immigrant.
Do you live in a country (non-U.S.) where you have faced or fear persecution, either by the government or by someone the government can't control—and is that persecution because of your race, religion, nationality, political opinion, or membership in a particular social group?	You may qualify as a refugee, which would allow you to travel to the United States and apply for a green card after one year.	See Chapter 13 for more information on obtaining refugee status from overseas.
Are you in the United States now, but fear returning to your home country because you have faced or still fear persecution, either by the government or someone the government can't control—and is that persecution because of your race, religion, nationality, political opinion, or membership in a particular social group?	You may qualify for political asylum, which would allow you to stay in the United States, and apply for a green card after one year.	See Chapter 13 for more information on obtaining political asylum.
Have you lived in the U.S. continuously since January 1972?	You may be eligible for a green card based on registry.	See a lawyer for more information on obtaining a registry-based green card.
Have you said "no" to all of the above questions?		See an immigration attorney to reevaluate whether you qualify for any type of green card.

PERMANENT GREEN CARDS

Immigration Eligibility Self-Quiz (cont'd)

Question	Possible rights to a visa	For more information
Are you interested in a short trip to the U.S., for pleasure, business, or medical care?	You may qualify for a B-1 or B-2 visitor visa.	See Chapter 15 for more information on obtaining B visas.
Has a U.S. employer offered you a job requiring highly specialized knowledge gained from a university degree or equivalent work experience?	You may qualify for an H-1B work visa (good for up to six years).	See Chapter 16 for more information on obtaining H-1B visas.
Has a U.S. employer offered you a temporary or seasonal nonagricultural job, whether skilled or unskilled?	You may qualify for an H-2B work visa (good for up to one year).	See Chapter 17 for more information on obtaining H-2B visas.
Does a U.S. company plan to offer you on-the-job training in order to help your career in your home country?	You may qualify for an H-3 visa (good for the length of the training, up to two years).	See Chapter 18 for more information on obtaining H-3 visas.
Does your company, which has offices both inside and outside the U.S., want to transfer you to the U.S. as an owner, executive, manager, or an employee with special knowledge?	You may qualify for an L-1 visa (usually good for five to seven years).	See Chapter 19 for more information on obtaining L-1 visas.
Are you a part owner or key employee of a company that trades with the U.S., and coming to the U.S. to trade or help develop or direct the company's operations?	You may qualify for an E-1 treaty trader visa (initially good for up to two years).	See Chapter 20 for more information on obtaining E-1 visas.
Are you a part owner or key employee of a U.S. company supported by investment from natives of your home country, and coming to the U.S. to work for that company?	You may qualify for an E-2 treaty investor visa (initially good for up to two years).	See Chapter 21 for more information on obtaining E-2 visas.
Have you been accepted to study at an academic or vocational school in the U.S.?	You may qualify for an F-1 (academic student) or M-1 (vocational student) visa (good for the length of your studies).	See Chapter 22 for more information on obtaining F-1 and M-1 visas.
Have you been accepted to participate in an exchange program in the U.S.?	You may qualify for a J-1 exchange visitor visa (good for the length of the program).	See Chapter 23 for more information on obtaining J-1 visas.
Has a U.S. employer offered you a job based on either your extraordinary ability in the arts, sciences, education, business, or athletics; or as a religious worker?	You may qualify for an O, P, or R visa (good for between one and five years in the case of O and P visas, and five years in the case of R visas).	See Chapter 24 for more information on obtaining O, P, or R visas.
Have you said "no" to all of the above questions?		See an attorney to see whether you have overlooked any possibility.

TEMPORARY VISAS

Which Government Office Will Be Handling Your Immigration Application

Getting your green card or nonimmigrant visa may require dealing with more than one U.S. government agency, and maybe more than one office within that agency. The possibilities include the following:

- The **U.S. Department of State** (DOS, at www.state.gov), through U.S. embassies and consulates located around the world. If you're coming from outside of the U.S., you'll be dealing primarily with a U.S. consulate—and if you're currently in the U.S., you, too, may have to travel to a consulate to complete your application. Not all U.S. consulates provide visa-processing services. To find more information about the U.S. consulate nearest to your home, either check the phone book of your country's capital city, or go online at http://usembassy.state.gov. Note that you cannot normally apply for an immigrant visa (permanent residence) in a U.S. embassy or consulate *outside* your home country, unless the U.S. has no diplomatic relationship with the government of your homeland. You can apply for *nonimmigrant* visas (such as tourist visas) in third countries, so long as you have never overstayed your permitted time in the United States, even by one day.

- The **National Visa Center** (NVC), a private company under contract to the DOS for the purpose of handling case files during certain intermediate parts of the green card application process. After US-CIS approves a visa petition by a U.S.-based family member or company, the NVC is given the file, and hangs onto it until it's time for the NVC to send the first set of forms and instructions to the foreign-born applicant. The NVC then forwards the file to the appropriate U.S. consulate or USCIS district office.

- **U.S. Citizenship and Immigration Services** (USCIS, formerly called INS, at www.uscis.gov), an agency of the Department of Homeland Security (DHS). Even if you're living outside the United States, you may have to deal with USCIS, particularly if you're applying for a green card rather than a temporary visa—most green card applications must be started by a U.S.-based family member or company filing a visa petition with a USCIS service center. USCIS has various types of offices that handle immigration applications, including service

Which Government Office Will Be Handling Your Immigration Application (continued)

centers (large processing facilities that serve a wide region, which you cannot visit in person), district offices (about 33 nationwide, which interact with the public by providing forms and information, accepting certain applications, and holding interviews), suboffices (like district offices, but smaller and with more limited services), Application Support Centers (where you go to have fingerprints taken and in some cases pick up forms or turn in applications) and asylum offices (where interviews on applications for political asylum are held).

- **Customs and Border Protection** (CBP), also under DHS, responsible for patrolling the U.S. borders. This includes meeting you at an airport or other U.S. entry point when you arrive with your visa, and doing a last check to make sure that your visa paperwork is in order and that you didn't obtain it through fraud or by providing false information.

- The **U.S. Department of Labor**, (DOL), through its Employment and Training Administration, at www .doleta.gov. If your visa or green card application is based on a job with a U.S. employer, certain parts of the paperwork may have to be filed with and ruled on by the DOL. The DOL's role is to make sure that hiring immigrant workers doesn't make it harder for U.S. workers to get a job, and that you're being paid a fair wage (one that doesn't act to bring down the wages of U.S. workers).

Although you needn't learn a lot about these various agencies, it's important to keep track of which one has your application as it makes its way through the pipeline. This is especially true if you ever change your address, because you'll have to advise the office that actually has control of your application. (These offices don't communicate well with each other—if you tell one place about your change of address, it may not tell the one that actually has your file, and you may not hear about important requirements or interviews.)

C. The Typical Application Process

Now let's assume that you are not inadmissible, and that you have what it takes to be eligible for either a permanent green card or a temporary U.S. visa. Although we'll give you more detail about the application processes later in this book, here's a preview. Your main steps will include:

- deciding whether you'll need legal help to complete your application
- if you're applying for a permanent green card, waiting while your U.S. family member or employer fills out what's called a "visa petition," proving either that you are the person's family member or have been offered a job; and then waiting even longer for the U.S. immigration authorities to approve the petition
- if, in the category under which you're applying, only limited numbers of visas or green cards are given out every year, waiting until the people in line ahead of you have received their green cards (which often takes years)
- filling out your own set of application forms, collecting documents, and submitting them to either a U.S. consulate in your home country or to the U.S. immigration authorities
- tracking your application to make sure it doesn't get lost in the system
- attending an interview at a consulate outside of the U.S. or a U.S. immigration office, at which your application is reviewed and you answer questions
- receiving either a visa to enter the U.S., or a green card or other right to stay in the U.S. (unless you are denied, in which case you may want to reapply), and finally
- entering the United States, protecting your status, and working toward the next step, if any (if you received a green card, you may want to work toward U.S. citizenship, the highest and most secure status you can receive).

One issue that will make a big difference in how your application proceeds is whether you are currently living in the United States or in another country. U.S. government offices have been set up to handle U.S. immigration applications both outside the U.S. (at U.S. consulates) and within the United States (at USCIS district offices and service centers). However, not all of these offices handle all types of immigration applications—you can't just walk into one and expect it to handle yours. See "Which Government Office Will Be Handling Your Immigration Application," above.

What's more, many of the people who would most prefer to file their immigration applications in the United States—because they have been living here for many years, perhaps illegally—will find that they are not allowed to do so. We will discuss this at length in Chapter 3.

The short explanation is that, if you either entered the United States illegally (not with a visa or other entry document or right), or you have worked here illegally, you cannot (with a few exceptions), use the services of a USCIS immigration office. Instead, you must leave the U.S. and go to a U.S. consulate to make your visa or green card request. That creates a huge problem for people who have lived illegally in the United States for more than six months after January 1, 1997. Once you leave, you can be prevented from returning for three years if your illegal stay was between six months and one year. If your illegal stay in the U.S. lasted more than one full year, you can be prevented from returning for ten years. Some people can apply for waivers to return earlier, but not everyone can apply for them and the waivers are frequently denied.

In fact, this problem creates a trap for many people who, although they are technically eligible for a green card, can't actually get a green card because they are living in the United States illegally.

> **EXAMPLE:** Maria crossed the border illegally from Mexico in the year 2002. She married David, a U.S. citizen, in 2007. However, because of Maria's illegal entry, she cannot apply for a green card at a local USCIS office. She would have to go to a U.S. consulate in Mexico to file her green card application—and then potentially be barred from returning to the U.S. for three or ten years.

Now that you have some idea whether there's a visa or green card that you qualify for, please go on to read either Chapter 2 (if you have parents or grandparents who were U.S. citizens) or Chapter 3, concerning inadmissibility. Then proceed straight to the chapter concerning the visa or green card you're interested in. If, after reading the detailed eligibility requirements, you confirm that you qualify, don't forget to read Chapter 4, with crucial advice on handling the paperwork and dealing with bureaucrats, and Chapter 6, on when and how to find a good lawyer.

Icons Used in This Book

 The caution icon warns you of potential problems.

 This icon indicates that the information is a useful tip.

 This icon refers you to helpful books or other resources.

 This icon indicates when you should consider consulting an attorney or other expert.

 This icon refers you to a further discussion of the topic somewhere else in the book.

 Look for related information in another part of this book. ■

Chapter 2

Are You Already a U.S. Citizen?

Most people who are U.S. citizens already know it, either because they were born in the U.S. or because they successfully applied to become naturalized citizens. However, U.S. citizenship can be obtained in two additional, less well-known ways, including:

- birth outside the U.S. to U.S. citizen parents (acquisition), or
- citizenship or naturalization of parents after the child has obtained a green card in the U.S. (derivation).

Many people born or living outside the U.S. are already U.S. citizens but don't know it. The key to acquisition of citizenship is having U.S. citizens in your direct line of ancestry. Even though you were born elsewhere and your U.S. ancestors have not lived in the U.S. for a long time, U.S. citizenship may have still been passed down the line.

Derivation of citizenship helps people who do live in the U.S., but who didn't realize that minor children with green cards can acquire citizenship automatically, without having to apply for naturalization.

 You can't lose your citizenship just by living outside of the U.S. for too long. People who were born in the U.S. but have lived most of their lives in other countries sometimes believe that their long absence from the U.S. and voting or military activities elsewhere have stripped them of U.S. citizenship. That's not the case—anyone born with U.S. citizenship will retain it for life unless he or she performs some act to intentionally lose it, such as filing an oath of renunciation.

 This book does not describe how people who have already gotten their green card can apply to become naturalized citizens. For complete information on your eligibility and the process, see *Becoming a U.S. Citizen: A Guide to the Law, Exam & Interview*, by Ilona Bray (Nolo).

What If You Were Born "Out of Wedlock" to a U.S. Citizen Father?

In many cases, your right to U.S. citizenship may depend on your relationship to a U.S. citizen father. However, if your parents weren't married at the time you were born, the laws of the time may refer to you as "illegitimate," meaning in legal terms that you have no recognized father. As you'll see in the sections below, your right to claim citizenship may depend on you providing evidence that your father took the actions necessary to satisfy the legitimation law of your birth country. Legitimation laws require fathers to legally acknowledge their children.

A. Acquisition of Citizenship Through Birth to U.S. Citizen Parents

In many circumstances, even though a child is born outside the U.S., if at least one parent was a U.S. citizen at the time of the child's birth, he or she automatically "acquires" U.S. citizenship. When this child marries and has children, those children may also acquire U.S. citizenship at birth.

The laws governing whether or not a child born outside U.S. boundaries acquires U.S. citizenship from his or her parents have changed several times. The law that was in effect on the date of the child's birth determines whether he or she acquired U.S. citizenship from a parent or grandparent. If there is anyone in your direct line of ancestry whom you believe may be a U.S. citizen, it is worth your time to read what the U.S. laws were on the date of your birth and theirs.

Most laws controlling the passage of U.S. citizenship from parent to child require that the parent, the child, or both have a period of living in the United States ("residence"). Sometimes the residence is required to be for a specified length of time (like five years) and sometimes it is not. When the law doesn't say exactly how long the residence period must be, you can assume that even a brief time, such as a month, might be enough. The key element is often not the amount of time but wheth-er or not USCIS or the State Department believes it was a residence and not a visit. If the period of stay has the character of a residence, the length of time doesn't matter.

1. Birth Prior to May 24, 1934

If you were born before 1934, the law provided that only your U.S. citizen father (not mother) could pass citizenship on to you. The rules were very simple. In order to pass on U.S. citizenship, the father must have resided in the U.S. at some time before the child's birth. The law didn't require any particular length of time or dates when the residence took place. Technically, a day or a week would be enough if it could be regarded as a residence and not just a visit. Once a child obtained U.S. citizenship at birth through a U.S. citizen father, there were no conditions to retaining it. These rules also applied to so-called illegitimate children (children born to unmarried parents), provided the U.S. citizen father had at some time legally legitimated the child (acknowledged his paternal responsibility). U.S. citizenship was then acquired at the time of legitimation, without regard to the child's age.

This law has been challenged several times as discriminatory, with some courts holding that citizenship could also be passed by the mother to the children. Congress finally addressed this issue in 1994 and amended the law, retroactively, to provide that either parent could pass his or her U.S. citizenship to children.

Consider that if you were born before May 24, 1934, and either of your parents was a U.S. citizen, that citizenship might have been passed on to you. Consider also, that if either of your parents was born before May 24, 1934, they may have acquired U.S. citizenship from either of their parents, which they then passed on to you under laws in existence at a later date. A check of the family tree may well be worth your while.

2. Birth Between May 25, 1934, and January 12, 1941

If you were born between May 25, 1934, and January 12, 1941, you acquired U.S. citizenship at birth on the conditions that both your parents were U.S. citizens and at least one had resided in the U.S. prior to your birth. The law at this time placed no additional conditions on retaining U.S. citizenship acquired in this way.

You could also get U.S. citizenship if only one of your parents was a U.S. citizen, as long as that parent had a prior U.S. residence. If your U.S. citizenship came from only one parent, you too would have been required to reside in the U.S. for at least two years between the ages of 14 and 28 in order to retain the citizenship you got at birth. Alternately, you could retain citizenship if your noncitizen parent naturalized before you turned 18 and you began living in the U.S. permanently before age 18. Oth-

erwise, your citizenship would be lost. If the one U.S. citizen parent was your father and your birth was illegitimate (took place while your parents weren't married), the same rules applied provided your father legally legitimated you (acknowledged paternal responsibility). Citizenship was passed at the time of legitimation without regard to your age, so long as you had met the retention requirements.

3. Birth Between January 13, 1941, and December 23, 1952

If you were born between January 13, 1941, and December 23, 1952, both your parents were U.S. citizens and at least one had a prior residence in the U.S., you automatically acquired U.S. citizenship at birth, with no conditions to retaining it.

If only one parent was a U.S. citizen, that parent must have resided in the U.S. for at least ten years prior to your birth, and at least five of those years must have been after your parent reached the age of 16. With a parent thus qualified, you then acquired U.S. citizenship at birth, but with conditions for retaining it. To keep your citizenship, you must have resided in the U.S. for at least two years between the ages of 14 and 28. Alternately, you could retain citizenship if your noncitizen parent naturalized before you turned 18 and you began living in the U.S. permanently before age 18. As a result of a U.S. Supreme Court decision, if you were born after October 9, 1952, your parent still had to fulfill the residence requirement in order to confer citizenship on you, but your own residence requirements for retaining U.S. citizenship were abolished—you need not have lived in the U.S. at all.

If your one U.S. citizen parent was your father and your birth was illegitimate (took place while your parents weren't married), the same rules applied provided you were legally legitimated (your father acknowledged paternal responsibility) prior to your 21st birthday and you were unmarried at the time of legitimation.

4. Birth Between December 24, 1952, and November 13, 1986

If at the time of your birth both your parents were U.S. citizens and at least one had a prior residence in the U.S., you automatically acquired U.S. citizenship, with no other conditions for retaining it.

If only one parent was a U.S. citizen at the time of your birth, that parent must have resided in the U.S. for at least ten years, and at least five of those years must have been after your parent reached the age of 14. If your one U.S. citizen parent is your father and your birth was illegitimate (took place while your parents weren't married), the same rules apply provided you were legally legitimated (your father acknowledged paternal responsibility) prior to your 21st birthday and you were unmarried at the time of legitimation.

5. Birth Between November 14, 1986, and the Present

If at the time of your birth, both your parents were U.S. citizens and at least one had a prior residence in the U.S., you automatically acquired U.S. citizenship, with no conditions for retaining it.

If only one parent was a U.S. citizen at the time of your birth, that parent must have resided in the U.S. for at least five years and at least two of those years must have been after your parent reached the age of 14. Even with only one U.S. citizen parent, there are still no conditions to retaining your citizenship. If your one U.S. citizen parent is your father and your birth was illegitimate (took place when the parents weren't married), the same rules apply provided you were legally legitimated (your father acknowledged paternal responsibility) prior to your 18th birthday. Additionally, your father must have established paternity prior to your 18th birthday, either by acknowledgment or by court order, and must have stated, in writing, that he would support you financially until your 18th birthday.

6. Exception to Requirements for Retaining Citizenship

It is not unusual for a child born and raised outside the U.S. to have acquired U.S. citizenship at birth from parents or grandparents without knowing it. The child, ignorant of the laws and circumstances affecting his or her birthright, then proceeds to lose U.S. citizenship by failing to fulfill U.S. residency requirements.

Congress sought to address this by adding a law for people who once held U.S. citizenship but lost it by failing to fulfill the residency requirements that were in effect before 1978. Such persons can regain their citizenship by simply taking the oath of allegiance to the United States. It is not necessary that the person apply for naturalization. Contact a U.S. consulate or USCIS office for more information. The relevant statute is 8 U.S.C. § 1435(d)(1), I.N.A. § 324(d)(1).

B. Automatic Derivation of U.S. Citizenship Through Naturalized Parents

When one or both parents are or become naturalized U.S. citizens (by applying for citizenship and passing an exam), the children may, under certain circumstances, become U.S. citizens automatically. The law calls this derivation of citizenship. Becoming a U.S. citizen in this way has a special benefit because the child does not have to participate in a naturalization ceremony and can thereby avoid taking an oath renouncing allegiance to any country but the United States.

There are a number of people whose parents have been naturalized who do not realize they are U.S. citizens because

they never went through a naturalization ceremony themselves. The laws on automatic naturalization of children have varied over the years. Once again, whether or not you achieved U.S. citizenship in this manner is determined by the laws as they were when your parents' naturalization took place.

1. Parents Naturalized Before May 24, 1934

If either parent naturalized prior to your 21st birthday and you held a green card at the time, you automatically derived U.S. citizenship. This applied to you if you were either an illegitimate child of your U.S. citizen father (your parents weren't married when you were born) and had been legally legitimated (your father acknowledged paternal responsibility); or you were an illegitimate child of your U.S. citizen mother, whether legitimated or not. Adopted children and stepchildren did not qualify.

2. Parents Naturalized Between May 24, 1934, and January 12, 1941

If both parents became naturalized prior to your 21st birthday and you held a green card at the time, you automatically derived U.S. citizenship. This applied to you if you were an illegitimate child of your father (born when your parents weren't married) and had been legally legitimated. It also applied if you were an illegitimate child of your mother, whether legitimated or not. Adopted children did not qualify.

If only one parent became naturalized prior to your 21st birthday, you acquired U.S. citizenship automatically if you had held a green card for at least five years. The five years could have taken place before or after your parent was naturalized (as long as the years started before you turned 21), so if you hadn't held a green card for that long when the naturalization occurred, you automatically became a U.S. citizen whenever you finally accumulated the five-year total.

3. Parents Naturalized Between January 13, 1941, and December 23, 1952

You derived U.S. citizenship if you held a green card and both parents were naturalized prior to your 18th birthday (or if, when one parent naturalized, the other parent was dead, or your parents were legally separated and the parent with legal custody of you naturalized). At this time, the law did not permit either so-called illegitimate (born to unmarried parents) or adopted children to derive citizenship in this manner.

4. Parents Naturalized Between December 24, 1952, and October 4, 1978

You derived U.S. citizenship if you were unmarried and both parents were naturalized prior to your 16th birthday. You must also have received a green card before your 18th birthday. If only one parent naturalized, you can derive citizenship only if the other parent was dead, or if they were legally separated and the naturalized parent had custody of you. This applied to you if you were either an illegitimate child of your U.S. citizen father (born while your parents weren't married) and had been legally legitimated (your father accepted paternal responsibility); or if you were an illegitimate child of your mother, whether legitimated or not. Adopted children and stepchildren did not qualify.

5. Parents Naturalized Between October 5, 1978, and February 26, 2001

You derived U.S. citizenship if one of your parents was a U.S. citizen when you were born and never ceased to be a citizen, and your other parent was naturalized prior to your 18th birthday, or the naturalization of both parents occurred before your 18th birthday. In either case, you need to have been unmarried at the time, and have been lawfully admitted to the U.S as a permanent resident (had a green card). This applies to all children, including those who are illegitimate (born while their parents weren't married) and those who were adopted (so long as the adoption took place before you turned 18, and the naturalization(s) took place while you were living in the

U.S. in the legal custody of your adoptive parent(s)). However, adopted children born prior to December 29, 1981, or after November 14, 1986, derived U.S. citizenship only if the adoption occurred prior to their 16th birthday.

6. Parent Born in U.S. or Naturalized Between February 27, 2001, and the Present

You derived U.S. citizenship if one of your parents was born in the U.S. or if one of your parents naturalized prior to your 18th birthday while you were living in the U.S., in the legal and physical custody of that parent. You must also have had a green card (permanent residence). This law applies to both natural and adopted children.

Notice that, for the first time in the history of this law, children may derive citizenship through a parent who was born in the U.S. rather than only through a parent who later naturalizes. This has the practical effect of turning many children into citizens the instant that they obtain a green card through one U.S. citizen parent. In recognition of this instant citizenship, USCIS does not require Affidavits of Support (Form I-864) to be submitted with such children's green card applications.

Naturalization for Certain Children Living Outside the United States

Children who live outside of the U.S. can also gain citizenship through a citizen parent. The child must be under 18 and the parent must have lived in the U.S. for at least five years, at least two of which were after the age of 14. In addition, children in this situation must enter the U.S. on a nonimmigrant visa (a tourist visa, for example) and submit an application to USCIS for a certificate of citizenship (the child's citizenship is not automatic in this situation).

If you plan to apply for this, get started as soon as possible—the entire process, including interview and approval of the certificate, must be completed before the child's 18th birthday. This can be difficult, with many USCIS offices backed up for years with these applications.

C. Obtaining Proof of U.S. Citizenship

If you have a legitimate claim to U.S. citizenship, in order to establish that claim you must apply for some kind of citizenship document. If your birth took place outside the territorial U.S, and you acquired U.S. citizenship at birth from your parents or derived it through your parents' naturalization, the following types of documents will be recognized as proof of U.S. citizenship:

- U.S. passports
- certificates of citizenship, or
- certificates of consular registration of birth.

1. U.S. Passports

If you were born abroad to U.S. citizen parents, you can apply for a U.S. passport in the same way as someone born in the United States. However, you will have the added requirement of establishing your citizenship claim. Passports are available from passport offices in the U.S. (run by the U.S. Department of State) and at U.S. consulates outside the U.S., but experience shows that you have a better chance at a U.S. consulate. Wherever you apply, you will be required to present proof of your parents' U.S. citizenship and evidence that they, and you, complied with any applicable U.S. residency requirements. Review the sections on birth to a U.S. citizen for what you must prove under these circumstances.

You will need to present documents such as birth or citizenship records of your parent or grandparent and work or tax records establishing U.S. residency for your parent or grandparent.

2. Certificates of Citizenship

Certificates of citizenship are issued only inside the U.S. by USCIS offices. Anyone with a claim to U.S. citizenship can apply for a certificate of citizenship. In most cases it is more difficult and takes much longer to get a certificate of citizenship than a U.S. passport. However, in situations where your U.S. citizenship was obtained automatically through the naturalization of a parent, certificates of citizenship applications are the best choice. In fact, at the time a parent is naturalized, the children can, upon the parent's request, be issued certificates of citizenship simultaneously with their naturalization certificates.

Certificates of citizenship not requested simultaneously with a parent's naturalization must be applied for later, on Form N-600. (Except that a slightly different form, numbered N-600K, must be used by children living outside of the U.S. who apply for citizenship through their parents, as described in "Naturalization for Certain Children Living Outside of the United States," above.) The current fee for both the N-600 and the N-600K is $460, or $420 for minor adopted children. Copies of these forms and detailed instructions are available on the USCIS website.

We recommend that you also prepare a cover letter explaining the basis of your claim to U.S. citizenship and describing the documents you are offering as proof. These should include your parents' birth certificates, marriage certificate, and citizenship or naturalization certificates. You should also present your own birth certificate, marriage certificates, and any divorce decrees to show legal changes in your name since birth. If you are not applying as the child of a naturalized citizen, your letter should also list whatever evidence you will be presenting to show that you have met any residency requirements as described in the section in this chapter on birth to a U.S. citizen.

Form N-600 or N-600K, the documents, and the cover letter should be submitted to the USCIS local office having jurisdiction over your place of residence in the United States. You will most likely be called in for an interview on your application. In the busier USCIS offices, it can take up to a year to get a decision on an application for certificate of citizenship.

3. Certificates of Consular Registration of Birth

Certificates of consular registration of birth are issued by a U.S. consulate abroad. If your parents were U.S. citizens but were not physically in the U.S. when you were born, they may have registered your birth with a U.S. consulate to establish your right to U.S. citizenship and create an official birth record. For you to have acquired a certificate of consular registration of birth, your parents must have registered your birth at a consulate within five years after you were born.

Multiple copies can be issued at the time of registration but duplicates cannot be obtained later. Therefore, parents should request at least several copies. In issuing the certificate, the consulate asks to see evidence that any residence requirements the law placed on your parents were fulfilled. The consular registration is conclusive proof of U.S. citizenship, but if your parents did not take the steps to get one when you were a child, there is no way of obtaining one now.

If your parents did not register your birth in time, you may either apply for a passport through a passport office in the U.S. or at a U.S. consulate abroad, or you may apply for a certificate of citizenship through the USCIS in the United States. You can typically get the passport much faster than the certificate of citizenship.

D. Dual Citizenship

If a child is born on U.S. soil and either or both parents are citizens of another country, it is quite possible that the child may have dual citizenship. Whether or not dual citizenship is created depends on the laws of the parents' country or countries. A child born in the U.S. is always a U.S. citizen in the eyes of the U.S. government, no matter what the laws of the parents' homelands say. (The only exception to this rule is children born of foreign diplomats.) However, if the foreign country recognizes the child as a citizen, the U.S. will recognize the non-U.S. citizenship as well.

Whenever a child is born to U.S. citizen parents but the birth takes place outside U.S. territory, again, the child may acquire dual citizenship. In this situation, the child will, depending on the laws of the country where the birth took place, usually have the nationality of the country in which he or she was actually born, in addition to U.S. citizenship through the nationality of the parents. U.S. law recognizes dual citizenship under these circumstances, and if you have acquired dual citizenship in this manner, under U.S. law you will be entitled to maintain dual status for your lifetime.

In addition, a person who becomes a U.S. citizen through naturalization can retain his or her previous citizenship if his or her original country allows dual citizenship.

■

Chapter 3

Can You Enter or Stay in the U.S. at All?

Let's say you've found a category of visa or green card that you think you're eligible for—for example, a college has accepted you and you're hoping to get a student visa, or your mother has become a U.S. citizen, and you're hoping to get a green card through her. The sad truth is that the U.S. immigration authorities still have the power to tell you "no" and deny your application if they decide that you're "inadmissible."

But what is it to be inadmissible? It means that you have a condition or characteristic that the U.S. government has decided is undesirable or would threaten the health and safety of people living in the United States. For example, if someone applying to immigrate is infected with tuberculosis, or the person once committed a violent crime, giving him or her the right to be in the United States might cause harm to U.S. citizens and residents.

The U.S. government keeps a list of the conditions and characteristics that make a person inadmissible. (See I.N.A. § 212, 8 U.S.C. § 1182.) The list includes affliction with various physical and mental disorders, commission of crimes, participation in terrorist or subversive activity, likelihood of needing welfare or other public assistance, and more. If you're found to match one of the items on this list, then you won't ordinarily be allowed to enter the United States. Or, if you've already entered, you won't be allowed to receive a green card or most other immigration benefits.

The government is stricter with green card applications than with applications for temporary visas. Although technically, your application for almost any temporary immigration benefit (such as a student visa) can be denied based on inadmissibility, in reality, inadmissibility is checked less closely when it comes to nonimmigrant applications, and certain grounds don't apply to certain visas. Also, a waiver of a ground of inadmissibility is easier to get for a nonimmigrant visa—the law doesn't attach the same requirements as it does for a green card application. (See I.N.A. § 212(d)(3), 8 U.S.C. § 1182(d)(3).)

You may be wondering how the government finds out that you're inadmissible. All green card and visa application forms ask questions designed to find out whether any grounds of inadmissibility apply in your case. Although some people obviously give false answers, those who are caught lying will have their immigration application denied for sure, and probably lose their chance to apply for any other visa or green card in the future. What's more, many of the applications—particularly those for green cards, as opposed to temporary visas—require you to supply your fingerprints or police reports as well as the results of medical examinations. If the results show that you have certain crimes on your record or communicable medical conditions, you will be found inadmissible.

Falling into one of the categories of inadmissibility doesn't mean you are absolutely barred from getting a green card or otherwise entering the United States. Some—though not all—grounds of inadmissibility may be legally excused or, in lawyer-speak, waived. But applying for a waiver is complicated, and you should consult with an attorney if you think you'll need one.

Below is a chart summarizing the grounds of inadmissibility, whether or not a waiver is available, and the special conditions you must meet in order to get a waiver. Unless otherwise indicated, the waivers described on the chart apply to people applying for green cards, not nonimmigrant visas. If you're applying for a nonimmigrant visa, you can request a waiver of many (but not all) of the grounds of inadmissibility if the consular officer recommends that you receive the waiver and USCIS approves it. (See I.N.A. § 212(d)(3), 8 U.S.C. § 1182(d)(3).) In deciding whether to recommend or approve your waiver, the officials will consider and balance three things:

- the risk of harm to society if you are allowed to enter the U.S.
- the seriousness of your criminal or immigration violation or other ground of inadmissibility, and
- your reason for wanting to come to the United States.

Risk of Being Stopped at the Border

Even if a U.S. consular officer in your home country didn't notice that you were inadmissible to the United States, the inspector who meets you at the U.S. airport, border, or other entry point might. Using a power called summary exclusion, the inspector can demand that you return home immediately if either of the following is true:

- The inspector thinks you are misrepresenting (lying about) practically anything connected to your right to enter the U.S., such as your purpose in coming, intent to return, prior immigration history, or use of false documents.
- You do not have the proper documentation for entry in the category you're requesting.

EXAMPLE: Boris arrives from Russia with a B-2 tourist visa. Although his visa stamp is the real thing, the border inspector discovers a ring and love letters describing wedding plans in his luggage. Upon questioning, Boris admits that he plans to marry his U.S. citizen girlfriend and apply for a green card. That makes his use of the tourist visa fraudulent, and the inspector sends him right back to Russia.

If the inspector excludes you, you may not request entry again for five years, unless a special waiver is granted. If the inspector intends to find you inadmissible, you may ask to withdraw your application to enter the U.S. in order to prevent having the five-year order on your record. The inspector may allow you to do so in some cases.

Summary of Grounds of Inadmissibility

Ground of Inadmissibility	Waiver Available	Conditions of Waiver
Health Problems		
Persons with communicable diseases of public health significance, in particular tuberculosis and HIV (AIDS).	Yes	Waiver available to the spouse or the unmarried son or daughter or the unmarried minor lawfully adopted child of a U.S. citizen or permanent resident, or of an alien who has been issued an immigrant visa; or to an individual who has a son or daughter who is a U.S. citizen, or a permanent resident, or an alien issued an immigrant visa, upon compliance with USCIS's terms and regulations. HIV-positive business and tourist visitors coming for up to 60 days also receive an automatic ("categorical") waiver.
Persons with physical or mental disorders which threaten their own safety or the property, welfare, or safety of others.	Yes	Special conditions required by USCIS, at its discretion.
Drug abusers or addicts.	No	(But doesn't include single-use experimentation.)
Persons who fail to show that they have been vaccinated against certain vaccine-preventable diseases.	Yes	The applicant must show either that he or she subsequently received the vaccine; that the vaccine is medically inappropriate as certified by a civil surgeon; or that having the vaccine administered is contrary to the applicant's religious beliefs or moral convictions.
Criminal and Related Violations		
Persons who have committed crimes involving moral turpitude.	Yes	Waivers are not available for commission of crimes such as attempted murder or conspiracy to commit murder, or murder, torture, or drug crimes. Also, no waivers are available to persons previously admitted as permanent residents, if they have been convicted of aggravated felony since such admission or if they have fewer than seven years of lawful continuous residence before removal proceedings were initiated against them. Waivers for all other offenses are available only if the applicant is a spouse, parent, or child of a U.S. citizen or green card holder; or the only criminal activity was prostitution; or the actions occurred more than 15 years before the application for a visa or green card is filed and the alien shows that he or she is rehabilitated and is not a threat to U.S. security.
Persons with two or more criminal convictions.	Yes	"
Prostitutes or procurers of prostitutes.	Yes	"

Summary of Grounds of Inadmissibility (continued)

Ground of Inadmissibility	Waiver Available	Conditions of Waiver
Diplomats or others involved in serious criminal activity who have received immunity from prosecution.	Yes	"
Drug offenders.	No	Except for simple possession of less than 30 grams of marijuana. There may also be an exception for simple possession or use by juvenile offenders.
Drug traffickers.	No	
Immediate family members of drug traffickers who knowingly benefited from the illicit money within the last five years.	No	But note that the problem "washes out" after five years.
National Security and Related Violations		
Spies, governmental saboteurs, or violators of export or technology transfer laws.	No	
Persons intending to overthrow the U.S. government.	No	
Persons intending to engage in unlawful activity.	No	
People subject to special registration who fail to have their departure confirmed and recorded are presumed to fall into this category	No	
Terrorists and members or representatives of foreign terrorist organizations.	No	
Persons whose entry would have adverse consequences for U.S. foreign policy, unless the applicant is an official of a foreign government, or the applicant's activities or beliefs would normally be lawful under the U.S. constitution.	No	
Voluntary members of totalitarian parties.	Yes	An exception is made if the membership was involuntary, or is or was when the applicant was under 16 years old, by operation of law, or for purposes of obtaining employment, food rations, or other "essentials" of living. An exception is also possible for past membership if the membership ended at least two years prior to the application (five years if the party in control of a foreign state is considered a totalitarian dictatorship). If neither applies, a waiver is available for an immigrant who is the parent, spouse, son, daughter, brother, or sister of a U.S. citizen, or a spouse, son, or daughter of a permanent resident.

Summary of Grounds of Inadmissibility (continued)

Ground of Inadmissibility	Waiver Available	Conditions of Waiver
Nazis	No	
Economic Grounds		
Any person who, in the opinion of a USCIS or consular official, is likely to become a public charge, that is, receive public assistance or welfare in the United States. The official can consider factors such as the person's age, health, family and work history, and previous use of public benefits.	No	However, the applicant may cure the ground of inadmissibility by overcoming the reasons for it or obtaining an Affidavit of Support from a family member or friend.
Family-sponsored immigrants and employment-sponsored immigrants where a family member is the employ-ment sponsor (or such a family member owns 5% of the petitioning business) whose sponsor has not executed an Affidavit of Support (Form I-864).	No	But an applicant may cure the ground of inadmissibility by subsequently satisfying Affidavit of Support requirements.
Nonimmigrant public benefit recipients (where the individual came as a nonimmigrant and applied for benefits when he or she was not eligible or through fraud). Five-year bar to admissibility.	No	But ground of inadmissibility expires after five years.
Labor Certifications and Employment Qualifications		
Persons without approved labor certifications, if one is required in the category under which the green card application is made.	No	But see Chapter 8, for a discussion of the national interest waiver.
Graduates of unaccredited medical schools, whether inside or outside of the U.S., immigrating to the U.S. in a second or third preference category based on their profession, who have not both passed the foreign medical graduates exam and shown proficiency in English. (Physicians qualifying as special immigrants, who have been practicing medicine in the U.S., with a license, since January 9, 1978 are not subject to this exclusion.)	No	
Uncertified foreign health care workers seeking entry based on clinical employ-ment in their field (not including physicians).	Yes	But applicant may show qualifications by submitting a certificate from the Commission on Graduates of Foreign Nursing Schools or the equivalent.

Summary of Grounds of Inadmissibility (continued)

Ground of Inadmissibility	Waiver Available	Conditions of Waiver
Immigration Violators		
Persons who entered the U.S. without inspection by the immigration authorities (INS or CBP).	Yes	Available for certain battered women and children who came to the U.S. escaping such battery or who qualify as self-petitioners. Also available for individuals who had visa petitions or labor certifications on file before January 14, 1998, or before April 30, 2001, with proof of physical presence in the U.S. on December 21, 2000. ($1,000 penalty required for latter waiver.) Does not apply to applicants outside of the U.S.
Persons who were deported after a hearing and seek readmission within ten years.	Yes	Discretionary with USCIS.
Persons who have failed to attend removal (deportation) proceedings (unless they had reasonable cause for doing so). Five-year bar to reentry.	Yes	Advance permission to apply for readmission. Discretionary with USCIS.
People who have been summarily excluded from the U.S. and again attempt to enter within five years	Yes	Discretionary with USCIS.
Persons who made misrepresentations during the immigration process.	Yes	The applicant must be the spouse or child of a U.S. citizen or green card holder. A waiver will be granted if the refusal of admission would cause extreme hardship to that relative. Discretionary with USCIS.
Persons who made a false claim to U.S. citizenship.	No	
Individuals subject to a final removal (deportation) order under the Immigration and Naturalization Act § 274C (Civil Document Fraud Proceedings).	Yes	Available to permanent residents who voluntarily left the U.S., and for those applying for permanent residence as immediate relatives or based on other family petitions, if the fraud was committed solely to assist the person's spouse or child and provided that no fine was imposed as part of the previous civil proceeding.
Student visa abusers (persons who improperly obtain F-1 status to attend a public elementary school or adult education program, or transfer from a private to a public program except as permitted). Five-year bar to admissibility.	No	

Summary of Grounds of Inadmissibility (continued)

Ground of Inadmissibility	Waiver Available	Conditions of Waiver
Certain individuals twice removed (deported or removed after aggravated felony). Twenty-year bar to admissibility for those twice deported.	Yes	Discretionary with USCIS (advance permission to apply for readmission).
Individuals unlawfully present (time counted only after April 1, 1997 and after the age of 18). Presence for 180–364 days results in three-year bar to admissibility. Presence for 365 or more days creates ten-year bar to admissibility. Bars kick in only when the individual departs the U.S. and seeks reentry after a period of unlawful presence.	Yes	A waiver is provided for an immigrant who has a U.S. citizen or permanent resident spouse or parent to whom refusal of the application would cause extreme hardship. There is also a complex body of law concerning when a person's presence can be considered "lawful," for example if one has certain applications awaiting decision by USCIS or is protected by battered spouse/child provisions of the immigration laws.
Individuals unlawfully present after previous immigration violations. (Applies to persons who were in the U.S. unlawfully for an aggregate period over one year, who subsequently reenter without being properly admitted. Also applies to anyone ordered removed who subsequently attempts entry without admission.)	No	
Stowaways.	No	This is a permanent ground of inadmissibility. However, after being gone for ten years an applicant can apply for advance permission to reapply for admission.
Smugglers of illegal aliens.	Yes	Waivable if the applicant was smuggling in persons who were immediate family members at the time, and either is a permanent resident or is immigrating under a family-based visa petition as an immediate relative; the unmarried son or daughter of a U.S. citizen or permanent resident; or the spouse of a U.S. permanent resident.
Document Violations		
Persons without required current passports or visas.	No	Except certain limited circumstance waivers. Under new "summary removal" procedures, CBP may quickly exclude for five years persons who arrive without proper documents or make misrepresentations during the inspection process.

Summary of Grounds of Inadmissibility (continued)		
Ground of Inadmissibility	Waiver Available	Conditions of Waiver
Draft Evasion and Ineligibility for Citizenship		
Persons who are permanently ineligible for citizenship.	No	
Persons who are draft evaders, unless they were U.S. citizens at the time of evasion or desertion.	No	
Miscellaneous Grounds		
Practicing polygamists.	No	
Guardians accompanying excludable aliens.	No	
International child abductors. (The exclusion does not apply if the applicant is a national of a country that signed the Hague Convention on International Child Abduction.)	No	
Unlawful voters (voting in violation of any federal, state, or local law or regulation).	No	
Former U.S. citizens who renounced citizenship to avoid taxation.	No	

A. Particularly Troublesome Grounds of Inadmissibility

Below is a discussion of some of the grounds that create the most trouble for people planning to either immigrate or obtain nonimmigrant visas.

1. Likely to Become a Public Charge (Receive Government Assistance)

One of the leading reasons for green card denials is a finding that the im-migrant is "likely to become a public charge" (receive welfare or government assistance in the U.S.). In fact, the law requires almost all visa applicants, whether coming for a temporary or a permanent stay, to prove either that they will be self-supporting or that someone else will be responsible for supporting them.

To determine whether a person is likely to become a public charge, the government traditionally looks at the "totality of the circumstances," in other words, the whole picture. They may consider your age, health, family assets, resources, financial status, education, and skills. They may also require you to provide documentary proof of your ability to support yourself, or of other persons' promises to support you.

 A few immigrants need not worry about the public charge requirement. These include:

- refugees or political asylees
- people granted cancellation of removal
- Cubans or Nicaraguans applying for adjustment of status under the Nicaraguan Adjustment and Central American Relief Act of 1997 (NACARA)
- applicants for adjustment of status under the Haitian Refugee Immigration Fairness Act of 1998
- Cubans applying for adjustment under the Cuban Adjustment Act who were paroled as refugees before April 1, 1980
- Amerasian immigrants when they are first admitted to the U.S.
- "Lautenberg" parolees (certain Soviet and Indo-Chinese parolees applying for adjustment of status)
- registry applicants (people who've lived in the U.S. since before January 1, 1972), and
- special immigrant juveniles.

a. Support Requirement for Temporary, Nonimmigrant Visa Applicants

If you plan to come to the U.S. on a temporary visa, you must also plan how you'll prove you are going to support yourself. If you're coming on a work-based visa, this won't normally require any extra documentation or proof—your job will usually be presumed to be enough to support you. If, however, you're coming to the U.S. on some other type of visa, chances are you won't even be allowed to work here, in which case how you'll support yourself becomes a major issue.

For example, if you're hoping to get a tourist or a student visa, expect a major part of your application to involve proving that you have enough money—or can get it from someone else, such as a family member—to cover the costs of your entire U.S. stay.

Tourists (B-2 visa). A tourist will have to show that he or she knows how much this trip is going to cost—including hotel stays, rental cars, food, tickets, and other items—and has a way to pay for it. The more family members go with you, the more expensive the trip will be. But leaving family members at home may not be the answer. If you are the principal wage earner for your spouse and children and they are not traveling with you, you'll have to show that they will be provided for while you're away—particularly if you're planning a long trip. If it looks like your family will be going hungry while you're traveling, the official deciding your case may assume that there's more to your trip than meets the eye—perhaps that you are hoping to find employment in the United States.

Visitors for medical care (B-2 visa).
People who have arranged to come to
the United States for medical care—
usually specialized—are allowed to apply
for a visitor visa to do so. However,
showing that the care will be paid for
is particularly tricky, since U.S. medical
costs are extremely high. If a doctor has
agreed to see you at no cost, and you
can provide a letter proving this, that's
a good start. But if there's a chance that
the doctor will then refer you to a hospital for emergency treatment, your visa
may be denied, because the consulate
knows that the hospital would have to
treat you for free, thus putting a strain on
the U.S. health care system.

Students. If you're applying for a student visa, you must show that your education will be fully financed and all your
day-to-day living expenses (including the
expenses of your spouse or children if
they plan to come with you) will be paid
without your having to work in the United States. (And, if your family will not be
coming with you, and you normally support them, you may also be asked how
they'll be supported while you're gone.)
Although some students will be permitted to work during their student years,
you cannot rely on this work to prove
your visa eligibility. In fact, you probably
won't know until you get to the United
States what type of work you'll be able to
get. The permitted work will probably be
low-paying or a small part of your study
program. That means your financing will

need to come from your own resources
or from family, friends, or scholarships.

Fiancés. If you're planning to come to
the United States as the fiancé of a U.S.
citizen (on a K-1 or K-3 visa), you are
considered to be a nonimmigrant. (This
is despite the fact that you plan to apply
for a green card after arriving in the United States.) That's good news, because
it means that you probably won't be
asked to prove financial support in the
way someone applying for a green card
through the consulate would. Your U.S.
citizen fiancé will probably be asked to
fill out an affidavit of support, promising
to care for you financially and repay any
government assistance that you receive
(Form I-134). However, it's a short, fairly
simple form, much easier than a similar
one that your spouse will have to fill out
after you're married and applying for the
green card.

b. Support Requirement for Immigrant Visa and Green Card Applicants

If you plan to apply for a green card, the
U.S. immigration authorities will want
to see that you'll be taken care of financially for many years to come. If you're
immigrating based on employment, this
is fairly easy to prove, since you'll obviously have a job. However, if you're
immigrating through family, or through
employment where your own relatives
submitted the visa petition or own at
least 5% of the petitioning company, the

requirements get stiffer. Whichever family member signed your visa petition (to start your immigration process) will also need to submit a lengthy document called an Affidavit of Support on Form I-864.

Form I-864 is many pages long, and complicated—though fortunately, if you are the only person your petitioner is sponsoring, and your petitioner can meet the sponsorship requirements based upon his or her income alone, your petitioner can use a shorter version of the form, called I-864EZ. Note that Form I-864 is not required for most employment-based petitions or nonimmigrant visas, although

2007 Poverty Guidelines

2007 Poverty Guidelines*
Minimum Income Requirement for Use in Completing Form I-864.

For the 48 Contiguous States, the District of Columbia, Puerto Rico, the U.S. Virgin Islands and Guam:

Sponsor's Household Size	100% of Poverty Guidelines* For sponsors on active duty in the U.S. Armed Forces who are petitioning for their spouse or child.	125% of Poverty Line For all other sponsors
2	$13,690	$17,112
3	17,170	21,462
4	20,650	25,812
5	24,130	30,162
6	27,610	34,512
7	31,090	38,862
8	34,570	43,212
	Add $3,480 for each additional person.	Add $4,350 for each additional person.

Sponsor's Household Size	For Alaska: 100% of Poverty Line For sponsors on active duty in the U.S. Armed Forces who are petitioning for their spouse or child	125% of Poverty Line For all other sponsors	For Hawaii: 100% of Poverty Line For sponsors on active duty in the U.S. Armed Forces who are petitioning for their spouse or child	125% of Poverty Line For all other sponsors
2	$17,120	$21,400	$15,750	$19,687
3	21,470	26,837	19,750	24,687
4	25,820	32,275	23,750	29,687
5	30,170	37,712	27,750	34,687
6	34,520	43,150	31,750	39,687
7	38,870	48,587	35,750	44,687
8	43,220	54,025	39,750	49,687
	Add $4,350 for each additional person	Add $5,437 for each additional person.	Add $4,000 for each additional person.	Add $5,000 for each additional person.

* These poverty guidelines remain in effect for use with Form I-864, Affidavit of Support, from April 1, 2007 until new poverty guidelines go into effect in the spring of 2008.

some of these applicants may need to fill out a shorter, simpler Form I-134.

How much support is required? The Affidavit of Support on Form I-864 basically promises that your relatives will pay your living expenses so that you, the immigrant, do not have to rely on government assistance. Your sponsoring family member must show that he or she earns (or has assets worth) at least 125% of the income needed for his or her own family plus you, the immigrant (plus your spouse and children if they're immigrating with you). Just how much income is needed to support a certain size family is computed every year by the federal government and published in a document called the *Poverty Guidelines*. See, for example, the *2007 Poverty Guidelines*, above. You'll need to meet the guidelines for the year when your Affidavit of Support is filed—don't worry if the required income levels get raised later, it won't affect you.

What if the U.S. sponsor lives overseas, too? An additional problem for sponsors required to sign Form I-864 is that they must be domiciled (which usually means "live") in the United States or a U.S. territory or possession. That means that the sponsoring relative will have to return to the United States by the time Form I-864 is submitted (which usually happens some months before or at your consular interview, the last step in the immigration process). And, of course, if the sponsor is giving up a job overseas, he or she

will need to find a new job in the United States to replace the lost income.

There are, however, alternate ways of meeting the domicile requirement. As the U.S. State Department says on its website, "[m]any U.S. citizens and lawful permanent residents reside outside the United States on a temporary basis, usually for work or family considerations. 'Temporary' may cover an extended period of residence abroad. The sponsor living abroad must establish the following in order to be considered domiciled in the United States:

- He/she left the United States for a limited and not indefinite period of time,
- He/she intended to maintain a domicile in the United States, and
- He/she has evidence of continued ties to the United States."

For more information, see the State Department website at www.state.gov.

Who can avoid filling out Form I-864? Even among people who would ordinarily have to fill out a Form I-864, two exceptions apply. First, if the immigrating person has already worked *legally* in the U.S. for a total of 40 "quarters" (as defined by the Social Security Administration) or about ten years, no I-864 needs to be submitted on his or her behalf. In fact, in an interesting twist, immigrants can be credited with work done by their U.S. citizen spouse while they were married. So if your U.S. citizen spouse worked 40 quarters in the U.S. during your marriage, and he or she would be the one signing your Form I-864, the support obligation is taken care of, and your spouse need not even fill out the form—but should instead fill out Form I-864W, which explains why he or she falls within an exception. Of course, it's the rare married couple who will have gone this many years (approximately ten) without applying for a green card for the immigrant. Nevertheless, for those to whom this exception applies, it's highly useful.

The second major exception is that if the immigrant beneficiary is a child who will become a U.S. citizen immediately upon approval or entry to the U.S. for a green card (as discussed in Chapter 7), no I-864 needs to be submitted for the child, but an I-864W should be.

Others who don't need to fill out Form I-864, and should fill out an I-864W to prove it, include self-petitioning widows or widowers of U.S. citizens, and self-petitioning battered spouses or children (both explained in Chapter 7).

How long does Form I-864 bind the person who signs it? A family member who signs a Form I-864 is promising a long-term commitment. This Affidavit is legally enforceable by the government for any means-tested public benefits utilized by the sponsored immigrant. In other words, if the immigrant were to go on welfare, the government could make the family member who signed the Affidavit of Support pay the money back. The immigrant can also use the Affidavit

to demand support from his or her family member. The obligation does not end until the immigrant becomes a U.S. citizen, has earned 40 work quarters, dies, or permanently leaves the United States.

 A sponsor remains legally obligated even after a divorce. Yes, a divorced immigrant spouse could decide to sit on a couch all day and sue his or her former spouse for financial help. The sponsor may wish to have the immigrant sign a separate contract in advance agreeing not to do this, but it's not clear whether courts will enforce such a contract.

What if the family member helping you immigrate doesn't have enough money? The person who signs the immigrant's visa petition (to start the process) must file Form I-864 even if his or her income as shown on his or her tax returns doesn't meet the 125% of Poverty Guidelines level. If the immigrant can get a better job before submitting the Form I-864, then it's important to prove the resulting higher income using a combination of a letter from the employer (stating the sponsor's name, dates of employment, position and title, wages or salary, number of hours worked per week, prospects for long-term employment, marital status, dependents claimed, and emergency contact information) and copies of recent pay stubs, preferably up to six months' worth.

However, another person (a joint sponsor) who meets the 125% income

requirement for his or her own household plus the immigrant's may add that
income to the sponsor's if he or she is:

- willing to be jointly liable
- a U.S. legal permanent resident or
  citizen (they need not be family
  members)
- over 18 years old, and
- residing in the U.S.

The joint sponsor files a separate Form
I-864 Affidavit of Support. You can have
up to two joint sponsors per family, but
no more than one per immigrant.

In addition, other household members
may join their income to that of the main
sponsor to help reach the 125% level,
but only if they have been living with
the sponsor and they agree to be jointly
liable by filing Form I-864A (Contract Between Sponsor and Household Member).
And the immigrant him- or herself can
add income to the mix if already living
with the petitioner in the U.S. and working legally at a job that will continue after getting the green card.

Personal assets of the sponsor or
the immigrant or the sponsor's household members (such as property, bank
account deposits, and personal property
such as automobiles) may also be used
to supplement the sponsor's income. The
assets must be readily convertible to cash
within one year. If using assets owned
by the sponsor's household members or
the immigrant, those people must submit
a Form I-864A. The assets (minus any
debts or liens) will be counted at only

one-fifth their value for most immigrants.
That changes to one third their value
if the immigrant is the spouse of a U.S.
citizen or the child, over age 18, of a U.S.
citizen. And it changes to the full value
of the assets in orphan adoption cases.

You'll also need to attach proof of
these assets' ownership, location, and
value, such as bank statements or title
deeds.

**What else does Form I-864 require of
people who sign it?** Sponsors must notify
USCIS within 30 days of the sponsor's
change of address, using Form I-865.
Failure to do so is punishable by fines of
$250 to $5,000.

If you are a sponsor and have questions about meeting the eligibility requirements, or about the scope of your legal
responsibility (which may last ten or
more years or until the immigrant permanently leaves the country, dies, or naturalizes), consult an immigration attorney.

**How should the sponsor fill out Form
I-864?** You don't need to read this yet,
but come back to it after reading later
chapters describing your green card application procedures. Here are some tips
for the trickier questions on the form:

In **Part 1**, the main sponsor checks
box a if it's purely a family immigration
case. If the sponsor is an employer/fam-
ily petitioner, he or she must check box
b or c. Nice friends who agree to fill in
this form as joint sponsors check either
box d or e.

In **Part 3**, note that there's a place to list children. You don't need to name children who were born in the United States, because the sponsor has no obligation to support them (at least not under the immigration laws, though they will be counted elsewhere within this form to test the sponsor's overall financial capacity). The form also says "Do not include any relatives listed on a separate visa petition," which they would be, for example, if they're immediate relatives of the petitioner. The reasoning is that anyone with their own visa petition will also need their own Form I-864, filled out just for them, rather than a photocopy of their mother or father's form. (For example, if a U.S. citizen father petitions for his wife and stepchildren, they're all immediate relatives, will all need separate visa petitions, and therefore will all need separate Form I-864s. But if a lawful permanent resident father petitions for his wife and stepchildren, the children are allowed to accompany the mother on her visa petition without having visa petitions separately filed for each of them, and they therefore won't need separate Form I-864s prepared on their behalf.)

In **Part 4**, remember that the sponsor's place of residence must be in the United States in order to be eligible as a financial sponsor. If your sponsor is living overseas and doesn't want to return to the United States until you, the immigrant, can enter as well, your sponsor must still prepare and sign this Affidavit of Support. However, your sponsor will have no choice but to find a joint sponsor who lives in the United States and will submit an additional Affidavit.

Part 5, Sponsor's household size

This section is self-explanatory. Remember not to count anyone twice!

Part 6, Sponsor's income and employment

Question 22: The sponsor needs to fill in information about his or her employment here. Self-employment is fine. Be aware that if a self-employed sponsor has underreported income in the past, the earnings shown may not be sufficient to support you. In that case, the sponsor will need to file an amended tax return and pay a penalty before the newly reported income is accepted as meeting the guidelines for sponsorship.

Question 23: Here, the sponsor is supposed to enter the income shown on his or her most recent tax return. But what if the sponsor's income has risen since filing those taxes? In that case, the sponsor should enter the more recent income figure, but put an asterisk (an *) next to it. Then find some white space somewhere on the page and write "This figure reflects present earnings, not earnings shown on tax return; see supporting documentation." Then the sponsor should attach such documentation as an employer letter and pay stubs, as described earlier, to show current income.

Question 24: This question is important for sponsors whose income is not enough by itself, but who will be using the income of members of their household to help meet the *Poverty Guidelines* minimum requirements. First, every sponsor must state his or her own income. Then, if the sponsor wants other people's income counted, they must be mentioned in Question 24b. Unless any one of these household members is the actual immigrant, they must plan to complete a separate agreement with the sponsor, using Form I-864A. The total income from the sponsor and household members goes in Question 24c.

Part 7, Use of assets to supplement income

The sponsor needs to complete this section only if his or her income wasn't enough by itself to meet the *Poverty Guidelines* requirements. See the earlier instructions on how assets are counted, and remember to attach documents proving their existence.

If the combination of the sponsor's household available income and assets don't yet meet the *Poverty Guidelines* minimum, you'll still need to hand in this Affidavit. But you'll definitely want to look for a joint sponsor.

Part 8, Sponsor's Contract

Unlike earlier versions of the form, the sponsor's signature no longer needs to be witnessed by a notary public. Put that $15 to another use!

2. Having Committed Crimes or Security Violations

You're probably not a "criminal"—but you might be surprised at how a few or seemingly minor arrests or blotches on a person's record can ruin his or her chances of immigration. Criminal grounds are often the number one factor making temporary visa applicants inadmissible, but they affect many green card applicants, too.

Because this is such a large problem, do not be surprised or offended if, in working with an immigration attorney, the attorney asks you to have your fingerprints taken and checked against the U.S. Federal Bureau of Investigation files. The immigration authorities will eventually check the same files, so it's best to know in advance what they'll find.

Among the many crimes that make you inadmissible are:

- any crime of moral turpitude, such as theft (which could include passing a bad check), fraud, assault, murder, rape, arson, or drunk driving with a suspended license
- virtually any drug crime more serious than simple possession of less than 30 grams of marijuana
- prostitution or procuring a prostitute, or
- any combination of two criminal convictions that weren't part of the same scheme of criminal misconduct (for example, convictions for

shoplifting and resisting the subsequent arrest wouldn't make you inadmissible, but convictions for shoplifting one day and then stealing a car the next day would).

Kids under 18 get a break. If your case was handled in the juvenile courts, it won't result in a conviction, so you won't be inadmissible (unless you admit to a category of admissibility that doesn't require an actual conviction). Also, even if your case is handled in the adult court system, you may get help from what's called the "youthful offender exception." This exception says that a single crime of moral turpitude committed while under the age of 18 doesn't make you inadmissible if the crime itself and your release from prison occurred over five years before your immigration application. (See I.N.A. § 212(a)(2)(A)(ii)(I).)

If you've been convicted of a crime involving alcohol, you may have double trouble. Even if the crime itself doesn't make you inadmissible, USCIS can, and often does, argue that it's a sign that you have a physical or mental disorder associated with harmful behavior—in other words, that you're inadmissible on health, rather than criminal grounds. This is most often a problem for people with convictions for DUI or DWI (driving under the influence, or driving while intoxicated). Other crimes, such as assaults or domestic violence, where alcohol or drugs were contributing factors can lead to the same result.

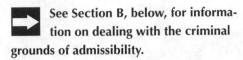 **See Section B, below, for information on dealing with the criminal grounds of admissibility.**

A related area of concern is whether you are considered a security risk, because you are affiliated with a terrorist or other such group. If you have any connection with any group that might conceivably be suspected of terrorism, hire a lawyer and look into this further. Under recent changes to the law within the U.S. Patriot Act, even fundraising for or supporting the humanitarian projects of a group that the U. S. government calls a terrorist organization can make you inadmissible. For more information and lists of attorneys specializing in this area, see the website of the National Immigration Project of the National Lawyers Guild at www.nationalimmigrationproject.org.

3. Having Spent Too Much Time in the U.S. Unlawfully

If you have ever lived in the United States unlawfully—perhaps because you crossed the border illegally or you stayed past the expiration date on your I-94 card—you must read this section. People become inadmissible if they've been "unlawfully present" in the U.S. for 180 days (about six months) after April 1, 1997, subsequently left the U.S., and then request admission by applying for an immigrant or nonimmigrant visa from overseas. This category of inadmissibility won't keep you out of the U.S. forever—but it will bar your reentry for a very long time. If you've spent between 180 days and 365 days (one year) in the U.S. unlawfully and then left, you won't be allowed to reenter for three years. The period becomes ten years if you were unlawfully present for one year or more.

If you're not in the U.S. now, but spent time in the U.S. unlawfully before you left, this could be a problem for you—though luckily, the longer you wait, the better, because you're already working off your three-year or ten-year bar on returning.

Even if you're in the U.S. now, however, this ground of inadmissibility may give you trouble—because you may have no choice but to leave the United States in order to finish the application for your green card. The only people who can stay in the United States to apply for the green card are those who are eligible to use a procedure called adjustment of status. Those few people have it lucky—by not leaving the United States, they can't be barred from reentering the United States. However, the adjustment of status procedure is mainly available to people who entered the U.S. legally and continued to maintain their legal status. If you entered illegally, or under the Visa Waiver Program, or are here in unlawful status, chances are you aren't eligible to adjust status; see Section 4, below, for details.

If you aren't eligible to adjust status, your only choice is to complete your green card application through a U.S. consulate in another country. The consulate will schedule an interview for you and review your file. But after your interview, the consulate will probably tell you that you can't return to the U.S. for a full three years or ten years. There is a waiver you can apply for, but it's hard to get, as discussed in Subsection b, below.

EXAMPLE: Soo-Yun came to the U.S. from South Korea on a student visa in 2002. After she finished her studies and her permitted stay expired (in 2005), she didn't go home. She worked as a freelance computer programmer for two years. Then she found an employer willing to give her a job and help her get a green card. Unfortunately, because she is not on a valid visa, and because of her unauthorized work, she cannot adjust status in the United States. Even more unfortunately, because of her two-year overstay, there is no point in her leaving to apply for the green card at a U.S. consulate overseas—they would simply tell her that because of her overstay, she must stay in Korea (or any other country outside the U.S.) for ten years before returning to the United States. Soo-Yun has no choice but to turn down the job.

Again, this bar does not apply to someone who stays in the U.S. to adjust status—so anyone eligible to adjust status should take advantage of this and not leave the U.S. until they get their green card. If you're not sure, consult an attorney.

a. When Your Stay May Be Lawful

If you have no choice but to apply for your green card overseas, through consular processing, it will become very important to calculate exactly how many of the days you spent in the U.S. were okay, and how many were unlawful. Any periods of your time in the United States will be considered lawful (or at least, not unlawful) for purposes of the three-year and ten-year bars if you were:

- under the age of 18
- in the U.S. prior to April 1, 1997 (only your time after that date, when the new law took effect, counts)
- in the U.S. only for short periods of time, less than three months each stay. Periods of unlawful presence are not counted in the aggregate for purposes of the three-year and ten-year bars—in other words, you have to be present for a block of time; USCIS will not add up 90 days during one stay and 90 days during another stay to find that you were unlawfully present for 180 days.
- a bona fide asylum applicant (including while your administrative or judicial review was pending), unless you were employed without authorization
- under Family Unity protection (a status that you would have applied for on Form I-817) based on being

a family member of a Special Agricultural Worker

- a battered spouse or child who can show a substantial connection between the status violation or unlawful entry and the abuse
- lawfully admitted to the United States but were waiting for a USCIS decision on a valid and timely filed application for a change or extension of status (as long as you did not work without authorization), but only up to a maximum of 120 days
- awaiting a USCIS decision on a properly filed application for adjustment of status
- admitted to the U.S. as a refugee
- granted asylum
- granted withholding of deportation/ removal
- granted Deferred Enforced Departure (DED)
- granted Temporary Protected Status (TPS)
- Cuban or Haitian and meet certain other criteria
- admitted for "duration of status" (D/S) (such as a student or exchange visitor)—however, you may have begun to accrue unlawful presence if either an immigration judge found you to have violated your status and become deportable (removable), or USCIS, in the course of reviewing an application, determined that you had violated your status

- on a valid visa—assuming you were admitted until a specified date, you will begin to accrue unlawful presence only when the date on the I-94 (or any extension) has passed, or USCIS or an immigration judge finds that you violated your status, whichever comes first.

A couple of other rules apply mainly to people who have been in removal (immigration court) proceedings:

- Where the unlawful presence determination is based on a USCIS or immigration judge finding of a status violation, the unlawful presence clock starts to run from the date determined to be when the status violation began.
- A grant of voluntary departure (V/D or V/R for voluntary return) constitutes a period of authorized stay. This includes the period between the date of the V/R order and the date by which the alien must depart. If you fail to depart by the date specified in the V/D order, the unlawful presence clock starts running.

However, there are many circumstances under which your stay is definitely unlawful. In some cases, you may be legally allowed to stay in the United States—for example, while waiting for a decision on your application for cancellation of removal or withholding of removal—but still be considered unlawfully present. People who were granted deferred action status are also considered unlawfully present. This is a complicated and evolving area of the law, so see a lawyer for a full analysis of your case.

b. Waiver of Three-Year or Ten-Year Bars

A waiver is available to an applicant who is the spouse, son, or daughter of a U.S. citizen or permanent resident, if the applicant can show that being kept out of the U.S. for three or ten years would cause the U.S. citizen extreme hardship. Note that hardship to the immigrant applicant doesn't count.

Extreme hardship usually means more hardship than is normally experienced by family separation; economic hardship is not usually sufficient to meet this requirement. These waivers are hard to get; and some U.S. consulates are more willing to grant them than others. See a lawyer for help.

4. Can You Get Around the Time Bars by Adjusting Status?

The rules concerning who is allowed to remain in the United States to adjust status (get a green card without having to leave for an interview at a consulate outside the U.S.) are complicated. If you entered the U.S. properly—by being inspected by a USCIS official—and maintained your nonimmigrant status (in particular, didn't let your visa expire or do anything unauthorized), you can get your green card without leaving the

United States. However, this doesn't work for people who entered the U.S. using a visa waiver (that is, who came from one of the countries that doesn't require an advance visa to visit the U.S., and didn't in fact apply for an actual tourist or other visa)—unless they will be adjusting status as the immediate relative of a U.S. citizen. (See I.N.A. § 245.1(b)(8), 8 U.S.C. § 212.)

Also, immigrants who marry U.S. citizens or are the parent or unmarried child, under age 21, of a U.S. citizen (referred to as immediate relatives) can adjust their status here even if they have fallen out of status or worked without authorization, as long as they did not enter without being properly inspected, or as a crewman or stowaway.

People who've been granted political asylum can also adjust status one year after their approval, under a separate provision of the law, without worrying about the usual bars on adjusting status. (See 8 C.F.R. § 209.2.)

Most everyone else, however, will be technically unable to adjust status. If, for example, you entered the United States without being inspected by a border guard or other official; under the Visa Waiver Program; or you have fallen out of lawful status or worked without authorization, you will not ordinarily be allowed to apply for your green card without leaving the United States first. (See I.N.A. § 245(c)(2).) A few rare exceptions exist, however, referred to as the penalty and grandfather clauses, described below.

a. The Penalty and Grandfather Clauses

If you are otherwise ineligible to apply get your green card by adjusting status in the U.S., your last hope might be the possibility that you were "grandfathered," or included within an old law (I.N.A. § 245(i)) that allowed people to pay a $1,000 penalty fee in order to adjust status. (The old § 245(i) law expired in the fall of 1997.)

Presently, the only people who may still adjust status by paying a penalty fee are those who either:

- had a visa petition or labor certification on file by January 14, 1998, or
- had a visa petition or labor certification on file by April 30, 2001, and can also prove that they were physically in the U.S. on December 21, 2000.

It doesn't matter who filed the visa petition or labor certification that you use as your ticket to adjust status. For example, if your U.S. citizen brother filed a visa petition on your behalf, but he died before you could get a green card, you are still allowed to use that petition as a basis to adjust status—even if you're now applying for your green card through an employer, a U.S. citizen spouse, or some other petitioner. The one catch is that the visa petition has to have been "approvable" when it was filed. In other words, if your best U.S.-citizen friend filed a visa petition on your behalf, that petition would not have been approvable, because no visa category exists allowing U.S. citizens to petition for other people based solely on friendship—so the petition wouldn't help you adjust status later.

Unmarried children younger than 17 years old and the spouses or unmarried children younger than 21 years old of legalized aliens who are qualified for and have applied for benefits under the Family Unity program can adjust status without paying the penalty fee.

 Don't believe the news reports that call § 245(i) an "amnesty." Every time Congress considers bringing back this useful law, the anti-immigrant forces rally people against it by claiming that it is an "amnesty" that will let in many illegal immigrants. In fact, § 245(i) doesn't give anyone a right to immigrate who didn't already have that right—it simply allows them to get around the three-year and ten-year time bars, by staying in the U.S. and adjusting status instead of leaving for a consulate.

b. Special Exception for Certain Employment-Based Green Card Applicants

If you are getting your green card through the first, second, or third preference employment category (as a priority worker, advanced degree professional, person of exceptional ability, skilled worker, professional, or other worker)

or as a special immigrant, you can have worked without authorization or fallen out of status for up to 180 days and still apply to adjust status.

This exception applies only if at the time of filing the green card application, your last entry to the U.S. was legal, you have maintained continuous legal status, and you have not violated the terms of your status or other terms of admission, other than during a 180-day aggregate period.

5. Having Entered Illegally More Than Once: The Permanent Bar

In addition to the three-year and ten-year bars described above, a separate and more serious provision punishes certain people who've entered the U.S. illegally. If illegal entrants spend a total of one year's unlawful time in the U.S. or are ordered deported by an immigration judge (even after spending less than one year in the U.S.), and they then leave and return or attempt to return to the United States illegally, they become permanently inadmissible. This so-called permanent bar is found at I.N.A. § 212(a)(9)(C), 8 U.S.C. § 1182(a)(9)(C).

Unlike the three-year and ten-year time bars, you can accumulate a year's unlawful time through various short stays—your unlawful time doesn't have to be continuous to count against you. Like the three-year and ten-year bars, however, no unlawful time before April 1, 1997 (the date the law took effect) counts.

> **EXAMPLE:** Sandra entered the U.S. illegally in 2000 and lived there until 2003, when she returned to Mexico. In 2004, she illegally crossed the border to the U.S., met a U.S. citizen with whom she fell in love, and got married in 2007. When she tried to apply for a green card based on her marriage, however, she was told that she was permanently barred from applying. The reason: She had entered illegally and spent more than a year in the U.S. illegally after April 1, 1997, then left and returned by entering illegally.

You can request a waiver if you're otherwise eligible for a green card, but only after a full ten years have passed since leaving the United States. In any case, see an attorney for a full analysis—especially if you live in one of the Western United States, where a case called *Acosta v. Gonzales* (439 F.3d 550 (9th Cir. 2006)) says that 245(i) eligible people who left the U.S. and returned illegally are not subject to the permanent bar.

6. Having Violated Immigration Laws or Used Fraud

Although you'll have to provide a lot of documents to back up any immigration application, at times the immigration officials will have to rely on your word alone. For that reason, it's very important to them that they be able to trust your word. If you have ever been caught lying to an immigration official, using fraud, or otherwise violating the immigration laws, you are inadmissible.

> **EXAMPLE:** Krystof's mother wins the visa lottery, and can apply for U.S. green cards for herself, her husband, and any unmarried children under the age of 21. Krystof, though age 20, has secretly married. The U.S. consulate finds out, and denies him the visa. Three years later, he himself wins the visa lottery. However, his past visa fraud makes him inadmissible to the United States.

A fraud waiver is available—but, if you're applying for a green card (as opposed to a nonimmigrant visa), the waiver is available only if you have a husband, wife, or parent who is a U.S. citizen or lawful permanent resident (green card holder). That person is your "qualifying relative." Also, you must establish that your qualifying relative would suffer "extreme hardship" if you were denied admission or forced to leave the United States. (History note: Prior to the enactment of the Immigration Reform Act of 1996, children could serve as qualifying relatives for parents who needed a waiver for having made misrepresentations or used false documents, but no longer.)

EXAMPLE: Graciela, a trained nurse, enters the U.S. on a tourist visa. One week later, she starts working caring for a disabled person in her home. Two months later, she finds a nursing home employer willing to sponsor her for a green card. However, because Graciela started working within 30 days of entry on a tourist visa, the law presumes that she misrepresented her intention in coming to the United States. What's more, Graciela has no qualifying relatives in the U.S., so she cannot apply for a fraud waiver.

A similar ground of inadmissibility applies to immigrants who were assessed a civil penalty for committing document fraud under Section 274C of the I.N.A (8 U.S.C. § 1324c). This is most likely to affect people who lived in the U.S. illegally and bought or sold fake green cards, Social Security cards, or other immigration-related documents. The penalty itself is usually a cease and desist order, sometimes with a money penalty of between $250 and $2,000. Document fraud means forging, counterfeiting, altering, or making any document to satisfy an immigration requirement; using, attempting to use, possessing, or receiving any such document; or using someone else's valid document.

Although a waiver is available for the document fraud ground of inadmissibility (for humanitarian purposes or to assure family unity), it's hard to get. For one thing, it's available only to applicants who have either already been approved for green cards and simply took a temporary trip out of the U.S. (and got stopped trying to come back into the country) or who are applying for family-based green cards and committed the fraud solely to assist, aid, or support their husband, wife, or child. But the waiver is completely unavailable if you were ordered to pay a civil fine for the document fraud. (See I.N.A. § 212(d)(12), 8 U.S.C. § 1182(d)(12).)

B. Avoiding or Reversing an Inadmissibility Finding

The U.S. immigration authorities may decide you are inadmissible any time after you have filed an application for a green card, nonimmigrant visa, or other immigration status. Typically, they won't notice the problem until you arrive for your visa or green card interview—at which time they'll often alert you to the issue, then give you more time to either prove that their suspicion that you are inadmissible is wrong, or to apply for a waiver.

Assuming your case is not denied outright, there are four ways to deal with the immigration authorities' possible denial of your application based on inadmissibility:

- In the case of physical or mental illness, you may be able to treat and cure the condition.

- You can prove that you really don't fall into the category of inadmissibility. For example, in the case of a criminal ground of inadmissibility, you may be able to go back to the criminal court and have the court set aside the criminal conviction.
- You can prove that the accusations of inadmissibility against you are a mistake and completely false.
- You can apply for a waiver of inadmissibility.

If, even after you have presented more evidence, you are found inadmissible, your application will be denied. Some people manage to hide their inadmissibility long enough to receive a green card or visa and be admitted into the United States—however, if the problem is ever discovered, for example when they apply for U.S. citizenship, they can be deported.

Other people become inadmissible after entering the United States but before becoming a U.S. citizen. If they leave the country for six months or more and try to come back, even though they have a green card, they can be stopped and denied entry.

> **EXAMPLE:** Maria, who is from Mexico, marries a U.S. citizen and successfully obtains a green card. Three years later however, the two of them divorce. Maria, who by now has one child, is unable to find a job that pays enough to cover child

care. Also, she has no medical insurance. When her daughter becomes ill with leukemia, she drives to Mexico where she can afford to see a doctor. They stay for seven months. Upon return, however, the border officials discover the situation and deny Maria entry on grounds that she is likely to become a public charge (receive government assistance) and is therefore admissible.

1. Curing the Condition That Makes You Inadmissible

If you have had a physical or mental illness that is a ground of inadmissibility and you have been cured of the condition by the time you submit your green card application, you will no longer be considered inadmissible. Unfortunately, however, some of the physical conditions that make you admissible are not curable, such as HIV. If the condition is not cured by the time you apply, you may still be given more time to seek a cure, or you may apply for a waiver of inadmissibility.

2. Proving That You're Not Really Inadmissible

Proving that you're not really inadmissible is mainly useful for overcoming criminal and ideological grounds of inadmissibility. Both the type of crime committed and the nature of the punishment must be examined to see whether your criminal activity really constitutes a ground of inadmissibility. For example, with some crimes, only actual convictions are grounds of inadmissibility. If you have been charged with a crime and the charges were then dropped, or if the case is still on appeal, you can argue that you weren't in fact convicted. Sometimes a conviction can be "vacated" if you can show it was unlawfully obtained—in essence, that you were wrongly convicted. On the other hand, a crime that has been expunged or erased from your record (which some states allow if you, for example, successfully complete your probation and other requirements), still counts for immigration purposes.

Another example involves crimes of moral turpitude. Crimes of moral turpitude are those showing dishonesty or immoral conduct. There is no set list of which crimes involve moral turpitude, particularly because it partly depends on the precise wording of each U.S. state's criminal laws. However, crimes where the person intended to commit theft, fraud, great bodily harm, or lewd acts, or the person acted with recklessness or malice, are usually considered to fit the moral turpitude description. Committing acts that amount to a crime of moral turpitude can be a ground of inadmissibility, even if you weren't actually arrested or convicted.

EXAMPLE: During her green card interview, Sonya is asked why she no longer has her I-94 card. She explains that, after an argument with her husband about him spending all his time fixing up his old Chevy, she left the house and angrily lit a match to the garage, which ended up burning the whole house down. Sonya has now basically confessed to arson, which is a crime of moral turpitude. She can be denied the green card on this basis.

Crimes with no element of moral turpitude, however, are often not considered grounds of inadmissibility.

Still other factors that may help you are the length (hopefully short) of any prison terms, how long ago the crime was committed, the number of convictions in your background, conditions of plea bargaining, and available pardons.

 As you can see, proving that a criminal ground of inadmissibility does not apply in your case is a complicated business. You need to have a firm grasp not only of immigration law, but the technicalities of criminal law as well. If you have a criminal problem in your past, you may be able to get a green card, but not without the help of an experienced immigration lawyer.

3. Proving That a Finding of Inadmissibility Is Factually Incorrect

You can also try to prove that the suggestion that you are inadmissible is just plain wrong. For example, if a USCIS medical examination shows that you have certain medical problems, you can present reports from other doctors stating that the first diagnosis was wrong and that you are free of the problem condition. Or, if you are accused of lying on a visa application, you can present evidence proving that you told the truth, or that your false statements were made unintentionally.

4. Applying for a Waiver

If you have no choice but to admit that the ground of inadmissibility applies to you, there's one last hope in some cases: applying for a waiver. In obtaining a waiver, you don't try to get rid of or disprove the ground of inadmissibility. Instead you ask the immigration authorities to overlook the problem and give you a green card or visa anyway. Not all grounds of inadmissibility can be waived, however. For example, people who have abused, trafficked in, or been addicted to drugs have no opportunity to apply for a waiver.

When the contents of your application clearly show that you're inadmissible, and a waiver is generally available for that ground of inadmissibility, you may submit an application for a waiver at the same time you submit the rest of your application.

In most cases, however, the issue won't come up until your final visa interview at a USCIS office or consulate. You will then be given additional time to file your waiver request. Unfortunately, having to file for a waiver at that point will slow down the process greatly—waivers can take many months to process. In many cases, the person reviewing your case does not make the final decision—it is sent to a supervisor, or even to another office. For example, if you file your waiver application with a U.S. consulate abroad, you will have to wait for the consulate to send your application to a USCIS office. The consulate cannot approve the waiver on its own.

Waiver applications are made on Form I-601 and must include a filing fee ($545 at the time this book was published). The form and fee are just the beginning of the waiver application process, however. For USCIS to evaluate your case, it will also need to see convincing evidence that you deserve the waiver. For example, in cases where your waiver eligibility depends on having a qualifying relative, you'd need to include a birth or marriage certificate showing that you are truly related to that person, as well as proof that your relative is a U.S. citizen or permanent resident. If the waiver requires that you show hardship to the U.S. citizen or permanent resident if you aren't allowed to immigrate to the U.S., you'd need to provide reports from doctors, psychiatrists, or others who can testify how important you are to that person (simply being emotionally close or in love is usually not enough). In a medical waiver, you'd normally need to prove that your health costs will be covered and that the nature of your condition and your personal behavior make it unlikely that you'll pass the disease to others.

Once again, many technical factors control whether or not your application for a waiver of inadmissibility is granted. You stand the best chance of success by hiring a good immigration lawyer. A good lawyer may have some creative strategies to help you. For example, a lawyer may be able to bring you to the United States on a temporary, nonimmigrant visa (for which it's easier to obtain a waiver), giving you more time to deal with the ground of inadmissibility before applying for a green card. ■

Chapter 4

Dealing With Paperwork, Government Officials, Delays, and Denials

Remember the application bog that we discussed early in the book? No matter what type of visa or green card you apply for, your application process will involve a lot of paperwork—forms that you fill out, birth certificates and other documents that you collect, filing fees, and more. Then you'll have to wait while your carefully prepared application gets shuffled along with hundreds of thousands of others through a maze of government offices. You'll also need to meet in person with government officials. In order to prevent any or all of your work—and your hopes—from getting mishandled, misunderstood, or lost, you're going to have to:

- set up a system for organizing your personal paperwork (see Section A, below)
- make sure that all your forms and documents are of a type that USCIS and the consulates will accept (see Section B, below)
- locate and translate some of the documents that you'll need to support your application (see Section C, below)
- protect your application before you mail it from being lost by the U.S. government (see Section D, below)
- track your application's progress and write letters or perform other follow-up in case of delays (see Section E, below)
- prepare to present yourself and your case to a government official

(see Section F, below, regarding consular interviews, Section G regarding USCIS interviews in the U.S., and Section H on how to handle interviews that go badly)

- know your options when an application is denied (see Section I, below), and
- know how to contact a U.S. congressperson for help (see Section J, below).

A. Getting Organized

Start by setting up a good system to keep track of all the forms and documents that you'll need during this application process. There is no feeling worse than being in front of an impatient government official while you desperately go through piles of stuff looking for that one vital slip of paper. And sometimes when the government loses your file, you'll be asked to provide copies of what you originally sent it. If you're working with an attorney, he or she will hopefully keep good files on your case, but you should ask for copies of everything, and carefully keep these yourself as well.

We suggest using manila file folders and putting them in a box or drawer (or use a series of large envelopes or an accordion file). Label one folder or envelope Original Documents, for things like your birth certificate, marriage certificate, and USCIS or consular approval notices. Keep this file in a very safe place (such as a safe deposit box at your local bank). Be sure to remember to retrieve your originals in time to take them to your interview.

Label the other files or envelopes according to which sets of forms or documents they contain. If you're applying for a green card within the United States, for example, you might label one folder Visa Petition; another Adjustment of Status Packet; another Interview Materials (containing copies of the documents you'll want to take to your interview); and another Old Drafts/Copies. Similarly, if you're applying from a country outside of the U.S., one folder might be labeled Visa Petition, another Mailed to Consulate, another Affidavit of Support and Financial Documents, another Interview Materials, and the rest as described above.

You should also keep a separate file for correspondence from USCIS or the consulate. Include in this file your handwritten notes on any phone conversations you've had with USCIS or consular personnel. Don't forget to write the date on your notes, so you can refer to them later in further correspondence.

When you've finished filling a folder or envelope, take out some of the old drafts or items you've decided not to use and move them to the Old Drafts/Copies folder, so as not to clutter up the materials you'll take to your interview. Carefully write "final copy, mailed xx/xx/20xx" (you fill in the date) on the top of the

copy of the application or petition you've mailed to USCIS or the consulate.

B. How to Obtain and Prepare Immigration Application Forms

The first step in virtually every immigration application process is to fill out a government form. We haven't included copies of these forms in this book, because the government revises them frequently and you'll want to make sure you have the latest version. The forms are easy to obtain on your own, and some of them will be sent to you automatically once the process is underway.

1. Where to Get the Forms You'll Need

The forms you'll need will come from up to three sources:

- **USCIS**, which produces the forms for any application being sent to a USCIS service center, district office, or other U.S.-based office
- the **U.S. State Department**, which produces the forms for any application being handled by a U.S. consulate in another country, or
- the **U.S. Department of Labor**, which produces the forms for certain parts of the application for an employment-based visa or green card.

How Nightmarish Can It Get?

Maybe you'll turn in your application and everything will go like clockwork: USCIS and consular files all in order, approval received on time. Educating yourself about the process and preparing everything carefully certainly improves your chances. But we wouldn't be doing our job if we didn't warn you about how the government bureaucracy can chew up and spit out even the best-prepared application.

Every immigration lawyer has his or her favorite horror stories. For instance, there was the client whose visa petitions were lost by USCIS—so after many months, the lawyer filed new petitions and cancelled the checks that went with the lost ones. But USCIS then found, and tried to cash, the "lost" checks—and to collect the bank charges from the client when the checks bounced.

Then there was the woman who waited over six months for USCIS to approve her work permit—only to have it finally send her a work permit with someone else's name and photo. By the time that finally got straightened out, the work permit had expired and USCIS forced her to apply, and pay again, for a new one.

And let's not forget the woman who nearly got stuck outside the United States because USCIS refused to renew her Refugee Travel Document on the nonsensical grounds that she hadn't provided a valid address in the application. (She had, and it was the same address that USCIS had been using to correspond with her for years.)

What can you do about such absurd and Orwellian horrors? Mostly, just know in advance that they may happen to you, leave time to deal with them, and keep copies of everything.

The government, your immigration lawyer, and others will refer to forms not by their name or title, but by the tiny numbers in the lower-left or upper right-corner. For example, if you apply for a family-based green card, you'll start the process with a form entitled Petition for Alien Relative—usually called an I-130, which number you'll see at the bottom of the form.

USCIS forms are recognizable because they usually start with the letter "I" (such as in Form I-129 or I-130). Most USCIS forms can be downloaded from its website, at www.uscis.gov. (Click "Immigration Forms" and scroll down until you find the form number.) If you prefer not to deal with a computer, call 800-870-3676, and USCIS will mail you the forms.

It usually takes a few weeks for the mailed forms to arrive. You can also pick up forms at a USCIS district office—however, many offices require you to make appointments before you go.

Visiting USCIS Offices

You may, at some point, wish to visit USCIS in person, whether to ask something about it's handling of your case or to pick up a form (but never to ask legal advice!). However, because of the long lines to get in, the agency now requires visitors to most offices to make appointments online, before they arrive. The system is called "InfoPass," and it's accessible at www. uscis.gov (click the InfoPass link on the left side of the page). You'll be asked to enter information and can request an appointment date. Look for a computer with a printer—you'll need a printout of your appointment notice when you go. Also, be sure to bring photo identification and any paperwork associated with your immigration case to your appointment. You can use this same website to cancel your appointment, if necessary.

State Department forms usually start with the letters "DS." Most State Department forms are best obtained directly from the particular consulate handling your application. Once you've begun your immigration application process, the forms will be mailed to you without your asking. However, if you're just beginning an application involving the consulate, or need an extra copy of a form, go to your consulate's website via www.usembassy. state.gov—many consulates put their forms online. If you can't find it on your consulate's website, check the State Department's website at www.travel.state.gov/visa and click on "Forms" in the left column.

Department of Labor forms usually start with the letters "ETA." They can be downloaded from its website at www. doleta.gov. (Click the "Workforce Professionals" tab, then click "Hiring Guest Workers," then follow the links for the type of application you're interested in.)

When you print forms from a government website, you'll see that some of them print out many copies of the same page. This isn't a mistake. You're getting multiple copies because you're supposed to submit the page in triplicate, quadruplicate, or another number. (In other words, the government wants to receive multiple, but identical, copies.) It may be easier for you to complete only one set, then use a photocopy machine to make the required number of copies and attach them to the original.

2. Making Sure You're Using the Most Recent Form

Besides the form number, the upper-right or lower-left corner usually tells you the date the form was issued. That's an important date, because once the government issues a later version (which they're doing a lot of these days), you'll usually need to use the later one. For every form you plan to submit (except for ones that were sent to you by a consulate you're dealing with), you should check the appropriate website just before actually mailing it. Sometimes the website will tell you a date upon which the government will stop accepting the old version of the form.

After you have submitted the form, you can stop worrying—you won't need to redo it even if the government issues a new form before your application has been decided.

3. Reading the Instructions That Come With the Forms

Most immigration-related forms come with an extensive set of instructions. It's worth reading these closely. However, realize that immigration laws and procedures change quickly, while revisions of the form instructions tend to lag behind. If you see contradictory information on the government's website or a later news item, that's usually the information you should act upon.

Save yourself a little postage and don't send the instruction pages back when the time comes to submit your application. The immigration authorities want only the part of the form you fill in.

4. Paying the Appropriate Filing Fees

Many of the immigration forms require you to pay a fee in order to file them. (No, you can't get your money back if your case is not approved.) Don't go by the fees listed on the form instructions; they're often out of date. And even the forms in this book may be out of date by the time you read this. Current USCIS fees are displayed on the "Immigration Forms" portion of its website at www.uscis.gov. (USCIS fees are based on which forms you submit, so you'll need to add up the fees yourself if you submit a combination of forms.) Alternately, you can call the USCIS information line at 800-375-5283.

The consulate will tell you the latest fees for visa processing, usually in the written instructions that it will mail to you.

You must pay the fees by personal check or money order, made out to the Department of Homeland Security. Don't send cash through the mail!

For some applications, you may find yourself submitting more than one petition or application at the same time. For example, in a marriage case where your spouse is here in the U.S., you can file Form I-130 and Form I-485 simultaneously. Or, you may file applications for your spouse and your stepchild in the same envelope. In any of these situations, resist the temptation to combine all the filing fees into a single check.

If you submit separate, individual checks for each filing fee, then if you make a mistake on the check (for example, you forget to sign it, or you make it for the wrong amount), USCIS will reject only the filing that is affected by that check. But if you submit a single check covering all fees, you will ruin all of the filings at once if you make a mistake. It's a pain to have to write more than one check for forms and applications being submitted in the same package, but most of the time it's worth it.

5. Using a Typewriter or Ink?

An increasing number of immigration forms can be filled out online—though it's not always convenient, since you can't save your work and come back to it. If you prefer to do the forms by hand, this isn't the time to express your individuality with purple ink. Fill in all immigration forms using a typewriter, if you can find one in this age of computers. If you must prepare the forms by hand, use black ink.

6. Inapplicable Questions

If a question on a form just doesn't fit your situation, write "N/A" (not applicable) rather than leaving the space blank. Or, if the answer is "none," as in "number of children," answer "none." Try not to mix these two up—it irritates the government officials reading your application. But if you're not sure how or whether to answer a question, seek skilled legal help. (Chapter 6 gives you information on finding a good lawyer.)

7. Telling the Truth

There will be many temptations to lie in this process—to hide a ground of inadmissibility, ignore a previous marriage, or avoid questions about previous visits to the United States, for example. But lying to the government can get you in bigger trouble than the problem you are lying about. And you've never seen anyone angrier than a government official who discovers that you've lied to him or her.

If you feel you just can't complete the form without hiding a certain piece of information—or you really don't know how to answer or explain a key question—see a lawyer. The lawyer may be able to show you how to be truthful in a way that doesn't risk having your application denied.

 What if you're asked for an address and you're living in the U.S. illegally? One piece of information that frequently causes concern to immigrants living illegally in the United States is their address. Many of them wonder whether they shouldn't use a friend's address as a "mailing address." However, this could be interpreted as lying on an immigration form, which could disqualify your application by itself. You are expected to supply your actual address. Fortunately, USCIS has, so far, shown very little interest in using these addresses to track down people living here illegally. (However, we can't guarantee that this will continue in the future.)

8. What's Your Name?

The easiest thing on a form should be filling out your name, right? Not in this bureaucratic morass. The immigration authorities will want not only your current name, but on certain of its forms, "other names used." Here are some important things to get straight before you start writing your name(s) in the forms to follow:

- **Current name.** When your current name is requested, it is best to insert the name you currently use for legal purposes. This will normally be the name on your bank account, driver's license, and passport. If you've always gone by a nickname (for example, your name is Richard but you always use the common nickname "Dick"), it's okay to fill in the application as "Dick," as long as you list "Richard" where the form asks for other names used. This will avoid confusion when someone compares your application form with the accompanying documents (your employer, for example, might write a letter on your behalf saying "Dick worked here . . ."). But there's no way to avoid a little confusion, since your birth certificate will still say Richard.

- **Legal name changes.** If you've actually done a court-ordered legal name change, include a copy of the court order, to help dispel some

of the inevitable confusion. If you have changed your name without a court order (by simply beginning to use a different name and using it consistently, which is legal in many states) and you use your changed name for all legal purposes, list it as your current name.

- **Married name.** If you've just married and changed your last name as part of your marriage, use your married name. But women shouldn't feel pressured into taking on a married name. By now the U.S. immigration authorities are well aware that not all women change their names when they marry. Nor does having different last names seem to cause any confusion in the processing of your application (after all, the government tends to think of you as a number, not a name).

- **Other names used.** The category for "other names used" could include nicknames. The immigration authorities will want to know about nicknames that might have made their way onto your various legal documents (or criminal record). You should also include names by which you have been commonly known, especially as an adult.

- **Previous married names.** If you have been married previously, and used a married name then, don't forget to list that name in the boxes requesting other names used.

9. Being Consistent

You will more than likely be filling out many forms in connection with your immigration application—and many of them ask for exactly the same pieces of information. If you're not consistent in filling these out, you may cause confusion. At worst, not getting your facts straight can cause the person reviewing your application to think you cannot be believed. If, for example, you live with your parents but sometimes stay with a friend and receive mail there, make up your mind which address to use and then stick to it.

C. How to Obtain Needed Documents

You would be lucky if forms were the only paperwork you had to worry about—but no, there are documents, too. For example, you often need your birth and marriage certificates to complete your visa or green card application. You may also need other documents, such as school transcripts, employment records, death or divorce certificates, or the birth certificate or U.S. passport of a U.S. citizen relative who is petitioning for you to immigrate.

When it's time for your visa or green card approval, you will need a passport from your own country (either to travel to the United States or to hold a stamp showing your residence status).

Within the United States, official copies of birth, death, marriage, and divorce certificates can usually be obtained from the vital records office (called the registrar's or recorder's office in some areas) of the appropriate county or locality. Even if you already have your own copy of these items, it's a good idea to request a copy from the vital records office. That's because your copy may not have been given all the official governmental stamps necessary for the immigration authorities to accept it as authentic. You can find more details on the National Center for Health Statistics website at www.cdc.gov/nchs. (Look under the "Top 10 Links" heading, and click "Help obtaining birth, death, marriage, or divorce certificates.") Or, check the blue pages of a U.S. phone book. There are also services that will order your vital records for a small fee, such as www.vitalchek.com.

U.S. passports are available to U.S. citizens through the State Department; see www.state.gov (under "Travel & Business," see "Passports (U.S. Citizens)") or the federal government pages of a U.S. phone book.

Outside of the United States, records should be obtained from official, government sources wherever possible. The sources that USCIS and the State Department consider acceptable are listed in the State Department's *Foreign Affairs Manual* (FAM), the contents of which are accessible at http://travel.state.gov/visa/

reciprocity/index.htm (use the alphabet at the top of the page to click on the letter which your country starts with, then scroll down to where it describes the acceptable documents). U.S. law libraries may also be able to locate copies of the FAM for you.

In the FAM, you can discover such fun (and relevant) facts as that the Ascension Islands don't grant divorce certificates because of the lack of a supreme court, and that the place to obtain vital documents in Lithuania is called the Marriage Palace. If you are outside of the U.S. and do not have Web access, talk to your local U.S. consulate about what form of record will be acceptable, particularly if you need to document an event for which your government does not issue certificates.

1. Translating Non-English Documents

If the documents you are submitting are in a language other than English, you will need to submit both a copy of the original document and a certified, word-for-word translation (summaries are not acceptable). This is particularly true if you're submitting the document to a USCIS office; consulates can often deal with documents that are in the language of that country (their instructions will usually tell you if they can't).

There is no need to spend big bucks to obtain certified translations. Any trustworthy friend who is fluent in English

and the language of the document and is not your close relative can do the certified translation. That person should simply type out the translated text, then add at the bottom:

I certify that I am competent to translate from [the language of the document] *to English and that the above* [identify the document and to whom it pertains] *is a correct and true translation to the best of my knowledge and belief.*

Signed: ___[translator's full name]___

Address: _____

Telephone: _____

Date: _____

If you prefer, you can hire a professional translator, who should also add the same certification at the bottom of the translation.

2. Substituting for Unavailable Documents

If you cannot obtain a needed document, the immigration authorities may, under some circumstances, accept another type of evidence. For example, if your birth certificate was destroyed in a fire, you may be able to use school records or sworn statements by people who knew you to prove your date of birth.

The instructions included with various government forms usually outline the other types of evidence that will be accepted. If you substitute a new type of evidence for a missing document, you should also include a statement from the local civil authorities explaining why the original document is unavailable.

3. Creating Substitute Documents

One form of substitute document that you may need to use is a sworn declaration. For example, you might need to ask a friend or family member to prepare one affirming your date and place of birth. If so, emphasize to the person that fancy legal language is not as important as detailed facts when it comes to convincing an immigration official to accept his or her word in place of an official document.

Someone could write, for example, "I swear that Francois was born in Paris in 1962 to Mr. and Mrs. Marti." But it would be much more compelling for them to write, "I swear that I am Francois's older brother. I remember the morning that my mother brought him home from the hospital in 1962 (I was then five years old), and we grew up together in our parents' home (Mr. and Mrs. Xavier Marti) in Paris."

The full declaration should be longer and contain more details than this example. The more details that are offered, the more likely USCIS or the consulate is to accept the declaration as the truth.

To start the declaration, the person should state his or her complete name and address, as well as country of citizenship. At the bottom of the declaration, the person should write:

> *I swear, under penalty of perjury, that the foregoing is true and correct to the best of my knowledge.*
>
> *Signed: _____*
> *Date: _____*

If preparing sworn declarations seems like too much to accomplish, you could hire a lawyer for this task only. Below is a sample of a full sworn declaration, written to prove that an immigrant who is applying through marriage is no longer married to his first wife, due to her death. (Remember, when writing your own declaration, tailor it to your situation—don't follow the wording of the sample too closely—except for the sworn statement part, which should be verbatim.)

Declaration in Support of Application of Guofeng Zheng

I, Shaoling Liu, hereby say and declare as follows:

1. *I am a U.S. permanent resident, residing at 222 Rhododendron Drive, Seattle, WA 98111. My telephone number is 206-555-1212. I have been living in the United States since January 2, 1997.*

2. *I am originally from Mainland China, where I grew up in the same town (called Dahuo, in Suzhou province) as Guofeng Zheng.*

3. *I knew Guofeng's first wife, Meihua. I attended their wedding, and had dinner at their home several times. I also remember when Meihua fell ill with cancer. She was sick for many months before passing away on October 31, 1996.*

4. *I received the news of Meihua's death a few days later, in early November of 1996. I knew the doctor who had treated her, and he was very sad that his treatments had failed. I also attended Meihua's funeral on November 7th. Her ashes are buried in the local cemetery.*

5. *I am also aware that the municipal records office, where all deaths are recorded, burnt down in the year 2000. I myself had difficulty with this, when I tried to get a copy of my mother's birth certificate last year.*

I swear, under penalty of perjury, that the foregoing is true and correct to the best of my knowledge.

Signed: *Shaoling Liu*

Date: *August 4, 2007*

Don't Confuse a Declaration With an Affidavit

An affidavit is very similar to a declaration—it's a written statement that the author dates and signs—but it has one additional feature. Affidavits are notarized, which means that they are signed in front of someone who is authorized by the government to attest to, or certify, the authenticity of signatures. When you bring an affidavit to a notary, that person will ask for identification, such as your passport or driver's license, to make sure that you are the person whose signature is called for on the affidavit. You sign the affidavit in the presence of the notary, who makes a note of this in his or her notary book. The notary also places a stamp, or seal, on your document.

As you can see, affidavits are more formal and more trouble than simple declarations. An affidavit is not required for substitute documents such as we're describing now—but if you want to make the document look more official, and know where to find a notary, you might want to take the extra trouble. If an immigration process described in this book requires an affidavit, we'll alert you.

Need a Copy of USCIS's Files on Your Case?

If you've submitted past applications to USCIS, and either lost your copies or want to see whether they added any notes to the paperwork, you can ask for a copy of your file. The procedure for doing this is to file what's called a Freedom of Information Act or FOIA request. There is no fee, and the first 100 pages of copies are free.

To file your request, fill out Form G-639 (available on the USCIS website) and submit it to the central office listed on the form. Unfortunately, because these requests are now processed centrally (unlike in past years), you'll probably wait several weeks at least for a reply.

D. Before You Mail an Application

Most applications must be mailed to USCIS, a consulate, or other office, rather than delivered in person. There are three important rules to follow when mailing:

- Make copies.
- Mail your applications by a traceable method.
- Don't mail anything that you can't replace.

We'll explain the reasons for these maxims—and how to follow them.

1. Make Complete Copies

When you've at last finished filling out a packet of required immigration forms, your first instinct will be to seal them in an envelope, pop them in the mail, and forget about them for awhile. That could waste all of your hard work.

Find a photocopy machine and make copies of every page of every application, as well as any photos, documents, checks, and money orders. Carefully keep these in your records. This will help you recreate these pages and items if they're lost in the mail or in the overstuffed files of some government office. It may also help convince USCIS or the consulate to take another look for the lost items.

2. Mail by a Traceable Method

In any government agency, things get lost. The sorting of newly arrived applications seems to be a common time for them to disappear. If this happens to your application, it can become important to prove that you mailed it in the first place.

In the United States, it's best to go to the post office and use certified mail with a return receipt for all your applications or correspondence with USCIS or the consulates. When you request a return receipt, you will prepare a little postcard that is attached to your envelope and will be signed by the person at USCIS or the consulate who physically receives your envelope. The postcard will be mailed to you, and will be your proof that the envelope was received. You can use this postcard to convince USCIS or the consulate to look for the application if it gets misplaced.

If you're mailing something from outside of the U.S., you'll have to find the most reliable method, such as a courier service. However, courier services can't deliver to a post office box, and many USCIS addresses (in particular those of the service centers) are at post office boxes. You'll have to use regular mail if mailing to a P.O. box. Some service centers provide alternate addresses for delivery by courier.

3. If You Want It Back, Don't Send It

Many immigration applications require that certain documents be attached (paper-clipping them to the form is fine). Some documents must be included in packets of forms you must file and others must be brought to interviews. Whatever you do, *don't send originals* to USCIS or the consulate.

Instead, simply photocopy any document (as long as the original is the official version), and send the copy to USCIS or the consulate. The USCIS or consular officer will have a chance to view the originals when you bring them to your interview. (Of course, if they make a special request that you mail them the original, you'll want to comply—but make copies for yourself first!) It's best to add the following text, right on the front of the copy, if there's room:

> *Copies of documents submitted are exact photocopies of unaltered original documents, and I understand that I may be required to submit original documents to an immigration or consular official at a later date.*
>
> *Signature: _____*
>
> *Typed or printed name: _____*
>
> *Date: _____*

Always make photocopies for US-CIS on one-sided, 8½-by-11-inch paper. Some applicants have been known to try to create exact copies of things by cutting the image out of the full page of paper—creating, for example, a tiny photocopied green card. The government doesn't appreciate these minicopies.

By the same token, 8½-by-14-inch paper (or larger) doesn't fit well into the government's files—use a photocopy machine that will reduce your document image to 8½-by-11 inches, if possible.

4. Some Applications Can Be Filed Online ("e-Filing")

USCIS recently started an e-filing program for some (but not all) petitions and applications. USCIS says that the benefits of e-filing include your being able to file petitions and applications from anywhere

with an Internet connection, pay your fees with a credit card or directly through your checking or savings account, and get immediate confirmation that your application has been received by USCIS.

However, the program is still somewhat cumbersome—for example, you must still mail photocopies of documents such as birth certificates and passports. USCIS promises that the program will improve over time. If you're a procrastinator, or you worry about whether every "i" has been dotted and "t" crossed in your paperwork, you might especially appreciate the "instant confirmation" feature of e-filing. More information about e-filing is available at www.uscis.gov (click "Immigration Forms," then "Electronic Filing").

E. Dealing With Delays

In view of the number of people applying for visas and green cards, it's almost guaranteed that your application will spend some months, or even years in processing limbo. Even the relatively short eight months that most USCIS service centers were taking to decide on initial petitions for employment-based green cards can also seem like a long time if you're the one waiting. Although you can't prevent delays, you can anticipate them and be ready to deal with them when the time comes.

⚠️ **Don't even think of bribing a U.S. government official.** Although there are countries where the only way to get anything from a government official is to offer cash or other gifts, the United States is not one of them. Personnel at USCIS and the consulates may sometimes be difficult, but it's generally not because they're expecting money. In fact, most of them are proud of the fact that the United States operates strictly according to the rule of law. Offering a bribe will most likely hurt your chances of getting a green card or visa.

1. Asking Questions by Mail

If your application drags on too long or some other problem arises, write courteous, clear letters asking for action, as shown in the example below. All correspondence should include any processing number assigned to you by the office with which you're corresponding and your A-number, if you've already been assigned one. (Your A-number is the letter A—for Alien—followed by eight digits.)

If you're dealing with a USCIS service center, your receipt notice will show your processing number—something like "CSC 07 202 50007." You'll recognize it because it starts with a three-letter abbreviation—the main ones are CSC, LIN, EAC, SRC, or TSC. These abbreviations refer to the service center handling your application: California uses CSC (formerly WAC), Nebraska uses LIN, Vermont uses EAC,

and Texas uses SRC or TSC. The 07 represents the fiscal year (October 1, 2006 through September 30, 2007) in which the case was received. The 202 refers to the computer workday on which the fee was collected. The 50007 represents your particular case number.

If you haven't been assigned any processing number, or haven't even gotten a receipt notice, include copies of previous correspondence and/or certified mail receipts when you write your inquiry letters.

Keep your letters clear and to the point. The people at the other end don't want to read long passages about how you've been checking your mail every day and can't sleep at night for worry. Answers to inquiry letters usually take at least six weeks.

2. When Should You Start Inquiring About Delays?

When it comes to delays, how long is too long? That is the million-dollar question. Processing times for immigration applications vary, depending on the number of people applying. If you're waiting for an initial receipt, such as one for an I-130 or I-140 visa petition that your family member or employer filed with a USCIS service center, six weeks is the longest you should wait. After that, your family member or employer should write a letter similar to the one below.

Sample Letter for No Receipt Notice

222 Snowy Road
Buffalo, New York 14221
(716) 555-1212
March 31, 20xx

Department of Homeland Security
U.S. Citizenship and Immigration Services
Vermont Service Center
75 Lower Welden St.
Saint Albans, Vermont 05479

RE: Petitioner: Charlie Citizen
*   Beneficiary: Greta German*
*   Delayed Receipt Notice*

Dear Sir/Madam:

I filed an I-130 visa petition for the above-named beneficiary on January 14, 20xx. According to my certified mail receipt, the petition arrived in your office on January 16 (a copy of that notice is enclosed). It has now been over six weeks and I have not gotten a receipt notice from you.

Please advise me of the status of my visa petition at the above address or phone number. I look forward to your response.

Very truly yours,

Charlie Citizen
Charlie Citizen

Encl. (Copy of Return Receipt)

3. Emergency Attention

If there is some reason that your application really should be given immediate attention—that is, put ahead of all the other waiting applications—be sure to highlight this in a letter. But limit your cries for help to true emergencies, such as:

- a family member is very ill or dying in your home country and you need permission to leave the country during your green card processing to visit them, or

- you have scheduled surgery on the same day as an important USCIS appointment.

If possible, include proof of any claimed emergency, such as a letter from a doctor. Remember, they won't change the laws to accommodate you—for example, if you are waiting in line for a family-based visa, and the government has already given out the maximum number that year, nothing you can do will convince them to give you a visa out of next year's allotment. But if you're simply waiting for the government to act on something that it could do any time, but for being backed up with excess work, you can legitimately ask for quicker attention.

4. USCIS Time Estimates for Application Approval

Sooner or later, you'll get a receipt notice from the USCIS service center in response to your first inquiry or in the normal course of processing. The notice will give you your receipt number, which you can use to check the USCIS website for information on its processing. Look at the upper-left box in the sample receipt notice below—you'll see a number that begins "WAC." Go to the USCIS website (www.uscis.gov), and enter your number in the box under "Check Case Status."

Even without using your receipt notice, the USCIS website can tell you whether they're still dealing with applications filed earlier than yours—and

therefore can't be expected to decide on yours yet—or have moved on to applications filed after yours, in which case there's a problem. On the home page (www.uscis.gov), click "My case is pending," then "Processing Times and Case Status," then "Processing Times." Choose your Service Center, click "Processing Dates," and follow the instructions.

5. Delays Beyond USCIS Time Estimates

The service center won't want to hear from you with more inquiries about your application until the number of processing days predicted on its website has passed. But if that date passes with no results, it's time to write a letter like the one below.

If you hear nothing from USCIS after four weeks, write another, similar letter. Write another every two weeks until you get an answer. It's best to start with very polite, short letters, and then get more insistent as time goes on. Be careful, however—although eloquent and justified outrage may eventually get USCIS's attention, never insult or threaten a government official. This will get you nowhere and, if your letter is interpreted as a threat, may lead to a criminal prosecution as well as a quick denial.

Sample Receipt Notice for I-129F

Department of Homeland Security U.S. Citizenship and Immigration Services	**I-797C, Notice of Action**

THE UNITED STATES OF AMERICA

RECEIPT NUMBER WAC-05-041-00000		CASE TYPE I129F PETITION FOR FIANCE(E)
RECEIVED DATE November 18, 2004	PRIORITY DATE	PETITIONER ANDERSON, CHRISTA
NOTICE DATE December 1, 2004	PAGE 1 of 1	BENEFICIARY CUEVAS, BERNARDO

ILONA BRAY RE: BERNARDO CUEVAS 950 PARKER ST. BERKELEY, CA 94710	**Notice Type:** Receipt Notice Amount received: $ 165.00

Receipt notice - If any of the above information is incorrect, call customer service immediately.

Processing time - Processing times vary by kind of case.
- You can check our current processing time for this kind of case on our website at **uscis.gov**.
- On our website you can also sign up to get free e-mail updates as we complete key processing steps on this case.
- Most of the time your case is pending the processing status will not change because we will be working on others filed earlier.
- We will notify you by mail when we make a decision on this case, or if we need something from you. If you move while this case is pending, call customer service when you move.
- Processing times can change. If you don't get a decision or update from us within our current processing time, check our website or call for an update.

If you have questions, check our website or call customer service. Please save this notice, and have it with you if you contact us about this case.

Notice to all customers with a pending I-130 petition - USCIS is now processing Form I-130, Petition for Alien Relative, as a visa number becomes available. Filing and approval of an I-130 relative petition is only the first step in helping a relative immigrate to the United States. Eligible family members must wait until there is a visa number available before they can apply for an immigrant visa or adjustment of status to a lawful permanent resident. This process will allow USCIS to concentrate resources first on cases where visas are actually available. This process should not delay the ability of one's relative to apply for an immigrant visa or adjustment of status. Refer to **www.state.gov/travel** <http://www.state.gov/travel> to determine current visa availability dates. For more information, please visit our website at www.uscis.gov or contact us at 1-800-375-5283.

Always remember to call customer service if you move while your case is pending. If you have a pending I-130 relative petition, also call customer service if you should decide to withdraw your petition or if you become a U.S. citizen.

Please see the additional information on the back. You will be notified separately about any other cases you filed.
IMMIGRATION & NATURALIZATION SERVICE
CALIFORNIA SERVICE CENTER
P. O. BOX 30111
LAGUNA NIGUEL CA 92607-0111
Customer Service Telephone: (800) 375-5283

Form I-797C (Rev. 08/31/04) N

Sample Letter for Delayed USCIS Decision

344 Noview Drive
Fremont, CA 90000
(510) 555-1212
September 31, 20xx

USCIS/California Service Center
P.O. Box 10130
Laguna Niguel, CA 92607-0130

RE: Petitioner: Joe Citizen
      Beneficiary: Tana Tanzanian
      Processing Number: WAC 01-55-54321

Dear Sir/Madam:

I filed a visa petition for the above-named beneficiary on May 1, 20xx. I got your receipt notice on June 1, 20xx. According to the USCIS website, I could expect a decision from you within 90 days. A copy of my receipt notice is enclosed. It has now been approximately 120 days and I have received neither a decision nor any requests for further information.

Please advise me of the status of my visa petition at the above address or phone number. I look forward to your response.

Very truly yours,

Joe Citizen
Joe Citizen

Encl. (Copy of USCIS receipt)

6. Scheduling the Interview

After all your paperwork is submitted, you're ready for an interview—but you can't predict how long it will take before your interview is scheduled. For interviews in the United States, waits of a year or more are common; if you're outside of the U.S., it's not unusual to wait several months for an interview at the consulate.

There's no harm in trying to find out when you'll be scheduled, however. The information desk at your local USCIS or consulate may also be able to tell you about the usual wait, even if they can't access your application. Sample inquiry letters regarding delayed consular and USCIS interviews are shown below.

Note that the letter to the consulate was sent to an address in Texas, although the consulate is in Ciudad Juarez, Mexico. (The consulate picks up its mail in El Paso.) If you don't have the address of the consulate handling your case, you can locate your consulate via www.travel .state.gov/links.html; or call the State Department's Visa Services Office in Washington, DC, at 202-663-1225.

 Your case number is on the letter from the National Visa Center that you received with your packet of forms. It usually starts with the three-letter abbreviation for your consulate. In the case below, CDJ stands for Ciudad Juarez.

Sample Letter for Delayed Consular Interview

333 Plaintree Drive
Tucson, AZ 90000
(520) 555-1212
July 8, 20xx

Consulate General of the United States
Visa Unit
P.O. Box 10545
El Paso, TX 79995-0545
USA

RE: Case Number: CDJ 2000xxxxxxx
*   Petitioner Name: SMITH, Sandra*
*   Beneficiary Name: CARCAMO CAMPOS, Jorge*

Dear Sir/Madam:

I am the beneficiary named above. I mailed Forms DS-2001 and DS-230 Part I to the NVC in January of this year, over six months ago. I believe the NVC has transferred the case to your office. Please see the attached copy of the return receipt that I received after sending these forms by certified mail. I have still not received my visa appointment.

Enclosed is an additional copy of the previously submitted forms, in case the first set was misplaced. Please advise me if you need anything further. If not, please schedule me for my visa appointment as soon as possible. Thank you.

Very truly yours.

Jorge Carcamo Campos

Jorge Carcamo Campos

Encl. (Return receipt from post office and copy of forms and documents)

The sample letter below was mailed to the USCIS office in Chicago, to which applicants must send their adjustment of status applications.

Sample Letter for Delayed USCIS Interview

888 Windy Road
Boston, MA 02000
(617) 555-1212
January 5, 20xx

U.S. Citizenship and Immigration Services
P.O. Box 805887
Chicago, IL 60680-4120

RE: A#12345678
    Petitioner: Larry Local
    Beneficiary: Zelda Zelinski

Dear Sir/Madam:

I am the beneficiary named above. I turned in my application for adjustment of status in October of 20xx, approximately 16 months ago. Please see the attached copy of my receipt notice. Although I was called in for fingerprinting five months ago, I have still not received an interview appointment.

Please let me know the status of my application and schedule me for an interview as soon as possible. Thank you.

Very truly yours,

Zelda Zelinski

Zelda Zelinski

Encl. (Copy of U.S. Postal Service return receipt)

7. Telephone Calls

You'll no doubt be anxious to just pick up the phone to ask about the progress of your application. Unfortunately, phone calls often produce frustration instead of answers. You might get through to a consulate after many tries. But USCIS almost never gives out phone numbers, except to its main information line, which is probably miles away from where your application is stored.

The USCIS service centers, where most initial visa petitions are decided, are a unique case. The good news is that these service centers have their own telephone information lines. The bad news is that after you spend many hours trying to get through, the person (or machine) who picks up the phone usually has no access to your file. Usually, the most they will do is read from a computer screen, telling you that your case is pending. However, if the computer shows that the service center sent you a request for more documents or actually denied your case, the phone call will be worth the effort—but count on many hours of effort.

Lawyers can be helpful in this regard—they will sometimes have inside email or phone lines to use in case of extreme delays.

8. Incomplete or Lost Portions of Your Application

If USCIS or the consulate needs something to complete your application, such as further evidence of your bona fide marriage, or a missing financial document, they will usually mail you a request. If you receive a request for more documentation, try to gather whatever the immigration authorities have asked for and get it in the mail as soon as possible. Don't forget to include the notification form as a cover sheet—but make a copy for yourself first. A sample of the kind of notice a service center might send is shown

below (this sample is from a work permit application).

What should you do if you're asked for something that you know you've already sent? This is a surprisingly common occurrence—in fact, an investigative report by *The Oregonian* newspaper found that, "With 25 million case files in storage, the INS [as it was then called] misplaces tens of thousands of files each year ... and leaves immigrants to resubmit applications and pay fees all over again." (From "INS Bureaucracy, Blundering Create 'The Agency From Hell,'" by Brent Walth and Kim Christensen, *The Oregonian*, Monday, December 11, 2000.) If the requested item is something inexpensive or easy to come by, don't even try arguing with USCIS or the consulate—even if you have photocopies proving that you already sent the item. Just assume it's been lost and send another one.

Lost checks or money orders are a different matter. Don't send another check or money order until you've found out what happened to the first draft. If you sent a check and haven't received information about it with your monthly bank statement, ask your bank to tell you whether your check has been cashed. If so, get the check and send a copy of both sides, so that the officials can see their own stamp and processing number. If you sent a money order and kept the receipt with the tracer number, call the company that issued the money order to

Sample USCIS Rejection Notice—Page 1

Department of Homeland Security
U.S. Citizenship and Immigration Services

Notice of Action

THE UNITED STATES OF AMERICA

RECEIPT NUMBER			CASE TYPE	1765
WAC-06-013-99999			APPLICATION FOR EMPLOYMENT AUTHORIZATION	
RECEIPT DATE	PRIORITY DATE		APPLICANT	A99 999 999
			IVAN PLATOV	
NOTICE DATE	PAGE			
October 20, 2006	1 of 1			

IVAN PLATOV
2367 BROADWAY
NEW YORK, NEW YORK 20012

Notice Type: Rejection Notice

Your Application for Employment Authorization, Form I-765, is being rejected for incorrect fee.

To establish the correct fee, you must select one eligibility category and submit the fee according to the directions on the application.

Select one eligibility category from Part 2 on the instruction sheet and write it in Item 16 on the form. Return the completed Form I-765 with the correct fee as indicated on Part 5 of the instructions for processing.

Please see the additional information on the back. You will be notified separately about any other cases you filed.
IMMIGRATION & NATURALIZATION SERVICE
CALIFORNIA SERVICE CENTER
P. O. BOX 30111
LAGUNA NIGUEL CA 92607-0111
Customer Service Telephone: (949) 831 8427

Form I-797C (Rev. 09/07/93)N

Sample USCIS Rejection Notice—Page 2

U.S. Department of Homeland Security
U.S. Citizenship and Immigration Services
California Service Center
P.O. Box 10765
Laguna Niguel, CA 92607-0765

Ivan Platov
2367 Broadway
New York, New York 20012

Date: 8/13/06
Form: I-765
"A" #: 12345678

Dear Applicant:

Your application(s) is/are being returned to you for the following reason(s):

1. ___   You have failed to correctly or properly complete the portion of your application which begins "I AM APPLYING FOR _____". Please check the proper box and return to the above address.

2. ___   You have improperly completed or failed to complete Item #16 of your application. Please read the instruction marked "ELIGIBILITY" on the back of the application. Complete Block #16 and return.

3. ___   Please sign your I-765 application.

4. ✗   The I-765 application fee is $100.00

5. ___   Please go to your local INS office nearest you for assistance

6. ___   You failed to submit the required "Form I-765 signature card" with your application. Attached is the I-765 signature card. Sign this card in the blue box marked "signature". **Your signature must fit within the blue box.**

7. ___   You have indicated one of the following eligibility codes in block 16 of your I-765: (a)(3), (a)(4), (a)(5), (a)(7), (a)(8). These eligibility codes are not processed in the California Service Center. Please forward your I-765 to the **Nebraska Service Center**, P.O. Box 82521, Lincoln, NE 68501-2521.

8. ___   A fee is not required for the application or petition you submitted. Your fee, in the amount of _____ is being returned to you.

9. ___   The Form I-765 you submitted has been revised. You must submit the Form I-765 with a revision dated of **4/11/91 or later** to this office.

10. ___   Please complete Section 1 (NAME) or section 3 (ADDRESS).

11. ___   You may ONLY apply for an employment authorization document under one eligibility classification on the application you are submitting.

12. ___   OTHER _____

**IF YOU WISH TO FILE UNDER THE TEMPORARY PROTECTED STATUS AVAILABLE TO HONDURANS AND NICARAGUANS, PLEASE SUBMIT FORM I-765 UNDER (C)(19) ELIGIBILITY CODE FILED TOGETHER WITH FORM I-821, SUPPORTING EVIDENCE AND CORRECT FEES. CALL 1-888-557-5398 FOR MORE INFORMATION. FOR FORMS, CALL 1-800-870-3676.

IMPORTANT NOTE: Please review the instructions carefully to be sure all required documentation is attached to your application (i.e., copy of INS decision notice, copy of your current I-94 or copy of your current EAD card).

IF YOU NEED ASSISTANCE, PLEASE VISIT THE INS OFFICE NEAREST YOUR PLACE OF RESIDENCE. PLACE THIS NOTICE ON TOP OF THE APPLICATION AFTER COMPLETING THE REQUESTED ACTION(S) AND RETURN IT TO THE SERVICE CENTER AT THE ABOVE ADDRESS.

ID#
INS Conc. ____
rev 9/27/00 fm I 765

find out whether it's been cashed. Ask for a copy of the cashed money order or other evidence that you can use to prove who cashed it. If you can't get a copy of the cashed money order, send a copy of your receipt and an explanation. Hopefully, they will stop bugging you for the money.

F. Attending Interviews With USCIS or Consular Officials

The final step in obtaining your visa or green card is—with very few exceptions—to attend an interview with a U.S. consular or USCIS official. Until the date of your interview, it's quite possible that you will not have had any personal contact with any immigration official. For that reason, many applicants approach the interview with needless fear. Below, we coach you on what to expect and how to treat the interview as important—without suffering it as an ordeal.

With all the paperwork you've submitted by now (especially if you're applying for a green card, not a temporary visa), you might think the government should be able to approve your request without having to meet you face to face. However, the government views the interview as its opportunity to confirm the contents of your application after you've sworn to tell the truth (even though you represented that the answers on your application forms were true and correct when you

signed them). The interview also allows the government to ask additional questions—for example, in a marriage-based green card case, to ask personal questions that will test whether your marriage is real or a sham.

1. Who Must Attend an Interview?

Almost every hopeful immigrant or visitor can count on having to attend an interview, whether for a temporary visa or a green card. If you're applying for a family-based green card at a USCIS office, your petitioning family member will usually be required to attend the interview with you.

If you're applying for a family-based visa/green card from outside of the U.S., however, your U.S. petitioner is not usually required to attend the interview—but it's an excellent idea for them to do so. After all, one of the main topics of discussion will be a form your family member filled out—the Affidavit of Support—showing his or her financial situation. If your family member can confirm the contents of the affidavit in person, so much the better.

2. Preparing for Your Interview

The key to a smooth interview is preparation. Prepare all the appropriate forms and documents as described in the appropriate chapter of this book. The USCIS or consular office will send you a list with your appointment notice, but you should also prepare your own set of documents, for you to refer to during the interview.

a. What to Review

In order to prepare for the oral part of the interview, your most important homework task is to review your paperwork. Look at the questions and answers on every form that you've submitted or that has been submitted for you, including the ones filled out by your U.S. petitioner. Though they seem to contain only boring, dry bits of information, this information is loaded with meaning to a USCIS or consular official. The dates of your visits to different places, the financial figures, and your immigration history can all add up to a revealing picture in the official's eyes.

> **EXAMPLE:** Leticia hates dealing with money issues, so she didn't read the Affidavit of Support that her husband filled out. And she didn't notice that her husband wrote on the form that he has "no dependents." At the interview, the officer observed, "It looks like your husband doesn't earn much. How will you be supported?" Leticia replied, "Oh, I'm sure we'll make do financially. After all, my husband's aging parents and orphan nephew all live with him and don't work and he seems to support them just fine." Leticia just created a huge problem. It's now apparent that her

husband lied on his Affidavit of Support and has several dependents. He is clearly less capable of supporting Leticia than it originally appeared. As a result, the consular officer may find Leticia inadmissible as a potential public charge.

The example above shows why you and your petitioner should review all the paperwork and forms carefully to be sure both of you understand them completely. If there have been any changes or if you've noticed any errors since filling out the forms, be prepared to explain the changes and provide documents confirming the new information, if appropriate.

b. What to Wear

The interviewing officer's decision rests almost entirely on whether he or she believes that you're telling the truth. You'll come across as more sincere if you're dressed neatly, professionally, and even conservatively. Avoid T-shirts or jewelry with slogans or symbols that might make the officer wonder about your lifestyle or morals.

> **EXAMPLE:** Jon showed up at his interview wearing expensive leather shoes and, around his neck, a chain with a solid gold marijuana leaf dangling from it. The officer took one look at this and went right into questioning him as to whether he had ever tried, abused, or sold drugs. When Jon wouldn't admit to any-

Sample Interview Appointment Notice

AMERICAN CONSULATE GENERAL
IMMIGRANT VISA UNIT
GIESSENER STRASSE 30
60435 FRANKFURT, GERMANY

Date: 19 Jun 2007

BRAY, ILONA
950 PARKER STREET
BERKELEY, CA 94710

Dear KHAN, JAWHAR MAKIN

This office is ready to begin final processing of the immigrant visa applicant(s) named below in this case. We have scheduled an appointment for a visa interview in the Immigrant Visa section on the date printed below. This letter must be presented upon your arrival at this office on the appointment date.

Please see the enclosed information for further instruction about the medical examination required for all intending immigrants. Be sure to read all the enclosed information and follow the instructions very carefully. Your case is filed under your name as shown below. When communicating with this office either by telephone or letter, please provide your name and case number exactly as shown in this letter. If they are wrong or incomplete, please inform us.

Sincerely,

Thomas J. Wallis
Vice-Consul

Chief, Immigrant Visa Branch

Visa Appointment		Medical Appointment	
Date	Time	Date	Time
*************************************		*************************************	
05-Jul-2007	09:30	05-Jul-2007	07:30

Case Number: FRN199412345
Name (P)   : KHAN, JAWHAR MAKIN
Preference Category: F2B - IRAN

Traveling Applicants:
(P) KHAN, JAWHAR MAKIN   05 JULY 1972

Packet 4

thing, she referred him for another medical exam. The doctor found evidence of drug use in Jon's bloodstream, and he was denied the visa.

3. Procedures for Consular Interviews

If you're coming from a country outside of the U.S., and are interested in a temporary visa, check your consulate's website or call it to find out its appointment procedures—you may need an advance appointment, or you may simply be able to arrive and stand in line. If you're applying for a fiancé visa or an immigrant (green card) visa, the consulate will mail you an interview notice telling you where and when to go for your visa interview. The appointment notice will look much like the one above.

a. Getting There Safely and on Time

If you don't live in the same city as the consulate, you'll want to arrive at least a few days in advance. You will need time to complete your medical exam (at a clinic designated by the consulate) and to get the test results back.

On the day of your interview, it's best to arrive early, in case there's a line. Don't be surprised if you have to wait beyond your scheduled appointment time—the consulates often schedule applicants in large groups, telling all the members of each group to show up at the same time.

⚠ Beware of crime around U.S. consulates. Criminals know where the U.S. consulates are and they know that many people going for interviews are carrying large sums of money for visa fees. Take whatever precautions you think are appropriate in your country. Watch out for con artists who hang around the consulate, trying to convince people that they won't get through the front door unless they hand over some money first.

b. What the Consular Officials Will Do and Say

Here's what will happen when you arrive at the consulate for your interview. First, a clerk will check the packet of forms and other items that you've brought, to make sure you've brought all that's needed. You'll pay any application fees that you haven't already paid by mail. (Although the many of the applications have basic processing fees, the government has added surcharges to some of these, for example a $45 security surcharge for all immigrant visas and a $375 visa surcharge for all diversity visa (lottery) green card applicants.) You can pay in U.S. dollars or in the currency of the country where the consulate is located. Some consulates accept payment only by certified check, money order, or traveler's check. Others accept cash. You'll be told the proper method of payment in your appointment packet.

After these preliminaries, a consular officer will meet with you, place you under oath (have you swear to tell the truth), and review the contents of your entire application. Don't expect a cozy fireside chat in the official's office. Many consulates now conduct interviews through bulletproof glass windows that make you feel like you're in a bank or a prison.

The officer will probably start by reviewing your forms and documents. He or she may ask you questions that are identical to the ones on your forms. Since you will have reviewed these carefully, this shouldn't be a problem—but if you can't remember something, it's much better to say so than to guess at the answer.

You'll probably also have to answer other questions designed to test whether your family relationship, job offer, or other basis for going to the U.S. is the real thing. For example, if you're applying for a student visa, the consular officer will be testing to see whether your true intention is actually to look for a job and stay in the United States permanently (in which case, you don't qualify for a student visa). If you're applying for a fiancé visa or marriage-based immigrant visa, the officer may ask questions about how you and your U.S. citizen fiancé or spouse met, when you decided to get married, and other facts regarding your visits or correspondence. If you're already married, the official may ask questions such as how many people attended the ceremony and how you've visited or corresponded with one another in recent years.

The interview can take as few as 20 or 30 minutes, assuming your basis for going to the United States is obviously real, all documents are in order, and you don't fall into any of the grounds for inadmissibility. Don't panic if it lasts longer. If you find yourself getting nervous, remember to curb that understandable instinct to start babbling. Many applicants have gotten themselves into deep trouble by being unable to stop talking.

c. Delayed Approvals

Consular officers rarely deny applications on the spot. If there are problems that can be corrected, or if you are inadmissible but are eligible to apply for a waiver, they will normally ask you to provide additional materials. Politely ask that the officer put any requests for more materials in writing, stating exactly what is needed and why. If there are any questions having to do with your petitioner in the United States, the consular officer may send your file back to the United States for investigation.

> **EXAMPLE:** A U.S. consular officer in Guatemala told Estela that he couldn't approve her immigrant visa until she brought in her "sister's tax returns." What was the problem? No such tax returns existed because the sister (who was helping sponsor Estela financially) hadn't even been working long enough to reach a tax deadline. Her lawyer in the United States wrote a letter explaining this,

but the consulate continued to ask for these tax returns. Because Estela didn't have the consulate's original request in writing, this led to months of arguing back and forth, with the consular officials continually changing or forgetting what it was they were looking for.

The consulate probably won't approve your visa on the spot, either. First, your name must be checked against various security databases to see whether you have a history of criminal or terrorist behavior. This can add many weeks to the approval of your application, particularly if you come from a country that the U.S. government has identified as sponsoring terrorism. Usually you have to return to the consulate later to pick up your visa—which will in some cases actually be a thick envelope stuffed full of all your supporting documents.

⚠️ **Do not open the visa envelope!** You will give the envelope to the U.S. border officer when you arrive. The officer will examine the contents and do a last check for any problems. The border official, not the consulate, will place a stamp in your passport indicating that you are either a visa holder or a permanent resident or conditional resident.

G. Procedures for USCIS Interviews

Approximately 12 months after you submit your adjustment of status packet to a USCIS service center, USCIS will schedule your interview at one of its local offices, hopefully near where you live. If the interview goes well—for example, your relationship to your family or employee petitioner is obviously the real deal, you don't fall into any of the grounds for inadmissibility, and your documents are in order—the interview can take as few as 20 minutes.

At the end, you will be approved for permanent residence. The exception is if you either entered on an investor visa or are applying for a marriage-based green card and you've been married for less than two years (which automatically applies to anyone who entered the United States on a fiancé visa). These two categories of people receive what's called conditional residence, which is much like permanent residence except that it expires after two years. You must apply, within the three months before the expiration date, to turn your conditional residence into permanent residence.

The interview appointment notice will look much like the one below. Read the notice carefully—there's a chance that your local USCIS office has added requirements that were not covered in this book.

Sample Interview Notice

Department of Homeland Security
U.S. Citizenship and Immigration Services

I-797C, Notice of Action

REQUEST FOR APPLICANT TO APPEAR FOR INITIAL INTERVIEW			NOTICE DATE January 31, 2007
CASE TYPE FORM I-485, APPLICATION TO REGISTER PERMANENT RESIDENCE OR ADJUST STATUS			A# A 099 909 909
APPLICATION NUMBER MSC0712345678	RECEIVED DATE January 12, 2007	PRIORITY DATE January 12, 2007	PAGE 1 of 1

HAI-ZI ZHANG
c/o ILONA BRAY
950 PARKER ST.
BERKELEY, CA 94710

You are hereby notified to appear for the interview appointment, as scheduled below, for the completion of your Application to Register Permanent Residence or Adjust Status (Form I-485) and any supporting applications or petitions. *Failure to appear for this interview and/or failure to bring the below listed items will result in the denial of your application.* *(8 CFR 103.2(b)(13))*

Who should come with you?

☐ **If your eligibility is based on your marriage, your husband or wife must come with you to the interview.**
☐ **If you do not speak English fluently, you should bring an interpreter.**
☐ Your attorney or authorized representative may come with you to the interview.
☐ If your eligibility is based on a parent/child relationship and the child is a minor, the petitioning parent and the child must appear for the interview.

NOTE: Every adult (over 18 years of age) who comes to the interview must bring Government-issued photo identification, such as a driver's license or ID card, in order to enter the building and to verify his/her identity at the time of the interview. You do not need to bring your children unless otherwise instructed. Please be on time, but do not arrive more than 45 minutes early. We may record or videotape your interview.

YOU MUST BRING THE FOLLOWING ITEMS WITH YOU: (Please use as a checklist to prepare for your interview)

☐ This Interview Notice and your Government issued photo identification.
☐ A completed medical examination (Form I-693) and vaccination supplement in a sealed envelope (unless already submitted).
☐ A completed Affidavit(s) of Support (Form I-864) with all required evidence, including the following, for each of your sponsors (unless already submitted):
    ☐ Federal Income Tax returns and W-2's, or certified IRS printouts, for the past 3 years;
    ☐ Letters from each current employer, verifying current rate of pay and average weekly hours, and pay stubs for the past 2 months;
    ☐ Evidence of your sponsor's and/or co-sponsor's United States Citizenship or Lawful Permanent Resident status.
☐ All documentation establishing your eligibility for Lawful Permanent Resident status.
☐ Any immigration-related documentation ever issued to you, including any Employment Authorization Document (EAD) and any Authorization for Advance Parole (Form I-512).
☐ All travel documents used to enter the United States, including Passports, Advance Parole documents (I-512) and I-94s (Arrival/Departure Document).
☐ Your Birth Certificate.
☐ Your petitioner's Birth Certificate and your petitioner's evidence of United States Citizenship or Lawful Permanent Resident Status.
☐ If you have children, bring a Birth Certificate for each of your children.
☐ If your eligibility is based on your marriage, in addition to your spouse coming to the interview with you, bring:
    ☐ A certified copy of your Marriage Document issued by the appropriate civil authority.
    ☐ Your spouse's Birth Certificate and your spouse's evidence of United States Citizenship or Lawful Permanent Resident status;
    ☐ If either you or your spouse were ever married before, all divorce decrees/death certificates for each prior marriage/former spouse;
    ☐ Birth Certificates for all children of this marriage, and custody papers for your children and for your spouse's children not living with you;
☐ Supporting evidence of your relationship, such as copies of any documentation regarding joint assets or liabilities you and your spouse may have together. This may include: tax returns, bank statements, insurance documents (car, life, health), property documents (car, house, etc.), rental agreements, utility bills, credit cards, contracts, leases, photos, correspondence and/or any other documents you feel may substantiate your relationship.
☐ Original and copy of each supporting document that you submitted with your application. Otherwise, we may keep your originals for our records.
☐ If you have ever been arrested, bring the related Police Report and the original or certified Final Court Disposition for each arrest, even if the charges have been dismissed or expunged. If no court record is available, bring a letter from the court with jurisdiction indicating this.
☐ A certified English translation for each foreign language document. The translator must certify that s/he is fluent in both languages, and that the translation in its entirety is complete and accurate.

YOU MUST APPEAR FOR THIS INTERVIEW- If an emergency, such as your own illness or a close relative's hospitalization, prevents you from appearing, call the U.S. Citizenship and Immigration Services (USCIS) National Customer Service Center at 1-800-375-5283 as soon as possible. Please be advised that rescheduling will delay processing of application/petition, and may require some steps to be repeated. It may also affect your eligibility for other immigration benefits while this application is pending.

If you have questions, please call the USCIS National Customer Service Center at 1-800-375-5283 (hearing impaired TDD service is 1-800-767-1833).

PLEASE COME TO: U.S. Citizenship and Immigration Services 630 SANSOME ST 2ND FLOOR - ADJUSTMENT OF STATUS SAN FRANCISCO CA 94111	ON: Wednesday, March 28, 2007 AT: 02:15 PM
3	REPRESENTATIVE COPY

1. Arrange for an Interpreter

USCIS doesn't provide interpreters at interviews in the United States. A few of their officers speak Spanish or other languages, but you can't count on getting a bilingual officer, nor can you request one. If you're not comfortable in English, you'll need to bring a friend or hire an interpreter to help.

The interpreter must be over 18 and fluent in both your language and in English. Some officers also require that the interpreter be a legal resident or citizen of the United States (of course, if they're here illegally, they'd be foolish to walk into a USCIS office).

2. What the USCIS Officials Will Do and Say

In spite of the fact that hundreds of very different people are interviewed each day across the United States, these interviews tend to follow a pattern. Here's what will probably happen at your adjustment interview, step by step.

1. After sitting in the waiting room with dozens of other immigrants for so long that you're sure they've forgotten you, you'll be summoned to the inner rooms of the USCIS adjustments unit.

2. You'll be brought to the USCIS officer's desk, where your identification will be checked. Just when you're seated comfortably, you, your petitioner, and your interpreter (if you've brought one) will have to stand up again, raise your right hands, and take oaths to tell the truth.

3. The officer will start by going through your written application, asking you about the facts and examining the medical and fingerprint reports for factors that might make you ineligible for a green card. As discussed earlier, this is one of the most important parts of the interview. You'll sign the application to confirm its correctness.

4. The officer will ask you and your petitioner about facts relating to your basis for immigrating. You'll get the most questions if you're applying based on marriage, in which case expect questions about where you met, when and why you decided to get married, how many people attended your wedding, or what you did on your most recent birthday or night out. You'll back up your answers with documents that illustrate the genuine nature of your marriage, such as rental agreements and joint utility bills.

5. If there's a problem in your application that you can correct by submitting additional materials, the officer may put your case on hold and send you home with a list of additional documents to provide by mail within a specified time. For example, if your family petitioner's

earnings are insufficient, the officer may suggest you find another family member to sign an I-864 Affidavit of Support. However, USCIS is showing an increasing tendency to deny applications on the spot, in which case your case will be referred to immigration court.

6. If you're applying based on marriage, and the officer suspects that your marriage is fraudulent, a whole new step will be added to the process. You will meet the Fraud Unit. There, an officer will interview you and your spouse separately—and intensively. The officer will compare the results of your two interviews.

At the end of the adjustment of status interview, if you are approved, a stamp will be placed in your passport as evidence of your conditional or permanent residence. With this stamp, you acquire all the rights of a green card holder, including the right to work, and freedom to travel in and out of the United States. You will receive your permanent green card by mail several months later.

If your fingerprints have not cleared yet, your application will be approved only provisionally, pending FBI clearance. In those cases, no stamp will be placed in your passport at the interview. Instead, you should receive a written notice of approval within a month or two.

That written notice serves as your proof of U.S. residency until you receive your green card, which normally takes several weeks. If you need to travel outside the U.S. before your green card arrives, however, you must go back to the USCIS office, with your passport and the written notice of approval, and get a temporary stamp in your passport, enabling you to return after your trip. Never leave the U.S. without either your green card or a temporary passport stamp.

H. What to Do If an Interview Is Going Badly

Your chances of a smooth interview will be greatly increased by the advance preparation and organizing you're doing by using this book. Unfortunately, your efforts can't entirely guarantee a successful interview. A lot will hinge on the personality or mood of the government official.

It's important to have a balanced view of the USCIS and consular officers who will be interviewing you. They're human —and they have seen a lot of fraudulent applicants along with the worthy ones.

Certain immigration officers have been known to go out of their way to help people—for example, spending hours searching for something in a room full of old files; or fitting a person's interview into their schedule even when the person arrived two hours late. On the other hand, some officers can get downright rude or hostile. Remember that they hold much of the power—getting angry will get you nowhere fast. Remain respectful and answer honestly if you don't know or remember something. Never guess or lie.

Some immigrant applicants have heard wild rumors about how to win over a U.S. government official. One showed up for his USCIS interview wearing a loud tie covered with American flags. He interjected comments about America's greatness and what a terrific member of society he would be. Not surprisingly, the officer rolled her eyes and got irritated. Most USCIS officers just want to see someone who won't waste their time, has an orderly, clean case, and is legally eligible for the green card or other benefit.

Try to get the officer's name. USCIS and consular officers often don't tell you their name, but it may be shown on their desk. The best thing to do is politely ask the person's name at the beginning of the interview (not when things have already started to go badly, when he or she may get defensive). Then write the name down. This tidbit of information may become important later. For example, if you need to file a complaint, discuss the matter with a supervisor, or consult with an attorney, you'll have an edge if you know whom you dealt with. (An experienced attorney will know all the local USCIS officers by name and can better understand your description of what happened when he or she learns who was involved.)

Some officers are irate no matter how the applicant behaves. You might encounter an officer who makes irrelevant ac-

cusations, acts in a discriminatory manner based on your race or gender, becomes uncontrollably angry, or persists with a line of questions or statements that is completely inappropriate. If any of these things happens, ask to see a supervisor.

If things are going badly, you don't have to let the situation go from bad to worse, ending with an on-the-spot rejection of your application. To avoid letting the officer make a final, negative decision, offer to supply any information that the officer asked for, so that your case will be postponed ("pended" in USCIS lingo). When you get home, write down as many details as you can remember of the interview, while it's fresh in your mind. Then, consider consulting an attorney about your experience to learn what you can do to improve the reaction to your application. Even if you don't speak with a lawyer, write a letter, asking that a supervisor consider the interviewer's conduct when making his or her final review of your case. Supervisors review all cases, but they will assume the officer acted appropriately unless you tell them otherwise.

I. What to Do If an Application Is Denied

First, a word of reassurance: Neither USCIS nor the consulates like to deny visas to eligible applicants. Unless you are clearly ineligible, they will usually give you many chances to supplement your application and make it worthy of approval. Maybe this is the good side of a slow-moving bureaucracy—every decision takes time, even a negative one. (But don't use this as an excuse to be sloppy in putting your application together the first time.)

 If your visa or green card has been denied, and you didn't use a lawyer, it's time to hire one. This advice is particularly important if the denial was due to something more serious than a bureaucratic mistake or a lack of documentation on your part. You'll definitely need a lawyer for the complicated procedures mentioned below, including removal proceedings and motions to reopen or reconsider. See Chapter 6 on finding a lawyer.

1. Denial of Initial Visa Petition

If the USCIS service center denies your initial visa petition (I-129F, I-130, or I-140), the best thing for your petitioner to do is to start over and file a new one. This is true even if a lawyer is helping. There is an appeal process, but hardly anyone ever uses it. You'll probably spend less time starting over, and the fee is about the same. Besides, no government agency likes to admit it was wrong, so there is a tactical advantage to getting a fresh start.

2. Denial of Visa or Green Card

If USCIS or the consulate denies an application farther along in the process, your response will depend on where you are—in the U.S. or in another country.

a. Denial of Green Card After Adjustment of Status Application in the U.S.

If you are applying for adjustment of status in the United States, there is technically no appeal after a denial. If, as is likely, you have no other legal right to be in the United States when the application is denied (such as a pending political asylum application), you will be placed in removal proceedings in Immigration Court. There, you will have the opportunity to renew your green card application before an immigration judge. In rare circumstances, you might need to file a motion to have your case reopened or reconsidered; or you may need to file a separate suit in federal court.

Never ignore a notice to appear in Immigration Court. Attorneys regularly receive questions from immigrants who were scheduled for a hearing in Immigration Court and either forgot, couldn't make it, or just hoped the problem would go away. Failing to appear for a court date is the worst thing you can do to your hopes of immigrating. It will earn you an automatic order of removal (deportation), which means that DHS can pick you up and put you on a plane home anytime, with no more hearings. You'll also be hit with a ten-year prohibition on returning to the United States and further punishments if you return illegally.

b. Denial of Nonimmigrant Visa at U.S. Consulate

If you are applying for a nonimmigrant (temporary) visa through a consulate outside the United States, you have no appeal after a denial. The consulate is at least required to tell you the reason for the denial, and often the fastest thing is to fix the problem and reapply. For example, if it appears that you have insufficient funds to support yourself while you're in the United States, you might find an additional person to fill out an Affidavit of Support on your behalf. You can reapply, but must usually wait a certain amount of time first, for example three months. Ask the consulate for details.

c. Denial of Immigrant Visa at U.S. Consulate

If you are applying for an immigrant (permanent residence) visa, the consulate will give you up to one year after the denial of your visa application to provide information aimed at reversing the denial. At the end of the year, your application will close and you must start all over again. There is no appeal from the denial or the closure.

⚠ Don't attempt multiple, inconsistent applications. The U.S. government keeps a record of all your applications for visas and green cards. If you come back a few years later with a new basis for immigrating, USCIS or the consulate will be happy to remind you of any past fraud or other reasons for inadmissibility. (Changing your name won't work—by the end of the application process, the U.S. immigration authorities will have your fingerprints.)

J. When All Else Fails, Call Your U.S. Congressperson

If your case turns into a true bureaucratic nightmare or a genuine miscarriage of justice, your U.S. citizen or permanent resident petitioner or employer can ask a U.S. congressperson for help. Some of them have a staff person dedicated to helping constituents who have immigration problems. A simple inquiry by a congressperson can end months of USCIS or consular stonewalling or inaction. In rare cases, the congressperson's office might be willing to put some actual pressure on USCIS or the consular office.

EXAMPLE: Rodrigo, a U.S. citizen, was trying to get permission for his daughter Sandra to immigrate from Mexico. She attended her visa interview and was told to come back with more proof that she would be financially supported and not become a public charge. Although Rodrigo's income was already over the *Poverty Guidelines*, he found a joint sponsor, who submitted an additional Affidavit of Support for Sandra. The consulate still wasn't willing to grant the visa. Rodrigo consulted with an attorney, who wrote letters to the consulate—but got no reply. Finally his attorney wrote a letter to Rodrigo's congressperson asking for help. They submitted copies of all the relevant documents so that the congressperson would fully understand the problem. The visa was granted—with no explanation—a week after the congressperson's inquiry.

Your congressperson probably won't be surprised to hear from you. Illinois Congresswoman Janice Schakowsky reported that eight out of ten calls from her constituents were complaints about the INS (as USCIS was then called). (See "Unchecked Power of the INS Shatters American Dream," by Kim Christensen, Richard Read, Julie Sullivan, and Brent Walth, *The Oregonian*, Sunday, December 20, 2000.) ■

Chapter 5

Special Rules for Canadians and Mexicans

Many Canadian and Mexican citizens believe they **are disfavored by the U.S. immigration** system. Actually, the exact opposite is true, as the following descriptions of special rules show.

A. Canadian Visitors and Nonimmigrants

Canadian citizens do not have to have visas to enter the U.S. For the casual tourist or business visitor, this is a big benefit. With the exception of E-1 and E-2 treaty traders and investors, and fiancé(e)s and their children (K-1 and K-2), Canadians have no need to go to a U.S. consulate and get nonimmigrant visas. They will, however, need to present a valid passport.

⚠ **Despite the benefits, you must still prove that you don't fall into one of the inadmissibility categories, which bar U.S. entry.** Anyone coming into the U.S. can be examined regarding his or her health, criminal, and other history to see whether the person falls into one of the grounds of inadmissibility described in Chapter 3.

Even though a nonimmigrant visa is not usually required, Canadians still must show that they are eligible to enter the United States. For visitors, this may mean something as simple as answering a few questions from a Customs and Border Protection (CBP) inspector at a U.S. port of entry. On other occasions, a Canadian visitor might be asked to prove that he or she has enough money to last during the U.S. trip. Visitors may also have to show that they still keep Canadian residences to which they can return.

Canadian tourist visitors are not normally issued I-94 cards as are people from all other countries. This is another advantage. Canadians are not expected to have this document on hand for purposes of proving status in the United States. If you want an I-94, however, you can request one.

B. Special Work Privileges for Canadian and Mexican Visitors

Canadians and Mexicans are granted some special work privileges.

1. Working Without a Visa

The North American Free Trade Agreement (NAFTA) includes a program permitting Canadian and Mexican visitors who are coming to the U.S. to do certain kinds of work in the U.S. without having work visas. There are no other countries whose citizens are granted these privileges.

To take advantage of this opportunity, you must show written proof that you are engaging in one of the occupations included in the program. A letter from your employer verifying the work to be done will serve this purpose. If relevant, you should also offer evidence that you are qualified for the job, such as copies of diplomas or licenses. These documents are presented to a U.S. immigration officer on your entry to the United States. No fee or special application is needed for Canadians. However, Mexican nationals must obtain a valid entry document (Form I-186 or Form I-586) prior to arriving at the port of entry.

The types of work that Canadians and Mexicans may do in the U.S. without work visas are:

- performing research and design functions for a company located in Canada or Mexico
- supervising a crew harvesting agricultural crops; only the owner of the company qualifies
- purchasing for a company located in Canada or Mexico
- conducting other commercial transactions for a company located in Canada or Mexico
- doing market research for a company located in Canada or Mexico.
- attending trade fairs
- taking sales orders and negotiating contracts for a company located in Canada or Mexico
- transporting goods or passengers into the U.S
- picking up goods and passengers in the U.S., only for direct transport back to Canada or Mexico

- performing normal duties as a customs broker. The goods must be exports from the U.S. to Canada or Mexico
- servicing equipment or machinery after sales
- performing any professional services, provided no salary is paid from within the U.S.
- performing financial services for a company located in Canada
- consulting in the fields of public relations and advertising
- conducting tours that originate or have significant portions taking place in Canada, and
- performing language translation and acting as an interpreter for a company located in Canada

2. Simplified Procedures for L Visas (Canadians and Mexicans)

If you are seeking a visa as an L-1 intracompany transferee, and you are a citizen of Canada or Mexico, a simplified application process is available to you. Instead of going through the USCIS petition process, you can choose to take all your L-1 paperwork, both petition forms and documents, along with the required fee, directly to a port of entry. There, an immigration officer will decide on the spot whether you qualify for L-1 status (you cannot send them your paperwork in advance). Your accompanying spouse and children will be admitted on show-ing proof of their family relationship to you. This requires presenting a marriage certificate for your spouse and long-form birth certificates for your children.

When your status is approved, you will be given an I-94 card and admitted to the U.S. immediately. The petition is then forwarded to the appropriate ser-vice center in the U.S. and the final deci-sion on the petition is made in about 60 days, and mailed to you.

⚠️ **If you're flying to the U.S., you may have to submit your paperwork to a preflight inspector before you board the plane.** In that case, plan to arrive several hours before your flight to make sure you're approved before the plane departs.

Although this method is much faster than going through normal USCIS peti-tion procedures, if you are denied entry, your rights of appeal are limited. In addition, border inspectors are usually less experienced in deciding cases than USCIS office personnel, and therefore, may be reluctant to approve a more diffi-cult case. When your situation is compli-cated, you are probably better off having your petition approved in advance at the service center and not using this alterna-tive procedure.

3. H-1 Visa Alternative: TN Status

For Canadian and Mexican citizens who practice certain professional occupations, an alternative to filing a USCIS petition is available for H-1 cases as well. This is called TN status. TN status lasts one year, and can be renewed in one-year increments, with no limit on renewals. You don't always have to be coming for a job—TN status can also be used by people coming for temporary training related to their profession, or to conduct seminars.

At present, only the occupations listed below qualify for TN status. A bachelor's or licensure degree from a college or university is required, unless an alterna-tive is shown in parentheses. You must have a U.S. employer; TN status is not available for self-employment in the United States. For some professions, there are requirements in addition to a degree. These, too, are shown in paren-theses. Whenever a license is required, either a federal Canadian, Mexican, or a U.S. licensing agency from any province or state is acceptable. The occupations are:

- accountant
- architect (degree or license)
- computer systems analyst
- disaster relief claims adjuster (degree or three years' experience)
- economist
- engineer (degree or license)
- forester (degree or license)

- graphic designer (degree and three years' experience)
- hotel manager (licensure degree or diploma or certificate plus three years' experience)
- industrial designer (degree or certificate or diploma plus three years' experience)
- interior designer (degree or certificate or diploma plus three years' experience)
- land surveyor (degree or license)
- landscape architect
- lawyer (member of Canadian, Mexican, or U.S. bar)
- librarian (Master's degree)
- management consultant (degree or five years' experience)
- mathematician (including statistician)
- medical professions:
  - clinical lab technologist
  - dentist (professional degree or license)
  - dietitian (degree or license)
  - medical lab technologist (degree or certificate or diploma plus three years' experience)
  - nutritionist
  - occupational therapist (degree or license)
  - pharmacist (degree or license)
  - physician (teaching or research position only)
  - physio/physical therapist (degree or license)
  - psychologist
  - recreational therapist
  - registered nurse (license)
  - veterinarian (professional degree or license)
- range manager
- research assistant (for colleges or universities only)
- scientific technician (degree not required if you are working with professionals in: agricultural sciences, astronomy, biology, chemistry, engineering, forestry, geology, geophysics, meteorology, physics)
- scientist working as:
  - agronomist
  - agriculturist
  - animal breeder
  - animal scientist
  - apiculturist
  - astronomer
  - biochemist
  - biologist
  - chemist
  - dairy scientist
  - entomologist
  - epidemiologist
  - geneticist
  - geochemist
  - geologist
  - geophysicist
  - horticulturist
  - meteorologist
  - pharmacologist
  - physicist
  - plant breeder
  - poultry scientist
  - soil scientist

- ■ zoologist
- • social worker
- • silviculturist
- • teacher (at a college, university, or seminary only)
- • technical publications writer (degree, diploma, or certificate plus three years' experience)
- • urban planner, and
- • vocational counselor.

The person seeking TN status must be coming temporarily, to engage in business activities at a professional level. A person who intends to separately apply for a green card while in the U.S. can be denied TN status, because he or she violates the requirement that he or she intends to stay only temporarily. The person must also meet the minimum requirements for the profession or occupation in question, as set forth in Appendix 1603.D.1 to Annex 1603 of NAFTA (also found at 8 C.F.R. § 2145.6(c)). Furthermore, the person must not be self-employed in the United States. Although the basic requirements are the same for Canadians and Mexicans, the procedures are distinct.

a. TN Procedures for Canadians

There is no annual limit for Canadian TNs. A Canadian professional worker may be admitted to the U.S. without advance petition approval or labor certification. In order to apply, the applicant merely goes straight to any U.S. port of entry (border, airport, or preflight inspection station). There, an immigration or NAFTA officer will adjudicate the application, and you'll need to proceed directly to the United States. Although no formal application form is required, you must pay a fee (currently $50, or $56 if you're crossing the border by car). Your spouse and unmarried minor children may accompany you, but may not work in the United States. Family members must bring proof of the family relationship, such as a marriage or birth certificate. They will be given TD status.

If the applicant is already in the U.S., he or she can apply for a change of status. The employer makes this application on Form I-129, and sends it to USCIS.

A Canadian applicant will need to supply the following documents to be given TN status:

- • evidence of Canadian citizenship, such as a birth certificate, citizenship identification card, certificate of citizenship, or passport
- • a job offer letter describing the proposed employment activity at a professional level, including your daily job duties, the job requirements (such as educational level or license), your salary and benefits, and how long your services will be needed, for up to one year
- • evidence of your qualifications to perform at a professional level, as demonstrated by degrees, licenses, memberships, or other relevant credentials that establish professional status, and a resume (optional), and

- evidence of the particular profession as one listed in Appendix 1603.D.1 to Annex 1603 of NAFTA.

The application should include a letter from the prospective employer, confirming that the applicant will perform the professional activity for the employer. The letter should also state:

- that the work will be temporary
- how long the work will last
- the employer's need for professional services
- the job duties, salary, and other essential terms of the employment offer
- how the applicant's educational and work experience confirm his or her professional status, and
- how the applicant's qualifications comply with any state licensing or other requirements.

When admitted, the TN professional will be given an I-94 card indicating authorized status for up to one year. This period can be extended in one-year increments without leaving the United States. An extension may be requested by your employer on Form I-129 and filed at the Northern Service Center in Nebraska (regardless of where you live). Or, it may be requested by departing the U.S. prior to the first status expiration and reentering at the port of entry by presenting the above-listed documents.

b. TN Procedures for Mexicans

There is no longer an annual cap on TNs from Mexico and the application procedures have recently gotten easier. As of January 2004, Mexican TN applicants no longer need to obtain an approved Labor Condition Application (LCA). Nor do their employers have to file a petition with USCIS.

Applicants who are outside of the U.S. can simply present themselves at a U.S. consular post to apply for TN status and an entry visa. The applicant will need to bring a Mexican passport, plus the same types of documents as described in Subsection a, above.

If the applicant is already in the U.S., he or she can apply for a change of status. The employer makes this application on Form I-129, and sends it to USCIS.

Applicants can also bring their spouses and children to the U.S. (in TD status) by providing proof of the family relationship, such as a birth or marriage certificate. Family members with TD status cannot legally work in the United States.

Upon entering the U.S., the Mexican TN professional will be given an I-94 card indicating an authorized stay of up to one year. This period can be extended in one-year increments without leaving the United States. To file for an extension, your employer must send Form I-129, together with the same types of documents used for your initial application, to the USCIS Nebraska Service Center. If you don't mind leaving the U.S., you can also request an extension by departing before your status has expired and revisiting a U.S. consulate.

c. Advantages and Disadvantages of TN Status

The advantages of the treaty professional procedure are that you avoid potentially long delays from filing a petition in the United States. TN status is also useful for Canadians and Mexicans who have used up their six years of H-1B status, but wish to continue working in the United States. Similarly, it's helpful for H-1B applicants who find that the annual supply of H-1B visas has run out. And, because the list of professions qualifying for TN status is fairly broad, it's useful for some people whose profession could never qualify them for an H-1B visa in the first place.

The main disadvantage is that professional workers using the TN instead of a standard H-1 visa must intend to return to Canada or Mexico when their work in the U.S. is finished, and they may receive only one-year periods of status at a time. Therefore, if you plan to apply for a green card, you should, if possible, get a standard H-1 visa, which does not have these restrictions. (Unfortunately, not all categories of TN status qualify for an H-1B visa.)

In addition, if you have a difficult case and you are denied entry as a treaty professional, there is no avenue of appeal. When a standard H-1 visa petition is denied, or if you apply for a TN status extension or change of status by filing an application with the service center, you have the ability to appeal the decision through both USCIS and, eventually, the U.S. courts.

4. Treaty Traders and Treaty Investors

NAFTA allows Canadians to obtain E-1 and E-2 visas. Canadians wishing to get E-1 or E-2 status are treated exactly like persons of all other nationalities. This means that you must obtain an actual visa stamp in your passport before you can enter the U.S. with an E-1 or E-2 status. Therefore, you should follow all of the procedures discussed in Chapters 20 and 21. This is the only nonimmigrant category where a visa is required of Canadians.

Although getting an E visa could formerly be done in one day at a U.S. consulate in Canada, consulates are now requiring that you attend an interview on one day, then return on a later day to pick up your passport and visa.

5. Fiancés

See Chapter 8 for instructions on obtaining a fiancé visa. Your other option, of course, is to enter the U.S. with no visa, get married, and then file for a green card within the United States. You would risk, however, a finding that you had used fraud when you entered the U.S. as a supposed nonimmigrant, with the actual intent of staying permanently.

C. Simplified Procedures for Canadian Students and Exchange Visitors

Canadians entering the U.S. as F-1 students, M-1 students, or J-1 exchange visitors also have a simplified way of getting status. First you must get an approved Certificate of Eligibility form. The Certificate of Eligibility for F-1 and M-1 students is Form SEVIS I-20. For J-1 exchange visitors it is Form SEVIS DS-2019. These are described in Chapters 22 and 23.

Once you have a Certificate of Eligibility, you may go directly to a port of entry and present it to a U.S. immigration inspector together with proof of your Canadian citizenship. You should also have available evidence of how you will be supported financially while in the United States. On showing these documents, you will be admitted as a student or exchange visitor. Your accompanying spouse and children will be admitted on showing proof of their family relationship to you. This requires presenting a marriage certificate for your spouse and long-form birth certificates for your children.

When you enter the U.S., you will receive an I-94 card indicating your immigration status and giving the dates of the period for which you may remain in the country. Your stay will usually be for duration of status, marked "D/S" on the I-94 card. This means you can stay until your studies are completed. If you leave the U.S. before your status expires and want to return, you need only present the I-94 card and Certificate of Eligibility at the port of entry and you will be admitted again.

D. Preflight Inspections for Canadians

Another benefit Canadians enjoy is access to the procedure known as preflight inspection. There are U.S. immigration offices located at most of the Canadian international airports. When Canadians fly to the U.S., they clear U.S. immigration and customs before boarding the plane. This service is considered to be a timesaving advantage.

There is a negative side to preflight inspection. In situations where a Canadian's eligibility to enter the U.S. is questionable, if the U.S. immigration inspector does not believe the Canadian traveler should be admitted, the inspector can prevent the Canadian from boarding the plane. Without preflight inspection, travelers to the U.S. can at least land on U.S. soil and are usually granted enough time in the country to stay and argue their case. However, the law punishes those individuals who arrive without the proper documentation and those who make a misrepresentation to a CBP inspector by making them inadmissible for a visa and unable to request entry for five years. Because of this, you should be extremely cautious about presenting yourself for inspection.

Chapter 6

How and When to Find a Lawyer

You are not required to have a lawyer when applying for a U.S. visa or green card. If you have a straightforward case, you may be able to proceed all the way to a visa or green card without a lawyer. In fact, if you are outside of the U.S., lawyers cannot attend consular interviews with you, though they are allowed to prepare the paperwork and have follow-up communications with the consulates.

Unfortunately, however, there are times when you'll need a lawyer's help. Because immigration law is complicated, even a seemingly simple case can suddenly become nightmarish. If so, you'll need good legal help, fast. In this chapter, we'll explain:

- when applicants typically need to consult an attorney (Section A)
- how to find suitable counsel (Sections B, C, and D)
- how to hire, pay, and (if necessary) fire your lawyer (Sections E, F, and G), and
- how to do some legal research on your own (Section H).

If you are, or have ever been, in deportation (removal) proceedings, you must see a lawyer. If the proceedings aren't yet over or are on appeal, your entire immigration situation is in the power of the courts—and you are not allowed to use most of the procedures described in this book. Even if the court proceedings are over, you should ask a lawyer whether the outcome affects your current application.

A. When Do You Need a Lawyer?

The most common legal problem encountered by would-be immigrants is the claim by USCIS or the consulate that they are inadmissible for one or more of the reasons listed in Chapter 3, such as having committed a crime or previously lied to the U.S. government. If you know that any of these grounds apply to you, it makes sense to get legal help before you begin the application process.

Another important role for lawyers is helping explain your case to the immigration authorities. As you read the various chapters of this book, you'll find that the eligibility criteria for U.S. visas and green cards tend to be quite complicated. Depending on your situation, you may, for example, be trying to convince an immigration officer that you have no secret plans to stay in the U.S. permanently; are getting married for love, not for a green card; fled your country because you received verbal death threats; or are an acknowledged expert in your field. You'll be required to submit various documents to prove such things, which an attorney can help you choose and prepare. But an experienced immigration attorney will often add an item that's not required—a cover letter or memo explaining what all the evidence adds up to, and making clear how your case fits within the legal requirements. Such written materials are difficult to produce if you are not experienced in immigration law. And the lawyer may also be able to argue some of these points in person, for example at your green card interview.

Yet another circumstance that often drives people to lawyers is the failure of USCIS or the consulate to act on or approve the application for reasons that have more to do with bureaucracy than law. For example, an applicant who moves from Los Angeles to San Francisco after filing a green card application might find that the application has disappeared into a bureaucratic black hole for several months. Delays at the USCIS service centers are also ridiculously common.

Lawyers don't have as much power as you—or the lawyers—might wish in such circumstances. True, the lawyer may have access to inside fax or email inquiry lines, where they (and only they) can ask about delayed or problematic cases—but even lawyers may have trouble getting answers to such inquiries. An experienced lawyer may have contacts inside USCIS or the consulate who can give information or locate a lost file. But these lawyers can't use this privilege on an everyday basis, and long delays are truly an everyday occurrence.

The bottom line is that a lawyer in most cases has no magic words that will force the U.S. government into taking action. So you'll have to decide whether it's worth it to pay a lawyer for this limited help. After all, the lawyer will in many instances be doing what you can probably do yourself—repeatedly calling or writing to USCIS or the consulate until they come up with an answer.

The exception to this advice would be if you are applying for something where you'll lose your rights if USCIS or a consulate doesn't act quickly. For example, a lottery winner must get the immigration authorities to approve his or her green card before the supply has run out, and before the end of that fiscal year, or his or her chance will be lost forever. Similarly, an immigrating child about to turn 21 may, in certain circumstances, lose rights or be delayed in his or her immigration process. A good lawyer will know the latest tactics for alerting USCIS or the consulates to such issues.

Don't rely on advice by USCIS information officers. Would you want the receptionist in your doctor's office to tell you whether to get brain surgery? Asking USCIS information officers for advice about your case (beyond basic procedural advice such as where to file an application and what the fees are) is equally unsafe. The people who staff USCIS phone and information services are not experts. USCIS takes no responsibility if their advice is wrong—and won't treat your application with any more sympathy. Even following the advice of officials higher up in the agency may not be safe—always get a second opinion.

A final reason to consult with an immigration lawyer is if you've researched the law and feel like you have no hope of getting a U.S. visa or green card.

Before giving up, it's worth checking with a lawyer to make sure you haven't missed anything. This is particularly true if you have some urgent reason for needing to come to or stay in the United States—for example, you developed a serious illness while visiting the U.S., and might die if transported home. Some unusual (and hard-to-get) remedies, with names like "humanitarian parole" and "deferred action" may help you. However, you'll definitely need a lawyer's assistance to apply for and obtain these remedies.

B. Where to Get the Names of Good Immigration Lawyers

Finding a good lawyer can involve a fair amount of work. Immigration law is a specialized area—in fact it has many subspecialties within it. So you will want to find a lawyer who specializes in immigration—you obviously don't want to consult the lawyer who wrote your best friend's will. And whatever you do, don't just open the telephone book and pick the immigration lawyer with the biggest advertisement. Even bar association referral panels (lawyer listing services run by groups of lawyers) tend not to be very helpful. Such services tend to assume that any one of their lawyer members is qualified to handle your case, and they

may simply refer you to the next lawyer on their list with no prescreening.

It is far better to ask a trusted person for a referral. Perhaps you know someone in the United States who is sophisticated in practical affairs and has been through an immigration process. This person may be able to recommend his or her lawyer, or can ask that lawyer to recommend another.

Local nonprofit organizations serving immigrants can also be excellent sources for referrals. A nonprofit organization is a charity that seeks funding from foundations and individuals to help people in need. Since they exist to serve others rather than to make a profit, they charge less and are usually staffed by people whose hearts and minds are in the right places. In the immigrant services field, examples include the Albuquerque Border City Project (New Mexico), Northwest Immigrant Rights Project (Seattle), El Rescate Legal Services (Los Angeles), the International Institutes (nationwide), and Catholic Charities (nationwide). For a list of USCIS-approved nonprofits, ask your local USCIS office or court or check the Department of Justice website at www.usdoj.gov/eoir (then click "EOIR Legal Orientation and Pro Bono Program," then "Recognition & Accreditation"). You don't need to use a nonprofit from this list, but it may be safer to do so—supposed nonprofit organizations can be unscrupulous too, or they may actually be for-profit businesses. Most nonprofits keep lists of lawyers who they know do honest immigration work for a fair price.

Yet another good resource is the American Immigration Lawyers Association (AILA)—call them at 800-954-0254 or find them on the Internet at www.aila .org. AILA offers a lawyer referral service. Their membership is limited to lawyers who have passed a screening process, which helps keep out the less-scrupulous practitioners. But not all good immigration lawyers have joined AILA (membership is a bit pricey).

Try to get a list of a few lawyers who you've heard do good work, then meet or talk to each and choose one. If you're living in another country now, you may have to communicate with a U.S.-based lawyer primarily by email. In major cities of some countries with high levels of immigration such as Canada and England, U. S. immigration firms have set up offices.

! **Don't contact lawyers expecting free advice.** The good immigration lawyers are extremely busy and under a lot of deadline pressure. Yet many of them receive supposed "quick questions," particularly via email, from people who are not their clients, and whom they've never met. It's unfair to expect a response to such contacts, and also unrealistic to assume that you'll get valid advice without a full analysis of your situation.

C. How to Avoid Sleazy Lawyers

There are good and bad immigration lawyers out there. Some of the good ones are candidates for sainthood—they put in long hours dealing with a difficult bureaucracy on behalf of a clientele that typically can't pay high fees. They are also active in the community, advocating for immigrants' rights when no one else does.

The bad immigration lawyers are a nightmare—and there are more than a few of them out there. They typically try to do a high-volume business, churning out the same forms for every client regardless of their situation. Such lawyers can get clients into deep trouble by overlooking critical issues in their cases or failing to submit applications or court materials on time. But the one thing they never seem to forget is to send a huge bill for their supposed help. Some signs to watch for are:

- **The lawyer approaches you in a USCIS office or other public location and tries to solicit your business.** This is not only against the lawyers' rules of professional ethics, but is also an indication that the lawyer may be incompetent— no competent lawyer ever needs to find clients this way.
- **The lawyer makes big promises, such as "I guarantee I'll win your case," or "I've got a special contact**

who will put your application at the front of the line." The U.S. government is in ultimate control of your application, and any lawyer who implies that he or she has special powers is either lying or may be involved in something you don't want to be a part of.

- **The lawyer has a very fancy office and wears a lot of flashy gold jewelry.** A fancy office or a $2,000 outfit aren't necessarily signs of a lawyer's success at winning cases. These trappings may instead be signs that the lawyer charges high fees and counts on impressing his clients with clothing rather than results.

- **The lawyer encourages you to lie on your application.** This is a tricky area. On the one hand, a good lawyer can assist you in learning what information you don't want to needlessly offer up, and can help you present the truth in the best light possible. But a lawyer who coaches you to lie—for example, by telling you to pretend you lost your passport and visa when in fact you entered the United States illegally— isn't ethical. There's every chance that USCIS knows the lawyer's reputation and will scrutinize your application harder because of it.

You might think that the really bad lawyers would be out of business by now, but that isn't the case. Sad to say, neither the attorney bar associations nor the courts nor even the police take much interest in going after people who prey on immigrants. Occasionally, nonprofits devoted to immigrants' rights will attempt to get the enforcement community interested in taking action. Unfortunately, this threat of official scrutiny isn't much of a deterrent.

 If you are the victim of an unscrupulous lawyer, complain! Law enforcement won't go after lawyers who prey on immigrants until there is enough community pressure. If a lawyer, or someone pretending to be a lawyer, pulls something unethical on you, report it to the state and local bar association and the local district attorney's (D.A.'s) office. Ask your local nonprofits if anyone else in your area is collecting such information.

D. How to Choose Among Lawyers

Once you've got your "short list" of lawyers, you'll want to speak to each one. How much a lawyer charges is bound to be a factor in whom you choose (see Section F, below), but it shouldn't be the only factor. Here are some other important considerations.

1. Familiarity With Cases Like Yours

Some immigration lawyers spend much of their time in subspecialties, such as helping people obtain political asylum or employment-based visas. To learn how much experience a lawyer has in the type of visa or green card you're interested in, ask some very practical questions, such as:

- How long do you expect my case to take?
- What is the reputation of the officers at the USCIS or consular office who will handle my case?
- How many cases like mine did you handle this year?

2. Client Rapport

Your first instinct in hiring a lawyer may be to look for a shark—someone you wouldn't want to leave your child with, but who will be a tough fighter for your case. This isn't necessarily the best choice in the immigration context. Since you may need to share some highly confidential issues with your lawyer, you'll want to know that the person is discreet and thoughtful. Also, realize that a lawyer's politeness goes a long way in front of immigration officials—sharks often produce a bureaucratic backlash, whereas the lawyers with good working relations with USCIS may have doors opened to them.

3. Access to Your Lawyer

You'll want to know that you can reach your lawyer during the months that your application winds its way through the USCIS or consular bureaucracy. A lawyer's accessibility may be hard to judge at the beginning, but try listening to the lawyer's receptionist as you wait in his or her office for the first time. If you get the sense that the receptionist is rude and trying to push people off or give them flimsy excuses about why the lawyer hasn't returned their calls or won't talk to them, don't hire that lawyer.

Many immigration lawyers are sole practitioners and use an answering machine rather than a receptionist. In that case, you'll have to rely on how quickly they answer your initial calls. In your first meeting, simply ask the lawyer how quickly he or she will get back to you. If the lawyer regularly breaks promises, you'll have grounds on which to complain.

Of course, you, too, have a responsibility not to harass your lawyer with frequent calls. The lawyer should be available for legitimate questions about your case, including inquiries about approaching deadlines.

4. Explaining Services and Costs

Take a good look at any printed materials the lawyer gives you on your first visit. Are they glitzy, glossy pieces that look more like advertising than anything useful? Or are they designed to acquaint you with the process you're getting into and the lawyer's role in it? Think about this issue again before you sign the lawyer's fee agreement, described in the section immediately below. Being a good salesperson doesn't necessarily make someone a good lawyer.

E. Signing Up Your Lawyer

Many good lawyers will ask you to sign an agreement covering their services and the fees you will pay them. This is a good idea for both of you, and can help prevent misunderstandings. The contract should be written in a way you can understand; there's no law that says it has to be in confusing legal jargon. The lawyer should go over the contract with you carefully, not just push it under your nose, saying, "Sign here." Some normal contract clauses include:

- **Scope of work.** A description of exactly what the lawyer will do for you.
- **Fees.** Specification of the amount you'll pay, either as a flat fee (a lump sum you pay for a stated task, such as $1,500 for an adjustment of status application) or at an hourly rate, with a payment schedule. If you hire someone at an hourly rate, you can ask to be told as soon as the hours have hit a certain limit.

Don't pay a big flat fee up-front. Since the lawyer already has your money, he or she will have little incentive to please you. And if you don't like the lawyer later on, chances are you won't get any of your money back. Instead, pay for a few hours' service—then if you don't like the lawyer's work, end the relationship.

- **Responsibility for expenses.** Most lawyers will ask you to cover the incidental expenses associated with the work that they do, such as phone calls, postage, and photocopying. This is fair. After all, if your case requires a one-hour phone call to the consulate in Brunei, that call shouldn't eat up the lawyer's fee. But check carefully to be sure that the lawyer charges you the actual costs of these items. Some lawyers have been known to turn a tidy profit by charging, for example, 20 cents a page for a photocopy job that really costs only three cents a page.
- **Effect of nonpayment.** Many lawyers charge interest if you fail to pay on time. This is normal and probably not worth making a big fuss about. If you have trouble paying on time, call the lawyer and ask for more time—he or she may be willing to forgo the interest if it's clear you're taking your obligation seriously.

- **Exclusion of guarantee.** The lawyer may warn you that there's no guarantee of winning your case. Though this may appear as if the lawyer is looking for an excuse to lose, it is actually a responsible way for the lawyer to protect against clients who assume they're guaranteed a win; or who later accuse the lawyer of having made such promises. After all, USCIS or the consulate is the ultimate decision maker on your case.
- **Effect of changes in case.** Most lawyers will warn you that if there is something you didn't tell them about (for example, that you are still married to your first wife while trying to get a green card through your second wife) or a significant life change affects your case (for instance, you get arrested), they will charge you additional fees to cover the added work these revelations will cause. This, too, is normal; but to protect yourself against abuse, make very sure that the contract specifies in detail all the work that is already included. For example, a contract for a lawyer to help you

---

Watch Out for Nonlawyers Practicing Immigration Law

Because much of immigration law involves filling in forms, people assume it's easy. They're wrong. Be careful about whom you consult with or hand your case over to. Unless the person shows you certification that they are a lawyer, an accredited representative, or a paralegal working under the direct supervision of a lawyer, they should be thought of as typists. (An accredited representative is a nonlawyer who has received training from a lawyer and been recognized by USCIS as qualified to prepare USCIS applications and represent clients in court.) And this is true even though they may go by fancy names such as "immigration consultant" or "notary public"—these people do not have a law degree. To check on whether someone is really a lawyer, ask for his or her bar number and call the state bar association.

Hiring a nonlawyer or nonaccredited representative is appropriate only if you want help with the form preparation, and no more. But even seemingly minor details asked for on a form, like your date of entry to the U. S. or your address, can have legal consequences. Don't just turn your case over and let the consultant make the decisions.

If you feel you've been defrauded by an immigration consultant, you may want to sue in small claims court; see *Everybody's Guide to Small Claims Court,* by Ralph Warner (Nolo).

with a green card application within the United States might specify that the lawyer will be responsible for "preparation of visa petition and adjustment of status packet, filing all applications with USCIS, representation at interview, and reasonable follow-up with USCIS." If the lawyer agrees to include work on any special waivers or unusual documents, make sure these are mentioned in the contract (for example, an HIV waiver or an extra Affidavit of Support from a joint sponsor).

F. Paying Your Lawyer

You may have to pay an initial consultation fee as well as a fee for the lawyer's services. The initial consultation fee is usually around $100. Some good lawyers provide free consultations. But many have found that they can't afford to spend a lot of their time this way, since many immigrants have no visa or remedy available to them, which means the lawyer gets no work after the initial consultation. Be ready to pay a reasonable fee for your initial consultation, but do not sign any contracts for further services until you're confident you've found the right lawyer. This usually means consulting with several lawyers before signing a contract with the one you like best.

Many lawyers charge flat rates for green card applications. That means you can compare prices. If the lawyer quotes an hourly rate instead, expect to pay between $100 and $300 per hour.

A higher rate doesn't necessarily mean a better lawyer. Those who charge less may be keeping their overhead low, still making their name in the business, or philosophically opposed to charging high fees. But an extremely low fee may be a sign that the person isn't really a lawyer, as covered in "Watch Out for Nonlawyers Practicing Immigration Law," above.

If the prices you are being quoted are beyond your reach but you definitely need legal help, you have a couple of options. One is to ask the lawyer to split the work with you. With this arrangement, the lawyer consults with you solely about the issue causing you difficulty, reviews a document, or performs some other key task at the hourly rate, while you do the follow-up work, such as filling out the application forms and translating or writing documents, statements, letters, or more.

Be forewarned, though, that while many lawyers will sell you advice on an hourly basis, most won't want to get into a mixed arrangement unless they are sure they won't end up cleaning up anything you might do wrong. For example, a lawyer might not agree to represent you in a USCIS interview if the lawyer wasn't hired to review your forms and documents before you submitted them to USCIS.

Another option is to look for a nonprofit organization that helps people with cases like yours. A few provide free services, while most charge reduced rates.

But don't get your hopes too high. The U.S. government does not fund organizations that provide services to immigrants (except for very limited types of services), which means that most nonprofits depend on private sources of income, and are chronically underfunded. The result is that many nonprofits will have long backlogs of cases and may not be able to take your case at all.

G. Firing Your Lawyer

You have the right to fire your lawyer at any time. But before you take this step, make sure that your disagreement is about something that is truly the lawyer's fault. Many people blame their lawyer for delays that are actually caused by USCIS or the consulates. You can always consult with another lawyer regarding whether your case has been mishandled. Ask your lawyer for a complete copy of your file first—you have a right to your file at any time. If it appears that your case was mishandled, or if relations with your lawyer have deteriorated badly, firing the lawyer may be the healthiest thing for you and your immigration case.

You will have to pay the fired lawyer for any work that has already been done on your case. If you originally paid a flat fee, the lawyer is permitted to keep enough of the fee to cover the work already done, at the lawyer's hourly rate, limited by the total flat fee amount. Ask for a complete list of hours worked and how those hours were spent. Don't count on getting any money back, however—flat fees are often artificially low, and it's very easy for a lawyer to show that he or she used up your fee on the work that was done.

Firing your lawyer will not affect the progress of your applications with USCIS or the consulate. However, you should send a letter to the last USCIS or consular office you heard from, directing them to send all future correspondence directly to you (or to your new lawyer).

H. Do-It-Yourself Legal Research

With or without a lawyer, you may at some point wish to look at the immigration laws yourself. If so, we applaud your self-empowerment instinct—but need to give you a few warnings. A government spokesperson once called the immigration laws a "mystery, and a mastery of obfuscation" (spokeswoman Karen Kraushaar, quoted in *The Washington Post,* April 24, 2001), and they've only gotten worse since her quote. One is tempted to think that the members of the U.S. Congress who write and amend the immigration laws deliberately made them unreadable, perhaps to confuse the rest of the representatives so they wouldn't understand what they were voting on.

The result is that researching the immigration laws is something even the experts find difficult—which means you may be wading into treacherous waters if you try it on your own. Figuring out local USCIS office procedures and policies can be even more difficult. Lawyers learn a great deal through trial and error and through the experiences of other lawyers who tried new tactics or who learned important information from USCIS or State Department cables, memos, or other instructions. Unfortunately, you won't have access to these sources.

Does all this mean that you shouldn't ever do your own legal research? Certainly not. Some research inquiries are quite safe—for instance, if we've cited a section of the law and you want to read the exact language or see whether that section has changed, there's no magic in looking up the law and reading it. But in general, be cautious when researching, and look at several sources to confirm your findings. Immigration laws are federal, meaning they are written by the U.S. Congress and do not vary from one state to another (though procedures and priorities for carrying out the laws may vary among USCIS offices in different cities or states). Below we give you a rundown on the most accessible research tools. Not coincidentally, lawyers often use these tools as well.

1. The Federal Code

The federal immigration law is found in Title 8 of the United States Code. Any law library (such as the one at your local courthouse or law school) should have a complete set of the U.S. Code (traditionally abbreviated as U.S.C.). The library may also have a separate volume containing exactly the same material, but called the Immigration and Nationality Act, or I.N.A.

Unfortunately, the two sets of laws are numbered a bit differently, and not all volumes of the I.N.A. cross-reference back to the U.S. Code, and vice versa. For this reason, when code citations are mentioned in this book, we include both the U.S.C. and I.N.A. numbers. You can also access the U.S. Code via Nolo's website at www.nolo.com. Go to the bottom of the home page, and click Site Map. Under "Legal Research," choose Federal Statutes, then U.S. Code. If you already know the title (which is 8) and section, you can enter them and pull up the text immediately.

2. USCIS and State Department Regulations and Guidance

Another important source of immigration law is the Code of Federal Regulations, or C.F.R. Federal regulations are written by the agencies responsible for carrying out federal law. The regulations are meant to explain in greater detail just how the federal agency is going to carry out the law. You'll find the USCIS regulations at Title 8 of the C.F.R.; the Department of State regulations (relevant to anyone whose application is being decided at a U.S. consulate) at Title 22 of the C.F.R.; and the Department of Labor regulations at 20 C.F.R. The regulations are helpful, but certainly don't have all the answers. Again, your local law library will have the C.F.R.s, and you can find them at www.nolo.com in the Legal Research area as well.

If you are applying from outside of the U.S., you may also wish to look at the State Department's *Foreign Affairs Manual*. This is primarily meant to be an internal government document, containing instructions to the consulates on handling immigrant and nonimmigrant visa cases. However, it is available for public researching as well. Your local law library may be able to find you a copy, or see the State Department's website, at http://foia.state.gov/REGS/Search.asp.

3. Information on the Internet

If you have Internet access, you will want to familiarize yourself with the USCIS, State Department, and Labor Department websites. The addresses are www.uscis.gov, www.state.gov, and www.doleta.gov (for the Employment & Training Administration).

The USCIS website offers advice on various immigration benefits and applications (though the advice is so brief as to sometimes be misleading), downloads of most immigration forms, and current fees.

On the State Department website, some of the useful information is found under "Travel & Business," including the monthly *Visa Bulletin*. Another useful entry address is www.travel.state.gov, from which you can access descriptions of visa types and procedures.

The Department of Labor website contains descriptions of programs for hiring foreign workers, application forms, FAQs, and more. (Click on the "Business & Industry" tab, then follow the links for "Hiring Guest Workers" or "Hiring Foreign Workers.")

The Internet is full of sites put up by immigration lawyers as well as immigrants. Because the quality of these sites varies widely, we don't even attempt to review them here. Many of the lawyers' sites are blatant attempts to give out only enough information to bring in business. The sites by other immigrants are well-meaning and can be good for finding out about the experiences of others; but they're not reliable when it comes to hard legal or procedural facts.

That said, a couple of lawyer sites that contain useful information include www.shusterman.com (by attorney Carl Shusterman, with regular news updates); www.visalaw.com (run by the firm of Siskind Susser, and including regular updates on immigration law matters); and www.ilw.com (a privately run website called The Immigration Portal, which includes articles and various chat room opportunities).

4. Court Decisions

Immigrants who have been denied visas or green cards often appeal these decisions to the federal courts. The courts' decisions in these cases are supposed to govern the future behavior of USCIS and the consulates. However, you should never need to discuss court decisions with a USCIS or State Department official. For one thing, the officials are not likely to listen until they get a specific directive from their superiors or until the court decision is incorporated into their agency's regulations (the C.F.R.). For another thing, such discussions probably mean that your case has become complicated enough to need a lawyer. We do not attempt to teach you how to research federal court decisions here.

5. Legal Publications

Two high-quality and popular resources used by immigration lawyers are *Interpreter Releases*, a weekly update published by Federal Publications Inc. (a West Group company), and *Immigration Law and Procedure*, a multivolume, continually updated looseleaf set by Charles Gordon, Stanley Mailman, and Stephen Yale-Loehr (LEXIS Publishing). Again, you should be able to find both at your local law library. Both are very well indexed. However, they are written for lawyers, so you'll have to wade through some technical terminology.

Internet Resources

This list summarizes the useful Internet sites that have been mentioned in this book.
- U.S. Citizenship and Immigration Services (USCIS): www.uscis.gov
- The U.S. Department of State: www.state.gov or www.travel.state.gov
- U.S. Department of Labor, Employment & Training Administration: www.doleta.gov
- U.S. consulates and embassies abroad: http://usembassy.state.gov
- List of approved nonprofit agencies: www.usdoj.gov/eoir
- Attorney Carl Shusterman: www.shusterman.com
- Siskind Susser: www.visalaw.com
- The Immigration Portal website: www.ilw.com.

Part II

Introduction to Permanent U.S. Residence (Green Cards)

This portion of the book introduces the topic of U.S. lawful permanent residence, otherwise known as a green card. People all over the world have heard of green cards. It is the unofficial term for the Alien Registration Receipt Card, which years ago were green in color. (Today they're pink.)

A lot of people mistakenly believe that green cards are nothing more than work permits. While a green card does give you the right to work legally in the U.S. where and when you wish, that is just one of its features. Identifying the holder as a permanent resident of the U.S. is its main function.

When you have a green card, you are required to make the U.S. your permanent home. If you don't, you risk losing your card. This does not mean your ability to travel in and out of the U.S. is limited. Freedom to travel as you choose is an important benefit of a green card. However, no matter how much you travel, your permanent home must be in the U.S., or your card will be revoked. It's wise not to spend more than six months at a time outside the United States.

All green cards issued since 1989 carry expiration dates of ten years from the date of issue. This does not mean that the residency itself expires in ten years, just that the card must be replaced.

A. Categories of Green Card Applicants

There are nine categories of people who can apply for green cards. In some of the categories you are immediately eligible for a green card, in others you must wait until one is available. We briefly describe the categories here, but you should refer to the appropriate chapter of this book for details.

1. Immediate Relatives

An unlimited number of green cards can be issued to immigrants who are immediate relatives of U.S. citizens. Immediate relatives are defined as:

- spouses of U.S. citizens, including recent widows and widowers
- unmarried people under the age of 21 who have at least one U.S. citizen parent
- parents of U.S. citizens, if the U.S. citizen child is over the age of 21
- stepchildren and stepparents, if the marriage creating the stepparent/stepchild relationship took place before the child's 18th birthday, and
- parents and children related through adoption, if the adoption took place before the child reached the age of 16. All immigration rules governing natural parents and children apply to adoptive relatives but there are some additional procedures.

Immediate relatives are discussed in Chapter 7.

2. Other Relatives

Certain other family members of U.S. citizens or permanent residents are also eligible for U.S. green cards. However, only a limited number of green cards are available to these applicants, based on their place in the preference categories, as outlined below.

- **Family first preference.** Unmarried people, any age, who have at least one U.S. citizen parent.
- **Family second preference.**
  2A: Spouses of green card holders and unmarried children under age 21; **2B:** unmarried sons and daughters (who are over age 21) of green card holders.
- **Family third preference.** Married people, of any age, who have at least one U.S. citizen parent.
- **Family fourth preference.** Sisters and brothers of U.S. citizens where the citizen is over 21 years old.

Family preference categories are discussed in Chapter 7.

3. Employment-Based Green Cards

People with job skills wanted by U.S. employers are also eligible for green cards as outlined below. However, only a limited number of green cards are available to these applicants, based on their place in the preference categories, as outlined below.

- **Employment first preference.** Priority workers, including the following three groups:
  - persons of extraordinary ability in the arts, sciences, education, business, or athletics
  - outstanding professors and researchers, and
  - managers and executives of multinational companies.
- **Employment second preference.** Professionals with advanced degrees or exceptional ability.
- **Employment third preference.** Professionals and skilled or unskilled workers.
- **Employment fourth preference.** Religious workers, various miscellaneous categories of workers, and so-called Special Immigrants.
- **Employment fifth preference.** Individual investors willing to invest $1,000,000 in a U.S. business (or $500,000 if the business is in an economically depressed area).

Employment-based green cards are discussed in Chapter 9.

4. How the Numerical Limits Affect Your Wait for a Green Card

If a family member or employer petitions for you in a preference category—that is, a category with annual limits on the number of visas—your wait could be several years long. Although it's possible to estimate the likely wait in your category, this will be only an estimate. You will need to learn to track it, month by month, based on the *Visa Bulletin* published by the U.S. State Department. This system can be confusing at first. You might want to read this explanation now, to get an idea of how it works, then refer back to it after you are deeper into the application process.

Every government fiscal year (which starts October 1), a fresh supply of visa numbers is made available. How many depends on the numbers of people that Congress has said can get green cards in the preference categories in any one year. (For purposes of this explanation, a visa or visa number means the same thing as a green card.)

There's just one problem. Thousands of people who applied in previous years are probably still waiting for their visa. So you won't be able to make use of this fresh crop of visas right away.

Instead, the State Department (DOS) has devised a system where the people who have been waiting longest have the first right to a visa. DOS keeps track of your place on the waiting list using the date that your family member or employer first submitted a visa petition indicating that they'd like to help you immigrate. That date is called your Priority Date.

You will need to know your Priority Date, because the whole system of figuring out where you are in your wait for a green card depends on it. The DOS's *Visa Bulletin* gives you only one clue about the length of your wait: a list of the Priority Dates of other people who are now getting visas and green cards. By comparing your Priority Date to theirs, you'll be able to track your progress.

Let's take a closer look at how this works, by examining the sample chart from the *Visa Bulletin*, below. (It's the one for family-based applicants; there is another for employment-based applicants.) This chart is from March 2007. To access a current *Visa Bulletin*, go to www.state.gov. Click the "Travel & Business" tab, then under "Visas (Foreign Citizens)," click "Visa Bulletins."

 You can ask to have the *Visa Bulletin* sent to you monthly, by email. This is a great way to make sure you don't forget to check how your Priority Date is advancing. Complete instructions for how to subscribe to this service can be found toward the bottom of any *Visa Bulletin*.

You'll see on the chart below that the preference categories are listed in the column on the left and the countries of origin are listed in the row across the top. The rest of the squares contain the "current" Priority Dates—also called the visa cutoff dates. Anyone whose date

March 2007 Family Preferences				
	All Chargeability Areas Except Those Listed	CHINA-mainland born	INDIA	MEXICO	PHILIPPINES
Family					
1st	01MAY01	01MAY01	01MAY01	01JAN94	22JAN92
2A	22MAR02	22MAR02	22MAR02	15AUG00	22MAR02
2B	01JUL97	01JUL97	01JUL97	01MAR92	01OCT96
3rd	01MAR99	01MAR99	01MAR99	01AUG94	01SEP90
4th	22MAR96	22AUG95	08NOV95	01MAY94	01SEP84

shows up on this chart has finished their wait and is eligible for a green card.

Let's say you are the brother of a U.S. citizen and you're from the Philippines. Let's also imagine that your brother files a petition for you to immigrate, in March 2007. To find out what the waits are like now, as you begin the process, you will need to locate your preference category in the left column (4th Preference, on the bottom line), and your country on the top row, then find the square that corresponds to both—it's the square at the bottom right.

The Priority Date listed in that square is 01SEP84 (September 1, 1984). That tells you that brothers of U.S. citizens who started this process on September 1, 1984, became eligible for green cards in the month this *Visa Bulletin* came out (March 2007). To estimate your wait, figure out how long they waited—about 23 years. That's more or less how long you can expect to wait, starting from your March 2007 Priority Date.

The waiting periods for people from the Philippines tend to be longer than from other countries, because there are so many applicants and a limit on how many can come from any one country. Most people will wait less time. For example, if you were from Brazil and were the spouse of a lawful permanent resident, you would look at the row for category 2A, under the first box saying "All Chargeability Areas Except Those Listed." The corresponding current Priority Date there is March 22, 2002—meaning you could expect a wait of about five years if you applied in March 2007 (the date this *Visa Bulletin* was published).

These waits are frustrating, but there is truly nothing you can do to move them along (unless your family petitioner can become a U.S. citizen, which will often put you into a higher preference category or make you an immediate relative).

As you track these dates over the years, you'll notice they don't advance smoothly. Sometimes they get stuck on one date for months at a time. Other times your square will just say "U" for unavailable, meaning no one is eligible for a green card in that category until further notice—usually when a new fiscal year begins, in October. But if you're really lucky, you may see a "C," meaning that everyone who has a visa petition on file is immediately eligible for a green card, regardless of Priority Date.

Most likely you will eventually see your own Priority Date (or a later date) on the *Visa Bulletin* chart. Then you'll know you're ready for the next step in obtaining your green card, as discussed in the relevant chapter of this book.

5. Diversity Visa: Green Card Lottery

Approximately 50,000 green cards are offered each year to people from countries that in recent years have sent the fewest immigrants to the United States. The purpose of this program is to ensure a varied ethnic mix among those who immigrate to the U.S. (although applicants must also meet certain educational requirements). Therefore, green cards in this category are said to be based on ethnic diversity. The method used for choosing people who can apply for these green cards is a random selection by computer, so the program is popularly known as the green card lottery. This visa is discussed in Chapter 10.

6. Refugees and Political Asylees

Every year, many people seek political asylum in the U.S. or try to get green cards as refugees. The two are often thought of as the same category, but there are some technical differences. A refugee receives permission to come to the U.S. in refugee status before actually arriving. Political asylum is granted only *after* someone has physically entered the U.S., usually either as a nonimmigrant or an undocumented alien, and then submitted an application.

The qualifications for refugee status and political asylum are similar. You must have either been persecuted or fear future persecution in your home country on account of your race, religion, nationality, membership in a particular social group, or political opinion. If you are only fleeing poverty or general violence, you do not qualify in either category. Both refugees and political asylees can apply for green cards one year after their approval (asylees) or entry into the U.S. (refugees). (See Chapter 13 for details.)

7. Temporary Protected Status

The U.S. Congress may decide to give citizens of certain countries temporary safe haven in the U.S. when conditions in their homeland become dangerous. This is called Temporary Protected Status (TPS). TPS is similar to political asylum except that it is always temporary, and will never turn directly into a green card. (See Chapter 13 for more details.)

8. Long-Term Residents and Other Special Cases

The law also allows certain people who have lived illegally in the U.S. for more than ten years to obtain permanent legal residence, through a procedure known as cancellation of removal. They must show that their spouse or children—who are U.S. citizens—would face "extraordinary and exceptionally unusual hardship" if the undocumented alien were forced to leave the country.

If you believe that you meet this requirement, consult with a lawyer before going to the immigration authorities. Otherwise, you might ultimately cause your own deportation by making your presence known. Even if you fall within this category, applying is difficult, because there is no regular process unless you are in deportation proceedings. For this reason, we do not cover the application procedures in this book.

Another category, known as registry allows people to adjust status if they have lived in the United States since January 1, 1972. See a lawyer if you believe you qualify for registry—we do not cover it in this book.

Individual members of Congress have, on occasion, intervened for humanitarian reasons in extraordinary cases, helping an individual obtain permanent residence even if the law would not allow it. How-ever, this is a last resort, and you should explore all other possible options first.

⚠ **This book does not discuss green card programs whose application deadlines have passed.** For example, we do not cover the amnesty and special agricultural worker (SAW) programs of the 1980s, or the so-called NACARA program—despite the fact that ongoing litigation means that many of these cases are not over. For more information, consult an experienced immigration attorney.

The remaining chapters of this Part II, organized by type of green card, will give you details on your eligibility, the advantages and disadvantages of each type of green card, application procedures, and strategies for success.

B. How Many Green Cards Are Available?

There are no limits on the number of green cards that can be issued to immediate relatives of U.S. citizens. For those who qualify in any other category, there are annual quotas. Both family and employment preference-based green cards are affected by quotas.

Green cards allocated annually to employment-based categories, including investors and Special Immigrants, number 140,000 worldwide. Approximately 480,000 green cards worldwide can be issued each year in the family categories.

Only 7% of all worldwide preference visas can be given to persons born in any one country. There are, therefore, two separate quotas: one for each country and one that is worldwide. This produces an odd result, because when you multiply the number of countries in the world by seven (the percentage allowed to each country) you get a much larger total than 100. What this means from a practical standpoint is that the 7% allotment to each country is an allowable maximum, not a guaranteed number. Applicants from a single country that has not used up its 7% green card allotment can still be prevented from getting green cards if the worldwide quota has been exhausted. Right now, there are, in fact, waiting periods in many preference categories, caused by the limits of the worldwide quota.

In addition to the fixed worldwide totals, 50,000 extra green cards are given each year through the ethnic diversity or lottery category. Qualifying countries and the number of green cards available to each are determined each year according to a formula. ∎

Chapter 7

Getting a Green Card Through Family Members in the U.S.

I f you have close family members in the United States, they may, if they are willing, be able to help you immigrate. It depends first on what relation they are to you—the closer the relation, the more rights you have under immigration law. It also depends on whether your relatives are U.S. citizens or lawful permanent residents (green card holders). U.S. citizens can bring more distant relatives than green card holders can—their parents and brothers and sisters, for example. Also, U.S. citizens' relatives are allowed, in many cases, to immigrate faster than lawful permanent residents' relatives are. This chapter will explain who is eligible for a green card through their family members and how to apply for it.

Do you need a lawyer? Many people are able to handle the application process for a family-based visa on their own, without a lawyer. However, if you have trouble dealing with paperwork or understanding the instructions, or have any complications in your case (such as a criminal record, including by the U.S. petitioner, particularly if he or she has committed offenses against a minor; past visa overstays in the U.S.; an abusive spouse upon whom you are relying to help you immigrate; or an immigrating child who will turn 21 soon), a lawyer is well worth the price. See Chapter 6 for tips on finding a good one.

Key Features of Family-Based Green Cards

Here are some of the advantages and disadvantages of permanent residence obtained through U.S. family members:

- Unlike many other green cards, your educational background or work experience do not matter.
- Your spouse and unmarried children under the age of 21 are in many cases also eligible for green cards, as derivative, accompanying relatives.
- As with all green cards, yours can be taken away if you misuse it—for example, you live outside the U.S. for too long, commit a crime, or even fail to advise the immigration authorities of your change of address. However, if you successfully keep your green card for five years (or three years if you're married to and still living with a U.S. citizen), you can apply for U.S. citizenship.

A. Are You Eligible for a Green Card Through a Relative?

You may qualify for a green card through relatives if you fall into one of the following categories:

- immediate relative of a U.S. citizen
- preference relative of a U.S. citizen or green card holder, or
- accompanying relative of someone in a preference category.

1. Immediate Relatives

These people qualify as immediate relatives:

- spouses of U.S. citizens. This includes widows and widowers of U.S. citizens if they were married to the U.S. citizen for at least two years and are applying for a green card within two years of the U.S. citizen's death.
- unmarried children of a U.S. citizen, under the age of 21, and
- parents of U.S. citizens, if the U.S. citizen child is age 21 or older. If the U.S. citizen child was abusing a parent, and then either died, or lost citizenship status as a result of the abuse, the parent can file his or her own immigration petition on USCIS Form I-360. (This is a 2005 legal change, amending a portion of the immigration laws known as VAWA.) The abused parent must prove that

he or she has good moral character, lives or has lived with the U.S. citizen child, and has been battered or subject to extreme cruelty by the child.

Immediate relatives may immigrate to the U.S. in unlimited numbers. They are not controlled by any annual limit or quota.

Stepparents and stepchildren qualify as immediate relatives if the marriage creating the parent/child relationship took place before the child's 18th birthday.

Parents and children related through adoption may, in some cases, qualify as immediate relatives. (See section 2, below, for information on adopting a foreign-born child. If an adopted U.S. citizen child wants to petition for foreign-born parents to immigrate, the requirements are similar to those described below, in that the adoption must have been finalized before the child's 16th birthday, the parent must have had legal custody of the child for two years before or after the adoption, and the child must have lived with the adoptive parent for two years before or after the adoption.)

2. Adopting a Foreign-Born Child

People hoping for green cards often ask their attorneys whether they could become eligible by having a U.S. citizen adopt them. Unfortunately, this rarely works—for one thing, anyone over the age of 16 is already too old for a green card through adoption. For another thing, adopted children who are not orphaned must live in the petitioning parents' legal custody for two years before applying for the green card, which is all but impossible unless the parents live outside the United States.

Orphan adoptions are a bit easier, which is the reason that many U.S. citizen parents seeking to adopt look to foreign orphanages. As a practical matter, the parents usually use the help of adoption agencies in the U.S., which are better versed in the procedures than many attorneys. For this reason, this book will not discuss adoption procedures at length, beyond the following introduction to the basic rules.

Even with an agency, expect the process to take at least six to 12 months. Although we can't provide you with a list of reputable agencies, two California-based groups that Nolo lawyers have had good experiences with are Adopt International, at 415-934-0300, www.adoptinter.org; and Adoption Connection, at 800-972-9225, 415-359-2494, www.adoptionconnection.org.

Be selective in choosing an adoption agency—look for one that has been doing adoptions for a number of years, successfully completes a comparatively large number per year, serves the countries in which you're interested, and is happy to show you evidence that it's licensed and comes with good references. The U.S. government also provides a centralized information source, the Child Welfare Information Gateway, at www.childwelfare.gov.

a. Orphan Eligibility

Orphan means a child whose natural parents are either deceased, have disappeared, or have permanently and legally deserted or abandoned the child. Or if only one parent is absent, the other parent hasn't remarried and is incapable of providing child care that meets the standard of living in their country.

Be careful: Some parents may put a child into an orphanage temporarily, without giving up all of their parental rights, in which case the child isn't eligible to immigrate. In the case of a birth to nonmarried parents, if the law of the native country confers equal benefits to illegitimate and legitimate children, both parents must relinquish their rights.

In addition, the orphan child must be living outside the U.S. and, if not already adopted by the U.S. parents, must either be in the U.S. parents' custody or in the custody of an agent acting on their behalf in accordance with local law. You cannot get a green card for a child you've adopted while the child was already in the U.S., whether the child is here on a visa or is undocumented. Finally, the child must be under 16 years of age when the initial visa petition (that starts the green card process) is filed.

The adopting parents themselves must also meet certain criteria. First, at least one of the parents must be a U.S. citizen; and if the other parent is not a U.S. citi-

International Adoption for Lesbians and Gays

Currently, no foreign country allows adoption by same-sex couples or by any openly gay person. Most countries strongly prefer that the adopting parents be married. In fact, some won't allow adoption by single people at all, and there's an unfortunate trend in that direction. If a country requires adoptive parents to be married, then neither a same-sex couple nor a lesbian or gay individual can adopt there. Although many states in the U.S. have expanded the rights of same-sex couples to adopt, it's doubtful that such change in the U.S. will have any impact on the host country's policy.

At least one country (China) is so determined not to grant adoptions to lesbians and gays that it requires adoptive parents to sign an affidavit swearing that they are heterosexual. Apparently undeterred by signing such a form, a large number of same-sex couples have successfully adopted Chinese girls who were being raised in orphanages.

As a result, if you are not heterosexual and are proceeding with a foreign adoption, you will need to keep your sexual orientation—and your relationship with your partner—hidden from the host country. It is a judgment call whether or not you tell the agency helping you with the adoption about your sexual orientation. Many agencies operate on a wink-and-nod basis—they are fully aware of the nature of your relationship with your partner, but refer to the partner as a "roommate" in their reports to the host country, and simply ignore the issue of sexual orientation.

No agency will advertise that it works with same-sex couples or lesbian/gay individuals on international adoptions, so word of mouth is the best way to find an agency to help you.

For more about adoption and parenting for same-sex couples, check out *A Legal Guide for Lesbian & Gay Couples,* by Hayden Curry, Denis Clifford, and Frederick Hertz (Nolo).

---

zen, he or she must be legally present in the United States. If an adopting parent is single, he or she must be at least 25 years of age. There are no age restrictions if the petitioner is married.

b. Orphan Immigration Procedures

Procedurally, the orphan adoption process begins when the U.S. citizen parents submit a visa petition to a USCIS service center. Which form they use, and the precise procedures that follow, depend upon whether or not they've actually identified the child.

Parents who already have a particular child in mind would use USCIS Form I-600, accompanied by documents proving the petitioner's U.S. citizen status and qualifications to adopt, his or her marriage to the other parent, completion of a home study (by the state government or an approved agency) and any preadoption requirements in the state where they live, and the child's age, orphan status, legal custody status, and availability for adoption. The petition must be accompanied by an application fee (currently $750) and a fingerprinting or biometrics fee ($80). The parents may submit the visa petition either before or after the legal adoption is completed; and if it has been completed, they should also include the adoption certificate.

To save time, some parents can simply figure out which country they'll be adopting from, satisfy any preadoption requirements existing in the laws of the U.S. state where they live, and then start the process with a slightly different immigration form, I-600A, plus relevant documents and a $750 application fee and $80 biometrics fee. They would then submit Form I-600 with the remaining documents after the child has been identified, but without needing to pay the fees again. Eventually, the parents will have to meet the child in person, before or during the adoption proceedings.

After the parents have submitted the Form I-600, they will be called in for fingerprinting, and USCIS will evaluate whether they meet the various requirements. Once the petition has been approved, the procedures will follow the usual consular processing procedures described in Section E, below.

c. Nonorphan Eligibility

A nonorphan may qualify for a green card if his or her adoption was finalized before his or her 16th birthday. It doesn't matter how old the child is when the initial visa petition is filed (to start a green card application process). In addition to being legally adopted, the child must have been in the legal custody of, and physically residing with, the adopting parents for at least two years before applying for a green card. It doesn't matter whether those two years were before or after the adoption took place.

As a practical matter, however, the residency requirement usually means that at least one of the parents must live outside of the U.S. with the child for two years. USCIS doesn't offer any temporary visas allowing the child to come to the U.S. to fulfill the two-year requirement before applying for the green card. (Though in rare cases usually amounting to emergencies, it might allow something called humanitarian parole.) Most U.S. parents who don't already have a particular child in mind find it easier to locate an orphan to adopt.

Unfortunately, the combination of limited number of visas per year and the two-year residency requirement can make it impossible for a permanent resident parent or parents to be united with a newly adopted child. Here's why: The child won't be able to legally enter the U.S. until he or she has a green card. (As an "intending immigrant," the child is not going to be allowed a tourist visa.) But the child can't get a green card unless he or she has already lived in the U.S. parent's legal custody for two years. If the child had been adopted before his or her parent(s) came to the U.S., and they had lived together outside of the U.S. for two years, this would not be a problem. But if the child has recently been adopted, the family is stuck in an impossible situation. The permanent resident parent can't even choose to live outside of the U.S. for the two years, since by doing so he or she may be considered to have abandoned, or given up, his or her U.S. residence and green card.

For a nonorphan to get a green card, it is also necessary that the adopting parents meet certain requirements. They must be investigated by a U.S. state public or government-licensed private adoption agency. Such an investigation is usually part of standard adoption procedure in most U.S. states. If, however, the adoption takes place outside the U.S., or an investigation is not compulsory in the particular U.S. state where the adoption occurs, this study must now be satisfactorily completed. The age of the petitioning parent is irrelevant in filing a nonorphan petition, even if the parent is unmarried.

d. Nonorphan Immigration Procedures

If a child adopted by a U.S. citizen parent or green card holder falls into the category of nonorphan, the procedures for obtaining a green card are exactly the same as those for blood-related children of parents who are U.S. citizens or green card holders. See the remainder of this chapter for further instructions. Note that for an adopted child, either a consular or U.S. filing is possible, depending on the physical location of the child when the application is submitted.

 You'll also need to follow the rules of the country you're adopting from. Not every country allows international adoptions, and those that do usually impose various requirements on the parents. For example, some countries refuse to allow single-parent adoptions, or require that adopting parents be of a certain age. You'll need to research these international requirements on your own or with the help of your adoption agency.

3. Preference Relatives

You may qualify for a green card through relatives if you fall into one of the categories below; but, depending on demand, you'll have to wait in line, possibly for many years, before claiming your green card:

- **Family first preference.** Unmarried children, any age, of a U.S. citizen.
- **Family second preference. 2A:** Spouses and unmarried children (under 21 years old) of green card holders; and **2B:** unmarried sons and daughters of green card holders, who are at least 21 years old.

Moving Between the Visa Categories

During the long wait for a green card, people's life circumstances change. This may mean they move from one preference category to another, move up to immediate relative, or even lose eligibility for a green card altogether. Here's a summary of the changes that most commonly affect applicants:

- **Immediate relatives:**
  - If the spouse of a U.S. citizen divorces before being approved for a green card, he or she loses eligibility (except in cases where the U.S. citizen was abusive).
  - If the minor child of a U.S. citizen marries, she drops from immediate relative to family third preference.
  - If the unmarried child of a U.S. citizen turns 21 after the visa petition is filed, she is protected, under the 2002 Child Status Protection Act (CSPA), from changing visa categories ("aging out")—she will remain an immediate relative.
- **Family first preference relatives:** If the child of a U.S. citizen gets married, he or she drops to family third preference, but keeps the same Priority Date.

- **Family second preference relatives:**
  - If the child of a permanent resident (category 2A) marries, he or she completely loses green card eligibility under this petition.
  - If a child in category 2A turns 21 *before* his or her Priority Date is current, the child drops into category 2B and faces a longer wait (but if the child turns 21 *after* his or her Priority Date is current, he or she can retain 2A status by filing for a green card within one year, under the CSPA; the child can also subtract from his or her age the number of days it took the former INS or USCIS to make a decision on the initial visa petition).
  - In cases where the petitioning spouse or parent of a second preference beneficiary becomes a U.S. citizen, the immigrant spouse or children in category 2A become immediate relatives and the children in category 2B move up to family first preference, keeping the same Priority Date.
- **Family third preference:** If the child of a U.S. citizen divorces (for real reasons, not just to get a green card), he or she moves up to family first preference and retains the same Priority Date.

- **Family third preference.** Married children of a U.S. citizen, any age.
- **Family fourth preference.** Sisters and brothers of U.S. citizens, where the U.S. citizen is at least 21 years old.

4. Bringing Your Spouse and Children

If you are getting a green card as a preference relative and you are married or have unmarried children below the age of 21, your spouse and children can get green cards as accompanying relatives by proving their family relationship to you and filling out some applications of their own—it takes only one Form I-130 visa petition to start the process. If, however, you qualify as an immediate relative, they cannot. Ordinarily, this doesn't cause problems—for example, a U.S. citizen petitioning his or her spouse can simply file separate visa petitions for each child (on Form I-130) so that they don't have to ride on their parent's visa application.

This difference may, however, create some real problems in cases involving parents immigrating through their adult children or stepparents and stepchildren who wish to immigrate as a family (as illustrated in the examples below). This is probably one of the most difficult areas in immigration to understand. If you don't have adult children or stepchildren involved in your immigration plans, skip these examples.

EXAMPLE 1: Suppose your daughter is over age 21 and is a U.S. citizen. You are applying for a green card as an immediate relative (her mother), with your U.S.-citizen daughter acting as petitioner. Suppose also that your husband, the child's father, has died, and last year (when your child was 20) you married someone else. In that case, your spouse has a problem. He or she can't get a green card automatically as an accompanying relative, because you are an immediate relative, not a preference relative, and only preference relatives can bring accompanying relatives. But your child cannot petition for your new husband or wife directly, because they are not related. Any children you may have, even if they are minors, cannot be accompanying relatives either, for the same reason. You will have to wait until you get your own green card and are living in the U.S., at which time you can petition for your spouse and children under the family second preference category (as the relative of a green card holder).

If your present marriage had taken place before your U.S. son or daughter reached the age of 18, your new husband's problem would be solved, because he would, according to immigration law, be your child's stepparent. Likewise, if your husband adopted your U.S. citizen child before the child's 16th birthday, he would qualify as an adopting parent. Stepparents and adopting parents count as immediate relatives of a U.S. citizen, and your child can petition for a stepparent or adopting parent just as if he or she were a natural parent.

Suppose instead that your spouse did not die, but is the father or mother of your U.S. citizen child. In that case, your child may file petitions for each parent at the same time, as immediate relatives, but the two filings will be completely separate. The marriage between you and your spouse will not be relevant when the USCIS considers your cases.

Your U.S citizen child may also sponsor his or her brothers and sisters under the family fourth preference category. Again, however, the fact that you qualify for a green card will not help your children. There is a long wait under the quota for family fourth preference applicants, while there is no wait at all for immediate relatives. Members of the same family may be forced to immigrate on different time schedules. (On the other hand, after you get your green card, you can file a separate visa petition for your children—even if your U.S. citizen child has already filed a visa petition for them—and see which waiting period goes by the fastest.)

EXAMPLE 2: Suppose you are unmarried and under age 21. Your parent is a U.S. citizen and is petitioning for you to get a green card. You are in the unique situation of being able to choose between classifications. You qualify either as an immediate relative or in the family first preference category. It would seem logical for you to choose the immediate relative category, because preference relatives are subject to annual limits, and therefore long waits, while immediate relatives are not.

But this may not be the right choice if you have a child of your own. In that case, it's more logical to place yourself in the preference category, because then your child could automatically be eligible for a green card as an accompanying relative. Without this option, your child will have to wait until you have become a green card holder living in the U.S., and can petition for him or her in Category 2A (which will take several years to complete).

5. Marriage to a U.S. Citizen

Almost everyone knows that there are immigration advantages to marrying a U.S. citizen. It's also no secret that many who are not fortunate enough to have

U.S. citizen relatives try to acquire one through a marriage of convenience.

For a fuller discussion of all aspects of applying for a green card through marriage to a U.S. citizen or permanent resident, see *Fiancé & Marriage Visas: A Couple's Guide to U.S. Immigration*, by Ilona Bray (Nolo).

a. Two-Year Testing Period for Marriage-Based Green Cards

Because suspicions are so high regarding foreign nationals who marry U.S. citizens, they face extra hurdles in getting a green card through marriage to a U.S. citizen. If you have been married for less than two years when your application is approved, the card will be issued only conditionally. These conditional green cards last for two years. When that time is up, you must apply to USCIS to have the condition removed and your green card made permanent. If you are still married, you and your U.S. spouse should file an application together. Then, if the USCIS continues to believe your marriage was for real, not just for immigration purposes, you will receive a permanent green card.

Sham Marriages and the Law

By law, green cards are not available to people who marry only for immigration purposes. Such marriages, even though they may be legal in every other way, are regarded by immigration officials as shams. Of course, it can be very difficult for U.S. government officers to tell which marriages are shams and which are not. However, USCIS and the Department of State have been heard to assert that more than half of all the marriage applications they process are fake. It is not surprising, then, that they are especially careful about investigating marriage cases.

It is a criminal offense to file a green card application based on a sham marriage. If you attempt to qualify for a green card in this way, you will risk money penalties and a long jail sentence as well as deportation. In addition, you will almost certainly be permanently barred from getting a green card. The U.S. citizen also risks being charged a fine and/or going to jail.

If, however, your marriage has ended or your U.S. spouse simply refuses to cooperate, you must file for removal of the condition yourself. Under these circumstances you can still keep your green card if you can show one of the following things:

- your spouse has died, but you entered into the marriage in good faith: in other words, your marriage was not a sham
- you are now divorced, but you originally entered into the marriage in good faith
- your eventual deportation will cause you extreme hardship, greater than that suffered by most people who are deported, or
- you were abused or subjected to extreme cruelty by your U.S. citizen or green card holder spouse.

A green card approved after two years of marriage is permanent, with no condition attached. If you have been married for close to two years, and have a green card marriage interview scheduled shortly before your anniversary, you may want to consider postponing the interview until afterward. If your interview is at a U.S. consulate in another country, there is no need to delay it if you will reach your two-year anniversary before you actually use your visa to enter the United States.

Even when you stay married for two years or more and get your permanent green card, if you divorce at a later time, your immigration benefits are still restricted. Although you can keep the green card, if you remarry within five years and petition for your next husband or wife to get a green card, USCIS will assume that your first marriage was one of convenience, unless and until you prove

through convincing documentation that it was not. If you can make such a showing, you may sponsor your new spouse within five years of the first marriage. Otherwise, you have to wait until the five years has passed.

b. Marriages to Abusive U.S. Spouses

If you are the battered or abused spouse or child (unmarried, under age 21) of a U.S. citizen and he or she refuses to petition on your behalf, you can petition for yourself. (This comes from the 1994 Violence Against Women Act, or VAWA, at I.N.A. § 204(a), 8 U.S.C. § 1154.) You must be physically inside the U.S. to take advantage of this opportunity. Children between ages 21 and 25 can still petition if they can prove that the child abuse was at least one central reason for the filing delay.

You must also prove all of the following:

- that you were either battered or subjected to extreme cruelty by the U.S. spouse during the marriage
- that you have good moral character (note that having a prior removal order on your record is no longer a bar to establishing good moral character, thanks to amendments to VAWA passed in 2005)
- that you resided with your spouse or parent inside the U.S., or that you lived with the spouse or parent outside of the U.S. and the abuser is an employee of the U.S. government or Armed Forces, and

- if you're a spouse, that the marriage was entered into in good faith—that is, not just to get a green card.

USCIS recognizes that a wide range of behavior can constitute battery or extreme cruelty, such as threats, beatings, sexual use or exploitation, threats to deport the immigrant or turn him or her over to immigration authorities, forcible detention, or threatened or committed acts of violence against another person in order to mold the immigrant's behavior.

⚠️ **If the abuser loses his or her immigration status, you lose your right to submit a self petition.** For example, if he or she had a green card, and is removed or deported from the U.S., you are considered to have no basis to apply for residency. If you've already submitted the petition, however, you're okay. Also, an exception has been carved out for cases where the abuser loses his or her status during the two years immediately before you file your self petition for a reason that is related to or due to an incident of domestic violence. (The crime of domestic violence is a ground of removal.) The purpose of this is to make sure that you don't hesitate to call the police out of fear that you'll lose your right to self petition.

Children of the abuser can either submit their own self petition or, if their parent is self petitioning, they can gain legal status by being included on the parent's petition.

The self-petition application is done on a different form than most family petitions: USCIS Form I-360. As important as the form, however, is the collection of documents you must assemble to prove your case, including your own statement, describing the situation in detail. For some applicants, one of the toughest documents to come up with is one proving that the abuser was a U.S. citizen or lawful permanent resident (such as a copy of a U.S. passport, birth certificate, or green card). If you can't locate any such document, and if your spouse or parent obtained a green card or naturalization certificate through the USCIS, it is willing to check its computer records to help you.

The completed packet must be sent to the USCIS Vermont Service Center (no fee). Also, you can, if you are married to a U.S. citizen, or are the unmarried child under age 21 of the U.S. citizen, apply to adjust status (get a green card), at the same time, using the document list in this chapter. (But you'd still send the whole packet to the Vermont Service Center.) If you are instead married to, or the unmarried child under age 21 of, a lawful permanent resident, you must wait for a visa to become available before applying for adjustment of status.

Get professional help. It's worth trying to find a free or low-cost attorney at a nonprofit organization to help you with the self petition and subsequent green card application.

c. Marriage During Removal Proceedings

If you marry a U.S. citizen or green card holder while you are in the middle of removal (deportation) proceedings, you may still apply for a green card. However, an even stricter standard will be applied when your motives for marriage are examined. You will be required to produce clear and convincing evidence that your marriage is not a sham. Expect a very detailed marriage interview. Definitely hire an immigration attorney.

d. Widows and Widowers

If your U.S. citizen husband or wife dies before filing a petition for you to get a green card, what happens? You may still apply, but only if you were married for at least two years before the U.S. spouse's death occurred. To do so, file a petition on Form I-360. This petition must be filed no more than two years after the death of the U.S. citizen. If you remarry before you are approved for your green card, then you lose your right to it. However, if you remarry after getting a green card, it will not be taken away.

These rules apply only to the surviving spouses of U.S. citizens. Husbands and wives of green card holders may get green cards themselves only if the petitioner remains alive until the permanent residence is actually approved. In extraordinarily sympathetic circumstances, however, you can write a letter asking USCIS to grant the green card even though the petitioner died. This is called humanitarian reinstatement. You should get a lawyer's help for this.

B. Quick View of the Application Process

Getting a green card through a relative is a two- to four-step process. Certain parts of this process are technically the responsibility of your sponsoring relative, who is referred to as the petitioner. Other parts are meant to be done by you.

 You're allowed to help the petitioner fill out the forms for you. As we give you step-by-step instructions for getting a green card, we will discuss each task according to who has the legal responsibility for carrying it out. However, even if the law presumes your relative is performing a particular task, there is nothing to stop you from helping your relative with the paperwork. In fact, we recommend that you do so. For example, you can fill out forms intended to be completed by your relative and simply ask him or her to check them over, fill in whatever is left, and sign them.

The main steps are as follows:

- Your U.S. citizen or permanent resident relative starts the process by filing what's called a visa petition (on USCIS Form I-130). If you are a widow or abused spouse or child, however, you would self-petition, by filing Form I-360. The object of the petition is to establish that you are what you say you are: namely, the qualifying relative of a qualifying sponsor.

- If you're in a preference relative category, then after USCIS approves the petition, you wait until a visa becomes available (based on your Priority Date, when your petitioner turned in the visa petition).

- Once your visa petition has been approved, and a visa is available to you, you submit an application for permanent residence (an immigrant visa and green card), either at a U.S. consulate outside the United States, or through a process called adjustment of status at a USCIS office inside the United States.

- If you applied at a U.S. consulate, you use your immigrant visa to enter the United States and claim your permanent residence status.

⚠️ **An approved visa petition does not by itself give you any right to be present, enter, or work in the United States.** It is only a prerequisite to submitting the application for a green card. Your petition must be approved and your Priority Date must be current before you are eligible for a green card. (On the other hand, if you are already living in the United States illegally and know you are eligible for adjustment of status, you will lose that eligibility if you leave.) Consult an attorney for a personal analysis of your case.

C. Step One: Your U.S. Relative Files the Visa Petition

To start the process of immigrating through a family member, your U.S.-based family member must submit what's called a visa petition to USCIS, on Form I-130. The visa petition asks USCIS to acknowledge that your family relationship exists, and to let you go forward with green card processing. Approval of the visa petition does not mean you're guaranteed approval of your green card, however. This is only the first step in the process. Like every immigrant, you will have to file your own, extensive portion of the green card application. At that time, the U.S. immigration authorities will take a hard look at your financial situation and other factors that might make you inadmissible.

Form I-130 is available at www.uscis .gov—and it comes with extensive instructions. Aside from asking for some basic biographical information, the form takes care of some other details, like informing USCIS whether you will be continuing with your application through a U.S. consulate outside the United States or a U.S.-based USCIS office. (If you're not sure, choose the consulate—if you change your mind later, all you need to do is file an application at a USCIS office. Doing the reverse, and transferring your case from a USCIS office to a consulate, requires filing a separate application.)

The I-130 also provides space to list your spouse and children (who may want to immigrate along with you). Be sure not to leave anyone off the list, even if that person doesn't want to immigrate now. USCIS wants to know about all your family members, and if someone who wasn't on the list decides to immigrate later, you may have trouble convincing USCIS that he or she is really a member of your family.

The checklist below provides a complete list of what should go into your visa petition.

⚠️ **A petitioner who has been convicted of any "specified offense against a minor" is not eligible to file Form I-130.** It doesn't matter whether the immigrant is an adult or a child. See an attorney for more information or for help in requesting a waiver to this rule.

Checklist of Forms and Documents for I-130 Visa Petition

Your family petitioner will need to assemble the following:

Forms

❑ Form I-130 (needed in all family cases except those involving widows and widowers or battered spouses).

❑ Fee for Form I-130 (currently $355; checks and money orders made out to Department of Homeland Security are accepted—do not send cash).

❑ Form I-360 (used by widows and widowers or battered spouses only, in place of Form I-130).

❑ Fee for Form I-360 (no fee for self-petitioning battered or abused spouse, parent, or child of a U.S. citizen or permanent resident; Amerasians or special immigrant juveniles; all others pay $375).

❑ Form G-325A (needed only in marriage cases; one form is required for each spouse).

Documents

❑ Petitioner's proof of U.S. citizenship or green card status.

❑ Your long-form birth certificate.

❑ Marriage certificate, if you're applying based on marriage to a U.S. citizen or permanent resident.

❑ If either the petitioner or you has been married before, copies of all divorce and death certificates showing termination of all previous marriages.

❑ If you are applying as a battered spouse, evidence of physical abuse, such as police reports, medical or psychiatric reports, or affidavits from people familiar with the situation, such as friends, landlords, and shelter staff.

❑ If you are a father petitioning for a child, certificate showing marriage to child's mother.

❑ If you are either a father petitioning for an illegitimate child, or an illegitimate child petitioning for your father, documents proving both paternity and either legitimation or a genuine parent/child relationship.

❑ If the petition is for an adopted (nonorphan) child:

  ❑ adoption decree, or child's new birth certificate showing you are the parent

  ❑ evidence you and the child have lived together for at least two years, and

  ❑ evidence you have had legal custody of the child for at least two years.

❑ If the petition is for a U.S. citizen's brother or sister, a copy of the parents' marriage certificate and the brother or sister's birth certificate.

❑ If you are either a stepchild petitioning for your stepparent, or a stepparent petitioning for a stepchild, the stepparent's marriage certificate as well as divorce decrees or death certificates indicating that all prior marriages of the stepparent or the natural parent were legally terminated. You must also present a stepchild's long-form birth certificate to show the names of his or her natural parents.

❑ In marriage cases, one photograph of each spouse.

❑ If you are filing a petition as a widow(er), your marriage certificate, proof that any previous marriages were legally ended, and your spouse's death certificate showing that the death occurred within the last two years.

Married Beneficiaries Living Outside of the U.S. Can Use Fiancé Visas (K-3)

Before December 2000, there was a clear split between the types of visas available to foreign-born persons living outside the U.S. but intending to immigrate through their U.S. citizen fiancé or spouse. Those who were engaged to U.S. citizens could use a fiancé visa to enter the United States (after which they could marry and apply for their green card), while the already-married persons had to go through the whole green card application process outside of the U.S. and use a marriage-based visa to enter the United States. The problem was, the fiancé visa application process was simpler, and therefore unmarried couples were being reunited in the United States faster than the already-married ones.

To address this unfairness, in December 2000, Congress passed legislation providing a new visa option to immigrating spouses of U.S. citizens. These spouses are now able to use a variety of the fiancé visa to enter the United States, even though they are already married. (However, if the marriage took place outside the U.S., note that you can apply for the K-3 visa only at a consulate in the country where the marriage took place.) Like the fiancé visa, their visa is coded with the letter K—the new spouse visa is called a K-3 visa (and accompanying children receive K-4 visas), while the regular fiancé visa is still called a

K-1 (and the children receive K-2s). The reason that this new visa can be faster is that the immigrant spouse doesn't have to wait outside the U.S. through the entire green card application process. It's sort of like cutting the process into two halves, the second of which will be conducted in the United States. Although this may (depending on how backed up the relevant offices are) allow the couple to be together sooner than they otherwise would have, the new visa is no savings on overall paperwork. The married immigrant using a fiancé visa will still have to go through the full application process for a green card (adjustment of status) once he or she is in the United States. (The immigrant also has the option of returning to the U.S. consulate for final green card processing.)

To apply, the petitioning U.S. spouse should file a single Form I-129F (the fiancé visa petition, covered in Chapter 8; include the proper fee and proof of having submitted Form I-130 as well) and a separate Form I-130 for the immigrating spouse. Forms I-130 should also be submitted for each accompanying child, unless the child is between ages 18 and 21, in which case filing an I-130 would destroy their eligibility to enter the U.S. using a fiancé visa. (Form I-130 is covered in this chapter. Form I-129F is usually used for regular fiancés—USCIS may eventually design a new form for

Married Beneficiaries Living Outside of the U.S. Can Use Fiancé Visas (K-3) (continued)

K-3/K-4 visas.) On Question 22 of Form I-130, the petitioner should find a place to write *"applicant plans to obtain a K-3/K-4 visa abroad and* [either: *adjust status in the United States* or *return to the U.S. consulate for consular processing*, whichever one you choose]."

The applications must be mailed to USCIS service centers in the United States; see the form or www.uscis.gov for the addresses.

You can submit these two applications almost simultaneously, but start with the Form I-130 petition—you'll need to make a copy of it and get proof of its mailing (such as a delivery service receipt) to include with the Form I-129F fiancé visa petition. (Eventually USCIS may start insisting that you wait for the USCIS notice indicating its receipt of your Form I-130 petition to include with your Form I-129F petition, but so far USCIS has been willing to accept lesser forms of proof that you filed Form I-130.)

After your Form I-129F petition is approved, the case will be transferred to a U.S. consulate. The consulate will follow up with you, but the procedures should return to the normal steps for fiancé visas as described in Chapter 8. By the way, if your Form I-130 is approved before your consular interview for the K-3 visa, you'll have a choice of how to proceed. You can either ask that the approval be forwarded to the consulate,

and then apply for an immigrant visa, allowing you to become a permanent resident as soon as you enter the U.S.; or you can proceed with the K-3 visa, and then apply for adjustment of status after arriving in the United States. Many people prefer to continue with the K-3 visa, because it tends to get you into the U.S. faster, where you can complete the harder part of the application, potentially with the help of a lawyer. After entering the U.S., you won't need to wait for approval of the Form I-130 to submit the green card (adjustment of status) application at a USCIS office. When you file for adjustment, the USCIS office handling your file will simply request your I-130 file from wherever it's then being processed. (Nevertheless, the K-3/K-4 visas will cover a two-year stay in the U.S. Children who will turn 21 within those two years, however, will be issued K-4 visas that are good only until their 21st birthday. To make sure that the green card application can be submitted and approved before the birthday, keep writing to the USCIS office handling the Form I-130 and ask it to expedite, or speed up its decision.)

Holders of K-3 and K-4 visas can apply for work authorization. Use Form I-765 (available on the USCIS website). Send it with two photos and the proper fee (currently $340), to the USCIS office that handled the fiancé visa application.

A few of the items on this checklist require extra explanation:

Proof of the petitioner's status. All I-130 petitions must be filed with evidence that the petitioner is either a U.S. citizen or a U.S. lawful permanent resident (green card holder). (Send copies, not originals.)

If the petitioner is a U.S. citizen by birth, a birth certificate is the best proof. Only birth certificates issued by a U.S. state government agency are acceptable. Hospital birth certificates cannot be used. When the petitioner is a U.S. citizen born outside U.S. territory, a certificate of citizenship, naturalization certificate, or U.S. consular record of birth abroad are best. An unexpired U.S. passport can also serve as proof. If the petitioner is a U.S. citizen but does not have any of these documents, read Chapter 4 to learn how to obtain them.

If the petitioner is not a U.S. citizen but is a permanent resident, his or her status can be proven with the petitioner's green card (make a copy of both sides), unexpired reentry permit, or passport with an unexpired stamp indicating admission to the U.S. as a permanent resident. (The unexpired stamp in a foreign passport is used only in the few cases where the petitioner has just been approved for a green card but is still waiting to receive the card itself. The card typically arrives by mail several months later.) When green card holders act as petitioners, USCIS will not check its own records to establish the exis-

tence of the green card. Your petitioning relative is responsible for supplying this evidence.

Marriage certificate. If the basis of the petition is your marriage to a U.S. citizen or green card holder, you must establish that you are lawfully married to the petitioner. Do this by showing a valid civil marriage certificate. Church certificates are generally insufficient. You may have married in a country where marriages are not customarily recorded. Tribal areas of Africa are an example. See Chapter 4 of this book for more information, or call the nearest consulate or embassy of your home country for help with finding acceptable proof of marriage.

Proof of termination of prior marriages. If either you or your spouse has been married before, you must prove that all prior marriages were legally terminated. This requires either a divorce decree or death certificate ending every prior marriage. Where a death certificate is needed, it must be an official document issued by a government. Certificates from funeral homes are not acceptable. Divorce papers must be official court or government documents. If the death or divorce occurred in one of those few countries where such records are not kept, call the nearest consulate or embassy of your home country for advice on getting acceptable proof of death or divorce.

Birth certificates. Usually, you may verify a parent/child relationship simply by presenting the child's birth certificate.

Many countries, including Canada and England, issue both short- and long-form birth certificates. Where both are available, the long form is needed because it contains the names of the parents, while the short form does not.

1. Mailing the Visa Petition

When ready, your petitioning family member must submit the visa petition (Form I-130 or I-360, accompanying documents, and fee) to the USCIS regional service center that serves the area where your family member lives. See the USCIS website for the proper address and P.O. box. USCIS regional service centers are not the same as USCIS local offices. For one thing, you cannot visit regional service centers in person—service centers process applications but they do not see applicants. There are several USCIS regional service centers spread across the United States, and other USCIS offices overseas, to serve U.S. citizen petitioners who live there.

If you are in the United States, and you have a valid, unexpired visa, you may be able to file your green card application (as described in Section E, below) at the same time, or concurrently, with your family member's visa petition. But you can only file concurrently under two circumstances—one, if you are an immediate relative, or two, if you're a preference relative and a visa is already available in your category, as described in Section E, below. Concurrent filing

offers many advantages, including giving you the right to stay in the U.S. while the application is pending (useful if you are on a temporary visa that has expired or is due to expire soon) and the right to apply for work permits for you and your immediate family members. Unfortunately, the possibility of concurrent filing is fading away, as the waits for green cards in most categories have recently stretched to many months and years long.

2. Awaiting USCIS Approval of the Visa Petition

After filing Form I-130 (or I-360) (assuming you didn't file it concurrently with your green card application), you will have to wait for the petition to be approved, which can take several months or even years by itself. (See Chapter 4 for how to track the length of time USCIS is taking to decide on visa petitions, and how to track your own application online.)

Within a few weeks after mailing the petition, your family petitioner should receive a written confirmation that the papers are being processed, together with a receipt for the fees. This notice will also give your case file number and tell you your Priority Date and approximately when to expect a decision on the petition. Current USCIS policy is to act more quickly on petitions whose Priority Dates are likely to become current sooner—which means that people in preference categories with long waits may literally wait years to find out whether or not their visa petition was approved. It all works out, however (assuming the petition is approved), because your Priority Date—which is set as soon as your family petitioner files the I-130 for you—protects your place in line.

> **EXAMPLE:** Dante, who is from the Philippines, has a brother who is a U.S. citizen. The brother files a visa petition for Dante on March 1, 2003. That puts Dante in the fourth preference category. However, Dante waits a full four years—until March of 2007—for the visa petition to be approved. Although frustrating, this doesn't hurt Dante any, because his March 1, 2003 Priority Date is still years away from being current—visas are at that time only just becoming available to people who applied years before him, with Priority Dates of September 1, 1984.

If USCIS wants further information before acting on your case, it will send you a Request for Evidence (RFE) on Form I-797. The I-797 tells your family petitioner what corrections, additional pieces of information, or additional documents are expected. Your family member should make the corrections or supply the extra data and mail them back to the USCIS regional service center with the request form on top.

Once your petition is approved, USCIS will advise your family petitioner using a Notice of Action, also on Form I-797 (see the sample below). If you plan to attend your visa interview at a U.S. consulate abroad, USCIS will forward the file to the National Visa Center (NVC), located in Portsmouth, New Hampshire. The NVC will then send a packet of forms and instructions to you so that you may proceed with consular processing, described later in this chapter.

D. Step Two: Preference Relatives Wait for an Available Visa

If you're an immediate relative, you can skip this section. But because there are annual limits on the number of people who can receive green cards in certain categories (the preference categories), preference relatives may have to wait in line until a visa/green card becomes available. Your place in the line is tracked by a number called your Priority Date. It comes from the date on which your family petitioner filed your visa petition.

It's impossible to say exactly how long you will have to wait—it all depends on how many people are in line before you. See the explanation of how to track your wait in the Part II Introduction, Section A4.

If you have an approved petition but your Priority Date is not yet current, you

Sample I-130 Approval Notice

Department of Homeland Security U.S. Citizenship and Immigration Services	**I-797, Notice of Action**

THE UNITED STATES OF AMERICA

RECEIPT NUMBER WAC-06-047-00000	CASE TYPE I130 IMMIGRANT PETITION FOR RELATIVE, FIANCE(E), OR ORPHAN
RECEIPT DATE December 15, 2000	PRIORITY DATE December 14, 2000	PETITIONER MANCINI, ALBERTO
NOTICE DATE April 11, 2007	PAGE 1 of 1	BENEFICIARY MANCINI, TERESE

ILONA BRAY RE: TERESE MARIA MANCINI 950 PARKER ST. BERKELEY, CA 94710	**Notice Type:** Approval Notice Section: Husband or wife of permanent resident, 203(a)(2)(A) INA

The above petition has been approved. We have sent the original visa petition to the **Department of State National Visa Center (NVC), 32 Rochester Avenue, Portsmouth, NH 03801-2909.** NVC processes all approved immigrant visa petitions that need consular action. It also determines which consular post is the appropriate consulate to complete visa processing. NVC will then forward the approved petition to that consulate.

The NVC will contact the person for whom you are petitioning (beneficiary) concerning further immigrant visa processing steps.

If you have any questions about visa issuance, please contact the NVC directly. However, please allow at least 90 days before calling the NVC if your beneficiary has not received correspondence from the NVC. The telephone number of the NVC is **(603) 334-0700.**

THIS FORM IS NOT A VISA NOR MAY IT BE USED IN PLACE OF A VISA.

Please see the additional information on the back. You will be notified separately about any other cases you filed.
U.S. CITIZENSHIP & IMMIGRATION SVC
CALIFORNIA SERVICE CENTER
P. O. BOX 30111
LAGUNA NIGUEL CA 92607-0111
Customer Service Telephone: (800) 375-5283

Form I-797 (Rev. 01/31/05) N

must wait until it is current to take the next step and file your green card application. The immigration authorities will advise you by mail when your Priority Date finally comes up (so make sure to send them any change of address!). It's also worth tracking your Priority Date on your own, in case they forget to notify you.

If you're in the United States on a temporary visa, be careful that your status does not expire before your Priority Date becomes current and you can apply for a green card—possessing an approved visa petition does not give you any right to live in the United States. If this looks like it might become a problem, consult as soon as possible with an immigration attorney.

E. Step Three: You Submit the Green Card Application

After your visa petition has been approved and your Priority Date has become current, it's time for you to play a more active role in the application process: You'll need to file your application for permanent residence or a green card. If your spouse or children will be accompanying you, they must each file their own green card applications. And if you're coming from outside of the U.S., remember that you'll first receive an immigrant visa from a U.S. consulate, which

you will trade in for your permanent residence upon entering the United States.

The most important question at this point is where you file the application and attend your interview—at a USCIS office in the United States or at a U.S. consulate outside the United States? You should have already made this choice on your Form I-130, but you're allowed to change your mind, so it's worth revisiting this question.

If you're living outside of the United States now. The answer is fairly easy for people living in countries other than the U.S.—you'll file at a local U.S. consulate and attend an interview there before entering the United States. (This method is called consular processing.) If you're sure you'll use this method, skip straight to Section 2, below.

If you're living in the U.S. now. The answer is a bit more complicated for applicants already in the United States. The easiest thing for you would probably be to "adjust status" without leaving—that is, send your application to the nearest USCIS Service Center and attend your interview at a local USCIS office. If you're one of the few people legally allowed to use this option, it's a great one. Once your application is filed, your stay in the United States will be considered legal, and you can apply for permission to work. Should problems arise in your case, you will be able to wait for a decision in the United States. Also, if your application for a green card is turned down, you have greater rights of appeal inside the U.S. than you do at a U.S. consulate.

The catch is that you are allowed to adjust status only if you're already in the U.S. legally, that is, on a valid, unexpired visa or other form of permission. (There are a few exceptions, discussed in Chapter 3. Most notably, immediate relatives of U.S. citizens who entered the U.S. legally—for example, with a visa or on a visa waiver—do not have to worry about whether their visa has expired or whether

they've worked illegally when they apply for adjustment of status in the United States.) You might, for example, already be legally in the United States on a temporary visa such as an H-1B work visa, or an F-1 student visa, in which case you're welcome to apply for adjustment of status before your visa expires. Unfortunately, that's the rare case—many family members in preference categories have already been out of status for a long time and should see an attorney for help.

Marriage Interviews After Filing I-130

The USCIS sometimes requires petition interviews in marriage cases, especially if the marriage recently took place or if there are great age or cultural differences between the spouses. Interviews are less common if the application is being filed at a U.S. consulate.

Marriage interview procedures vary with the individual personality of the examining officer, and you should be prepared to adjust to that officer's interviewing style. You and your U.S. spouse may be brought into the interviewing room separately. Each of you may then be questioned about your life together, how you met, what sorts of things you do as a couple, daily routines, common friends, favorite places to go, what the inside of your home looks like, and so on. These questions are intended

to reveal whether or not you and your U.S. spouse actually share a life—or whether you're committing immigration fraud. You may refuse to answer some or all questions, but doing so could result in the petition being denied.

Many couples wonder if they will be asked about the more intimate details of their relationship. USCIS policy states that the interviewers should not ask embarrassingly personal questions, but sometimes USCIS officials believe it is necessary to ask intimate questions in an attempt to uncover a fraudulent case. Most USCIS offices now videotape all interviews, so the likelihood of abuse has been diminished. The best advice we can offer is be prepared for anything and cooperate as much as possible.

⚠ **You may be accused of visa fraud if you got married soon after entering the U.S. on a temporary visa.** Many people misread the rules and think that they can enter the U.S. on, for example, a tourist visa, get married, and then apply for a green card in the United States. Unfortunately, this scenario often leads to accusations that you committed visa fraud—that is, pretended to be coming temporarily with the secret intent of staying permanently. If you marry within 60 days of your entry on a temporary visa, you will be presumed to have committed visa fraud.

If you're living in the United States with no legal status, or have worked without authorization, or you entered legally without a visa under the Visa Waiver Program, you are ordinarily barred from filing your green card application inside the United States. See Chapter 3 for information on whether you might be one of the rare few people allowed to adjust status regardless, due to an exception. If not, you'll probably need to consult with an experienced immigration attorney.

Whether or not you are eligible to adjust status, you may instead decide to leave the United States and apply for your green card at a U.S. consulate abroad. If the consulates are issuing visas more quickly than your local USCIS office is handling adjustment of status applications (which is common), leaving to apply at a consulate outside of the U.S. could be a smart strategic move.

However, if you have already spent six months or more in the U.S. out of legal status, or crossed the border without inspection, be sure you are not inadmissible or subject to a three-year or ten-year bar on reentering the U.S. before you go. (See Chapter 3.) Otherwise, you could find yourself stuck outside the United States for three or ten years. Fortunately, hardship-based waivers are available for certain family members of U.S. citizens and permanent residents; get an attorney's help for this.

1. What Happens When Adjusting Status in the U.S.

The process of adjusting your status to permanent resident involves preparing a set of forms and documents (a separate set for you and each of your accompanying spouse and children), mailing these to a USCIS office called the Chicago Lockbox, waiting for some weeks or months until you're called in to have your fingerprints taken, and then waiting a few weeks or months longer until you're called in for your final green card interview at a local USCIS office (not the one to which you sent your application). You should be approved for your green card at or soon after the interview. See Chapter 4 for information on tracking the progress of your application.

As part of your adjustment of status application, you and your family members may apply for permission to work (an Employment Authorization Document or EAD).

⚠️ **Security checks are a likely cause of delays.** As part of your adjustment of status application, the FBI must run both a fingerprint check and a name check on you, and the CIA must run a separate name check. These name checks can take months or even years, especially because many applicants have similar names. If you've been informed that your case is stalled due to security checks, get the name of a person you can keep in touch with for updates, or hire a lawyer to help with this task.

a. Paperwork to Prepare for Adjustment of Status Application

The basic form used in the U.S. adjustment of status application is Form I-485, Application for Permanent Residence. However, a handful of other forms must be prepared to accompany this main one, and you must collect various documents.

An easy way to get all these forms is to call the USCIS forms line at 800-870-3676 or go to a local USCIS office and ask for an Adjustment of Status Packet. Or, you can obtain the forms online at www.uscis.gov (click "Immigration Forms," and scroll down and select the forms you need one by one based on the checklist below.)

The following checklist will help you assemble and keep track of the appropriate forms and documents. A complete set of the items below must also be prepared for your accompanying spouse and children.

Checklist for Adjustment of Status Application

Forms

❑ Form I-485, with filing fee (currently $1,010 for applicants ages 14 to 78 or under 14 and not filing with the I-485 of at least one parent, $600 for other applicants under age 14, and $930 for applicants age 79 or older). Checks and money orders are accepted, but do not send cash through the mail. This includes your fingerprinting or "biometrics" fee. You'll be notified of where and when to appear. Double check all fees at www.uscis.gov.

❑ Form I-485A (only if you'll be paying the $1,000 penalty fee in order to adjust status).

❑ Form G-325A (if you're between ages 14 and 79).

❑ Form I-765 (optional, if you want a work permit; include a separate filing fee, currently $340. Your answer to Question 16 of the form should be "(c)(9)").

❑ Form I-864 Affidavit of Support, with supporting documents (including the most recent year's federal tax returns, or transcripts, with all attachments, and proof of assets, if any are being used to prove financial ability). Accompanying spouses or children can submit a photocopy of the main form.

❑ I-131, Application for Travel Document (Advance Parole), for use if you think you'll need to travel outside the United States while your application is processed. This also requires a separate filing fee, currently $305.

Documents

❑ Copy of your I-130 approval notice.

❑ Copy of a long-form birth certificate for you and each accompanying relative (this mainly serves as a form of identification). If the birth certificate is in another language, it must be accompanied by a full English translation.

❑ Copy of I-94 card for you and each accompanying relative (the small white or green card placed in your passport). Failure to submit this may result in a conclusion that you entered or remained in the U.S. illegally and either are not eligible to adjust status or are subject to the $1,000 penalty described in Chapter 3.

❑ Two photographs of you and two photographs of each accompanying relative in U.S. passport style (it's best to have a professional do these). Write your name and A-number (if you've received one from USCIS) in pencil on the back of each photo.

❑ Medical exam report for you and for each accompanying relative (on Form I-693).

A few of the items on this checklist need additional explanation:

Form I-485. While most of the form is self-explanatory, a few items typically raise concerns. If a particular question does not apply to you, answer it with "None" or "N/A." The questions on this form requiring explanation are as follows:

Part 1. This asks for general information about when and where you were born, your present address, and immigration status. If you don't have a Social Security number, say "none." If you've used a fake number or one belonging to someone else, consult a lawyer. The form also asks for an A number, that is, an eight-digit "Alien number." Normally, you will not have an A number unless you previously applied for a green card or have been in deportation proceedings (in which case you should see a lawyer).

The form also asks for your I-94 number. This is the number on the little white or green card that was tucked into your passport when you entered the United States. (Green means you entered on a visa waiver, and can adjust status only if your petitioner is an immediate relative such as a U.S. citizen spouse.) If you entered illegally, write "none" here (but double check whether you're allowed to adjust your status in the U.S.—see Chapter 3). Under Current USCIS Status, write the type of visa you're on, such as F-1 student or H-1B worker—or if your visa has expired, write "OOS," which stands for out of status.

Part 2. Mark Box "a" if you are the principal applicant; Box "b" if your spouse or parent is the principal applicant. Choose Box "c" if you entered the U.S. on a K-1 fiancé(e) or on a K-2 child of fiancé(e) visa. Do not mark any other box.

Part 3. Under Place of Last Entry into the United States, be sure to name the city through which you most recently entered—even if it was after a short trip and you'd spent time in the U.S. before. The question about whether you were "inspected" by an immigration officer simply asks whether you entered legally. The nonimmigrant visa number is the number that appears on the very top of your visa stamp. It is not the same as your visa classification.

The questions in Part 3, Section C, are meant to identify people who are inadmissible. With the exception of certain memberships in terrorist, Communist Party, or similar organizations, you will not be considered inadmissible just because you joined an organization. However, if your answer to any of the other questions is "yes," you may be inadmissible; see Chapter 3 for more information, or consult an attorney. Don't lie on your answers, because you will probably be found out, especially if you have engaged in criminal activity. Many grounds of inadmissibility can be legally overcome, but once a lie is detected, you will lose the legal right to correct the problem. In addition, a false answer is grounds for denying your application in itself and may result in your being permanently barred from getting a green card.

Form I-485A. This form is required only if you are subject to the $1,000 penalty fee for residing in the U.S. illegally and are eligible to file for adjustment of status. You would be eligible only if you had a visa petition or labor certification on file before January 14, 1998, or before April 30, 2001, so long as you were in the United States on December 21, 2000. The form is self-explanatory, and is intended only to determine if you are subject to the penalty.

Form G-325A. This Biographic Data Form must be filled out for you and for each accompanying relative. You need not file a G-325A for any child under the age of 14 or any adult over the age of 79. If the basis of your immigration case is marriage to a U.S. citizen, a G-325A must be completed for both you and your U.S. spouse (despite the fact that you may have already submitted one with your visa petition). This is the only type of case where full biographic data is requested on someone who is already a U.S. citizen.

Form I-864. See Chapter 3 of this book for more explanation of this form. Also pay close attention to the detailed instructions that come with the form itself.

Medical exam. You and your accompanying relatives will be required to submit medical examination reports on Form I-693. You must take this form to a USCIS authorized physician or medical clinic. The USCIS local office will provide you with the form as well as a list of approved physicians in your area, or you can call 800-375-5283 and write them down by hand. The fees are around $150 per exam, depending on the doctor. The exam itself involves taking a medical history, blood test, chest X-ray, and vaccinations, if required. Pregnant women can refuse to be X-rayed until after the pregnancy. The vaccination requirement may be waived for religious, moral, or medical reasons.

 Some fiancés can skip most of the exam. If you had an exam overseas within the last year, all you need is a vaccination "Supplemental Form to I-693," also completed by a USCIS-designated doctor. The exception is if medical grounds of inadmissibility were noted during your exam or when you entered the United States.

After completion of the medical exam, and upon obtaining the test results, the doctor will give you the report in a sealed envelope. Do not open the envelope.

The main purpose of the medical exam is to verify that you are not medically inadmissible. The primary medical grounds of inadmissibility are tuberculosis and HIV (AIDS). Some medical grounds of inadmissibility can be overcome with treatment or by applying for a waiver. (See Chapter 3 for details.)

Dealing With Delays in Approval of Your Work Authorization

If you want to work before your application for a green card is approved, you must file a separate application for employment authorization. To do so, fill out Form I-765 and file it together with your adjustment of status application. To accompany Form I-765, submit a copy of your I-94 card and pay a separate filing fee. Be sure to keep the fee receipt that USCIS gives you, so you can prove that the I-765 was filed. Normally, you will file the application for employment authorization at the same time as your adjustment of status application papers.

Legally, USCIS does not have to make a decision on your employment authorization application for up to 90 days after the notice date on the receipt it sends you. If, for some reason, you are not given a decision within 90 days, you are supposed to be granted an interim employment authorization, which will last 240 days. Unfortunately, claiming this right has recently become impossible.

The idea used to be that you could go to your local USCIS office and apply for the interim EAD, which the local office could quickly produce. However, USCIS declared in an April 2006 memo that local offices would no longer do this—at best, they'll contact the service center for you to find out why your EAD has been delayed. Lawsuits were being filed against USCIS at the time this book went to print. In the meantime, you may need an attorney's help if your EAD approval has been delayed.

If you receive an interim EAP, but 240 days pass and you still have not received a final decision on the I-765, you must stop working. Interim work authorization cards cannot be renewed. However, if you reach this point, you have the option to file a new I-765 application. If you do not get a decision on the new application within 90 days, you will then be entitled to another interim work authorization card.

b. Where to Send Your Adjustment of Status Packet

As a family visa applicant, you'll need to mail your application, consisting of both forms and documents, to the appropriate USCIS service center; check the website for the exact address, as USCIS was about to change it when this book went to print.

After filing your adjustment of status application, you will receive a receipt that estimates the processing time for your application. If USCIS requires additional evidence or information, it will send you a Request for Evidence (I-797). You will also receive, after some weeks or months, a notice advising you where to go to have your fingerprints taken. These will then be used to check whether you have any history of arrests (whether by the police, FBI, DHS, or other authority). See Chapter 4 for information on how to track USCIS's progress toward your interview.

Planning to Leave the U.S. Before Your Adjustment Interview?

Once your application for adjustment of status has been filed, you *must not* leave the U.S. for any reason before you have applied for and received advance permission to reenter the U.S. (Advance Parole). Any absence without this permission will be viewed as a termination of your application for a green card—which means that, upon return, you will be told that your green card application is dead and you have no right to enter the United States.

However, if you were out of status for six or more months after April 1, 1997, you should not depart the U.S., even with Advance Parole. You're inadmissible, and may be stuck outside the U.S., with a three-year or ten-year bar against reentering.

Many people simply apply for Advance Parole at the same time they apply to adjust status, just in case. Or, you can wait until you're sure you have to leave, and apply at the same service center where you sent your adjustment of status application—but you're taking a risk this way, because USCIS may take many weeks to approve your Advance Parole application.

Your application for Advance Parole should include Form I-131, together with the filing fee, three passport-type photographs, a copy of your adjustment of status filing receipt (if you've already sent in that application), and a short explanation of why you want to leave— you will need a bona fide personal or business reason, though it need not be an emergency.

If approved, you will be allowed to leave the U.S. and return again with no break in the processing of your application.

c. Your Adjustment of Status Interview

You will most likely be called in for a personal interview, which will be held at a USCIS office near you. USCIS will send you and any accompanying relatives an appointment notice, usually about two weeks in advance of the interview. If you have an attorney, he or she may come with you to the interview. (Even if you don't have an attorney, you could consult with or hire one at this point.)

Checklist: Documents to Bring to Your Adjustment Interview

Prepare all of the following to take with you to your USCIS interview:

❑ A complete photocopy of your green card application. This is for your use—you may want to follow along as the officer asks you questions about the material you filled out on the forms, or you may find that the officer is missing something that you have.

❑ Photo identification or passport for you and every one of your family members. (It's best to bring your passport, because if you are approved for your green card on the day of the interview, USCIS can place a stamp in your passport demonstrating this—and you can use this stamp as proof when you work or travel.)

❑ Originals of all documents that you made copies of for submission with your application. For example, if you submitted a photocopy of an I-94, divorce decree, a birth certificate, or another official document, a USCIS officer may want to examine the originals. Similarly, your petitioner must bring original proof of U.S. citizen or green card status. Naturalized citizens are asked to bring their certificate of citizenship rather than a passport.

❑ Any documents received from USCIS or other immigration authorities. For example, if you left the country on Advance Parole, bring this permit.

❑ Documents proving the petitioner's continued employment, including a letter from the employer stating the petitioner's dates of employment, position and title, salary, marital status, dependents claimed, and emergency contact information; plus the last three pay stubs.

❑ Any updates to the material in your application. For example, if you have given birth to another child, bring the birth certificate. If you've been arrested, bring a full explanation (and consult with an attorney to make sure that the arrest doesn't make you inadmissible).

❑ If you're applying based on marriage, evidence that it's the real thing, such as joint bank account statements, apartment leases, utility bills, love letters, wedding invitations, photos, and more.

See Chapter 4 for detailed information on what expect during your adjustment of status interview. If your adjustment of status application is denied, also see Chapter 4. Also, for information on how to protect your green card holder status after you're approved, see Chapter 14.

2. What Happens During Consular Processing

If you're outside the U.S., you'll need to submit your application at a U.S. consulate, usually in the capital city of your country. At the beginning, consular processing involves a lot of paper being sent in various directions. First, after USCIS approves your visa petition, it will forward your file to the National Visa Center (NVC) in Portsmouth, New Hampshire. At the same time, it will send a Notice of Approval directly to your relative. Also, either at the same time or, if you're a preference relative, when your Priority Date is close to becoming current, the NVC will send a bill (currently $70) for reviewing the Affidavit of Support (Form I-864 or I-864EZ) to your petitioning relative. It will send you a form called an Agent of Choice and Address (DS-3032), which simply asks where you want the rest of your visa-related mail sent; for example, to your attorney rather than to you.

Once your petitioning relative has paid the I-864 processing fee, the NVC will send him or her the I-864 forms and instructions, with instructions on what to do with the completed version (either send it back to the NVC for review or to you, to hand carry to your interview). The petitioner/sponsor will need to prove the contents of the affidavit by attaching supporting documents, including the most recent year's tax returns, and proof of assets, if any are being used to prove financial ability. For further discussion of the requirements when filling out the Affidavit of Support, see Chapter 3.

Once the NVC receives your form DS-3032, it will mail you (or your attorney or agent) an Immigrant Visa (IV) fee bill (currently $335) plus a $45 security surcharge. Once you've paid that bill, the NVC will send you what's called an instruction packet of forms and information. The exact contents of the instruction packet will depend on where you'll be interviewed for the visa. Around this time, the NVC will forward your file to the U.S. consulate that will be handling your case (if the NVC asked the petitioner to send it the Affidavit of Support for review, it won't forward your file until it has reviewed and approved the affidavit).

You'll need to prepare your forms and documents according to the instructions, notify the consulate when you are ready, wait until you receive a notice scheduling you for an interview at a U.S. consulate, undergo a medical exam, prepare additional forms and documents for the interview, and finally, attend the interview. There, if all goes well, you will be approved (subject to final security checks) for a visa to enter the United States.

Much of your job at this point involves convincing the consulate that you are not inadmissible for health, criminal, security, or financial reasons.

3. Paperwork to Prepare for Consular Processing

After the initial back-and-forth of correspondence, the main paperwork involved in consular processing falls into two parts. The first part is the instructional packet (formerly called Packet 3). The second will be sent to you as part of your interview notification from your local U.S. consulate.

a. Handling the Instructional Packet

The instructional packet actually contains both forms and instructions. Some of these forms are for you to fill out and return in order to keep the process moving—namely Form DS-230 Part I and Form DS-2001. The forms are normally designated by a DS preceding a number, and copies of many of them are available on the State Department website at www.state.gov. However, it's better to wait for the ones the consulate sends you, because some of them are slightly different than the ones on the website—for example, many of the consulates use forms with bilingual translations into the language of your country.

 Keep the process moving. You don't really need to have all your documents in hand when you send in Form DS-2001. Although the form asks you to sign it only after you're ready with the listed forms, many people simply sign as soon as they know they can get the forms together, to speed up their application.

After you've sent in the necessary forms, and your petitioner's Affidavit of Support has been approved, your local U.S. consulate will start communicating with you directly. It will provide you with additional forms to fill out, a list of documents to collect in preparation for your interview, and other tasks to take care of.

b. Preparing Forms and Documents for Your Interview

The checklist below provides a brief explanation of some of the documents you'll need to gather in preparation for your immigrant visa interview. Keep your eyes open for any special requirements that your consulate may add to this list. Bring the originals and a set of copies with you to your interview (the consular officer may want to examine the originals to make sure they're not fraudulent, but keep copies for your files). Do not mail your paperwork to the consulate!

Checklist: Documents and Forms for Your Consular Interview

Forms

❑ DS forms (DS-230 Part II and any others sent to you by the NVC and U.S. consulate).

Documents

❑ Original notice of your visa petition approval (for the consulate's review).

❑ Long-form birth certificate (original and photocopy) for you and each accompanying relative as well as for any unmarried minor children who are not immigrating with you.

❑ Marriage certificate (original and photocopy) if you are married and bringing your spouse.

❑ If either you or your spouse has been previously married, copies of divorce and death certificates showing termination of all previous marriages (originals and photocopies.

❑ Documents proving the petitioner's continued employment, including a letter from the employer stating his or her dates of employment, position and title, salary, marital status, dependents claimed, and emergency contact information; plus the last three pay stubs.

❑ Passport for you and each accompanying relative, valid for at least six months beyond the date of the interview.

❑ Police certificates from every country (except the U.S.) in which you and each accompanying relative has lived for at least six months since age 16.

❑ Fingerprints, if requested by the consulate. The current fingerprinting fee is $85.

❑ Military records for you and each accompanying relative.

❑ Two color photographs of you and three photographs of each accompanying relative.

❑ Medical exam report for you and each accompanying relative.

❑ Form I-864 Affidavit of Support, if it hasn't already been submitted.

Here's some additional explanation regarding some of the items on the checklist above:

Police clearance. You personally must collect police clearance certificates from each country you have lived in for one year or more since your 16th birthday. Additionally, you must have a police certificate from your home country or country of last residence, if you lived there for at least six months since the age of 16. You do not need to obtain police certificates from the United States.

Contact the local police department in your home country for instructions on how to get police certificates. To obtain police certificates from nations other than your home country, contact the nearest consulate representing that country for instructions. Some nations refuse to supply police certificates, or their certificates are not considered reliable, and so you will not be required to obtain them from those locations. The U.S. consulate will tell you which countries police certificates are not required from.

Some countries will send certificates directly to U.S. consulates but not to you personally. Before they send the certificates out, however, you must request that it be done. Usually this requires filing some type of request form, together with a set of your fingerprints.

Photos. You and each accompanying relative must bring two photographs taken in compliance with the consulate's instructions (U.S "passport style"). Often your information packet will contain a list of local photographers who take this type of picture. If your religious beliefs require wearing a head covering, you should be able to keep it on for the photo. However, your eyes and face must still be visible, and you must submit a written statement explaining why you can't submit a standard photograph.

Medical exam. Immediately before your visa interview, you and your accompanying relatives will be required to have medical examinations. Some consulates conduct the medical exams up to several days before the interview. Others schedule the medical exam and the interview on the same day. You will be told where to go and what to do in your appointment letter.

The medical examinations are conducted by private doctors. The fees vary from $50 to more than $150 per exam, depending on the country. The fee will be stated in your appointment letter. The exam itself involves taking a medical history, blood test, chest X-ray, and vaccinations, if required. Pregnant women can refuse to be X-rayed until *after* the pregnancy. The vaccination requirement may be waived for religious, moral, or medical reasons.

The main purpose of the medical exam is to verify that you are not medically inadmissible. The primary medical grounds of inadmissibility are tuberculosis and HIV (AIDS). Some medical grounds of inadmissibility can be overcome with treatment or by applying for a waiver. (See Chapter 3 for more details.) If you need a medical waiver, you will be given complete instructions by the consulate at the time of your interview, but should also consult an experienced immigration attorney.

4. Your Consular Interview

A written notice of your interview appointment will be sent to you a few weeks before the appointment date. The appointment package will tell you what to bring to your interview, including your completed forms, photographs, passports, and the like. See the checklist in Section 3, above, for the items usually requested, but also read the consular list carefully for any additions or changes.

For details on what to expect during your consular visa interview, see Chapter 4. Chapter 4 also contains information on what to do if your visa is denied.

F. Step Four: You Enter the U.S. With Your Immigrant Visa

Your immigrant visa allows you to request entry to the United States at a border post, airport, or other arrival point. It's good for six months after you get it. You acquire the full status of green card holder only after you have been inspected and admitted into the United States. If you are bringing any accompanying relatives, they must enter at either the same time or after you do in order to become permanent residents.

The inspection process involves a U.S. border officer opening the sealed envelope containing your visa documents, and doing a last check to make sure you haven't used fraud. The border officer has "expedited removal" powers, which means he or she can turn you right around and send you home if anything appears wrong in your packet or with your answers to the officer's questions. Be polite and careful in answering.

When the officer is satisfied that everything is in order, he or she will stamp your passport to show that you're now a U.S. permanent resident (or conditional resident if you've been married less than two years and got your residence based on this marriage). You are immediately authorized to work.

You won't receive an actual green card yet, however. Cards for you and your accompanying relatives will be ordered for you, and will come to you by mail several weeks later.

G. Removing Conditional Residence in Marriage Cases

As we've already mentioned, green cards based on recent marriage to a U.S. citizen (within the last two years) are issued only conditionally, meaning they will expire after two years. This is true of cards issued both to spouses and stepchildren of U.S. citizens.

After holding your conditional green card for two years, if you are still married, you and your U.S. spouse must file a joint petition (Form I-751) to remove the condition, allowing you to receive permanent residence. The condition should be removed not only from your green card but from those of any children who came with you. If you are divorced, or your spouse has died or refuses to join in the petition, you must file for a waiver of the requirement.

1. Filing a Joint Petition With Your Spouse

You may file the joint petition even if you are separated or a divorce is in progress, as long as you remain legally married and your U.S. citizen spouse agrees to sign the I-751 petition.

Nevertheless, you will need to check box "d" in Part 2, and expect to be called into your local USCIS office for an interview. Also, if your divorce is finalized before the joint petition has been decided on, you, the immigrant, are expected to send in a written request to withdraw that joint petition and file a new I-751 petition (plus fee) on your own, checking box "d" and requesting a waiver of the joint filing requirement.

You must file the petition 90 days or fewer before the expiration of the two-year conditional period. If you fail to meet this deadline, be prepared to show an extremely good reason why you could not file on time. Otherwise you will lose your U.S. residence and could be deported.

The petition to remove the conditional status of your green card is made by filling out Form I-751, available on the USCIS website. Where stepchildren are involved, one form may be used for the entire family. It must be signed by both you and your U.S. spouse, unless, of course, you are filing on your own because your spouse has died, you are divorced, or your spouse is abusive.

Together with your form, you must also supply documents to show that your marriage was not entered into only for immigration purposes. Look for documents that prove that you and your spouse have been living together and sharing your financial and other matters, such as joint bank accounts, credit card statements, automobile and insurance policies in both names, and leases or contracts showing you rent or purchased your home in both names. Sworn affidavits from people who know both you and your U.S. spouse, stating that they observed you living together during a particular period are also helpful. If you wish, you may bring witnesses to the interview (if you are called in for one) who can testify to observing that you and your U.S. spouse are truly married.

Forms and documents should be mailed together with a filing fee (currently $545, including biometrics) for any dependent children included in the application to the USCIS regional service center nearest your home. Check the USCIS website for the appropriate address, fee, and P.O. box number.

Within a few weeks of mailing your petition to the regional service center, you will receive a written receipt (Form I-797) by return mail. The receipt is very important—it will be your only proof of legal status in the U.S. until your application is approved. Make a copy for your files, and use the original, together with your expired card, to prove your status to employers. Carefully note the expiration date on the receipt. It normally expires one year after USCIS received your application.

If you plan to travel in and out of the U.S. for that one year, you'll need to take your conditional green card, and this receipt. Be careful not to leave the U.S. after your receipt has expired if you haven't yet received a USCIS decision. Unfortunately, the USCIS may take more than a year to make its decision. If you need to take a trip outside the U.S., or if your employer is asking for proof that you're allowed to work, visit your local USCIS office. USCIS can give you either a temporary I-551 stamp in your passport or an I-94 card, either of which will extend the expiration date of your conditional residence by another year.

Eventually, you will be sent an appointment notice stating when and where you must appear for biometric processing. (It's usually at a USCIS Application Support Center.) Biometric processing includes taking your photograph, signature, and index fingerprint, for use in generating your new green card. If you're between ages 14 and 79, it also includes taking your fingerprints, in order to do another criminal background check. Later, you will either get a decision approving your petition or be asked to come to the USCIS local office for an interview. The interview is at the USCIS's discretion and does not necessarily indicate a problem. If your interview is successful, you will usually be approved at that time. After approval, your permanent green card will be sent to you by mail (months later).

2. Getting a Waiver of the Requirement to File a Joint Petition

If you are unable to file a joint petition with your U.S. spouse to remove the condition on your residency, either because of divorce or because he or she died or refuses to cooperate, you must then file for a waiver of the requirement to file the joint petition. This waiver will be granted in only three circumstances:

- you entered into a good faith marriage but the marriage is legally terminated (death or divorce)
- your deportation will cause you extreme hardship (one greater than that normally experienced by someone who is deported) and the marriage was originally entered into in good faith, or
- you were battered or subjected to extreme cruelty by your U.S. spouse and the marriage was originally entered into in good faith.

Like the joint petition, an application for a waiver must ordinarily be filed before your two-year conditional residency expires. However, if you are forced to file late because you were abused, or for another good reason—especially a reason connected to your waiver request—USCIS may excuse the delay.

Waiver applications, like joint petitions, are filed on Form I-751. Where stepchildren are involved, one form may be used for the entire family.

Together with your form, you must also supply documents showing that your marriage was not entered into only for immigration purposes. Proving that a marriage lasting less than two years was not a sham can be very difficult. First, you are not likely to have the cooperation of your ex-spouse, who in fact may even testify against you. In this situation, any other proof you can present to show that you married for love and not to get a green card can help.

This is best accomplished by submitting records that you and your spouse held joint bank accounts and credit cards, had automobile and insurance policies in both names, and rented or purchased your home in both names. Sworn affidavits from people who know both you and your U.S. spouse, stating that they observed you living together during a particular period of time, are also helpful. If you had children together, this too is excellent evidence that your marriage was not a sham—include their birth certificates or your hospital records.

If you are divorced, you should also provide a copy of your divorce decree. If you have separated or if divorce proceedings have been started but aren't yet finished, you are not eligible to submit a waiver request, and you may be placed in removal proceedings. Don't panic,

however—the immigration judge should be willing to postpone your case until the divorce proceedings are done and you can ask for a waiver. If your spouse died, provide a copy of the death certificate.

Proving extreme hardship is more difficult. Situations that might qualify include serious illness, other close family members living in the U.S., financial loss such as vested pension benefits or lost career opportunities, and serious political or economic problems in your home country. You should submit a detailed, written statement in your own words explaining the circumstances of your marriage, what you gave up to come to the U.S, and what you will lose by returning to your home country. The statement should be supported by written documentation.

If the basis of your waiver is that you were abused by your U.S. spouse, you must supply evidence such as police reports, medical or psychiatric reports, photographs, or affidavits from witnesses. If you are in divorce proceedings, court records including pleadings and depositions may be used. Your own personal written statement explaining the details of the abuse should also be submitted.

Your forms and documents must be mailed, together with a filing fee, to the USCIS regional service center nearest your home. See the USCIS website for the correct address, fee, and P.O. box. Within a few weeks, you will receive a written receipt by return mail. The receipt is very important—it will be your only proof of legal status in the U.S. until your application is approved. Make a copy for your files, and use the original, together with your expired card, to prove your status to employers. Carefully note the expiration date on the receipt. It normally expires one year after USCIS received your application.

If you plan to travel in and out of the U.S. during that one year, you'll need to present your conditional green card and this receipt at a local USCIS office and get a temporary I-551 stamp in your passport.

Many applications for waivers will require a personal interview before being approved. If an interview is required in your case, you will be notified by mail. The interview will be held at the USCIS local office nearest your home.

Get a lawyer. Due to the complexity of waiver applications and the severe consequences if they fail, we strongly recommend that you hire an experienced immigration lawyer to assist you. ∎

Chapter 8

Getting a K-1 Visa to Marry Your U.S. Citizen Fiancé

I f you intend to marry a U.S. citizen, your fiancé may bring you to the U.S. for the wedding, with a K-1 visa. (See I.N.A. § 214, 8 U.S.C. § 1184, 8 C.F.R. § 214.2(k).) Although it is a nonimmigrant (temporary) visa—lasting only 90 days—we have included it with the chapters on green cards because after you get married, you can apply for a green card. If you are already in the U.S., or if your fiancé lives outside of the U.S. with you, getting a K-1 visa is unnecessary. Instead, you should get married and then apply for a green card as outlined in Chapter 7.

 This chapter doesn't cover K-3 so-called fiancé visas for people who are already married. In fact, even if you're not yet married, but think you might prefer to hold your wedding in your home country, the K-3 visa is worth considering. See Chapter 7 for information on K-3 visas for married couples.

This chapter covers who is eligible for a K-1 visa and how to apply. Fiancés are fortunate in that there are no annual limits on K-1 visas, and thus no long waiting periods. The first step, fiancé visa petition approval, normally takes three to seven months. After the petition has been approved, it will take an additional two to five months for the U.S. consulate to issue a visa.

Note: Although the accurate way to generally refer to both male and female fiancés is "fiancé(e)," we are using the term "fiancé" for simplicity's sake.

Key Features of Fiancé Visas

Here are some of the advantages and disadvantages of using a fiancé visa to enter the United States:

- A fiancé visa may be your only option if your U.S. citizen fiancé is unable to travel to your home country to marry you.
- Fiancé visas last for 90 days, which should, if you act reasonably quickly, give you enough time to get married and prepare your green card application. However, the fiancé visa cannot be renewed.
- You can use a K-1 visa to enter the U.S. more than once.
- You may apply for permission to work immediately upon arriving in the United States.
- After using a fiancé visa to go to the United States and get married, you have a choice of either returning to your home country or staying and applying for a U.S. green card.
- Your unmarried children under the age of 21 are eligible to accompany you on your fiancé visa (as K-2 visa holders).

 Do you need a lawyer? Many people are able to handle the application process for a fiancé visa on their own, without a lawyer. However, if you have trouble dealing with paperwork or understanding the instructions, or have any complications in your case (such as a criminal record, past visa overstays in the U.S., or an immigrating child who will turn 18 soon and therefore no longer qualify as your spouse's stepchild), a lawyer is well worth the price. See Chapter 6 for tips on finding a good one.

U.S. Citizen Petitioners Must Disclose Criminal Records

Recently Congress became concerned that immigrating fiancés were particularly susceptible to domestic violence and abuse—particularly those whose engagements were arranged through a marriage broker (sometimes called "mail order brides"). In response, Congress passed the International Marriage Brokers Regulation Act of 2005 (IMBRA). As a result of IMBRA, the fiancé visa petition (Form I-129F) now asks whether you and your fiancé or spouse met through an international marriage broker. If you did, the immigrant will be asked, at the visa interview, whether the broker complied with new legal requirements that he or she collect information on the U.S. fiancé or spouse's criminal record and pass it to the immigrant. In addition, Form I-129F now asks all U.S. citizen petitioners whether they have a history of violent crime and crime relating to alcohol or controlled-substance abuse.

A. Do You Qualify for a K-1 Visa?

The main eligibility criteria for getting a K-1 visa are that:

- your intended spouse is a U.S. citizen (not a permanent resident or green card holder)
- both members of the couple are legally able to marry (single and of legal age)
- you must have a genuine intention of marrying the U.S. citizen petitioner after arriving in the U.S., and
- the two of you must have met and seen each other in person within the past two years.

This visa is not for use by couples who are simply considering marriage. You'll have to show that you have made actual wedding plans for your 90-day stay. It doesn't have to be a fancy wedding, but you'll need to have made some basic plans, for example a place, a date, a type of ceremony or proceedings (even if it's only in front of a judge), and the like.

For some couples, the requirement that they have already met is difficult or violates their religious principles. If you practice a religion in which marriages are customarily arranged by families and premarital meetings are prohibited, you can ask that a meeting requirement be waived. You'll have to show that both parties will be following all the customs of marriage and weddings that are part of the religion.

It is also possible to get a waiver of the personal meeting requirement if such a meeting would cause an extreme hardship to the U.S. citizen member of the couple. Only the most extreme situations involving medical problems are likely to be regarded as a good enough reason for the waiver to be granted. Economic problems alone are not usually acceptable.

Bringing Your Children

When you get a K-1 visa, any of your unmarried children under the age of 21 can be issued K-2 visas. This will enable them to accompany you to the U.S. They, too, will be able to apply for green cards once you get married.

 You'll need to separately apply for a green card after the marriage. Once you marry, if the 90-day validity period of the K-1 visa has not yet expired, you may file for a green card without leaving the United States. Simply follow the directions for adjustment of status in Chapter 7. Because you have already gotten a K-1 visa, you are excused from the normal first step in this process (the I-130 visa petition). You will, however, be subject to the two-year conditional residency placed on green cards obtained through marriage to a U.S. citizen. This, too, is covered in Chapter 7. Read it carefully before applying for a fiancé visa.

B. Quick View of How to Apply for a K-1 Visa

Getting a K-1 visa is a four-step process:
- First, your U.S. citizen fiancé mails a visa petition on USCIS Form I-129F to a USCIS regional service center in the United States.
- Second, after the petition is approved, you fill out forms sent to you by the National Visa Center (NVC).
- Third, you fill out more forms and collect documents, and bring them to an interview at a U.S. consulate in your home country.
- Fourth, you use your fiancé visa to enter the United States.

C. Step One: Your U.S. Citizen Fiancé Submits a Visa Petition

To start the process, your U.S. citizen fiancé will need to file what's called a fiancé visa petition. The object of the petition is to prove that:
- you have a bona fide intention of marrying a U.S. citizen within 90 days after you arrive in the United States
- both of you are legally able to marry, and
- you have physically met each other within the past two years—or can prove that this requirement should be waived based on religion or extreme hardship.

The Form I-129F itself is mostly self-explanatory, but here are some tips regarding certain tricky portions. On the first page, the left-hand column is for information about the U.S. citizen, and the right-hand column is for information about the immigrant. In Question 6 (both in Part A and B), check only one box, and make sure it is not the one that says "married." In Part A Question 11, the U.S. citizen must state whether he or she has filed petitions for other immigrant fiancés or husband/wives before. If the answer is yes, USCIS will take a closer look at their and your cases to make sure this isn't a pattern that indicates fraud.

In Part B (the immigrant's column), Question 8 asks for a Social Security number. You won't have one unless you've lived in the U.S.; write "N/A" if you don't. Question 9 asks for an "A#," which means an "Alien Registration Number." You won't have unless you've previously applied for permanent or in some cases temporary residency, or been in deportation/removal proceedings (see a lawyer if that's the case). If you have a number, you must enter it here.

All of the questions about past spouses are designed to make sure both of you are free to marry now.

On Question 14, the address where you intend to live in the U.S. should be the same as your U.S. citizen petitioner's, or you'll raise questions. If there's a compelling reason to live apart (for example, you plan to move in together only after you marry), attach a separate document explaining that.

On Question 17, if the two of you are blood relations, you'll have to make sure that a marriage between you is allowed in the U.S. state where you plan to marry.

For Question 18, it's best to attach a separate statement fully explaining the details of how you met and decided to get married. This is a good opportunity to convince USCIS that your relationship is the real thing, not just a fraud to get you a green card. See the sample below.

Question 19 is a new question, a result of recent concern by Congress that so-called "mail-order" spouses (who meet through the services of an international matchmaking agency) are especially susceptible to domestic violence and abuse. In response, Congress passed the International Marriage Brokers Regulation Act of 2005 (IMBRA). IMBRA requires you to state here whether you met your fiancé or spouse through an international marriage broker, and if so, to give information about the broker.

In Question 20, try to name the U.S. consulate with a visa processing office in your country. (Don't worry—if you get it wrong, USCIS will figure it out.)

Part C refers to the U.S. citizen petitioner. Questions 2 and 3 require the U.S. citizen petitioner to reveal to USCIS any history of violent crime, crime relating to alcohol, or controlled substance abuse. This is for your, the immigrant's protection—you will be told of any relevant history. The petitioner should see an attorney if there is any question about whether this section applies.

Sample Fiancé Meeting Statement – Attachment to Form I-129F

Filed by Sandra Beach on Behalf of Nigel Hollis

Question 18

I met my fiancé 18 months ago, while visiting a college friend who has settled in England. My friend Carrie had been telling me for months that she wanted to introduce me to Nigel, because of our offbeat senses of humor and shared interest in long-distance swimming. I've had bad experiences with friends trying to set me up before, so I didn't take it very seriously. But when vacation plans took me to England, I let her arrange for me and Nigel to meet over lunch at a pub.

To my amazement, we clicked right away. We had a lot to talk about—he had completed an English Channel swim a few months before, and I'm hoping to swim the Channel next year. Both of us have built our lives around swimming, which sometimes leaves little time for other things, including relationships. We compared notes on training techniques, equipment, dealing with cold water, rip tides, and more.

Our lunch lasted all afternoon and into the evening. By the end of that evening, I considered Nigel a friend, and someone I could very easily fall in love with.

Nigel and I spent almost all my remaining week's vacation together. Poor Carrie joked that her plan had backfired, because I spent embarrassingly little time at her house. By the end of the week, we both knew this was headed toward a serious relationship.

Since then, Nigel and I have corresponded almost constantly by email, and call each other twice a week. During one long phone call, we decided to get married.

It was difficult deciding where we would live after marrying—Nigel has a beautiful cottage in Cornwall, and I could happily live in England. However, my mother is in poor health, and ever since my father passed away last year, she has relied on my help, so we agreed to make our home in New York.

As proof that Nigel and I are in love and plan to marry, I am attaching copies of his plane tickets to New York; photos of the two of us together; copies of our telephone bills and some of our emails; copies of catering and other contracts showing that the two of us plan to marry in July; and copies of our travel itinerary for New Zealand, where we will honeymoon.

Signed: _Sandra Beach_____
          Sandra Beach

Date: _8/20/2007_____

The checklist below will help your U.S. citizen fiancé prepare and assemble the various forms and documents. A note on word usage: Your U.S. citizen fiancé will now be known as your "petitioner." You are the "beneficiary."

Checklist for Fiancé Visa Petition

Forms

❑ Form I-129F, with accompanying fee (currently $455; send a check or money order, not cash). If you have children, make sure they are listed on this form, which is necessary if you want them to accompany you.

❑ Form G-325A (biographical data) filled out for you, the visa applicant.

❑ Form G-325A (biographical data) filled out for your U.S. citizen fiancé.

Documents

❑ Proof of your fiancé's U.S. citizenship, such as a copy of his or her birth certificate, U.S. passport, certificate of citizenship, naturalization certificate, or consular record of birth abroad.

❑ Proof that you and your fiancé can legally marry, such as your birth certificate to show that you are over 18 (or whatever the age of consent is in the U.S. state where you plan to marry); and if either of you has been married before, proof that all prior marriages were legally terminated, such as a divorce decree or death certificate.

❑ Proof of your intent to marry, such as wedding announcements, catering contracts, a letter or affidavit from your pastor or justice of the peace stating that he or she has been contacted about performing your marriage ceremony, and a statement by your fiancé petitioner explaining how you met each other, why he or she cannot travel to your home country to marry you there, and describing your wedding plans.

❑ Proof that you have met in person, such as photographs of the two of you together, letters you have written to each other indicating that there has been a meeting, and copies of plane tickets, credit card receipts, and hotel receipts.

❑ If you have not met each other for religious reasons, evidence of your membership in such a religion, including a letter from an official in your religious organization verifying that you and your fiancé are members, and a detailed statement from a clergyperson explaining the religious laws concerning marriage. A letter from your parents would also be helpful.

❑ If you have not met each other because it would impose an extreme hardship on your U.S. citizen petitioner, a written statement explaining in detail why you cannot meet. If there is a medical reason why the U.S. citizen can't travel to meet you, include a letter from a medical doctor explaining the condition.

❑ One photograph of you and one photograph of your U.S. citizen fiancé, in U.S. passport style, in color. Write your name in pencil on the back of your photo.

1. Mailing the Fiancé Visa Petition

Once your U.S. citizen petitioner has finished the fiancé visa petition, he or she must mail it to the USCIS regional service center serving his or her area. USCIS service centers are not the same as local offices—for one thing, you cannot visit service centers in person. Check the USCIS website at www.uscis.gov to get the appropriate address and P.O. box for this application. (Look up Form I-129F and follow the accompanying links.)

2. Awaiting Approval of the Visa Petition

Within a few weeks after mailing your petition, your fiancé should get back written confirmation that the papers are being processed, together with a receipt for the fees. This notice will also contain your immigration file number, which is useful if the decision gets delayed.

If USCIS wants further information before acting on your case, the petition papers, forms, and documents may be returned to your U.S. citizen petitioner, together with another form known as an I-797 Request for Evidence. This form will tell the citizen what additional pieces of information or documents are expected. He or she should supply the extra data and mail the whole package back to the service center.

Sometimes, USCIS will request a personal interview with the U.S. citizen petitioner prior to approving a fiancé petition. The purpose is to make sure a marriage will really take place after you arrive in the U.S. and to confirm that you have previously met each other. All interviews are held at USCIS local offices. The service center will forward the file to the USCIS local office nearest the petitioner's home before the interview. The USCIS local office will send the petitioner a notice of when and where to appear for the interview and instructions to bring additional documentation, if any is required.

Once your petition is approved, USCIS will send a Form I-797 Notice of Action to your U.S. citizen fiancé, indicating the approval. (See the sample notice below.) At the same time, USCIS will send a copy of the notice to an office called the National Visa Center, which will assign you a case number and transfer the file to the appropriate U.S. consulate in your country.

 Don't use the approved fiancé visa petition to try to enter the United States! An approved petition does not by itself give you any immigration benefits. It is only a prerequisite to the next step, submitting your application at a U.S. consulate.

Sample I-797 Notice of Action

Department of Homeland Security U.S. Citizenship and Immigration Services	I-797, Notice of Action

THE UNITED STATES OF AMERICA

RECEIPT NUMBER WAC-05-041-00000	CASE TYPE I129F PETITION FOR FIANCE(E)
RECEIPT DATE November 30, 2006	PRIORITY DATE	PETITIONER BEACH, SANDRA
NOTICE DATE April 13, 2005	PAGE 1 of 1	BENEFICIARY HOLLIS, NIGEL

ILONA BRAY
RE: NIGEL IAN HOLLIS
950 PARKER ST.
BERKELEY, CA 94710

Notice Type: Approval Notice

Valid from 04/13/2005 to 08/13/2005

The above petition has been approved. We have sent the original visa petition to the Department of State National Visa Center (NVC), 32 Rochester Avenue, Portsmouth, NH 03801-2909. The INS has completed all action; further inquiries should be directed to the NVC.

The NVC now processes all approved fiance(e) petitions. The NVC processing should be complete within two to four weeks after receiving the petition from INS. The NVC will create a case record with your petition information. NVC will then send the petition to the U.S. Embassy or Consulate where your fiance(e) will be interviewed for his or her visa.

You will receive notification by mail when NVC has sent your petition to the U.S. Embassy or Consulate. The notification letter will provide you with a unique number for your case and the name and address of the U.S. Embassy or Consulate where your petition has been sent.

If it has been more than four weeks since you received this approval notice and you have not received notification from NVC that your petition has been forwarded overseas, please call NVC at (603) 334-0700. Please call between 8:00am-6:45pm Eastern Standard Time. You will need to enter the INS receipt number from this approval notice into the automated response system to receive information on your petition.

THIS FORM IS NOT A VISA NOR MAY IT BE USED IN PLACE OF A VISA.

Please see the additional information on the back. You will be notified separately about any other cases you filed.
U.S. CITIZENSHIP & IMMIGRATION SVC
CALIFORNIA SERVICE CENTER
P. O. BOX 30111
LAGUNA NIGUEL CA 92607-0111
Customer Service Telephone: (800) 375-5283

Form I-797 (Rev. 01/31/05) N

D. Step Two: You Follow Instructions From the National Visa Center

After the visa petition has been approved, you'll receive a follow-up application and further instructions from the National Visa Center (NVC). (This collection of items was formerly referred to as "Packet 3" but now it's called the instruction packet.) One important item it will contain is Biographical Information Form DS-2001.

To keep the process moving, you'll need to fill out and mail certain of the forms received in your instruction packet fairly quickly. Don't delay, since the approval of your fiancé visa petition is good for only four months (although the consulate can give you one four-month extension). In fact, many people send in Form DS-2001 before they have actually collected all the documents listed on the form.

E. Step Three: You Apply at a U.S. Consulate

The consulate will next contact you by mail, sending an appointment letter with the necessary forms and detailed instructions for your application. This will include instructions for obtaining a medical exam and your fingerprints. Some consulates conduct the medical exams the day before the interview. Others schedule the medical exam and the interview on the same day. You will be told where to go and what to do in your appointment letter.

1. Preparing for Your Interview

See the checklist below to help you organize the forms and documents necessary for your fiancé visa interview.

Here's some additional information regarding some of the items on the checklist below:

Police clearance. Unlike applications made in the U.S., you personally must collect police clearance certificates from each country you have lived in for one year or more since your 16th birthday. Additionally, you must have a police certificate from your home country or country of last residence, if you lived there for at least six months since the age of 16. You do not need to obtain police certificates from the United States.

Contact the local police department in your home country for instructions on how to get police certificates. To obtain police certificates from nations other than your home country, contact the nearest consulate representing that country for instructions. Some nations refuse to supply police certificates, or their certificates are not considered reliable, and so you will not be required to obtain them from those locations. The U.S. consulate will tell you from which countries police certificates are not required.

Checklist for Fiancé Visa Interview

Forms

❑ State Department Forms, potentially including Form DS-156, DS-156K, and DS-230 Part II (depending upon which of these you were already asked to mail in).

❑ USCIS Form I-134, Affidavit of Support, if the consulate requests it (signed by your petitioner, stating that he or she will reimburse the government if you receive public assistance or welfare).

❑ State Department Form DS-1858, Sponsor's Financial Responsibility Under the Social Security Act.

Documents

❑ Original USCIS Notice of Action approving your fiancé visa petition.

❑ Originals of documents submitted in connection with the visa petition, such as your fiancé's U.S. birth certificate and proof that any previous marriages were legally ended.

❑ Documents to accompany Form I-134, such as proof of U.S. citizen's employment, copy of U.S. citizen's most recent federal tax return, and letter from U.S. citizen's bank(s) confirming the account(s).

❑ A valid passport from your home country, good for at least six months.

❑ Your original birth certificate.

❑ An original police clearance certificate, if available in your country (the instructions from the consulate will tell you).

❑ Two additional photographs of you, the immigrating fiancé (according to the consulate's photo instructions).

❑ Results of your medical examination, in an unopened envelope.

❑ Additional documents proving your relationship (to cover the time since you submitted the fiancé visa petition), such as phone bills showing calls to one another, copies of emails and other correspondence, and photos taken during recent joint vacations.

❑ Application fee: Currently $100 for the visa.

❑ Fingerprinting fee: $85 if required.

Some countries will send certificates directly to U.S. consulates but not to you personally. Before they send the certificates out, however, you must request that it be done. Usually this requires filing some type of request form, together with a set of your fingerprints.

Fingerprints. A few consulates require you to submit fingerprints, though most do not. Consulates wanting fingerprints will send you instructions.

Photos. You must bring to the interview two photographs of you and two photographs of each accompanying child. They must be taken in compliance with the consulate's instructions (U.S "passport style"). Often your information packet will contain a list of local photographers who take this type of picture. If your religious beliefs require wearing a head covering, you should be able to keep it on for the photo. However, your eyes and face must still be visible, and you must submit a written statement explaining why you can't submit a standard photograph.

Medical exam. Immediately before your visa interview, you and your accompanying children will be required to have medical examinations. Some consulates conduct the medical exams up to several days before the interview. Others schedule the medical exam and the interview on the same day. You will be told where to go and what to do in your appointment letter.

The medical examinations are conducted by private doctors. The fees vary from $50 to more than $150 per exam, depending on the country. The fee will be stated in your appointment letter. The exam itself involves taking a medical history, blood test, chest X-ray, and vaccinations, if required. Pregnant women can refuse to be X-rayed until after the pregnancy. The vaccination requirement may be waived for religious, moral, or medical reasons.

The main purpose of the medical exam is to verify that you are not medically inadmissible. The primary medical grounds of inadmissibility are tuberculosis and HIV (AIDS). Some medical grounds of inadmissibility can be overcome with treatment or by applying for a waiver. (See Chapter 3 for details.) If you need a medical waiver, you will be given complete instructions by the consulate at the time of your interview, but should also consult an experienced immigration attorney.

Affidavit of support. As part of overcoming the grounds of inadmissibility, you will have to show that you will not become a public charge (go on welfare) in the United States. Normally, the consulate will ask your fiancé to fill out an Affidavit of Support on Form I-134. You actually have a choice between two forms: Form I-134 and a much longer one, Form I-864. The only reason to consider submitting the longer one at this stage is that all K-1 visa applicants will eventually have no choice but to submit Form I-864 with their green card application in the United States.

In cases where the level of financial support is clearly not a problem, you could submit the I-864 in support of the K visa to avoid duplicating your efforts. On the other hand, there are advantages to using the old I-134 initially, and then using the I-864 during the U.S. green card application. The main advantage is that Form I-134 is not considered legally enforceable. In other words, the U.S. government is very unlikely to go after whoever signs the I-134 for reimbursement if the immigrant ends up needing public benefits. That's a particular advantage if your U.S. citizen fiancé can't satisfy the financial requirements to be a sponsor and you need to convince a friend or family member to sign an additional affidavit of support on your behalf.

See Chapter 3 for more information on filling out Form I-864 and overcoming the public charge ground of inadmissibility.

2. Attending Your Interview

After the medical exam, you and your accompanying children will report to the consulate for the interview. Bring with you to the interview the items on the checklist above, and anything else the consulate requested. The interview process involves verification of your application's accuracy and an inspection of your documents.

For details on what to expect during your consular visa interview, see Chapter 4. Also see Chapter 4 if your visa is denied.

F. Step Four: You Enter the U.S. on Your Fiancé Visa

Normally, you must use the visa to enter the U.S. within six months, though the consulate can extend this period if necessary. The inspection process involves a U.S. border officer opening the sealed envelope containing your visa documents, and doing a last check to make sure you haven't used fraud. The border officer has expedited removal powers, which means he or she can turn you right around and send you home if anything appears wrong in your packet or with your answers to the officer's questions. Be polite and careful in answering.

When the officer is satisfied that everything is in order, he or she will stamp your passport to show that you're now a K-1 visa holder, and you will be authorized to remain in the U.S. for 90 days. If you are bringing accompanying children, they must enter the U.S. at either the same time or after you do. You can apply for a work permit once you're in the U.S.—see "Employment Authorization," below.

If you're planning to apply for a green card, your most important task at this point is to get married. You can't apply for the green card until you have an official government certificate of your marriage, which sometimes takes weeks after the wedding to be prepared. For more information on applying to adjust status based on your marriage, see Chapter 7.

 For a fuller discussion of all aspects of applying for a fiancé visa and for your green card after you've arrived in the U.S. and gotten married, see the latest edition of *Fiancé & Marriage Visas: A Couple's Guide to U.S. Immigration*, by Ilona Bray (Nolo).

Employment Authorization

To file an application for employment authorization for the 90 days you're on a fiancé visa, complete Form I-765 and file it with a USCIS service center, according to the instructions on the USCIS website. Answer Question 16 of the form "(a)(6)." Together with Form I-765, you must submit a copy of your I-94 card. The filing fee is $340.

You can also apply for a work permit when you submit your green card application. This may be worth waiting for—you're unlikely to get the work permit approved before your 90 days are up and the permit would expire anyway. The work permit you receive after applying to adjust status will also last a lot longer.

Chapter 9

Getting a Green Card Through Employment

Every year, 140,000 green cards are made available to people whose labor or work skills are needed to fill gaps or needs in the U.S. workforce. Before you can even think about getting an employment-based green card, however, two lucky things need to happen:

- you need to receive a job offer from a U.S. employer (unless you have exceptional abilities), and
- the employer must (with a few exceptions) be willing to sponsor you for a green card—including a long process known as labor certification, which involves advertising and interviewing other people for the job you've been offered, and ultimately rejecting all of them for good reasons.

Many people would love to come to the U.S. in order to look for a job and stay permanently, but realistically, employment-based green cards are mainly available to people who have advanced job skills, higher education, or extraordinary abilities. Unskilled workers needn't give up entirely—there is a subcategory of this type of green card available to them—but far more unskilled workers are looking for green cards than the number of green cards available, so the wait for them can be years long. Not many employers are willing to wait this long to hire an unskilled worker.

Do you need a lawyer? Once you have successfully found a job, your employer will normally hire and pay for the services of a lawyer to help both the employer and you prepare and submit the necessary application materials. In fact, 2007 Department of Labor rules require the employer to pay all attorney's fees and other costs associated with a part of the process call "labor certification." Many large companies have experienced staff people who will take care of immigration matters for highly desirable employees. However, it is often the employee who is most interested in having the green card issued, and to some U.S. employers, the red tape of hiring a foreign employee can be an unfamiliar nuisance. If your prospective employer doesn't hire you a lawyer, it's worth paying for one on your own. The lawyer's help is particularly important right now, because many of the government rules concerning the application process have recently changed and are very confusing.

A. Are You Eligible for a Green Card Through Employment?

In order to qualify for a green card through employment:

- The type of work you'll be doing must fit within one of the five categories (preferences) of employment listed under the law.

Key Features of an Employment-Based Green Card

Here are some of the advantages and limitations of an employment-based green card:

- You must start out working full-time for the company through which you obtained the green card—however, after your green card is approved, you may switch jobs or choose not to work at all, so long as your original intention wasn't to take advantage of your employer and leave as soon as you could.
- Your spouse and your unmarried children under the age of 21 may also be eligible for green cards as accompanying relatives.
- The job through which you get your green card must be for full-time work, and not self-employment (with some exceptions, depending on which category of work you apply under).
- As with all green cards, yours can be taken away if you misuse it—for example, you live outside the U.S. for too long, commit crimes, or even fail to advise the immigration authorities of your change of address. However, if you successfully keep your green card for five years, you can apply for U.S. citizenship.

- You must have an offer of full-time, permanent, U.S.-based work from an employer that is also permanently located in the United States. (See 20 C.F.R. § 656.3 for a full discussion of what types of employers qualify—for example, neither visiting diplomats nor foreign media companies can sponsor you for a green card.)
- You must have the correct background (education and work experience) for the job you've been offered.
- There must be no qualified U.S. worker willing or able to take the job—except in categories of green cards where labor certification is not required.

1. Do You Fit Within One of the Five Employment Preference Categories?

Green cards through employment are divided into five preference categories. In each category, only a limited number are given out each year. Often, more people apply in a year than there are green cards available. When that happens, the people who applied latest must wait, and receive their green cards in a later year, as they become available.

The five employment preference categories are:

- **Employment first preference (EB-1).** Priority workers
- **Employment second preference (EB-2).** Workers with advanced degrees or exceptional ability

- **Employment third preference (EB-3).** Skilled or unskilled workers without advanced degrees
- **Employment fourth preference (EB-4).** Religious workers and various miscellaneous categories of workers and other individuals; also called special immigrants
- **Employment fifth preference (EB-5).** Individual investors willing to invest $1,000,000 in a U.S. business (or $500,000 in a business in an economically depressed area).

a. Employment First Preference (EB-1) Category

First preference, or "priority" workers, are divided into three subcategories:

- workers of extraordinary ability
- outstanding university professors or researchers, and
- transferring executives or managers of multinational companies.

Applying as a priority worker is easier than applying in most of the other employment categories, because your employer doesn't need to start out by seeking labor certification on your behalf. In fact, in the subcategory for workers of extraordinary ability, you do not even need a job offer. (People applying as professors or researchers, however, do need job offers. And transferring executives or managers must, obviously, already be employed by the company that's transferring them.)

i. EB-1: Workers of Extraordinary Ability Subcategory

You may qualify for a green card as a priority worker if you have extraordinary ability in the sciences, arts, education, business, or athletics. Your achievements must have been publicly recognized, and resulted in a period of sustained national or international acclaim. For example, top-rated amateur athletes or Nobel Prize winners would qualify in this category.

A further condition of this subcategory is that your entry into the U.S. will substantially benefit the United States in the future. USCIS doesn't focus much attention on this particular requirement, but it is taken to mean that you must still be at the top of your field when you apply, not in a decline, or retiring.

You do not need a specific job offer in this subcategory so long as you will continue working in your field of expertise once you arrive in the United States. If, however, you have been offered a job, your employer can help with your application by filing the initial petition for you.

ii. EB-1: Outstanding Professors and Researchers Subcategory

You may qualify for a green card as a priority worker under the outstanding professors and researchers' subcategory if you have an international reputation for being outstanding in a particular academic field. You need three years' minimum of either teaching or research experience in that field. You must also be entering the U.S. to accept a specific tenured or tenure-track teaching or research position at a university or institution of higher learning.

Alternatively, you may accept a job conducting research in industry or with a research organization. The U.S. company or institution employing you should have a history of making significant achievements in research and must employ at least three other full-time research workers. Research positions must not be temporary, but rather be expected to last for an unlimited or indefinite duration.

iii. EB-1: Multinational Executives and Managers Subcategory

You may qualify for a green card as a priority worker under the multinational executives and managers subcategory if you have been employed as an executive or manager by a qualified company outside the U.S. for at least one out of the past three years. Or, if you're already in the U.S. on a temporary visa, for one of the three years before you arrived here. You must now be going to take a similar position with a U.S. branch, affiliate, or subsidiary of the same company. The U.S. office must have been in business for at least one year. (The qualifications needed are similar to those for L-1 intracompany transfer visas, discussed in Chapter 19.)

Not only do you need to meet the various qualification requirements under this subcategory, but the foreign and U.S.-based offices of your employer must either be:

- different branches of the same company
- a joint venture where the parent company owns half or has equal control and veto power
- related so that one company is a majority-controlled subsidiary of the other, or
- an affiliation in which both companies are under the control of the same person, persons, company, or group of companies.

Because your own job position, both in and out of the U.S., must be "executive" or "managerial" in nature, the exact meaning of these terms is important. A manager is defined as a person who:

- manages the organization or a department, subdivision, function, or component of the organization
- supervises and controls the work of other supervisory, professional, or managerial employees, or manages an essential function of the organization
- has the authority to hire and fire those persons supervised, or if none are supervised, works at a senior level within the organization, and
- has the authority to make decisions concerning the day-to-day operations of the activities or function of the organization over which he or she has authority.

Note that all four of the above criteria must be met for someone's job to be considered managerial. A supervisor below the level of middle management, often called a first-line supervisor, is not normally considered a manager for green card qualifying purposes—unless the employees being supervised are professionals. The word professional here means a worker holding a university degree.

An executive is defined as a person who:

- directs the management of the organization or a major part or function of the organization
- sets the goals and policies of the organization or a part or function of the organization
- has extensive decision-making authority, and
- receives only general supervision or direction from higher level executives, a board of directors, or the stockholders of the organization.

b. Employment Second Preference (EB-2) Category

The second preference category of green cards through employment is for:

- professionals holding advanced university degrees, and
- persons of exceptional ability in the sciences, arts, or business.

To qualify in this category, you must be coming to the U.S. specifically to work full-time in your field of expertise. With limited exceptions, you must have a definite, permanent job offer from a U.S. employer. Your entry must substantially benefit the United States' economic,

cultural, or educational interests or welfare. Labor certifications are normally required for this category. (For exceptions, see Subsection iii, below.) This is another preference category that is divided into subcategories.

i. EB-2: Advanced Degree Professionals Subcategory

To be a professional means, under the immigration laws, that you work in an occupation requiring, at a minimum, a baccalaureate (B.A. or B.S.) degree or its equivalent from a college or university. Therefore, to qualify as an advanced degree professional for this subcategory takes something more. Specifically, you must hold a graduate level degree, or a professional degree requiring postgraduate education, such as is standard in U.S. law or medicine. You must also be internationally recognized or outstanding in your field.

Many people who qualify for temporary, H-1 visas in professions like nursing and engineering do not qualify for green cards in this subcategory unless they have completed postgraduate degrees.

There is a substitute for having an advanced degree. You can also qualify if you have a baccalaureate degree followed by five years of work experience in a professional position. Your work experience can be either in the U.S. or abroad. The level of responsibility you exerted and knowledge you gained in that position must have increased progressively over the course of the five years.

Academic Credential Evaluations

Not every country in the world operates on the same academic degree and grade level system found in the United States. If you were educated in some other country, USCIS, as part of judging your eligibility, will usually ask you to provide an academic credential evaluation from an approved consulting service to determine the U.S. equivalent of your educational level.

After USCIS receives the evaluation report from the consulting service, it doesn't have to believe what the report says. USCIS considers these reports "nonbinding" on its decision—but such reports can be very persuasive nonetheless. When the results are favorable, they strengthen your case. If, however, the

evaluation shows that your credentials do not equal those required for advanced degree professionals, you will not qualify in this subcategory.

A list of these accreditation services can be found at www.naces.org/members.htm.

If you were educated outside the United States, it's best to get an evaluation before USCIS asks for it. If it's favorable, include it with your petition. This strengthens your case and saves time if USCIS decides to request it later. If your evaluation is unfavorable, submit the results only if USCIS insists you do. You may also wish to consider applying in a different category, because your application in this one is likely to fail.

ii. EB-2: Persons of Exceptional Ability Subcategory

The exceptional ability subcategory of the employment second preference covers people in the sciences, arts, and business. It's easily confused with the employment first preference priority worker subcategory for persons of extraordinary ability described above, but the requirements are slightly less narrow. (However, people with jobs in education and athletics are left out of this second preference subcategory.) Typical

cases might include economists, lawyers, obstetricians, veterinarians, physicists, market research analysts, geographers, mental health workers, and marriage and family therapists.

The main benefit of this subcategory is that you don't need to have received international acclaim in your field. Proven sustained national acclaim will meet the required standard. You must, however, still be considered significantly more accomplished than the average person in your profession.

iii. EB-2 Applicants Who Can Use a National Interest Waiver Instead of Labor Certification

If you're applying in the second preference category and your presence will benefit the U.S. in the future, you may be able to apply without having a job offer or labor certification, through what's called a national interest waiver. In order to "benefit" the U.S., you'll have to show that your coming will have a favorable impact on its economic, employment, educational, housing, environmental, or cultural situation, or on some other important aspect of U.S. life. The impact must be national in scope—in other words, a public health researcher at a federal agency or a university would probably pass, while the same person coming to provide services at a local clinic would probably not.

You'll also have to show that the field in which you'll be working has "substantial intrinsic merit"—in other words, that it's a good thing in and of itself. In addition, you'll need to demonstrate that you will prospectively benefit the national interest to a substantially greater degree than a similarly qualified, available U.S. worker would. (Unfortunately, USCIS often reinterprets this requirement to mean that you must show that forcing you to go through the labor certification process would actually have an adverse impact on the U.S. national interest. A local labor shortage is not considered to be an adverse impact.)

Because the combination of the above criteria is difficult to satisfy, obtaining a national interest waiver is very rare, and you will definitely need a lawyer's help. The key case that the lawyer will refer to is *Matter of NYSDOT*, Int. Dec. 3363.

c. Employment Third Preference (EB-3) Category

Employment third preference is the third broad category of green cards through employment. You'll need a job offer and a labor certification under all of its subcategories. (No national interest waiver is available for the third preference.) The work cannot be temporary or seasonal. The subcategories include:

- professional workers
- skilled workers, and
- unskilled workers.

You may wonder what difference it makes whether you are classified as a professional worker, skilled worker, or unskilled worker. Indeed, all three categories require labor certifications and draw green cards from the same 40,000 annual allotment.

The answer is that of those 40,000 green cards available each year, only 10,000 are for unskilled workers. Accordingly, those classified as unskilled often have to wait much longer for green cards than workers in the other subcategories, depending on how many other people apply. The wait has been as long as ten years.

i. EB-3: Professional Workers (No Advanced Degree) Subcategory

Are you a professional? Immigration law is always vague about the definition of this word, stating only that professionals include such occupations as architects, lawyers, physicians, engineers, and teachers. Other occupations that have routinely been approved as professional include accountants, computer systems analysts, physical therapists, chemists, pharmacists, medical technologists, hotel managers (large hotels only), fashion designers, certain upper-level business managers, and commercial airline pilots of 747s or other large aircraft.

If you hold only a bachelor's degree and have fewer than five years of work experience, this may be the subcategory for you. The job you've been offered must be in a field of work that normally requires a bachelor's degree. As long as you have the necessary degree, proving eligibility in this category is fairly simple.

ii. EB-3: Skilled Workers Subcategory

Workers engaged in occupations that normally do not require college degrees, but do need at least two years of training or experience, qualify in the subcategory of skilled workers. For example, the EB-3 category may be used for some computer and technical workers (not researchers or managers), chefs, construction first-line supervisors, stonemasons, reporters and journalists, graphic designers, and fashion designers. Relevant postsecondary training can be counted as training.

How much experience or training may be necessary for a specific job is not always clear. Your local state labor department office can tell you the exact number of years of education and experience it considers a minimum for the particular job you have been offered. Or you can look it up on the Department of Labor's website at http://online.onetcenter.org.

iii. EB-3: Unskilled Workers Subcategory

Any job not falling into one of the subcategories already described goes into the subcategory of unskilled workers. This usually includes occupations requiring less than two years' training or experience. Housekeepers, nannies, janitors, yard workers, nurse's aides, and farm workers are among the likely applicants. Of course, your own qualifications must satisfy whatever requirements the job does normally have, or you will not succeed in getting a green card using this subcategory. For example, if you've been offered a job requiring a one-year vocational training program, you must have completed such a program before you can begin applying for a green card on the basis of that job.

d. Employment Fourth Preference (EB-4) Category

This is the fourth category of employment-based workers, also called special immigrants. One of its subcategories is religious workers, which include ministers and religious professionals. The fourth preference also includes various miscellaneous subcategories of people, from former U.S. government workers to children dependent on the U.S. foster care system. (See Chapter 12 for a full discussion of this category.)

e. Employment Fifth Preference (EB-5) Category

This employment category is for investors willing to invest a minimum of $500,000 to $1,000,000 in a new U.S. business that will create jobs. The minimum amount depends on the location of the enterprise. (See Chapter 11 for a full discussion of the employment fifth preference category.)

2. Do You Have a Job Offer From a U.S. Employer?

You need a specific job offer from a U.S. employer in order to get a green card through employment.

Two groups of people don't need job offers. The first includes people who can qualify as workers of extraordinary ability. This is a small subgroup of the first preference *priority workers* category. The second exception is for workers with exceptional ability, under the second preference category. This exception is usually allowed when USCIS agrees that it's in the national interest to do so. Both categories are described earlier in this chapter.

The employer who offers you a job may be a company, institution, organization, or individual, located in the United States. If you yourself own a U.S. business, you cannot normally act as your own employer to get yourself a green card. The only situation in which you may be able to hire yourself is where you own a corporation employing many others as well.

If you have an agent who books your talents for a variety of jobs, as is common in the entertainment industry, the agent may also be the source of your job offer. For an agent to act as if he or she were your employer, you must receive your salary directly from the agent.

What's the reason behind the job offer requirement? Many people are surprised to learn that they need a job offer *before* applying for a green card. The idea behind it is that you are getting a green card only because your services are essential to a U.S. employer. Put another way, the U.S. government is issuing a green card not for your benefit, but to help a U.S. company or institution.

It may be hard for you to find an employer willing to offer you a job, because the employer probably realizes that before you can start work, the employer must spend a lot of time and effort to help get you a green card. The application process includes something called labor certification, during which your employer must prove that no qualified U.S. workers are available to take the job being offered to you. The employer will also need to assemble or produce numerous other documents, including company financial records and tax returns.

Your prospective employer should also have the patience to wait, because unless you already have a nonimmigrant work visa, you cannot legally start the job until your green card application is approved. This can take anywhere from several months to several years, depending on your qualifications and nationality. However, when a potential employer badly needs your skills, it will usually cooperate with the various requirements.

3. Do You Have the Correct Background?

You must have the correct background in terms of experience, training, and education for the job you have been offered. For example, if you are a qualified nuclear scientist, but are offered a job managing a U.S. bakery, you cannot use that job offer to get a green card, because you have no background in bakery management. It is irrelevant that your native intelligence and general knowledge of business may make you quite capable of handling the bakery job. Likewise, reliability, honesty, or willingness to work hard—characteristics that are much in demand by real-world employers—will not help you in the eyes of USCIS. A match between your background and the job is the main concern.

What to Tell Your Potential Employer

When you are trying to find a U.S. job, it may help if you can assure the employer that he or she is taking limited legal risks by participating in your green card application. The employer assumes absolutely no financial responsibility for you during the application process or after you enter the U.S., except that it guarantees to pay you the market wage for the position during the time you are actually employed. The employer also has the right to withdraw its petition for your green card for any reason and at any time. Once you receive a green card and begin working, your employer is free to fire you at will.

Prospective employers will be asked to supply business and financial records to USCIS. Many are afraid to do this. You can reassure them by explaining that USCIS checks these records for the main purpose of proving that the business has enough money to pay your salary, not to report its findings to other federal agencies.

Your employer cannot, on the other hand, simply write a job offer that pulls in all your unusual qualifications, and thereby eliminates other candidates from the running. For example, if the employer hopes to hire you as an art therapist, but claims that you must also have expertise in Renaissance art history, the DOL is likely to suspect that the employer has gone too far. In fact, unless the employer can give a good reason based on business necessity, the stated job requirements must be those normally required for the occupation and cannot exceed a measurement known as the Specific Vocational Preparation level, found in the government's O*NET Job Zones database, available online at http://online.onetcenter.org. (See 20 C.F.R. § 656.17(h).) In line with these requirements, the employer must not have hired workers with less training or experience for jobs substantially comparable to that involved in your job opportunity. (See 20 C.F.R. § 656.17(i)(2).)

Employers often tag special requirements onto the job description to help the applicant get a green card—the most common being a foreign language requirement. Unfortunately, the U.S. government knows that employers will use such a requirement for the singular purpose of excluding U.S. applicants. As a result, the regulations specifically say that a language requirement cannot be included in the job description unless it is justified by business necessity. (See 20 C.F.R. § 656.17(h)(2).) The situation is not hopeless, however. An employer can show business necessity for a foreign language requirement based upon such factors as the nature of the job (a translator's job, for instance) or a demonstrable need to communicate with a large majority of the employer's customers, contractors, or employees.

4. Can Your Employer Find No Qualified U.S. Workers for the Job?

Politicians in the U.S. are under a lot of pressure to show that they aren't giving away green cards to foreigners who take jobs away from U.S. citizens. To help relieve the pressure, the law requires most employers wanting to hire and get a green card for a foreign worker to complete a process called labor certification. (Certain types of jobs, however, are considered so desperately in need of workers that labor certifications will not be required—see Section 5a, below, for these "Schedule A" jobs.)

Labor certification involves proving to the U.S. Department of Labor that there are no able, qualified U.S. workers available and willing to take the job you have been offered, in the region where the job is offered. This is not an abstract requirement. Your prospective employer will have to advertise the job and conduct interviews. If your employer finds someone who fits the job requirements (even if the employer doesn't actually give that person the job), you won't be granted labor certification.

Even if you're better than all the other applicants, that may not be enough. If your employer finds a U.S. worker who simply meets the minimum qualifications for the job, that may push you out of the running for a green card. Also, if the U.S. worker can acquire the skills necessary to perform the job during a reasonable period of on-the-job training, that's enough to qualify him or her. (See 20 C.F.R. § 656.17(g)(2).)

If you're a college professor or a person of exceptional ability in the arts and sciences, getting a green card through employment is a little easier. It will be enough for you to show that you're *more qualified* than any suitable U.S. college and university faculty applicants, even if you're not the only one available. This difference may seem small, but since it normally takes only one minimally qualified U.S. job applicant to ruin a person's chances for a green card, it could make all the difference in the world.

Believe it or not, there are a fair number of jobs where the employer cannot find a minimally qualified U.S. worker to fill the position—that may be why the employer would be willing to help you get a green card in the first place. How much competition you have depends on what kind of job it is and where the job is located. For example, in some remote parts of the United States, employers have trouble attracting anyone to work there, while you'd probably face a lot of competition in a major city like New York or San Francisco.

Jobs that typically make successful opportunities for green card applications are those requiring workers with a college education, special knowledge, or unusual skills. Unskilled jobs that have odd working hours or other undesirable factors are also good possibilities for green card applicants.

5. Schedule A Jobs: No Formal Labor Certification Required

The U.S. labor department keeps track of types of jobs for which U.S. workers are in short supply. It regularly publishes a list of these jobs, called Schedule A. If the type of job you've been offered is on Schedule A, that means your employer can avoid going through the whole labor certification procedure to test the market for the availability of U.S. workers. Your employer will, however, still need to obtain a prevailing wage determination from a state workforce agency (SWA). (See 20 C.F.R. § 656.15 (b)(1).) Most of the jobs that make it onto Schedule A are in the second preference category.

Note that Schedule A is not a separate green card category. You still have to fit within one of the five employment preferences listed above. However, even if you'll be applying within a category that normally requires labor certification, the idea is that your employer can skip this step, because shortages of such workers are already a recognized fact.

The Schedule A list is not permanent. It changes as U.S. labor needs change.

Below are the occupations presently on the Schedule A list. To check the latest version of Schedule A yourself, see 20 C.F.R. § 656.5.

a. Group I: Certain Medical Occupations

The first part of Schedule A, called Group I, covers only people in medical jobs. Those currently on the list include:

- **Physical therapists.** You must be qualified for a license in the state where you intend to practice, but you need not be licensed already.
- **Professional nurses.** This includes only registered nurses. Licensed practical nurses do not qualify. You must have passed either the Commission on Graduates of Foreign Nursing Schools (CGFNS) examination or the National Council Licensure Examination for Registered Nurses (NCLEX-RN), which is administered by the National Council of State Boards of Nursing. Alternatively, you qualify for Schedule A if you are licensed by the U.S. state in which you intend to practice.

b. Group II: People With Exceptional Ability in Arts or Sciences

The second part of Schedule A, called Group II, covers only people with exceptional ability in the arts or sciences. It is difficult to qualify in this category. Instead of just matching an entry on a list of jobs, you must prove that you are internationally recognized for your out-standing, well-above-standard, work in the arts or sciences. You must also show that you have been practicing your science or art for at least the year prior to your application and intend to continue practicing it in the United States.

The category specifically includes college or university teachers. Other likely candidates under this category are internationally famous scientists, writers, or fine artists such as painters and sculptors. Performing artists may also qualify if their work during the past 12 months required exceptional ability, and their intended work in the United States will also require such ability.

If you try to avoid labor certification by applying under Group II, your employer must submit extensive supporting documentation proving your qualifications.

 Schedule B, which was a list of occupations for which there were already enough U.S. workers, was eliminated in 2005. This is good news—usually labor certifications were denied for any job listed on Schedule B.

B. Quick View of the Application Process

Once you've received a suitable job offer (if you need one under your green card category), getting a green card through employment is normally a seven-step process. It will involve:

- your employer requesting what's called a prevailing wage determination (PWD) from the workforce agency in its state (SWA), stating how much money is normally paid to people in jobs like the one you've been offered
- your employer advertising and recruiting for the job you've been offered, and ultimately determining that there are no qualified U.S. workers available to take the job
- your employer filing a labor certification application (unless you're applying in a category that doesn't require labor certification)
- within 180 days of the labor certification approval, your employer filing a visa petition (or, if you're in one of the few categories that don't require a job offer, your filing your own petition)
- after USCIS approves the petition, waiting until your Priority Date becomes current and a visa is available
- your filing a green card application, in connection with which you may attend an interview, either at a U.S. consulate outside of the U.S. or at a USCIS office within the United States, and
- if your interview is at a consulate, your entering the U.S. with your immigrant visa, at which time you become a permanent resident.

! **These application procedures were changed dramatically in 2005.** In an effort to streamline the process of applying for a green card based on work, USCIS issued new regulations changing the application form, the recruiting requirements, and many other parts of the process. These regulations are popularly called PERM, although their official name is Labor Certification for the Permanent Employment of Aliens in the United States. Don't rely on advice from fellow immigrants who went through this process before 2005, or on written materials published before that date.

If you're married or have children below the age of 21 and you qualify for a green card through employment, your spouse and children can get green cards as accompanying relatives by providing proof of their family relationship to you. They must also, like any intending immigrant, prove that they are not inadmissible. (See Chapter 3 for details on the kinds of things that might make your relative inadmissible.)

C. Step One: The Prevailing Wage Determination

Before your employer starts the immigration application process for you, it must make sure that the salary or wages it plans to pay you are normal for the local job market. The purpose is to make sure that hiring low-cost immigrant labor doesn't weaken the wages and in conditions of U.S. workers. To find this out, the employer must submit a request, called a prevailing wage determination (PWD), to its local SWA (state workforce agency). The SWA's response will tell the employer how much is normally paid to people in jobs equivalent to the one you've been offered.

Each U.S. state has its own form for making this request. To find contact information for your state's SWA, go to the DOL website at www.foreignlaborcert .doleta.gov/contacts.cfm. Finding out the prevailing wage is important, because your employer must offer you 100% or more of the prevailing wage—a change from the 95% that was acceptable before.

D. Step Two: Employer Advertising and Recruitment

Next, your employer can begin recruiting for the job. (Actually, your employer can start recruiting before this, but must be especially careful to offer a salary that's at least as high as the prevailing wage.)

⚠ For you to get a green card, your employer must fail at this recruiting attempt. If the employer finds a U.S. worker who is suited for the job and willing to accept it, the government presumes that your services are no longer needed—even if you are the employer's first choice. Nevertheless, your employer must make an honest effort at advertising and interviewing

for the job. If the DOL suspects any funny business, it may insist on directly supervising additional recruitment efforts by your employer. (See 20 C.F.R. § 656.21(a).)

The necessary types of advertising depend first on whether you are applying for a professional or a nonprofessional job. However, there are special requirements for college or university teachers selected under what's known as a competitive recruitment and selection process (your employer should see 20 C.F.R. § 656.18, Schedule A occupations (20 C.F.R. §§ 656.5 and 656.15)). Special recruiting requirements also apply to hiring sheepherders (see 20 C.F.R. § 656.16).

1. Recruiting Requirements for Nonprofessional Jobs

If the application is for a nonprofessional job, your employer must, at a minimum, place a job order with the SWA and publish two newspaper advertisements. These steps must be conducted at least 30 days but no more than six months before the employer files the labor certification application.

Placing a job order with an SWA requires no fee, and minimal effort from the employer. First, the SWA will enter a description of the position, identified by the job order number, in its statewide computer bank. For 30 days, anyone throughout the state who contacts the state labor department will have an opportunity to apply for the job. The state will collect the applications and resumes and forward them to the employer.

The employer must carefully choose which newspaper to advertise in. The government requires that the ads appear on two different Sundays in a newspaper of general circulation, which workers likely to apply for the job would be expected to read in an appropriate geographic area. If the job is located in a rural area with no Sunday paper, the employer may publish on whatever day has the widest circulation.

For exactly what information should go into the advertisements, the employer should see 20 C.F.R. § 656.17(f), which sets the requirements out quite clearly. One of the most important requirements is that the ad not state wages or terms and conditions of employment worse than those being offered to you. In other words, if the employer hopes to turn people away by announcing that the job will require regularly taking a night shift, but the employer doesn't really plan to make you work the night shift, the government will consider that ad insufficient.

2. Recruiting Requirements for Professional Jobs

If the job you've been offered is for a professional (someone with experience and an advanced degree), then your employer must start by following the two steps required for nonprofessionals (a job order and two print ads). However, instead of one of the Sunday advertisements ordinarily required, the employer can, if a professional journal normally would be used to advertise the job, place one advertisement in the professional journal most likely to bring responses from able, willing, qualified, and available U.S. workers.

In addition, employers recruiting for professional workers must conduct three additional steps chosen from a list published in the regulation. The list includes: (1) job fairs; (2) the employer's website; (3) a job-search website other than the employer's, which can include a Web page created by the same publisher to which the employer submitted a print ad; (4) on-campus recruiting; (5) trade or professional organizations, for example via their newsletters or trade journals; (6) private employment firms or placement agencies; (7) an employee referral program, if it includes specific incentives; (8) a notice of the job opening at a campus placement office, if the job requires a degree but no experience; (9) local and ethnic newspapers, so long as they're appropriate for the job opportunity; and (10) radio and television advertisements. (See 20 C.F.R. § 656.17(e)(ii).)

Unlike the pre-2005 system, all recruiting must be completed before your employer submits any part of the actual request for labor certification.

3. Handling Job Applications

If anyone applies for the job, the employer must then review the resumes. If the candidates do not meet the minimum qualifications for the job as described in the advertisement, the employer can refuse to interview them—but must be prepared to state in writing why not. Even if a single requested qualification is missing from the resume, that's enough reason for the employer to reject a U.S. job candidate in favor of you, if the employer wishes to do so.

However, when some acceptable resumes do turn up, the employer must interview those people within a reasonable time (it's best to contact them within ten days of their application being submitted). Neither you nor your attorney is permitted to attend these interviews. (20 C.F.R. § 656.10 (b)(2).)

After the interviews, the employer will hopefully still be unsatisfied and wish to employ you. If so, your employer must prepare what's called a recruitment report. (See 20 C.F.R. § 656.17(g).) The report must describe the recruitment steps undertaken and the results achieved, the number of hires, and, if applicable, the number of U.S. workers rejected, categorized by the lawful job-related reasons for such rejections. The employer must sign the report (despite the fact that, like the other supporting documents, this need not be turned in unless requested). The DOL may, if it reviews the recruitment report, also request the U.S. workers' resumes or applications.

Once an interview has been held, the employer is no longer limited to rejecting candidates only because they do not meet the job description as stated in the ad or the labor certification application. Poor health or work habits, lack of job stability, questionable character, and similar business considerations, if legitimate, are also satisfactory reasons. In addition, it sometimes comes out in an interview that the prospective worker's qualifications are not in fact what they appeared to be on the resume, or that the worker is not willing to relocate or is not otherwise willing to accept the job. This provides still another reason to turn down the U.S. candidate.

Your employer must complete all recruiting before submitting any part of the actual request for labor certification.

E. Step Three: Your Employer Seeks Labor Certification

If, after the recruiting has been completed, your employer hasn't found a qualified, willing, available, and able U.S. worker to take the job, it can submit what's called a labor certification application to the U.S. Department of Labor.

(However, if your employer takes too long in the recruiting process, the prevailing wage determination results may expire.) An application for labor certification can be filed only by your U.S. employer, not by you on your own. The purpose of labor certification is to satisfy the U.S. government that there are no qualified U.S. workers available and willing to take the specific job that has been offered to you.

Employment first preference priority workers and those with occupations appearing on Schedule A do not have to go through the labor certification procedures. They may move directly to the visa petition step described in Section G, below. Still, they'll have to prove that they're allowed to skip labor certification, by providing forms and documents showing that they qualify as either priority workers or for Schedule A.

In order to apply for labor certification, your employer must complete a ten-page form (ETA-9089), available on the DOL website at www.foreignlaborcert. doleta.gov. The form can be submitted either online or by mail. (If it's submitted online, your employer must make sure to sign it as soon as it receives approval.)

Many of the questions on the form ask for simple yes or no answers.

Your employer will not be required to submit any documentation with the ETA-9089, but will be expected to keep supporting documentation on hand, in case its application is selected for audit or the reviewing officer requests it. If your application is selected for an audit—that is, a full review by USCIS—it may either be because something in your paperwork looked suspicious, or it may simply be that your application was randomly selected.

No fee is required with the labor certification application, although a fee might be added in the future.

The Department of Labor is supposed to make a decision on the labor certification in 45 to 60 days. Unfortunately, the reality is that this can take more like six months.

If all goes well, the labor certification will eventually be approved. Be aware, however, that an approved labor certification does not, by itself, give you any right to live or work in the U.S. It is only a prerequisite to submitting the petition and application for a green card. If the labor certification is denied, your employer has 30 days in which to request reconsideration.

Checklist of Labor Certification Documents

Below are the documents your employer must keep on hand in case of an audit after submitting Form ETA-9089.

❑ Documents justifying any unusual or restrictive job requirements, including foreign language abilities.

❑ Copies of all advertisements and other recruitment-related documents, such as notices of on-campus recruitment or contracts with a private recruiting firm. If your employer uses a website as a recruitment medium, the employer should print out dated copies of the relevant pages. If your employer uses radio or television to advertise, this can be documented with a copy of the employer's text of the employer's advertisement along with a written confirmation from the radio or TV station stating when the ad was aired.

❑ Evidence that notice was provided to the bargaining representative of the employer's employees, if any, or that the job opportunity was posted conspicuously at the employer's workplace.

❑ Report from the employer of advertising results saying why each U.S. job candidate was turned down.

❑ Any additional documents required for special cases, such as sheepherders, live-in domestics, physicians, or college and university teachers.

F. Step Four: Your Employer Files the Visa Petition

At last, your U.S. employer can approach the U.S. immigration authorities, by filing what's called a visa petition on Form I-140. It must do so before the approved labor certification expires, that is, within 180 days. During this part of the process, your employer is known as your "petitioner," and you are the "beneficiary." In a few rare cases, you yourself can file the petition (and become your own petitioner), but only if your skills are so high-level that you don't need a job offer to immigrate through employment—more specifically, if you either:

- have extraordinary ability in the sciences, arts, education, business, or athletics (a subcategory of the first preference category described earlier), or

- are a professional holding an advanced degree, or have exceptional ability in the sciences, arts, or business, and you're claiming that you qualify for a national interest waiver (a subcategory of the second preference category described earlier).

Form I-140 is available at www.uscis .gov—and it comes with extensive instructions. The object of the petition is to prove that you or your employer have successfully completed any steps that were required so far, and to alert USCIS that your employer, or you on your own wish to start the immigration process. The form also takes care of some other details, like informing USCIS whether you will be continuing with your application through a consulate outside of the U.S. or through a U.S.-based USCIS office. (If you're not sure, choose the consulate. If you change your mind later, all you need to do is file an application at a USCIS office. Doing the reverse, and transferring your case from a USCIS office to a consulate, requires filing a separate application.)

The I-140 also provides space to list your spouse and children (who may want to immigrate along with you). Be sure your employer doesn't leave anyone off the list, even if that person doesn't want to immigrate now. USCIS wants to know about all your family members now, and if someone who wasn't on the list decides to immigrate later, you may have trouble convincing USCIS that he or she is really a member of your family.

The following checklist will help you keep track of all the forms and documents that you and your employer will need to collect and prepare in order to file the visa petition.

Checklist of Forms and Documents for Visa Petition

Your employer will need to assemble the following:

❑ Form I-140.

❑ Fee (currently $475).

❑ Approved labor certification or evidence of qualifying as a priority worker of extraordinary ability, Schedule A, or as a second preference worker of exceptional ability.

❑ Evidence that your employer can actually pay the wage it's offering you. If you're already employed there (on a nonimmigrant visa), this will be enough by itself. If not, your employer must supply such evidence as federal tax returns, annual reports, or audited financial statements. This is to show that the company's net income or net current assets are equal to or greater than the offered wage.

❑ Evidence that you have the education necessary to perform your job, such as diplomas and transcripts from colleges or universities.

❑ Evidence that you have the training or experience necessary to perform your job, such as professional certificates or other documents proving previous job experience.

❑ If requesting quick (premium processing): Form I-907, with filing fee (currently $1,000).

If Applying as a Priority Worker (EB-1):

In the persons of extraordinary ability subcategory (EB-1A):

❑ Evidence that you have either received a major, internationally recognized award (like a Nobel or an Oscar), or at least three of the following:

    ❑ Evidence you have received several lesser nationally or internationally recognized prizes or awards in your field.

❑ Documentation of membership in associations that require outstanding achievements of their members, as recognized by national or international experts.

❑ Published material about you in professional or major trade publications or other major media relating to your work.

❑ Evidence of your participation as a judge of the work of others in your field or an allied field.

❑ Evidence of your original scientific, scholarly, artistic, athletic, or business-related contributions of major significance in your field.

❑ Evidence of your authorship (or coauthorship, though this carries less weight) of scholarly articles in professional or major trade publications or other major media.

❑ Evidence of the display of your work at artistic exhibitions or showcases.

❑ Evidence that you have performed in leading or critical roles for distinguished organizations or establishments.

❑ Evidence that you have commanded a comparatively high salary or other compensation.

❑ Evidence that you have achieved commercial success in the performing arts (box office receipts, evidence of sold-out clubs, concert halls, arenas, or stadiums, or sales data on your recordings or videos).

❑ If the above do not fit your occupation, comparable evidence.

❑ Copy of your U.S. employment contract, an employer letter, or a statement written by you, explaining how you will continue your extraordinary work in the United States.

In the outstanding professor and researcher subcategory (EB-1B):

❑ At least two of the following:

  ❑ Evidence that you have received major prizes or awards for outstanding achievement in your academic field.

  ❑ Evidence of your membership in associations in your academic field—associations that require outstanding achievements for membership.

  ❑ Published material in professional publications written by others about your work. Mere citations to your work in bibliographies are not sufficient.

  ❑ Evidence of your participation as a judge of the work of others in the same or an allied field.

  ❑ Evidence of your original scientific or scholarly research contributions to the academic field.

  ❑ Evidence of your authorship of scholarly books or articles in scholarly journals having international circulation.

❏ Evidence that you have at least three years of teaching or research experience in your field (such as letters from former employers).

❏ If it is a university position, a letter or contract from the university stating that the U.S. position is either a tenured, tenure-track, or permanent researcher position.

❏ If the employer is in private industry, evidence that it has a history of significant achievements in research, employs at least three other full-time research workers, and intends to hire you for a permanent research position.

In the multinational managers and executives subcategory (EB-1C):

❏ Notice of approval of an L-1 visa petition, if any (recommended, not required).

❏ Documents proving employment as an executive or manager with the parent company for at least one of the past three years outside of the U.S. (or, if you're already in the U.S., for one of the three years before you arrived).

❏ Documents proving that you will be working in an executive or managerial capacity, including a description of your duties.

❏ Documents proving that your U.S. employer is either the same legal entity or in an affiliate or subsidiary relationship with your overseas employer, and has been doing business for at least a year, including such documents as:

    ❏ Articles of incorporation or other legal charter or business license of the foreign business.

    ❏ Articles of incorporation or other legal charter or business license of the U.S. business.

    ❏ Legal business registration certificate of the foreign business.

    ❏ Legal business registration certificate of the U.S. business.

    ❏ Tax returns of the foreign business for the past two years, if available.

    ❏ Tax returns of the U.S. business for the past two years, if available.

    ❏ If the company is publicly held, annual shareholder reports of both the U.S. and foreign companies.

    ❏ Accountant's financial statements, including profit and loss statements, and balance sheets of both the U.S. and foreign company for the past two years.

    ❏ Payroll records of the foreign company for the past two years, if available.

    ❏ Promotional literature describing the nature of the employer's business, both U.S. and foreign.

    ❏ Copy of the business lease or deed for the premises of the U.S. business.

    ❏ If either company is publicly held, statements from the secretary of the corporation attesting to how the companies are related.

    ❏ For private companies, copies of all outstanding stock certificates.

    ❏ For private companies, a notarized affidavit from the corporations' secretaries verifying the names of the officers and directors.

- ❏ For private companies, copies of the minutes of shareholder meetings appointing the officers and directors.
- ❏ If a joint venture, copy of the joint venture agreement.

If Applying as a Second-Preference Worker (EB-2):

If you are a second preference applicant filing your own visa petition based on a requested national interest waiver of the job offer and labor certification requirements:

- ❏ DOL Form ETA-750, Part B only, and
- ❏ Written statement, support letters from colleagues and experts in your field, and other documentation explaining why an exemption from the job requirement is in the U.S. national interest.

In the professional of exceptional ability in the sciences, arts, or business subcategory (EB-2B), either:

- ❏ An official academic record, showing that you have either a U.S. advanced degree or an equivalent foreign degree, or a U.S. baccalaureate (B.A.) or equivalent foreign degree together with letters from your current or former employers showing that you have at least five years of progressive postbaccalaureate experience in your specialty; or
- ❏ At least three of the following:
  - ❏ Evidence that you have an academic degree, diploma, certificate, or similar award from an institution of learning relating to your area of exceptional ability.
  - ❏ Evidence that you have at least ten years of full-time experience in your field (letters from current or former employers).
  - ❏ A license or certification to practice your profession.
  - ❏ Evidence that you have commanded a comparatively high salary or other compensation.
  - ❏ Evidence of your membership in professional associations.
  - ❏ Evidence of your recognition for achievements and significant contributions to your industry or field. This recognition should come from your peers, governmental entities, or professional or business organizations.

If none of the above types of evidence fits your occupation, submit comparable evidence of your eligibility.

If Applying as a Third-Preference Worker (EB-3):

In the professional workers subcategory (EB-3A):

- ❏ Evidence that you have a U.S. baccalaureate (B.A.) degree or equivalent foreign degree
- ❏ Evidence that a B.A. is required for your job.

In the skilled worker subcategory (EB-3B):

- ❏ Evidence that you meet the educational requirements, and the minimum two years' training or experience requirements for the job.

In the unskilled worker subcategory (EB-3C):

❑ Evidence that you meet any educational, training, or experience requirements of the job.

IF YOU DID NOT SEEK A LABOR CERTIFICATION BECAUSE YOU'VE BEEN OFFERED A SCHEDULE A JOB:

❑ An original and one copy of Application for Permanent Employment Certification (Form ETA-9089), including a prevailing wage determination from the SWA. The form need not be certified, but must be signed by an authorized official of the petitioning company.

❑ Evidence of compliance with the posting/union notification requirements, including a copy of the posted notice and of any in-house postings via electronic or other media.

Group I: Medical Occupations:

❑ Evidence that notice of filing the Application for Permanent Employment Certification was provided to the bargaining representative of the employer's employees.

Physical Therapists (subcategory of Group I):

Either:

❑ Copy of a U.S. state physical therapist license, or

❑ Letter from the state physical therapy licensing agency stating that you meet all the qualifications to sit for the state exam.

Registered Nurses (subcategory of Group I):

Either:

❑ Copy of a full and unrestricted state nursing license to practice in the state where you will be employed

❑ Copy of your certificate of having passed the Commission on Graduates of Foreign Nursing Schools (CGFNS) exam, or

❑ Evidence that you have passed the National Council Licensure Examination for Registered Nurses (NCLEX-RN).

Group II: Exceptional Ability in the Arts or Sciences:

❑ Documentary evidence showing the widespread acclaim and international recognition accorded you by recognized experts in your field.

❑ Documentation showing that your work in your artistic or scientific field during the past year did, and your intended work in the United States will, require exceptional ability.

❑ At least two of the following:

   ❑ Documents proving that you have won internationally recognized prizes or awards in your field of work.

   ❑ Documents showing membership in selective international associations— associations that require outstanding achievement of their members, as judged by recognized international experts.

❑ Articles about your work appearing in relevant professional publications, including the title, date, and author of such published material.

❑ Documents proving that you have acted as a judge in international competitions in your field or an allied field.

❑ Evidence of your original scientific or scholarly research contributions, which were of major significance in your field.

❑ Copies of scientific or academic articles by you that have been published in international journals (including professional journals with international circulation).

❑ Documents proving that your artistic work has been exhibited in at least two different countries.

Performing artists must additionally provide:

❑ Documentary evidence that your work experience during the past 12 months did require, and your intended work in the United States will require, exceptional ability; with documentation to show this exceptional ability, such as:

❑ Documentation showing your current widespread acclaim and international recognition, and your receipt of internationally recognized prizes or awards for excellence.

❑ Published material by or about you, such as critical reviews or articles in major newspapers, periodicals, and/or trade journals (including the title, date, and author of such material).

❑ Documentary evidence that your earnings have been commensurate with your claimed level of ability.

❑ Playbills and star billings.

❑ Documents showing the outstanding reputation of the theaters, concert halls, night clubs, and other establishments in which you've appeared or are scheduled to appear.

❑ Documents showing the outstanding reputation of theaters or repertory companies, ballet troupes, orchestras, or other organizations in which or with which you've performed during the past year in a leading or starring capacity.

1. Mailing the Visa Petition

Your employer must submit the visa petition—Form I-140, accompanying documents, and the fee—to the USCIS regional service center that serves your employer's place of business. (Currently, either the Texas or Nebraska Service Center; the USCIS website provides the proper address and P.O. box number.) USCIS regional service centers are not the same as USCIS local offices. For one thing, you cannot visit regional service centers in person—they process applications but they do not see applicants. There are several USCIS regional service centers spread across the United States.

If, however, you are in the United States, and you have a valid, unexpired visa, you may be able to file your green card application (Step 6, below) at the same time, or concurrently, with your employer's visa petition. But you can do so only if a visa is already available in your category, as described in Section G, below. Concurrent filing offers many advantages, including giving you the right to stay in the U.S. while the application is pending (useful if your temporary visa has expired or is due to expire soon) and the right to apply for work permits for you and your immediate family members. Unfortunately, the possibility of concurrent filing is fading away, as the waits for green cards in most categories have recently stretched to many months and years long.

2. Awaiting USCIS Approval of the Visa Petition

After filing Form I-140, you will have to wait for the petition to be approved, which can take several months by itself. (See Chapter 4 for how to track the length of time USCIS is taking to decide on visa petitions, and how to track your own application online.)

Faster processing—at a price. For $1,000 over and above the regular filing fees, USCIS promises "premium processing" of the visa petition, including a decision within 15 days. To use the service, the employer must fill out an additional application (Form I-907) and submit the application to a special USCIS Service Center address. For complete instructions, see the USCIS website at www.uscis.gov. Within a few weeks after mailing the petition, your employer should receive a written confirmation that the papers are being processed, together with a receipt for the fees. This notice will also contain your case file number. If USCIS wants further information before acting on your case, it will send your employer a request for evidence (RFE) Form I-797. The I-797 tells your employer what corrections, additional pieces of information, or additional documents are expected. Your employer should make the corrections or supply the extra data and mail them back to the USCIS regional service center with the request form on top.

The filing procedure is the same for all work-based green card petitions, but your employer must indicate which employment preference and subcategory is being requested. If you are turned down for one category, the petition will not automatically be considered for a lower category. However, your employer may always submit a new petition under a different employment preference or subcategory. For example, if you have a job offer that might fall under the skilled worker subcategory of the third preference, but you are not sure, consider filing two petitions, one as a skilled worker and another as an unskilled worker. This will save some time if the petition under the higher-level subcategory is turned down.

Once your petition is approved, USCIS will advise your employer using a Notice of Action, also on Form I-797. If you plan to attend your visa interview at a U.S. consulate abroad, USCIS will forward the file to the National Visa Center (NVC), located in Portsmouth, New Hampshire. The NVC will then send a packet of forms and instructions to you so that you may proceed with consular processing, described later in this chapter.

Like the labor certification, an approved petition does not by itself give you any right to immigrate to, or live in the United States. It is only a prerequisite to the next steps, including submitting your own application for a green card.

G. Step Five: You Wait for an Available Visa Number

Because there are annual limits on the number of people who can receive green cards through employment, you will most likely have to wait in line until a visa number becomes available. (You can't get a green card until you're given a visa number, regardless of whether you're coming from outside or inside the United States.) Your place in the line is tracked by your Priority Date. It comes from the date on which your employer filed your labor certification. (Where formal labor certification is not required, your Priority Date is the date your application was filed at USCIS.)

It's impossible to say exactly how long you will have to wait—it all depends on how many people are in line before you. In general, waiting periods tend to be longer for people from China, India, Mexico, and the Philippines, especially for non-skilled workers. This is not because of any discrimination against those countries—it merely reflects the fact that more people from those countries apply for visas than from other countries, and there is a per-country limit. The supply of visas for those countries is regularly less than the number of people applying for them, so the waiting list keeps getting longer.

Although you can't predict how long you will wait, you can track the progress of your own Priority Date through the system, and get some sense of the rate at which it is moving. To do so, you first

March 2007 Priority Dates for Employment-Based Visas

	All Chargeability Areas Except Those Listed	CHINA-mainland born	INDIA	MEXICO	PHILIP-PINES
Employment-Based					
1st	C	C	C	C	C
2nd	C	22APR05	08JAN03	C	C
3rd	01AUG02	01AUG02	08MAY01	15MAY01	10AUG02
Other Workers	01OCT01	01OCT01	01OCT01	01OCT01	01OCT01
4th	C	C	C	C	C
Certain Religious Workers	C	C	C	C	C
Iraqi & Afghani Translators	18SEP06	18SEP06	18SEP06	18SEP06	18SEP06
5th	C	C	C	C	C
Targeted Employment Areas/Regional Centers	C	C	C	C	C

need to look at the State Department's monthly *Visa Bulletin*, which lists the Priority Dates of people who are allowed to get visas that month. It's available on a recorded message at 202-663-1541, or at its website at www.state.gov (under "Travel & Business," click "Visa Bulletins"). The State Department updates this chart around the middle of every month, but not on any exact day.

When you look at the *Visa Bulletin*, look for the chart like the one above:

Here's how to read the *Visa Bulletin* chart:

1. Locate your preference category in the first column. For example, if you're applying as an unskilled worker, you're in the third preference category, which is the third row down.

2. Locate your country across the top. If you don't see it listed, look in the column called "All Chargeability Areas Except Those Listed."

3. Draw lines across from your preference category and down from your country of origin. The box where your two lines cross is the one containing what's called your Visa Cutoff Date. Sometimes, it contains a letter instead of a date. The letter "C" is good news—it means that no one needs to wait, and all applicants are considered current, that is, immediately eligible for a visa or green card. The letter "U" is bad news—it means that all the visas have been used up for that year, and more will not become available until October

(when the federal government starts its new fiscal year).

4. If, instead of a letter, your box contains a Visa Cutoff Date, compare it with your Priority Date. If the Visa Cutoff Date is the same as your Priority Date, or is even later, great—you can now apply for your green card. However, if the cutoff date is earlier than your Priority Date, you still have to wait—because only people who applied some time before you now have the right to apply for their visa or green card.

EXAMPLE: Sarita is a citizen of India, who has been offered a job as a medical researcher in a U.S. pharmaceutical company. This puts her in the second preference visa category. Her employer files a visa petition for her on August 4, 2006. In March of 2007, she decides to check her Priority Date. As you'll see on the March 2007 chart above, her Visa Cutoff Date was then January 8, 2003. That means that people from India whose employers filed visa petitions for them on January 8, 2003 (or before that) were finally allowed to continue with the process and apply for a green card in March 2007. Their wait was approximately four years—which suggests that Sarita may wait a similar length of time.

If you have an approved petition but your Priority Date is not yet current, you must wait until it is current to take the next step and file your green card application. The immigration authorities will advise you by mail when your Priority Date finally comes up (so make sure to send them any change of address!).

If you're in the United States on a temporary work visa, be careful that your status does not expire before your Priority Date becomes current and you can apply for a green card—possessing an approved visa petition does not give you any right to live in the United States. If this looks like it might become a problem, consult as soon as possible with an immigration attorney.

H. Step Six: You Submit the Green Card Application

After your visa petition has been approved and your Priority Date has become current, it's time for you to play a more active role in the application process: You'll need to file your application for permanent residence or a green card. (In fact, the timing works a little differently if you're in the U.S. and visa numbers are immediately available in your category. In that case, you don't have to separate the visa petition and green card application steps, because you can file the two concurrently.) If your spouse or children will be accompanying you, they must each file their own green card applications. And if you're coming from outside of the U.S., remember that you'll first receive an immigrant visa from a U.S. consulate, which you will trade in for your permanent residence upon entering the United States.

The most important question at this point is where you file the application—in the United States or at a U.S. consulate in another country? You should have already made this choice on your Form I-140, but you're allowed to change your mind, so it's worth revisiting this question.

If you're living outside of the United States now. The answer is fairly easy for people living outside of the U.S.—you'll file at a local U.S. consulate and attend an interview there before entering the United States. (This method is called consular processing.)

If you're living in the U.S. now. The answer is a bit more complicated for applicants already in the United States. The easiest thing for you would probably be to adjust status without leaving —that is, send your application to the nearest USCIS Service Center and attend your interview at a local USCIS office. If you're one of the few people legally allowed to use this option, it's a great one. Once your application is filed, your stay in the United States will be considered legal, and you can apply for permission to work. Should problems arise in your case, you will be able to wait for a decision in the U.S., a circumstance most green card applicants prefer. Also, if your application for a green card is turned down, you have greater rights of appeal inside the U.S. than you do at a U.S. consulate.

The catch is that you are allowed to adjust status only if you're already in the U.S. legally, that is, on a valid, unexpired visa or other form of permission (with a few exceptions). You might, for example, already be working for your employer on a temporary visa such as an H-1B. If, however, you're living in the United States with no legal status, or have worked without authorization, or you entered legally without a visa under the Visa Waiver Program, you are barred from filing your green card application inside the United States. See Chapter 3 for information on whether you might be one of the rare few people allowed to adjust status regardless, due to an exception. If not, you'll probably need to consult with an experienced immigration attorney.

Whether or not you are eligible to adjust status, you may instead decide to leave the United States and apply for your green card at a U.S. consulate abroad. If the consulates are issuing visas more quickly than your local USCIS office is handling adjustment of status applications (which is common), leaving to apply at a consulate in your home country could be a smart strategic move. However, if you have already spent 180 days or more in the U.S. out of legal status, or crossed the border without inspection, be sure you are not inadmissible or subject to the three-year or ten-year reentry bar before you go. (See Chapter 3.) Otherwise, you could find yourself stuck outside the United States for three or ten years.

1. What Happens When Adjusting Status in the U.S.

The process of adjusting your status to permanent resident involves four steps. First, you prepare a set of forms and documents—one set for you and separate sets for your accompanying spouse and for each of your accompanying children. Second, you mail those packets to a USCIS service center. Then you wait for some weeks or months until the USCIS calls you and your family members in to have your fingerprints taken. You then wait weeks or months longer until the USCIS finally calls you and your family members in for your final green card interview at a local USCIS office (not the one to which you sent your application). You should be approved for your green card at or soon after the interview. Nowadays, the interview is often waived, in which case you'll get a letter in the mail telling you you've been approved. See Chapter 4 for information on tracking the progress of your application at the service center and at your local office.

⚠ **Remember, you may not apply to adjust status until you have an approved labor certification, if one is required, and an approved visa petition (unless you can file it concurrently).** You must also be eligible to adjust status in the U.S.—see Chapter 3 if you haven't yet researched this.

As part of your adjustment of status application, you and your family members may apply for permission to work (an Employment Authorization Document or EAD).

💡 **Are you here on an H-1B visa?** If so, and if your H-1B status won't expire for a while, there's no need for you to apply for separate work permission. In fact, some lawyers specifically advise continuing to renew your H-1B status and not using an EAD, just in case your adjustment of status

application is denied (for example, because your employer goes out of business). With your H-1B still valid, you could simply switch to another employer, start a new green card application, and avoid a lot of trouble.

2. Paperwork to Prepare for Adjustment of Status Application

The basic form used in the U.S. adjustment of status application is Form I-485, Application for Permanent Residence. However, a handful of other forms must be prepared to accompany this main one, and you'll need to collect various documents as well.

An easy way to get all the necessary forms is to call the USCIS forms line at 800-870-3676 and ask for the Adjustment of Status Packet. Or, you can obtain the forms online at www.uscis.gov. (Click "Immigration Forms," then scroll down and select the forms you need one by one.)

 Filing the visa petition and green card application concurrently? To prevent confusion at the service center, it's best to label the outside of the package "I-140/I-485 concurrent filing," and explain it in a cover letter, as well.

The checklist below will help you assemble and keep track of the appropriate forms and documents. A complete set of the below must also be prepared for your accompanying spouse and children.

You'll need to mail your application, consisting of both forms and documents, to the USCIS service center nearest the place you are living. Check for the appropriate address and P.O. box number at www.uscis.gov.

Checklist for Adjustment of Status Application

Forms

❑ Form I-485.

❑ Filing fee: Currently $1,010 for applicants between ages 14 and 79, $600 for applicants under age 14 who are filing with a parent, and $930 for applicants age 79 and over or under age 14 but not filing with a parent. Includes fee for biometrics (fingerprinting). You'll be notified of where and when to appear. In addition, if you're in the U.S. illegally, but allowed to adjust status under old laws, you must pay a $1,000 penalty fee. Double check all fees at www.uscis.gov.

❑ Form I-485A (only if you'll be paying the $1,000 penalty fee in order to adjust status).

❑ Form G-325A.

❑ Form I-765 (optional, if you want a work permit; include a separate filing fee, currently $340).

❑ Form I-134 (Affidavit of Support on behalf of your spouse and children).

❑ Form I-864 (more complicated Affidavit of Support used if a relative of yours owns 5% or more of the business that petitioned for you).

❑ I-131, Application for Travel Document (Advance Parole), for use if you think you'll need to travel outside the United States while your application is processed. This also requires a separate filing fee, currently $305.

Documents

❑ Notice of approval of the visa petition—or, if you're filing the visa petition concurrently with the adjustment of status application, Form I-140 and all supporting documents as described in Section F, above.

❑ Copy of a long-form birth certificate for you and each accompanying relative. If this certificate is in another language, it must be accompanied by a full English translation.

❑ Marriage certificate if you are married and bringing your spouse.

❑ If you or your spouse was married before, copies of divorce and death certificates.

❑ Copy of I-94 card for you and each accompanying relative (the small white or green card placed in your passport).

❑ Two photographs of you and two photographs of each accompanying relative, in U.S. passport style (it's best to have a professional do these). Write your name and A-number (if you've received one from USCIS) in pencil on the back of each photo.

❑ Letter from the petitioning employer verifying the job is still open.

❑ Medical exam report for you and each accompanying relative (Form I-693, filled out and signed by a USCIS-certified doctor, and presented in an unopened envelope).

❑ If you're a nurse, a Visa Screen certificate showing that you've met the exam and English language requirements.

Dealing With Delays in Approval of Your Work Authorization

If you want to work before your application for a green card is approved, you must file a separate application for employment authorization. To do so, fill out Form I-765 and file it with your adjustment of status application. To accompany Form I-765, you must submit a copy of your I-94 card and pay a separate filing fee.

Legally, USCIS does not have to make a decision on your employment authorization application for up to 90 days. If, for some reason, you are not given a decision within 90 days, you can request an interim employment authorization that will last 240 days. To request an interim card, make an appointment to visit your local USCIS office. Be aware, however, that lawsuits are currently underway, due to USCIS failure to provide interim EADs.

If 240 days pass and you still have not received a final decision on the I-765, you must stop working. Interim work authorization cards cannot be renewed. However, if you reach this point, you have the option to file a new I-765 application. If you do not get a decision on the new application within 90 days, you will then be entitled to another interim work authorization card.

After filing your adjustment of status application, you will receive a receipt that estimates the processing time for your application. If USCIS requires additional evidence or information, it will send you a Request for Evidence (I-797). You will also receive, after some weeks or months, a notice advising you where to go to have your fingerprints taken. These will then be used to check whether you have any history of arrests (whether by the police, FBI, DHS, or other authority).

3. Your Adjustment of Status Interview

Personal interviews are usually not required in applications for green cards through employment. You should simply receive an approval letter in the mail, usually several months (or years) after you filed the application. Your approval notice will instruct you where to go to a local USCIS office for your green card or so-called ADIT processing.

If required, the interview will be held at a USCIS office near you. You and your accompanying relatives will be sent an appointment notice, usually about two weeks in advance. If you have an attorney, he or she may come with you to the interview. Even if you don't have an attorney, you could consult with or hire one at this point, particularly if you're worried about why you've been called in for an interview.

When to Apply for Advance Parole

Once your application for adjustment of status has been filed, you must not leave the U.S. for any reason before you have applied for and received advance permission to reenter the U.S. (Advance Parole). Any absence without this permission will be viewed as a termination of your application for a green card—which means that, upon return, you will be told that your green card application is dead and you have no right to enter the United States.

Many people simply apply for Advance Parole at the same time they apply to adjust status, just in case. Or, you can wait until you're sure you have to leave, and apply at the same service center where you sent your adjustment of status application—but you're taking a risk this way, because USCIS may take many weeks to approve your Advance Parole application. Your application for Advance Parole should include Form I-131, together with the filing fee, two passport-type photographs, a copy of your adjustment of status filing receipt (if you've already sent in that application), and a short explanation of why you want to leave—you will need a bona fide personal or business reason, though it need not be an emergency.

If approved, you will be allowed to leave the U.S. and return again with no break in the processing of your application. However, if you were out of status for 180 days or more after April 1, 1997, you should not depart the U.S. even on the basis of an Advance Parole, as this may subject you to the three-year or ten-year bars to reentry (discussed in Chapter 3). Note that if you have an H-1 or L-1 visa, you're not required to apply for Advance Parole.

Checklist: Documents to Bring to Your Interview

Prepare all of the following to take with you to your USCIS interview:

❑ A complete photocopy of your green card application. This is for your use—you may want to follow along as the officer asks you questions about the material you filled out on the forms, or you may find that the officer is missing something that you have.

❑ Photo identification or passport for you and for every one of your family members. (It's best to bring your passport, because if you are approved for your green card on the day of the interview, USCIS can place a stamp in your passport demonstrating this—and you can use this stamp as proof when you work or travel.)

❑ Originals of all documents that you made copies of for submission with your application. For example, if you submitted a photocopy of a birth certificate or other official document, a USCIS officer may want to examine the original.

❑ Any documents received from USCIS or other immigration authorities. For example, if you left the country on Advance Parole, bring this permit.

❑ Any updates to the material in your application. For example, if your employer has changed its name, bring proof of this change. If you've been arrested, bring a full explanation (and consult with an attorney, to make sure that the arrest doesn't make you inadmissible).

See Chapter 4 for detailed information on what expect during your adjustment of status interview. If your adjustment of status application is denied, also see Chapter 4. And for information on how to protect your status as a green card holder after you're approved, see Chapter 14.

4. What Happens During Consular Processing

Consular processing involves a standard series of events. First, you prepare some forms and documents according to instructions. Then you notify the consulate when you are ready with these, and wait until you receive a notice scheduling you for an interview at a U.S. consulate. You will then undergo a medical exam, prepare additional forms and documents for the interview, and finally attend the interview. There, if all goes well, you will be approved (subject to final security checks) for a visa to enter the United States.

Much of your job at this point involves convincing the consulate that you are not inadmissible for health, criminal, security, or financial reasons. You will be asked to undergo a medical exam and possibly provide evidence that you have no criminal record. Luckily, since you have a job offer, proving that you can support yourself financially should not be a problem. (However, the law says that if one of your relatives owns 5% or more of the business that is petitioning for you, you need to file Form I-864, an Affidavit of Support signed by a relative—see Chapter 3 for a full discussion of this affidavit. The I-864 usually needs to be separately sent to the NVC for review before you continue your case with the consulate.)

If you don't need to fill out an I-864 but your spouse and children will be accompanying you, you yourself will need to fill out a Form I-134 Affidavit of Support. The purpose is to show that you are willing and able to support your family once you're all living in the United States. If you are in the subcategory of priority workers that aren't required to have a job offer in order to get a green card, you have already submitted documents showing your intent to continue working. These documents will be enough to substitute for Form I-134.

5. Paperwork to Prepare for Consular Processing

At the beginning, consular processing involves a lot of paper being sent in various directions. First, after USCIS approves your visa petition, it will forward your file to the National Visa Center (NVC) in Portsmouth, New Hampshire. It will send you a form called an Agent of Choice and Address (DS-3032), which simply asks where you want the rest of your visa-related mail sent; for example, to your attorney rather than to you.

Once the NVC receives your form DS-3032, it will mail you (or your attorney or agent) an Immigrant Visa (IV) fee bill (currently $335) and a security fee (currently $45). Once you've paid that bill, the NVC will send you what's called an instruction packet of forms and information (formerly called Packet 3). It will send you a second packet as part of your interview notification from.

a. Handling the Instructional Packet

The instructional packet sent to you by the NVC will include forms and materials for you to read. To keep the process moving, you must fill out and return some of the forms as soon as possible— namely Form DS-230 Part I and Form DS-2001 (formerly called OF-169). The forms are normally designated by a DS preceding a number, and copies of many of them are available on the State Department website at www.state.gov. However, it's better to wait for the ones the consulate sends you, because some of them are slightly different than the main State Department forms. For example, many of the consulates use forms with bilingual translations into the language of your country.

 You don't really need to have all your documents in hand when you send in Form DS-2001. Although the form asks you to sign it only after you're ready with the listed forms, many people simply sign as soon as they know they can get the forms together, to keep the process moving.

After you've sent in the necessary forms, your local U.S. consulate will start communicating with you directly. It will provide you with additional forms to fill out, a list of documents to collect, and other tasks to take care of.

b. Preparing Forms and Documents for Your Interview

The checklist below provides a brief explanation of some of the documents you'll need to gather in preparation for your immigrant visa interview. Keep your eyes open for any special requirements that your consulate may add to this list. Bring the originals and a set of copies with you to your interview (the consular officer may want to examine the originals to make sure they're not fraudulent, but keep copies for your files). Do not mail your paperwork to the consulate!

Checklist: Documents and Forms for Your Consular Interview

Forms

❑ DS forms (sent to you by the NVC and U.S. consulate).

❑ Form I-134 (Affidavit of Support for family members immigrating with you).

❑ Form I-864 (Affidavit of Support to be used if a relative owns 5% or more of the business that petitions for you).

Documents

❑ Notice of approval of your visa petition.

❑ Long-form birth certificate for you and each accompanying relative as well as for any unmarried minor children who are not immigrating with you.

❑ Marriage certificate if you are married and bringing your spouse.

❑ If either you or your spouse have been previously married, copies of divorce and death certificates showing termination of all previous marriages.

❑ Passport for you and for each accompanying relative, valid for at least six months beyond the date of the final interview.

❑ Police certificates from every country in which you and each accompanying relative has lived for at least six months since age 16.

❑ Fingerprints, if specifically requested by the consulate.

❑ Military records for you and each accompanying relative.

❑ Two photographs of you and two photographs of each accompanying relative.

❑ Letter from the petitioning employer verifying the job is still open.

❑ Medical exam report for you and each accompanying relative.

❑ If you're a nurse, a Visa Screen certificate showing that you've met the exam and English language requirements.

Here's some additional explanation regarding some of the items on the checklist above:

Police clearance. Unlike with applications made in the U.S., you personally must collect police clearance certificates from each country you have lived in for one year or more since your 16th birthday. Additionally, you must have a police certificate from your home country or country of last residence, if you lived there for at least six months since the age of 16. You do not need to obtain police certificates from the United States.

Contact the local police department in your home country for instructions on how to get police certificates, or visit http://travel.state.gov/visa/reciprocity/index.htm. To obtain police certificates from nations other than your home country, contact the nearest consulate representing that country for instructions. Some nations refuse to supply police certificates, or their certificates are not considered reliable, and so you will not be required to obtain them from those locations. The U.S. consulate will tell you which countries police certificates are not required from.

Some countries will send certificates directly to U.S. consulates but not to you personally. Before they send the certificates out, however, you must request that it be done. Usually this requires filing some type of request form, together with a set of your fingerprints.

Photos. You and each accompanying relative must bring to the interview two photographs taken in compliance with the consulate's instructions (U.S "passport style"). Often your information packet will contain a list of local photographers who take this type of picture. If your religious beliefs require wearing a head covering, you should be able to keep it on for the photo. However, your eyes and face must still be visible, and you must submit a written statement explaining why you can't submit a standard photograph.

Fingerprints. A few consulates require you to submit fingerprints, though most do not. Consulates wanting fingerprints will send you blank fingerprint cards with instructions. The current fingerprinting fee is $85.

Medical exam. Immediately before your visa interview, you and your accompanying relatives will be required to have medical examinations. Some consulates conduct the medical exams up to several days before the interview. Others schedule the medical exam and the interview on the same day. You will be told where to go and what to do in your appointment letter.

The medical examinations are conducted by private doctors. The fees vary from $50 to more than $150 per exam, depending on the country. The fee will be stated in your appointment letter. The exam itself involves taking a medical history, blood test, and chest X-ray, and vaccinations, if you need them. Although pregnant women can refuse to be X-rayed until after the pregnancy, the requirement to have an X-ray taken cannot be waived entirely. The vaccination requirement may be waived for religious, moral, or medical reasons.

The main purpose of the medical exam is to verify that you are not medically inadmissible. The primary medical grounds of inadmissibility are tuberculosis and HIV (AIDS). Some medical grounds of inadmissibility can be overcome with treatment or by applying for a waiver. (See Chapter 3 for more details.) If you need a medical waiver, you will be given complete instructions by the consulate at the time of your interview, but should also consult an experienced immigration attorney.

 Bring copies of everything you and your employer have submitted up to this point. Such copies will help you answer questions from the consular officer. They may also come in handy in case any items got lost in the transfer between the U.S. immigration offices and the U.S. consulate.

6. Your Consular Interview

Consulates hold interviews on all green card applications. A written notice of your interview appointment will be sent to you a few weeks before the appointment date. The appointment package will tell you what to bring to your interview, including your completed forms, photographs, passports, and the like. See the checklist in Section 5, above, for the items usually

requested, but also read the consular list carefully for any additions or changes.

 For details on what to expect during your consular visa interview, see Chapter 4. For information on what to do if your visa is denied, also see Chapter 4.

I. Step Seven: Entering the U.S. With Your Immigrant Visa

Your immigrant visa allows you to request entry to the United States, at a border post, airport, or other arrival point. You acquire the full status of green card holder only after you have been inspected and admitted into the U.S. If you are bringing any accompanying relatives, they must enter at either the same time or after you do in order to become permanent residents.

The inspection process involves a U.S. border officer opening the sealed envelope containing your visa documents, and doing a last check to make sure you haven't used fraud. The border officer has expedited removal powers, which means he or she can turn you right around and send you home if anything appears wrong in your packet or with your answers to the officer's questions. Be polite and careful in answering.

When the officer is satisfied that everything is in order, he or she will stamp your passport to show that you're now a U.S. permanent resident and are immediately authorized to work. You won't receive an actual green card yet, however. Cards for you and your accompanying relatives will be ordered for you, and will come to you by mail several weeks later.

■

Chapter 10

Getting a Green Card Through the Diversity Visa Lottery

The Immigration Act of 1990 created a new green card category, technically known as the diversity visa, to benefit persons from countries that in recent years have sent the fewest numbers of immigrants to the U.S. (See I.N.A. § 203(c), 8 U.S.C. §1153(c).) You can enter the lottery if you are a native of one of these countries and meet certain educational and other requirements. Different qualifying countries are selected each year, based on how many of their citizens immigrated to the U.S. during the previous five years, in proportion to the size of their populations.

The total number of diversity visa winners every year is 50,000 (it was formerly 55,000, but 5,000 of these are now reserved for applicants under a different program called NACARA). These 50,000 are distributed by dividing up the world into regions and allocating varying percentages of the total green cards to each region. Additionally, each qualifying country within each region is limited to no more than 7% of the available lottery green cards per year (or 3,850).

Because the method used to select winners of the diversity visa is a random drawing, it is popularly known as the green card lottery. However, this name is somewhat misleading, because not all winners succeed in receiving a U.S. green card. The problems are usually due to delays or because the lottery winners are found to be inadmissible to the United States. This chapter will explain who can become eligible for a green card based on the diversity visa lottery, how to apply, and how to increase your chances of success.

The diversity visa rules and deadlines change every year, usually around September. To make sure you're getting the latest version, check the State Department website at www.state.gov.

Key Features of the Diversity Visa

Here are some of the advantages and disadvantages of the diversity visa:

- The minimal entry requirements help people who might not fit into any other green card eligibility category.
- Winning the diversity visa doesn't guarantee you a green card—you must still show that you're not inadmissible, including that you'll be able to support yourself in the United States.
- If you win, your spouse and unmarried children under the age of 21 may also get green cards as accompanying relatives.
- As with all green cards, yours can be taken away if you misuse it—for example, you live outside the U.S. for too long, commit a crime, or even fail to advise the immigration authorities of your change of address. However, if you successfully keep your green card for five years, you can apply for U.S. citizenship.

Do you need a lawyer? Entering the lottery is fairly simple and doesn't usually require a lawyer's help. You may, however, need to pay someone for help with some of the technological parts of completing the application, which requires Internet access and digital photos. Once you win the lottery, a lawyer's help can be well worth the investment, to make sure that government delays don't end up wasting your winning lottery ticket.

A. Are You Eligible for a Green Card Through the Lottery?

In order to enter the lottery, you must be from one of the qualifying countries, and must have either a high school diploma or a minimum of two years' experience in a job that normally requires at least two years of training or experience. U.S. job offers are not a requirement. Whether the type of work you've been doing for two years qualifies will be determined based on a U.S. Department of Labor database at www.onetcenter.org.

Only the lottery winner—not his or her spouse or children—needs to meet the educational requirements. However, a spouse or child who does meet these requirements should apply separately (it's okay to be listed on a parent or spouse's application at the same time you file your own). There is no minimum age to enter the lottery. However, the requirement of a high school diploma or

two years' experience usually keeps out anyone under the age of 16.

The lottery requirements are different from the green card requirements. Entering the lottery is just the first step. When it comes time to claim your green card, you will have to show that you are not inadmissible, which includes showing that you can support yourself financially in the U.S. or that someone there is willing to support you. It also includes showing that you haven't committed certain crimes, been involved in terrorist or subversive activities, or become afflicted with certain physical or mental defects. Also, if you are living in the United States illegally, it may be impossible for you to collect your green card anytime soon. Procedurally, you would (unless you fall into an exceptional category) have to leave the U.S. for an interview at a consulate outside of the United States. At that point, however, you could be barred from reentering the U.S. for three or ten years, depending on the length of your illegal U.S. stay. (See Chapter 3 on inadmissibility.)

There is a new application period every year, usually occurring in late winter or early spring. The most recent application deadline was December 3, 2006. Registrations submitted one year are not held over to the next, so if you are not selected one year you need to reapply the next year to be considered. For the 2006 lottery (technically called DV-2008, because 2008 is the year in which the visas will actually be given out), the only countries not qualified were:

Brazil

Canada

China (mainland-born)

Colombia

Dominican Republic

El Salvador

Haiti

India

Jamaica

Mexico

Pakistan

Peru

Philippines

Poland

Russia

South Korea

United Kingdom (except Northern
Ireland) and its dependent
territories, and

Vietnam.

If you are from a country not named on the list above, you could have applied for the lottery that took place in 2006. Most of these countries reappear on the list year after year. Winners of the DV-2008 were notified by mail between May and July of 2007.

B. Quick View of the Application Process

Getting a green card through the lottery is a three-step process:

- First, you register, which simply means filling out an online application that places your name among those who may be selected through the lottery drawing system. If you've

won, you will be notified within approximately eight months. (If you don't win, you will receive no further communications.)

- Second, winners can proceed to filing a green card application, together with their accompanying relatives, if any.
- Third, if your interview was at a U.S. consulate in another country, you must enter the U.S. with your immigrant visa, at which time you become a permanent resident.

If your permanent residence cannot be approved by the end of the lottery (fiscal) year (September 30), your application becomes invalid and you lose your chance at a green card. This happens to thousands of people every year. It may not be within your control.

C. Step One: Registering for the Lottery

The rules for registering yourself in the lottery drawing change every year. For the latest, check the State Department website at http://travel.state.gov (click "Travel & Business," then look under "Visas for Foreign Citizens" for the latest announcement). There is no fee to register.

For the 2006 deadline (DV-2008) applicants were asked to fill out an application form online and to attach digital photographs meeting certain specifications. The information requested in the online form included the following:

Sample Lottery Application

1. FULL NAME - Last/Family Name, First Name, Middle Name

2. DATE OF BIRTH - Day, Month, Year

3. GENDER - Male or Female

4. CITY WHERE YOU WERE BORN

5. COUNTRY WHERE YOU WERE BORN - The name of the country should be the one currently in use for the place where you were born (for example, Slovenia rather than Yugoslavia, or Kazakhstan rather than Soviet Union).

6. COUNTRY OF ELIGIBILITY OR CHARGEABILITY FOR THE DV PROGRAM - Normally your country of birth, unless you can use a spouse or parent's birthplace (see separate description).

7. ENTRY PHOTOGRAPH(S) - (according to photo specifications; include photos of spouse and children)

8. MAILING ADDRESS - Address, City/Town, District/Country/Province/State, Postal Code/Zip Code, Country

9. COUNTRY WHERE YOU LIVE TODAY

10. PHONE NUMBER - (optional)

11. EMAIL ADDRESS - (optional)

12. WHAT IS THE HIGHEST LEVEL OF EDUCATION YOU HAVE ACHIEVED, AS OF TODAY? - Choose either (1) Primary school only, (2) High school, no degree, (3) High school degree, (4) Vocational school, (5) Some university courses, (6) University degree, (7) Some graduate level courses, (8) Master's degree, (9) Some doctorate level courses, and (10) Doctorate degree.

13. MARITAL STATUS - Unmarried, Married, Divorced, Widowed, Legally Separated

14. NUMBER OF CHILDREN - Give the name, date, and place of birth of all natural children, legally adopted children, and stepchildren, who are unmarried and under age 21. It doesn't matter whether you're married to the child's other parent, nor whether the child lives with you or will immigrate with you— put their names down anyway. (You don't need to mention children who are already U.S. legal permanent residents or citizens.)

15. SPOUSE INFORMATION - Name, Date of Birth, Gender, City/Town of Birth, Country of Birth, Photograph

16. CHILDREN INFORMATION - Name, Date of Birth, Gender, City/Town of Birth, Country of Birth, Photograph

Failure to list your spouse and all eligible children will result in disqualification for the visa. In fact, you'll need to fill in every answer on the form, or your entry will be disqualified.

Send only one registration per person (if you submit more than one application you'll be disqualified). However, husbands and wives can each submit a separate application. Do not send separate registrations for children unless they qualify on their own and are willing to immigrate without you. Although unmarried children under 21 automatically qualify to immigrate with their parents, if selected, the opposite is not true. If a child is selected, the parents will not get green cards unless they are selected separately.

Once you've successfully registered online, the State Department will issue you a notice of receipt. The notice will contain your name, date of birth, country of chargeability, and a time/date stamp. Don't be confused into thinking that acceptance of your registration means you've won the lottery. It means only that you appear to come from a qualifying country and didn't make any mistakes in the registration process.

Using a Family Member's Birthplace as Your Native Country

To enter the lottery, an applicant must be able to claim what the law describes as nativity in an eligible country. Nativity in most cases is determined by the applicant's place of birth. However, if you were born in an ineligible country but your spouse was born in an eligible country, you can claim your spouse's country of birth rather than your own (so long as your spouse will be immigrating with you and you'll be entering the U.S. together). Also, if you were born in an ineligible country, but neither of your parents was born there or resided there at the time of your birth, you may be able to claim nativity in one of your parents' country of birth.

⚠ **Paying someone won't help your application.** Some immigration consultants claim they can get special attention for your lottery registration if you pay them to handle it. Such claims are false. There's nothing wrong with paying a lawyer or qualified paralegal to help you complete the registration according to the instructions, but recognize that that's the only type of help you'll be getting.

D. Step Two: The Green Card Application

If you receive notification that your name has been drawn in the lottery, you must act quickly to apply for your green card. If your spouse or children will be accompanying you, they must each file their own green card applications. A big part of the green card application is

---

Dealing With the "Public Charge" Ground of Inadmissibility

You must convince USCIS that once you receive a green card you are not likely to go on public assistance or welfare. A source of support must be shown for your accompanying relatives as well. You have three alternatives: You can submit a written job offer from a U.S. employer. You can also submit your own personal current financial documents showing you have sufficient savings and investment income to support yourself. The third possibility is to have a U.S. friend or relative sign an I-134 Affidavit of Support on your behalf. If this form is filed, then no further documentation is required. The form I-134 guarantees that the signer is willing to take financial responsibility for you. USCIS offices normally insist that the person signing the Form I-134 be both your close relative and a U.S. resident.

If you can show that you are financially independent or have a job offer in the U.S., an I-134 need not be filed for you. You should still, however, fill out Form I-134 for any accompanying relatives. Because you will have an income, you should be the one to sign the Form I-134, taking financial responsibility for each of them.

When you request a family member or friend to sign an Affidavit of Support on your behalf, he or she will doubtless wish to know the legal extent of the financial obligation. In signing the Affidavit of Support, the signer does not promise to support you. What he or she does promise to do is reimburse the U.S. government for the sum total of any government support payments you receive if you go on welfare. The Affidavit of Support binds the person signing it to this obligation for three years. After that, his or her responsibility to both you and the U.S. government comes to an end.

proving that you are not inadmissible to the United States. Review Chapter 3 regarding the grounds of inadmissibility.

One of the most problematic issues for lottery visa applicants is proving that you will not become a public charge (receive government assistance). See "Dealing With the "Public Charge" Ground of Inadmissibility," above.

The most important question at this point in the process is where you file the application—at a USCIS office in the United States or at a U.S. consulate outside of the United States? You should have already made this choice on your Form I-140, but you're allowed to change your mind, so it's worth revisiting this question.

If you're living outside of the United States now. The answer is fairly easy for people currently living outside of the U.S.—you'll file at a local U.S. consulate and attend an interview there before entering the United States. (This method is called consular processing.)

If you're living in the U.S. now. The answer is a bit more complicated for applicants already in the United States. Ordinarily, the most convenient choice would probably be for you to adjust status without leaving—that is, send your application to the nearest USCIS service center and attend your interview at a local USCIS office. Once your application is filed, your stay in the United States will be considered legal, and you can apply for permission to work. Should problems arise in your case, you'll be able to wait for a decision in the U.S.,

a circumstance most green card applicants prefer. Also, if your application for a green card is turned down, you have greater rights of appeal inside the U.S. than you do at a U.S. consulate.

One catch is that you are allowed to adjust status only if you're already in the U.S. legally, that is, on a valid, unexpired visa or other form of permission (with a few exceptions). You might, for example, already be on a temporary visa such as a student, F-1 visa. If, however, you're living in the United States with no legal status, or have worked without authorization, or you entered legally without a visa under the Visa Waiver program, you are barred from filing your green card application inside the U.S. See Chapter 3 for information on whether you might be one of the rare few people allowed to adjust status regardless, due to an exception. If not, you'll probably need to consult with an experienced immigration attorney.

Whether or not you are eligible to adjust status, you may instead decide to leave the United States and apply for your green card at a U.S. consulate abroad. If the consulates are issuing visas more quickly than your local USCIS office is handling adjustment of status applications (which is common), leaving to apply at a consulate outside of the U.S. could be a smart strategic move. Remember, time is all-important in a lottery-based green card application. However, if you have already spent 180 days or more in the U.S. out of legal status, or crossed the border without inspection, see an attorney to be sure you are not inadmissible or subject to a three-year or ten-year waiting period before you go. (See Chapter 3.) Otherwise, you could find yourself stuck outside the United States for three or ten years.

The need for speed. Let's look a little closer at why it's so important to submit your green application in an office that's not too slow or backed up. If your immigrant visa isn't issued before the end of the fiscal year for which you were selected, your registration becomes void and you lose your chance for the green card. The deadline is the end of the fiscal year *for*, and not *in*, the year you were picked. The government fiscal years begin on October 1 and end on September 30. This means that if you were selected after the registration period that took place between October and December of 2006, and were notified between May and July of 2007, your deadline for receiving an approval of either your immigrant visa (if you're processing outside of the U.S.) or your adjustment of status (if you're processing in the U.S.) would be September 30, 2008.

Although that gives you just over a year to apply, attend your interview, and receive an approval, that's actually less time than it sounds like. In fact, it's the typical processing time in many consular and USCIS offices, so if one small thing goes wrong, you could be out of the running. You must, therefore, file as soon as you possibly can to be sure the processing is completed in time.

Another reason for speed is that the U.S. government notifies twice as many people as there are green cards available. It assumes some of these people either will not qualify or will change their minds about immigrating. If the assumption is wrong and everyone selected does mail in applications, the green cards will be given on a first-come, first-served basis. It is, therefore, possible that even though you win the lottery, if that year's green card allotment is used up before your own interview is scheduled, you will not get a green card. Once again, the normally speedier consular processing may offer some protection.

If you have any children who will turn 21 soon, you have yet another reason to want the process to go quickly. Once the child turns 21, he or she technically loses eligibility for the diversity visa. Fortunately, children have some protection from this difficulty under a law called the Child Status Protection Act (CSPA). This law allows you to subtract from the child's actual age the number of days which passed between the first day people were allowed to register for the program that year and the date your family received a notification that your registration had been selected.

EXAMPLE: Sven, from Sweden, registers for the DV-2008 program. The registration period opened on October 4, 2006. He receives a congratulatory letter dated June 6, 2007, notifying him that he's been selected. Accordingly, Sven's diversity visa petition has been pending for 243 days. His appointment to receive his immigrant visa is scheduled for September 1, 2008. By that time, Sven's daughter has turned 21 (on August 1, 2008). Fortunately, because she has been 21 for fewer than 243 days, the CSPA allows her to proceed with her application.

Only a U.S. consulate or embassy in your home country is required to accept your lottery green card application. You can ask a consulate located elsewhere to accept your application, but it has the option to say "no," and, in fact, will turn down most such requests.

1. What Happens When Adjusting Status in the United States

The process of adjusting your status to permanent resident involves preparing a set of forms and documents (a separate set for you, your spouse, and each of your accompanying children), mailing these to a USCIS service center, waiting for some weeks or months until you're called in to have your fingerprints taken, and then waiting a few weeks or months longer until you're called in for your final green card interview at a local USCIS office (not the one to which you sent your application). You should be approved for your green card at or soon after the interview. See Chapter 4 for information on tracking the progress of your application at the service center and at your local office.

As part of your adjustment of status application, you and your family members may apply for permission to work (an Employment Authorization Document or EAD).

Security checks are the most likely cause of delays. As part of your adjustment of status application, the FBI must run both a fingerprint check and a name check on you, and the CIA must run a separate name check. These name checks can take several months or even years, especially because many applicants have similar names. If you've been informed that your case is stalled due to security checks, get the name of a person you can keep in touch with for updates, or hire a lawyer to help.

2. Paperwork to Prepare for Adjustment of Status Application

The basic form used in the U.S. adjustment of status application is Form I-485, Application for Permanent Residence. However, a handful of other forms must be prepared to accompany this main one.

An easy way to get all these forms is to call the USCIS forms line at 800-870-3676 and ask for the Adjustment of Status Packet. Or, you can obtain the forms online at www.uscis.gov (click "Immigration Forms," then scroll down and select the forms you need one by one, based on the checklist below).

The following checklist will help you assemble and keep track of the appropriate forms and documents. A complete set of the below must also be prepared for your accompanying spouse and children.

Checklist for Adjustment of Status Application

Forms

❑ Form I-485.

❑ Filing fee. Currently $1,010 for applicants between ages 14 and 79, $600 for applicants under age 14 who are filing with a parent, and $930 for applicants over age 79 or under age 14 but not filing with a parent. The fee includes fingerprinting (biometrics); you'll be notified of where and when to appear. In addition, if you're in the U.S. illegally, but allowed to adjust status under old laws, you must pay a $1,000 penalty fee, described in Chapter 3. Checks and money orders are accepted, but don't send cash through the mail. Double check all fees at www.uscis.gov.

❑ Form I-485A (only if you'll be paying the $1,000 penalty fee in order to adjust status).

❑ Form G-325A.

❑ Form I-765 (optional, if you want a work permit; include a separate filing fee, currently $340).

❑ Form I-134 or other proof of financial support.

❑ I-131, Application for Travel Document (Advance Parole), for use if you think you'll need to travel outside the United States while your application is processed. This also requires a separate filing fee, currently $305.

Documents

❑ Copy of the official notice that your lottery registration was selected.

❑ Proof of education. The lottery green card program requires applicants to have either a high school diploma or the equivalent, or job skills needing at least two years of experience or training to learn. Appropriate evidence would be either a copy of your high school diploma or proof of job skill training, such as a vocational school certificate, and proof of at least two years of skilled employment verified by letters from past employers.

❑ Copy of a long-form birth certificate for you and each accompanying relative. If this is in another language, it must be accompanied by a full English translation.

❑ Marriage certificate if you are married and bringing your spouse.

❑ If you or your spouse was married before, copies of divorce and death certificates.

❑ Copy of I-94 card for you and each accompanying relative (the small card in your passport). If you don't submit this, it will look like you entered the U.S. illegally and either are not eligible or are subject to the $1,000 penalty described in Chapter 3.

❑ Two color photographs of you and two of each accompanying relative in U.S. passport style (it's best to have a professional do these). Write your name and A-number (if you've received one from USCIS) in pencil on the back of each photo.

❑ Medical exam report for you and for each relative (Form I-693, filled out by a USCIS-certified doctor, presented in an unopened envelope). The fee is around $150 per exam. The doctor will take your medical history, do a blood test and chest X-ray, and give vaccinations if needed. Pregnant women may refuse to be X-rayed until after the baby's birth.

Dealing With Delays in Approval of Your Work Authorization

If you want to work before your application for a green card is approved, you must file a separate application for employment authorization. To do so, fill out Form I-765 and file it together with your adjustment of status application. To accompany Form I-765, submit a copy of your I-94 card and pay a separate filing fee. Be sure to keep the fee receipt that USCIS gives you, so you can prove that the I-765 was filed. Normally, you will file the application for employment authorization at the same time as your adjustment of status application papers.

Legally, USCIS does not have to make a decision on your employment authorization application for up to 90 days. If, for some reason, you are not given a decision within 90 days, you have the right to an interim employment authorization that will last 240 days. Unfortunately, claiming this right has recently become impossible. The idea used to be that you could go to your local USCIS office and apply for the interim EAD, which the local office could quickly produce. However, USCIS declared in an April 2006 memo that local offices would no longer do this—at best, they'll contact the service center for you to find out why your EAD has been delayed. Lawsuits were being filed against USCIS at the time this book went to print. In the meantime, you may need an attorney's help if your EAD approval has been delayed.

If 240 days pass and you still have not received a final decision on the I-765, you must stop working. Interim work authorization cards cannot be renewed. However, if you reach this point, you have the option to file a new I-765 application. If you do not get a decision on the new application within 90 days, you will then be entitled to another interim work authorization card.

Tips for filling out Form I-485:
You'll notice on the first page of the form, under Part 2: Application, it asks you to choose the basis upon which you're applying for a green card. Mark Box "a" if you are the principal applicant. Also mark Box "h" (other basis of eligibility) and write in "Diversity Lottery Winner." Leave the other boxes in Part 2 blank. Form I-485 also asks for an A number. Normally, you will not have an A number unless you previously applied for a green card or have been in deportation proceedings (in which case you should see a lawyer). It also asks for your I-94 number. This is the number on the little white or green card that was tucked into your passport when you entered the U.S. (Green means you entered on a visa waiver, and probably cannot adjust status.)

Read This If You Plan to Leave the U.S. Before Your Adjustment Interview

Once your application for adjustment of status has been filed, you must not leave the U.S. for any reason before you have applied for and received advance permission to reenter the U.S. (Advance Parole). Any absence without this permission will be viewed as a termination of your application for a green card—which means that, upon return, you will be told that your green card application is dead and you have no right to enter the United States.

Many people simply apply for Advance Parole at the same time they apply to adjust status, just in case. Or, you can wait until you're sure you have to leave, and apply at the same service center where you sent your adjustment of status application—but you're taking a risk this way, because USCIS may take many weeks to approve your Advance Parole application.

Your application for Advance Parole should include Form I-131, together with the filing fee, three passport-type photographs, a copy of your adjustment of status filing receipt (if you've already sent in that application), and a short explanation of why you want to leave—you will need a bona fide personal or business reason, though it need not be an emergency.

If approved, you will be allowed to leave the U.S. and return again with no break in the processing of your application. However, if you were out of status for six or more months after April 1, 1997, you should not depart the U.S. even on the basis of Advance Parole, as this may subject you to a three-year or ten-year bar against reentering.

As a diversity visa applicant, you'll need to mail your application, consisting of both forms and documents, to a USCIS service center. Check the website for the exact address; USCIS was about to change it at the time this book went to print.

After filing your adjustment of status application, you will receive a receipt that estimates the processing time for your application. If USCIS requires additional evidence or information, it will send you a Request for Evidence (I-797). You will also receive, after some weeks or months, a notice advising you where to go to have your fingerprints taken. These will then be used to check whether you have any history of arrests (whether by the police, FBI, DHS, or other authority).

3. Your Adjustment of Status Interview

You will be called in for a personal interview, which will be held at a USCIS office near you. USCIS will send you and your accompanying relatives an appointment notice, usually about two weeks in advance of the interview. If you have an attorney, he or she may come with you to the interview. (Even if you don't have an attorney, you could consult with or hire one at this point.)

See Chapter 4 for detailed information on what expect during your adjustment of status interview. If your adjustment of status application is denied, also see Chapter 4. And for information on how to protect your status as a green card holder after you're approved, see Chapter 14.

Checklist of Documents to Bring to USCIS Adjustment of Status Interview

- ❑ A complete photocopy of your green card application. This is for your use—you may want to follow along as the officer asks you questions about the material you filled out on the forms, or you may find that the officer is missing something that you have.
- ❑ Photo identification or passport for you and every one of your family members. (It's best to bring your passport, because if you are approved for your green card on the day of the interview, USCIS can place a stamp in your passport demonstrating this—and you can use this stamp as proof when you work or travel.)
- ❑ Originals of all documents that you made copies of for submission with your application. For example, if you submitted a photocopy of a birth certificate or other official document, a USCIS officer may want to examine the original.
- ❑ Any documents received from USCIS or other immigration authorities. For example, if you left the country on Advance Parole, bring this permit.
- ❑ Any updates to the material in your application. For example, if you have given birth to another child, bring the birth certificate. If you've been arrested, bring a full explanation (and consult with an attorney, to make sure that the arrest doesn't make you inadmissible).
- ❑ Whoever signed the Affidavit of Support should bring proof of recent employment.

4. What Happens During Consular Processing

Consular processing requires you to prepare some forms and documents according to instructions, pay fees, notify the consulate when you are ready with these, wait until you receive a notice scheduling you for an interview at a U.S. consulate, undergo a medical exam, prepare additional forms and documents for the interview, and finally attend the interview. There, if all goes well, you will be approved (subject to final security checks) for a visa to enter the United States.

Much of your job at this point involves convincing the consulate that you are not inadmissible for health, criminal, security, or financial reasons. You will be asked to undergo a medical exam and possibly provide evidence that you have no criminal record.

5. Paperwork to Prepare for Consular Processing

There are two main sets of paperwork involved in consular processing. The first will be sent to you after your notification in an instructional packet (formerly called Packet 3). The second will be sent to you as part of your interview notification from your local U.S. consulate.

a. Handling the Instructional Packet

When you are selected for the lottery, your notification will include a packet containing both forms and instructions.

Some of these forms are for you to fill out and return in order to keep the process moving—namely Form DS-230 Part I and Form DS-2001.

The forms are normally designated by a DS preceding a number, and copies of many of them are available on the State Department website at www.state.gov. However, it's better to wait for the ones the consulate sends you, because some of them are slightly different than the ones on the website—for example, many of the consulates use forms with bilingual translations into the language of your country. You'll also be asked to pay visa and security fees.

 Keep the process moving. You don't really need to have all your documents in hand when you send in Form DS-2001. Although the form asks you to sign it only after you're ready with the listed forms, many people simply sign as soon as they know they can get the forms together, to speed matters toward their consular interview.

After you've sent in the necessary forms, your local U.S. consulate will start communicating with you directly. It will provide you with additional forms to fill out, a list of documents to collect, and other tasks to take care of.

b. Preparing Forms and Documents for Your Interview

The checklist below provides a brief explanation of some of the documents you'll need to gather in preparation for your immigrant visa interview. Keep your eyes open for any special requirements that your consulate may add to this list. Bring the originals and a set of copies with you to your interview (the consular officer may want to examine the originals to make sure they're not fraudulent, but keep copies for your files). Do not mail your paperwork to the consulate!

Checklist of Documents and Forms for Consular Interview

Forms
- ❑ DS forms (sent to you by the NVC and U.S. consulate).
- ❑ Form I-134 (Affidavit of Support signed by a relative in the United States, or signed by the primary source of financial support for family members immigrating with you).

Documents
- ❑ Notice of your selection for the diversity visa lottery.
- ❑ Long-form birth certificate for you and each accompanying relative as well as of any unmarried minor children who are not immigrating with you.
- ❑ Marriage certificate if you are married and bringing your spouse.
- ❑ If either you or your spouse has been previously married, copies of divorce and death certificates showing termination of all previous marriages.
- ❑ Proof that your education or training meets the requirements for the diversity visa.
- ❑ Passport for you and each accompanying relative, valid for at least six months beyond the date of the final interview.
- ❑ Police certificates from every country (except the U.S.) in which you and each accompanying relative has lived for at least six months since age 16.
- ❑ Fingerprints, if specifically requested by the consulate.
- ❑ Military records for you and each accompanying relative.
- ❑ Two color photographs of you and two photographs of each accompanying relative, in U.S. passport style.
- ❑ Letter from the petitioning employer verifying the job is still open.
- ❑ Medical exam report for you and each accompanying relative.
- ❑ Diversity Visa Lottery surcharge (per person applying as a result of the lottery program): $375.

Here's some additional explanation regarding some of the items on the checklist above:

Proof of education. The lottery green card program requires applicants to have either a high school diploma or the equivalent, or job skills needing at least two years of experience or training to learn. Appropriate evidence would be either a copy of your high school diploma or proof of job skill training, such as a vocational school certificate, and proof of at least two years of skilled employment verified by letters from past employers. A specific job offer in the U.S. is not required.

Police clearance. You personally must collect police clearance certificates from each country you have lived in for one year or more since your 16th birthday. Additionally, you must have a police certificate from your home country or country of last residence, if you lived there for at least six months since the age of 16. You do not need to obtain police certificates from the United States.

Contact the local police department in your home country for instructions on how to get police certificates. To obtain police certificates from nations other than your home country, contact the nearest consulate representing that country for instructions. Some nations refuse to supply police certificates, or their certificates are not considered reliable, and so you will not be required to obtain them from those locations. The U.S. consulate will tell you which countries police certificates are not required from.

Some countries will send certificates directly to U.S. consulates but not to you personally. Before they send the certificates out, however, you must request that it be done. Usually this requires filing some type of request form, together with a set of your fingerprints.

Fingerprints. A few consulates require you to submit fingerprints, though most do not. Consulates wanting fingerprints will send you blank fingerprint cards with instructions. The current fingerprinting fee is $85.

Photos. You and each accompanying relative must bring to the interview two color photographs taken in compliance with the consulate's instructions (U.S passport style). Often your information packet will contain a list of local photographers who take this type of picture. If your religious beliefs require wearing a head covering, you should be able to keep it on for the photo. However, your eyes and face must still be visible, and you must submit a written statement explaining why you can't submit a standard photograph.

Medical exam. Immediately before your visa interview, you and your accompanying relatives must visit a doctor for medical examinations. Some consulates conduct the medical exams up to several days before the interview. Others schedule the medical exam and the interview on the same day. You will be told where to go and what to do in your appointment letter.

The medical examinations are conducted by private doctors. The fees vary from $50 to more than $150 per exam, depending on the country. The fee will be stated in your appointment letter. The exam itself involves taking a medical history, blood test, chest X-ray, and vaccinations, if you need them. Pregnant women can refuse to be X-rayed until after the pregnancy. The vaccination requirement may be waived for religious, moral, or medical reasons.

The main purpose of the medical exam is to verify that you are not medically inadmissible. The primary medical grounds of inadmissibility are tuberculosis and HIV (AIDS). Some medical grounds of inadmissibility can be overcome with treatment or by applying for a waiver. (See Chapter 3 for details.) If you need a medical waiver, the consulate will give you complete instructions at your interview, but you should also consult an experienced immigration attorney.

6. Your Consular Interview

Consulates hold interviews on all green card applications. A written notice of your interview appointment will be sent to you a few weeks before the appointment date. The appointment package will tell you what to bring to your interview, including your completed forms, photographs, passports, and the like. See the checklist in Section 5, above, for the items usually requested, but also read the

consular list carefully for any additions or changes.

For details on what to expect during your consular visa interview, see Chapter 4. And for information on what to do if your visa is denied, see Chapter 4 as well.

E. Step Three: Entering the U.S. With Your Immigrant Visa

Your immigrant visa allows you to request entry to the United States at a border post, airport, or other arrival point. It's good for six months after you get it—and once you have the visa, you no longer have to worry about the September 30 deadline of the government's fiscal year.

You acquire the full status of green card holder only after you have been inspected and admitted into the United States. If you are bringing any accompanying relatives, they must enter at either the same time or after you do in order to become permanent residents.

The inspection process involves a U.S. border officer opening the sealed envelope containing your visa documents, and doing a last check to make sure you haven't used fraud. The border officer has expedited removal powers, which means he or she can turn you right around and send you home if anything appears wrong in your packet or with your answers to the officer's questions. Be polite and careful in answering.

When the officer is satisfied that everything is in order, he or she will stamp your passport to show that you're now a U.S. permanent resident and are immediately authorized to work. You won't receive an actual green card yet, however. Cards for you and your accompanying relatives will be ordered for you, and will come to you by mail several weeks later.

Ready for information on how to protect your status as a green card-holder? See Chapter 14. ■

Chapter 11

Getting a Green Card as an Investor

Like many countries, the U.S. provides an avenue for entry to wealthy people who will pump money into its economy. (See I.N.A. § 203(b)(5), 8 U.S.C. § 1153(b)(5).) However, it's not like buying a ticket to get in. Applicants for a green card through investment (Employment Fifth Preference or EB-5) must not only invest between $500,000 and $1 million in a U.S. business, they must take an active role in that business (though they don't need to control it). This chapter will discuss who is eligible for a green card through investment and how to apply.

Green cards for investors are limited to 10,000 per year, with 3,000 of those reserved for persons investing in rural areas or areas of high unemployment. If more than that number of people apply per year (which hasn't happened lately), you will be placed on a waiting list, based on your Priority Date (the day you filed the first portion of your application). Fortunately, only principal applicants are counted toward the 10,000 limit. Accompanying relatives are not. Therefore, in reality, many more than 10,000 people per year can be admitted with green cards through investment.

The trouble is, USCIS rejects many more applications than it accepts in this category, partly because the eligibility requirements are narrow, and partly because of the category's history of fraud and misuse. In fact, some lawyers encourage their clients to use their wealth to fit themselves into another category with a greater chance of success. For example, by investing in a company outside the United States that has a U.S. affiliate, the person might qualify to immigrate as a transferring executive or manager (priority worker, in category EB-1).

 Do you need a lawyer? If you can afford an investment-based green card, you can afford the services of a high-quality immigration lawyer. It's well worth the investment. USCIS has a history of denying the majority of these applications. If you try the application once on your own and fail, you may damage your chances of success in the future. What's more, because you are expected to make the investment first, and apply for the green card later, you could waste a lot of money.

A. Are You Eligible for a Green Card Through Investment?

Green cards through investment are available to anyone who invests a minimum of $1 million in creating a new U.S. business or restructuring or expanding one that already exists. It doesn't matter where you got the money—gifts and inheritances, for example, are fine—so long as you obtained it lawfully. The business must employ at least ten full-time workers, produce a service or product, and benefit the U.S. economy.

Key Features of an Investment-Based Green Card

Here are some of the advantages and limitations to an investment-based green card:

- As long as you have money to invest and can demonstrate that you are in the process of investing it in a for-profit business, you yourself do not need to have any particular business training or experience. Nor does it matter which country you come from, although the immigration authorities are more suspicious about fraud with applicants from certain countries.
- You can choose to invest your money in a business anywhere in the U.S., so long as you maintain your investment for at least three years and are actively engaged with the company you invest in.
- After approximately the first three years, you can work for another company or not work at all.

- You must actually live in the United States—you may not use the green card only for work and travel purposes.
- Your unmarried children under the age of 21 can get green cards as accompanying relatives.
- Your green card will initially be only conditional—that is, it will expire in two years, after which you will need to apply to renew it and make it permanent.
- As with all green cards, yours can be taken away if you misuse it—for example, you live outside the U.S. for too long, commit a crime, or even fail to advise the immigration authorities of your change of address. However, if you successfully keep your green card for five years (and yes, your two years as a conditional resident count), you can apply for U.S. citizenship.

Full-time employment is defined as requiring at least 35 hours of service per week.

The investor, his or her spouse, and their children may not be counted among the ten employees. Other family members may be counted, however. The ten workers don't necessarily have to be U.S. citizens, but they must have more than a temporary (nonimmigrant) visa—

U.S. green card holders, conditional residents, temporary residents, asylees, refugees, and recipients of remedies known as "suspension of deportation" and "cancellation of removal" can all be counted. Independent contractors do not count toward the ten employees. (See 8 C.F.R. § 204.6(e).)

The required dollar amount of the investment may be reduced to $500,000 if the business is located in a rural area or in an urban area with an unemployment rate certified by the state government to be at least 150% of the national average. Rural areas are defined as any location not part of an official metropolitan statistical area or not within the outer boundaries of any city having a population of 20,000 or more. State governments will identify the parts of the particular state that are high in unemployment, and will notify USCIS of which locations qualify. Even if you know that the area of your intended investment has extremely high unemployment, it will not qualify for the lesser dollar amount unless the state government has specifically designated it as a high-unemployment area for green card through investment purposes.

Also, the investor must be actively engaged in the company, either in a managerial or a policy forming role. (See 8 C.F.R. § 204.6(j)(5).) Passive investments such as land speculation do not ordinarily qualify you for a green card in this category—except under the pilot program described next.

Under a temporary pilot program (currently set to expire in 2008), 3,000 of the visas for high-unemployment areas are set aside for immigrants who invest in "designated regional centers." Regional centers are designated by USCIS, but run privately, and work to promote economic growth through increased export sales, improved regional productivity, creation of new jobs, and increased domestic capital investment. Investors in regional centers need not prove that they themselves provided new jobs for ten U.S. workers, only that the regional center created ten or more jobs, directly or indirectly, or that it increased regional productivity.

Some immigration attorneys report that regional centers offer one of the most desirable ways to pursue an investor visa, because they allow a wealthy investor to make a cash investment without creating or managing a new enterprise. The key, however, is to make sure that it's a well-managed regional center—the fact that USCIS has designated the center does not protect the investor from the risk of losing the investment. And don't forget that this program will end in 2008 unless Congress votes to renew it.

USCIS also has the authority to require a greater amount of investment than $1 million. This may occur when the investor chooses to locate the business in an area of low unemployment. At present, USCIS has adopted the policy of not raising dollar investment requirements on this basis.

The investment must be an equity investment (ownership share), rather than a loan. Also, you must place your investment at risk of partial or total loss if the business does badly. However, the entire investment does not have to be made in cash. Cash equivalents such as certificates of deposits, loans, and notes can count in the total. So can the value of equipment, inventory, or other tangible property. (See 8 C.F.R. § 204.6(e).) Borrowed funds may be used as long as the investor is personally liable in the event of a default, and the loan is adequately secured (and not by assets of the business being purchased). This means that mortgages on the business assets disqualify the amount borrowed from being calculated into the total investment figure.

A number of investors may join together in creating or expanding a U.S. business and each may qualify for a green card through the single company. However, the individual investment of each person must still be for the minimum qualifying amount, and each investor must be separately responsible for the creation of ten new jobs. For example, if five individuals each invest $1 million in a new business that will employ at least 50 U.S. workers, all five investors qualify for green cards.

Although it is expected that the investment will be well under way when the green card application is made, the law does require the investment to be in a new commercial enterprise. However, the enterprise does not need to have been established by the applicant. And "new" means only that the business was established after November 29, 1990.

There is also an exception to the new enterprise rule. The investor can purchase an existing business if he or she increases either its net worth or the number of employees by at least 40%. The rules requiring a $1 million investment and ten employees still apply, however. Therefore, the existing business must be large enough so that a 40% increase will amount to the fixed required dollar and employment minimums in the category.

If the existing business purchased is in financial trouble, an investment designed to save that business will qualify the investor for a green card in this category. Purchasing a troubled business releases the investor from having to increase the net worth or the number of employees. It does not, however, excuse the $1 million minimum investment requirement. To qualify as a troubled business, the company must have been in operation for at least two years, and have had an annual loss during those two years equal to at least 20% of the company's net worth. An investor buying a troubled business is prohibited from laying off any employees. And, if the business fails within the first two years, the investor may not be approved for a permanent green card.

1. Two-Year Testing Period for Investor-Based Green Cards

A green card for an investor is first issued only conditionally. The conditional green card is granted for two years. When the two years are over, the investor will have to file a request with USCIS to remove the condition and make his or her U.S. residence "permanent."

In deciding whether the condition should be removed, USCIS will investigate whether or not the full investment has actually been completed, whether ten full-time U.S. workers have been hired, whether or not the business is still operating, and whether the business is still owned by the investor who got the green card.

When any of the required factors cannot be established to the satisfaction of USCIS; or if the petition for removal of the condition is not filed within the final 90 days of the two-year conditional period, the investor will lose his or her green card and be subject to removal from the U.S. (deportation). If, on the other hand, USCIS is satisfied that the investment still meets all requirements, USCIS will remove the condition and issue a permanent green card.

2. Bringing Your Spouse and Children

If you are married or have unmarried children below the age of 21 and you acquire a green card through investment, your spouse and children can get green cards as accompanying relatives by providing proof of their family relationship to you and submitting other required paperwork and documents. Their green cards will also be issued conditionally and will become permanent when yours does.

3. Inadmissibility

If you have ever committed a crime, been involved in a terrorist organization, lied on an immigration application, lied to an immigration officer, suffered particular physical or mental illness as specified by USCIS, or are otherwise inadmissible, you may be unable to receive a green card unless you can qualify for what is known as a waiver of inadmissibility. (See Chapter 3 to find out exactly who is inadmissible and how you can overcome these problems.) Your family members will also have to show that they are not inadmissible.

B. Quick View of the Application Process

Getting a green card through investment is a two- to four-step process. Unlike many other types of green card applications, you perform all the steps on your own, without needing someone in the U.S. to file a petition on your behalf. The steps include:

- First, you mail what's called a visa petition to a USCIS regional service center, to show that you either have made or are in the process of making a qualifying business investment in the United States.
- Second, if the number of petitions is greater than the number of available investor visas when you apply, you wait until your Priority Date

is current and a visa is available to you. (Fortunately, there is rarely a wait in this category.)

- Third, after your petition has been approved, you and your accompanying relatives submit your applications for green cards, either at a U.S. consulate outside the United States, or possibly at a USCIS office within the United States (an option mainly available to people who are already legally in the United States).
- Fourth, if your interview was held at a U.S. consulate in another country, you enter the U.S. with your immigrant visa, at which time you become a permanent resident.

C. Step One: You File a Visa Petition

To begin your immigration process, you must file what's called a visa petition on Form I-526. The purpose of this form is to show that you're actively making an investment in a qualified U.S. business. Form I-526 is available at www.uscis. gov—and it comes with extensive instructions about what documentation to include with your form.

The form also takes care of some other details, like informing USCIS whether you will be continuing with your application through a consulate outside of the U.S. or through a U.S.-based USCIS office. (If you're not sure, choose the consulate—if you change your mind later, all you need to do is file an application at a USCIS office. Doing the reverse, transferring your case from a USCIS office to an consulate outside of the U.S., requires filing a separate application.)

The following checklist will help you keep track of all the forms and documents that go into your initial visa petition.

Checklist of Forms and Documents for Visa Petition

- ❑ Form I-526.
- ❑ Application fee (currently $1,435; checks or money orders are accepted, but not cash).
- ❑ Evidence that you've established a lawful, active business entity in the U.S., or else invested enough in an existing business to make its net worth or number of employees go up by at least 40%, such as:
    - ❑ Articles of incorporation, partnership agreement, or other legal charter or business license of the company, together with a notarized affidavit from an official of the company certifying who owns the business and in what percentages
    - ❑ Copies of all outstanding stock certificates, if the business is a corporation

- ❏ Notarized affidavit from the secretary of the corporation, or, if the business is not a corporation, from the official record keeper of the business, stating the names of each owner and percentages of the company owned
- ❏ Credit agreements with suppliers
- ❏ Evidence that you transferred capital resulting in a 40% or higher gain in number of employees or net worth, and
- ❏ Payroll records of the company for the past two years, if available.
- ❏ If applicable, evidence certifying that the business is located in a rural or high-unemployment area, such as a letter from your state government.
- ❏ Evidence that you came by the capital lawfully, such as tax returns of the company for the past two years (from the U.S. or elsewhere), if available.
- ❏ Evidence that you are in the process of making an investment, such as:
  - ❏ Accountant's financial statements, including profit and loss statements and balance sheets of the company for the past two years
  - ❏ Bank wire-transfer memos showing the amount of money sent to the U.S. from abroad
  - ❏ Letters from banks or bank statements indicating the average account balance of the business
  - ❏ Evidence of deposits of funds in the business's bank account
  - ❏ Comprehensive business plan with cash flow projections for the next three years
  - ❏ Contracts for purchase and bills of sale for the purchase of capital goods and inventory, and
  - ❏ Lease agreements for the business premises, contracts to purchase, deeds for business real estate, or construction contracts and blueprints for building the business premises.
- ❏ Evidence that you will be in a managerial or policymaking role, such as a written statement explaining your duties or documentation showing your position within the company or on its board of directors.
- ❏ Evidence that the business will create at least ten full-time positions for U.S. citizens, permanent or conditional residents, or immigrants with permission to work, such as tax records, Forms I-9 (filled out upon hiring), or a business plan showing future hires.
- ❏ Detailed written statement summarizing the business, where the investment is coming from, how the investment will be used, and an itemization of full-time positions that will be filled with qualifying workers, including duties, salaries, and when each job will become available.

If you are in the process of starting up the business, you may be unable to produce all of the items on the checklist. In that case, at a minimum you will have to present evidence that you have sufficient funds to invest, such as bank statements or lines of credit sufficient to purchase the business, and a written contract legally committing you to make the investment. You must also include a detailed written explanation of the nature of the business, containing statements of how much will be invested, where the funds for investment will come from, how the funds will be used, and a list of the specific job openings you expect to have over the first two years of the business, including job title, job description, salary, and when these jobs will become available. Finally, you should submit a comprehensive business plan supporting all of these documents.

1. Mailing the Visa Petition

You must mail the visa petition to one of two USCIS regional service centers in the U.S. having jurisdiction over your place of business. USCIS regional service centers are not the same as USCIS local offices—for one thing, you cannot visit them in person. There are four USCIS regional service centers spread across the U.S., but you will send yours to either the Texas or the California Service Center. The USCIS website will tell you which one serves your state. The Texas Service Center's address (for use with I-526 applications only) is: USCIS TSC, P.O. Box 852135, Mesquite, TX 75185-2135. The California Service Center's address for this application is: USCIS California Service Center, P.O. Box 10040, Laguna Niguel, CA 92607-0526.

2. Awaiting USCIS Approval of the Visa Petition

Within a few weeks after mailing the petition, you should receive a written confirmation that the papers are being processed, together with a receipt for the fees. This notice will also give your immigration case file number.

If USCIS wants further information before acting on your case, it will return all petition papers, forms, and documents to you, together with another form known as an I-797 Request for Evidence. The I-797 tells you what corrections, additional pieces of information, or additional documents are expected. You should make the corrections or supply the extra data and mail the whole package back to the regional service center, with a copy of the I-797 on top.

After filing Form I-526, you will have to wait for the petition to be approved, which can take several months by itself. (See Chapter 4 for how to track the length of time USCIS is taking to decide on visa petitions, and how to track your own application online.)

Once your petition is approved, a Notice of Action Form I-797 will be sent to you, indicating the approval. If you plan to apply for your green card at a U.S. consulate abroad, USCIS will forward the file to the National Visa Center (NVC) located in Portsmouth, New Hampshire. The NVC will then send a packet of forms and instructions to you so that you may proceed with the next step, described later in this chapter.

An approved petition does not by itself give you any right to immigrate to, or live in the United States. It is only a prerequisite to the next step, submitting your own application for a green card.

D. Step Two: You Await an Available Visa Number

Because there are annual limits on the number of people who can receive green cards through investment, it's possible—though unlikely—that you will have to wait in line until a visa/green card becomes available. Your place in the line is tracked by a number called your Priority Date. It comes from the date on which you filed your I-526 visa petition.

It's impossible to say exactly how long you might have to wait—it all depends on how many people are in line before you. In general, waiting periods for all visas tend to be longer for people from China, India, Mexico, and the Philippines. This is not because of any discrimination against those countries—it merely reflects the fact that more people from those countries apply for visas than from other countries, and there is a per-country limit. The supply of visas for those countries is often less the number of people applying for them, so the waiting list gets longer and longer.

Although you can't predict how long you will wait, you can track the progress of your own Priority Date through the system, and get some sense of the rate at which it is moving. To do so, you first need to look at the State Department's monthly *Visa Bulletin*, which lists the Priority Dates of people who are allowed to get visas that month. It's available on a recorded message at 202-663-1541, or at its website at www.state.gov (under "Travel & Business," click "Visa Bulletins"). The State Department updates this chart around the middle of every month, but not on any exact day.

When you look at the *Visa Bulletin*, look for the chart like the one below, which is from March 2007.

Here's how to read the *Visa Bulletin* chart:

1. Locate the "5th preference" box in the first column (or the "Targeted Employment Areas/Regional Centers" box, if applicable.

2. Locate your country in one of the boxes across the top. If you don't see it listed, look in the column called "All Chargeability Areas Except Those Listed."

March 2007 Priority Dates for Employment-Based Visas				
	All Chargeability Areas Except Those Listed	**CHINA-mainland born**	**INDIA**	**MEXICO**	**PHILIP-PINES**
Employment-Based					
1st	C	C	C	C	C
2nd	C	22APR05	08JAN03	C	C
3rd	01AUG02	01AUG02	08MAY01	15MA701	01AUG02
Other Workers	01OCT01	01OCT01	01OCT01	01OCT01	01OCT01
4th	C	C	C	C	C
Certain Religious Workers	C	C	C	C	C
Iraqi & Afghani Translators	18SEP06	18SEP06	18SEP06	18SEP06	18SEP06
5th	C	C	C	C	C
Targeted Employment Areas/Regional Centers	C	C	C	C	C

3. Draw lines across from your preference category and down from your country of origin. The box where your two lines cross is the one containing what's called your Visa Cutoff Date. Often, it contains a letter instead of a date. The letter "C" is good news—it means that no one needs to wait, and all applicants are considered current, that is, immediately eligible for a visa or green card. The letter "U" would be bad news—it means that all the visas have been used up for that year, and more will not become available until October (when the federal government starts its new fiscal year).

4. If, instead of a letter, your box contains a Visa Cutoff Date, compare it with your Priority Date. If the Visa Cutoff Date is the same as your Priority Date, or is even later, great—you can now apply for your green card. However, if the cutoff date is earlier than your Priority Date, you still have to wait—because only people who applied some time before you are now receiving the right to apply for an immigrant visa or green card.

EXAMPLE: Martha is a citizen of South Africa, who is investing in a U.S. jewelry-making company. She files a visa petition in May of 2006. In March of 2007, her petition is approved, and she checks her Priority Date. As you'll see on the March 2007 chart above, it says "C," meaning all applicants can continue right away with the green card process. Let's say, however, that the Visa Cut-off Date was then March 1, 2006. That means that people who filed visa petitions on March 1, 2006 (or before that) were finally allowed to continue with the process and apply for a green card in March 2007. Their wait was approximately one year—which would suggest that Martha would have to wait a similar length of time.

If you have an approved petition but your Priority Date is not yet current, you must wait until it is current to take the next step and file your green card application. The immigration authorities will advise you by mail when your Priority Date finally comes up (so make sure to send them any change of address!).

If you're in the United States on a temporary work visa, be careful that your status does not expire before your Priority Date becomes current and you can apply for a green card—possessing an approved visa petition does not give you any right to live in the United States. If this looks like it might become a problem, consult an immigration attorney as soon as possible.

E. Step Three: You Apply for a Green Card

Once your visa petition has been approved, and your Priority Date becomes current, you can apply for a green card. If your spouse or children will be accompanying you, they must each file their own green card applications. A big part of the green card application is proving that you are not inadmissible to the United States. Review Chapter 3 regarding the grounds of inadmissibility.

The most important question at this point in the process is where you file the application—in the United States or at a consulate outside of the United States? You should have already made this choice on your Form I-526, but you're allowed to change your mind, so it's worth revisiting the question.

If you're living outside of the U.S. now. The answer is fairly easy for people living outside of the United States—you'll file at a local U.S. consulate and attend an interview there before entering the United States. (This method is called consular processing.)

If you're living in the U.S. now. The answer is a bit more complicated for applicants already in the United States. Ordinarily, the most convenient choice would probably be for you to adjust status without leaving—that is, send your application to the nearest USCIS Service Center and attend your interview at a local USCIS office. Once your application is filed, your stay in the United States will be considered legal, and you can apply for permission to work. Should problems arise in your case, you'll be able to wait for a decision in the U.S., a circumstance most green card applicants prefer. Also, if your application for a green card is turned down, you have greater rights of appeal inside the U.S. than you do at a U.S. consulate.

One catch is that you are allowed to adjust status only if you're already in the U.S. legally, that is, on a valid, unexpired visa or other form of permission (with a few exceptions). You might, for example, already be on a temporary visa such as a treaty investor, E-2, visa. If, however, you're living in the United States with no legal status, or have worked without authorization, or you entered legally without a visa under the Visa Waiver program, you are barred from filing your green card application inside the United States. See Chapter 3 for information on whether you might be one of the rare few people allowed to adjust status regardless, due to an exception. If not,

you'll probably need to consult with an experienced immigration attorney.

Whether or not you are eligible to adjust status, you may instead decide to leave the United States and apply for your green card at a U.S. consulate abroad. If the consulates are issuing visas more quickly than your local USCIS office is handling adjustment of status applications (which is common), leaving to apply at a consulate outside of the U.S. could be a smart strategic move. However, if you have already spent 180 days or more in the U.S. out of legal status, or crossed the border without inspection, be sure you are not inadmissible or subject to a three-year or ten-year waiting period before you go. (See Chapter 3.) Otherwise, you could find yourself stuck outside the U.S. for three or ten years.

1. What Happens When Adjusting Status in the U.S.

The process of adjusting your status to permanent resident involves preparing a set of forms and documents (a separate set for you, your spouse, and each of your accompanying children), mailing these to a USCIS service center, waiting for some weeks or months until you're called in to have your fingerprints taken, and then waiting a few weeks or months longer until you're called in for your final green card interview at a local USCIS office (not the one to which you sent your application). You should be approved for your green card at, or soon after, the interview. Nowadays, the interview is often waived, in which case you'll get a letter in the mail telling you you've been approved. See Chapter 4 for information on tracking the progress of your application at the service center and at your local office.

As part of your adjustment of status application, you and your family members may apply for permission to work (an Employment Authorization Document or EAD).

⚠️ **Security checks are a likely cause of delays.** As part of your adjustment of status application, the FBI must run both a fingerprint check and a name check on you, and the CIA must run a separate name check. These name checks can take months or even years, especially because many applicants have similar names. If you've been informed that your case is stalled due to security checks, get the name of a person you can keep in touch with for updates, or hire a lawyer to help with this task.

2. Paperwork to Prepare for Adjustment of Status Application

The basic form used in the U.S. adjustment of status application is Form I-485, Application for Permanent Residence. However, a handful of other forms and documents must be prepared to accompany this main one.

An easy way to get all these forms is to call the USCIS forms line at 800-870-3676 and ask for the Adjustment of Status Packet. Or, you can obtain the forms online at www.uscis.gov. (Click "Immigration Forms," then scroll down and select the forms you need one by one based on the checklist below.)

The following checklist will help you assemble and keep track of the appropriate forms and documents. A complete set of the items on the checklist must also be prepared for your accompanying spouse and children.

Checklist for Adjustment of Status Application

Forms

❑ Form I-485, with filing fee (currently $1,010 for applicants between ages 14 and 79, $600 for applicants under age 14 who are filing with a parent, and $930 for applicants under age 14 who are not filing with a parent). Checks and money orders are accepted, but don't send cash through the mail.

❑ Form I-485A (only if you'll be paying the $1,000 penalty fee in order to adjust status).

❑ Form G-325A.

❑ Form I-765 (optional, if you want to a work permit; include a separate filing fee, currently $340). On I-765 Question 16, answer the question "(c)(9)."

❑ Form I-134 signed by the investor on behalf of any accompanying family members, promising to support them financially.

❑ I-131, Application for Travel Document (Advance Parole), for use if you think you'll need to travel outside the United States while your application is processed. This also requires a separate filing fee, currently $305.

Documents

❑ Copy of your I-526 approval notice.

❑ Copy of a long-form birth certificate for you and each accompanying relative. If this is in another language, it must be accompanied by a full English translation.

❑ Marriage certificate if you are married and bringing your spouse.

❑ If either you or your spouse have been previously married, copies of divorce and death certificates showing termination of all previous marriages.

❑ Copy of I-94 card for you and each accompanying relative (the small white card placed in your passport). Failure to submit this may result in a conclusion that you entered or remained in the U.S. illegally and either are not eligible or are subject to the $1,000 penalty described earlier.

❑ Two photographs of you and two photographs of each accompanying relative, in U.S. passport style (it's best to have a professional do these). Write your name and A number (if you've received one from USCIS) in pencil on the back of each photo.

❑ Medical exam report for you and each accompanying relative (Form I-693, filled out and signed by a USCIS-certified doctor, and presented in an unopened envelope). The fee is usually around $150 per exam, depending on the doctor. The exam itself involves taking a medical history, blood test, chest X-ray, and administering vaccinations if applicable and/or recommended for you. Pregnant women may refuse to be X-rayed until after the baby is born.

Dealing With Delays in Approval of Your Work Authorization

If you want to work before your application for a green card is approved, you must file a separate application for employment authorization (or ("EAD"). To do so, fill out Form I-765 and file it together with your adjustment of status application. To accompany Form I-765, submit a copy of your I-94 card and pay a separate filing fee. Be sure to keep the fee receipt that USCIS gives you, so you can prove that the I-765 was filed. Normally, you will file the application for employment authorization at the same time as your adjustment of status application papers.

Legally, USCIS does not have to make a decision on your employment authorization application for up to 90 days from the date on your receipt notice.

If, for some reason, you, are not given a decision within 90 days, you can request an interim EAD that will last 240 days. To request an interim card, make an appointment to visit your local USCIS service center. Be aware, however, that USCIS is currently being sued over its unwillingness to issue interim EADs.

If 240 days pass and you still have not received a final decision on the I-765, you must stop working. Interim work authorization cards cannot be renewed. However, if you reach this point, you have the option to file a new I-765 application. If you do not get a decision on the new application within 90 days, you will then be entitled to another interim work authorization card.

Tip for filling out Form I-485: You'll notice on the first page of the form, under "Part 2: Application," it asks you to choose the basis upon which you're applying for a green card. Mark Box "a" if you're the investor; Box "b" if you're a spouse or child.

A few items on the above checklist could use extra explanation:

Form I-134, Affidavit of Support. All immigrants must convince USCIS that once they receive a green card they are not likely to go on public assistance or welfare. Since your application is based on a large business investment, that

alone should be sufficient proof that you have a way to support yourself. You should still, however, fill out Form-134, the Affidavit of Support, for any accompanying relatives. Because the consulate knows you will have an income, you must sign the I-134 form and take financial responsibility for each of them.

In signing the I-134 Affidavit of Support, you are not actually promising to support your accompanying relatives. What you do promise is to reimburse the U.S. government for the sum total of any government support payments they

Read This If You Plan to Leave the U.S. Before Your Adjustment Interview

Once your application for adjustment of status has been filed, you must not leave the U.S. for any reason before your approval without first applying for and receiving advance permission to reenter the U.S. (Advance Parole). Any absence without this permission will be viewed as a termination of your application for a green card—which means that, upon return, you will be told that your green card application is dead and you have no right to enter the United States.

Many people simply apply for Advance Parole at the same time they apply to adjust status, just in case. Or, you can wait until you're sure you have to leave, and apply at the same service center where you sent your adjustment of status application—but you're taking a risk this way, because USCIS may take many weeks to approve your Advance

Parole application.

Your application for Advance Parole should include Form I-131, together with the filing fee, two passport-type photographs, a copy of your adjustment of status filing receipt (if you've already sent in that application), and a short explanation of why you want to leave—you will need a bona fide personal or business reason, though it need not be an emergency.

If approved, you will be allowed to leave the U.S. and return again with no break in the processing of your application. However, if you were out of status for 180 days or more after April 1, 1997, you should not depart the U.S. even on the basis of Advance Parole, as this may subject you to a three-year or ten-year bar to reentry.

might receive should they go on welfare. The I-134 Affidavit of Support supposedly binds you to this obligation for three years (though many lawyers say it would never hold up in court). Your responsibility to the government then comes to an end.

Medical exam. You must submit a Medical Examination Report for each applicant. This is done on Form I-693, which you must take to a USCIS-authorized physician or medical clinic. You'll have to pay a fee. The USCIS local office will provide you with the form as well as a list of approved physicians in your area.

After completion of the medical exam, and upon obtaining the test results, the doctor will give you the results in a sealed envelope. Do not open the envelope.

3. Mailing the Adjustment Packet

After you have finished preparing the adjustment of status paperwork, you must mail it to a USCIS service center.

(Do so by certified mail, return receipt requested, and keep a complete copy of everything you send in.) At the time this book went to print, all investor visa adjustments were required to be sent to the Nebraska Service Center, P.O. Box 87485, Lincoln, NE 68501-7485. However, check the USCIS website for any changes to this policy.

Generally, after filing your green card application, you will not hear anything from USCIS for several months. Then you should receive notices of your fingerprint and interview appointments. The interview notice will also tell you whether any further documentation is needed.

4. Your Adjustment of Status Interview

You may be called in for a personal interview, which will be held at a USCIS office near you. However, personal interviews are often waived in green-card-through-investment applications. If USCIS requires you to attend an interview, it will send you and your accompanying relatives an appointment notice, usually about two weeks in advance of the interview. If you have an attorney, he or she may come with you to the interview. (Even if you don't have an attorney, you could consult with or hire one at this point.)

Checklist of Documents to Bring to Your Adjustment Interview

Prepare all of the following to take with you your USCIS interview:

❏ A complete photocopy of your green card application. This is for your use—you may want to follow along as the officer asks you questions about the material you filled out on the forms, or you may find that the officer is missing something that you have.

❏ Photo identification or passport for you and every one of your family members. (It's best to bring your passport, because if you are approved for your green card on the day of the interview, USCIS can place a stamp in your passport demonstrating this—and you can use this stamp as proof of your status when you work or travel.)

❏ Originals of all documents that you made copies of for submission with your application. For example, if you submitted a photocopy of a birth certificate or other official document, a USCIS officer may want to examine the original.

❏ Any documents received from USCIS or other immigration authorities. For example, if you left the country on Advance Parole, bring this permit.

❏ Any updates to the material in your application. For example, if you have given birth to another child, bring the birth certificate. If you've been arrested, bring a full explanation (and consult with an attorney, to make sure that the arrest doesn't make you inadmissible).

See Chapter 4 for details on what to expect during your adjustment of status interview. If your adjustment of status application is denied, also see Chapter 4. For information on how to protect your status as a green card holder after you're approved, see Chapter 14.

If everything is in order, your application will be approved at the conclusion of the interview, or soon after. Your passport will be stamped to show that you have been admitted to the U.S. as a conditional resident, and your green card will be ordered.

The green card will come to you in the mail several weeks after the interview. It will show a two-year expiration date. (See Section G, below, "Converting Your Conditional Residence Into Permanent Residence," for how to become a permanent resident after two years.)

If you need to travel outside the U.S. before your green card arrives, however, you must go back to the USCIS office with your passport and the written notice of approval. A temporary stamp will be placed in your passport, enabling you to return after your trip. Never leave the U.S. without either your green card or a temporary stamp in your passport.

5. What Happens During Consular Processing

Consular processing requires you to prepare some forms and documents according to instructions, notify the consulate when you are ready with these, wait until you receive a notice scheduling you for an interview at a U.S. consulate, undergo a medical exam and prepare additional forms and documents for the interview, and finally attend the interview. There, if all goes well, you will be approved (subject to final security checks) for a visa to enter the United States.

Much of your job at this point involves convincing the consulate that you are not inadmissible for health, criminal, security, or financial reasons. You will be asked to undergo a medical exam and possibly provide evidence that you have no criminal record.

6. Paperwork to Prepare for Consular Processing

At the beginning, consular processing involves a lot of paper being sent in various directions. First, after USCIS approves your visa petition, it will forward your file to the National Visa Center (NVC) in Portsmouth, New Hampshire. It will send you a form called an Agent of Choice and Address (DS-3032), which simply asks where you want the rest of your visa-related mail sent; for example, to your attorney rather than to you.

Once NVC receives your form DS-3032, it will mail you (or your attorney or agent) an Immigrant Visa (IV) fee bill (currently $335) and a security fee (currently $45). Once you've paid that bill, the NVC will send you what's called an instruction packet of forms and information (formerly called Packet 3). It will send you a second packet as part of your interview notification form.

a. Handling the Instructional Packet

The NVC will send you an instructional packet, which includes some forms and material for you to read. Some of the forms are for you to fill out and return in order to keep the process moving—namely Form DS-230 Part I and Form DS-2001 (formerly called OF-169). (The forms are normally designated by DS preceding a number, and copies of many of them are available on the State Department website at www.state.gov. However, it's better to wait for the ones the consulate sends you, because some of them are slightly different than the main State Department forms—for example, many of the consulates use forms with bilingual translations into the language of your country.)

 You don't really need to have all your documents in hand when you send in Form DS-2001. Although the form asks you to sign it only after you're ready with the listed forms, many people simply sign as soon as they know they can get the forms together, to keep the process moving.

After you've sent in the necessary forms, your local U.S. consulate will start communicating with you directly. It will provide you with additional forms to fill out, a list of documents to collect, and other tasks to take care of.

b. Preparing Forms and Documents for Your Interview

The checklist below provides a brief explanation of some of the documents you'll need to gather in preparation for your immigrant visa interview. Keep your eyes open for any special requirements that your consulate may add to this list. Bring the originals and a set of copies with you to your interview (the consular officer may want to examine the originals to make sure they're not fraudulent, but keep copies for your files). Do not mail your paperwork to the consulate!

Checklist of Documents and Forms for Your Consular Interview

Forms

❑ DS forms (sent to you by the NVC and U.S. consulate).

❑ Form I-134 Affidavit of Support, signed by the investor on behalf of family members immigrating with him or her.

Documents

❑ Copy of I-526 approval notice from USCIS (it should have been sent directly to the consulate, but bring a copy just in case).

❑ Long-form birth certificate for you and for each accompanying relative as well as for any unmarried minor children who are *not* immigrating with you.

❑ Marriage certificate if you are married and bringing your spouse.

❑ If either you or your spouse have been previously married, copies of divorce and death certificates showing termination of all previous marriages.

❑ Passport for you and for each accompanying relative, valid for at least six months beyond the date of the final interview.

❑ Police certificates from every country in which you and each accompanying relative has lived for at least six months since age 16.

❑ Fingerprints, if specifically requested by the consulate (current cost: $85).

❑ Military records for you and for each accompanying relative.

❑ Passport-type photographs, two of you and two of each accompanying relative.

❑ Medical exam report for you and for each accompanying relative.

Here's some additional explanation regarding some of the items on the checklist above:

Form I-134. All immigrants must convince the consulate that once they receive a green card they are not likely to go on public welfare. Since your application is based on a large business investment, that alone should be sufficient proof that you have a way to support yourself. You should still, however, fill out the Form-134 Affidavit of Support for any accompanying relatives. Because the consulate knows you will have an income, you must sign the I-134 form and take financial responsibility for each of them.

In signing the I-134 Affidavit of Support, you are not actually promising to support your accompanying relatives. What you do promise is to reimburse the U.S. government for the sum total of any government support payments they might receive should they go on welfare. The I-134 Affidavit of Support supposedly binds you to this obligation for three years (although many lawyers say it would never hold up in court). Your responsibility to the government then comes to an end.

Police clearance. Unlike applications made in the U.S., you personally must collect police clearance certificates from each country you have lived in for one year or more since your 16th birthday. Additionally, you must have a police certificate from your home country or country of last residence, if you lived there for at least six months since the age of 16. You do not need to obtain police certificates from the United States.

Contact the local police department in your home country for instructions on how to get police certificates, or visit http://travel.state.gov/visa/reciprocity/index.htm. To obtain police certificates from nations other than your home country, contact the nearest consulate representing that country for instructions. Some nations refuse to supply police certificates, or their certificates are not considered reliable, and so you will not be required to obtain them from those locations. The U.S. consulate will tell you which countries police certificates are not required from.

Some countries will send certificates directly to U.S. consulates but not to you personally. Before they send the certificates out, however, you must request that it be done. Usually this requires filing some type of request form, together with a set of your fingerprints.

Photos. You and each accompanying relative must bring to the interview two photographs taken in compliance with the consulate's instructions (U.S passport style). Often your information packet will contain a list of local photographers who take this type of picture. If your religious beliefs require wearing a head covering, you should be able to keep it on for the photo. However, your eyes and face must still be visible, and you must submit a written statement explaining why you can't submit a standard photograph.

Medical exam. Immediately before your visa interview, you and your accompanying relatives will be required to have medical examinations. Some consulates schedule the medical exams up to several days before the interview. Others schedule the medical exam and the interview on the same day. You will be told where to go and what to do in your appointment letter.

The medical examinations are conducted by private doctors. The fees vary from $50 to more than $150 per exam, depending on the country. The fee will be stated in your appointment letter. The exam itself involves taking a medical history, blood test, chest X-ray, and vaccinations, if you need them. Although pregnant women can refuse to be X-rayed until after the pregnancy, the requirement to have an X-ray taken cannot be waived entirely. The vaccination requirement may be waived for religious, moral, or medical reasons.

The main purpose of the medical exam is to verify that you are not medically inadmissible. The primary medical grounds of inadmissibility are tuberculosis and HIV (AIDS). Some medical grounds of inadmissibility can be overcome with treatment or by applying for a waiver. (See Chapter 3 for more details.) If you need a medical waiver, you will be given complete instructions by the consulate at the time of your interview, but should also consult an experienced immigration attorney.

7. Your Consular Interview

Consulates hold interviews on all green card applications. A written notice of your interview appointment will be sent to you a few weeks before the appointment date. The appointment package will tell you what to bring to your interview, including your completed forms, photographs, passports, and the like. See the checklist in Section 5, above, for the items usually requested, but also read the consular list carefully for any additions or changes.

For details on what to expect during your consular visa interview, see Chapter 4. And for information on what to do if your visa is denied, see Chapter 4 as well.

F. Step Four: You Enter the U.S. Using Your Immigrant Visa

Your immigrant visa allows you to request entry to the United States at a border post, airport, or other arrival point. You acquire the status of green card holder only after you have been inspected and admitted into the United States. If you are bringing any accompanying relatives, they must enter at either the same time or after you do in order to become permanent residents.

The inspection process involves a U.S. border officer opening the sealed envelope containing your visa documents, and doing a last check to make sure you haven't used fraud. The border officer has expedited removal powers, which means he or she can turn you right around and send you home if anything appears wrong in your packet or with your answers to the officer's questions. Be polite and careful in answering.

When the officer is satisfied that everything is in order, he or she will stamp your passport to show that you're now a U.S. permanent resident and are immediately authorized to work. You won't receive an actual green card yet, however. Cards for you and your accompanying relatives will be ordered for you. They will come to you by mail several weeks later, and will show a two-year expiration date. (See Section G, below, for how to become a permanent resident after two years.)

G. Converting Your Conditional Residence Into Permanent Residence

As we've stated, green cards through investment are first issued conditionally, for two years. After the two years are up, in order to make the green cards permanent, you must then go through a procedure for removing the conditions on your residence. Give your full attention to this part of the process—an astonishing number of these applications are denied.

File the items on the checklist below with the USCIS service center with jurisdiction over the area where your company is located. You can file this application up to 90 days prior to the second anniversary of your admission to the United States. Your spouse and children should be included on the form.

Checklist for Removal of Conditions on Residence

- ❑ USCIS Form I-829, with filing fee (currently $2,930).
- ❑ Biometrics fee for each dependent (spouse or child) included in your application (currently $80).
- ❑ Copies of your and your family members' green cards.
- ❑ Evidence that you actually established the commercial enterprise (such as federal income tax returns).
- ❑ Evidence that you actively invested the required capital (such as articles of incorporation, a business license, and financial statements).
- ❑ Evidence that you have substantially met and maintained the capital investment requirement throughout your conditional residence (such as bank statements, invoices, receipts, contracts, tax returns, etc.).
- ❑ Evidence that the enterprise has generated employment (or will soon do so) for ten U.S. workers, such as payroll records, tax documents, and Forms I-9. (If the investment was in a "troubled business," submit evidence that the preinvestment level of employees was maintained during the two-year conditional residence period.)

Failure to submit the I-829 and documentation within the 90-day window period will cause USCIS to terminate your resident status, and it may start removal (deportation) proceedings against you and your family members. If you miss the deadline you can still file the removal petition for "good cause and extenuating circumstances" up to the time USCIS commences removal proceedings. After your case arrives at the immigration court, the judge may terminate proceedings and restore permanent resident status, but only if the USCIS agrees to this.

After USCIS receives your I-829 application, it will send you a receipt notice. Guard this notice carefully—it is also proof that your status has been extended for the months that USCIS will take to approve your permanent residence. If you leave the U.S., you'll need to take both this notice and your expired green card to your local USCIS office and get what's called an I-551 stamp in your passport in order to be allowed back in. If the extension expires before you've gotten an answer from USCIS, go to your local USCIS office with your passport for a stamp further extending your status.

During this time period, you will also be sent an appointment notice stating when and where you must appear for biometric processing. (It's usually at a USCIS Application Support Center.) Biometric processing includes taking your photograph, signature, and index fin-gerprint, for use in generating your new green card. If you're between ages 14 and 79, it also includes taking your fingerprints, in order to do another criminal background check.

USCIS may or may not interview you in connection with the I-829 filing. If your accompanying documentation makes it clear you have fulfilled the requirements for the green card, you should be approved without an interview.

If USCIS requires an interview, it will be held at a local USCIS office near where your commercial enterprise is located. If you fail to appear for the interview, USCIS regulations specify that USCIS should put you, the petitioner-entrepreneur, into removal proceedings. (If that happens, you can still write USCIS and request that the interview be rescheduled or waived. If it is rescheduled or waived, your conditional resident status is restored. Otherwise, the petition has to be considered in Immigration Court as discussed above.)

Upon approval of your request to remove the conditions on your residence, your U.S. residency will become permanent. A new green card will be sent to you, with no expiration date.

Ready for information on how to protect your status as a green card-holder after you're approved? See Chapter 14. ■

Chapter 12

Getting a Green Card as a Special Immigrant

This chapter covers six categories of so-called special immigrants. The name is somewhat misleading—it actually refers to the employment fourth preference category, which encompasses religious workers, foreign medical graduates, employees of the U.S. consulate in Hong Kong, former foreign U.S. government workers, retired employees of international organizations, juveniles declared dependent on a U.S. juvenile court, and more. (There are other categories of special immigrants that we don't cover in this book because they apply to so few people, such as former employees of the Panama Canal Zone and international broadcasting employees.)

A total of 10,000 green cards are available each year for all special immigrant categories taken together. No more than 5,000 of that total can go to nonclergy religious workers.

A. Do You Qualify for a Green Card as a Special Immigrant?

Occasionally, laws are passed making green cards available to people in special situations. Special immigrant green cards are available to the following people:

- workers for recognized religious organizations
- foreign medical graduates who have been in the U.S. a long time
- foreign workers who were formerly longtime employees of the U.S. government
- retired officers or employees of certain international organizations who have lived in the U.S. for a certain time
- foreign nationals who have been declared dependent on juvenile courts in the United States
- persons who served honorably for 12 years on active U.S. military duty after October 15, 1978
- Panama Canal Treaty employees (a little-used category that is not discussed further in this chapter)
- NATO civilian employees (a little-used category that is not discussed further in this chapter), and
- persons coming to work as broadcasters for the International Broadcasting Bureau of the Broadcasting Board of Governors, or for its grantee (a little-used category that is not discussed further in this chapter).

Do you need a lawyer? If you think you might fit into one of the more obscure categories that we don't cover in this chapter, you'll probably want to seek an immigration lawyer's help. In any case, a lawyer can help you prove that you fit into the category you're seeking, and navigate the often difficult bureaucratic requirements.

Key Features of a Special-Immigrant-Based Green Card

If you qualify for this type of green card, here are some of its advantages and limitations:

- Although not many green cards are available in this category, the eligibility criteria are so narrowly defined that if you fit them, you have a good chance of getting a green card.
- You must actually live in the United States—you must not use the green card only for work and travel purposes.
- Your unmarried children under the age of 21 can get green cards as accompanying relatives.
- As with all green cards, yours can be taken away if you misuse it—for example, you live outside the U.S. for too long, commit a crime, or even fail to advise the immigration authorities of your change of address. However, if you successfully keep your green card for five years, you can apply for U.S. citizenship.

1. Religious Workers

There are two subcategories of religious workers: clergy and other religious workers. Clergy is defined as a person authorized by a recognized religious denomination to conduct religious activities. This includes not only ministers, priests, and rabbis, but also salaried Buddhist monks, commissioned officers of the Salvation Army, practitioners and nurses of the Christian Science Church, and ordained deacons. Usually, to be considered a member of the clergy, you must have formal recognition from the religion in question, such as a license, certificate of ordination, or other qualification to conduct religious worship.

The subcategory of "other religious workers" covers people who are in a "religious vocation" or "religious occupation," and are authorized to perform normal religious duties, but are not considered part of the clergy. This includes anyone performing a traditional religious function in a professional capacity, such as liturgical workers, religious instructors, religious counselors, cantors, catechists, workers in religious hospitals or religious health care facilities, missionaries, religious translators, or religious broadcasters. It does not cover workers involved in purely nonreligious functions such as janitors, maintenance workers, clerical staff, fundraisers, or even singers. It also does not cover volunteers. Internal USCIS decisions have added that religious workers must have had some formal religious training or theological education—training that was established by the governing body of their denomination. (This issue is being fought out in federal courts, so the USCIS position may eventually change.) USCIS also requires that religious workers be working in a traditionally permanent salaried position within the denomination and be assigned only religious duties.

To qualify for a green card in either of the two religious subcategories, you must have been a member for at least the past two years of a recognized religion that has a bona fide nonprofit organization in the United States. During those two years, you must have been employed continuously (though not necessarily full-time) by that same religious group. Your sole purpose in coming to the U.S. must be to work as a minister of that religion (and your denomination must need additional ministers), or, at the request of the organization, to work in some other capacity related to the religion's activities in the United States. Spouses and children may apply with you.

This provision of the law has been the subject of some controversy and there have been efforts in Congress to eliminate it as a way of getting permanent residence. In the year 2003, Congress extended the law to September 30, 2008.

2. Foreign Medical Graduates

If you are a graduate of a foreign medical school who came to the U.S. before January 10, 1978, on either an H or J visa, you qualify as a special immigrant if you can meet all of the following conditions:

- you were permanently licensed to practice medicine in some U.S. state on or before January 9, 1978
- you were physically in the U.S. and practicing medicine on January 9, 1978
- you have lived continuously in the U.S. and practiced medicine since January 9, 1978, and
- if you came to the U.S. on a J-1 visa and were subject to the two-year home residency requirement, you got a waiver of the home residency requirement, or you have a "no objection letter" from your home government.

3. Former International U.S. Government Workers

If you have been employed abroad by the U.S. government for at least 15 years, you may apply for a green card as a special immigrant. Your spouse and children may apply with you. To qualify, you must have the recommendation of the principal officer-in-charge of the U.S. government foreign office in which you were employed. The U.S. Secretary of State must also approve the recommendation. In addition, certain employees of the American Institute in Taiwan can qualify under this category. The director of the Institute must recommend you.

4. Retired Employees of International Organizations

If you are a retired employee of an international organization, you qualify for a green card under the following conditions:

- you have resided in the U.S. for at least 15 years prior to your retirement, on a G-4 or N visa
- you lived and were physically present in the U.S. for at least half of the seven years immediately before applying for a green card, and
- you apply to receive a green card within six months after your retirement.

If you are the unmarried child of an officer, employee, former officer, or former employee of an international organization, you qualify for a green card if all of the following are true:

- you have a G-4 or N visa
- you lived and were physically present in the U.S. for at least half of the seven-year period before applying for a green card
- you lived in the U.S. for at least a total of seven years while you were between the ages of five and 21, and
- you apply for a green card before your 25th birthday.

If you are the spouse of an officer or employee in this special immigrant class, you qualify for a green card as an accompanying relative. However, if you were married to a qualifying officer or employee who has died, you can still get a green card if you lived in the U.S. for at least 15 years on a G-4 or N visa before the death of your spouse, you have lived in the U.S. for at least one half of the seven years before your application, and you apply within six months after your spouse's death.

5. Persons Declared Dependent on a Juvenile Court

A foreign national child can qualify for a green card as a special immigrant if:

- he or she is under age 21 and unmarried (and remains both under 21 and unmarried all the way through approval of the green card, meaning you should act quickly in the case of a child who is nearing age 21)
- he or she has been declared dependent on a juvenile court located in the U.S.
- that court says the child is either eligible for long-term foster care, or has committed the child to the care of a state agency, due to abuse, neglect, or abandonment, and
- the court has determined that it is in the minor's best interest to remain in the United States.

(See I.N.A. § 203(b)(4), 8 U.S.C. § 1153(b)(4); I.N.A. § 101(a)(27), 8 U.S.C. § 1101; 8 C.F.R. § 204.11.)

If the child is already in DHS custody, DHS must specifically consent to the court proceedings before they begin. Even if the child is not in custody, you must obtain DHS's express consent to the dependency order. DHS will only give its consent if it's persuaded that the main purpose of the effort is to relieve the child from abuse, neglect, or abandonment, rather than to get a green card for the child.

⚠️ **Unlike other immigrants, those who get their permanent residency as a special immigrant juvenile may not petition for their natural or prior adoptive parents to immigrate to the United States.** This is because the U.S. offers this special green card to juvenile immigrants with the understanding that the children need to get away from their homeland parents—so it would make little sense for them to be reunited with those parents.

6. Servicepeople With 12 Years' Duty

If you have served a total of 12 years of active duty with the U.S. armed services after October 12, 1978, you may qualify for special immigrant status. You need to have enlisted outside the U.S. under the terms of a treaty between the U.S. and your country. If you've served six years and have reenlisted for another six, you also qualify. Your spouse and child are eligible to apply with you.

7. Your Spouse and Children

If you are married or have children below the age of 21 and you get a green card as a special immigrant, your spouse and children can get green cards as accompanying relatives simply by providing proof of their family relationship to you. In a few special immigrant categories, they must additionally prove other factors, such as how long they lived with you.

⚠️ **Anyone can be refused a green card based on inadmissibility.** If you have ever been arrested for a crime, lied on an immigration application, lied to an immigration officer, or you suffer from a particular physical or mental illness, you may be inadmissible from receiving a green card. In some cases, a waiver of inadmissibility may be available. (See Chapter 3.)

B. Quick View of the Application Process

Unlike many other types of green card applications, you perform all the steps on your own, without needing someone in the U.S. to file a petition on your behalf. The steps include:

- First, you mail what's called a visa petition to a USCIS regional service center, proving that you fit one of the special immigrant categories.

- Second, if the number of petitions is greater than the number of available EB-4 visas when you apply, you wait until your Priority Date is current, and a visa is available to you. (Fortunately, there is rarely a wait in this category.)
- Third, after your petition has been approved, you and your accompanying relatives submit your applications for a green card, either at a U.S. consulate outside the United States, or possibly at a USCIS office within the United States (an option mainly available to people who are already legally in the United States).
- Fourth, if your interview was held at a U.S. consulate in another country, you enter the U.S. with your immigrant visa, at which time you become a permanent resident.

 Certain types of special immigrants can combine some of these steps. Children of international organization employees, as well as special immigrant juveniles, are allowed to file their visa petition concurrently with their green card application (assuming there is no wait for their Priority Dates to become current). This exception attempts to protect them from becoming too old to qualify for the green card. Religious workers and others, however, cannot file concurrently.

C. Step One: You File the Visa Petition

To begin your immigration process, you must file what's called a visa petition on Form I-360. The purpose of this form is to show that you meet the eligibility criteria for your special immigrant category— for which you'll normally have to supply supporting documents.

Form I-360 is available at www.uscis .gov—and it comes with extensive instructions about what documentation to include with your form. The form also takes care of some other details, like informing USCIS whether you will be continuing with your application through a consulate outside of the U.S. or through a U.S.-based USCIS office. If you're not sure, choose the consulate. If you change your mind later, all you need to do is file an application at a USCIS office. Doing the reverse, transferring your case from a USCIS office to a consulate, requires filing a separate application.

The following checklist will help you keep track of all the forms and documents that go into your initial visa petition.

Checklist of Forms and Documents for Visa Petition

❑ Form I-360.

❑ Application fee (currently $375, but free to special immigrant juveniles; checks or money orders are accepted, but not cash).

Religious Workers:

❑ Diplomas and certificates showing your academic and professional qualifications (the minimum requirement is a bachelor's degree (B.A.); if you're a minister, include proof of your ordination).

❑ Detailed letter from the U.S. religious organization, fully describing the operation of the organization both in and out of the U.S., including the number of followers in both your home country and the United States.

❑ If you are a minister, the letter above should also describe why your services are needed, including details regarding the current number of ministers, the congregation size, your duties, and what they've done before to meet the need.

❑ Letter from the U.S. organization giving details of your U.S. job offer, including title, duties, qualifications, and your salary and other compensation.

❑ Written verification that you have been a member of and worked (for pay) outside the U.S. for that same organization for at least two years.

❑ Evidence that the religious organization in the U.S. is eligible for tax-exempt (§ 501(c)(3)) status under the Internal Revenue Code.

❑ Evidence that the organization is able to pay you.

Foreign Medical Graduates:

❑ A copy of your original I-94 card (even if it has expired) or your passport with a visa stamp showing you were admitted to the U.S. with a J or H visa prior to January 9, 1978.

❑ Copy of your medical license issued by any U.S. state prior to January 9, 1978, or a letter from the medical board of a state verifying you were licensed.

❑ Evidence that you have been employed as a physician since January 9, 1978, such as a letter from your employer, or your personal income tax returns, including W-2 forms, for all years from 1977 to the present.

❑ Evidence of your continuous residence in the U.S. since entry. Proof of this can include your personal income tax returns for each year, your children's school records, your utility bills, bank records, letters from employers, and the like.

❑ If you had a J-1 visa, a copy of your Certificate of Eligibility (DS-2019 or IAP-66) and, if it indicated you were subject to the foreign residence requirement, a "no objection" letter from the embassy of your home country.

Former U.S. Government Workers:

☐ Verification of at least 15 years of U.S. government employment outside the U.S. or with the American Institute in Taiwan (for example, copies of your personal tax returns or a letter of verification from the U.S. government agency that employed you).

☐ Letter of recommendation for a green card from the principal officer-in-charge of the agency where you worked.

☐ Letter of recommendation from the U.S. Secretary of State. The agency you worked for should be able to assist you in getting this.

Retired Employees of International Organizations:

☐ Evidence you have lived in the U.S. on a G-4 or N visa for the past 15 years, such as copies of passports, I-94 cards, or U.S. tax returns; or if these are not available, a detailed letter from the international organization in the U.S. stating your periods of employment and visa status.

☐ Evidence that you lived in the U.S. for at least half of the seven-year period prior to filing for a green card. Copies of your passport and I-94 cards during the past seven years would again be the best proof. You need to make a complete copy of your passport to show your entries and departures. If unavailable, other acceptable proofs of your physical presence in the U.S. are a letter from your employer stating the number of days you worked in the U.S. and bank statements showing regular deposits and withdrawals during this time.

☐ A letter from the U.S. employer or other written verification of your retirement date (which must have occurred within the six months before submitting this application).

Children of International Organization Retirees:

☐ Letter from the international organization in the U.S. employing your parent, verifying his or her position and period of employment.

☐ Your long-form birth certificate showing the names of your parents.

☐ Evidence that you have been physically present in the U.S. for at least half of the seven-year period immediately before applying for a green card. A complete copy of your passport and all I-94 cards issued is usually sufficient.

☐ If your passport and I-94 cards are unavailable or do not show your entries and departures for at least the past seven years, other evidence of your presence in the U.S. for one half of the past seven years, such as letters from employers stating the number of days you worked in the U.S., or school records.

Persons Employed at the U.S. Consulate in Hong Kong:

❑ Written recommendation to grant you a green card from the consul general of the U.S. consulate in Hong Kong, which includes an explanation of how your welfare in Hong Kong will be threatened because you are working for the U.S. government.

❑ Your own written statement explaining how your welfare in Hong Kong will be threatened because you worked for the U.S. government there.

❑ Written evidence that you were employed at the U.S. consulate in Hong Kong for at least three years, such as tax returns or a letter from the consulate itself.

Persons Declared Dependent on a Juvenile Court:

❑ Copy of a juvenile court decree declaring the child's dependency on the court or placing the juvenile under the custody of a state agency or department.

❑ The court order should also state that the child is eligible for long-term foster care due to abuse, neglect, or abandonment.

❑ If it is not specifically stated in the court decree, and the court will not amend the decree to include it, a letter from the juvenile court judge stating the following:

   ❑ That the child is eligible for long-term foster care, and

   ❑ That it would not be in the child's best interest to return him or her to the home country.

❑ Proof of the child's age, such as a birth certificate, passport, or foreign document (such as a cedula or cartilla).

Servicepeople:

❑ Certified proof of your active duty status for 12 years, or of six years' duty plus re-enlistment, and

❑ Your birth certificate showing that you are a native of a country that has a treaty with the U.S. covering military service.

1. Submitting the Visa Petition

Where you'll submit or send your visa petition depends on what subcategory of special immigrant you are applying under. Here is some information from the USCIS website; you'll need to go there (www.uscis.gov) to check for changes, and to get the exact address and P.O. box number of the service center that is right for you.

Where to File Your Visa Petition	
Your Subcategory	**Where to File**
Religious worker	File at the service center with jurisdiction over the state where you will be residing.
Military	If you are filing with an I-485, and are in the U.S., file at the local office with jurisdiction over your place of residence. If you are filing without an I-485, and are in the U.S., file at the service center with jurisdiction over your place of residence. If you are filing without an I-485 and are outside the U.S., file at the foreign USCIS office with jurisdiction over your place of residence.
Juvenile	File petition with the local office with jurisdiction over the child's place of residence.
Amerasian	If you are living in the U.S., file your petition with the local office with jurisdiction over your place of residence; if you are living outside of the U.S., you can either file your petition with the foreign USCIS office that has jurisdiction over your current place of residence, or you can file your petition with the local office that has jurisdiction over your intended place of residence in the United States.
Physician	File your petition with the service center with jurisdiction over your place of residence.
International organization officer or employee and family members: I-360 only	Nebraska Service Center P.O. Box 87360 Lincoln, NE 68501-7360
International organization officer or employee and family members whose Form I-360 was previously approved, or is being filed concurrently with Form I-485	Nebraska Service Center P.O. Box 87485 Lincoln NE 68501-7485

If your petition can be submitted to a local USCIS office, you may be able to deliver it in person. Check your local office's procedures to be sure.

2. Awaiting Approval of the Visa Petition

If you mail the petition in to a service center, within a few weeks after mailing it, you should receive a written confirmation that the papers are being processed, together with a receipt for the fees. This notice will also contain your immigration case file number.

If USCIS wants further information before acting on your case, it will return all petition papers, forms, and documents to you, together with an I-797 Request for Evidence. This will tell you what corrections, additional pieces of information, or additional documents USCIS expects. You should make the corrections or supply the extra data and mail the whole package back to the regional service center, with a copy of the I-797 on top.

After filing Form I-360, you will have to wait for the petition to be approved, which can take several months by itself. (See Chapter 4 for how to track the length of time USCIS is taking to decide on visa petitions, and how to track your own application online.)

Once your petition is approved, a Notice of Action (also on Form I-797) will be sent to you, indicating the approval. If you plan to apply for your green card at a U.S. consulate abroad, USCIS will forward the file to the National Visa Center (NVC) in Portsmouth, New Hampshire. The NVC will then send a packet of forms and instructions to you so that you may proceed with the next step, described later in this chapter.

An approved petition does not by itself give you any right to immigrate to or live in the United States. It is only a prerequisite to the next step, submitting your own application for a green card.

D. Step Two: You Await an Available Visa Number

Because there are annual limits on the number of people who can receive green cards as special immigrants, it's possible—though unlikely—that you will have to wait in line until a visa number (allowing you to apply for an immigrant visa or green card) becomes available. Your place in the line is tracked by your Priority Date. It comes from the date on which you filed your I-360 visa petition.

It's impossible to say exactly how long you might have to wait—it all depends on how many people are in line before you. In general, waiting periods for all visa numbers tend to be longer for people from China, India, Mexico, and the Philippines. This is not because of any discrimination against those countries—it merely reflects the fact that more people from those countries apply for visas than from other countries, and there is a per-country limit. The supply of visas for those countries is often less than the number of people applying for them, so the waiting list gets longer and longer.

Although you can't predict how long you will wait, you can track the progress of your own Priority Date through the system, and get some sense of the rate at which it is moving. To do so, you first need to look at the State Department's monthly *Visa Bulletin*, which lists the Priority Dates of people who are allowed to get visas that month. It's available on a recorded message at 202-663-1541, or at its website at www.state.gov (under "Travel & Business" click "Visa Bulletins"). The State Department updates this chart around the middle of every month, but not on any exact day.

When you look at the *Visa Bulletin*, look for the chart like the one below.

Here's how to read the *Visa Bulletin* chart:

1. Locate the 4th "preference" category in the first column (notice that there is a separate entry for "Certain Religious Workers").

2. Locate your country across the top. If you don't see it listed, look in the column called "All Chargeability Areas Except Those Listed."

3. Draw lines across from your preference category and down from your country of origin. The box where your two lines cross is the one containing what's called your Visa Cutoff Date. Often, it contains a letter instead of a date. The letter "C" is good news—it means that no one

needs to wait, and all applicants are considered current, that is, immediately eligible for a visa or green card. The letter "U" would be bad news—it means that all the visas have been used up for that year, and more will not become available until October (when the federal government starts its new fiscal year).

4. If, instead of a letter, your box contains a Visa Cutoff Date, compare it with your Priority Date. If the Visa Cutoff Date is the same as your Priority Date, or is even later, great—you can now apply for your green card. However, if the cutoff date is earlier than your Priority Date, you still have to wait—because only people who applied some time before you are now receiving the right to immigrate.

EXAMPLE: Amanda is a citizen of Somalia who is a retired U.S. government employee. She files a visa petition on May 5, 2006. In March of 2007, her petition is approved, and she checks her Priority Date. As you'll see on the March 2007 chart below, it says "C," meaning all applicants can continue right away with the green card process. Let's say, however, that the Visa Cutoff Date was then March 1, 2006. That means that people who filed visa petitions on March 1, 2006 (or before that) were finally allowed to continue with the process and apply for a green card in March 2007.

March 2007 Priority Dates for Employment-Based Visas					
	All Chargeability Areas Except Those Listed	CHINA-mainland born	INDIA	MEXICO	PHILIP-PINES
Employment-Based					
1st	C	C	C	C	C
2nd	C	22APR05	08JAN03	C	C
3rd	01AUG02	01AUG02	08MAY01	15MAY01	01AUG02
Other Workers	01OCT01	01OCT01	01OCT01	01OCT01	01OCT01
4th	C	C	C	C	C
Certain Religious Workers	C	C	C	C	C
Iraqi & Afghani Translators	18SEP06	18SEP06	18SEP06	18SEP06	18SEP06
5th	C	C	C	C	C
Targeted Employment Areas/Regional Centers	C	C	C	C	C

Their wait was approximately one year—which suggests that Amanda would have to wait a similar length of time.

If you have an approved petition but your Priority Date is not yet current, you must wait until it is current to take the next step and file your green card application. The immigration authorities will advise you by mail when your Priority Date finally comes up (so make sure to send them any change of address!).

If you're in the United States on a temporary work visa, be careful that your status does not expire before your Priority Date becomes current and you can apply for a green card—possessing an approved visa petition does not give you any right to live in the United States. If this looks like it might become a problem, consult as soon as possible with an immigration attorney.

E. Step Three: You Apply for a Green Card

Once your visa petition has been approved, and your Priority Date has become current, you can apply for a green card. If you are in a category where your spouse or children can accompany you, they must each file their own green card applications. A big part of the green card application is proving that you are not inadmissible to the United States. Review Chapter 3 regarding the grounds of inadmissibility. Note, however, that special immigrant juveniles are exempted from many of the grounds of inadmissibility, including those regarding the likelihood of becoming a public charge, and the need for a proper immigrant visa or labor certification. (See I.N.A. § 245(h)(2), 8 U.S.C. § 1255(h)(2).)

The most important question at this point in the process is where you file the application—in the United States or at a U.S. consulate in another country? You should have already made this choice on your Form I-360, but you're allowed to change your mind, so it's worth revisiting the question.

If you're living outside of the U.S. now. The answer is fairly easy for people living outside of the United States—you'll file at a local U.S. consulate and attend an interview there before entering the United States. (This method is called consular processing.)

If you're living in the U.S. now. The answer is a bit more complicated for applicants already in the United States. Ordinarily, the most convenient choice would probably be for you to adjust status without leaving—that is, send your application to the nearest USCIS service Center and attend your interview at a local USCIS office. Once your application is filed, your stay in the United States will be considered legal, and you can apply for permission to work. Should problems

arise in your case, you'll be able to wait for a decision in the U.S., a circumstance most green card applicants prefer. Also, if your application for a green card is turned down, you have greater rights of appeal inside the U.S. than you do at a U.S. consulate.

One catch is that you are allowed to adjust status only if you're already in the U.S. legally, that is, on a valid, unexpired visa or other form of permission (with a few exceptions). You might, for example, already be on a temporary visa. If, however, you're living in the United States with no legal status, or have worked without authorization, or you entered legally without a visa under the Visa Waiver Program, you are barred from filing your green card application inside the United States. See Chapter 3 for information on whether you might be one of the rare few people allowed to adjust status regardless, due to an exception. If not, you'll probably need to consult with an experienced immigration attorney.

Special immigrant juveniles, foreign medical graduates, unmarried sons or daughters of international organization officers, and servicepeople will be able to adjust status. The law exempts them from various grounds of inadmissibility, including the requirement that they have entered with a proper immigrant visa. In addition, special immigrant juveniles are deemed to have been "paroled" into the United States (a legal form of entry; and one that causes them not to accrue unlawful status). (See I.N.A. § 245(a),(h), 8 U.S.C. § 1255(a),(h).)

Whether or not you're eligible to adjust status, you may instead decide to leave the United States and apply for your green card at a U.S. consulate abroad. If the consulates are issuing visas more quickly than your local USCIS office is handling adjustment of status applications (which is common), leaving to apply at a U.S. consulate in another country could be a smart strategic move. However, if you have already spent 180 days or more in the U.S. out of legal status, or crossed the border without inspection, be sure you are not inadmissible or subject to a three-year or ten-year reentry bar before you go. (See Chapter 3.) Otherwise, you could find yourself stuck outside the U.S. for three or ten years.

1. What Happens When Adjusting Status in the U.S.

The process of adjusting your status to permanent resident involves preparing a set of forms and documents (a separate set for you, your spouse, and each of your accompanying children), mailing these to a USCIS service center, waiting for some weeks or months until you're called in to have your fingerprints taken, and then waiting a few weeks or months longer until you're called in for your final green card interview at a local USCIS office (not the one to which you sent your application). You should be approved for your green card at or soon after the interview. Nowadays, the interview is often waived, in which case you'll get a letter in the mail telling you you've been approved. See Chapter 4 for information on tracking the progress of your application at the service center and at your local office.

As part of your adjustment of status application, you and your family members may apply for permission to work (an Employment Authorization Document or EAD).

! Security checks are a likely cause of delays. As part of your adjustment of status application, the FBI must run both a fingerprint check and a name check on you, and the CIA must run a separate name check. These name checks can take months or even years, especially because many applicants have similar names. If you've been informed that your case is stalled due to security checks, get the name of a person you can keep in touch with for updates, or hire a lawyer to help with this task.

2. Paperwork to Prepare for Adjustment of Status Application

The basic form used in the U.S. adjustment of status application is Form I-485, Application for Permanent Residence. However, a handful of other forms and documents must be prepared to accompany this main one.

An easy way to get all these forms is to call the USCIS forms line at 800-870-3676 and ask for the Adjustment of Status Packet. Or, you can obtain the forms online at www.uscis.gov. (Click "Immigration Forms," then scroll down and select the forms you need one by one based on the checklist below.)

The following checklist will help you assemble and keep track of the appropriate forms and documents. A complete set of the items on this list must also be prepared for your accompanying spouse and children.

Checklist for Adjustment of Status Application

Forms

❑ Form I-485.

❑ Form I-485A (only if you'll be paying the $1,000 penalty fee in order to adjust status).

❑ Form G-325A.

❑ Form I-765 (optional, if you want a work permit; include a separate filing fee, currently $340). On I-765 Question 16, answer "(c)(9)."

❑ Form I-134 Affidavit of Support , signed by the principal applicant, if employed, on behalf of any accompanying family members, promising to support them financially. (Special immigrant juveniles need not submit this.) If the principal family member is not employed, either Form I-134 signed by a friend or relative in the U.S., or other proof of financial support such as a written offer of employment from a U.S. employer or financial documents showing sufficient income and assets to support the principal applicant and accompanying relatives without employment.

❑ I-131, Application for Travel Document (Advance Parole), for use if you think you'll need to travel outside the United States while your application is processed. This also requires a separate filing fee, currently $170.

Documents

❑ Copy of your I-360 approval notice (unless you're filing the I-360 concurrently).

❑ Copy of a long-form birth certificate for you and each accompanying relative. If this is in another language, it must be accompanied by a full English translation.

❑ Marriage certificate if you are married and bringing your spouse.

❑ If either you or your spouse has been previously married, copies of divorce and death certificates showing termination of all previous marriages.

❑ Copy of I-94 card for you and each accompanying relative (the small white card placed in your passport). Failure to submit this may result in a conclusion that you entered or remained in the U.S. illegally and either are not eligible or are subject to the $1,000 penalty described earlier.

❑ Filing fee (currently $1,010 for applicants between ages 14 and 79, $600 for applicants under age 14 who are filing with a parent, and $930 for applicants age 79 and older or applicants under age 14 fiing alone). In addition, if you are in the U.S. illegally, but are allowed to adjust status under old laws, you must pay a $1,000 penalty fee. Checks and money orders are accepted, but we advise against sending cash through the mail. Double check all fees at www.uscis.gov.

❑ Two photographs of you and two photographs of each accompanying relative, in U.S. passport style (it's best to have a professional do these). Write your name and A number (if you've received one from USCIS) in pencil on the back of each photo.

❑ Medical exam report for you and for each accompanying relative (Form I-693, filled out and signed by a USCIS-certified doctor, and presented in an unopened envelope). The fee is usually around $150 per exam, depending on the doctor. The exam itself involves taking a medical history, blood test, and chest X-ray, and administering vaccinations if applicable and/or recommended for you. Pregnant women may refuse to be X-rayed until after the baby is born.

Tip for filling out Form I-485: You'll notice on the first page of the form, under "Part 2: Application," it asks you to choose the basis upon which you're applying for a green card. Mark Box "a" if you're the primary applicant; Box "b" if you're a spouse or child.

A few items on the above checklist could use extra explanation:

Form I-134, Affidavit of Support. All immigrants must convince USCIS that once they receive a green card they are not likely to go on public assistance or welfare. If your application is based on employment, that alone should be sufficient proof that you have a way to support yourself. If, however, a spouse or child will be accompanying you, you will need to fill out a Form I-134 Affidavit of Support for them.

Special immigrant juveniles need not submit an Affidavit of Support or other evidence of financial capacity, because the public charge ground of inadmissibility is waived in their case. (See I.N.A. § 245(h)(2), 8 U.S.C. § 1255(h)(2); I.N.A. § 212(a)(4), 8 U.S.C. § 1182 (a)(4).)

In signing the I-134 Affidavit of Support, you are not actually promising to support your accompanying relatives. What you do promise is to reimburse the U.S. government for the sum total of any government support payments they might receive should they go on welfare. The I-134 Affidavit of Support binds you to this obligation for three years. Your responsibility to the government then comes to an end.

If the principal applicant is not employed and therefore cannot sign an I-134, he or she will need to find some other source of financial support for the family—either an affidavit signed by a U.S.-based friend or relative, a job offer, or proof of assets and investments.

Medical exam. You must submit a Medical Examination Report for each applicant. This is done on Form I-693, which must be taken to a USCIS authorized physician or medical clinic. You'll have to pay a fee. The USCIS local office will provide you with the form as well as a list of approved physicians in your area. After completion of the medical exam, and upon obtaining the test results, the doctor will give you the results in a sealed envelope. Do not open the envelope.

Dealing With Delays in Approval of Your Work Authorization

If you want to work before your application for a green card is approved, you must file a separate application for employment authorization. To do so, fill out Form I-765 and file it together with your adjustment of status application. (Answer Question 16 of the form "(c)(9).") To accompany Form I-765, submit a copy of your I-94 card and pay a separate filing fee. Be sure to keep the fee receipt that USCIS gives you, so you can prove that the I-765 was filed. Normally, you will file the application for employment authorization at the same time as your adjustment of status application papers.

Legally, USCIS does not have to make a decision on your employment authorization application for up to 90 days. If for some reason you are not given a decision within 90 days, you can request an interim employment authorization, which will last 240 days. To request an interim card, make an appointment to visit your local USCIS office.

If 240 days pass and you still have not received a final decision on the I-765, you must stop working. Interim work authorization cards cannot be renewed. However, if you reach this point, you have the option to file a new I-765 application. If you do not get a decision on the new application within 90 days, you will then be entitled to another interim work authorization card.

3. Mailing the Adjustment Packet

After you have finished preparing the adjustment of status paperwork, you must mail it to a USCIS service center serving your geographic region. (Addresses are on the USCIS website, www.uscis.gov. Submit your application by certified mail, return receipt requested, and keep a complete copy of everything you send in.

Generally, after filing your green card application, you will not hear anything from USCIS for several months. Then you should receive notices of your fingerprint (biometrics) and interview appointments. The interview notice will also tell you whether any further documentation is needed.

Read This If You Plan to Leave the U.S. Before Your Adjustment Interview

Once your application for adjustment of status has been filed, you must not leave the U.S. for any reason before you have applied for and received advance permission to reenter the U.S. (Advance Parole). Any absence without this permission will be viewed as a termination of your application for a green card—which means that, upon return, you will be told that your green card application is dead and you have no right to enter the United States.

Many people simply apply for Advance Parole at the same time they apply to adjust status, just in case. Or, you can wait until you're sure you have to leave, and apply at the same service center where you sent your adjustment of status application—but you're taking a risk this way, because USCIS may take many weeks to approve your Advance

Parole application.

Your application for Advance Parole should include Form I-131, together with a filing fee (currently $305), two passport-type photographs, a copy of your adjustment of status filing receipt (if you've already sent in that application), and a short explanation of why you want to leave—you will need a bona fide personal or business reason, though it need not be an emergency.

If approved, you will be allowed to leave the U.S. and return again with no break in the processing of your application. However, if you were out of status for 180 days or more after April 1, 1997, you should not depart the U.S. even on the basis of an Advance Parole, as this may subject you to the three- or ten-year bars to reentry.

4. Your Adjustment of Status Interview

You may be called in for a personal interview, which will be held at a US-CIS office near you. However, personal interviews are often waived in special immigrant applications. If USCIS requires you to attend an interview, it will send you and your accompanying relatives an appointment notice, usually about two weeks in advance of the interview. If you have an attorney, he or she may come with you to the interview. (Even if you don't have an attorney, you could consult with or hire one at this point.)

Checklist: Documents to Bring to Your Interview

Prepare all of the following to take with you to your USCIS interview:

❏ A complete photocopy of your green card application. This is for your use—you may want to follow along as the officer asks you questions about the material you filled out on the forms, or you may find that the officer is missing something that you have a copy of.

❏ Photo identification or passport for you and every one of your family members. (It's best to bring your passport, because if you are approved for your green card on the day of the interview, USCIS can place a stamp in your passport demonstrating this—and you use this stamp as proof when you work or travel.)

❏ Originals of all documents that you made copies of for submission with your application. For example, if you submitted a photocopy of a birth certificate or other official document, a USCIS officer may want to examine the original.

❏ Any documents received from USCIS or other immigration authorities. For example, if you left the country on Advance Parole, bring this permit.

❏ Any updates to the material in your application. For example, if you have given birth to another child, bring its birth certificate. If you've been arrested, bring a full explanation (and consult with an attorney, to make sure that the arrest doesn't make you inadmissible).

See Chapter 4 for detailed information on what expect during your adjustment of status interview. If your adjustment of status application is denied, also see Chapter 4.

If everything is in order, your application will be approved at the conclusion of the adjustment of status interview, or soon after. Your passport will be stamped to show that you have been admitted to the U.S. as a permanent resident, and your green card will be ordered. The green card will come to you in the mail several weeks after the interview. If you need to travel outside the U.S. before your green card arrives, however, you must go back to the USCIS office with your passport and the written notice of approval, and a temporary stamp will be placed in your passport, enabling you to return after your trip. Never leave the U.S. without either your green card or a temporary stamp in your passport.

Ready for information on how to protect and renew your green card status after you're approved? See Chapter 14.

5. What Happens During Consular Processing

Consular processing requires you to prepare some forms and documents according to instructions, notify the consulate when you are ready with these, wait until you receive a notice scheduling you for an interview at a U.S. consulate, prepare additional forms and documents for the interview, and finally attend the interview. There, if all goes well, you will be approved (subject to final security checks) for a visa to enter the United States.

Much of your job at this point involves convincing the consulate that you are not inadmissible for health, criminal, security, or financial reasons. You will be asked to undergo a medical exam and possibly provide evidence that you have no criminal record.

6. Paperwork to Prepare for Consular Processing

At the beginning, consular processing involves a lot of paper being sent in various directions. First, after USCIS approves your visa petition, it will forward your file to the National Visa Center (NVC) in Portsmouth, New Hampshire. It will send you a form called an Agent of Choice and Address (DS-3032), which simply asks where you want the rest of your visa-related mail sent; for example, to your attorney rather than to you.

Once the NVC receives your form DS-3032, it will mail you (or your attorney or agent) an Immigrant Visa (IV) fee bill (currently $335) and a security fee (currently $45). Once you've paid that bill, the NVC will send you what's called an instruction packet of forms and information (formerly called Packet 3). It will send you a second packet as part of your interview notification from.

a. Handling the Instructional Packet

The instructional packet includes some forms and material for you to read. Some of the forms are for you to fill out and return in order to keep the process moving—namely Form DS-230 Part I and Form DS-2001 (formerly called OF-169). (The forms are normally designated by DS preceding a number, and copies of many of them are available on the State Department website at www.state. gov. However, it's better to wait for the ones the consulate sends you, because some of them are slightly different than the main State Department forms—for example, many of the consulates use forms with bilingual translations into the language of your country.)

Keep the process moving. You don't really need to have all your documents in hand when you send in Form DS-2001. Although the form asks you to sign it only after you're ready with the listed forms, many people simply sign as soon as they know they can get the forms together, to save time.

After you've sent in the necessary forms, your local U.S. consulate will start communicating with you directly. It will send you an interview notice, including additional forms to fill out, a list of documents to collect, and other tasks to take care of.

b. Preparing Forms and Documents for Your Interview

The checklist below provides a brief explanation of some of the documents you'll need to gather in preparation for your immigrant visa interview. Keep your eyes open for any special requirements that the local consulate may add to this list. Bring the originals and a set of copies with you to your interview (the consular officer may want to examine the originals to make sure they're not fraudulent, but keep copies for your files). Do not mail your paperwork to the consulate!

Checklist of Documents and Forms for Your Consular Interview

Forms

❏ DS forms (sent to you by the NVC and U.S. consulate).

❏ Form I-134 Affidavit of Support, signed by the principal applicant, if employed, on behalf of any accompanying family members, promising to support them financially. (Special immigrant juveniles need not submit this.) If the principal family member is not employed, either a Form I-134 signed by a friend or relative in the U.S., or other proof of financial support such as a written offer of employment from a U.S. employer or financial documents showing sufficient funds and investments to support the principal applicant and accompanying relatives without employment.

Documents

❏ Notice of approval of your visa petition.

❏ Long-form birth certificate for you and each accompanying relative as well as of any unmarried minor children who are not immigrating with you.

❏ Marriage certificate if you are married and bringing your spouse.

❏ If either you or your spouse has been previously married, copies of divorce and death certificates showing termination of all previous marriages.

❏ Passport for you and each accompanying relative, valid for at least six months beyond the date of the final interview.

❏ Police certificates from every country in which you and each accompanying relative has lived for at least six months since age 16.

❏ Fingerprints, if specifically requested by the consulate (current cost: $85).

❏ Military records for you and each accompanying relative.

❏ Two photographs of you and two photographs of each accompanying relative.

❏ Medical exam report for you and for each accompanying relative.

Here's some additional information regarding some of the items on the checklist above:

Form I-134, Affidavit of Support. All immigrants must convince the U.S. immigration authorities that once they receive a green card they are not likely to go on public assistance or welfare. If your application is based on employment, that alone should be sufficient proof that you have a way to support yourself. If, however, a spouse or child will be accompanying you, you will need to fill out a Form I-134 Affidavit of Support for them.

Special immigrant juveniles need not submit an Affidavit of Support or other evidence of financial capacity, because the public charge ground of inadmissibility is waived in their case. (See I.N.A. § 245(h)(2), 8 U.S.C. § 1255(h)(2); I.N.A. § 212(a)(4), 8 U.S.C. § 1182(a)(4).)

In signing the I-134, you are not actually promising to support your accompanying relatives. What you do promise is to reimburse the U.S. government for the sum total of any government support payments they might receive should they go on welfare. The I-134 binds you to this obligation for three years (although many lawyers say it would never hold up in court). Your responsibility to the government then comes to an end.

If the principal applicant is not employed and therefore cannot sign an I-134, he or she will need to find some other source of financial support for the family—either an affidavit signed by a U.S.-based friend or relative, a job offer, or proof of assets and investments.

Police clearance. Unlike applications made in the U.S., you personally must collect police clearance certificates from each country you have lived in for one year or more since your 16th birthday. Additionally, you must have a police certificate from your home country or country of last residence, if you lived there for at least six months since the age of 16. You do not need to obtain police certificates from the United States.

Contact the local police department in your home country for instructions on how to get police certificates, or visit http://travel.state.gov/visa/reciprocity/index.htm. To obtain police certificates from nations other than your home country, contact the nearest consulate representing that country for instructions.

Some nations refuse to supply police certificates, or their certificates are not considered reliable, and so you will not be required to obtain them from those locations. The U.S. consulate will tell you which countries police certificates are not required from.

Some countries will send certificates directly to U.S. consulates but not to you personally. Before they send the certificates out, however, you must request that it be done. Usually this requires filing some type of request form, together with a set of your fingerprints.

Photos. You and each accompanying relative must bring to the interview two photographs taken in compliance with the consulate's instructions (U.S passport style). Often your information packet will contain a list of local photographers who take this type of picture. If your religious beliefs require wearing a head covering, you should be able to keep it on for the photo. However, your eyes and face must still be visible, and you must submit a written statement explaining why you can't submit a standard photograph.

Medical exam. Immediately before your visa interview, you and your accompanying relatives will be required to have medical examinations. Some consulates conduct the medical exams up to several days before the interview. Others schedule the medical exam and the interview on the same day. You will be told where to go and what to do in your appointment letter.

The medical examinations are conducted by private doctors. The fees vary from $50 to more than $150 per exam, depending on the country. The fee will be stated in your appointment letter. The exam itself involves taking a medical history, blood test, chest X-ray, and vaccinations, if you need any. Although pregnant women can refuse to be X-rayed until after the pregnancy, the requirement to have an X-ray taken cannot be waived entirely. The vaccination requirement may be waived for religious, moral, or medical reasons.

The main purpose of the medical exam is to verify that you are not medically inadmissible. The primary medical grounds of inadmissibility are tuberculosis and HIV (AIDS). Some medical grounds of inadmissibility can be overcome with treatment or by applying for a waiver. (See Chapter 3 for more details.) If you need a medical waiver, you will be given complete instructions by the consulate at the time of your interview, but should also consult an experienced immigration attorney.

F. Step Four: You Enter the U.S. With Your Immigrant Visa

Your immigrant visa allows you to request entry to the United States at a border post, airport, or other arrival point. It's good for six months after you get it—and once you have the visa. You acquire the full status of green-card holder only after you have been inspected and admitted into the U.S. If you are bringing any accompanying relatives, they must enter at either the same time or after you do in order to become permanent residents.

The inspection process involves a U.S. border officer opening the sealed envelope containing your visa documents, and doing a last check to make sure you haven't used fraud. The border officer has expedited removal powers, which means he or she can turn you right around and send you home if anything appears wrong in your packet or with your answers to the officer's questions. Be polite and careful in answering.

When the officer is satisfied that everything is in order, he or she will stamp your passport to show that you're now a U.S. permanent resident and are immediately authorized to work. You won't receive an actual green card yet, however. Cards for you and your accompanying relatives will be ordered for you, and will come to you by mail several weeks later.

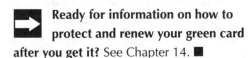 **Ready for information on how to protect and renew your green card after you get it?** See Chapter 14. ■

Chapter 13

Humanitarian Protection: TPS, DED, Asylee, and Refugee Status

For some immigrants, getting out of their home country and finding safe haven in a country like the United States is literally a matter of life and death. The immigration laws offer help to such people, although the door is not as open as you might wish. This chapter covers both temporary and permanent rights to take shelter in the U.S., including Temporary Protected Status (TPS), Deferred Enforced Departure (DED), refugee status, and political asylum.

Do you need a lawyer? Yes! This chapter will give you an outline of how to apply for TPS, refugee, or asylee status. However, given the risks you'll face if your application is denied, and that preparing an asylum application is more like writing a book than filling out a form, it's worth trying to get additional help. An experienced lawyer can show you how to highlight the important parts of your story in a way that turns your case from a loser into a winner. Within the U.S., a number of organizations offer free or low-cost help to refugees and asylees. See, for example, the searchable directory on www.asylumlaw.org.

Any inadmissible person may be denied U.S. entry or status. If you have ever committed a serious crime, been involved in a terrorist group, lied on an immigration application, lied to an immigration officer, or suffered one of a few specific physical or mental illnesses, you may be inadmissible. That can cause a denial of your initial application, and is even more likely to cause a denial of your application for permanent resident status after being given refugee status or political asylum. However, most grounds of inadmissibility can be waived (forgiven) for refugees, political asylees, and persons seeking TPS or DED, except those grounds concerning the commission of serious crimes, persecution of others, or participation in subversive or terrorist activities such that you are considered a possible threat to U.S. security. (Unlike the normal waiver of inadmissibility, this waiver does not require you to have a family member who is already a permanent resident or U.S. citizen.)

A. Do You Qualify for Temporary Protected Status (TPS)?

Temporary Protected Status (TPS) is much what its name sounds like: It lets people who are from countries that are currently in turmoil, and therefore unsafe, apply to live in the U.S. with a work permit until conditions in their home country improve. (See I.N.A. § 244, 8 U.S.C. § 1254.) For example, countries in the midst of civil war, or that have recently experienced a huge natural disaster such as an earthquake may be put on the TPS list by the U.S. government. In creating this list, however, the government always puts an expiration date on each country's TPS designation.

TPS does not help people currently living in the affected countries. You must be in the U.S. when TPS is established for your country in order to qualify, and you must submit an application to USCIS (see Section B, below). When your country's TPS designation runs out, so does your right to stay in the United States. (The U.S. government may, however, if the disaster continues, renew your country's TPS designation, in which case you'll need to reregister.) TPS status does not lead to a green card.

TPS is currently available for citizens of Burundi, El Salvador, Honduras, Liberia, Nicaragua, Somalia, and Sudan.

Whenever a new country is named, a notice will be published in the *Federal Register*, stating the time period for which the protection is granted (a minimum of six months and a maximum of 18 months), and the dates and procedures for registering. Also see the USCIS website (www.uscis.gov) for this information (click "Services and Benefits," then "Humanitarian Benefits," then "Temporary Protected Status").

 TPS does not include rights to travel outside the United States. If you travel, your TPS will probably be canceled unless you apply for Advance Parole on Form I-131 (see the USCIS website for the form and instructions).

B. How to Apply for Temporary Protected Status

Applying for Temporary Protected Status is a one-step process. You'll need to fill out two USCIS forms, Form I-765 and Form I-821. Copies of these forms may be found on the USCIS website at www.uscis.gov. The forms are simple and self-explanatory. The I-821 asks for your name, address, birth date, nationality, and the date you began living in the United States. The I-765 is an application for a work permit. You will mark Box (a)(11) in Question 16.

In addition to the above forms, you must also submit documents showing you really come from the country that you say you do (such as a copy of your passport or birth certificate) and that you have lived in the U.S. for the time required under the TPS rules for your particular country. Evidence of your stay in the U.S. could include copies of your passport and I-94 card, employment records, and school records.

Applicants must pay an application fee, plus separate fees for fingerprinting and photographs, and for work authorization (see the checklist below, but double check fees at www.uscis.gov). If you don't plan to work, you don't need to pay the work authorization fee—but you still need to submit Form I-765.

Checklist for Temporary Protected Status Application

Use this checklist to help organize your TPS application.

Forms

☐ Form I-821, with appropriate fee (currently $130 including biometrics, or $50 for applicants age 14 and younger) .

☐ Form I-765, with appropriate fee (currently $175).

☐ Fee for fingerprints (biometrics) if renewing or reregistering (currently $80).

Documents

☐ Evidence of your presence during the necessary time period in the United States.

☐ Evidence of your identity and nationality (birth certificate, passport, etc.).

TPS applicants are subject to the grounds of inadmissibility (see Chapter 3), though some can be waived.

You'll need to submit your completed TPS application to a USCIS office in Chicago, referred to as the Chicago Lockbox. However, the exact address depends on which country you are from, so check the USCIS website for this information.

After submitting your application, you will first be sent an appointment to have your photos and fingerprints taken, and later be called for an interview before an immigration officer. At your interview, or soon after (for example, if your fingerprints need time to clear) an immigration officer will approve or deny your TPS application.

C. What Is Deferred Enforced Departure?

Another possible basis for remaining in the U.S. if you're from a country in the midst of political or civil conflict is called Deferred Enforced Departure (DED). This temporary form of relief allows you to work and stay in the U.S. for a certain period of time. DED works much like TPS, except that a decision to grant DED comes directly from the U.S. president, as a foreign relations consideration, rather than from the Department of Homeland Security.

Under present policy, no countries are designated for DED, but this could change at any time.

DED protection does not extend to anyone:

- who has been convicted of an aggravated felony
- who is a persecutor of others
- whose removal, in the opinion of the attorney general, is in the interest of the United States
- whose presence or activities in the U.S. are found by the secretary of state to have potentially serious adverse foreign policy consequences for the United States
- who voluntarily returned or returns to his or her country of last habitual residence outside the United States
- who was deported, excluded, or removed before December 23, 1997, or
- who is subject to extradition.

D. Do You Qualify as a Refugee or Asylee?

People who are fleeing persecution in their home country may be granted either refugee or political asylum status—which allows them to stay in the U.S. until it's safe to return to their home country. If, after a year, conditions are no safer, both refugees and asylees can apply for a U.S. green card (permanent residence).

To qualify as a refugee or asylee, you must have experienced persecution in the past or have a well-founded fear of persecution in the future in your home country. Persecution is defined generally as a serious threat to your life or freedom. It needs to be a nationwide threat—you won't be thought to have a well-founded fear of persecution if you could avoid the problem simply by relocating to another part of the country. The fact that you are suffering economically is not considered a reason for granting refugee or asylee status. Nor is it enough if someone has a grudge against you, or has committed crimes against you for random or personal reasons.

The main difference between asylees and refugees is where they start their application process. People physically outside the U.S. must apply for refugee status. Even if you have been designated as a refugee by the United Nations High Commissioner for Refugees (UNHCR), you will still need to apply separately to the U.S. government, which will make its own decision about whether to accept you. As a refugee applicant, you must also have a financial sponsor inside the U.S. before your application can be approved. The U.S. government gives out only a limited number of refugee visas each year (a decision made by the U.S. president).

You cannot apply for political asylum until you have reached U.S. soil. Asylees do not need financial sponsors to be granted asylum. There is no annual limit on the number of people granted asylum.

 If you file an asylum application that USCIS decides is frivolous (has no basis), you will be permanently ineligible for any benefits under U.S. immigration law. That means that you will never be given any U.S. visa or green card, even if you were to marry a U.S. citizen, get a U.S. job offer, or the like. Don't worry that your application will be deemed frivolous if it is denied for any reason—USCIS will find your application frivolous only if you had no business even considering political asylum as an option.

Beyond these differences, the qualifying requirements for refugees and asylees are the same.

Do not leave the United States after submitting your asylum application. If you do, USCIS will assume you've lost interest in your application, and cancel it. You can, however, prevent this by applying for and receiving what's called "Advance Parole," on Form I-131. (The form and instructions are available at www.uscis.gov.) Note, however, that Advance Parole does not give you an automatic right to reenter the United States. You'll need a separately valid visa or other entry document for that.

1. Persecution or Well-Founded Fear of Persecution

To establish eligibility for asylum or refugee status, you must prove you are either the victim of past persecution or in fear of future persecution. In the case of past persecution, you must prove that you were persecuted in your home country or last country of residence. The persecution must be based on at least one of five grounds: your race, religion, nationality, political opinion, or membership in a particular social group. Proving this connection between the persecution and one of these five grounds is one of the most difficult parts of an application for asylee or refugee status—and it got more difficult in 2005, when the REAL ID Act added a requirement that one of the five grounds was or will be a "central reason" for your persecution.

Although the law does not specifically list types of persecution, it does, in one section (added in 1996) specify that refugees and asylees can include people who have undergone or fear a "coercive population control program" (such as forced abortion or sterilization—this pro-

vision was directed primarily at mainland China).

Persecution may also in some cases be based on your gender, including cultural practices such as female genital cutting or forced marriage. Lawyers have also been fighting for years to have domestic violence, honor killing, and trafficking (sexual or labor) recognized as bases for asylee status, particularly in cases where the police and government compound the problem by failing to protect the women or prosecute the perpetrators. For more on these developing areas of the law, see the website of the Center for Gender & Refugee Studies, based at Hastings College of the Law, at http://cgrs.uchastings.edu.

The persecution doesn't only need to come from your country's government or other authorities. Refugee law also recognizes persecution by groups that the government is unable to control, such as guerrillas, warring tribes, or organized vigilantes. Again, however, the persecution must have some political or social basis—a member of a criminal network who comes after you just because you haven't paid him off is not persecuting you according to refugee law.

 You will not be granted asylum or refugee status if you have persecuted others. For example, if a policeman committed abuses in tracking down guerrillas, his claim that the guerrillas were in turn sending him death threats will not be sufficient to qualify him for asylum.

If you have not actually suffered persecution in the past, you can still qualify for political asylum or refugee status if you have a genuine fear of future persecution in your home country or last country of residence. For example, if you were the secretary of a student dissident group, and undercover agents sent you death threats, or killed the treasurer and president of your group, you could probably show a reasonable fear of persecution. Again, a "central" reason for your persecution must be your race, religion, nationality, membership in a particular social group, or political opinion. You do not have to prove that you are likely to be singled out for persecution from the members of a generally persecuted group. You need only show a pattern or practice, where groups of persons who are similar to you are being persecuted. Then, you must show that you either belong to or would be identified with the persecuted group.

2. Evidence Showing Persecution

One of the most difficult parts of an asylum applicant's case can be proving that your story is true. In the past, it was enough to present convincing and consistent testimony, supported by newspaper articles, reports from human rights organizations, and other general evidence of the conditions in your country. As of 2005, however, the decision maker in your case may require you to present "corroborating evidence" of your own claim, unless you "[do] not have the evidence and cannot reasonably obtain the evidence"—and it will be up to the decision maker to decide whether or not that is the case. (See REAL ID Act of 2005 § 101.)

In addition, the 2005 legal changes allow the decision maker to decide whether or not you look like you're telling the truth based on your demeanor, candor, inherent plausibility, and the consistency of your written and oral statements. In a worst-case scenario, the fact that you wrote one address on your asylum application and then remembered the address differently during your interview could be held against you. If the decision maker thinks you're lying, your case will, of course, be denied.

Cultural differences can make it difficult for some people to convince the judge that they're telling the truth. For example, in some cultures it is not polite to look someone like the judge in the eye—while in the United States, failing to look someone directly in the eye is considered a sign of dishonesty. Victims of torture or trauma may also find it difficult to make eye contact or openly discuss—or even sometimes remember—the details of their persecution. (If you work with a lawyer, he or she will help you practice telling your story, and may help arrange a psychiatrist's report to help explain how your difficulties were caused by your persecution.)

3. No Firm Resettlement in Another Country and Unavailability of Safe Haven Elsewhere

Though you may clearly be fleeing persecution, you generally cannot come to the U.S. as a refugee or asylee if you have already been granted or offered a permanent status in another country. You may prefer coming to the U.S., but that makes no difference. The availability of permanent status in another country is known as firm resettlement.

If you've lived in another country before coming to the U.S., however, you can still qualify for refugee or political asylum status in the U.S. if you entered the other country while fleeing persecution, stayed there only as long as was necessary to arrange your continued travel, and did not establish significant ties to that country. In addition, if your rights there with respect to living conditions, employment, holding of property, and travel were significantly less than those of actual citizens or full residents, you may still apply for refugee status or political asylum in the United States.

4. No Improvement of Circumstances in Your Home Country

If you prove that you've been persecuted in the past, you are assumed to have a well-founded fear of persecution in the future. However, if USCIS sees that circum-stances in your home country have fun-damentally changed since you filed your application, it may decide that you don't actually have a well-founded fear anymore, and deny you asylum or refugee status. For example, USCIS could argue that because the civil war in your country has ended and peace accords have been signed, you have nothing more to fear from either side of the conflict. It could make a similar ar-gument if something has changed in your personal circumstances—if, for example, you were once persecuted because you were thought to be the illegitimate daugh-ter of a high-ranking political figure, but your country's newspapers have since reported that DNA tests showed that some-one else was your father.

Still, asylum is sometimes granted even after an improvement in country conditions, for humanitarian reasons.

5. One-Year Time Limit for Asylum Application

You must file an asylum application within one year after you arrive in the U.S. to be eligible for asylum.

There are a few exceptions. You can apply for asylum after one year if you can show either changed circum-stances that have a major effect on your eligibility for asylum or extraordinary circumstances explaining why your ap-plication wasn't filed on time. Changed circumstances can include changes in conditions in your country; for example if you're a member of an ethnic or religious group that a new government has begun targeting. Extraordinary circumstances can include events or factors beyond your control that caused the late filing, such as a medical problem.

Also, informal USCIS policy is to not count the time you spend on a valid visa (as a student, for example) toward the one year. However, you must apply within a "reasonable time" of the visa's expiration—don't wait a whole year!

6. Alternate Remedies to Asylum: Withholding of Removal, U.N. Torture Convention

Even if you don't qualify for political asylum, you may, by showing that you'd be "more likely than not" to face persecution if returned to your country, qualify for a remedy called withholding of removal. This is a harder standard to meet than the standard for asylum, but it's useful in cases where, for example, you missed the one-year deadline for applying for asylum, or you've committed minor crimes that make you ineligible for asylum but not ineligible for withholding.

Withholding of removal isn't the best of remedies—it essentially means that although you won't be granted asylum or the right to later get a green card, you won't be removed from the U.S. and you'll be allowed to work while you're here. However, if you leave the U.S. on your own, you won't be permitted to return, because you'll have an order of removal in your file.

Another alternate remedy, for those who can show that it is more likely than not that they would be tortured if returned to their home country, is available under an international treaty called the U.N. Convention Against Torture. While you don't have to show that the persecution you experienced or fear is on account of one of the five protected grounds—race, religion, nationality, membership in a particular social group, or political opinion—these cases are not often granted, because it's hard to prove that you're more likely than not to face torture. Like withholding, however, it's helpful for people who missed the one-year asylum filing deadline, or have committed crimes—even serious crimes won't bar you from Torture Convention relief, though you may be kept in detention if you appear to be a danger to the United States.

You don't need to separately apply for these remedies—applying for political asylum on Form I-589 will automatically include them.

7. Numerical Limits on Refugees

Refugees (but not asylees) have an annual quota set each year by the U.S. president. The quota may vary by country.

The president also decides how the total will be divided among the various regions of the world, such as Latin America, Southeast Asia, Eastern Europe, and Africa. Recently, the annual quota has gone down to 70,000. However, even after setting the quota, the U.S. government makes no guarantees that it will allow this many people in—in fact, it admitted only around 42,000 refugees in the year 2006. Applications are approved on a first-come, first-served basis. It is not unusual for qualified refugees to end up on a waiting list.

The refugee quota cannot be accurately forecast, because the number of slots available each year changes. Some countries get many refugee numbers in a given year while others receive practically none. Refugee applications can take from several months to a year or more for approval.

8. Financial Sponsorship— Refugees

Your refugee application will not be approved unless you can show that you have a way to pay for your transportation to the U.S. and a means of support once you arrive. (This rule doesn't apply to asylum applicants, who are already in the U.S.) This is usually done by finding a financial sponsor, such as relatives already in the U.S. or a private charitable group such as a church or refugee assistance organization. Occasionally, the U.S. government itself allocates money for refugee assistance.

9. Alternate Refugee Entrance as Parolees

If you qualify for refugee status but the quota has been exhausted for the year, you may be permitted to come to the U.S.

as a parolee without a visa. Parolees are permitted to work and live indefinitely in the U.S., but their futures are less certain than those of refugees. Parolee status can be revoked at any time and does not lead to a green card. A parolee may apply for political asylum after arriving in the U.S., but there is no guarantee asylum will be granted.

A request for parole status must be made in writing to the USCIS central office in Washington, DC. Such applications are most likely to be approved if you will be joining family already in the U.S., or if you cannot remain temporarily in the country where you filed your refugee application. There is no special form to file in requesting parole status. The USCIS office that handles your refugee application can help you with the procedures.

10. Bringing Your Spouse and Children

If you are married or have children under the age of 21 and you get either refugee or political asylee status, your spouse and children can also be granted refugee or asylee status by providing proof of their family relationship to you. Accompanying relative status allows your family to live and work in the United States.

If you're a refugee traveling with your family, or an asylee whose family is already in the U.S. with you, simply including your family members' names and information on your application will be enough to get them granted refugee or asylee status along with you. If you are traveling separately from your spouse and children when you are granted refugee status, or they are outside the U.S. when you are granted asylum, you will need to submit a separate application to a USCIS Service Center asking that they be allowed to join you. This is done on Form I-730. See the USCIS website at www.uscis.gov for the form and more information.

E. How to Apply for Refugee Status

Anyone physically outside the U.S. who qualifies as a refugee may apply for refugee status at a USCIS office outside of the United States. These USCIS offices are not the same as U.S. embassies or consulates, although most are located within consulate or embassy buildings. There are very few of these foreign USCIS offices; not all countries have one.

You cannot apply for refugee status by mail. You must do so in person. In fact, USCIS will not accept your application for refugee status (on Form 1-590) until you have first been found eligible for a refugee interview. If you can make contact with the nearest UNHCR representative, this organization can help link you up with USCIS. Any U.S. consulate can help guide you to a USCIS office or contact person as well.

You may apply for refugee status at any USCIS office outside of the United States, provided you are physically able to remain in that location while your case is being processed. Since many refugees do not have passports, they may have difficulty gaining entry into a country where a USCIS office or contact person is located. Depending on what country you're in, you may need to start with an office of the U.S. Refugee Program (USRP) or the U.N. High Commissioner for Refugees (UNHCR). These offices may put you through an initial screening before you're allowed to file your application with USCIS.

You will also have to have a medical exam done by a doctor designated by USCIS. Procedures among USCIS offices vary, so you should call in advance to find out the policies of the office where you intend to apply. However, be prepared for a long wait—getting through all the bureaucratic requirements can take anywhere from two months to two years. USCIS has increased its attention to security checks, and this has resulted in a seemingly endless wait for some refugees.

1. Step One: Preparing and Submitting Your Refugee Application

It is common for refugee applicants to have fled their home countries hurriedly, without time to gather many personal documents. Frequently, refugees also have been denied passports by their home countries. Therefore, USCIS does not insist on any specific documentation to support a refugee application. You should provide some type of personal identification, however.

For each accompanying relative, you should bring documents proving their family relationship to you. You may verify a parent/child relationship using the child's long-form birth certificate. Many countries issue both short- and long-form birth certificates. Where both are available, the long-form is needed because it contains the names of the parents while the short form does not.

If you are accompanied by your spouse, you must show that you are lawfully married. This is best shown by a civil marriage certificate. If any of these documents are unavailable, the USCIS office may, at its own discretion, accept other kinds of proof, including notarized affidavits from you or other people familiar with your family situation.

Additionally, you must provide documents to support your claim of persecution in your home country. Again, due to the varied circumstances under which refugees flee persecution, USCIS requires no specific types of documents to prove this qualification. However, the burden is on you to show your eligibility. One important document proving persecution is your detailed sworn statement describing your fear and any past persecution. This statement should be in your own words and need not be in any special form.

Additional documents may include:
- newspaper articles describing the type of persecution you would

encounter if you returned to your home country
- affidavits from people who know of, or have personally experienced, similar persecution in your home country, and
- written human rights reports about your country supplied by organizations, such as Amnesty International or Human Rights Watch, or the U.S. State Department's *Country Reports*.

If the persecution is based on your membership in a particular social group, you must supply evidence that the group as a whole is experiencing persecution. You must also prove that you are a member of that group.

Finally, you must present documents showing you have a financial sponsor. If a relative is sponsoring you, the relative should fill out an Affidavit of Support, on USCIS Form I-134, available from www.uscis.gov. If you are being sponsored by an organization, the organization will supply you with a written sponsorship agreement.

Documenting your eligibility for refugee status can be extremely difficult. If, after reading this chapter, you believe you have a realistic chance of qualifying for refugee status, you may want to consider getting help with preparing your documents from one of the many refugee assistance organizations that exist both in the U.S. and abroad. Many of these organizations will help you without charge. Your church, mosque, or synagogue can show you how to find such an organization, or see www.asylumlaw.org.

Refugee Application Checklist

Use this checklist to help you assemble the needed forms and documents:

Forms

❏ Form I-590.

❏ Form G-325C.

Documents

❏ Personal identification for each applicant.

❏ Long-form birth certificate for you and each accompanying relative.

❏ Marriage certificate if you are married and bringing your spouse.

❏ If either you or your spouse have ever been married, copies of divorce and death certificates showing termination of all previous marriages.

❏ Personal sworn affidavit describing in detail your reasons for seeking refugee status.

❏ Newspaper articles describing the conditions of persecution in your home country.

❏ Affidavits from knowledgeable people describing the conditions of persecution in your home country.

❏ Written human-rights reports about your country supplied by organizations such as Amnesty International or the Americas Watch Committee, or the U.S. State Department's *Country Reports*.

❏ Documents showing you have a financial sponsor in the U.S., such as a completed Form I-134.

❏ Three photographs of you and three photographs of each accompanying relative.

❏ Medical examination report for each applicant.

---

2. Step Two: Attending Your Interview for Refugee Status

All refugee applications require personal interviews. Procedures vary from one USCIS office to the next, but usually you will be told the time and place of your interview through an appointment letter sent by mail. Immediately before the interview, you and your accompanying relatives must have medical examinations. The proce-

dures for these examinations will be explained in your appointment letter.

The exam itself involves the taking of a medical history, blood test, and chest X-ray, and proof of vaccination. Pregnant women may refuse to be X-rayed until after the pregnancy.

The main purpose of the medical exam is to verify that you are not medically inadmissible. The primary medical exclusions are HIV (AIDS) and tuberculosis. Some medical grounds of inadmissibility can be overcome with treatment. (See Chapter 3 for more details.) If you need a medical waiver, you will be given complete instructions by USCIS at the time of your interview.

After the medical exam, you and your accompanying relatives will report to the USCIS office for the interview. Your application will be reviewed, information verified, and you will be questioned in detail about your claim of persecution in your home country.

If your application is approved, you will be issued what is known as a travel document. This document will allow you to enter the U.S. as a refugee. You must enter the U.S. within four months after the date your application was approved, or you will lose your refugee status.

3. Submitting an Appeal When Refugee Status Is Denied

When a USCIS office outside of the U.S denies a refugee application, there is no formal appeal available, although you are free to reapply as often as you like. When your application is denied, the reasons will be explained. The most common reason is failure to show that you have been either subject to persecution or have a reasonable fear of being persecuted if you remain in your home country. Sometimes presenting more evidence on an unclear fact can bring about a better result.

If the USCIS office still refuses to approve your refugee application, your chances for further appeals are severely limited. There is no right to appeal through the U.S. courts and there is no formal appeal procedure through any U.S. government agency.

4. Entering the U.S. After Refugee Status Is Granted

On entering the U.S. as a refugee, you will be met at the border by an officer of Customs and Border Protection (CBP). The officer will examine your paperwork and ask you some questions to make sure everything is in order. Assuming you're approved for entry, the officer will give you an I-94 card. (This is a portion of the form you are asked to fill out when you arrive.) It will be stamped with a date showing for how long your refugee status has been approved. It will also state that you are authorized to work in the United States. Normally, you are granted refugee status for one year, after which you can apply for a green card.

F. How to Apply for Political Asylum

If you are physically present in the U.S. in either legal or undocumented status, and you are otherwise qualified, you may apply for political asylum. If you are not presently in removal proceedings, you must submit your application by mail to a USCIS regional service center. You will then be called in for an interview, and you will receive a decision in writing a few weeks later. (See Section 2, below.)

If your case is denied, unless you are in valid status at the time, you will end up in removal proceedings. This means that you will be "referred" to an immigration judge. If you are already in removal proceedings, your application must be filed with the court and immigration judge presiding over your case, and you should seek a lawyer's help.

Earning money to afford a lawyer will be difficult. You cannot apply for work authorization until either your asylum request has been approved or your application has been pending for five months (150 days) without a decision.

1. Step One: Preparing and Submitting Your Asylum Application

Your application for political asylum will consist of Form I-589 and documents, as indicated on the checklist below. You must file the application in triplicate (three copies), by mail, at a USCIS regional service center. There is no filing fee. The proper regional service center address for filing asylum cases is given on the USCIS website.

The regional service center will initially review your application to determine whether any legal prohibition prevents your application being approved, such as a serious criminal conviction, or an indication that you have persecuted others. (If

that is the case, your application will be denied quickly and you will be placed in deportation (removal) proceedings.)

Assuming you pass that hurdle, you will later receive an appointment to have your fingerprints taken. These will be used to check your police and immigration record.

New Rules for Asylum Applicants

In our post-9/11 world, Congress has been concerned that terrorists could use our asylum application process to gain a "safe harbor" in the United States. In response to this and other concerns, Congress passed the REAL ID Act of 2005. Among other things, REAL ID:

- requires asylum applicants to prove at least one of the central motives of their persecutors
- obliges asylees to at least attempt to obtain corroborating evidence of their persecution, and
- allows judges to take into account the asylees' demeanor when testifying about their experiences, as well as their statements not made under oath, when making their decisions.

Many immigration advocates believe these changes will make asylum much harder to obtain in the future. However, it remains to be seen how REAL ID will truly affect our asylum process.

Requesting Asylum at a U.S. Border, Airport, or Other Entry Point

If you can get a U.S. visa, such as a tourist visa, you can apply for political asylum when you arrive, by telling the inspections officer that you fear returning to your country and wish to apply for asylum. However, it's best not to mention this unless the officer is acting like he or she doesn't plan to let you into the U.S. anyway. If you start the application process now, you'll have very little time in which to find a lawyer or prepare.

In fact, someone requesting entry to the U.S. can be quickly found inadmissible and deported for five years. This can happen if an inspector believes that you are making a misrepresentation (committing fraud), or misrepresented the truth when you got your visa, or if you do not have the proper travel or visa documents at the time you request entry. This quick deportation procedure is known as "summary exclusion." It can be applied to everyone except people entering the United States under the Visa Waiver Program (according to a 1999 decision by the Board of Immigration Appeals).

There is an exception to the summary exclusion process for people who fear persecution and request asylum.

So, even if you do not have the proper documents or you have made a misrepresentation, you could still be allowed to enter the U.S. if you make clear that your reason is to apply for asylum and you can show that you'd be likely to win asylum.

After you have said you want to apply for asylum, you'll immediately be given a "credible fear" interview by an asylum officer. The purpose of this interview is to make sure you have a significant possibility of winning your case. Most importantly, the officer will want to be sure that your request is based on a fear of persecution as described earlier in this section. This interview is supposed to be scheduled quickly, within one or two days, but it has been taking longer.

If the officer isn't convinced of your fear, you must request a hearing before an immigration judge, or you will be deported for five years. The judge must hold the hearing within seven days in person or by telephone.

If the judge finds that you have a credible fear of persecution, you'll be scheduled for a full hearing, and should seek an attorney. This proceeding will progress much like a normal asylum proceeding as described in this chapter (except that it will be in court, which we don't cover). Most asylum applicants are held in detention at this point, although you can and should request release. If you fail the credible fear test before the immigration judge, you will be deported.

Asylum Application Checklist

Forms (original and two copies)

❑ Form I-589.

❑ Form G-325A for you and each accompanying relative over the age of 14.

Documents (three copies)

❑ Copies of personal identification (such as a passport or birth certificate) for you and each accompanying relative.

❑ Copies of all immigration documents, such as I-94 cards.

❑ Copy of long-form birth certificate for you and each accompanying relative.

❑ Copy of marriage certificate if your spouse is included in your application.

❑ If either you or your spouse have ever been married, copies of divorce and death certificates showing termination of all previous marriages.

❑ Personal sworn affidavit describing in detail your reasons for seeking political asylum.

❑ Newspaper articles describing the conditions of persecution in your home country.

❑ Affidavits from knowledgeable people describing the conditions of persecution in your home country.

❑ Written human rights reports about your country supplied by organizations, such as Amnesty International or Human Rights Watch, or the U.S. State Department's *Country Reports*.

❑ Color passport photos—one of you, one of your spouse, and one of each of your children, with the person's name (and A number, if any) written in pencil on the back.

a. Filling Out Form I-589

Be sure to answer all questions on Form I-589 as fully as possible. USCIS or an immigration judge will closely review your answers for inconsistencies and will be doubtful about new information that arises during an interview or hearing unless you can show good reasons why such information was not initially included in your written application. If there isn't enough space to answer a question on the form, write "see attached sheet."

Then prepare your own statement—as lengthy as you want.

The statement should be in your own words and be reasonably detailed (though not so detailed that you'll get confused in retelling it at your interview). For example, USCIS will not be convinced if you say only "I was persecuted by the government and am afraid to go back." But an applicant who explains that "I was tortured by the local security forces after I joined the union and am terrified that if I go back they'll kill me in the same way they killed many other union members" has a much better chance. (And this is only the beginning —this applicant, for example, should include a history of his union involvement, a description of the torture, and an account of what happened to other union members.)

Part A Section I.

Questions 1-2. Question 1 asks for your Alien Registration Number or "A #." Normally, you will not have an A-number unless you have previously applied for a green card, were paroled into the U.S., or are already in removal (deportation) proceedings. And you won't have a Social Security Number unless you've been in the U.S. with the right to work, and applied for one. If you do not have these numbers, leave the questions blank.

Questions 3-12. These questions are self-explanatory.

Question 13. This question asks for your nationality. If you are stateless, say how you became stateless. You are not stateless unless your nationality has been taken away from you and you have no legal right to live in any country. The fact that you might be arrested if you return to your home country does not make you stateless.

Questions 14-16. These are self-explanatory. Be sure that this information is consistent with your asylum claim; if you are claiming persecution based on your religion, race, or nationality, this section should reflect that fact.

Question 17. Check the box ("a," "b," or "c") to indicate whether you have ever been before an immigration judge.

Question 18. Box "b" asks for your I-94 number, which is the number on the white or green entry card you received if you entered the U.S. legally, at a border, airport, or seaport.

Questions 19-24. Self-explanatory.

Part A Section II.

This section asks for information about your family members. Mention all of them, whether or not they are applying for asylum. Be aware that you must be legally married to your current spouse for him or her to be granted asylum under your application. Your children will be given asylum along with you only if they are unmarried and under 21 years old at the time of the asylum grant.

Part A Section III.

If your prior address was in a third country (not your home country) for an extended period of time, you will be required to show that you were not firmly resettled—that is, you were not granted permanent residence or otherwise entitled to substantial benefits and privileges in that country.

Part B.

Question 1. This question asks what basis you are seeking asylum on—that is, why your persecutor was motivated to single you out. In the top part of Question 1, you can check more than one box. If the first four boxes (race, religion, nationality, political opinion) don't seem to fit—for example, you're disabled or HIV positive, a female subject to female genital cutting, or a member of a non-political club—your best choice may be "particular social group." Try to avoid checking nothing but the Torture Convention box—this means that you won't actually be applying for political asylum, but only to be spared from removal (deportation) for awhile.

For Questions A and B, your answers should be "yes," otherwise you don't qualify for asylum. Instead of trying to fit your answer into the spaces on the form, it is best to put down "see my attached affidavit" and write your entire response on a separate sheet of paper (with your name at the top to avoid the possibility of part of your answer getting misplaced).

Question B is intended to find out what you think will happen to you if you return to your home country. Be as specific as you can, explaining how you will be arrested, tried by the military, sentenced to jail, put to death, or whatever consequence you might suffer. You should also write "See my attached affidavit and supporting documentation" (and then give more details in your affidavit).

Question 2. This question asks whether you have been accused, charged, arrested, detained, interrogated, convicted, sentenced, or imprisoned in any country.

Your answer to this question can help your case if the action against you was a violation of your human rights, for example if you were arrested and beaten for taking part in a lawful, nonviolent protest march. However, your answer can hurt your case if it shows that you are a criminal and the government was merely taking appropriate, lawful action against you.

Question 3. This question asks about your and your family's involvement in organizations and groups, such as political parties, guerrilla groups, labor unions, and paramilitary organizations. It is very helpful to your claim if you can identify some group to which you belong. To succeed in your claim for asylum, you must have been persecuted for a reason—and that reason must be your connection with some identifiable group. However, if you identify yourself with a group that is known to commit acts of terrorism or persecute others, then your asylum application will likely be denied.

You must identify a group of which you are a member. If your persecution wasn't because of your race, religion, nationality, or political opinion, you must define a "particular social group" of which you are a member. Describe the group as specifically as possible, such as "women who refuse to wear the veil," "people who have the HIV virus," "people with olive-colored skin," or "people who live on the poor side of town." It should be a group whose history of experiencing discrimination or persecution you can explain and document.

Question 4. This question asks whether you fear being tortured in your home country. The answer may be based on what happened to you in the past or what is happening to persons who are in similar circumstances.

Part C.

Questions 1-2. These questions request information about any prior asylum applications and whether you were firmly resettled in another country before coming to the United States. If you answer "yes" to any of these questions, consult with an asylum expert or attorney before filing your Form I-589.

Questions 3-6. If you answer "yes," consult with an asylum expert or attorney before filing your Form I-589, as one or more of your family members may be ineligible for asylum.

With regard to Question 5, see the discussion of the time limits that apply to application for asylum, above. If you answer "yes" to this question, you are ineligible for asylum unless you fall under one of the exceptions discussed above.

Parts D and E.

This section requests your signature and information about the person who prepared the application. Keep in mind that a person who files a fraudulent application may be subject to criminal penalties and barred from getting any applications or benefits approved by USCIS and will probably be deported. There are also criminal penalties for failure to disclose one's role in helping to prepare and/or submit an application which contains false information. Finally, USCIS may use the information on the application to deport you, if you are not granted asylum.

Parts F and G.

Leave these blank for now.

b. Creating and Collecting Documents to Accompany Form I-589

It is common for asylum applicants to have fled their home countries hurriedly, without time to gather many personal documents. Frequently, asylees also have been denied passports. Therefore, USCIS does not insist upon any specific documentation to support asylum applications. Some type of personal identification should be provided, however. If you entered the U.S. legally, you should present copies of your I-94 card and passport.

For each accompanying relative (spouse or unmarried children under age 21), provide copies of documents showing their family relationship to you. You may prove a parent/child relationship by presenting the child's long-form birth certificate. Many countries issue both short- and long-form birth certificates. Where both are available, the long-form is needed, because it contains the names of the parents while the short-form does not. If you are accompanied by your spouse, you must prove that you are lawfully married. This is best shown by a civil marriage certificate. If any of these documents are unavailable, the

Applying for a Work Permit If 150 Days Go by With No Decision

If, after submitting your asylum application, you receive no decision on your case within five months, you're in luck—you can apply for a work permit. However, USCIS works very hard to make sure you don't wait this long. Nevertheless, you should keep track of the days, because occasionally they don't meet their goal.

If you are able to apply for a work permit, fill out Form I-765 according to the instructions that come with the form. There will be no fee for your first work permit. Answer Question 16 "(c)(8)."

With your I-765 form, you'll need to enclose evidence that your asylum application was filed with USCIS (its receipt notice is best) and evidence that USCIS has made no decision on your application yet. Also, send a copy of the front and back of your I-94 card and two photos (the usual passport style). On the back of the photos, write your name and A number in pencil.

Send your work permit application to the USCIS service center indicated in the instructions or on the USCIS website (www.uscis.gov).

Additionally, you must provide documents to support your claim of persecution by the government of your home country. The burden is on you to prove your eligibility. One document proving fear of persecution is your own sworn statement explaining your persecution or fear of persecution. The statement should be in your own words and need not be in any special form—though at the end, above your signature, it's best to add the words "I swear that the foregoing is true and correct to the best of my knowledge." Additional documents may include:

- newspaper articles describing the type of persecution you would encounter if you returned to your home country
- affidavits from other people, preferably experts or people in positions of authority, who know you personally or have personally experienced similar persecution in your home country, and
- written human rights reports about your country supplied by organizations, such as Amnesty International, or Human Rights Watch, or the U.S. State Department's *Country Reports*.

If the persecution is based on your membership in a particular social group, you must not only supply evidence that the group is experiencing persecution, but also you must offer proof that you are a member of that group.

USCIS office may, at its discretion, accept other kinds of proof, including notarized affidavits from you or other people familiar with your family situation.

2. Step Two: Attending Your Asylum Interview

Assuming your application is not summarily denied by the service center, you will be asked to come to an asylum office for a personal interview. Asylum interviews are conducted at only a few locations, so you may be required to travel for the interview. You will receive notice of the time of your interview in the mail. Some applications for political asylum are sent by USCIS for review to the U.S. Department of State, which makes a recommendation on the application.

You can't choose the asylum officer who will interview you. However, if you're a woman, and your persecution involved experiences that you would feel uncomfortable describing in front of a man, you can ask to be interviewed by a female officer.

Expect the interview to last about a half hour. If you don't speak English, you must bring an interpreter with you. The officer will start by asking you to raise your right hand and swear to tell the truth. Then he or she will go over some of the basic information in your application.

Eventually, the officer will ask you to describe the persecution that you experienced, or the basis of your fear of persecution. Some officers may ask you a general question and invite you to talk at length, others may ask more specific questions based on the statement you submitted with your application. These officers are highly trained regarding the conditions in your country, and will also be asking questions to test whether you match their other knowledge about the country or its citizens, or whether you are who you say you are. For example, if you claim to be from a certain religious minority, the officer might ask you to describe in detail certain rituals done within that religion.

A few weeks after the interview, you'll have to return to the Asylum Office to get your decision. A clerk at the front desk will tell you the decision on your application in person and give you a written document confirming it.

3. If Your Asylum Is Approved

Once you've been granted asylum, whether by the USCIS Asylum Office or by an immigration judge, you'll be given a small card, called an I-94, that proves your status and should be kept with your passport. (Make a copy for your records, too, and keep it in a safe place.) With your I-94, you can obtain a Social Security number and driver's license, which is more than enough to show an employer that you have a right to work. If you wish, however, you can also apply for an employment authorization card, by mailing Form I-765 to the USCIS Nebraska Service Center. You'll find the form and instructions on the USCIS website. Answer Question 16 with "(a)(5)." There is no fee for your first work permit, but a $340 fee for renewals.

Protect your asylee status. Although there is no limit on how long you can stay in the United States as an asylee, your rights can be taken away, for example if conditions in your home country get better or you commit a crime. Plan to submit an application for a green card as soon as you can (exactly one year from your asylum approval date). And don't travel outside the United States without first getting a "refugee travel document" (which you apply for on Form I-131; the form and instructions are at www.uscis.gov). And whatever you do, *don't travel to your home country*—USCIS may see that as a sign that you don't really fear returning there, and deny you reentry to the U.S. after your trip, or later deny your application for a green card. (If your spouse or children got asylum based on your application, however, they can ordinarily travel to your home country without fear of being barred from returning to the U.S. But be cautious, particularly if, in your application, you claimed that they were a target as well.)

Did you leave a husband, wife, or child (unmarried, under age 21) in your home country when you fled to the United States? If so, that person may now be eligible to join you as a fellow asylee. This works only if you were married, or were the child's parent, before leaving your country. In other words, you can't now get married or adopt a child and apply to bring them here. To apply, fill out a separate Form I-730 for each person coming—it's available at www.uscis.gov. Also be aware that your family members

can be denied entry if they've committed serious nonpolitical crimes, been affiliated with terrorism, or otherwise violated other provisions of the immigration laws at I.N.A. § 208(b)(2), or 8 U.S.C. § 1158.

4. If Your Asylum Application Is Denied

If, after your interview, the officer expects to deny your asylum application, he or she may, in rare cases, send you a written notice by mail warning you and explaining the reasons. In that case, you have an opportunity to send the asylum officer additional materials or a personal statement to try to overcome his or her doubts.

More often, you'll simply receive your denial when you go to pick up your decision after your interview. You will be given what's called a Notice to Appear (NTA), which is the start of a removal proceeding. Such proceedings take place in immigration court, where your application may be considered again by an immigration judge. You can (and should) bring an immigration lawyer, who will help you fully present your story orally before the judge.

If your application is then turned down by the immigration judge, you may file an appeal with the Board of Immigration Appeals, in Washington, DC. If that appeal is unsuccessful, you may have your case reviewed in a U.S. Circuit Court of Appeals. You should not attempt such appeals without the assistance of an experienced immigration lawyer, because you are in serious danger of being deported.

G. How to Get a Green Card as a Refugee or Asylee

Refugees who get their statuses before entering the U.S. are entitled to apply for green cards one year or more after arriving in the United States. Political asylees are also eligible to apply for green cards one year or more after their asylee status is granted. You will not receive a notice to come in for a green card interview. You will have to keep track on your own of when you are eligible to apply, then assemble and submit your application.

It's worth applying for your green card as soon as you can. For one thing, if the conditions supporting your claim to asylum status end before you are approved for a green card, you may never receive a green card and you may have to leave the United States.

 The sooner you get your green card, the sooner you can apply for U.S. citizenship. Since citizenship is the most secure status the U.S. can offer, it's worth applying as soon as you're eligible.

The process of applying for your green card—that is, adjusting your status to permanent resident—involves preparing a set of forms and documents (a separate set for you and each of your accompanying spouse and children), mailing these to a USCIS service center, waiting for some weeks or months until you're called in to have your fingerprints taken, and then waiting a few weeks or months longer until you're called in for your final green card interview at a local USCIS office (not the one to which you sent your application). You should be approved for your green card at or soon after the interview. See Chapter 4 for information on tracking the progress of your application at the service center and at your local office.

As part of your adjustment of status application, you and your family members may apply for permission to work (an Employment Authorization Document or EAD). If you already have a work permit, you can renew it, when necessary, with the office processing your adjustment application.

Security checks are a likely cause of delays. As part of your adjustment of status application, the FBI must run both a fingerprint check and a name check on you, and the CIA must run a separate name check. These name checks tend to take several weeks, especially because many applicants have similar names. If you've been informed that your case is stalled due to security checks, get the name of a person you can keep in touch with for updates, or hire a lawyer to help with this task.

1. Step One: Preparing Your Adjustment of Status Application

The basic form used in the U.S. adjustment of status application is Form I-485, Application for Permanent Residence. However, a handful of other forms as well as documents must be prepared to accompany this main one.

An easy way to get all these forms is to call the USCIS forms line at 800-870-3676 and ask for the Adjustment of Status Packet (but throw out the Form I-864 Affidavit of Support—you won't need it). Or, you can obtain the forms online at www.uscis.gov. (Click "Immigration Forms," and scroll down and select the forms you need based on the checklist below.)

The following checklist will help you assemble and keep track of the appropriate forms and documents. A complete set must also be prepared for your spouse and for your children if they're in the U.S. and were also granted asylum or refugee status at least a year ago.

Dealing With Delays in Approval of Your Work Authorization

If you want to work before your application for a green card is approved, and don't have an existing work permit, you must file a separate application for employment authorization. To do so, fill out Form I-765 and file it with the Nebraska Service Center (which you can do together with your adjustment of status application). To accompany Form I-765, submit a copy of your I-94 card and pay a separate filing fee. Be sure to keep the fee receipt that USCIS gives you, so you can prove that the I-765 was filed.

Legally, USCIS does not have to make a decision on your employment authorization application for up to 90 days. If for some reason you are not given a decision within 90 days, you have a legal right to be granted an interim employment authorization that will last 240 days. Unfortunately, claiming this right has recently become impossible. The idea used to be that you could go to your local USCIS office and apply for the interim EAD, which the local office could quickly produce. However, USCIS declared in an April 2006 memo that local offices would no longer do this—at best, they'll contact the service center for you to find out why your EAD has been delayed. Lawsuits were being filed against USCIS at the time this book went to print. In the meantime, you may need an attorney's help if your EAD approval has been delayed.

If you receive an interim EAD, but 240 days pass and you still have not received a final decision on the I-765, you must stop working. Interim work authorization cards cannot be renewed. However, if you reach this point, you have the option to file a new I-765 application. If you do not get a decision on the new application within 90 days, you will then be entitled to another interim work authorization card.

Checklist for Adjustment of Status Application

Forms

❑ Form I-485.

❑ Form G-325A (but you need not file a G-325A for any child under the age of 14).

❑ Form I-765 (optional, if you want a work permit; include a separate filing fee, currently $340).

❑ I-131, Application for Travel Document (Advance Parole), for use if you think you'll need to travel outside the United States while your application is processed without abandoning your application. This also requires a separate filing fee, currently $305. *Do not travel to the country from which you gained asylum or refugee status, or you will lose your right to this status.*

Documents

❑ Copy of your I-94 card, showing approval of your asylum or refugee status; alternately, asylees can submit their approval letter and refugees can submit a copy of their work permit card.

❑ Copy of a long-form birth certificate for you and each accompanying relative. If this is in another language, it must be accompanied by a full English translation.

❑ Evidence that you've been physically present in the U.S. for one year. USCIS asks that you submit only a few of these documents, and choose ones that cover broad periods of time, such as a letter of employment, a lease, school enrollment records, or similar documentation.

❑ Proof of any absences from the U.S. since you have been granted asylum or entered as a refugee. For example: photocopies of pages in a refugee travel document or passport. (These absences subtract from your one year, so do the math and make sure you don't submit your adjustment of status application early.)

❑ A medical exam report done by a USCIS-approved doctor on Form I-693, in a sealed envelope.

❑ Marriage certificate if you are married and bringing your spouse.

❑ If either you or your spouse has been previously married, copies of divorce and death certificates showing termination of all previous marriages.

❑ Two photographs of you and two photographs of each accompanying relative in U.S. passport style (it's best to have a professional do these). Write your name and A number in pencil on the back of each photo.

❑ Filing fee for Form I-485 (asylees only, not refugees). Currently $1,010 for applicants between ages 14 and 79, $930 for applicants age 79 and over, or under age 14 and not filing with a parent, and $600 for applicants under age 14 who are filing with a parent. Checks and money orders are accepted, but we advise against sending cash through the mail. Double check all fees at www.uscis.gov.

Read This If You Plan to Leave the U.S. Before Your Adjustment Interview

Once your application for adjustment of status has been filed, you must not leave the U.S. for any reason before you have applied for and received advance permission to reenter the U.S. (Advance Parole). Any absence without this permission will be viewed as a termination of your application for a green card—which means that, upon return, you will be told that your green card application is dead and you have no right to enter the United States.

Many people simply apply for Advance Parole at the same time they apply to adjust status, just in case. Or, you can wait until you're sure you have to leave, and apply at the same service center where you sent your adjustment of status application—but you're taking a risk this way, because USCIS may take many weeks to approve your Advance Parole application.

Your application for Advance Parole should include Form I-131, together with the filing fee, three passport-type photographs, a copy of your adjustment of status filing receipt (if you've already sent in that application), and a short explanation of why you want to leave—you will need a bona fide personal or business reason, though it need not be an emergency.

If approved, you will be allowed to leave the U.S. and return again with no break in the processing of your application. *However, be sure not to return to the country from which you're claiming to have fled persecution, or you could lose your asylee or refugee status.*

Form I-485: This is the main form you'll fill out, and needs a bit more explanation.

Part 1. Part 1 asks for general information about when and where you were born, your present address, and your immigration status. It also asks for an A number. Everyone who enters the U.S. as a refugee or has applied for political asylum is given an A number.

Part 2. Mark Box "d" if you're an asylee; Box "h" if you're a refugee, and write "refugee" on the accompanying line.

Part 3. The questions in Sections A through C are self-explanatory. If you didn't use a visa to enter the U.S., write "N/A" for the related questions. The questions in Section C are meant to identify people who are inadmissible. With the exception of certain memberships in the Communist Party or terrorist organizations, you will not be deemed inadmissible simply because you joined an organization. However, if your answer to any of the other questions is "yes," you may be inadmissible. (See Chapter

3, which is intended to help you identify and overcome such obstacles.)

 What if you plan to travel, but your home country will not issue you a passport? You can apply to USCIS for what's called a Refugee Travel Document, which serves the same function as a passport. This is done using USCIS Form I-131 (the same form as you'd use to apply for Advance Parole), available with instructions on the USCIS website.

Medical exam. You and your accompanying relatives will be required to submit medical examination reports. You must take Form I-693 to a USCIS-authorized physician or medical clinic. Your local US-CIS office will give you the form and a list of approved physicians in your area, or you can call 800-375-5283 and write down the doctors' names by hand (quickly!).

The fees are around $150 per exam, depending on the doctor. The exam itself involves taking a medical history, blood test, chest X-ray, and vaccinations, if required. Pregnant women can refuse to be X-rayed until after the pregnancy. The vaccination requirement may be waived for religious, moral, or medical reasons.

 Some refugees (not asylees) can skip most of the exam. If you had an exam overseas, and are applying no more than one year after arriving in the U.S., all you need is a vaccination "Supplemental Form to I-693," also completed by a USCIS-designated doctor. The exception is if medi-cal grounds of inadmissibility were noted when you entered the United States.

After completion of the medical exam, and upon obtaining the test results, the doctor will give you the report in a sealed envelope. Do not open the envelope!

The main purpose of the medical exam is to verify that you are not medically inadmissible. The primary medical grounds of inadmissibility are tuberculosis and HIV (AIDS). Some medical grounds of inadmissibility can be overcome with treatment or by applying for a waiver (See Chapter 3 for details.)

As a refugee or asylum applicant, you'll need to mail your application, consisting of both forms and documents, to a USCIS service center. However, you'll need to check www.uscis.gov for the latest address; filing procedures were being changed when this book went to print. The P.O. box may differ slightly depending on whether you're a refugee or an asylee, as follows:

U.S. Department of Homeland Security
U.S. Citizenship and Immigration
   Services
Nebraska Service Center
P.O. Box [87209 for refugees, 87485
   for asylees]
Lincoln, NE [68501-7209 for refugees,
   68501-7485 for asylees]

After filing your adjustment of status application, you will receive a receipt notice. If USCIS requires additional evidence or information, it will send you a Request for Evidence (I-797). You will also receive, after some weeks or months, a notice advising you where to go to have your fingerprints taken. These will then be used to check whether you have any history of arrests (whether by the police, FBI, DHS, or other authority).

2. Step Two: Attending Your Adjustment of Status Interview

You will be called in for a personal interview, which will be held at a USCIS office near you. USCIS will send you and your accompanying relatives an appointment notice, usually about two weeks in advance of the interview. If you have an attorney, he or she may come with you to the interview. (Even if you don't have an attorney, you could consult with or hire one at this point.)

Be prepared to explain at your interview why you still fear returning to the country from which you fled. If you no longer fear returning there, you do not qualify for your asylee or refugee status, and therefore do not qualify for the green card. If any dramatic changes have occurred to supposedly improve conditions in your country—such as a regime change or peace treaty—you'll have some extra explaining to do. If possible, supply supporting documents under such circumstances. If you don't already have an attorney, this would be a good time to hire one.

The checklist below will help you prepare for your interview. Prepare all these items for yourself and your family members.

Checklist of Documents to Bring to Your Adjustment Interview

❑ A complete photocopy of your green card application. This is for your use—you may want to follow along as the officer asks you questions about the material you filled out on the forms, or you may find that the officer is missing something that you have.

❑ Photo identification or passport for you and every one of your family members. (It's best to bring your passport or Refugee Travel Document, because if you are approved for your green card on the day of the interview, USCIS can place a stamp in your passport demonstrating this—and you can use this stamp as proof when you work or travel.)

❑ Originals of all documents that you made copies of for submission with your application. For example, if you submitted a photocopy of a birth certificate or other official document, a USCIS officer may want to examine the original.

❑ Any documents received from USCIS or other immigration authorities. For example, if you left the country on Advance Parole, bring this permit.

❑ Any updates to the material in your application. For example, if you have given birth to another child, bring the birth certificate. If you've been arrested, bring a full explanation (and consult with an attorney, to make sure that the arrest doesn't make you inadmissible).

See Chapter 4 for detailed information on what expect during your adjustment of status interview—and what to do if your adjustment of status application is denied. Also, for information on how to protect your status as a green card holder after you're approved, see Chapter 14.

 Even after you get your green card, try not to return to your home country. Family emergencies are usually an acceptable reason to go, but making casual trips may cause the immigration authorities to reexamine your asylum application. They may decide that you are not really afraid to return there, and that your asylum application was therefore fraudulent—which could lead to cancellation of your green card. ■

After Your Approval for a Green Card

I f you're reading this after becoming a permanent or conditional resident, congratulations! But don't stop reading. This chapter will give you some important tips on how to protect and enjoy your new status.

A. How to Prove You're a U.S. Resident

Whether you came through a consulate outside the U.S. or applied for adjustment of status in the U.S., you won't get an actual green card right away. Until the card arrives, a temporary stamp in your passport will serve as evidence of your permanent resident status (or, for newly married or investor applicants, your conditional resident status). You can show this stamp to employers or use it to travel in and out of the United States.

You may have to wait several months for the actual green card. If you're over the age of 18, the law requires you to carry your green card or other evidence of your status at all times. But keep a photocopy of it in a safe place, in case it's lost or stolen—this will make it much easier to get a replacement card from USCIS.

If you applied to adjust status at a USCIS office in the States and were not approved in person, you'll receive a letter from USCIS. Unfortunately, this letter is rather unclear at first sight. Many immigrants who receive it don't understand what it means, and a few

have tossed it in the trash. This letter, however, is the official notice of approval for residency. A sample is shown below. When you receive it, make a copy for your records and take it with your passport to your local USCIS office, where they'll stamp your passport to show that you're a resident.

Don't let your passport stamp expire. The temporary stamp in your passport may expire before you get your green card. This doesn't mean you've lost your legal right to live in the United States, but it can be very inconvenient if you're working or you're traveling abroad. If you see that the stamp is about to expire, go to your local USCIS office for another stamp. They probably won't be able to tell you when your card will arrive, since the card is being manufactured in a USCIS factory elsewhere, but they can give you a form with which to make an inquiry.

B. Traveling Abroad

There's no question about it—travel outside the United States is one of your rights as a conditional or permanent resident. But don't stay away too long. As the term "resident" suggests, you are expected to reside—that is, make your home—in the United States. If you make your home outside the United States, you could lose your green card.

Border officers have the power to decide whether returning green card

Sample Notice of Action

Department of Homeland Security U.S. Citizenship and Immigration Services	**I-797, Notice of Action**

THE UNITED STATES OF AMERICA

RECEIPT NUMBER		CASE TYPE	
MSC07-010-33333		I485 APPLICATION TO ADJUST TO PERMANENT RESIDENT STATUS	
RECEIPT DATE October 12, 2006	**PRIORITY DATE**	**PETITIONER** A096 944-222 BOONMEE, LAWAN	
NOTICE DATE January 23, 2007	**PAGE** 1 of 1	**BENEFICIARY**	

ILONA BRAY 950 PARKER STREET BERKELEY, CA 94710	**Notice Type:** Approval Notice **Section:** Adjustment as direct beneficiary of immigrant petition COA: CR6

The above petition has been approved. We have sent the original visa petition to the Department of State National Visa Center (NVC), 32 Rochester Avenue, Portsmouth, NH 03801-2909. The INS has completed all action; further inquiries should be directed to the NVC.

The NVC now processes all approved fiance(e) petitions. The NVC processing should be complete within two to four weeks after receiving the petition from INS. The NVC will create a case record with your petition information. NVC will then send the petition to the U.S. Embassy or Consulate where your fiance(e) will be interviewed for his or her visa.

You will receive notification by mail when NVC has sent your petition to the U.S. Embassy or Consulate. The notification letter will provide you with a unique number for your case and the name and address of the U.S. Embassy or Consulate where your petition has been sent.

If it has been more than four weeks since you received this approval notice and you have not received notification from NVC that your petition has been forwarded overseas, please call NVC at (603) 334-0700. Please call between 8:00am-6:45pm Eastern Standard Time. You will need to enter the INS receipt number from this approval notice into the automated response system to receive information on your petition.

THIS FORM IS NOT A VISA NOR MAY IT BE USED IN PLACE OF A VISA.

Please see the additional information on the back. You will be notified separately about any other cases you filed.
U.S. CITIZENSHIP & IMMIGRATION SVC
CALIFORNIA SERVICE CENTER
P. O. BOX 30111
LAGUNA NIGUEL CA 92607-0111
Customer Service Telephone: (800) 375-5283

Form I-797 (Rev. 01/31/05) N

Applying for a Social Security Number

With your U.S. residency, you are eligible for a Social Security number. This is a number given to all people legally living and working in the United States, to identify them and allow them to pay into a system of retirement insurance. You may have already applied for a Social Security number if you received a work permit before getting your green card. If not, now is the time to apply. You'll need this number before you start work— your new employer will ask for it in order to file taxes on your behalf.

To apply for your number, visit your local Social Security office. You can find it in your phone book within the federal government pages (usually blue) or on the Social Security Administration's website at www.ssa.gov.

holders are living outside the country. The officer will ask when you left the United States, what you were doing while you were away, and where you make your home. Being away for longer than six months will raise suspicion; being away for more than a year guarantees that you will have to attend an Immigration Court hearing before you can reclaim your U.S. residency and green card.

Before deciding whether you have abandoned your residency, the border officer will look at other factors besides the length of time you were away. The officer may note whether you:

- pay U.S. taxes
- own a home or apartment or have a long-term lease in the United States
- were employed in the foreign country
- took your family to the foreign country
- are returning to the U.S. with a one-way ticket or a round-trip ticket back to the foreign country, and
- maintained other ties with the United States.

If you're coming back after a trip of several months, you can make your entry to the United States easier by bringing copies of documents that show that your home base is still in the United States. These documents could include your U.S. tax returns, home lease, evidence of employment, or other relevant documents.

Many immigrants mistakenly believe that to keep your green card, all you need to do is enter the U.S. at least once a year. The fact is that if you ever leave with the intention of making some other country your permanent home, you give up your U.S. residency when you go.

Get permission before leaving. If you know in advance that you're going to have to spend more than a year outside the United States, you can apply for a reentry permit. Use Form I-131, Application for Travel Document, available at your local USCIS district office or on the USCIS website at www.uscis.gov. You will want to check Box "a" in Part 2 for reentry permits. You will have to explain to USCIS the purpose of your trip and how much time you've already spent outside the United States. Make sure to submit this form before you leave the United States. You can either submit the whole packet by mail to USCIS Nebraska Service Center, P.O. Box 87131, Lincoln, NE 68501-7131; or submit the application form and fee online through the USCIS website. If you choose this online, "E-Filing" option, however, you will still have to submit the remainder of your documents (such as a copy of your green card) by mail, to an address that you'll get in your confirmation receipt. Reentry permits cannot be renewed, and can be applied for only inside the United States. Therefore, if you need a second reentry permit, you must return briefly and apply for it.

If you stay outside the U.S. for more than one year and do not get a reentry permit before leaving, then in order to come back again, you must apply at a U.S. consulate abroad for a special immigrant visa as a returning resident. To get this visa you will have to convince the consular officer that your absence from the U.S. has been temporary and you never planned to abandon your U.S. residence. You will have to show evidence that you were kept away longer than one year due to unforeseen

circumstances. Such evidence might be a letter from a doctor showing that you or a family member had a medical problem. If you do not have a very good reason for failing to return within one year, there is a strong chance you will lose your green card.

The Commuter Exception

Green card holders who commute to work in the U.S. from Canada or Mexico on a daily or seasonal basis may keep their cards even while actually living outside the country. USCIS will grant you commuter status if, when you get a green card, you advise them of your intention to live in Canada or Mexico. If you live in the U.S. with a green card but later move to the other side of the border, you will be given commuter status when you notify USCIS of your new address.

C. Your Immigrating Family Members' Rights

If children immigrated with you, their legal status will pretty much match yours. If you received conditional, rather than permanent residency, so did they— and they will also have to apply for permanent residency 90 days before the second anniversary of the date they won conditional residency.

If you got a green card through marriage to a U.S. citizen, some special rules apply. If your spouse was a permanent resident when you were approved, then you, as well as your children, must wait five years before applying for U.S. citizenship. However, if your spouse was a U.S. citizen when you were approved, and you're still living together three years after your approval, you can apply for citizenship after these three years—and when you're approved, your children under 18 become citizens automatically (as long as they are living in the U.S. citizen parent's custody).

This right comes from the Child Citizenship Act of 2000. To prove their citizenship, your children will automatically receive a certificate of citizenship from USCIS by mail, within about six weeks of entering the United States. Children who are over 18 when they become permanent residents will have to wait five years before applying for citizenship (despite the fact that you, their parent, need wait only three years).

D. Losing Your Permanent Resident Status

You can lose your U.S. permanent resident status by violating the law (committing a crime) or by violating the terms of your residency, such as by staying out of the United States and living abroad for too long, as explained above in Section B. If you are in the United States, such a violation could make you removable (formerly called deportable), in which case USCIS might start immigration court proceedings against you and eventually send you away. If you attempt to return to the United States, you could be found inadmissible and kept out.

For more on inadmissibility, see the discussion in Chapter 3 and I.N.A. § 101(a)(13)(C), 8 U.S.C. § 1101(a)(13)(c). The grounds of inadmissibility overlap with the grounds of removability or deportability, but they are set out separately in the immigration laws, and there are significant differences. See I.N.A. § 237(a), or 8 U.S.C. § 1227(a) for more on removability.

A full discussion of removability is beyond the scope of this book. In brief, you become removable if you:

- are involved in document fraud or alien smuggling
- go on welfare (become a public charge) within the first five years of entry, unless you need public support because of something beyond your control, such as a disabling accident (see I.N.A. § 237(a)(5), 8 U.S.C. § 1227(a)(5))
- fail to comply with a condition of your green card (such as failing to follow a course of treatment to cure an illness you had when you were approved for residency)
- commit a crime, or
- violate the immigration laws (for example, participate in a sham

marriage or help smuggle other aliens into the United States).

You probably aren't planning on a crime spree as soon as you get your green card. But the message to take from the criminal grounds of removability is that you have to be extra careful. Your U.S. citizen friends might not worry too much about engaging in certain illegal activities, such as shooting a gun at the sky on the Fourth of July or sharing a marijuana cigarette among friends. But if you are caught participating in these same activities, you could lose your green card and be deported.

Men 18-26 Must Register for the Military Draft

Lawful U.S. resident males (green card holders) between the ages of 18 and 26 are required to register for military service, otherwise known as the Selective Service. USCIS won't deport you if you don't register, but it will hold up your eventual citizenship application. As of the year 2000, immigrants who apply to adjust status in the United States are registered automatically. If you don't receive confirmation of your registration, or if you applied through a consulate outside of the United States, you can pick up the Selective Service form at any local Post Office.

E. How to Renew or Replace Your Green Card

This section is about the green card itself—the little laminated card that shows you're a resident. If something happens to the card—if it expires or gets lost—you don't ordinarily lose your status. (The only exception is that when the cards of conditional, not permanent residents expire, their status expires along with it, as discussed in the chapters concerning conditional residents.) However, the law requires you to have a valid green card in your possession, and it's not a bad thing to have on hand in case you travel, get a new job, or get picked up by an overeager immigration officer who thinks you "look" illegal.

1. Renewing Expiring Green Cards

If you are a permanent resident (not a conditional resident), your status does not expire—but your green card *does* expire, every ten years. When the expiration date on your green card is six months away, you will need to apply to renew it. Use Form I-90, available at your local USCIS office, by mail from 800-870-3676, or on the USCIS website at www.uscis.gov. You can also submit this form electronically, or through the USCIS website—though you'll still have to mail in the supporting documentation. Instructions are not included in this book, but Form I-90

You Can Be Deported for Not Telling USCIS You've Changed Your Address

In 2002, the Immigration and Naturalization Service (INS, now called USCIS) shocked immigrants and their advocates by starting to enforce little-known provisions of the immigration law that make it a crime for immigrants not to submit immediate notifications whenever they change their address. The potential punishments include fines, imprisonment, or deportation. While the immigration authorities largely ignored these legal provisions in the past, their post-September 11 security focus changed this. Unfortunately, a number of innocents may be caught in the trap.

As a green card holder, you must take steps to protect yourself. Within ten days of your move, send USCIS a notice on Form AR-11. Note that you can't just send one form per family—every member of your household needs to have a separate form submitted for him or her.

The form and the address to which it must be sent are on the USCIS website (in various languages) at http://uscis.gov (click "Immigration Forms," then scroll down to Form AR-11). This portion of the website will also provide instructions if you prefer to change your address online. Form AR-11 itself is fairly self-explanatory. The question about your "last address" refers only to your last address in the United States, not your last address in any other country. The address you supply should be where you actually live, not a P.O. box or work address. There is no fee for filing Form AR-11.

In addition, if you have any applications on file that are waiting for a USCIS decision—for example, if you've applied for citizenship—you need to separately file a change of address at whichever USCIS office is handling your application. Check with that office for its procedures—a letter may be enough.

What if more than ten days have already passed and you've only just discovered your responsibility to file Form AR-11? Most attorneys advise that you fill out the form now, to show USCIS you made an attempt to comply and to assure that it has your current address. USCIS can forgive a failure to notify if that failure wasn't willful (intentional).

As with everything you send to USCIS, there's a chance it will get lost. Be sure to make a photocopy of your Form AR-11 and any notifications you send to other USCIS offices. Then mail everything by certified mail with a return receipt. The return receipt is particularly important because USCIS won't send you any separate acknowledgment that it has received your Form AR-11. Put your copies and the return receipt in a safe place in case you ever need to prove to USCIS that you complied with the law.

comes with a fairly complete set of instructions.

Alternately, if you are ready and eligible to apply for U.S. citizenship, you can submit the citizenship application instead of renewing the green card. It will probably take you over a year to get your citizenship, but USCIS doesn't mind if you carry around an expired green card in this circumstance. If you need to change jobs or travel, however, you will probably want to renew the green card, to prove to the rest of the world that you are still a permanent resident.

2. Replacing Lost or Stolen Green Cards

If your green card is lost, stolen, accidentally dropped into a blender, or otherwise destroyed, you will need to apply for a new one. Like renewal, this is done using Form I-90 (see instructions in Section 1, above, on where to obtain the form).

Report all stolen green cards to the police. Green cards are a hot item, and there is always a possibility that yours will be stolen and sold. If this happens, be sure to file a police report. You may not get your card back, but when you apply for a replacement card, the report will help convince USCIS that you didn't sell your own card.

3. Correcting USCIS Errors on Your Green Card

When you receive your green card, take a close look at it—USCIS occasionally makes errors, such as your name or birth date. It's worth taking the time to correct these—and fortunately, USCIS has recently agreed that people should not be charged a fee for correcting the USCIS's own mistakes.

This procedure also requires filling out a Form I-90. Send it to whichever USCIS service or benefits center processed the application that led to your receiving the green card. (You are not allowed to use e-filing for this type of request.) In addition, you must send your actual green card (the one containing the incorrect information) along with documentation to prove the mistake. For example, if your name was spelled wrong, send a copy of your birth certificate or passport.

If USCIS decides that the mistake was your fault, perhaps because you filled out an application wrong, it will charge you a filing fee and fingerprint (called biometrics) fee.

4. Dealing With Green Cards That Never Arrive

Your green card is being produced in a seemingly very busy factory, and waits of three to six or more months are not uncommon. If yours is very late, your first step is to write a letter to the last office that you dealt with, asking them to look into the situation. You can also visit your local USCIS office—they may at least be able to tell you who exactly to write to.

If eight or more months have gone by and you still haven't received your green card, send Form I-90 with proof of your permanent residence approval and copies of any of your previous correspondence regarding the late green card to the USCIS service or benefits center where your permanent residence was approved. You do not need to pay any fees for this application. However, if USCIS finds that it's your own fault that you didn't receive the card, because you provided an incorrect address or you moved without advising the appropriate USCIS office, you will be charged.

F. Green Cards and U.S. Citizenship

Green-card holders can, after a certain time, apply for U.S. citizenship. Except in rare cases, no one can become a U.S. citizen without first receiving a green card. It is frequently said that green cards give all the benefits of U.S. citizenship except the rights to vote and hold public office. The differences between the two are actually greater. The most important distinction is that if you violate certain laws or abandon your U.S. residence, you can lose your green card. U.S. citizenship cannot be taken away, unless you acquired it fraudulently or voluntarily give it up. Another important difference is that U.S. citizenship allows you to petition for more of your family members to immigrate than a green card does, and their immigration will be faster.

The time period you have to wait before applying for U.S. citizenship ranges between three and five years— three years for people married to U.S. citizens, five years for everyone else—except that asylees can actually apply four years after their approval for permanent residence, because their one year as an asylee counts, and refugees can apply five years after entry to the U.S., no matter when they became permanent residents.

You must also meet other eligibility criteria before applying for citizenship. You'll have to have behaved in a way that shows your good moral character while you had your green card, and you must have lived in the U.S. for most of that time.

 For complete instructions on and how to apply for U.S. citizenship: See *Becoming a U.S. Citizen: A Guide to the Law, Exam & Interview*, by Ilona Bray (Nolo).

G. Green Cards and U.S. Taxes

Once you get a green card, you automatically become a U.S. tax resident. U.S. tax residents must declare their entire incomes to the U.S. government, even if part or all of that income has been earned from investments or business activities carried on outside U.S. borders. This does not necessarily mean that the U.S. government will tax all of your worldwide income. International treaties often regulate whether or not you must pay U.S. taxes on income earned elsewhere. However, green card holders have to at least report all income they have earned worldwide.

You may believe that the number of days you spend in the U.S. each year has some effect on whether or not you are a U.S. tax resident. This is true for people who have nonimmigrant (temporary) visas. It is not true for green card holders. If you have a green card, your worldwide income must be reported to the U.S. government, even if you remain outside the U.S. for an entire year.

As a green card holder, you must file U.S. tax return Form 1040 each year by April 15th. Failure to follow U.S. tax laws may be considered a crime. If you are found guilty of a tax crime, your green card can be revoked and you may be deported. To find out exactly how to follow U.S. tax laws, consult an accountant, a tax attorney, or the nearest office of the U.S. Internal Revenue Service (or see its website at www.irs. gov). ■

Part III

Nonimmigrant (Temporary) Visas

There are many kinds of nonimmigrant (temporary) visas. Each is issued for a different purpose and each is known by a letter-number combination as well as a name. You may be familiar with the more popular types of nonimmigrant visas such as B-2 visitors, E-2 investors, or F-1 students. All of these fall into the general nonimmigrant group.

When you get a nonimmigrant visa, the U.S. government assumes you will perform a specific activity while you are in the United States. You are therefore given a specialized visa authorizing that activity—and only that activity—for a specific, limited time.

How is a nonimmigrant visa different from a green card? The most basic difference is that all green cards are permanent while all nonimmigrant visas are temporary. If you hold a green card, you are considered a permanent resident of the United States. Your green card can be taken away only if you violate certain laws or regulations. The exact opposite is true of nonimmigrant visas—they're very easy for the government to take away from you. For example, if you travel to the U.S. on a nonimmigrant visa and the border authorities think you do not plan to go home after your stay is over, the visa will be taken away. After you've held a green card for a certain length of time, you can become a U.S. citizen; a nonimmigrant visa, however, will never lead to U.S. citizenship.

Never lie to get a visa. People who use fraudulent documents or make misrepresentations, or who attempt entry to the U.S. without proper documentation, can be refused entry at the U.S. border or airport, deported from the U.S., and prevented from returning for five years. Accordingly, it is extremely important to understand the requirements of the visa classification you are requesting, and not make any misrepresentations of your intent or qualifications for a particular visa.

A. Types of Nonimmigrant Visas

Nonimmigrant visas differ from each other in the kinds of privileges they offer, as well as how long they last. Here is a summary list of the various nonimmigrant visas available:

A-1. Ambassadors, public ministers, or career diplomats, and their immediate family members

A-2. Other accredited officials or employees of foreign governments, and their immediate family members

A-3. Personal attendants, servants, or employees, and the immediate family members of A-1 and A-2 visa holders

B-1. Business visitors

B-2. Tourist visitors. (Also, tourists from certain countries are permitted to come to the U.S. without B-2 visas under what is known as the Visa Waiver Program. See Chapter 15 for a description of this program and the countries included.)

C-1. Foreign travelers in immediate and continuous transit through the U.S.

D-1. Crewmen who need to land temporarily in the U.S. and who will depart aboard the same ship or plane on which they arrived

E-1. Treaty traders, their spouses and children

E-2. Treaty investors, their spouses and children

E-3. Nationals of Australia working in a specialty occupation that requires a bachelor's degree or higher education

F-1. Academic or language students

F-2. Immediate family members of F-1 visa holders

F-3. Citizens or residents of Mexico or Canada commuting to the U.S. as academic or language students

G-1. Designated principal resident representatives of foreign governments coming to the U.S. to work for an international organization, their staff members and immediate family members

G-2. Other accredited representatives of foreign governments coming to the U.S. to work for an international organization, and their immediate family members

G-3. Representatives of foreign governments, and their immediate family members who would ordinarily qualify for G-1 or G-2 visas except that their governments are not members of an international organization

G-4. Officers or employees of international organizations and their immediate family members

G-5. Attendants, servants, and personal employees of G-1 through G-4 visa holders, and their immediate family members

H-1B. Persons working in specialty occupations requiring at least a bachelor's degree or its equivalent in on-the-job experience, and distinguished fashion models

H-2A. Temporary agricultural workers coming to the U.S. to fill positions for which a temporary shortage of U.S. workers has been recognized by the U.S. Department of Agriculture

H-2B. Temporary workers of various kinds coming to the U.S. to perform temporary jobs for which there is a shortage of available qualified U.S. workers

H-3. Temporary trainees

H-4. Immediate family members of H-1, H-2, or H-3 visa holders

I. Bona fide representatives of the foreign press coming to the U.S. to work solely in that capacity, and their immediate family members

J-1. Exchange visitors coming to the U.S. to study, work, or train as part of an exchange program officially recognized by the U.S. Information Agency

J-2. Immediate family members of J-1 visa holders

K-1. Fiancé(e)s of U.S. citizens coming to the U.S. for the purpose of getting married

K-2. Minor, unmarried children of K-1 visa holders

K-3. Spouses of U.S. citizens who have filed both a fiancé visa petition and a separate application to enter the U.S

K-4. Minor, unmarried children of K-3 visa holders

L-1. Intracompany transferees who work in positions as managers, executives, or persons with specialized knowledge

L-2. Immediate family members of L-1 visa holders

M-1. Vocational or other nonacademic students, other than language students

M-2. Immediate families of M-1 visa holders

M-3. Citizens or residents of Mexico or Canada commuting to the U.S. to attend a vocational program

N. Children of certain special immigrants

NATO-1, NATO-2, NATO-3, NATO-4, and NATO-5. Associates coming to the U.S. under applicable provisions of the NATO Treaty and their immediate family members

NATO-6. Members of civilian components accompanying military forces on missions authorized under the NATO Treaty, and their immediate family members

NATO-7. Attendants, servants, or personal employees of NATO-1 through NATO-6 visa holders, and their immediate family members

O-1. Persons of extraordinary ability in the sciences, arts, education, business, or athletics

O-2. Essential support staff of O-1 visa holders

O-3. Immediate family members of O-1 and O-2 visa holders

P-1. Internationally recognized athletes and entertainers, and their essential support staff

P-2. Entertainers coming to perform in the U.S. through a government-recognized exchange program

P-3. Artists and entertainers coming to the U.S. in a group for the purpose of presenting culturally unique performances

P-4. Immediate family members of P-1, P-2, and P-3 visa holders

Q-1. Exchange visitors coming to the U.S. to participate in international cultural exchange programs

Q-2. Immediate family members of Q-1 visa holders

R-1. Ministers and other workers of recognized religions

R-2. Immediate family members of R-1 visa holders

S-1. People coming to the U.S. to supply critical information to federal or state authorities where it has been determined that their presence in the U.S. is essential to the success of a criminal investigation or prosecution

S-5 or S-6. People coming to the U.S. to provide critical information to federal authorities or a court, who will be in danger as a result of providing such information, and are eligible to receive a reward for the information

S-7. Immediate family members of S visa holders

T. Women and children who are in the United States because they are victims of trafficking, who are cooperating with law enforcement, and who fear extreme hardship (such as retribution) if returned home

TN. NAFTA professionals

TO. Spouses or children of TN visa holders

U. Victims of criminal abuse in the U.S., who are cooperating with law enforcement

V. Spouses and minor unmarried children of lawful permanent residents who have been waiting three or more years to get a green card, whose initial visa petition was submitted to the INS before December 21, 2000.

By looking at these categories, you can probably see that some will apply to much larger groups of people than others. In this book, we have covered in detail those nonimmigrant visas utilized by the greatest majority of people. If you wish information on some of the lesser-used nonimmigrant visas, contact your USCIS local office or U.S. consulate for more information, or see an attorney.

B. Difference Between a Visa and a Status

A nonimmigrant visa is something you can see and touch. It is a stamp placed on a page in your passport. Your nonimmigrant visa gives you certain privileges, most importantly the right to request entry to the United Stares. Visas are entry documents. There are, however, other privileges that come with visas, such as permission to work, study, or invest in the U.S. Different privileges are attached to different visas.

A visa stamp cannot be issued inside the U.S. It can be obtained only at a U.S. embassy or consulate in another country. But some people who are already in the U.S. gain immigration privileges without getting the matching visa first, by applying for a change of status. For example, you could enter on a tourist visa and apply for a change to student status.

Status is the name given to the particular privileges you receive once you're in the U.S. For example, if you're in student status, you have the privilege of attending school here. Again, different groups of privileges go with different types of statuses and visas. However, the ability to enter the U.S. is not part of the status. Only an actual, physical visa can be used to enter the U.S., so if you apply for a particular status and then leave the U.S., you'll have to visit a U.S. consulate and apply for a visa before you return.

C. Time Limits on Nonimmigrant Visas

Just as nonimmigrant visas vary in purpose, they also vary as to how long they last—that is, for how long you can use them to enter the United States.

When you arrive, the border official will give you a separate expiration date for your status, that is, how long you can stay.

To fully understand the limits on your rights to enter and then stay in the U.S., you'll need to look at:

- the expiration date of your petition or certificate of eligibility, if one is required
- the expiration date of your visa
- the number of entries permitted on your visa
- the date stamped on your I-94 card
- the expiration date of your passport (rules are different for Canadians—see Chapter 5), and
- the expiration date of your status.

1. Expiration Date of Your Visa Petition or Certificate of Eligibility

Most visas can be obtained by applying directly to your local U.S. consulate. However, to get H, L, O, P, and Q work visas, you must first have a petition approved by USCIS. And F student visas, M student visas, and J exchange-visitor visas require that you first obtain certificates of eligibility from a U.S. school or employer. Such petitions and certificates of eligibility will indicate the desired starting and expiration dates of the visa.

When you enter the U.S. with one of these visas, you should also bring the certificate of eligibility or Notice of Approval for the petition. The CBP officer who admits you into the country will then know from the petition or certificate of eligibility, not the visa in your passport, how long you are permitted to stay. The officer will give you an I-94 card, which will show the date by which you must leave.

2. Expiration Date of Your Visa

A visa serves two purposes: it allows you to request entry to the U.S., and it gives you the right to engage in certain activities once you have arrived. Permissible activities vary with the type of visa. The expiration date on your visa does not show how long you can stay in the U.S. once you arrive (see the I-94 for that date), but it does indicate how long you have the right to enter or reenter the U.S. with visa privileges.

Nonimmigrant visas can be issued for any length of time up to a certain maximum allowed by law, depending on the type of visa. Visitor's visas, for example, can last up to ten years. (Remember, this means only that you have entry privileges for ten years, not that you can stay for that long.) Many other nonimmigrant visas can be issued for up to five years.

Citizens of some countries can't get visas issued for the maximum period usually allowed by law. The shorter time limitation is based on the nationality of the applicant, not the location of the consulate that issues the visa.

Remember that the visa controls only how long you have the right to enter the U.S., not how long you can stay. Even nationals of those countries who receive visas of shorter duration can have petitions or certificates of eligibility approved for the maximum length of stay. Then, when they do make an entry, they may stay for the full length of time indicated on the approved petition or certificate of eligibility—even if it's beyond the expiration date of their visa—and that date will be written on the I-94 card.

If your visa expires before your petition or certificate of eligibility, you can renew your visa at a U.S. consulate the next time you travel outside of the United States. You can also choose to stay in the U.S. without traveling for the full term of your petition or certificate of eligibility. Then the fact that your visa may expire doesn't really matter.

3. Number of U.S. Entries Permitted on the Visa

Most visas are the multiple-entry type. This means that until the visa expires, you may use it to go in and out of the U.S. an unlimited number of times. Some visas are the single entry type. If you hold such a visa, you may use it to enter the U.S. only once. When you leave, you can't return again with that same

Limited Travel When Your Visa Has Expired

If you have an expired visa in your passport but a current I-94 card, you can still do some traveling on a limited basis. Specifically, you are permitted to go to Canada, Mexico, or an island adjacent to the U.S. (such as the Bahamas or Bermuda) for up to 30 days, and return to the U.S. without getting a new visa. However, there are some limitations on this privilege. For one thing, you cannot apply for a new visa while you're away, because this will set a new security check into motion and the State Department doesn't want to risk people entering the U.S. while security checks are pending. For another thing, you are not allowed to use this procedure if you're from a country that the U.S. government has identified as supporting terrorism. As of this book's printing, those countries included North Korea, Cuba, Syria, Sudan, and Iran.

The limited travel law is also very useful to Mexican nationals in the U.S. on work and study visas. This is because they are often hampered in simply visiting their homes by the fact that many types of visas to Mexican nationals are issued for only six months at a time.

Special Registration for Certain People Visiting the U.S.

USCIS imposes extra monitoring on certain people who come to the U.S. on nonimmigrant (temporary) visas. You won't necessarily know before you arrive whether you'll be subject to this additional monitoring; USCIS is trying to keep some of its criteria secret.

The USCIS officer who greets you at the border will look at what country you're from, whether you show up on a database of security risks, and whether your personal characteristics match USCIS's ideas of risk factors. If the officer decides that you are a risk:

- you will have to be fingerprinted, photographed, and interviewed about your plans in the U.S.
- if you stay in the U.S. for more than 30 days, you may be asked to report in person to a USCIS office between day 30 and day 40 of your U.S. stay, to show that you are following your earlier-stated travel plan. (Until 2003, every

person identified as subject to Special Registration had to do this; now, only selected ones will.)

- if you will stay in the U.S for more than one year, and if you were told when you entered that you would have to reregister, report in person to a USCIS office within ten days of having been here for a year
- you will have to send USCIS written notification if you change your address, your employer, or your school (unless you stay in the U.S. for fewer than 30 days)
- you will have to leave the U.S. only through a designated port of departure (there are currently about 55 such designated ports), and
- you will have to meet with a USCIS officer when you leave.

You will be given a packet of information more fully explaining these requirements when you enter the U.S.

visa, even if time still remains before its expiration date.

4. Date Stamped on Your I-94 Card

When you enter the U.S. on a nonimmigrant visa, you will be given a small white card called an I-94 card. A Customs and Border Protection (CBP) officer will stamp the card with a date as you enter the country. We have already mentioned that the date you get will come from either the immigration laws, or the date on your petition or certificate of eligibility, if you have one. It is this date and not the expiration date of the visa that controls how long you can stay.

U.S. government regulations state that when you enter the U.S., you should be admitted for the full amount of time remaining on your petition, if you have one. Normally, this is also the expiration date of your visa. In practice, the date on your I-94 card, the final date on your petition, and the expiration date of your visa will usually all be the same.

Occasionally, however, a CBP inspector will stamp the I-94 card giving you a shorter stay than the dates on your petition indicate. Although this is technically improper, it is best not to argue with the inspector. In such cases, if the date on your I-94 card is about to pass and you still wish to remain in the U.S., you can apply for an extension. Directions on how to apply for extensions are in the specific chapters on the various types of visas.

5. Expiration Date of Your Passport

You can't get into the U.S. without a valid passport. Mexicans with border crossing cards and Canadians are the only exceptions to this rule. Remember that visas are stamped inside your passport. When you are ready to receive the visa stamp, make sure you have a passport that is not about to expire. You will not normally be admitted to the U.S. with an expired passport, even if the visa inside is still current.

There is a simple solution to this problem. If your passport contains a visa that is still in effect but the passport itself has already expired, you should apply for a new passport but keep the old one with the current visa stamp. When entering the U.S, show both the new passport and the old one containing the valid visa. Then your visa will be honored for its full term.

6. Expiration of Your Status

In rare cases, your status might expire on a date that wasn't shown in your I-94 card. Students are the best example. Their I-94 might say "D/S," which stands for duration of status, and means that they can stay for as long as they are actively pursuing the academic program for which they entered the United States.

After graduation, however, students are expected to leave within a short time.

7. Extending Your Status

If you are presently in the U.S. in valid nonimmigrant status, but want to switch to another nonimmigrant category, you can change your status without leaving the United States, by submitting Form I-539 by mail to USCIS.

Make sure to apply before your stay expires. In that case, you will get a different nonimmigrant status but no new visa. For example, you could go from F-1 student status to H-1B specialty worker status in this way. Your new status will be written on a new I-94 card you receive when your request for change of status is approved. Your period of authorized stay will be extended to the time allowed in the new status category.

D. At the Border

Even after obtaining a nonimmigrant visa, you aren't guaranteed entry into the United States. When you arrive at a U.S. airport, seaport, or land border post, you must present your visa, along with any supporting paperwork such as your proof of financial support or school acceptance. The person who reviews these materials will be part of a different arm of the U.S. government than you've dealt with before—called Customs and Border Protection, or CBP. The CBP inspector will examine your paperwork, possibly search your luggage, and ask questions to make sure you deserved the visa in the first place.

CBP inspectors have the power to deport someone requesting admission to the U.S. if:

- the inspector believes you are making a misrepresentation about practically anything connected to your entering the U.S., such as your purpose in coming, intent to return, or prior immigration history, or
- you do not have the proper documentation to support your entry to the U.S. in the category you are requesting.

If the inspector decides not to let you in (called "summary exclusion"), you may not request entry for five years, unless you were entering under the Visa Waiver Program or the immigration authorities grant a special waiver. For this reason, it is extremely important to understand the terms of your requested status and to not make any misrepresentations.

If you are found inadmissible, you can ask to withdraw your application to enter the U.S. to prevent having the five-year bar on your record. The CBP may allow you to do so in some cases. You can also ask to see a judge if you fear you'd be persecuted after returning to your home country and deserve political asylum (see Chapter 13).

Assuming you don't have such problems, your passport will be stamped and you'll be given an I-94 card, as described in Section C, above. You may also be fingerprinted and photographed.

E. Heightened Security Measures

Responding to the September 11, 2001, terrorist acts on the United States, Congress and the State Department have been scrutinizing every part of the visa application process and adding new requirements and security checks. They will no doubt continue strengthening or adjusting these measures in the future. Everyone applying for a visa to the U.S. can now expect delays due to background and security checks. Nearly every applicant is now required to appear for a personal visa interview, resulting in even longer waits at the consulates. Same-day visa processing is virtually a thing of the past. The waits are made even longer by the U.S. consulates' new practice regarding suspicious cases —these are being forwarded to the U.S. Federal Bureau of Investigation (FBI), thus adding weeks or even months to the decision-making process.

In addition, all 16- to 45-year-old male visa applicants must now submit Form DS-157 in addition to the usual application materials. This will affect mainly those applying for student and tourist visas. A few visa categories,

mostly diplomatic ones, are exempted, including categories A-1, A-2, G-1, G-2, G-3, G-4, NATO-1, NATO-2, NATO-3, NATO-4, NATO-5, NATO-6, and TECRO E-1. This new form is mandatory for young men from all countries in the world, not just for men from countries suspected of terrorist links. However, men from Middle Eastern countries are facing longer waits for visas than other applicants.

For new requirements affecting specific visa categories, such as tourists and students, see the chapters that follow.

F. Effect of Nonimmigrant Visas on Green Cards

Many people ask, "How does getting a nonimmigrant visa affect my ability to get a green card?" The answer is that usually, there is no effect at all. From a strictly legal standpoint, getting a nonimmigrant visa will not help you to get a green card, nor will it hurt you.

If you must have a nonimmigrant visa so you can go to the U.S. right away, but are definitely planning to apply for a green card later, you should probably not begin the process of applying for a green card (for example, by having a relative or employer file a visa petition on your behalf) until you have less need to travel. When you can wait for the green card to come through without too much inconvenience, only then should you start applying for one. That's because you may be blocked from entering for your temporary stay if you appear to have an "immigrant intent"—that is, you plan to stay in the United States permanently.

There are certain nonimmigrant visa categories that allow you to apply for a green card without worrying about immigrant intent. By law, immigrant intent is not a factor for consideration in H-1A, H-1B, L, O, and P visa applications.

G. Nonimmigrant Visas and U.S. Taxes

Though nonimmigrants are, by definition, not permanent residents of the U.S., it is possible to become a tax resident simply by spending a certain amount of time in the U.S. each year. If you become a tax resident, your entire worldwide income must be reported to the U.S. government. It doesn't matter if a portion or all of that income was earned from investments or business activities carried on outside the United States. The income still must be reported.

Becoming a tax resident does not necessarily mean that the U.S. government will actually tax all of your worldwide income. International treaties control whether or not you must pay U.S. taxes on income earned elsewhere. However, if you stay in the U.S. long enough to become a tax resident, you will have to at least report all

income you have earned worldwide—a paperwork burden, if nothing else.

At what point do you become a tax resident? If you have been present in the U.S. for 183 days or more of the current year, you are a tax resident for the year. If you have been in the U.S. for a weighted total of 183 days during the previous three years, you are also a tax resident unless you spend fewer than 30 days in the U.S. in the current year. For determining the weighted total number of days, each day in the current year counts as one, each day in the previous year counts as only one-third of a day, and each day in the second previous year counts as only one-sixth of a day. This latter rule does not apply to certain foreign government employees, certain teachers, students, and professional athletes.

Provided you spend fewer than 183 days of the current year in the U.S., you will also avoid being classified as a tax resident if you maintain a tax home in another country and have a closer connection to that country than to the United States. There are other exceptions to these rules. A tax treaty between the U.S. and your home country may also alter these rules. If you are unsure of your situation, consult with a tax accountant or lawyer.

If you do become a tax resident, you must file U.S. tax return Form 1040 each year by April 15th. The good news is, if you've been working for a U.S. employer that's been withholding taxes from your paycheck, you may be due a refund. But failure to follow U.S. tax laws may be considered a criminal offense, and can make it more difficult for you to stay in the U.S. or ultimately obtain permanent residency. To find out exactly how to comply with U.S. tax laws, consult a tax professional or the nearest office of the Internal Revenue Service (IRS) or visit its website at www.irs.gov.

H. Status Overstays and Automatic Cancellation of Visas

Some people may wish to obtain a nonimmigrant visa at a consulate other than one in their home country. This is called third-country national, or TCN, processing.

TCN processing is prohibited if you have been unlawfully present in the U.S. under a prior visa status. Even if you overstayed your status by just one day, your visa will be automatically canceled, you will not be eligible for TCN processing and you will have to return to your home country to apply for a new visa.

If you were admitted on an A, F, G, or J visa for duration of status (indicated as "D/S" on your Form I-94) and you remain in the U.S. beyond the time for which your status was conferred, you still may be eligible for TCN processing. You will be barred only if the USCIS (or the former INS) or an immigration judge has determined that you were unlawfully present. Six or more months of unlawful presence acquired after April 1, 1997, is also a ground of inadmissibility if you leave the U.S. (See Chapter 3 for details.)

∎

Chapter 15

Getting a Business or Tourist (B-1 or B-2) Visa

During any typical year, over ten million people will come to the United States as tourists (B-2) or business (B-1) visitors. (See I.N.A § 101(a)(15)(B), 8 U.S.C. § 1101(a)(15)(B); 8 C.F.R. § 214.) The U.S. naturally wants to keep its doors open to these visitors, who will enjoy the country's scenic and cultural pleasures, and engage in business and other exchanges with people in the United States. As with every visa, however, some tension surrounds its distribution. No one wants to see this visa used by people intending to do harm in the United States or to stay and never leave. As a result, U.S. consulates around the world deny a surprising number of visitor visas—in many cases to people who just weren't prepared for the rigors of the application process.

This chapter explains who is eligible for a temporary visa for business or pleasure, and how to maximize the odds of success when you apply. Most consulates can approve and issue visitors' visas within days, although new security measures can delay their final decision by weeks or months.

Do you need a lawyer? Applying for a visitor visa is fairly simple, and doesn't usually require a lawyer's help. If, however, you've had trouble getting visas in the past, have ever overstayed a visa, or are from a country thought to sponsor terrorism, a lawyer's help can be well worth the investment.

Key Features of the Visitor Visa

Here are some of the advantages and disadvantages of the visitor visa:

- The application process is reasonably quick and straightforward.
- B-2 visitor visas are often multiple entry, meaning you can use them for many trips to the United States.
- Although you may make many trips to the U.S. on your visitor visa, the length of each visit is normally limited to between 30 days and six months. After that you must leave the U.S. or apply for an extension of your stay.
- Although if you're from certain countries you might not need a visa at all, getting one allows you to stay longer and gain rights to extend or change your status once in the United States.
- You may not be employed or operate a business on a B-1 or B-2 visitor visa.

A. Do You Qualify for a Visitor Visa?

You qualify for a B-1 visa if you are coming to the U.S. as a visitor for a temporary business trip. You qualify for a B-2 visa if you are visiting the U.S. temporarily, either as a tourist or for medical treatment. Often, these two visas are issued together in combination so you have all the options under both. You must have the intent to return to your home country after your visit is over. Usually, you must have a home abroad to which you will return.

 HIV-positive applicants need not worry that their illness will block their entry to the United States. Although it's a ground of inadmissibility for other visa applicants, business and tourist visitors coming to the U.S. for up to 60 days receive an automatic ("categorical") waiver.

A B-1 visa allows you to be in the U.S. for business purposes such as making investments, buying goods, attending seminars, or performing other temporary work for an employer located outside the United States. You may not, however, be employed or operate your own company. You may not be paid by a source inside the United States. It is sometimes difficult to draw the line between permissible business activities and illegal employment on a B-1 visa.

Unlike the B-1 visitor, the B-2 tourist may not engage in business-related activities at all. A condition of being admitted on a B-2 visa is that you are visiting solely for purposes of pleasure or medical treatment.

If you enter the U.S. with a B visa, your intention must be to come only as a temporary visitor. Tourists are usually given stays of up to six months and business visitors may stay as necessary

up to a maximum of one year. The date when your permitted stay will expire will be shown on your Form I-94, a little white card that the CBP officer at the border or airport will put into your passport. Theoretically, you may leave the U.S. at the end of your stay, return the next day, and be readmitted for another stay. Alternatively, when your permitted stay has expired, you can apply for an extension of stay without leaving. (See Section C, below.)

If your travel history shows that you are spending most of your time in the U.S., the CBP will assume you have the intent to be more than just a temporary visitor. On this basis, you can be denied entry altogether, even though you do have a valid visa. Some people, thinking that they have found a loophole in the system, try to live in the U.S. permanently on a visitor's visa by merely taking brief trips outside the country every time their permitted stay expires. Do not expect this tactic to work for very long. However, those who want to have vacation homes in the U.S. and live in them for about six months each year may do so legally.

1. Exception to the Visitor's Visa Requirement: The Visa Waiver Program

If you're planning to come to the U.S. for tourism or business, are willing to leave within 90 days, haven't been denied past visas or violated their terms, and come from a country that does not have a history of illegal immigration to the

U.S., you may be able to avoid formally applying for a visa before your trip. A so-called visa waiver is available to people from the 27 countries currently participating in the Visa Waiver Program, including: Andorra, Austria, Australia, Belgium, Brunei, Denmark, Finland, France, Germany, Iceland, Ireland, Italy, Japan, Liechtenstein, Luxembourg, Monaco, the Netherlands, New Zealand, Norway, Portugal, San Marino, Singapore, Slovenia, Spain, Sweden, Switzerland, and the United Kingdom. (Foreign media representatives, however, cannot use a visa waiver, as the purpose of their stay is not considered business. They must obtain a nonimmigrant media visa.)

Each visitor who enters under the Visa Waiver Program must arrive with a transportation ticket to leave the United States. They must also present what's called a machine readable passport, that is, one with two lines of scannable characters at the bottom of the biographical information page. The passport must be good for at least six months past the date of entry. Entry under the Visa Waiver Program is permitted on land through Canada or Mexico, but qualifying visitors must show evidence at the border of sufficient funds to live in the U.S. without working.

When you enter the U.S. under the Visa Waiver Program, you will not be allowed to change your status to another nonimmigrant classification or apply for a green card without first leaving the country. (The only exception is for persons who marry a U.S. citizen or are the unmarried children or parents of a U.S. citizen.)

Participation in the Visa Waiver Program is optional, not a requirement. People from countries qualifying for visa waivers can still get standard visitor's visas. You will have more flexibility and rights once you enter the U.S. if you come with a visa.

For more information, see the State Department website at http://travel.state. gov (click "Visas," then "Visa Waiver Program").

B. How to Apply for a Visitor Visa

Applying for a B visa is a two-step process, in which you:

- prepare an application, consisting of one or two government forms and some personal documents, and
- present your application at a meeting with an official at a U.S. consulate.

For additional information on these application procedures, see the State Department website at http://travel.state /gov/visa, and follow the links for "Temporary Visitors to the U.S."

1. Step One: Preparing Your Application

Your application will consist of government forms as well as documents that you collect yourself. You can either get the forms in advance (download them from the State Department website or pick them up from a U.S. consulate), or get your documents together, go to the consulate, pick up and fill out the forms, and submit your application on the same day.

Your application should consist of the items on the checklist below.

Checklist for Visitor Visa Application

Forms

- ☐ DS-156: Nonimmigrant Visa Application.
- ☐ Visa application fee (currently $100).
- ☐ Visa issuance fee (the amount depends on your country).
- ☐ DS-157: Supplemental Nonimmigrant Visa Application, if you're either a male applicant between 16 and 45 years of age or you come from a state that the U.S. believes sponsors terrorism and you are age 16 or older, whether male or female.
- ☐ USCIS Form I-134 (if you will depend on someone else for financial support).

Documents

- ☐ Your passport, valid for at least six months.
- ☐ One passport-type photo of you, 2 inches x 2 inches.
- ☐ Documents showing the purpose of your trip, such as an itinerary and hotel arrangements, and reasons that you'll return to your home country, such as ownership of real estate, relationships with close family members staying behind, and proof that a job will be waiting for you on your return.
- ☐ Proof of ability to cover your expenses, such as:
  - ☐ Form I-134, Affidavit of Support from a U.S. friend or relative.
  - ☐ Letter from a friend or relative inviting you to visit, stating you are welcome to stay with him or her.
  - ☐ Bank statements.
  - ☐ Personal financial statements.
  - ☐ Evidence of your current sources of income.
- ☐ If you are coming to the U.S. on business, a letter from your foreign employer describing your job and telling what you will be doing for them during your U.S. trip. The letter should explain that you will be paid only from sources outside the U.S., and state when you will be expected to return from your trip. If you'll be attending a trade show or similar business event, bring promotional materials, flyers, and proof that you are registered for it.

One of the items on the list above requires more explanation:

Form I-134. You must convince the consulate that once you arrive in the U.S. you are not likely to seek employment or go on public welfare. The Form I-134 Affidavit of Support shows that someone is willing to take financial responsibility for you. (There is a newer Affidavit of Support, Form I-864, which contains much stricter legal requirements. It is not meant for nonimmigrant visas, so don't use it.)

If possible, the person you will be visiting in the U.S. should sign Form I-134 on your behalf. That person must be a U.S. citizen or green card holder. If you can prove that you are financially independent or are employed in your home country, you don't need an I-134.

When you request someone in the U.S. to sign an I-134 Affidavit of Support, he or she will doubtless wish to know the legal extent of the financial obligation. In signing the I-134, the person does not promise to support you. By signing, he or she promises to repay the U.S. government for the total of any government support payments you might receive. The Affidavit of Support supposedly binds your relative to this obligation for three years, though most lawyers believe the form is flawed and no court would enforce it anyway.

2. Step Two: Applying at the Consulate

The first question is which consulate you will apply at. Hopefully, you didn't just decide you'd like to stop in the U.S. while already in the middle of your round-the-world tour. Although, technically, the law allows you to apply for a B visa at any U.S. consulate you choose, from a practical standpoint, your case will be given greatest consideration at the consulate in your home country. Applying in some other country creates suspicion about your motives for choosing their consulate. (Often, when an applicant is having trouble at a home consulate, he or she will seek a more lenient office in some other country.)

Furthermore, if you have ever been present in the U.S. unlawfully, you cannot apply outside your own country. Even if you overstayed your status in the U.S. by just one day, you must return to your home country and apply for the visa from that consulate. There is an exception: If you were admitted to the U.S. for the duration of your status (indicated by a "D/S" on your I-94 form) and you remained in the U.S. beyond that time or purpose for which your status was conferred, you may still be able to apply in a third country. In that situation, you will be barred from third-country national processing only if an immigration judge or USCIS (or INS) official officially determined that you were unlawfully present. You may find that your success in applying as a third-country national depends on your country, the consulate, and the relative seriousness of your offense.

Your next task is to research your local consulate's visa application procedures. Most consulates insist on advance appointments. Since procedures among the consulates vary, telephone or check the consulate's website in advance to find out about local policies.

The last step in your process will be attending an interview with a consular officer. During the interview, the officer will examine your application form for accuracy. He or she will ask you questions about your ties to your home country and the state of your financial resources. The officer will surely ask you how long you intend to remain in the United States. Any answer suggesting uncertainty about plans to return or an interest in applying for a green card is likely to result in a denial of your B visa. The typical interview lasts only a few minutes, and the officer is under intense pressure to make a quick decision on your case.

If all has gone well to this point, the officer will initiate various security checks to make sure you haven't been involved in criminal or terrorist activity. Because the U.S. is doing more comprehensive security checks than in the past, you are unlikely to receive a

decision on your visa the same day as the interview. Security checks can add weeks or months to the processing time.

You will have to return to the consulate to pick up your visa. Don't forget to bring your visa issuance fee and your passport to be stamped. While there is a definite difference between B-1 and B-2 visas, the two are frequently issued together.

On entering the U.S. with your new B visa, you will be given an I-94 card. It will be stamped with the dates showing your authorized stay. You are normally permitted to remain in the U.S. for six months. Each time you exit and reenter the U.S., you will get a new I-94 card with a new period of authorized stay.

If your visa was issued as both B-1 and B-2 together, you should make it clear to the immigration inspector which visa you are using. Your I-94 card will show whether you were admitted as a B-1 business visitor or a B-2 tourist.

 Even with a valid visitor visa, entry at the U.S. border can be unpleasant. Expect the immigration officials who greet you to again question you closely about the purpose of your stay and your plans to depart on time. For security reasons, you may be searched. See Chapter 3 for more on these officials' summary removal powers.

C. Extensions of Stay

Assuming you can show that you're not just trying to stay in the U.S. indefinitely, and your total stay will not exceed one year, USCIS may grant you an extension of your B-1 or B-2 visitor stay. (Extensions are not available to people who entered on visa waivers, except for outright emergencies—visit your local USCIS office in such a case.) Usually, six additional months is as long an extension as you can hope for.

You must submit your request for an extension before the date on your I-94 card has passed, but USCIS recommends submitting it 45 days before that. (Rules are different for Canadians. See Chapter 5.)

To apply for an extension of stay, mail the items on the checklist below to the USCIS regional service center having jurisdiction over the place you are visiting. (To access the form and its instructions, and get the exact USCIS address and P.O. box number, go to the USCIS website or call 800-870-3676.)

Checklist for Extension Application

Forms

❑ Form I-539, with application fee, currently $300. If you have a spouse or children coming with you, also complete the I-539 supplement (they don't need separate Forms I-539).

❑ Form I-134 (or proof of your independent sources of income).

Documents

❑ Your I-94 card(s); the originals, not copies.

❑ A written statement by you, explaining the reason you need to stay longer, why that extended stay will be temporary, what arrangements you've made to leave the U.S., and how you're dealing with your house and your job back in your home country.

❑ Financial documents to accompany Form I-134 or to show independent sources of income.

❑ Proof of the relationship between you and accompanying family members, such as a child's long-form birth certificate or your marriage certificate.

❑ If you are a business visitor, a letter from your foreign employer explaining why you need the extension of stay.

If USCIS wants further information before acting on your request, it will return all papers, forms, and documents to you, together with another form known as an I-797. The I-797 tells you what additional pieces of information or documents are expected. Supply the extra data and mail the whole package back to the USCIS regional service center.

Applications for extensions of stay for visitors are normally decided on within two to four months. (See Chapter 4 for information on how to track the progress of your application online.) Assuming you filed your application on time, you will be permitted to remain in the U.S. until receiving a decision, even if your authorized stay (as shown on your I-94 card) expires.

When your application is approved, you will receive a Notice of Action on Form I-797, indicating the approval with the new date on a tear-off card that's meant to serve as a new I-94 card.

If your application for an extension of stay is denied, you will be sent a written notice explaining the reasons for the negative decision. The most common reason for denial is that USCIS feels you are merely trying to prolong your U.S. stay indefinitely. When your application is denied, you will normally be given a period of 30 days to leave the U.S. voluntarily. Failure to leave within that time may result in removal proceedings and deportation. ■

Chapter 16

Getting a Temporary Specialty Worker (H-1B) Visa

Each year, a total of 85,000 H-1B temporary visas are made available to workers in occupations requiring highly specialized knowledge and to distinguished fashion models. (See I.N.A. § 101(a)(15)(H), 8 U.S.C. § 1101(a) (15)(H).) This visa is commonly used by workers in computer and other high-tech industries, but it's also available to people in other specialized fields, from accountants to attorneys to librarians to dietitians and other scientific or medical workers.

Unfortunately, there are never enough H-1B visas to supply all the workers who want them—and once the limit is reached in a given year, no more H-1B petitions can be approved until the start of the next fiscal year, October 1. Also, not all of the 85,000 total are freely available. Within that number, 20,000 are reserved for people with a minimum Master's level degree from a U.S. academic institution. (The good news is that these 20,000 are a recent addition, added with the H-1B Visa Reform Act of 2004.) And not all of the remaining 65,000 are available to everyone—a certain number are earmarked each year for countries that have signed free trade agreements with the U.S., such as Chile and Singapore. On the other hand, you're not subject to the numerical limits if you'll be working for an institution of higher education, a nonprofit research organization, or a government research organization.

Key Features of the H-1B Visa

Here are some of the advantages and disadvantages of the H-1B visa:

- You can work legally in the U.S. for your H-1B sponsor, up to a maximum of six years.
- Visas are available for your accompanying spouse and minor children, but they may not work, unless they qualify for a work visa in their own right.
- You may travel in and out of the U.S. or remain here continuously until your H-1B status expires.
- If your employer dismisses you before your authorized stay expires, the employer must pay for the trip back to your home country. This is true even if the cause of the firing was your own fault. This liability does not apply if you quit the job—only if you are fired.

Do you need a lawyer? You can't apply for an H-1B without having an employer first—and it's in your employer's interest to hire a lawyer to help. Because more people try to get H-1B visas every year than there are visas available, a lawyer can help make sure that your application gets done right the first time, and gets filed before the visas run out.

A. Do You Qualify for an H-1B Visa?

To qualify for an H-1B visa, you must first have a job offer from a U.S. employer for duties to be performed in the United States. In addition, the requirements for getting an H-1B visa include that:

- You are coming to the U.S. to perform services in a specialty occupation with a college degree or its equivalent in work experience, or to be a distinguished fashion model.
- You must have a job offer from a qualified U.S. employer for work to be performed in the U.S., and you must be offered at least the prevailing wage that is paid in the same geographic area for that type of job (or the actual wage paid to similar workers at that employer— whichever is the higher of the two wages).
- You must have the correct background to qualify for the job you have been offered.
- Your employer must have filed an attestation (LCA) with the Department of Labor (DOL).

Your job itself must also meet certain criteria, at least one of the following:

- A bachelor's degree or higher degree (or the equivalent) is the minimum requirement for entry into the position.

- The degree requirement is common to the industry in parallel positions among similar organizations, or the duties of the position are so complex that it can be performed only by a person with a degree.
- The employer normally requires a degree or its equivalent for the position.
- The nature of the specific duties is so specialized and complex that knowledge required to perform the duties is usually associated with a bachelor's or higher degree.

H-1B visas are available only to workers in occupations requiring highly specialized knowledge normally acquired through a college education, and to distinguished fashion models. To qualify for this visa, unless you are a fashion model, you need at least a bachelor's degree or substantial on-the-job experience that is the equivalent of a bachelor's degree. If you're qualifying through a bachelor's degree, it's preferable if it's not in a liberal arts or general business subject area, which USCIS tends to view as insufficiently specialized.

If you don't have a bachelor's degree but will be attempting to qualify through work experience, USCIS usually wants to see three years of specialized training and/or work experience for every year of college that you would have attended.

You must be coming to the U.S. to perform services in a so-called specialty occupation. If a license to practice your particular occupation is required by the U.S. state in which you will be working, then, in addition to your educational credentials, you must also have the appropriate license.

Fashion models need not meet the specialty occupation requirements. Instead, they must show that they are nationally or internationally recognized for their achievements, and will be employed in a position requiring someone of distinguished merit and ability. They must be renowned, leading, or well known.

 For more information on H-1B visas for fashion models: See the USCIS regulations at 8 C.F.R. § 214.2(h)(4)(vii). Because this is such a specialized area, this chapter does not provide details on applying as a fashion model, but the regulations do a good job of spelling out the documentary and other requirements.

To get an H-1B visa, not only do your job qualifications have to meet the standards mentioned above, it is also necessary to have the correct type of background for the job you are offered. If your academic and professional credentials are strong, but they do not match the job, then you are not eligible for an H-1B visa.

H-1B visas are often not given to prominent business people without college degrees, even though these people may have substantial on-the-job experience. (O-1 visas may be available to this group. See Chapter 24.) H-1B visas are likewise not given to athletes and entertainers, who should consider instead O or P visas (discussed in Chapter 24). Professional nurses are eligible for H-1B visas only if the position they will occupy actually requires an RN degree—usually because the job duties are complex or there are supervisory duties involved.

 Unlike many other nonimmigrant visas, you don't have to prove that you plan to return home at the end of your U.S. stay. In fact, you can (if you are separately eligible) have family members or employers submit applications for you to get a permanent green card at the same time that you're pursuing your H-1B visa—which would be the kiss of death for most other temporary visa applications. It's a different story, however, if you aren't eligible for a green card now but openly admit that you have no intention of leaving the U.S. after your visa expires—then your visa will be denied.

1. Job Criteria

Specialty occupations include, but are not limited to, accountants, architects, engineers, artists, dietitians, chiropractors, librarians, computer systems analysts, physical therapists, chemists, pharmacists, medical technologists, hotel managers (large hotels), and upper-level business managers.

Some occupations requiring licenses do not usually fall into the H-1B category because college degrees are not normally needed. Such occupations include many types of medical technicians, real estate agents, plumbers, and electricians. Unless a college degree is required, people in such occupations are limited to the more restrictive H-2B visa described in Chapter 17.

Limitations on Qualifying Physicians

Although physicians can qualify for H-1B visas, they must either pass a certifying exam (FLEX, NBME, or USMLE) and an English competency exam (TOEFL), or graduate from an accredited medical school. If they don't, they'll face limitations in the type of job they'll be allowed to perform in the United States. Specifically, physicians who don't pass one of the exams can only work at a teaching or research job in a public or nonprofit private educational or research institution or agency. Jobs that primarily involve patient care will not qualify this group for H-1B visas (although some patient care is allowed if necessary within the teaching or research context). See 8 C.F.R. § 214.2(h)(4)(viii).

2. Job Offer From a U.S. Employer for Work Performed Inside the U.S.

To get an H-1B visa, you need a specific job offer from a qualified employer for work to be performed inside the United States. The employer will act as your petitioner in getting your H-1B visa (and you become the beneficiary).

Many people are surprised to learn that they require an employment offer before applying for a work visa. The idea behind it is that you are being granted an H-1B visa only because your services have been recognized as essential to a U.S. enterprise. Put another way, the U.S. government is issuing the visa not for your benefit, but to help the U.S. economy.

The petitioner may be a company or an individual. Whether or not you can form your own corporation and have that corporation act as your sponsoring employer is not completely clear under the law. When the company you own is a legitimate business corporation and is not dependent on your presence to operate, there should be no trouble in using the company as a petitioner. If, however, the corporation appears to have been formed strictly for the purpose of getting you a visa, problems are likely to arise with the application.

The employer must also be offering you at least the prevailing wage that is paid for your type of job in that geographic area. The local job service or state labor department office does periodic surveys of salaries and can provide you with prevailing wage information. If your employer elects to rely on its own or a different survey, however, it will be required to identify the source of the information.

3. Specialty Occupation

The job offered can't be for just any type of work. The position must really require the skills of a highly educated person. For example, you may be a certified public accountant holding an advanced college degree. Public accounting clearly qualifies as a professional occupation. However, if you are offered a job as a bookkeeper, you will not get an H-1B visa, because it doesn't take a highly educated accountant to carry out standard bookkeeping tasks.

4. Correct Background

You must have the correct background for the job you have been offered. For example, if you are a qualified nuclear scientist, but are offered a position managing a U.S. automobile factory, you will not be granted an H-1B visa, because you have no background in automobile factory management. If, however, the job you are offered requires a background in nuclear science, then you would be eligible for the H-1B visa.

It is irrelevant that your native intelligence and general knowledge of business may make you quite capable of handling the automobile factory job. Likewise, reliability or willingness to work hard, characteristics difficult to find and much in demand by real-world employers, are not a USCIS consideration.

5. Approved Attestation

A business cannot sponsor you for an H-1B petition unless it first files an attestation, also known as a Labor Condition Application or LCA, with the DOL. The attestation is a document similar to a sworn declaration or written oath. It must include a number of statements ensuring that both U.S. and foreign workers are being treated fairly. These are discussed below in Section C.

6. Bringing Your Spouse and Children

When you qualify for an H-1B visa, your spouse and your unmarried children under age 21 can apply for H-4 visas by providing proof of their family relationship to you. H-4 visas authorize your family members to stay with you in the U.S., but not to work there. Like you, however, your family members will have to prove that they are not inadmissible to the United States. (See Chapter 3).

The Road to a Green Card

Having an H-1B visa gives you no legal advantage in applying for a green card. Realistically, however, it is probably easier to get an employer to sponsor you for an H-1B visa than a green card, and coming to the U.S. first with an H-1B gives you the opportunity to decide whether you really want to live in the U.S. permanently. Once you are in the U.S. with a work permit, it is also usually easier to find an employer willing to sponsor you for a green card—or to convince your current employer to do so.

B. Quick View of the H-1B Visa Application Process

Getting an H-1B visa is a two- to four-step process:

- First, your U.S. employer files a Labor Condition Attestation (LCA) with the U.S. Department of Labor (DOL)
- Second, your U.S. employer files what's called a visa petition on USCIS Form I-129. If you're already in the U.S. in lawful status, this petition can simultaneously ask that your status be changed to H-1B worker, in which case the process will successfully end here.

- Third, if you're outside the U.S., then after the visa petition is approved, you submit your own application for an H-1B visa to a U.S. consulate (unless you're from Canada, in which case you can skip this step), and
- Finally, you use either your visa or (if you're from Canada) the notice of your approved visa petition to enter the U.S. and claim your H-1B status.

 Nothing stops you from helping with the employer's tasks during this application process. For example, you can fill out forms intended to be completed by your employer and simply ask the employer to check them over and sign them. The less your U.S. employer is inconvenienced, the more likely it will be willing to act as sponsor for your visa.

C. Step One: Your Employer Files an LCA

No employer can sponsor you for an H-1B petition unless it first files a Labor Condition Attestation (LCA) with the DOL. The LCA can be submitted up to six months before you plan to start work. An LCA is similar to a sworn declaration or a written oath. It must include the following information and statements:

- a description of the job for which H-1B workers are needed

- a statement of the number of foreign workers to be hired in that job
- a statement of the wages to be paid the foreign worker, what the prevailing wage is for that job, and where the employer obtained the prevailing wage information
- a written promise that foreign nationals will be paid 100% of the prevailing market wage for the position, or the employer's actual wage, whichever is higher; and will receive the same benefits as the U.S. coworkers
- a statement that there are no strikes, lockouts, or work stoppages in progress involving the jobs to be filled by H-1B workers, and
- a statement that the employer has given notice of the filing of H-1B attestations to either the labor union representing the type of employee involved, or, if no union exists, that the employer has posted notice of filing in at least two conspicuous locations at the place of employment for a period of ten days.

Fortunately, the prevailing wage rules recognize that academic institutions can't always match salaries in private industry. Therefore, if you're applying for a job at an institution of higher education or an affiliated or related nonprofit, at a nonprofit research organization, or at a governmental research organization, your employer will need only show that it will pay the prevailing wage as compared to similar institutions.

The law frowns on employers who rely too heavily on H-1B workers, however. Employers who are "H-1B dependent," or who have committed certain labor-related violations in the last five years, will have to make additional statements on the attestation form (except in cases where they're paying the worker more than $60,000 or the worker has a Master's degree or higher). H-1B dependent means that their workforce includes either:

- 25 or fewer full-time employees and eight or more H-1B employees
- 26 to 50 full-time employees and 13 or more H-1B employees, or
- 51 or more full-time employees and at least 15% H-1B employees.

The additional attestations that such H-1B-dependent employers must make include that:

- The H-1B worker will not displace U.S. workers.
- If the employer places the employee with another employer or worksite, the original employer will first make certain that no U.S. workers will be displaced there.
- The employer has made good faith efforts to recruit U.S. workers for the job, at the prevailing wage.

A separate LCA must be filed for each type of job the company wishes to fill with H-1B workers.

Filing the LCA is a very simple matter. Form ETA-9035 is submitted online at www.lca.doleta.gov.

The form has all necessary statements already written out, with blanks to be filled in with the appropriate occupations, numbers of workers and salaries. The DOL will accept for filing all complete attestations; however, anyone, including other employees at the petitioning company, can file a complaint against it. The primary objective here is to require employers to pay H-1B workers at least the prevailing wage or average (weighted average) salary for that type of job in the particular geographic area.

When the attestation is accepted, your employer will receive a version of the ETA-9035 form that it filed, with a DOL endorsement. A copy of the endorsed ETA-9035 must then be submitted to USCIS as a supporting document to the visa petition.

Even after the attestation has been accepted, your employer must make available at its offices for public inspection a copy of each H-1B worker's attestation and supporting documents. The file must also contain information about the company's wage system, benefits plan, and more. Many employers seek the help of attorneys in complying with these requirements.

D. Step Two: Your Employer Files a Visa Petition

Your employer needs to submit a visa petition to USCIS, on Form I-129. The object of the petition is to prove four things:

- that you personally qualify for H-1B status
- that your future job is of a high enough level to warrant someone with your advanced skills
- that you have the correct background and skills to match the job requirements, and
- that your U.S. employer has the financial ability to pay your salary.

1. Simultaneous Change of Status If You're Already in the U.S.

If you're already in the U.S. in lawful status, such as on a student or other temporary visa, the petition can be used to ask your status be immediately changed to H-1B worker. (Part 2, Question 5 of Form I-129 offers choices addressing this issue.) You can't, however, take advantage of this option if you entered the U.S. on a visa waiver, or using a C (alien in transit), TWOV (alien in transit without a visa), D (crewman), K-1 (fiancé), K-2 (dependent of a fiancé), J-1 (exchange visitor), or M-1 (vocational student) visa. You must have:

- entered the U.S. legally
- never worked in U.S. illegally, and

- not passed the expiration date on your I-94 card.

There is another problem that comes up only in U.S. filings. It is the issue of what is called "preconceived intent." To approve a change of status, USCIS must believe that at the time you originally entered the U.S. as a visitor or with some other nonimmigrant visa, you did not intend to apply for a different status. If USCIS thinks you had a preconceived plan to use one visa to enter the U.S. with an eye to applying for a different status after getting there, it may deny your application. (You can get around the preconceived intent issue by leaving the U.S. and applying for your H-1B visa at a U.S. consulate in another country.)

Your spouse and children, if they are also in the U.S. with you, can't change their status by being mentioned on your Form I-129, but must submit separate Forms I-539. They can submit these either at the same time your employer submits Form I-129, or afterward. (If they submit them afterward, however, they will need to include either a copy of the USCIS receipt notice indicating that your petition is pending, or a copy of the petition approval notice.)

Your eligibility to apply in the U.S. has nothing to do with your overall eligibility for an H-1B visa. Many applicants who are barred from filing in the U.S., but otherwise qualify for H-1B status, may still apply successfully for an H-1B visa at a U.S. consulate in another country.

If you decide to apply for a change of status within the U.S., realize that you still don't have the H-1B visa that you'll need if you ever leave the U.S.—a change of status only gives you H-1B status. Visas are never given inside the United States. They are issued exclusively by U.S. consulates in other countries. If you file in the U.S. and you are successful, you will get to remain in the U.S. with H-1B privileges until the status expires. But should you leave the country for any reason before that time, you will have to apply for the visa itself at a U.S. consulate before returning to the United States. Moreover, the fact that your H-1B status has been approved in the U.S. does not guarantee that the consulate will also approve your visa. For these reasons, some people simply file through a consulate.

2. Assembling the Visa Petition

The checklist below will help you and your employer assemble the necessary items for the visa petition.

Checklist for H-1B Visa Petition

❏ Form I-129, H Supplement, and H-1B Data Collection and Filing Fee Exemption Supplement.

❏ Base filing fee: $320.

❏ Additional fee of either $750 or $1,500, depending on employer's answers to the questions on the H-1B Data Collection and Filing Fee Exemption Supplement form.

❏ Fraud prevention and detection fee (currently $500).

❏ If you will be applying in the United States and your family members are with you and need a change of status, Form I-539 with accompanying fee (currently $300) and copies of your family members' I-94s or other proof of lawful immigration status and of their relationship to you, the primary beneficiary (such as marriage and birth certificates). One Form I-539 and fee will cover your spouse and all your children. Your family members should fill out this form, not your employer.

❏ If you're in the U.S., a copy of your I-94 or other proof of your current lawful, unexpired immigration status (except Canadians just visiting the U.S., who are not expected to have I-94 cards).

❏ If you're outside the U.S., a copy of your passport.

❏ Copy of employer's certified attestation Form ETA-9035 or ETA-9035e.

❏ Proof of employer's ability to pay your salary, such as annual report, tax returns, and accounting statements.

❏ Either a written employment agreement with you or a written summary of an oral agreement. The terms of your employment, including job duties, hours, and salary, must be mentioned. It is acceptable that the employment be "at will" and not of any particular duration.

❏ Evidence that your job will be in a "specialty occupation."

❏ Evidence that you have the required degree, such as your college and university diplomas (and if they're from a foreign university, evidence that they're equivalent to U.S. degrees). If you attended a school but did not graduate, the transcript is required. If you attended any relevant training courses, include a copy of the certificate of completion.

❏ If you do not have a degree, evidence that your combined education and experience is equivalent to a degree.

❏ If the job requires a license or other permit to practice in the U.S. state where you'll be located, a copy of your license or permit.

❏ If your intended job is as a physician, proof that you have passed the appropriate exams and met state licensing requirements.

If requesting quick (premium) processing:

❏ Form I-907, with $1,000 filing fee.

A few items on this checklist require some extra explanation:

Form I-129 and H Supplement.
The basic form for the visa petition is immigration Form I-129 and its H Supplement. The I-129 form is used for many different nonimmigrant visas. In addition to the basic part of the form that applies to all types of visas, it comes with several supplements for each specific nonimmigrant category. Simply use the supplement that applies to you.

The employer may choose to list more than one foreign employee on a single I-129 petition. This is appropriate if the employer has more than one opening to be filled for the same type of job. Supplement-1, which is also part of Form I-129, should be completed for each additional employee.

Proof of specialty occupation.
Sometimes, as with positions for physicians, accountants, and similarly recognized professions, the highly specialized nature of the work is common knowledge. In such cases, the employment agreement will serve to prove both the existence and the level of the job. Where it is not evident that the position is a specialty occupation, additional documents are required. Your employer should write out and submit a detailed description of all job functions, with an explanation of how advanced knowledge and education are essential to their performance. If it remains unclear that the job requires

a high-level employee, your employer might need to get written affidavits from experts, such as educators in the field or other employers in similar businesses, stating that jobs of this kind are normally held by highly qualified and degreed individuals.

Proof of employer's ability to pay your salary. Your employer must be able to prove its existence and financial viability. If the employer is large and well known, it is usually enough to state the annual gross receipts or income, in the letter it submits describing the job opportunity and duties. If the employer is very small, USCIS may request documents to verify the existence and financial solvency of the employer's business. In that case, USCIS will specifically advise your employer of the documents it wishes to see, including tax returns, profit and loss statements, and the like.

Publicly held companies do not have to produce tax returns, accounting records, or bank statements. For them, annual reports of the past two years are accepted to prove ability to pay wages. Again, the larger the company, the less evidence the USCIS demands of its ability to pay additional salaries.

Special documents for physicians.
Graduates of medical schools outside the U.S. or Canada may not get H-1B visas as practicing physicians unless they have passed the USMLE licensing exam or an equivalent exam and satisfy the state licensing requirements if they

will provide direct patient care services. If patient care will be provided, the physician must also have an unrestricted license to practice in a foreign state, or have graduated from a U.S. medical school. Passing the exam, however, is not required of foreign medical graduates who come to the U.S. to work solely in teaching or research positions at a public or nonprofit institution. In those cases, any patient care activities must be incidental to the teaching or research functions.

Therefore, in addition to all other documents required from members of the professions, the petitioning employer must submit either a certificate showing you have passed the USMLE or an equivalent exam, or a statement certifying that you will be employed as either a teacher or researcher and that any patient care will be undertaken only as part of the teaching or research. This written statement does not have to be in any special form but simply in the petitioner's own words.

Foreign medical students attending medical school abroad may petition to be classified as H-3 trainees if the hospital is approved by the American Medical Association or American Osteopathic Association. A hospital submits the petition, for either a residency or internship, if the alien will engage in employment as an extern during his or her medical school training.

3. Mailing the Visa Petition

After assembling the visa petition, your U.S. employer must mail it to either the California Service Center or the Vermont Service Center, whichever has jurisdiction over the employer's place of business. If you'll be coming from outside the U.S., your employer must send duplicate versions of the form (two signed originals; copies are not acceptable).

USCIS regional service centers are not the same as USCIS local offices—for one thing, you cannot visit regional service centers in person. See the USCIS website at www.uscis.gov for the regional service centers' addresses and P.O. box numbers.

4. Awaiting a Decision on the Visa Petition

Within a few weeks after mailing in the petition, your employer should receive a written confirmation that the papers are being processed, as well as a receipt for the fee. This notice will also give your immigration file number. If USCIS wants further information before acting on your case, all petition papers, forms, and documents will be returned to your employer with a form known as a Request for Evidence. Your employer should supply the extra data requested and mail the whole package back to the service center.

H-1B petitions are normally approved within two to five months. When this happens, a Form I-797 Notice of Action will be sent to your employer, showing the petition was approved. If you plan to submit your visa application at a U.S. consulate abroad, USCIS will also notify the consulate of your choice, sending a complete copy of your file. Only the employer receives communications from USCIS about the petition, because technically it is the employer who is seeking the visa on your behalf.

Faster processing—at a price. For $1,000 over and above the regular filing fees, USCIS promises "premium processing" of the visa petition, including a decision within 15 days. To use this service, the employer must fill out an additional application (Form I-907) and submit the application to a special USCIS service center address. For complete instructions, see the USCIS website at www.uscis.gov.

Be aware that an approved petition does not by itself give you any immigration privileges. It is only a prerequisite to the next step, submitting your application for an H-1B visa.

E. Step Three: Applicants Outside the U.S. Apply to a U.S. Consulate

After the H-1B visa petition filed by your employer has been approved, USCIS will send a Form I-797B, with which you can apply for a visa at a U.S. consulate—normally in your home country. (Some consulates will insist upon waiting for formal notification directly from USCIS, but most will accept an original Form I-797B from you.) Check with your local U.S. consulate regarding its application procedures. Many insist on advance appointments. Just getting an appointment can take several weeks, so plan ahead.

If you're visa exempt, you can skip this step. Citizens of Canada and certain others need not apply to a U.S. consulate. Instead, they can proceed directly to the United States with Form I-797B and supporting documents to request entry. (See 8 C.F.R. § 212.1.) If you're risk-averse, however, applying at a consulate first might be the safer route.

Applying at a Consulate That's Not in Your Home Country

The law allows most people to apply for an H-1B visa at any U.S. consulate they choose—with one exception. If you have ever been present in the U.S. unlawfully, your visa will be automatically cancelled and you cannot apply as a third-country national (at a consulate outside your home country). Even if you overstayed your status in the U.S. by just one day, you must return to your home country and apply for the visa from that consulate. There is an exception. If you were admitted to the U.S. for the duration of your status (indicated by a "D/S" on your I-94 form and most common with student visas) and you remained in the U.S. beyond that time for which your status was conferred, you will be barred from third-country national processing only if an immigration judge or USCIS (or former INS) officer has determined that you were unlawfully present. You may find that your success in applying as a third-country national will depend on your country, the consulate, and the relative seriousness of your offense. Being unlawfully present is also a ground of inadmissibility if the period of unlawful presence is 180 days or more. (See Chapter 3.)

Even if you are eligible for third-country national processing, your case will be given the greatest consideration at the consulate in your home country. Applying in some other country creates suspicion in the minds of the consular officers there about your motives for choosing their consulate. Often, when an applicant expects trouble at a home consulate, he or she will seek a more lenient consular office in some other country. This practice of consulate shopping is frowned upon by officials in the system. Unless you have a very good reason for being elsewhere (such as a temporary job assignment in some other nation), it is often smarter to file your visa application in your home country.

 Have you been, or are you now, working or living illegally in the United States? If so, see Chapter 3 regarding whether or not you can still get an H-1B visa from a U.S. consulate. You may have become inadmissible or subject to a three-year or ten-year bar on reentry.

The following checklist will help you prepare your consular application.

H-1B Visa Application Checklist

❑ Form DS-156, Nonimmigrant Visa Application (available at U.S. consulates).

❑ Form DS-157, Supplemental Nonimmigrant Visa Application (also available at U.S. consulates; but it only needs to be filled out by male nonimmigrant visa applicants between the ages of 16 and 45).

❑ Notice showing approval of the H-1B petition.

❑ Valid passport for you and each accompanying relative.

❑ One U.S. passport-type photo of you and one of each accompanying relative. (This is best done by a professional photographer; the consulate can give you a list.)

❑ If your spouse and children will be accompanying you, documents verifying their family relationship to you, such as marriage and birth certificates.

❑ Visa application fee (currently $100).

❑ Visa issuance fee (depending on what country you're from; if the country of your nationality charges fees for visas to U.S. citizens who wish to work there, then the U.S. will charge people of your country a similar fee as well).

As part of your application, the consulate will require you and your family members to attend an interview.

See Chapter 4 for what to expect during consular interviews, and what to do if your application is denied.

F. Step Four: You Enter the U.S. With Your H-1B Visa

You have until the expiration date on your H-1B visa to enter the United States. The border officer will examine your paperwork, ask you some questions, and if all is in order, approve you for entry. He or she will stamp your passport and give you a small white card called an I-94 card. It will be stamped with a date showing how long you can stay. Normally, you are permitted to remain up to the expiration date on your H-1B petition. (However, if your passport will expire before the petition's expiration date, some CBP officers will issue the I-94 until only the date of the passport's expiration.) Each time you exit and reenter the U.S., you will get a new I-94 card authorizing your stay up to the final date indicated on the petition.

Watch Out for Summary Exclusion

The law empowers a CBP inspector at the U.S. airport or border to summarily (without allowing judicial review) bar entry to someone requesting admission to the U.S. if either of the following is true:

- The inspector thinks you are lying about practically anything connected with entering the U.S., including your purpose in coming, intent to return, and prior immigration history. This includes the use or suspected use of false documents.
- You do not have the proper documentation to support your entry to the U.S. in the category you are requesting.

If the inspector excludes you, you cannot be readmitted to the U.S. for five years, unless USCIS grants a special waiver. For this reason it is extremely important to understand the terms of your requested status, and to not make any misrepresentations. If you are found to be inadmissible, you may ask the CBP inspector to withdraw your application to enter the U.S. in order to prevent having the five-year deportation order on your record. The CBP may allow this in some exceptional cases.

G. Extending Your U.S. Stay

H-1B visas can be extended for three years at a time, but you may not hold an H-1B visa for longer than a total of six years. Although an extension is usually easier to get than the H-1B visa itself, it is not automatic. USCIS has the right to reconsider your qualifications based on any changes in the facts or law, and your employer must maintain a valid attestation for your position. As always, however, good cases that are well prepared will be successful.

To extend your H-1B visa, the petition and visa stamp will both have to be updated. As with the original application, you can file either in the U.S. or at a consulate.

Under legislation enacted in 2000, H-1B visa holders who are awaiting a decision on their green card application can get additional extensions of one year at a time. Either your application for a labor certification or your immigrant visa petition must have been pending 365 days or more. Also, H-1B visa holders who are waiting for their Priority Dates to become current (as described in Chapter 9) can get additional extensions of three years at a time.

Extension procedures are identical with the procedures followed in getting the initial visa, except that less documentation is required. In addition to a copy of the previous employer's LCA (if it is valid for the extension

Working While Your Extension Petition Is Pending

If you file your petition for an extension of H-1B status before your authorized stay expires, you are automatically permitted to continue working for up to 240 days while you are waiting for a decision. If, however, your authorized stay expires after you have filed for an extension but before you receive an approval, and more than 240 days go by without getting a decision on your extension petition, your work authorization ceases and you must stop working. You will not be able to continue working until your extension is finally approved.

period requested—or a new LCA if the old one is expired), you need submit only your I-94 card, a copy of the Form I-797 approval from your first H-1B visa petition, a letter from the employer requesting your visa be extended and stating that you will continue to be employed in a specialty occupation as previously described, and a copy of your U.S. income tax returns for the previous two years, including the W-2 forms. (Be sure the tax returns reflect only H-1B employment before submitting them.)

If you extend your H-1B status while you're in the U.S., and travel outside the U.S. before your H-1B stay is over, you'll need to go to a U.S. consulate for a new H-1B visa before you return. Read (or reread) the procedures in Section E, above. The procedures for consular extensions are identical. If possible, try to schedule filing your extension application so that you can remain in the U.S. until it is complete.

H. Your Rights as an H-1B Worker

Once you've got H-1B status, the law offers you various forms of protection. For example, your employer is required to pay you, as a new H-1B employee, within 30 days of your entry into the United States. If you are already in the U.S., your employer must pay you within 60 days of your approval as an H-1B worker. The employer is also prohibited from "benching" you, that is, putting you on involuntary, unpaid leave. This prohibition holds true even if the employer has insufficient work for you or you lack a permit or license. Employees must be paid for any time spent in nonproductive status due to a decision by the employer.

If you lose your job, then as long as you entered the U.S. lawfully, have never worked without permission, and haven't stayed past the date when your original H-1B status was to expire, you can accept a new job as soon as your new employer files an I-129 petition on your behalf. It's not a perfect system—

you'll still have to leave the U.S. to get a new visa after the I-129 is approved, because people whose old visas have become invalid are not allowed to apply to change status within the United States. But at least you won't be sitting around unemployed and out of status or out of the country while USCIS is making its decision on the new I-129 petition.

Employers are prohibited from trying to keep hold of H-1B employees by forcing them to pay a penalty if they leave the job prior to a certain date. The employer can be fined up to $1,000 for this violation. ■

Chapter 17

Getting an H-2B (Temporary Nonagricultural Worker) Visa

The H-2B visa was created to allow people to come to the U.S. temporarily to fill nonagricultural jobs for which U.S. workers are in short supply. A total of 66,000 H-2B visa petitions may be approved during the government year (fiscal year), which ends on September 30. (See I.N.A. § 101(a)(15)(H), 8 U.S.C. § 1101(a)(15)(H).) Recent law effectively divided the fiscal year in two, however, so that no more than 33,000 visas can be passed out during the first six months. Although the 66,000 total doesn't include returning workers or accompanying spouses and children, lately the annual quota has not been enough to meet the demand. This chapter will explain who is eligible for an H-2B visa and how to apply.

Key Features of the H-2B Visa

Here are some of the advantages and disadvantages of the H-2B visa:

- You can work legally in the U.S. for your H-2B sponsor, up to a maximum of three years.
- Visas are available for your accompanying spouse and minor children, but they may not work, unless they qualify for a work visa in their own right.
- You may travel in and out of the U.S. or remain here continuously until your H-2B status expires.

Do you need a lawyer? You can't apply for an H-2B without having an employer first—and it's in your employer's interest to hire a lawyer to help. Because more people have recently been trying to get H-2B visas than there are visas available, a lawyer can help make sure that your application gets done right the first time, and gets filed before the visas run out.

A. Do You Qualify for an H-2B Visa?

H-2B visas are aimed at skilled and unskilled workers, as compared to H-1B visas, which are intended for college-educated workers. There are four requirements for obtaining an H-2B visa:

- You must have a job offer from a U.S. employer to perform work that is either temporary or seasonal.
- You must have the correct background to qualify for the job you have been offered.
- There must be no qualified U.S. workers willing or able to take the job. A temporary labor certification is required.
- You must intend to return home when your visa expires.

The term temporary refers to the employer's need for the duties performed by the position, regardless of whether the underlying position is permanent or temporary. Seasonal laborers, workers on short-term business projects, and those who come to the U.S. as trainers of other workers commonly get H-2B visas. A job can be deemed temporary if it is a one-time occurrence, meets a seasonal or peak-load need, or fulfills an intermittent but not regular need of the employer.

H-2B visas are also frequently used for entertainers who cannot meet the criteria for O or P visas. H-2B visas enable such entertainers to come to the U.S. for specific bookings. These bookings are considered temporary positions.

Other jobs that have met the criteria include athletes, camp counselors, craftpersons, ski instructors, and home attendants for terminally ill patients. Although we've just given you some examples of jobs that meet the USCIS's definition of temporary, be aware that most jobs do not.

1. Job Offer From a U.S. Employer

You need a specific job offer from a U.S. employer to get an H-2B visa. The employer will have to act as the petitioner in getting your H-2B visa. Many people are surprised to learn that they require an employment offer before applying for a work visa. The idea behind it is that you are being granted an H-2B visa because your services are essential to a U.S. company. Put another way, the U.S. government issues the visa to help your U.S. employer, not for your benefit.

The petitioner may be a company or an individual. Generally, you cannot act as your own employer. An agent who books your talents for a variety of jobs can be the source of the job offer if the salary is paid to you directly by the agent and not by the individual places where you perform. This is a common arrangement for entertainers.

The job you are offered can't be just any position. First, it must be one that meets the legal definition of temporary. To be considered temporary, the period of the employer's need for services should be one year or less, absent unusual circumstances.

Second, the employer's need must be either one-time, seasonal, based on a peak-load need, or based on an intermittent need. An example of a one-time need would be a specific project, such as building a housing development. Seasonal needs are fairly self-explanatory—workers at a ski resort would be a good example. Peak-load needs often occur around tourist or holiday seasons, when employers bring in extra workers whom they let go afterwards. Intermittent needs are ones where the employer needs workers occasionally for short periods, but not for long enough to justify hiring someone permanently. Professional minor-league baseball players are a common example of employees who do seasonal work. (Major-league players will usually qualify for O visas. See Chapter 24.)

Temporary Agricultural Worker: H-2A Visas

Under the 1986 amendments to the U.S. immigration laws, temporary agricultural workers are now treated differently from all other types of temporary workers. Agricultural workers are now issued H-2A visas while all other temporary workers receive H-2B visas.

The rules for getting temporary agricultural worker visas are extremely complex and beyond the scope of this book. The basic requirements are that before a non-U.S. agricultural worker may be granted an H-2A visa, the prospective employer must attempt to find U.S. agricultural workers. The employer must search for U.S. workers not just in the employer's own immediate geographical area, but throughout the entire adjacent region of the country. The employer must do this by undertaking a multistate recruitment effort.

Moreover, H-2A visas will not, as a practical matter, be issued to foreign workers who are already in the U.S. illegally. Due to the great amount of effort involved in obtaining H-2A visas, they will be attractive only to employers who urgently need to bring in a large crew of foreign laborers at one time to work on a particular harvest. Again, from a practical standpoint, the employer will either have to travel abroad or use the services of a foreign labor contractor to find these crews of temporary foreign workers. H-2A visas are not practical for bringing one temporary agricultural worker at a time to the United States.

2. Correct Background

You must have the correct background and abilities for the job you have been offered. For example, if you are a qualified insurance salesman but are offered a job supervising a catering project, you will not be granted an H-2B visa for that job because you have no background in catering. It is irrelevant that your native intelligence and general knowledge of business may make you quite capable of handling the catering job. Likewise, reliability or willingness to work hard, characteristics difficult to find and much sought after by real-world employers, are not a USCIS consideration. If you lack the required background in the job offered, the petition will fail.

H-2B visas can be issued to unskilled as well as skilled workers. If your job offer happens to be for employment as an unskilled worker, there are, by definition no specific background qualifications for you to meet. Under these circumstances, your natural abilities may be a consideration, but you do not need to be concerned about having the correct background.

3. No Qualified U.S. Workers

To obtain an H-2B visa, there must be no qualified U.S. workers available to take the job you have been offered. Your prospective employer must successfully complete a temporary labor certification to prove the unavailability of U.S. workers. This condition may or may not be hard to meet, depending on the type of job. Where the jobs are meant for skilled and unskilled workers rather than professionals, the competition factor can be a problem. Many employers do go begging, however, for want of either qualified or willing U.S. applicants, especially in businesses requiring unusual skills or with odd working hours or other undesirable features.

4. Intent to Return to Your Home Country

H-2B visas are meant to be temporary. At the time of applying, you must intend to return home when the visa expires. If you have it in mind to take up permanent residence in the U.S., you are legally ineligible for an H-2B visa. The U.S. government knows it is difficult to read minds. Expect to be asked for evidence showing that when you go to the United States on an H-2B visa, you are leaving behind possessions, property, or family members as incentive for your eventual return.

5. Bringing Your Spouse and Children

When you qualify for an H-2B visa, your spouse and unmarried children under age 21 can get H-4 visas by providing proof of their family relationship to you. Like you, your family members will also have to show that they are not inadmissible (see Chapter 3). H-4 visas authorize your accompanying relatives to stay with you in the U.S., but not to work there.

B. Possibilities for a Green Card From H-2B Status

Being in the U.S. on an H-2B visa gives you no advantage in applying for a U.S. green card. In fact, it will almost certainly prove to be a drawback. That is because H-2B visas, like most nonimmigrant visas, are intended only for those who plan to return home once their jobs or other activities in the U.S. are completed. However, if you apply for a green card, you are in effect making a statement that you never intend to leave the United States. Therefore, USCIS may allow you to keep H-2B status while pursuing a green card, but only if you can convince USCIS that you did not intend to get a green card when you originally applied for the H-2B visa and that you will return home if you are unable to secure a green card before your H-2B visa expires. Doing this can be difficult. If you do not succeed, your H-2B status can be taken away.

Entertainment Industry Workers: Special Considerations

Entertainment industry workers, both the performers and the many diversified workers it takes to make a movie or to stage a live performance, often need temporary U.S. work visas. H-1B visas are not available to entertainers or athletes. The better-known ones will qualify for O or P visas. (See Chapter 24.) The individual entertainment industry worker who is not well known, not part of a well-known group, or not part of an international production team is limited to an H-2B visa.

In these cases, there is a problem with both the temporariness of the job and the availability of similarly qualified U.S. workers. The definition of temporariness is narrow for entertainment industry jobs, as it is for positions in other occupations. If, for example, a Las Vegas nightclub wants to book an act for only one week, USCIS will still say that the job is not temporary because nightclubs are always employing acts to perform there. The conclusion is that the job is not temporary even if the booking is. On the other hand, jobs for performers on tour are considered temporary, as are jobs for workers on motion pictures. That is because tours and motion picture productions always end.

Even if the job is clearly temporary, your U.S. employer must still get a clearance from the Department of Labor (DOL) acknowledging that no U.S. workers are available to fill the job.

When such a clearance is requested, the DOL will, in turn, contact the appropriate U.S. entertainment industry union to see if the union can find a U.S. worker to fill the position or has some other objection to a non-U.S. worker taking the job. Since there are many competent U.S. entertainment industry workers looking for employment, getting union approval on an H-2B case may be difficult.

The availability of competing U.S. workers is not a problem in several situations. H-2B visas are readily available to all performing and non-performing members of lesser-known troupes coming to the U.S. on tour. We have already explained that in the view of USCIS, the touring factor makes a job temporary. Moreover, U.S. entertainment industry unions are usually reluctant to break up performing units. Therefore, an entire touring group, from performers to technicians and stage hands, can all get H-2B visas.

The offer of employment must be from a U.S. employer. The workers cannot be self-employed nor can they be working in the U.S. for a foreign company. Individual performers, therefore, normally have to get their H-2B visas through a central booking agent. This is acceptable, provided the booking agent acts as the employer in every respect, including being responsible for paying the salary.

Entertainment Industry Workers: Special Considerations (cont'd)

Foreign entertainment industry working units, such as film companies, that wish to get H-2B visas will need to do one of two things to supply themselves with the required U.S. employer. They can be sponsored for visas by an established U.S. company that will act as the employer of each individual foreign employee. Alternatively, the foreign group may form its own U.S. corporation and have it act as the employer. U.S. corporations are set up by state governments in the U.S. state where the business will be head-quartered. Forming a U.S. corporation is extremely simple and in most states can be accomplished in a matter of days. Information on how to form a U.S. corporation is available from the office of the secretary of state located in each state capital, and from Nolo's *Incorporate Your Business: A Legal Guide to Forming a Corporation in Your State*, by Anthony Mancuso.

It is also important to understand that even if you argue successfully and keep your H-2B status, the visa and the petition each carry a maximum duration of one year and will probably expire before you get a green card. Once you have made a green card application, you will be absolutely barred from receiving an extension of your H-2B status. Should you, for any reason, lose your H-2B status, it may affect your green card application.

Another problem comes up if it is your current H-2B sponsoring employer who also wants to sponsor you for a green card. USCIS regulations provide that if you have an approved permanent labor certification sponsored by the same employer who petitioned for your H-2B visa, the H-2B visa will automatically be revoked. The only way you can apply for a green card through employment and retain an H-2B visa, even until its expiration date, is to have a different sponsoring employer for the green card than you had for the H-2B visa.

If what you really want is a green card, apply for it directly and disregard H-2B visas. Although the green card is harder to get and may take several years, in the long run you will be happier with the results. Also, relatively few jobs qualify as temporary for H-2B visa purposes and you may actually have a better chance of getting a green card through a given job than an H-2B visa.

C. Quick View of the H-2B Visa Application Process

Once you have been offered a job, getting an H-2B visa is a two- to four-step process.

- First, your U.S. employer files an application for what's called temporary labor certification with the U.S. Department of Labor (DOL).
- Second, your U.S. employer files what's called a visa petition on USCIS Form I-129. If you're already in the U.S. in lawful status, this petition can simultaneously ask that your status be changed to H-2B worker, in which case the process will successfully end here.
- If you're outside the U.S., then after the visa petition is approved, you submit your own application for an H-2B visa to a U.S. consulate (unless you're from Canada, in which case you can skip this step).
- Finally, you use either your visa or (if you're from Canada) the notice of your approved visa petition to enter the U.S. and claim your H-2B status.

Nothing stops you from helping with the employer's tasks during this application process. For example, you can fill out forms intended to be completed by your employer and simply ask the employer to check them over and sign them. The less your U.S. employer is inconvenienced, the more likely it will be willing to act as sponsor for your visa.

D. Step One: Your Employer Applies for Temporary Labor Certification

Your U.S. employer starts the process by applying for what's known as temporary labor certification, on Form ETA-750 Part A (available, with instructions, at www.foreignlaborcert.doleta.gov/h-2b.cfm). The process may not begin more than 120 days before your services are needed. The object of the temporary labor certification is to satisfy the U.S. government that there are no qualified U.S. workers available to take the specific job that has been offered to you, and to determine whether the job is temporary in nature and therefore suitable for an H-2B visa. These things must be proven first to the DOL, and then to USCIS.

The judgment of the DOL on the temporary labor certification is only advisory in nature. USCIS has the final word. However, USCIS gives great weight to the DOL's opinion, and if the temporary labor certification is denied, it will be difficult to get a later approval from USCIS. Therefore, you will initially file temporary labor certification papers with the DOL.

Be aware that an approved temporary labor certification does not by itself give you any immigration privileges. It is only a prerequisite to the next steps, submitting your petition and application for an H-2B visa.

1. Which Government Agencies Handle the LCA Request

Temporary labor certifications, consisting both of forms and documents, are filed in the U.S. at the local state workforce agency (SWA) nearest the employer's place of business. We emphasize that this is an office of the state government, not the federal DOL. State government employment agencies assist the DOL in the temporary labor certification process by monitoring employers' efforts to locate U.S. workers. However, in keeping with the centralization of decision making implemented under the 2005 PERM regulations, the DOL's National Processing Center will handle the file after the state office finishes its work, and make the final decision on your temporary labor certification.

States differ about the exact place and procedures for filing temporary labor certifications. Some designate a single office to accept applications for the entire state while others use a system of several regional offices around the state. A call to the nearest office of the state employment agency in your employer's area of the country will tell your employer where and how to file the certification request.

There is no filing fee for a temporary labor certification. If possible, it is better for the employer to file in person so

you can be sure that the arrival of the papers is recorded. When filing the papers in person, ask for a dated written receipt. The receipt should be kept in a safe place together with a complete copy of everything submitted. Then your employer can prove when your temporary labor certification was filed and help to locate the papers should they get lost or delayed in processing.

When filing by mail, send the papers by certified mail, return receipt requested, and again keep a complete copy for your records.

Because there is no uniformity in operating methods among the various state employment agencies, the length of time it takes to get a temporary labor certification approved varies greatly from one state to another. However, all offices are supposed to give priority to temporary labor certification applications. The application cannot be filed more than 120 days before the worker is needed, and it is likely to take about four months to get approval. In some states, it may take longer.

If you have good reason, most DOL offices will expedite the processing of a temporary labor certification if you ask. Your employer must simply include a letter requesting expedited processing and explain why your presence on the job is needed immediately.

2. Advertising and Recruitment

The temporary labor certification is similar to the permanent labor certification process discussed in Chapter 9. Your U.S. employer must attempt to recruit U.S. workers for the position that has been offered to you. It is crucial to the success of the H-2B application that your employer fail at this attempt. To demonstrate that U.S. workers are in fact unavailable, the job must be publicly advertised. The employer must then wait to see whether any qualified U.S. candidates come forward. The DOL has established a specific procedure for this advertising.

The procedure begins when the employer files Form ETA-750 with the state labor department. The state labor department will send back a letter to the employer acknowledging receipt of the form and assigning an identification number known as a job order number to the case. The letter will also give instructions on how to advertise and will refer qualified candidates to the employer for interviews.

3. Handling Job Applications

If anyone applies for the job by responding to the advertisement or state labor department listing, the labor department will collect resumes from the candidates and forward them to the employer. The employer must then review the resumes and be prepared to state in writing why each candidate does not meet the minimum qualifications for the job as described in the advertisement and on Form ETA-750. The same must be done with candidates who respond directly to the employer (probably from

the posting of an in-house notice). Even if a single requested qualification is missing from the resume, that's enough reason for the employer to reject a U.S. job candidate in favor of you, if the employer wishes to do so. However, when some acceptable resumes do turn up, the employer must interview those people.

After the interview, if the employer is unsatisfied and still wishes to employ you, the employer must prepare a report stating why the U.S. job candidates were not suitable. Once an interview has been held, the employer is no longer limited to rejecting candidates only because they do not meet the job description as stated in the ad or the ETA-750 form. Poor work habits, lack of job stability, questionable character, and similar business considerations, if legitimate, are also satisfactory reasons. In addition, it sometimes comes out in an interview that the prospective worker's qualifications are not in fact what they appeared to be on the resume. This provides still another reason to turn down the U.S. candidate.

The DOL does not consider the fact that you may be more qualified than any other candidate to be a valid reason for rejecting a U.S. worker. Being the most qualified is not enough. You must be the only one who is qualified. The employer cannot be forced to hire a U.S. worker who happens to apply for the job as a result of the required advertising, but if a qualified U.S. worker does turn up and your prospective employer cannot

Foreign Language Requirements

According to the DOL, foreign language capability is not a valid requirement for most jobs, except perhaps the occupations of foreign language teacher or translator. By foreign language capability, we mean the ability to speak English plus at least one other language. Many temporary labor certification job descriptions contain a foreign language requirement because petitioning employers know it is a good way to decrease the chances that qualified U.S. workers if will apply for the job.

If your employer wants a foreign language capability in the job description, the employer must prove this need is real by preparing and submitting a signed statement explaining the business reasons why. The statement does not have to be in any particular form but it should answer obvious questions like: What is it about the employer's business that makes knowledge of a foreign language necessary? Why does this position require knowledge of a foreign language if someone else in the company already speaks that language? Why couldn't the company simply hire a translator as a separate employee or use a translator on a part-time basis when the need arises? The employer must show that the need for the employee to speak a foreign language is very great and that no alternative arrangement will be an adequate substitute.

A good example of how to approach this problem is an employer who owns a restaurant in a resort and is trying to justify a foreign language requirement for a seasonal waiter. Here, the employer can explain that a large percentage of the restaurant's customers speak the particular foreign language in question and expect to be addressed in that language when they come in to eat. If the restaurant's clientele demand it, it is reasonable that all employees of this restaurant who have contact with the public be able to speak the language of the customers.

The DOL doesn't like foreign language requirements, because it is well aware that most people who apply for temporary labor certification have the ability to speak a language other than English. The DOL regards this as a poor excuse to keep a U.S. worker from taking a job. Therefore, it is usually best not to include a language requirement, especially if the temporary labor certification is likely to be approved anyway. If, however, the occupation being certified is relatively unskilled, as in the case of the seasonal waiter, a language requirement supported by strong documents showing a real business need may mean the difference between success and failure of the temporary labor certification.

find a solid business reason to reject him or her, the temporary labor certification application filed on your behalf will fail.

If no suitable U.S. job candidates present themselves, the temporary labor certification will be approved. Then the stamped certification will be sent to your U.S. employer. Only the employer receives communications from the DOL because, technically, it is the company that is seeking temporary labor certification in order to fill a staff need.

4. Filling Out and Assembling the Temporary Labor Certification Application

The checklist below will help your employer assemble the forms and documents that make up the temporary labor certification application.

Temporary Labor Certification Checklist

- ❑ Form ETA-750, Part A only.
- ❑ Evidence of employer's advertising and recruitment efforts (such as clippings—not photocopies—of all newspaper ads).
- ❑ Employer's written statement of recruitment results.
- ❑ Employer's written statement explaining why the job is temporary or seasonal.
- ❑ If you are a touring entertainment industry worker, a written schedule of dates and cities where you will be working.

Although most of this form is fairly straightforward, a few of the questions require extra attention.

Question 13 asks the employer to describe the job being offered. This question should be answered with as much detail as possible. Daily duties, typical projects, supervisory responsibilities, the kinds and use of any machinery or equipment, foreign language skills needed, and so forth should all be thoroughly explained. If there are special job conditions, such as the requirement to live in the employer's home, or unusual physical demands, these too must be described. The employer should not fail to put down any skill or activity the job requires, no matter how obvious it may seem. The ability to reject U.S. workers will depend completely on how well the U.S. job candidates match up to the job description in Question 13. The more detailed the job description, the more possible reasons for rejecting U.S. candidates.

While the employer should do its best to describe the position and its demands fully, the employer should not invent aspects of the job that don't exist or seem excessive for the industry. For example, suppose the job opening is for a trainer of bakery managers, but in the job description the employer states that all applicants must have a background in nuclear science. This sort of illogical requirement makes it clear to the state employment agency reviewer that the job description is not legitimate, but deliberately made up to discourage U.S. workers from applying.

When the job description lacks real-world credibility, the ETA-750 will be sent back and the employer will be asked to justify the more unusual requirements. If the state employment agency reviewer cannot be convinced that the job description reflects the employer's true needs, the temporary labor certification will be denied.

The employer should also guard against asking for such a variety of requirements that the job seems more appropriate for two separate workers instead of one. For example, if the job is that of summer resort restaurant manager and the job description requires the applicant not only to manage the restaurant but to do the cooking as well, the reviewer might say the business really needs two people, a cook and a restaurant manager. Once again, this will result in the temporary labor certification being denied.

Question 14 asks for the minimum experience and education the job requires. The answer to this question should describe the demands of the job, not the personal qualifications of the potential H-2B visa recipient. For example, you may have a degree from a technical school representing two years of automotive mechanic's training, but if the position you have been offered is for a live-in housekeeper for the summer, being an automotive mechanic usually has nothing

to do with being a housekeeper and therefore should not be mentioned in the answer to this question. Remember, it is the job offer that is being described, not you.

When you count up how many years of relevant experience you have to offer, you may not include experience gained from working for your petitioning employer. You must be prepared to prove that you met the minimum experience and education requirements as stated in Question 14 of the ETA-750 before you started working for the petitioner, even if you have been employed there for some time.

As with salary levels, the DOL also has specific guidelines on what the minimum number of years of experience and education should be for a certain kind of job. The local state employment agency office can tell your employer exactly the number of years of education and experience it considers a normal minimum for the particular job you have been offered. This number comes from a Web-based database called O*NET (http://online.onetcenter.org). Keep in mind that the number of years of experience and education it lists for each job is the total allowable years of both experience and education.

Suppose the employer genuinely feels the company needs a person with more total years of education and experience than the O*NET database indicates. Then a letter from the employer should be submitted with the ETA-750 forms, giving the reason additional years of background are justified. The DOL will normally respect the employer's judgment if it seems reasonable. This letter does not have to be in any special form. A simple explanation in your employer's own words will do.

When a certain number of years appears in the box marked "Experience," it is understood that this means experience in the same occupation as the job being offered. If the experience is in a different but relevant field, it should go in the box marked "Related Occupations."

Question 15 asks the employer to state essential requirements for the job (over and above years of formal education or work experience). Any special knowledge or skills detailed in Question 13, such as foreign language ability, familiarity with certain types of machinery, or special physical capabilities (the strength to do heavy lifting, for example) should be repeated here. Later, you will have to prove in some way that you can perform the skills listed in Question 15, but you will not have to show an exact number of years of education or on-the-job experience as you will for the qualifications listed in Question 14.

Question 18 asks for the exact dates you wish to be able to work in the United States. Keep in mind that the H-2B status cannot be approved for more than 12 months at a time and therefore you should not request more than 12 months. The petition will be approved only through the dates requested on the temporary labor certification. Remember, the dates you ask for are the dates you will get, so choose a starting date three or four months after you begin filing your papers to allow some lead time for visa processing.

Question 21 asks your employer to describe past attempts to hire U.S. workers for the position being offered to you. At this stage, it is not essential that such efforts have already been made. If the U.S. employer has not yet tried to hire a worker for the job, he or she should write the following statement for Question 21:

Advertisements and job posting to begin upon receipt of job order number.

If, however, your employer has already made some attempt to hire a U.S. worker, the nature of these efforts (newspaper ads, use of employment agencies, and the like) and the results should be described here. Of course, we assume any prior efforts to fill the job have failed, or the employer would not be trying to hire you.

5. The Temporary Labor Certification Decision

After your employer has sent the temporary labor certification application to the SWA, the forms and documents will be initially reviewed, then eventually forwarded to the national processing center of the DOL for a decision. If the paperwork has been carefully prepared, the temporary labor certification should be approved on the first try. Sometimes, papers are returned to the employer with a request for additional information or instructions to remedy a defect in the advertising. After mistakes and deficiencies have been corrected, the papers should be returned to the DOL.

When your employer has finally gotten the paperwork the way the DOL wants it, the employer will receive a decision either granting or denying the temporary labor certification.

If the DOL thinks the temporary labor certification is unsatisfactory, it will be denied and the employer will receive a written decision explaining the reasons. The most common reason for denial is that the job is not temporary in nature. No appeal is available. The temporary labor certification, however, is considered to be only advisory and therefore an H-2B visa petition may be filed with USCIS even though the temporary labor certification is denied. You will have to convince USCIS, however, that the DOL was wrong.

E. Step Two: Your Employer Submits an H-2B Visa Petition

After receiving a decision on the temporary labor certification, your employer can shift focus to filing a visa petition with USCIS, on Form I-129. The object of the petition is to prove that:

- the job is temporary or seasonal in nature
- no qualified U.S. workers are available for the job
- you have the correct background, skills, and abilities to match the job requirements, and
- your U.S. employer has the financial ability to pay your salary.

Like the temporary labor certification, an approved petition does not by itself give you any immigration privileges. It is only a prerequisite to the next step, submitting your application.

1. Simultaneous Change of Status If You're Already in the U.S.

If you're already in the U.S. in lawful status, such as on a student or other temporary visa, the I-129 petition can be used to request that the USCIS immediately change your status to H-2B worker. (Part 2, Question 5, of Form I-129 offers choices addressing this issue.) However, you can't take advantage of this option if you entered the U.S. on a visa waiver, or if you entered using a C (alien in transit), TWOV (alien in transit without a visa), D (crewman), K-1 (fiancé), K-2 (dependent of a fiancé), J-1 (exchange visitor), or M-1 (vocational student) visa. You must have:

- entered the U.S. legally
- never worked in U.S. illegally, and
- not passed the expiration date on your I-94 card.

There is another problem that comes up only in U.S. filings. It is the issue of what is called "preconceived intent." To approve a change of status, USCIS must believe that at the time you originally entered the U.S. as a visitor or with some other nonimmigrant visa, you did not intend to apply for a different status. If USCIS thinks you had a preconceived plan to use one visa to enter the U.S. with an eye to applying for a different status after getting there, it may deny your application. (You can get around the preconceived intent issue by leaving the U.S. and applying for your H-2B visa at a U.S. consulate in another country.)

Your spouse and children, if they are also in the U.S. with you, can't change their status by being mentioned on your Form I-129, but must submit separate Forms I- 539. They can submit these either at the same time as your employer submits Form I-129, or afterward. (If they submit them afterward, however, they will need to include either a copy of the USCIS receipt notice indicating that your petition is pending, or a copy of the petition approval notice.)

 Your eligibility to apply in the U.S. has nothing to do with overall eligibility for an H-2B visa. Many applicants who are barred from filing in the U.S. but otherwise qualify for H-2B status may still apply successfully for an H-2B visa at a U.S. consulate in another country.

If you apply for a change of status within the U.S., you will receive only H-2B status, not the H-2B visa. The H-2B visa is a physical stamp in your passport that you will need if you ever want to reenter the United States. Visas are never given inside the United States. They are issued exclusively by U.S. consulates in other countries. If you file in the U.S. and you are successful, you may remain in the U.S. with H-2B privileges until the status expires. But should you leave the country for any reason before that time, you will have to apply for the visa itself at a U.S. consulate before returning to the United States. Moreover, the fact that your H-2B status has been approved in the U.S. does not guarantee that the consulate will also approve your visa. Therefore, if you have a choice of whether to file a change of status in the U.S. or apply through a U.S. consulate in your home country, you'll have to decide which is better for you, balancing the convenience of staying in the U.S. now versus the certainty of being allowed to return if you leave the United States before your H-2B status has expired.

2. Assembling the Visa Petition

The checklist below will help you and your employer assemble the necessary items for the visa petition.

H-2B Visa Petition Checklist

❑ Form I-129, H Supplement.

❑ Filing fee (currently $320).

❑ If you'll be applying in the U.S. and your family members are with you and need a change of status, Form I-539 with accompanying fee (currently $300) and copies of your family members' I-94 or other proof of lawful immigration status and of their relationship to you (marriage, birth certificates). One Form I-539 and fee will cover your spouse and all your children. Your family members should fill out and sign this form, not your employer.

❑ If you're in the U.S., a copy of your I-94 or other proof of your current lawful, unexpired immigration status (except that Canadian visitors aren't expected to have I-94s).

❑ If you're outside the U.S., a copy of your passport.

❑ If you're in the U.S., it's wise to supply evidence of your ties to your home country, strong enough to motivate your eventual return. Include any deeds verifying ownership of a house or other real property, written statements from you explaining that close relatives are staying behind, or a letter from a company in your home country showing that you have a job waiting when you return from the United States.

❑ Copy of documents submitted in connection with, as well as DOL recommendation on, the temporary labor certification application. If the recommendation was negative, add evidence to overcome its findings.

❑ Detailed written statement from the employer explaining why the position is temporary or seasonal. If the need is seasonal or intermittent, the statement should explain whether it is expected to occur again. If the job is temporary because it's tied to a specific project of the employer and will end upon its completion, attach a copy of the employer's contract for that project.

❑ Proof that you have the minimum education and experience called for in the advertisements and job description. If special requirements were added, you must prove you have those skills or abilities as well.

❑ If your employer asked for a specific type or amount of education, all your diplomas and transcripts. If you were educated outside the U.S., USCIS may request a credential evaluation.

❑ Proof of employer's ability to pay your salary, such as annual report, tax returns, and accounting statements.

❑ Either a written employment agreement with you or a written summary of an oral agreement. The terms of your employment, including job duties, hours, and salary, must be mentioned.

❑ If your job is as an entertainer touring the U.S., a copy of the touring route schedule, including cities and dates of performance.

If requesting quick ("premium") processing:

❑ Form I-907, with $1,000 filing fee.

A few items on this checklist require some extra explanation:

Form I-129 and H Supplement.
The basic form for the visa petition is immigration Form I-129 and its H Supplement. The I-129 form is used for many different nonimmigrant visas. In addition to the basic part of the form that applies to all types of visas, it comes with several supplements for each specific nonimmigrant category. Simply use the supplement that applies to you.

The employer may choose to list more than one foreign employee on a single I-129 petition. This is done if the employer has more than one opening to be filled for the same type of job. If more than one employee is to be included, Supplement-1, which is also part of Form I-129, should be completed for each additional employee.

Proof of your job qualifications.
Evidence of your job experience should include letters or notarized affidavits from previous employers. These do not have to be in any special form but simply in your former employer's own words. The letters should clearly indicate what your position was with the company, your specific job duties, and the length of time you were employed. If letters from previous employers are unavailable, you may be able to prove your work experience with your personal tax returns or by affidavits from former coworkers. Proof of special knowledge or skills can be supplied through

notarized affidavits, either from you or someone else who can swear you have the special ability (such as skill to use a particular machine or speak a foreign language) required. These, too, need not be in any special form.

3. Mailing the Visa Petition

After assembling the visa petition, your U.S. employer must mail it to either the California Service Center or the Vermont Service Center, whichever has jurisdiction over the employer's place of business. If you'll be coming from outside the U.S., your employer must send duplicate versions of the form (two signed originals; copies are not acceptable). USCIS regional service centers are not the same as USCIS local offices—for one thing, you cannot visit regional service centers in person. See the USCIS website at www.uscis.gov for the regional service centers' addresses and P.O. box numbers.

4. Awaiting a Decision on the Visa Petition

Within a few weeks after mailing in the petition, your employer should get back a written confirmation that the papers are being processed, together with a receipt for the fee. This notice will also contain your immigration file number. If USCIS wants further information before acting on your case, all petition papers, forms, and documents will be returned to your employer with a form known as

Academic Credential Evaluations

Not every country in the world operates on the same academic degree and grade level systems found in the United States. If you were educated in some other country, USCIS may ask for an academic credential evaluation from an approved consulting service to determine the U.S. equivalent of your educational level.

Evaluations from accredited credential evaluation services are not binding on USCIS. When the results are favorable (showing you have the equivalent of the educational level required by your U.S. employer) the evaluation strengthens your case.

We recommend obtaining a credential evaluation in every case where non-U.S. education is a factor. We also advise getting the evaluation before USCIS asks for it. If it's favorable, include it with your petition. If not, and your credentials are less than what your employer has asked for, do not submit the results unless USCIS insists. Discuss this with your employer, who may ask for less education in the job description. Also note that if the credential evaluation shows that you have the educational equivalent of a U.S. university bachelor's degree or more, you may be eligible for an H-1B visa and should consider applying for that instead. (See Chapter 16.)

Before sending an evaluation service your academic documents, you might call ahead to discuss your prospects. If your prospects are truly bleak, you may decide not to order the evaluation and save the service charge (typically upwards of $100).

Several qualified credential evaluation services are recognized by USCIS, among them International Education Research Foundation, www.ierf.org; and Educational Credential Evaluators, Inc., www.ece.org.

Credential evaluation companies will evaluate only formal education, usually not job experience. Some U.S. universities offer evaluations of foreign academic credentials and will recognize work experience as having an academic equivalent. Therefore, if you lack formal education but can show many years of experience, you are better off trying to get an evaluation from a U.S. college or university. When sending your credentials to a U.S. university, include documents showing your complete academic background, as well as all relevant career achievements. Letters of recommendation from former employers are good proof of work experience. Also submit evidence of any special accomplishments, such as awards or published articles. USCIS can be influenced, but not bound by, academic evaluations from U.S. colleges and universities.

a Request for Evidence. Your employer should supply the extra data requested and mail the whole package back to the service center.

H-2B petitions are normally approved within six weeks. When this happens, a Form I-797 Notice of Action will be sent to your employer, showing the petition was approved. If you plan to submit your visa application at a U.S. consulate abroad, USCIS will also notify the consulate of your choice, sending a complete copy of your file. Only the employer receives communications from USCIS about the petition, because technically it is the employer who is seeking the visa on your behalf.

Faster processing—at a price. For $1,000 over and above the regular filing fees, USCIS promises premium processing of the visa petition, including a decision within 15 days. To use this service, the employer must fill out an additional application (Form I-907) and submit the application to a special USCIS service center address. For complete instructions, see the USCIS website at www.uscis.gov.

Be aware that an approved petition does not, if you are overseas, give you any immigration privileges. It is only a prerequisite to the next step, submitting your application for an H-2B visa.

F. Step Three: Applicants Outside the U.S. Apply to a U.S. Consulate

After the H-2B visa petition filed by your employer has been approved, USCIS will send a Form I-797B, with which you can apply for a visa at a U.S. consulate— normally in your home country. (Some consulates will insist upon waiting for formal notification directly from USCIS, but most will accept an original Form I-797B from you.) Check with your local U.S. consulate regarding its application procedures. Many insist on advance appointments. Just getting an appointment can take several weeks, so plan ahead.

If you're visa exempt, you may be able to skip this step. Citizens of Canada and certain others need not apply to a U.S. consulate. Instead, they can proceed directly to the U.S. with Form I-797B and supporting documents to request entry. (See 8 C.F.R. § 212.1.) If you're risk-averse, however, applying at a consulate first might be the safer route.

Have you been, or are you now, working or living illegally in the United States? If so, see Chapter 3 regarding whether you can still get an H-2B visa from a U.S. consulate. You may have become inadmissible or subject to a three-year or ten-year bar on reentry.

The following checklist will help you prepare your consular application.

H-2B Visa Application Checklist

❑ Form DS-156, Nonimmigrant Visa Application (available from the U.S. consulate).

❑ Form DS-157, Supplemental Nonimmigrant Visa Application (also available from the U.S. consulate, but it needs to be filled out only by male nonimmigrant visa applicants between the ages of 16 and 45 and by applicants over age 16 (male or female) who come from countries that the U.S. believes sponsor terrorism).

❑ Notice showing approval of the H-2B petition.

❑ Valid passport for you and each accompanying relative.

❑ One U.S. passport-type photo of you and one of each accompanying relative. (This is best done by a professional photographer; the consulate can give you a list.)

❑ If your spouse and children will be accompanying you, documents verifying their family relationship to you, such as marriage and birth certificates.

❑ Documents establishing your intent to leave the U.S. when your status expires, such as deeds verifying ownership of a house or other real property, written statements from you explaining that close relatives are staying behind, or letters from a company showing that you have a job waiting when you return from the United States.

❑ Visa application fee (currently $100).

❑ Visa issuance fee (depending on what country you're from; if the country of your nationality charges fees for visas to U.S. citizens who wish to work there, then the U.S. will charge people of your country a similar fee).

As part of your application, the consulate will require you and your family members to attend an interview. During the interview, a consular officer will examine the data in your application for accuracy, especially regarding facts about your own qualifications. Evidence of ties to your home country will also be checked. During the interview, you will surely be asked how long you intend to remain in the United States. Any answer indicating that you are unsure about plans to return or have an interest in applying for a green card is likely to result in a denial of your H-2B visa.

See Chapter 4 for what else to expect during consular interviews, and what to do if your application is denied.

Applying at a Consulate That's Not in Your Home Country

The law allows most people to apply for an H-2B visa at any U.S. consulate they choose—with one exception. If you have ever been present in the U.S. unlawfully, your visa will be automatically cancelled and you cannot apply as a third-country national (at a consulate outside your home country). Even if you overstayed your status in the U.S. by just one day, you must return to your home country and apply for the visa from that consulate. There is an exception. If you were admitted to the U.S. for the duration of your status (indicated by a "D/S" on your I-94 form and most common with student visas) and you remained in the U.S. beyond that time for which your status was conferred, you will be barred from third-country national processing only if an immigration judge or USCIS (or former INS) officer has determined that you were unlawfully present. You may find that your success in applying as a third-country national will depend on your country, the consulate, and the relative seriousness of your offense. Being unlawfully present is also a ground of inadmissibility if the period of unlawful presence is 180 days or more. (See Chapter 3.)

Even if you are eligible for third-country national processing, your case will be given the greatest consideration at the consulate in your home country. Applying in some other country creates suspicion in the minds of the consular officers there about your motives for choosing their consulate. Often, when an applicant expects trouble at a home consulate, he or she will seek a more lenient consular office in some other country. This practice of consulate shopping is frowned upon by officials in the system. Unless you have a very good reason for being elsewhere (such as a temporary job assignment in some other nation), it is often smarter to file your visa application in your home country.

G. Step Four: You Enter the U.S. With Your H-2B Visa

You have until the expiration date on your H-2B visa to enter the United States. The border officer will examine your paperwork, ask you some questions, and if all is in order, approve you for entry. He or she will stamp your passport and give you a small white card called an I-94 card. It will be stamped with a date showing how long you can stay. Normally, you are permitted to remain up to the expiration date on your H-2B petition. (However, if your passport will expire before the petition's expiration date, some CBP officers will issue the I-94 until only the date of the passport expiration.) Each time you exit and reenter the U.S., you will get a new I-94 card authorizing your stay up to the final date indicated on the petition.

H. Extending Your U.S. Stay

H-2B visas may be extended for one year at a time, but you may not hold H-2B status for longer than a total of three years. Therefore, if your visa was first issued for the one-year maximum, you may be allowed two one-year extensions. Extensions are not automatic, nor are they easier to get than the original visa. In fact, extensions are sometimes more difficult to obtain because the longer you remain on a particular job, the less likely the DOL and USCIS are to believe that the job is truly temporary. Moreover, USCIS has

the right to reconsider your qualifications based on any changes in the facts or law. When the original application for an H-2B visa was weak, it is not unusual for an extension request to be turned down. As always, however, good cases that are well prepared will be successful.

To extend your H-2B visa, the temporary labor certification, petition and visa stamp will all have to be updated. As with the original application, you can file either in the U.S. or at a consulate.

1. Step One: Temporary Labor Certification

The process for getting an extension of the temporary labor certification is identical in every respect with the one used to obtain the original temporary labor certification. See Section D, above.

2. Step Two: Extension Petition

Extension procedures are nearly identical to the procedures followed in getting the initial visa petition approval. Fully document your application so that your case is not delayed if USCIS cannot locate your previous file. Submit the new Temporary Labor Certification and the Notice of Action indicating the approval that your employer received on the original petition. All your personal U.S. income tax returns and W-2 forms for the time period you have already been working in the U.S. on an H-2B visa are required as well. Once USCIS has these documents, it will notify the employer if any further data are needed.

Watch Out for Summary Exclusion

The law empowers a Customs and Border Protection (CBP) inspector at the U.S. airport or border to summarily (without allowing judicial review) bar entry to someone requesting admission to the U.S. if either of the following is true:

- The inspector thinks you are lying about practically anything connected with entering the U.S., including your purpose in coming, intent to return, and prior immigration history. This includes the use or suspected use of false documents.
- You do not have the proper documentation to support your entry to the U.S. in the category you are requesting.

If the inspector excludes you, you cannot be readmitted to the U.S. for five years, unless USCIS grants a special waiver. For this reason it is extremely important to understand the terms of your requested status, and to not make any misrepresentations. If you are found to be inadmissible, you may ask the CBP inspector to withdraw your application to enter the U.S. in order to prevent having the five-year deportation order on your record. The CBP may allow this in some exceptional cases.

Working While Your Extension Petition Is Pending

If you file your petition for an extension of H-2B status before your authorized stay expires, you are automatically permitted to continue working for up to 240 days while you are waiting for a decision. If, however, your authorized stay expires after you have filed for an extension but before you receive an approval, and more than 240 days go by without getting a decision on your extension petition, your work authorization ceases and you must stop working.

3. Step Three: Visa Revalidation

If you must leave the U.S. after your extension has been approved, you must get a new visa stamp issued at a consulate in order to return. Bring along all the documents you supplied for your U.S. extension. ■

Chapter 18

Getting a Temporary Trainee (H-3) Visa

The H-3 visa is useful for a limited group of people—those who have a job in their home country, but have been invited to participate in a training program in the United States. The training may be offered by a U.S. branch of their own company, or by an unrelated U.S. company. However, the training must be unavailable in the worker's home country. There are no limits on the number of people who can be granted H-3 visas each year.

The USCIS regulations recognize some specific types of trainees as potentially H-3 eligible. These include medical interns or residents who are attending a medical school abroad, if the student will engage in employment as an extern during his or her medical school vacation; and licensed nurses who need a brief period of training that is unavailable in their native country. (See 8 C.F.R § 214.2(h)(7).)

The H-3 visa can also be used by 50 special education exchange visitors per year—that is, people coming to the U.S. for a special education training program educating children who have physical, emotional, or mental disabilities. (See 8 C.F.R. § 214.2(h)(7)(iv).) The requirements for this group are slightly different than for other trainees.

Do you need a lawyer? You can't apply for an H-3 visa without having an employer first—and it's in your employer's interest to hire a lawyer to help. A lawyer can help make sure that your application gets done right the first time, and gets decided on before the training program begins.

A. Do You Qualify for an H-3 Visa?

You qualify for an H-3 visa if you are coming to the U.S. for on-the-job training to be provided by a U.S. company. Productive employment in the U.S. can be only a minor part of the total program. The purpose of the training should be to further your career in your home country. Similar training opportunities must be unavailable there. Be aware that very few training programs meet the USCIS's strict qualifications.

You must also possess the necessary background and experience to complete the U.S. training program successfully. Obviously, however, this should be the first time you'll receive this particular type of training. And, as with many nonimmigrant visas, you are eligible for an H-3 visa only if you intend to return to your home country when the visa expires.

Training programs supporting H-3 visas exist most often in two situations. A multinational company with branches in various countries might train employees in its U.S. branches before sending them to work elsewhere. Or, a U.S. company may wish to establish a beneficial business relationship with a foreign company. A good way to do this is by bringing in some of the foreign company's personnel and teaching them about the U.S. business. These people then develop personal ties with the U.S. company.

Key Features of the H-3 Visa

Here are some of the advantages and disadvantages of the H-3 visa:

- You can participate in a training program offered by a U.S. company and work legally in the U.S. for the company that is training you, so long as that work is incidental to the training program.
- You are restricted to working only for the employer who admitted you to the training program and acted as sponsor for your H-3 visa.
- Your visa can be approved for the length of time needed to complete the training program, although no more than two years are normally permitted. Extensions of one year

at a time may be allowed, but only if the original training has not yet been completed, and only within the overall two-year maximum.

- You can travel in and out of the U.S. or remain in the U.S. continuously while your H-3 visa is valid.
- Visas are available for your accompanying spouse and minor children (unmarried and under age 21), but they may not accept employment in the United States. Children are expected to attend school, and adults can attend school part-time under the terms of the H-4 visa.

1. Your Invitation to a Training Program

You need a specific offer to participate in a job training program from a U.S. company or U.S. government agency. The job training slot you are invited to fill can't be in just any occupation. It must be one that will further your career abroad. Many types of occupations qualify, however. For example, you could be coming for training in agriculture, commerce, communications, finance, government, industry, or virtually any other field. (However,

physicians are ineligible to use this category.) The training program must be formal in structure with a curriculum, books, and study materials.

2. Training Is Unavailable in Your Home Country

One of the more difficult requirements for getting an H-3 visa is that the training you will receive in the U.S. must be unavailable to you in your home country. This does not mean that the training cannot exist there, but only that you, personally, do not have access to it.

USCIS Suspicions About H-3 Visa Applicants

Here's a window into USCIS thinking, straight from their internal *Operations Instructions:*

"Operating experience has shown that when the alien is not of distinguished merit and ability or the petitioner cannot obtain a temporary labor certification, H-3 classification is sometimes requested to enable the alien to engage in actual employment under the guise of a training program. The regulations now list a number of restrictions on approval of training programs. Obviously, there may be unusual situations in which the restrictions may be inappropriate and careful review of the supporting documentation or a request for additional information from the petitioner may satisfactorily establish the bona fides of the proposed training program. However, all suspect petitions demand a careful review, and the examiner should be satisfied that the purpose of the program is genuinely to train the beneficiary for a career abroad (even though the petitioner may derive benefits from the alien's training), and that the beneficiary intends to return abroad for employment after termination of the training program." (See *Operations Instructions* (OI) 214.2(h)(6).)

3. Any Productive Employment Is Incidental

Although you can work in the U.S. while on your H-3 visa, the employment must be merely incidental and necessary to the training activities. If the employment aspect takes up so much time that the company could justify hiring a full-time U.S. worker to perform these duties, your H-3 visa will be denied. As a rule, if more than half of your time will be spent on productive employment, you will not qualify for an H-3 visa.

4. You Have the Correct Background

You must have the correct background for the training position you are offered. For example, for a training position as an intern with a U.S. law firm, intended to further your career as an international lawyer, you would have to show that you have a law degree.

5. You Intend to Return to Your Home Country

H-3 visas are meant to be temporary. At the time of applying, you must intend to return home when the visa expires. If you have it in mind to take up permanent residence in the U.S., you are ineligible for an H-3 visa. The U.S. government knows it is difficult to read minds. Expect to be asked for evidence showing that when you complete your training, you will go back home and use it there.

If you are training for work that doesn't exist in your home country, you'll have trouble. For example, if you will be in a training program for offshore oil drilling and you come from a country that is landlocked and has no oil, no one will believe you plan to take the skills learned in the U.S. back home.

You will also be asked for evidence that you are leaving behind possessions, property, or family members as incentives for your eventual return.

6. Bringing Your Relatives

When you qualify for an H-3 visa, your spouse and unmarried children under age 21 can get H-4 visas by providing proof of their family relationship to you. H-4 visas authorize your family members to stay with you in the U.S., but not to work there. They may, however, study at U.S. schools.

B. Quick View of the H-3 Visa Application Process

Once you have been offered a training position by a U.S. company, getting an H-3 visa is a one- to three-step process:

- First, the U.S. company where you will be trained files what's called a visa petition on USCIS Form I-129. If you're already in the U.S. in lawful status, this petition can simultaneously ask that your status be changed to H-3 worker, in which case, the process will successfully end here.
- If you're outside the U.S., then after the visa petition is approved, you submit your own application for an H-3 visa to a U.S. consulate (unless you're from Canada, in which case you can skip this step), and
- Finally, you use either your visa or (if you're from Canada) the notice of your approved visa petition to enter the U.S. and claim your H-3 status.

Nothing stops you from helping with the employer's tasks during this application process. For example, you can fill out forms intended to be completed by your employer and simply ask the employer to check them over and sign them. The less your U.S. employer is inconvenienced, the more likely it will be willing to act as sponsor for your visa.

C. Step One: Your Employer Submits an H-3 Visa Petition

The process starts when your U.S. employer/trainer sends a visa petition to USCIS on Form I-129. The object of the petition is to prove four things, including that:

Applying for a Green Card From H-3 Status

Being in the U.S. on an H-3 visa gives you no advantage in getting a green card, and, in fact, may prove to be a drawback. That is because H-3 visas, like most nonimmigrant visas, are intended only for those who plan to return home once their training or other activities in the U.S. are completed.

If you apply for a green card, you are in effect making a statement that you never intend to leave the U.S. In fact, if your method of applying for a green card is through employment, as discussed in Chapter 9, you are making it appear that you're really utilizing the H-3 visa to establish a career in the U.S. and so are no longer qualified for H-3 status. Therefore, although you are permitted to apply for the green card, your H-3 status may be revoked.

USCIS will allow you to keep H-3 status while pursuing a green card only if you are able to convince USCIS that you did not intend to get a green card when you originally applied for the H-3 visa

and that you will return home if you are unable to secure a green card before your H-3 visa expires. Proving these things can be difficult.

If you do not succeed, your H-3 status may be taken away. Should this happen, it will not normally affect your green card application. You will simply risk being without your nonimmigrant visa until you get your green card. However, if you are out of status for either 180 days or 12 months, or you work without authorization, you may not be able to get your green card. Read Chapter 3 regarding inadmissibility and bars to adjustment of status before you overstay 180 days or depart the United States.

If what you really want is a green card, apply for it directly and disregard H-3 visas. Although it may be more difficult to get a green card, which typically takes several years, in the long run you will be happier with the results—not to mention the fact that you will be obeying the law by not trying to hide your true intentions.

- a qualifying formal training position has been offered to you by a U.S. company
- you have the correct background for the training
- the training is unavailable to you in your home country, and
- the training will further your career in your home country.

1. Simultaneous Change of Status If You're Already in the U.S.

If you're already in the U.S. in lawful status, such as on a student or other temporary visa, the petition can be used to ask that your status be immediately changed to H-3 temporary trainee. (Part 2,

Question 5, of Form I-129 offers choices addressing this issue.) You can't, however, take advantage of this option if you entered the U.S. on a visa waiver, or if you entered using a C (alien in transit), TWOV (alien in transit without a visa), D (crewman), K-1 (fiancé), K-2 (dependent of a fiancé), J-1 (exchange visitor), or M-1 (vocational student) visa. Also, if you have already been in the U.S. for 18 months under any H or L status, you may not seek a change to H-3 status until you've lived outside the U.S. for six months.

Other than these restrictions, you're allowed to change status if you:

- entered the U.S. legally
- have never worked in U.S. illegally, and
- the expiration date on your I-94 card hasn't passed.

There is another problem that comes up only in U.S. filings. It is the issue of what is called "preconceived intent." To approve a change of status, USCIS must believe that at the time you originally entered the U.S. as a visitor or with some other nonimmigrant visa, you did not intend to apply for a different status. If USCIS thinks you had a preconceived plan to use one visa to enter the U.S. with an eye toward applying for a different status after getting here, it may deny your application. (You can get around the preconceived intent issue by leaving the U.S. and applying for your H-3 visa at a U.S. consulate in another country.)

Your spouse and children, if they are also in the U.S. with you, can't change their status by being mentioned on your Form I-129, but must submit separate Forms I-539. They can submit these either at the same time as your employer submits Form I-129, or afterward. (If they submit them afterward, however, they will need to include either a copy of the USCIS receipt notice indicating that your petition is pending, or a copy of the petition approval notice.)

 Your eligibility to apply in the U.S. has nothing to do with your overall eligibility for an H-3 visa. Many applicants who are barred from filing in the U.S., but otherwise qualify for H-3 status, may still apply successfully for an H-3 visa at a U.S. consulate in another country.

If you decide to apply for a change of status within the U.S., you will receive only H-3 status, not the H-3 visa. The H-3 visa is a physical stamp in your passport that you will need if you ever want to reenter the United States. Visas are never given inside the United States. They are issued exclusively by U.S. consulates in other countries. If you file in the U.S. and you are successful, you will get to remain in the U.S. with H-3 privileges until the status expires. But should you leave the country for any reason before that time, you will have to apply for the visa itself at a U.S. consulate before returning to the United States. Moreover, the fact that your H-3 status has been approved in the U.S.

does not guarantee that the consulate will also approve your visa. For these reasons, some people choose not to request a change of status on their Form I-129, but instead leave for a U.S. consulate and apply for their visa there.

2. Preparing the Visa Petition

The checklist below will help you and your employer assemble the necessary items for the visa petition.

H-3 Visa Petition Checklist

❑ Form I-129, H Supplement.

❑ Filing fee: $320.

❑ If you will be applying in the U.S. and your family members are with you and need a change of status, Form I-539, the fee (currently $300) and copies of your family members' I-94s or other proof of lawful immigration status and of their relationship to you (such as marriage and birth certificates). One Form I-539 and fee covers your spouse and all your children. Family members should fill out and sign this form, not your employer.

❑ If you're in the U.S., a copy of your I-94s or other proof of your current lawful, un-expired immigration status (except Canadian visitors, who are not expected to have I-94 cards).

❑ If you're in the U.S., we recommend that you supply evidence that ties to your home country are strong enough to motivate your eventual return. Proof of ties to your home country can include deeds for a house or other real property, your written statements explaining that close relatives are staying behind, or a letter from a company in your home country showing that you have a job waiting when you return.

❑ If you're outside the U.S., a copy of your passport.

All trainees except special education visitors:

❑ Detailed written statement from the employer describing the training program, in-cluding the number of hours per week in classroom study, on-the-job training, pro-ductive employment, and unsupervised work or study. Also, include a description of the curriculum, with names of any textbooks and the subjects to be covered.

❑ Additional explanation from the employer regarding why it is willing to incur the cost of your training without getting much productive work out of you in return.

❑ A summary of your prior relevant training and experience, such as diplomas and letters from past employers.

❑ Explanation of why you need the training, the absence of similar training in your country, and how the training will benefit you in your career in your home country.

Special education visitors only:

❑ a description of the training, staff, and facilities, and how you'll participate in the program

❑ evidence that any custodial care of children will be incidental to the training program, and

❑ evidence that you are almost done getting a B.A. degree in special education, or already have a B.A., or have extensive prior training in teaching children with disabilities.

If requesting quick (premium) processing:

❑ Form I-907, with $1,000 filing fee.

A few items on this checklist require some extra explanation:

Form I-129 and H Supplement.
The basic form for the visa petition is immigration Form I-129 and its H Supplement. The I-129 form is used for many different nonimmigrant visas. In addition to the basic part of the form that applies to all types of visas, it comes with several supplements for each specific nonimmigrant category. Simply use the supplement that applies to you.

The employer may choose to list more than one foreign trainee on a single I-129 petition. This is done if the employer has more than one opening to be filled for the same type of training position. If more than one trainee is to be included, Supplement-1, which is also part of Form I-129, should be completed for each additional person.

For purposes of Part 5, Question 8, of the Form I-129, note that the dates of intended training should not exceed a total of two years, which is the maximum

period of time for which an H-3 petition may be approved. The maximum reduces to 18 months if you are applying for a training program in special education of disabled children.

Section 4 of the H Supplement requires a written explanation of why the employer is willing to incur the cost of training you. There should be some logical way in which your training will financially benefit the U.S. employer, such as to help it with business abroad after you return to your home country.

Showing that training is unavailable in your home country. Your employer/trainer must prove that you cannot receive the same training in your home country. This is best shown by letters or affidavits from authorities in your home country who are leaders of industry, officials in government, or administrators in universities. The letters should give the names and positions of the writers. In such a letter, it should be stated that the writer is acquainted with the training program you intend to pursue in the U.S. and that similar training is not available in your home country. It may take a lot of effort to get these statements, but without them, your H-3 visa stands little chance of approval.

Showing how training will further your career. Ideally, the H-3 training program will be related to your current occupation at home. In that case, your U.S. employer can show the nature of your present job with a letter from your foreign employer explaining how the training will further your career in your home country. If you are not now employed in the occupation for which you hope to get U.S. training, it would be very helpful to your case to have a letter from a company in your homeland offering you a job based on the completion of your training in the United States. If you can't get a letter containing a specific job offer for the future, you will have to present evidence that jobs in the field for which you are training are available. Your U.S. employer must then submit a general statement from a leader in the industry for which you will be trained or an official of the government department of labor in your home country, confirming that there is a demand for persons with the type of training you will receive.

Proving you are qualified for the training program. If the nature of the training you will receive requires special background for entering the program, the employer must submit evidence showing that you have that background. For example, if the training is at a professional level, such as internships for lawyers or engineers, your employer must submit evidence that you are already qualified to practice law or engineering at home. The employer should also submit copies of your diplomas, and if you have previous professional work experience, letters from your foreign employers describing the nature and length of your previous employment.

3. Mailing the Visa Petition

After assembling the visa petition, your U.S. employer must mail it to either the California Service Center or the Vermont Service Center, whichever has jurisdiction over the employer's place of business. If you'll be coming from outside the U.S., your employer must send duplicate versions of the form (two signed originals; copies are not acceptable). USCIS regional service centers are not the same as USCIS local offices—for one thing, you cannot visit regional service centers in person. See the USCIS website at www.uscis.gov for the regional service centers' addresses and P.O. box numbers.

4. Awaiting a Decision on the Visa Petition

Within a few weeks after mailing in the petition, your employer should get back a written confirmation that the papers are being processed, together with a receipt for the fee. This notice will also contain your immigration file number. If USCIS wants further information before acting on your case, all petition papers, forms, and documents will be returned to your employer with a form known as a Request for Evidence. Your employer should supply the extra data requested and mail the whole package back to the service center.

H-3 petitions are normally approved within two to three months. When this happens, a Form I-797, Notice of Action, will be sent to your employer, showing the petition was approved. If you plan to submit your visa application at a U.S. consulate abroad, USCIS will also notify the consulate of your choice, sending a complete copy of your file.

Faster processing—at a price. For $1,000 over and above the regular filing fees, USCIS promises premium processing of the visa petition, including a decision within 15 days. To use this service, the employer must fill out an additional application (Form I-907) and submit the application to a special USCIS service center address. For complete instructions, see the USCIS website at www.uscis.gov.

Be aware that an approved petition does not, if you are overseas, give you any immigration privileges. It is only a prerequisite to the next step, submitting your application for an H-3 visa.

D. Step Two: Applicants Outside the U.S. Apply to a U.S. Consulate

After the H-3 visa petition filed by your employer has been approved, USCIS will send a Form I-797B, with which you can apply for a visa at a U.S. consulate— normally in your home country. (Some consulates will insist upon waiting for formal notification directly from USCIS, but most will accept an original Form I-797B from you.) Check with your local U.S. consulate regarding its application procedures. Many insist on advance appointments. Just getting an appointment can take several weeks, so plan ahead.

If you're visa exempt, you may be able to skip this step. Citizens of Canada and certain others need not apply to a U.S. consulate. Instead, they can proceed directly to the U.S. with Form I-797B and supporting documents to request entry. (See 8 C.F.R. § 212.1.) If you're risk-averse, however, applying at a consulate first might be the safer route.

Applying at a Consulate That's Not in Your Home Country

The law allows most people to apply for an H-3 visa at any U.S. consulate they choose—with one exception. If you have ever been present in the U.S. unlawfully, your visa will be automatically cancelled and you cannot apply as a third-country national (at a consulate outside your home country). Even if you overstayed your status in the U.S. by just one day, you must return to your home country and apply for the visa from that consulate. There is an exception. If you were admitted to the U.S. for the duration of your status (indicated by "D/S" on your I-94 form and most common with student visas) and you remained in the U.S. beyond the time for which your status was conferred, you will be barred from third-country national processing only if an immigration judge or USCIS (or formerly INS) officer has determined that you were unlawfully present. You may find that your success in applying as a third-country national will depend on your country, the consulate, and the relative seriousness of your offense. Being unlawfully present is also a ground of inadmissibility if the period of unlawful presence is 180 days or more. (See Chapter 3.)

Even if you are eligible for third-country national processing, your case will be given the greatest consideration at the consulate in your home country. Applying in some other country creates suspicion in the minds of the consular officers there about your motives for choosing their consulate. Often, when an applicant expects trouble at a home consulate, he or she will seek a more lenient consular office in some other country. This practice of consulate shopping is frowned upon by officials in the system. Unless you have a very good reason for being elsewhere (such as a temporary job assignment in some other nation), it is often smarter to file your visa application in your home country.

Have you been, or are you now, working or living illegally in the United States? If so, see Chapter 3 regarding whether you can still get an H-3 visa from a U.S. consulate. You may have become inadmissible or subject to a three-year or ten-year bar on reentry.

H-3 Visa Application Checklist

❑ Form DS-156, Nonimmigrant Visa Application (available from the U.S. consulate).

❑ Form DS-157, Supplemental Nonimmigrant Visa Application (also available from the U.S. consulate; but it needs to be filled out only by male nonimmigrant visa applicants between the ages of 16 and 45 and by applicants over age 16 (male or female) who come from countries that the U.S. believes sponsor terrorism).

❑ Notice showing approval of the H-3 petition.

❑ Valid passport for you and each accompanying relative.

❑ One U.S. passport-type photo of you and one of each accompanying relative. (This is best done by a professional photographer; the consulate can give you a list.)

❑ If your spouse and children will be accompanying you, documents verifying their family relationship to you, such as marriage and birth certificates.

❑ Documents establishing your intent to leave the U.S. when your status expires, such as deeds verifying ownership of a house or other real property, written statements from you explaining that close relatives are staying behind, or letters from a company showing that you have a job waiting when you return from the United States.

❑ Visa application fee (currently $100).

❑ Visa issuance fee (depending on what country you're from; if the country of your nationality charges fees for visas to U.S. citizens who wish to work there, then the U.S. will charge people of your country a similar fee as well).

The above checklist, will help you prepare your consular application.

As part of your application, the consulate will require you and your family members to attend an interview. During the interview, a consular officer will examine the data in your application for accuracy. Evidence of ties to your home country will also be checked. During the interview, you will surely be asked how long you intend to remain in the United States. Any answer indicating that you are unsure about plans to return or have an interest in applying for a green card is likely to result in a denial of your H-3 visa.

 See Chapter 4 for what else to expect during consular interviews, and what to do if your application is denied.

E. Step Three: You Enter the U.S. With Your H-3 Visa

You have until the expiration date on your H-3 visa to enter the United States. The border officer will examine your paperwork, ask you some questions, and, if all is in order, approve you for entry. He or she will stamp your passport and give you a small white card called

Watch Out for Summary Exclusion

The law empowers a Customs and Border Protection (CBP) inspector at the U.S. airport or border to summarily (without allowing judicial review) bar entry to someone requesting admission to the U.S. if either of the following is true:

- The inspector thinks you are lying about practically anything connected with entering the U.S., including your purpose in coming, intent to return, and prior immigration history. This includes the use or suspected use of false documents.
- You do not have the proper documentation to support your entry to the U.S. in the category you are requesting.

If the inspector excludes you, you cannot be readmitted to the U.S. for five years, unless USCIS grants a special waiver. For this reason it is extremely important to understand the terms of your requested status, and to not make any misrepresentations. If you are found to be inadmissible, you may ask the CBP inspector to withdraw your application to enter the U.S. in order to prevent having the five-year deportation order on your record. The CBP may allow this in some exceptional cases.

an I-94 card. It will be stamped with a date showing how long you can stay. Normally, you are permitted to remain up to the expiration date on your H-3 petition. (However, if your passport will expire before the petition's expiration date, some CBP officers will stamp the I-94 with the same expiration date as the passport has.) Each time you exit and reenter the U.S., you will get a new I-94 card authorizing your stay up to the final date indicated on the petition.

F. Extending Your U.S. Stay

H-3 visas can be extended only if your original permitted stay was less than two years, to bring your stay up to a total of two years' time spent in H-3 status. (Again, the total limit reduces to 18 months for special education exchange visitors.) Although an extension is usually easier to get than the status itself, it is not automatic. USCIS has the right to reconsider your qualifications based on any changes in the facts or law. When the original application for an H-3 visa was weak, it is not unusual for an extension request to be turned down. As always, however, good cases that are well prepared will generally be successful.

To extend your H-3 visa, the petition, I-94 card, and visa stamp will each have to be updated. As with the original application, you can file either in the U.S. or at a consulate.

Working While Your Extension Petition Is Pending

If you file your petition for an extension of H-3 status before your authorized stay expires, you are automatically permitted to continue working for up to 240 days while you are waiting for a decision. If, however, your authorized stay expires after you have filed for an extension but before you receive an approval, and more than 240 days go by without getting a decision on your extension petition, your work authorization ceases and you must stop working.

1. Step One: Extension Petition

Your employer will need to file another I-129 petition, fully documented in the same manner as the first petition. It should also include:

- a letter from the employer requesting your status be extended, with

an explanation of why the training has not yet been completed

- a copy of your U.S. income tax returns for the previous year, including W-2 forms (being sure that no employment other than that for your H-3 employer is reflected in your tax documents)
- a copy of your document I-94 card, and
- a copy of the first Notice of Action I-797.

If you have a spouse and children with you in the U.S., and would like to apply without leaving for a consulate in another country, they will need to submit Form I-539, as described in Section C, above

2. Step Two: Visa Revalidation

If you must leave the U.S. after your extension has been approved, you must get a new visa stamp issued at a consulate before you return. (Formerly, you could have your visa revalidated by applying to the U.S. State Department, but no longer.) Reread Section D, above. The procedures for consular extensions are identical.

⚠ Once your two-year (or 18-month) stay is over, you cannot use another H visa, or an L visa, until you have left the U.S. and stayed outside for six months.

■

Chapter 19

Getting an L-1 (Intracompany Transferee) Visa

The L-1 visa allows managers, executives, or especially knowledgeable employees who work at a company that has an affiliated entity inside the U.S. to come to the U.S. and perform services for the U.S. entity. There are no limits on how many people can get L-1 visas every year.

Do you need a lawyer? You can't apply for an L-1 visa without having an employer first—and it's in your employer's interest to hire a lawyer to help. A lawyer can help make sure that your application gets done right the first time, and deal with all the bureaucratic hurdles.

A. Do You Qualify for an L-1 Visa?

You qualify for an L-1 visa if you have been employed outside the U.S. as a manager or executive (L-1A) or as a person with specialized knowledge (L-1B) for at least one out of the past three years, and you are transferred to the U.S. to do a job that utilizes your special knowledge and skills.

The U.S. company to which you are transferring must be a branch, subsidiary, affiliate, or joint venture partner of your non-U.S. employer. The non-U.S. company must remain in operation while you have the L-1 visa. "Non-U.S. company" means that it is physically located outside the United States. Such

Key Features of the L-1 Visa

Here are some of the advantages and disadvantages of the L-1 visa:

- You can work legally in the U.S. for your L-1 sponsor for up to three years on your first visa. You may then apply for extensions of two years at a time, up to a maximum of seven years if you're a manager or executive, or five years if you're a person with specialized knowledge.
- You may work only for the U.S. employer who acted as your visa sponsor, and it must be a branch, subsidiary, affiliate, or joint venture partner of the company that currently employs you outside the United States.
- Visas are available for your accompanying spouse and minor children, and your spouse may accept employment in the United States.
- You may travel in and out of the U.S. or remain here continuously until your L-1 status expires.
- If you have an L-1 visa for an executive or managerial level position in the U.S. company, and you want to apply for a U.S. green card through employment, you can do so.

a company may be a foreign division of a U.S.-based business or it may have originated in a country outside the United States. Either one fits the definition of a non-U.S. company. The company must continue operations for the duration of your visa, and you should show that you can expect to be transferred back upon your return.

To get an L-1 visa, it is not necessary that either your non-U.S. or prospective U.S. employer be operating in a parti-cular business structure. Many legal forms of doing business are accepta-ble, including, but not restricted to, corporations, limited corporations, part-nerships, joint ventures, and sole pro-prietorships. The employer may also be a nonprofit or religious organization.

Although you are generally expected to work full-time in the U.S., you can work somewhat less if you dedicate a significant portion of your time to the job on a regular and systematic basis.

1. Manager, Executive, or Person With Specialized Knowledge

To be eligible for an L-1 visa, the job you hold with the non-U.S. company must be either that of a manager, executive, or person with specialized knowledge. Managers and executives receive L-1A visas and people with special knowledge receive L-1B visas. You must have worked in that position for a total of at least one year out of the past three years. That year must have been spent outside the United States. For immigration purposes, the definitions of "manager," "executive," and "specialized knowledge" are more restricted than their everyday meanings.

a. Managers

A manager is defined as a person who has all of the following characteristics:

- He or she manages the entire organization or else a department, subdivision, function, or component of the organization.
- He or she supervises and controls the work of other supervisory, professional, or managerial employees or manages an essential function, department, or subdivision of the organization.
- He or she has the authority to hire and fire or recommend these and other personnel decisions regarding the employees being supervised. If no employees are supervised, the manager must work at a senior level within the organization or function.
- He or she has the authority to make decisions concerning the day-to-day operations of the portion of the organization under his or her management.

First-line supervisors are lower management personnel who directly oversee nonmanagement workers. A first-line supervisor is not normally considered a manager unless the employees supervised are professionals.

The word "professional" here means a worker holding a university degree.

A manager coming to work for a U.S. office that has been in operation for at least one year also qualifies for a green card as a priority worker. See Chapter 9 for details.

b. Executives

An executive is defined as a person whose primary role includes that:

- He or she directs the management of the organization or a major function or component of it.
- He or she sets the goals or policies of the organization or a part or function of it.
- He or she has extensive discretionary decision-making authority.
- He or she receives only general supervision or direction from higher-level executives, a board of directors, or the stockholders of the organization.

An executive coming to work for a U.S. office that has been in operation for at least one year also qualifies for a green card as a priority worker. Again, see Chapter 9 for details.

c. Persons With Specialized Knowledge

The knowledge that is referred to in the term "specialized knowledge" must specifically concern the employer company, its products, services, research, equipment, techniques, management or other interests and its application in international markets, or advanced knowledge of the company's processes and procedures. The consular officers will be looking for knowledge that is not held commonly throughout the industry, but is truly specialized. They will also be looking to see that such knowledge is not readily available in the United States.

2. Branch, Subsidiary, Affiliate, or Joint Venture Partner

L-1 visas are available only to employees of companies outside the U.S. that have related U.S. branches, subsidiaries, affiliates, or joint venture partners. There is also a special category for international accounting firms. For visa purposes, these terms have specific definitions.

a. Branches

Branches are simply different operating locations of the same company. The clearest example of this is a single international corporation that has branch offices in many countries.

b. Subsidiaries

In a subsidiary relationship, one company must own a controlling percentage of the other company, that is, 50% or more. For L-1 purposes, when two companies are in the same corporate or limited form, and at least 50% of the stock of a company in the U.S. is owned by a non-U.S. company, or vice versa, this is a classic subsidiary relationship.

c. Affiliates

Affiliate business relationships are more difficult to demonstrate than those of branches or subsidiaries because there is no direct ownership between the two companies. Instead, they share the fact that both are controlled by a common third entity, either a company, group of companies, individual, or group of people.

There are two methods of ownership that will support an L-1 visa based on an affiliate relationship. The first is for one common person or business entity to own at least 50% of the non-U.S. company and 50% of the U.S. company. If no single entity owns at least 50% of both companies, the second possibility is for each owner of the non-U.S. company to also own the U.S. company, and in the same percentages. For example, if five different people each own 20% of the stock of the non-U.S. company, then the same five people must each own 20% of the U.S. company for an affiliate relationship to exist.

d. Joint Venture Partners

A joint venture exists when there is no common ownership between the two companies, but they have jointly undertaken a common business operation or project. To qualify for L-1 purposes, each company must have veto power over decisions, take an equal share of the profits, and bear the losses on an equal basis.

In a situation where both the U.S. and non-U.S. companies are in the corporate or limited form and the majority of the stock of both is publicly held, unless they are simply branches of the same company that wish to transfer employees between them, the joint venture relationship is the only one that is practical for L-1 qualifying purposes. The ownership of a publicly held company is too vast and diverse to prove any of the other types of qualifying business relationships.

e. International Accounting Firms

L-1 visas are available to employees and partners of international accounting firms. In the case of big accounting firms, the interests between one country and another are not usually close enough to qualify as affiliates under normal L-1 visa rules. Nevertheless, the law considers the managers of such companies qualified to support L-1 visa petitions for their employees. The firm must be part of an international accounting organization with an internationally recognized name. Ultimately, this option applies to a only limited number of very large and prominent firms.

3. Blanket L-1 Visas: Privileges for Large Companies

Large U.S. companies (other than nonprofits) that are branches, subsidiaries, or affiliates of non-U.S. companies may obtain what is known as a "blanket L-1 status." Blanket L-1 status enables qualified U.S. companies that require frequent transferring of non-U.S. employees to their related U.S. companies to do so easily. Instead of submitting individual petitions for each transferee, the company itself gets a general approval for transferring employees, which eliminates much of the time and paperwork involved in each individual case (though not all of it—individuals will still need a petition filed on their behalf, by using a simplified USCIS visa petition on Form I-129S). If a non-U.S. company has more than one U.S. branch, subsidiary, or affiliate, it need obtain only one blanket L-1 petition for all of its related U.S. companies.

It is the company itself and not the individual employee that qualifies for blanket status. Also, although the U.S. company must be a branch, subsidiary, or affiliate of a non-U.S. company to qualify, it is the U.S. company that petitions for and receives the blanket L-1 status.

Initially, a blanket L-1 petition can be approved for only three years. However, if the company continues to qualify, at the end of three years it can obtain an indefinite renewal.

The definitions for manager and executives under blanket L-1 visas are the same as for those who apply for individual L-1 visas. However, the specialized knowledge category differs from the one for individual L-1 applicants. For the blanket visa, they must not only be considered professionals, but have specialized knowledge as well.

If a company has the need and meets the following requirements, it should obtain a blanket L-1 petition:

- The petitioning U.S. company to which employees may be transferred must be a branch, subsidiary, or affiliate of a company outside the United States. (Note that a joint venture partnership is not a qualifying business relationship for blanket L-1 status purposes.)
- Both the U.S. company and its related non-U.S. company must be engaged in actual commercial trade or rendering of services.
- The U.S. company must have been engaged in business for at least one year.
- The U.S. company must have a total of at least three branches, subsidiaries, or affiliates, although all three need not be located in the United States.

The company and any related U.S. companies must either have:

- successfully obtained L-1 visas for at least ten of its employees during the past 12 months
- combined annual sales of at least $25 million, irrespective of the related company outside the U.S., or
- a total of at least 1,000 employees actually working in the United States.

4. Specialized Knowledge Professionals

This category is only for employees of companies with blanket L-1 status. It is a more stringent substitute for the specialized knowledge category available to individual L-1 applicants. USCIS's regulations require that an individual have specialized knowledge, as defined above, and that he or she further be a member of the professions as that term is defined in immigration law. The law specifically lists architects, engineers, lawyers, physicians, surgeons, and teachers in elementary and secondary schools, colleges, academies, or seminaries.

The term "profession," however, has been more liberally interpreted in other contexts. It may also include any occupation that requires theoretical and practical knowledge to perform the occupation in such fields as architecture, physical and social sciences, business specialties, and the arts. For these occupations, professional status requires completion of a university education reflected by at least a bachelor's degree in a specific occupational specialty, as long as that degree is the minimum requirement for entry to that occupation.

Under these criteria, the following occupations have also been found to be professional: accountant, computer systems analyst, physical therapist, chemist, pharmacist, medical technologist, hotel manager, fashion designer, commercial airline pilot of 747s or other large aircraft, and upper-level business managers.

Other occupations may also be considered professional, as long as they meet the criteria discussed above.

5. Bringing Your Relatives

When you qualify for an L-1 visa, your spouse and unmarried children under age 21 can get L-2 visas by providing proof of their family relationship to you. L-2 visas authorize your accompanying relatives to stay with you in the U.S., but only your spouse will be permitted to work there.

To take advantage of the right to work, after arriving in the U.S, your spouse should apply for a work permit. (Although the Social Security Administration says it's unnecessary, USCIS maintains that it is, so your safest bet is to apply.) This is done on Form I-765. In filling out the form, your spouse should write "spouse of L nonimmigrant" in Question 15, and "A-18" in Question 16.

Your spouse will need to mail this form, together with proof of your visa status, a copy of his or her I-94 card, the filing fee, and two photos, to the appropriate USCIS service center for your geographic region. For the address and other information, call USCIS Information at 800-375-5283 or see the USCIS website (www.uscis.gov).

B. Possibilities for a Green Card From L-1 Status

If you qualify for, or currently have, an L-1 visa as a manager or an executive, you may also be eligible for a green card through employment. (See Chapter 9.) In addition, you may also be able to get the green card without going through the rigorous procedures of labor certification, which is usually the first step required for those seeking green cards through employment. The purpose of the labor certification procedure is to show that there are no U.S. workers available to take the U.S. job that has been offered to you. However, if you qualify for L-1 status as a manager or executive, you also fall under a green card preference category called priority workers. This category is exempt from labor certification requirements.

In order to use L-1 eligibility to qualify for a green card, you need not have actually gotten an L-1 visa. Showing that you are eligible to get one is sufficient.

C. Quick View of the L-1 Visa Application Process

Once you have been offered a job transfer to the U.S., getting an L-1 visa as an individual is a one- to three-step process:

- First, the U.S. company to which you will be transferred files what's called a visa petition on USCIS Form I-129. If you're already in the U.S. in lawful status, this petition can simultaneously ask that your status be changed to L-1 transferee, in which case the process will successfully end here.
- If you're outside the U.S., then after the visa petition is approved, you submit your own application for an L-1 visa to a U.S. consulate (unless you're from Canada, in which case you can skip this step), and
- Finally, you use either your visa or (if you're from Canada) the notice of your approved visa petition to enter the U.S. and claim your L-1 status.

 Nothing stops you from helping with the employer's tasks during this application process. For example, you can fill out forms intended to be completed by your employer and simply ask the employer to check them over and sign them. The less your U.S. employer is inconvenienced, the more it may be willing to act as sponsor for your visa.

D. Step One: Your U.S. Employer Files a Visa Petition

The process starts when your U.S. employer sends a visa petition to USCIS on Form I-129. Your employer can choose to either submit an individual L-1 visa petition, just for you, or a blanket petition, if it expects to transfer a number

Academic Credential Evaluations

Because it is almost always necessary that you hold at least a bachelor's degree, evidence that you are personally eligible as a specialized knowledge professional should include copies of diplomas and transcripts from the colleges and universities you attended. However, not every country operates on the same academic degree and grade level systems found in the United States. If you were educated in some other country, USCIS or the U.S. consulate will often ask for an academic credential evaluation from an approved consulting service to determine the U.S. equivalent of your educational level.

When the results of a credential evaluation are favorable, they strengthen your case. If, however, the evaluation shows that your credentials do not equal at least a U.S. bachelor's degree, this can mean you will not qualify as a specialized knowledge professional.

We recommend obtaining a credential evaluation in every case where non-U.S. education is a factor. In addition, we advise getting the evaluation before USCIS or the consulate has the opportunity to ask for it. When the evaluation is favorable, include it with your application—it saves time if USCIS or the consulate decides to request it later.

Before sending a credential evaluation service your academic documents, you may want to call in advance to discuss your prospects over the telephone. Usually, you can get some idea of the likelihood for receiving good results. If your prospects are truly bleak, you may decide not to order the evaluation and to save the service charge, which is typically upwards of $100.

There are several qualified credential evaluation services recognized by USCIS. Two of them are International Education Research Foundation, at www.ierf.org, and Educational Credential Evaluators, Inc., at www.ece.org.

The credential evaluation companies listed above will evaluate only formal education. They will not evaluate job experience. Some U.S. universities also offer evaluations of foreign academic credentials but will recognize work experience as having an academic equivalent. Therefore, if you lack a university education but can show many years of responsible experience, you are better off trying to get an evaluation from a U.S. college or university.

When sending your credentials to a U.S. university, include documents showing your complete academic background, as well as all relevant career achievements. Letters of recommendation from former employers are the preferred proof of work experience. Evidence of any special accomplishments, such as awards or published articles, should also be submitted.

USCIS and the U.S. consulates can be influenced but not bound by academic evaluations from U.S. colleges and universities.

of employees on an ongoing basis. The object of the individual L-1 petition is to prove three things:

- that you have been employed outside the U.S. for at least one of the past three years as an executive, manager, or person with specialized knowledge
- that the company you worked for outside the U.S. has a branch, subsidiary, affiliate, or joint venture partner company in the U.S., and
- that the U.S. entity requires your services to fill a position of the same or similar level as the one you presently hold outside of the United States.

Blanket L-1 petitions are mainly useful for large corporations that transfer many employees to the U.S. each year. The object of the blanket L-1 petition is to prove five things:

- that the petitioning U.S. company is in a branch, subsidiary, or affiliate relationship with a company outside of the U.S.
- that the U.S. company has been engaged in actual trade or the rendering of services
- that the U.S. company has been in business for at least one year
- that the U.S. company has a total of at least three U.S. branches, subsidiaries, or affiliates, and
- that the U.S. company and its other U.S.-related business entities

- have successfully obtained L-1 visas for at least ten employees in the past year, and
- have combined total annual sales of at least $25 million, or a combined total of at least 1,000 employees working in the United States.

If your non-U.S. employer wants to transfer you to the U.S. and regularly transfers others, ask whether the company already has an approved blanket petition. If so, applicants outside of the U.S. who need an actual visa should ask their potential U.S. employer to fill out and send him or her a Form I-129S (original plus two copies) and also to send one copy of the earlier approval notice of the blanket L-1 petition. The applicant will include these documents with his or her visa application at a U.S. consulate in their home country (as described in Section E, below). If you are Canadian, or if you use some other exception allowing you to travel without a visa, your employer must nevertheless submit Form I-129S, with accompanying documents proving your qualifications, to a USCIS service center. Your employer must then receive and send you the approval before you leave for the United States. There is no fee for submitting Form I-129S.

For applicants already in the U.S., the employer will need to submit Form I-129 asking for a change of status, as described in Section 1, below.

If the U.S. company transfers many employees to the U.S. but has not obtained a blanket L-1 visa, you might suggest that it look into getting one.

1. Simultaneous Change of Status If You're Already in the U.S.

If you're already in the U.S. in lawful status, such as on a student or other temporary visa, the petition can be used to ask that your status be immediately changed to L-1 transferee. (Part 2, Question 5, of Form I-129 offers choices addressing this issue.) However, you can't take advantage of this option if you entered the U.S. on a visa waiver or if you entered using a C (alien in transit), TWOV (alien in transit without a visa), D (crewman), K-1 (fiancé), K-2 (dependent of a fiancé), J-1 (exchange visitor), or M-1 (vocational student) visa.

Other than these restrictions, you're allowed to change status if you:

- entered the U.S. legally
- have never worked in the U.S. illegally, and
- the expiration date on your I-94 card hasn't passed.

There is another problem that comes up only in U.S. filings. It is the issue of what is called "preconceived intent." To approve a change of status, USCIS must believe that at the time you originally entered the U.S., as a visitor or with some other nonimmigrant visa, you did not intend to apply for a different status. If USCIS thinks you had a preconceived plan to use one visa to enter the U.S.

with an eye to applying for a different status after getting there, it may deny your application. (You can get around the preconceived intent issue by leaving the U.S. and applying for your L-1 visa at a U.S. consulate in another country.)

Your spouse and children, if they are also in the U.S. with you, can't change their status by being mentioned on your Form I-129, but must submit a separate Form I-539 (one for the whole family). They can submit this either at the same time as your employer submits Form I 129, or afterward. (If they submit Form I-539 afterward, however, they will need to include either a copy of the USCIS receipt notice indicating that your petition is pending, or a copy of the petition approval notice.)

 Your eligibility to apply in the U.S. has nothing to do with overall eligibility for an L-1 visa. Many applicants who are barred from filing in the U.S., but otherwise qualify for L-1 status, may still apply successfully for an L-1 visa at a U.S. consulate in another country.

If you decide to apply for a change of status within the U.S., realize that you still won't have the L-1 visa that you'll need if you ever leave the United States. A change of status only gives you L-1 status with the right to stay in the U.S.; it does not give you the right to reenter. Visas are never given inside the United States. They are issued exclusively by

U.S. consulates in other countries. If you file in the U.S. and you are successful, you will get to remain in the U.S. with L-1 privileges until the status expires. But should you leave the country for any reason before that time, you will have to apply for the visa itself at a U.S. consulate before returning to the United States. Moreover, the fact that your L-1 status has been approved in the U.S. does not guarantee that the consulate will also approve your visa. For this reason, many people choose to leave the U.S. and apply through a consulate.

2. Preparing the Visa Petition

The checklist below will help you and your employer assemble the necessary items for the visa petition.

L-1 Visa Petition Checklist

- ❑ Form I-129, with L Supplement.
- ❑ Filing fee: $320.
- ❑ Fraud Prevention and Detection Fee: $500 (separate check or money order).
- ❑ Evidence of a qualifying relationship between the U.S. and foreign company, such as:
  - ❑ Articles of incorporation or other legal charter or business license of the non-U.S. company.
  - ❑ Articles of incorporation or other legal charter or business license of the U.S. company.
  - ❑ Legal business registration certificate of the non-U.S. company.
  - ❑ Legal business registration certificate of the U.S. company.
  - ❑ Tax returns of the non-U.S. company for the past two years.
  - ❑ Tax returns of the U.S. company for the past two years, if available.
  - ❑ Copies of all outstanding stock certificates, if the business is a corporation.
  - ❑ Notarized affidavit from the secretary of the corporation, or, if the business is not a corporation, from the official record keeper of the business, stating the names of each owner and percentages of the company owned.
  - ❑ If the business relationship is a joint venture, a copy of the written joint venture agreement.
  - ❑ Annual shareholder reports of the U.S. and non-U.S. companies, if publicly held.
  - ❑ Accountant's financial statements, including profit and loss statements and balance sheets of the non-U.S. company, for the past two years.
  - ❑ Accountant's financial statements, including profit and loss statements and balance sheets of the U.S. company for the past two years, if available.
  - ❑ If more than half the stock of either the U.S. or non-U.S. company is publicly held, statements from the secretary of the corporation describing how the companies are related.

Individual Petitions Only:

❑ If you will be applying in the U.S. and your family members are with you and need a change of status, Form I-539 with accompanying fee (currently $300) and copies of your family members' I-94s or other proof of lawful immigration status and of their relationship to you (such as marriage and birth certificates). One Form I-539 and fee will cover your spouse and all your children. This form is meant to be filled out and signed by your family members, not by your employer.

❑ If you're in the U.S., a copy of your I-94 or other proof of your current lawful, unexpired immigration status (except that Canadians who are just visiting are not expected to have I-94 cards).

❑ If you're outside the U.S., a copy of your passport.

❑ Documents proving one year of employment outside the U.S. during the last three years, such as copies of your wage statements and your personal income tax return filed in your home country for the most recent year. If tax returns are unavailable, submit a notarized statement from the bookkeeping department or accountant of your non-U.S. employer, with a statement explaining the situation.

❑ Documents proving employment outside of U.S. as an executive, manager, or person with specialized knowledge.

❑ A statement describing your proposed job's necessary qualifications, duties, salary, and dates of employment.

❑ Evidence that the proposed employment will be in an executive, managerial, or specialized knowledge capacity.

Blanket Petitions Only:

❑ Documents showing that the U.S. company is actively engaged in commercial trade or services, has been in business for at least one year, and has three or more domestic or foreign branches, subsidiaries, or affiliates. (Many of the documents you've already assembled to prove the qualifying relationship between the U.S. and foreign company will serve to prove this as well.)

❑ Either:

    ❑ Company income tax returns, audited accountant's financial statements, or the annual shareholders' report showing combined annual sales for all of the related U.S. employer companies totaling at least $25 million

    ❑ Copies of the Notice of Action Forms I-797 showing at least ten L-1 approvals during the past year, or

    ❑ The most recent quarterly state unemployment tax return and federal employment tax return Form 940 showing at least 1,000 employees for all of the related U.S. employer business locations.

If requesting quick (premium) processing:

❑ Form I-907, with $1,000 filing fee.

A few items on this checklist require some extra explanation:

Form I-129 and L Supplement. The basic form for the visa petition is immigration Form I-129 and its L Supplement. The I-129 form is used for many different nonimmigrant visas. In addition to the basic part of the form that applies to all types of visas, it comes with several supplements for each specific nonimmigrant category. Simply use the supplement that applies to you.

Proof that you are a manager, executive, or person with specialized knowledge. Your U.S. employer must submit evidence that your employment abroad fits the USCIS definition of manager, executive, or person with specialized knowledge, and that your employment in the U.S. will be of a similar type. To prove this, submit detailed statements from both the U.S. and non-U.S. employers explaining your dates of employment, qualifications, salary, and specific duties as well as the number and kind of employees you supervise. If the petition is based on specialized knowledge, the statements should also describe the nature of the specialized knowledge and how it will be used in your U.S. job. The statements should also include a description of the job you'll be doing in the U.S., including the duties, and evidence that the position is executive, managerial, or requires specialized knowledge. These statements may be in your employer's own words and do not have to be in any special form.

Proof that the U.S. and non-U.S. companies are engaged in trade or the rendering of services. For a blanket petition, the petitioning U.S. employer should submit as many documents as possible to show that both the U.S. and non-U.S. companies are financially healthy and presently engaged in trade or the rendering of services. Such documents could include:

- copies of the articles of incorporation or other legal charters
- any business registration certificates
- company tax returns for the past two years
- company annual reports or financial statements for the past two years, including balance sheets and profit/loss statements
- payroll records for the past two years
- letters of reference from chambers of commerce
- promotional literature describing the nature of the company
- letters from banks indicating average account balances, and
- copies of leases or deeds for business premises.

3. Mailing the Visa Petition

After assembling the visa petition, your U.S. employer must mail it to either the California Service Center or the Vermont Service Center, whichever has jurisdiction over the employer's place of business. If you'll be coming from outside the

U.S., your employer must send duplicate versions of the form (two signed originals; copies are not acceptable).

USCIS regional service centers are not the same as USCIS local offices—for one thing, you cannot visit regional service centers in person. See the USCIS website at www.uscis.gov for the regional service centers' addresses and P.O. box numbers.

4. Awaiting a Decision on the Visa Petition

Within a few weeks after mailing in the petition, your employer should get back a written confirmation that the papers are being processed, together with a receipt for the fee. This notice will also contain your immigration file number. If USCIS wants further information before acting on your case, all petition papers, forms, and documents will be returned to your employer with a form known as a Request for Evidence. Your employer should supply the extra data requested and mail the whole package back to the service center.

L-1 petitions are normally approved within six weeks. When this happens, a Form I-797 Notice of Action will be sent to your employer, showing the petition was approved. If you plan to submit your visa application at a U.S. consulate abroad, USCIS will also notify the consulate of your choice, sending a complete copy of your file. Only the employer receives communications from USCIS about the petition, because

technically it is the employer who is seeking the visa on your behalf.

 Faster processing—at a price. For $1,000 over and above the regular filing fees, USCIS promises premium processing of the visa petition, including a decision within 15 days. To use this service, the employer must fill out an additional application (Form I-907) and submit the application to a special USCIS service center address. For complete instructions, see the USCIS website at www.uscis.gov.

Be aware that an approved petition does not, if you are overseas, give you any immigration privileges. It is only a prerequisite to the next step, submitting your application for an L-1 visa.

E. Step Two: Applicants Outside the U.S. Apply to a U.S. Consulate

After the individual L-1 visa petition filed by your employer has been approved, USCIS will send a Form I-797B Notice of Action, with which you can apply for a visa at a U.S. consulate—normally in your home country. (Some consulates will insist upon waiting for formal notification directly from USCIS, but most will accept an original Form I-797B from you.) If your U.S. employer has already been approved for L-1 blanket status, the U.S. company will issue a Certificate of Eligibility directly to you. This is used as a substitute for the Notice of Action.

Check with your local U.S. consulate regarding its application procedures. Many insist on advance appointments. Just getting an appointment can take several weeks, so plan ahead.

 If you're visa exempt, you may be able to skip this step. Citizens of Canada and certain others need not apply to a U.S. consulate. Instead, they can proceed directly to the U.S. with Form I-797B and supporting documents to request

entry. (See 8 C.F.R. § 212.1.) If you're risk-averse, however, applying at a consulate first might be the safer route.

 Have you been, or are you now, working or living illegally in the United States? If so, see Chapter 3 regarding whether you can still get an L-1 visa from a U.S. consulate. You may have become inadmissible or subject to a three-year or ten-year bar on reentry.

Applying at a Consulate That's Not in Your Home Country

The law allows most people to apply for an L-1 visa at any U.S. consulate they choose—with one exception. If you have ever been present in the U.S. unlawfully, your visa will be automatically cancelled and you cannot apply as a third-country national (at a consulate outside your home country). Even if you overstayed your status in the U.S. by just one day, you must return to your home country and apply for the visa from that consulate. There is an exception. If you were admitted to the U.S. for the duration of your status (indicated by "D/S" on your I-94 form and most common with student visas) and you remained in the U.S. beyond the time for which your status was conferred, you will be barred from third-country national processing only if an immigration judge or USCIS (or formerly INS) officer has determined that you were unlawfully present. You may find that your success in applying as a third-country national will depend on your country, the

consulate, and the relative seriousness of your offense. Being unlawfully present is also a ground of inadmissibility if the period of unlawful presence is 180 days or more. (See Chapter 3.)

Even if you are eligible for third-country national processing, your case will be given the greatest consideration at the consulate in your home country. Applying in some other country creates suspicion in the minds of the consular officers there about your motives for choosing their consulate. Often, when an applicant expects trouble at a home consulate, he or she will seek a more lenient consular office in some other country. This practice of consulate shopping is frowned upon by officials in the system. Unless you have a very good reason for being elsewhere (such as a temporary job assignment in some other nation), it is often smarter to file your visa application in your home country.

The following checklist will help you
prepare your consular application.

L-1 Visa Application Checklist

❑ Form DS-156, Nonimmigrant Visa Application (available from the U.S. consulate).

❑ Form DS-157, Supplemental Nonimmigrant Visa Application (also available from the U.S. consulate; but it only needs to be filled out by male nonimmigrant visa applicants between the ages of 16 and 45).

❑ Notice showing approval of the L-1 petition.

❑ Valid passport for you and each accompanying relative.

❑ One U.S. passport-style photo of you and one of each accompanying relative. (This is best done by a professional photographer; the consulate can give you a list.)

❑ If your spouse and children will be accompanying you, documents verifying their family relationship to you, such as marriage and birth certificates.

❑ Visa application fee (currently $100).

❑ Visa issuance fee (depending on what country you're from; if the country of your nationality charges fees for visas to U.S. citizens who wish to work there, then the U.S. will charge people of your country a similar fee as well).

Additional documents required if applying under a blanket petition:

❑ Documents proving that you were employed outside of the U.S. by the non-U.S. company for at least one of the past three years, such as copies of your wage statements and your personal income tax return filed in your home country for the most recent year. If tax returns are unavailable, submit a notarized statement from the bookkeeping department or accountant of your non-U.S. employer, with a statement explaining the situation.

❑ Documents proving employment outside of the U.S. as an executive, manager, or person with specialized knowledge (see detailed suggestions for types of documents under Section D2, above).

❑ Documents showing that your employment in the U.S. will be of a similar type, such as a detailed statement from both the U.S. and non-U.S. employers explaining your specific duties as well as the number and kind of employees you will supervise; and, if your application is based on specialized knowledge, how that knowledge will be used in your U.S. job.

❑ Documents showing you meet the definition of a professional, such as copies of diplomas and transcripts from the colleges and universities you attended. If you attended a school but did not graduate, submit the transcript. If you were educated outside of the U.S., you need to supply a credential evaluation from an approved evaluation service as explained in "Academic Credential Evaluations," above.

As part of your application, the consulate will require you and your family members to attend an interview. During the interview, a consular officer will examine the data in your application for accuracy. See Chapter 4 for what else to expect during consular interviews, and what to do if your application is denied.

F. Step Three: You Enter the U.S. With Your L-1 Visa

You have until the expiration date on your L-1 visa to enter the United States. The border officer will examine your paperwork, ask you some questions, and if all is in order, approve you for entry. He or she will stamp your passport and give you a small white card called an I-94 card. It will be stamped with a date showing how long you can stay.

Normally, you are permitted to remain up to the expiration date on your L-1 petition or, in a blanket L-1 case, the Certificate of Eligibility. If you are coming to the U.S. on a blanket L-1 visa, your U.S. employer will provide you with Certificate of Eligibility Form I-129S in triplicate and a copy of the Notice of Action indicating approval of the blanket L-1 petition. In addition to the I-94 card, upon your entry the I-129S will be stamped by an immigration (CBP) inspector and you will be required to keep one copy, together with your I-94 card. Each time you exit and reenter the U.S., you will get a new I-94 card authorizing your stay up to the final date indicated on the petition or Certificate of Eligibility.

G. Extending Your U.S. Stay

L-1 visas can be extended for three years at a time, but you may not hold an L-1 visa for longer than a total of seven years if you are a manager or executive, or five years if you're a person with specialized knowledge. Although an extension is usually easier to get than the L-1 visa itself, it is not automatic. USCIS has the right to reconsider your qualifications based on any changes in the facts or law. As always, however, good cases that are well prepared will usually be successful.

To extend your L-1 visa, the petition and visa stamp will both have to be updated. Like the original application procedures, you can file either in the U.S. or at a consulate.

1. Step One: Extension Petition

Your employer must start your extension application by filing another Form I-129 visa petition, in much the same way as before, except that less documentation is generally required. However, the best practice is to fully document an extension application as well as the initial request, since USCIS will probably not have the original file and papers on site, and it could cause a long delay if they have to request the old file to decide the extension request. In addition to the same documents you filed with the first petition, you must submit your I-94 card. You should also submit a copy of the first Notice of Action I-797 (approval notice), a letter from your employer stating that your extension is required, a copy of your personal U.S. income tax returns for the past two years, including W-2 forms, and a copy of your employer's most recent U.S. income tax return.

Working While Your Extension Petition Is Pending

If you file your petition for an extension of L-1 status before your authorized stay expires, you are automatically permitted to continue working under the same terms of your L visa, for up to eight months (240 days) while you are waiting for a decision. If, however, your authorized stay expires after you have filed for an extension but before you receive an approval, and more than eight months (240 days) go by without getting a decision on your extension petition, you must stop working.

2. Step Two: Visa Revalidation

If you must leave the U.S. after your extension has been approved, but before your status expires, you must get a new visa stamp issued at a consulate in order to return. Read Section E, above. The

Watch Out for Summary Exclusion

The law empowers a Customs and Border Protection (CBP) inspector at the U.S. airport or border to summarily (without allowing judicial review) bar entry to someone requesting admission to the U.S. if either of the following is true:

- The inspector thinks you are lying about practically anything connected with entering the U.S., including your purpose in coming, intent to return, and prior immigration history. This includes the use or suspected use of false documents.
- You do not have the proper documentation to support your entry to the U.S. in the category you are requesting.

If the inspector excludes you, you cannot be readmitted to the U.S. for five years, unless USCIS grants a special waiver. For this reason it is extremely important to understand the terms of your requested status, and to not make any misrepresentations. If you are found to be inadmissible, you may ask the CBP inspector to withdraw your application to enter the U.S. in order to prevent having the five-year deportation order on your record. The CBP may allow this in some exceptional cases.

procedures for consular extensions are identical.

3. Blanket L-1 Extensions

This section briefly describes how a company can apply for an extension of its blanket L-1 status. (This is not an explanation of how an individual may extend his or her own L-1 visa if the person arrived in the U.S. under a company's blanket L-1 visa. Extensions for individuals who obtained visas under the blanket program are handled in the same manner as explained in Section 2 above, except that a Certificate of Eligibility Form I-129S must also be submitted.)

A company holding an approved blanket L-1 petition will have to extend that petition only one time. After the initial three-year approval period, the blanket L-1 visa petition can be extended with indefinite validity.

The company must begin by filing a new Form I-129 and L Supplement. The only documents required are:

- a copy of the previous Notice of Action, Form I-797, and
- a written list of the names of all transferees admitted under the blanket L-1 petition for the previous three years; for each person, include the position held, name of the specific company where the person worked, the date of initial admission, and the date of final departure.

⚠ Once you've spent your maximum amount of time on an L-1 visa, you probably won't be able to return to the U.S. for a while. The rules say that you have to spend one full year outside the United States before returning with another H or L visa. (See 8 C.F.R. § 214.2 (l)(12).) ∎

Chapter 20

Getting an E-1 (Treaty Trader) Visa

The United States has entered into trade treaties with several countries, and established the E-1 visa to help citizens of those countries more easily engage in international trading activities. (See I.N.A. § 101(a)(15)(E), 8 U.S.C. § 1101(a)(l5)(E); 8 C.F.R. § 214.2(e); 22 C.F.R. § 41.51.) If you are a businessperson from one of these countries, and you plan to either engage in substantial trade with the U.S. or work for an enterprise that does substantial trade with the U.S., then an E-1 visa may be the one for you.

Some people call this visa the next best thing to permanent residence, because of the possibility of self-employment, and the unlimited number of extensions. There is no limit on the number of E-1 visas that can be issued every year.

Do you need a lawyer? Simply figuring out whether you're eligible for a treaty trader visa can be difficult, and the procedural requirements are as complicated as most other U.S. visas. Hiring a lawyer might be a wise business expenditure.

Key Features of the E-1 Visa

Here are some of the advantages and disadvantages of the E-1 visa:

- You can work legally in the U.S. for a U.S. company if 50% of its business is with your home country, and your country has entered a trade treaty with the United States.
- You are restricted to working only for the U.S. employer or a self-owned business that acted as your visa sponsor.
- Your initial visa may extend up to two years, with unlimited possible two-year extensions.
- Visas are available for your accompanying spouse and minor children, but your children may not accept employment in the United States.
- Your spouse may accept U.S. employment.
- You may travel in and out of the U.S. or remain here continuously until your E-1 status expires.

A. Do You Qualify for an E-1 Visa?

To qualify for an E-1 visa, you must:
- be from a qualifying country
- work for a qualifying business
- be either a 50% owner or key employee, and
- most of your company's trade must be with the United States.

1. Citizen of a Treaty Country

E-1 visas are available to citizens of selected countries that have trade treaties with the United States. Those countries with treaties currently in effect are:

Argentina, Australia, Austria, Belgium, Bolivia, Bosnia and Herzegovina, Brunei, Canada, Chile, Colombia, Costa Rica, Croatia, Denmark, Estonia, Ethiopia, Finland, France, Germany, Greece, Honduras, Iran, Ireland, Israel, Italy, Japan, Jordan, Korea (South), Latvia, Liberia, Luxembourg, Macedonia, Mexico, The Netherlands, Norway, Oman, Pakistan, Paraguay, Philippines, Serbia and Montenegro, Singapore, Slovenia, Spain, Suriname, Sweden, Switzerland, Taiwan, Thailand, Togo, Turkey, and the United Kingdom.

Because treaty provisions are subject to change, be sure your country has one in force before proceeding with your application. The complete list is kept at Volume 9 of the *Foreign Affairs Manual* (FAM), § 41.51, Exh. 1. (You can find the FAM on the U.S. State Department website at http://foia.state.gov/regs/search.asp.)

2. Company Owned by Citizens of a Qualifying Country

At least 50% of the business with which you're associated must be owned by citizens of your treaty country. (See 9 FAM § 41.51, Note 3.1.) The company may be owned by you or by others. If the company is owned in part or in whole by others, and some or all of them already live in the U.S., those people may need to have E-1 visas themselves before the company can act as an E-1 sponsor for you. Specifically:

- at least 50% of the company must be owned by citizens of a single trade treaty country, and
- the owners from the single trade treaty country must either live outside the U.S. and be classifiable for E-1 status or live inside the U.S. with E-1 visas.

This second condition can be a little confusing. Some examples may help to make it clearer.

EXAMPLE 1: The company is owned 100% by one person. The owner is a citizen of a trade treaty country and lives outside the U.S. in his home country. He would qualify for E-1 status if he sought to enter the United States.

In this case the owner does not need to already have an E-1 visa for the company to support your E-1 visa application. He has already fulfilled the alternative condition by living outside the U.S. and being eligible for such status.

EXAMPLE 2: The company is owned in equal shares by two people. Each owner is a citizen of the same trade treaty country. One owner lives in the U.S. on a green card. The other still lives in his home country and is classifiable as an E-1.

In this case, neither owner needs an E-1 visa for the company to support your E-1 application, because 50% of the owners have fulfilled the qualifying conditions. If, however, we changed this example so that both owners lived in the U.S., at least one of them would need an E-1 visa to fulfill the required conditions. (Green card holders do not qualify as E-1 principals.)

EXAMPLE 3: The company is owned in equal shares by 100 people. Thirty owners are citizens of a particular trade treaty country but live in the United States. Thirty other owners are citizens of the same trade treaty country and they are living in their home country, but are eligible as E-1 visa holders. The remaining 40 owners are U.S. citizens.

In this situation, if the company is to act as an E-1 sponsor for others, 20 of the 30 owners who are citizens of the trade treaty country but live in the U.S. must hold E-1 visas. Remember that only 50 of the owners need to be citizens of the treaty country. Of those 50, each must either live outside the U.S. and be classifiable as E-1s, or live in the U.S. on an E-1 visa. In our example, 30 live outside the United States. Therefore, only 20 of the trade treaty country citizens living inside the U.S. need have E-1 visas to make up the necessary 50% total of qualifying owners.

Additionally, USCIS regulations allow a different test in the case of large multinational corporations in which it is difficult to determine ownership by stock ownership. In the situation where a corporation's stock is sold exclusively in the country of incorporation, it may be presumed to have the nationality of the country where the stocks are exchanged.

3. You Must Be Either a Supervisor or Manager, or a Key Employee

E-1 visas may be issued to people who are executives, supervisors, supervisory role executives, or person whose skills are essential to the enterprise.

a. Executives and Supervisors

The main duties of your position must be executive or supervisory, and give you ultimate control and responsibility for the operation of at least a major part of the enterprise. The immigration authorities will apply the following standards to determine whether a given position fits the bill:

- An "executive" position normally gives the employee great authority in determining the policy and direction of the enterprise.
- A "supervisory" position normally entails responsibility for supervising a major portion of an enterprise's operations and does not usually involve direct supervision of low-level employees.
- Your skills, experience, salary, and title should be on a par with executive or supervisory positions. The position should carry overall authority and responsibility in the context of the enterprise, such as discretionary decision making, policy setting, direction and management of business operations, and supervision of other professional and supervisory personnel.

b. Essential Employees

If you're not an executive or supervisor, you may still get an E-1 visa if you are an employee with special qualifications that make your services essential to the efficient operation of the enterprise. Your skills do not have to be unique or one of a kind, but they should be indispensable

to the success of the investment. USCIS evaluates employees' skills on a case-by-case basis. However, if your skills are commonplace or readily available in the U.S. labor market, showing that you are essential will be difficult.

The immigration authorities will consider the following to determine whether a nonexecutive, nonsupervisory person should be classified as an E-1 employee because his or her skills are essential:

- the degree of expertise in the area of operations involved
- the degree of experience and training with the enterprise
- whether U.S. workers possess the individual's skills or aptitude
- the length of time required to train an individual to perform the job duties of the position
- the relationship of the individual's skills and talents to the overall operations of the entity, and
- the salary the special qualifications can command.

Knowledge of a foreign language and/or culture will not by itself constitute the degree of essentiality required.

4. Fifty-One Percent of the Company's Trade Must Be Between the U.S. and Your Home Country

More than 50% of the company's trade must be between the U.S. and the treaty nation citizen's home country. For example, if you are from the U.K. and are in the business of importing English antiques to the U.S., more than 50% of your inventory, as measured by its cash value, must have been imported directly from the United Kingdom. If some other company does the importing and your business simply buys the British goods once they reach the U.S., you will not qualify for the visa because your company is not directly engaged in trade with the United Kingdom.

The law is liberal in its definition of what constitutes trade. The most straightforward example is the import or export of a tangible product, but exchange of monies or services can also qualify. For example, the transfer of technology through scientifically knowledgeable employees or the rendering of services have been recognized as trade. Activities other than the sale of goods that have been officially recognized by the U.S. Department of State as trade for E-1 purposes include international banking, insurance, transportation, communications, data processing, advertising, accounting, design and engineering, management consulting, tourism, technology and its transfer, and some news-gathering activities.

5. Substantial Trade

A company must be carrying on a substantial amount of trade between the U.S. and the home country in order for the company to successfully support your E-1 application. The term "substantial" is not defined in the law by a strict numerical measure. In fact it is not specifically defined at all, though USCIS regulations state that there must be a "continuous flow" of trade items between the two countries.

What is considered substantial depends on the type of business. For example, a business that imports heavy machinery may not have to show a huge number of sales, but will have to show a greater dollar volume of business than a business importing candy bars to meet the requirement of substantial trade.

There are three general tests— dollars, volume, and frequency—that can normally be relied on to measure substantiality. The company must be able to meet the minimum standards of all three.

a. Dollar Amount of Trade

The dollar amount (not the retail value) of the inventory, services, or other commodities purchased from or sold to the treaty country should exceed $200,000 per year. However, some consulates require the sales or purchases to equal or exceed as much as $500,000, while others may accept as little as $50,000. A specific sum is not written into the law. The individual consular officer has the authority to require varying amounts in different cases. However, experience shows that anything under the $200,000 mark is a weak case.

b. Volume

If the company sells products, to satisfy the volume test, its import or export trade must be enough to create full-time business in the United States. The company's initial shipment must fill at least an entire warehouse or retail store. If the company sells services, the volume should be large enough to support the E-1 visa holder and at least one other worker. Some businesses do not meet the volume test when they are first starting up, but grow to the required size as time goes on. Purchasing a growing business may be one way to fulfill the volume requirement immediately.

c. Frequency

The company must import to or export from the U.S. with sufficient frequency to maintain a full inventory at all times. One shipment is not enough. Importation or exportation must be ongoing.

⚠ These three measures have been partly derived from our own experience and not the immigration laws. It is possible for an E-1 visa to be approved with a smaller amount of trade than we have described in our three tests. With E-1 visas, a great deal is left to the judgment of the USCIS or consular officer evaluating the application.

6. Intent to Leave the U.S.

E-1 visas are meant to be temporary. At the time of your application, you must intend to depart the U.S. when your business there is completed. As previously mentioned, you are not required to maintain a foreign residence abroad.

The U.S. government knows it is difficult to read minds. Expect to be asked for evidence showing that when you go to the U.S. on an E-1 visa, you eventually plan to leave. In many nonimmigrant categories, you are asked to show proof that you will keep a house or apartment outside the U.S., indicating that you eventually intend to go back to your home country. You do not need to keep a home outside the U.S. to qualify for an E-1 visa—but it would help. You will certainly be asked to show that you have some family members, possessions, or property elsewhere in the world as an incentive for your eventual departure from the United States.

Possibilities for a Green Card From E-1 Status

If you have an E-1 visa, you can file to get a green card, but being in the U.S. on an E-1 visa gives you no advantage in doing so, and in fact may prove to be a drawback. That is because E-1 visas, like all nonimmigrant visas, are intended only for people who plan on leaving the U.S. once their jobs or other activities there are completed.

If you apply for a green card, you are in effect making a statement that you never intend to leave the United States. Therefore, the U.S. government may allow you to keep E-1 status while pursuing a green card, but only if you can convince it that you did not intend to get a green card when you originally applied for the E-1 visa, and that you will leave the U.S. if you are unable to secure a green card before your E-1 visa expires. Proving these things can be difficult. If you do not succeed, your E-1 visa may be taken away. Should this happen, it may affect your green card application, since being out of status or working without authorization may be a bar to getting a green card in the U.S., or may create a waiting period of three or ten years if you depart the U.S. and apply for a visa. (See Chapter 3.)

7. Bringing Your Spouse and Children

When you qualify for an E-1 visa, your spouse and unmarried children under age 21 can also get E-1 visas by providing proof of their family relationship to you. Your spouse will also be permitted to work in the United States.

To take advantage of the right to work, your spouse should, after arriving in the U.S., apply for a work permit. (Although the Social Security Administration says you don't need one, USCIS maintains that you do, so it's safest to apply.) This is done on USCIS Form I-765 (available on the USCIS website at www.uscis.gov). In filling out the form, your spouse should write "spouse of E nonimmigrant" in Question 15, and "A-17" in Question 16.

Your spouse will need to mail this form, together with proof of your visa status, a copy of his or her I-94 card, the filing fee (currently $340) and two passport-style photos, to the appropriate USCIS service center for your geographic region. For the address and other information, call USCIS Information at 800-375-5283 or see the USCIS website (www.uscis.gov).

B. Quick View of the E-1 Visa Application Process

Once you have opened a qualifying company engaged in trade between your home country and the United States, or been offered a job as a key employee of a qualifying company owned by others from your country, getting an E-1 visa is a one- or two-step process—although the nature of the step depends on where you are now:

- If you're outside the U.S., you file an application at a U.S. consulate there. (The vast majority of non-immigrant visa applications are filed at consulates, because most cases don't qualify for U.S. filing.)
- If you are already in the U.S. legally on some other type of nonimmigrant visa, you can, if you prefer, apply for a change to E-1 status at a USCIS office inside the United States. (However, if you were admitted without a visa, such as under the Visa Waiver Program, you may not carry out the application step in the United States.)
- If you're outside the U.S., step two is for you to use your visa to enter the U.S. and claim your E-1 status.

Nothing stops you from helping with your U.S. employer's tasks during this application process. For example, you can fill out forms intended to be completed by your employer and simply ask the employer to check them over and sign them. The less your U.S. employer is inconvenienced, the more it may be willing to act as sponsor for your visa.

C. How to Apply From Outside the U.S.

Applicants outside the U.S. must apply for an E-1 visa at a U.S. consulate in their home country. Check with your local U.S. consulate regarding its application procedures. Many insist on advance appointments. Just getting an appointment can take several weeks, so plan ahead.

Have you been, or are you now, working or living illegally in the United States? If so, see Chapter 3 regarding whether you can still get a visa from a U.S. consulate. You may have become inadmissible or subject to a three-year or ten-year bar on reentry.

1. Preparing Your Application Paperwork

When you file at a U.S. consulate abroad, the consular officials will provide you with certain forms, designated by "DS" preceding a number. Most consulates use Form DS-156 together with a supplemental form especially for E visa applicants called a DS-156E. Instructions for completing these forms, including what to do with them once they are filled out, will come with the forms. You can also get copies of the forms at www.state.gov.

The following checklist will help you prepare your consular application.

E-1 Visa Application Checklist

❑ Form DS-156, Nonimmigrant Visa Application.

❑ Form DS-156E, Nonimmigrant Treaty Trader/Investor Application.

❑ Form DS-157, Supplemental Nonimmigrant Visa Application (only needs to be filled out by male nonimmigrant visa applicants between the ages of 16 and 45).

❑ Valid passport for you and each accompanying relative (this proves both your identity and your right to travel, and that you are a citizen from one of the qualifying treaty countries).

❑ One U.S. passport-type photo of you and one of each accompanying relative. (This is best done by a professional photographer; the consulate can give you a list.)

❑ If your spouse and children will be accompanying you, documents verifying their family relationship to you, such as marriage and birth certificates.

❑ If either you or your spouse have ever been married before, copies of divorce and death certificates showing termination of all previous marriages.

❑ Proof of the nationality of the qualifying business owners.

❑ Proof that you are a key employee.

❑ Proof that your sponsoring company is a bona fide, active business.

❑ Proof that a majority of the company's trade is between the U.S. and your home country.

❑ Proof that the trade is substantial.

❑ Documents establishing your intent to leave the U.S. when your status expires, such as deeds verifying ownership of a house or other real property, written statements from you explaining that close relatives are staying behind, or letters from a company showing that you have a job waiting when you return from the United States.

❑ Visa application fee (currently $100).

❑ Visa issuance fee. (The amount of the fee depends on what country you're from. If the country of your nationality charges fees for visas to U.S. citizens who wish to work there, then the U.S. will charge people of your country a similar fee.)

Applying at a Consulate Outside of Your Home Country

The law allows most people to apply for an E-1 visa at any U.S. consulate they choose—with one exception. If you have ever been present in the U.S. unlawfully, your visa will be automatically cancelled and you cannot apply as a third-country national (at a consulate outside your home country). Even if you overstayed your status in the U.S. by just one day, you must return to your home country and apply for the visa from that consulate. There is an exception. If you were admitted to the U.S. for the duration of your status (indicated by a "D/S" on your I-94 form and most common with student visas) and you remained in the U.S. beyond the time for which your status was conferred, you will be barred from third-country national processing only if an immigration judge or USCIS (or formerly INS) officer has determined that you were unlawfully present. You may find that your success in applying as a third-country national will depend on your country, the consulate, and the relative seriousness of your offense. Being unlawfully present is also a ground of inadmissibility if the period of unlawful presence is 180 days or more. (See Chapter 3.)

Even if you are eligible for third-country national processing, your case will be given the greatest consideration at the consulate in your home country. Applying in some other country creates suspicion in the minds of the consular officers there about your motives for choosing their consulate. Often, when an applicant expects trouble at a home consulate, he or she will seek a more lenient consular office in some other country. This practice of consulate shopping is frowned upon by officials in the system. Unless you have a very good reason for being elsewhere (such as a temporary job assignment in some other nation), it is often smarter to file your visa application in your home country.

The following subsections provide further explanation of some of the items on the checklist.

a. Proof of the Nationality of the Qualifying Business Owners

You must show that the qualifying business is owned by citizens of one of the trade treaty countries. If you are not the owner yourself, you will need to show that both you and those who do own the company are citizens of the same treaty country, usually by showing copies of their passports.

Although you will be doing work for the qualifying company in the U.S., the company and its owners may or may not be located there. Therefore, you must provide documents showing where each of the owners is living currently. Affidavits from each of these owners stating their places of residence will serve this purpose. If any are living in the U.S., copies of their passports and I-94 cards are also needed to demonstrate that they hold valid E-1 visas. Remember, if the owners of the company live in the U.S., at least 50% must also hold E-1 visas for the business to support your own E-1 application.

You will need to prove that you or other nationals of your country own not just a small part, but a majority of the qualifying business. If the qualifying business is a corporation, you should submit copies of all stock certificates, together with a notarized affidavit from the secretary of the corporation listing the name of each shareholder and the number of shares each owns. The affidavit must account for all the shares issued to date. Remember that at least 50% must be owned by nationals of your treaty country.

If the qualifying business is not incorporated, instead of copies of stock certificates, you will need to present legal papers proving the existence and ownership of the company. These may be partnership agreements, business registration certificates, or business licenses, together with a notarized affidavit from an official of the company certifying who owns the business and in what percentages.

b. Proof That You Are a Key Employee

If you are not the majority owner of the company, you must submit evidence that your job in the U.S. will fit the USCIS definition of an executive or supervisor or supervisory role essential employee. To prove this, present detailed statements from the sponsoring business explaining your specific duties as well as the number and kind of employees you will supervise. If the application is based on your special position as an employee, the statements should also describe the nature of the essential knowledge or experience, how it will be used, and why it is essential in your U.S. job. These required statements may be in your employer's own words and do not have to be in any special form.

c. Proof of the Existence of an Active Business

You should submit documents to show that your E-1 visa application is based on a real, ongoing business. Such evidence should include:

- articles of incorporation or other business charter of the qualifying company
- bank statements for the qualifying company
- credit agreements with suppliers
- letters of credit issued
- leases or deeds for business premises and warehouse space
- tax returns filed in the past two years, if any, including payroll tax returns, and
- promotional literature or advertising.

If the business is newly formed, there will be no tax returns yet. You should then submit a detailed business plan including financial projections for the next five years.

d. Proof That a Majority of the Company's Trade Is Between the U.S. and Your Home Country

More than 50% of the company's total trade must consist of commerce between your treaty home country and the United States. This is best shown by presenting copies of all import or export documents from the previous 12 months, including purchase or sale orders, bills of lading and customs entry documents, contracts with suppliers outside of the U.S, and a balance sheet from the qualifying company showing the total amount of inventory for the same period. Comparison of the balance sheet with the import or export documents will show the percentage of the company's trade devoted to commerce between the U.S. and the trade treaty country. The dollar amount of the imports or exports between the U.S. and your home country must total more than 50% of the entire inventory.

e. Proof That the Trade Is Substantial

The qualifying company's trade between the U.S. and your home treaty country must be substantial, meeting the three tests previously described: dollar, volume, and frequency. The same documents presented to prove that the majority of the company's trade is between the U.S. and

your home treaty country will also serve to show that the trade is substantial.

2. Attending Your Consular Interview

As part of your application, the consulate will require you and your family members to attend an interview. During the interview, a consular officer will examine the data in your application for accuracy, especially regarding facts about the substantiality of the business and the nationality of the owners. Evidence of ties to your home country will also be checked. During the interview, you will surely be asked how long you intend to remain in the United States. Any answer indicating that you are unsure about plans to return or have an interest in applying for a green card is likely to result in a denial of your visa. (See Chapter 4 for what else to expect during consular interviews, and what to do if your application is denied.)

Once your E-1 visa is approved, you will probably be asked to return later to pick it up. However, your visa may be approved only provisionally, awaiting security checks, which can add weeks or months to the process.

D. How to Apply If You're in the U.S.

If you are physically present in the U.S., you may apply for E-1 status without leaving the country on the following conditions:

- you entered the U.S. legally and not on a visa waiver
- you have never worked illegally
- the date on your I-94 card has not passed, and
- you are admissible and none of the bars to changing status apply to you (see Chapter 3).

If you were admitted as a visitor without a visa under the Visa Waiver Program, you may not apply from within the United States. Similarly, you can't take advantage of this option if you entered the U.S. using a C (alien in transit), TWOV (alien in transit without a visa), D (crewman), K-1 (fiancé), K-2 (dependent of a fiancé), J-1 (exchange visitor), or M-1 (vocational student) visa.

 Your eligibility to apply in the U.S. has nothing to do with your overall eligibility for an E-1 visa. Many applicants who are barred from filing in the U.S. but otherwise qualify for E-1 status may still apply successfully for an E-1 visa at a U.S. consulate in another country.

There is another problem that comes up only in U.S. filings. It is the issue of what is called preconceived intent. To approve a change of status, USCIS must believe that at the time you originally entered the U.S. as a visitor or with some other nonimmigrant visa, you did not intend to apply for a different status. If USCIS thinks you had a preconceived plan to use one visa to enter the U.S. with an eye to applying for a different status after getting there, it may deny your application. (You can get around the preconceived intent issue by leaving the U.S. and applying for your E-1 visa at a U.S. consulate in another country.)

In technical terms, what you will be applying for in the U.S. is a change of status. To do so, you'll need to file an application with USCIS on Form I-129 (Petition for a Nonimmigrant Worker), with accompanying documents to prove your eligibility. If your spouse and children will be accompanying you, they must file for their change of status on a different form, called Form I-539.

If you decide to apply for a change of status within the U.S., you should realize that you still don't have the E-1 visa that you'll need if you ever leave the U.S.—a change of status only gives you E-1 status. Visas are never given inside the United States They are issued exclusively by U.S. consulates in other countries. If you file in the U.S. and you are successful, you will get to remain in the U.S. with E-1 privileges until the status expires. But should you leave the country for any reason before that time, you will have to apply for the visa itself at a U.S. consulate before returning to the United States. Moreover, the fact that your E-1 status has been approved in the U.S. does not guarantee that the consulate will also approve your visa. You'll have to present a whole new application, and they will evaluate it with little or no consideration for the previous USCIS decision. For this reason, many people find it easier to leave the U.S. and apply at a U.S. consulate from the start.

1. Preparing the Change of Status Application

The checklist below will help you prepare the documents and forms for your change of status application.

E-1 Change of Status Checklist

☐ Form I-129, with E Supplement (signed and submitted by you, if you're self-employed, or by your employer).

☐ Filing fee: $320.

☐ If your family members are with you and need a change of status, Form I-539 with accompanying fee (currently $300) and copies of your family members' I-94s or other proof of lawful immigration status and of their relationship to you, (such as marriage and birth certificates). One Form I-539 and fee will cover your spouse and all your children. This form is meant to be filled out and signed by your family members, not by your employer.

☐ If either you or your spouse have ever been married before, copies of divorce and death certificates showing termination of all previous marriages.

☐ A copy of your I-94 or other proof of your current lawful, unexpired immigration status (except Canadians visitors, who are not expected to have I-94 cards).

☐ Proof of the nationality of the qualifying business owners.

☐ Proof that you are a key employee.

☐ Proof of the existence of an active business.

☐ Proof that a majority of the company's trade is between the U.S. and your home country.

☐ Proof that the trade is substantial.

☐ Documents establishing your intent to leave the U.S. when your status expires, such as deeds verifying ownership of a house or other real property, written statements from you explaining that close relatives are staying behind, or letters from a company showing that you have a job waiting when you return from the United States.

☐ Cover letter (optional).

If requesting quick (premium) processing:

☐ Form I-907, with $1,000 filing fee.

For further explanation of some of the key items on this checklist, see Section C1, above.

Although it is not a requirement, one additional item that you may wish to add to the paperwork package is a cover letter. Cover letters act as a summary and index to the forms and documents, and are often used by immigration attorneys or U.S. companies that process many visas for their employees. Cover letters begin with a statement summarizing the facts of the case and explaining why the particular applicant is eligible for the visa. This statement is followed by a list of the forms and documents submitted. If it is carefully written, a cover letter can make the case clearer and easier to process for the consular or USCIS officer evaluating it. This is particularly important in an E-1 visa case where the documentation by itself may require explanation. Cover letters must be individually tailored to each case, so if you don't think you can write a good one, just leave it out and submit only your forms and documents; or hire an attorney to help.

2. Mailing the Change of Status Petition

After assembling the I-129 petition, mail it to the USCIS regional service center listed in the instructions to Form I-129. USCIS regional service centers are not the same as USCIS local offices—for one thing, you cannot visit regional service centers in person.

3. Awaiting a Decision on the Visa Petition

Within a few weeks after mailing in the petition, you or your employer should get back a written confirmation that the papers are being processed, together with a receipt for the fee. This notice will also contain your immigration file number. If USCIS wants further information before acting on your case, all petition papers, forms, and documents will be returned with a form known as a Request for Evidence. Supply the extra data requested and mail the whole package back to the service center.

E-1 petitions are normally approved within two to three months. When this happens, USCIS will send you a Form I-797 Notice of Action, showing that the change of status has been approved. A new I-94 card will be attached to the bottom of the form.

 Faster processing—at a price. For $1,000 over and above the regular filing fees, USCIS promises premium processing of the visa petition, including a decision within 15 days. To use this service, you must fill out an additional application (Form I-907) and submit the application to a special USCIS service center address. For complete instructions, see the USCIS website at www.uscis.gov.

E. Using Your E-1 Visa to Enter the U.S.

If you applied for your E-1 visa at a U.S. consulate abroad, you have until the expiration date on your E-1 visa to enter the United States. The border officer will examine your paperwork, ask you some questions, and if all is in order, approve you for entry. He or she will stamp your passport and give you a small white card called an I-94 card. It will be stamped with a date showing how long you can stay. Normally you are permitted to remain for two years at a time, without regard to when your visa actually expires (a visa is just an entry document—the I-94 shows the length of your E-1 status). Keep track of the whereabouts of this card, and make spare copies to keep in a safe place. You'll need it to prove your entry and to apply for extensions.

Each time you exit and reenter the U.S., you will get a new I-94 card authorizing your stay for an additional one- or two-year period. If you do not wish to leave the U.S. after that time, you can apply for extensions of stay, which are issued in two-year increments for as long as you maintain your E-1 status qualifications.

Watch Out for Summary Exclusion

The law empowers a Customs and Border Protection (CBP) inspector at the U.S. airport or border to summarily (without allowing judicial review) bar entry to someone requesting admission to the U.S. if either of the following is true:

- The inspector thinks you are lying about practically anything connected with entering the U.S., including your purpose in coming, intent to return, and prior immigration history. This includes the use or suspected use of false documents.
- You do not have the proper documentation to support your entry to the U.S. in the category you are requesting.

If the inspector excludes you, you cannot be readmitted to the U.S. for five years, unless USCIS grants a special waiver. For this reason it is extremely important to understand the terms of your requested status, and to not make any misrepresentations. If you are found to be inadmissible, you may ask the CBP inspector to withdraw your application to enter the U.S. in order to prevent having the five-year deportation order on your record. The CBP may allow this in some exceptional cases.

F. Extending Your U.S. Stay

E-1 visas can be extended for up to five years at a time and E-1 status stays can be extended for two years at a time. When you enter the U.S. with an E-1 visa, your authorized stay as indicated on your I-94 card, which is limited to two years at a time, may elapse before the expiration date of your visa. Therefore, depending on your situation, you may need to extend just your I-94 card, your visa, or both.

Although an extension is usually easier to get than the E-1 visa itself, it is not automatic. USCIS or the consulate has the right to reconsider your qualifications based on any changes in the facts or law. When the original application for an E-1 visa or status was weak, it is not unusual for an extension request to be turned down.

If you have received E-1 status in the U.S. but never applied for a visa, it's best to stay in the U.S. to apply for an extension of your status (in case the consulate disagrees with USCIS's original decision approving your E-1 status). However, if you have an E-1 visa that is still valid but your I-94 card is about to expire, it is generally better to leave the U.S. and return again instead of trying to extend your status in the United States. When you return to the U.S. on your valid E-1 visa, you will automatically receive a new I-94 card and a new one- or two-year period of authorized stay. By leaving and reentering, no extension application will be needed and there will be no reevaluation of your qualifications.

The general procedures for an E-1 extension from within the U.S. are the same as those described in Section D, above. The forms, documents, and fees are identical.

Working While Your Extension Application Is Pending

If you file your application for an extension of E-1 status before your authorized stay expires, you are automatically permitted to continue working for up to 240 days while you are waiting for a decision. If, however, your authorized stay expires after you have filed for an extension, but before you receive an approval, and more than 240 days go by without getting a decision on your extension application, your work authorization ends and you must stop working.

G. Visa Revalidation

If you leave the U.S. with an expired E-1 visa stamp, you must have a new visa issued at a consulate before returning (even if you've extended your E-1 status with USCIS). Reread procedures for consular filing in Section C, above. The procedures for consular visa extensions are identical. If you are outside the U.S. with a valid (unexpired) visa, you need only reenter and a new I-94 card authorizing your stay for one year will be given to you. ■

Chapter 21

Getting a Treaty Investor (E-2) Visa

An E-2 visa allows businesspeople from certain countries to work in the U.S. for a business in which people from their country have invested. (See I.N.A. § 101(a)(15)(E), 8 U.S.C. § 1101(a)(l5)(E); 8 C.F.R. § 214.2(e); 22 C.F.R. § 41.51.) Like the E-1 visa, some people call the E-2 the next best thing to permanent residence, because of the possibility of self-employment, and the unlimited number of extensions. There are no numerical limits on the number of E-2 visas that can be issued each year.

⚠ **Do not confuse E-2 treaty investor visas with green cards through investment, discussed in Chapter 11.** The E-2 visa is a completely different type of visa with completely different requirements. For one thing, it's a nonimmigrant visa. All nonimmigrant visas are temporary, while green cards are permanent. Moreover, a green card through investment requires a dollar investment of $1 million or more, while an E-2 visa has no dollar minimum. Again, see Chapter 11 to compare.

Key Features of the E-2 Visa

Here are some of the advantages and disadvantages of the E-2 visa:

- You can work legally in the U.S. for a U.S. business in which a substantial cash investment has been made by you or other citizens of your home country, so long as your country has a trade treaty with the U.S.
- You may travel in and out of the U.S. or remain here continuously until your visa and status expire.
- You are restricted to work only for the employer or self-owned business that acted as your E-2 visa sponsor.
- Your initial visa may last up to two years, with unlimited possible two-year extensions.
- Visas are available for your accompanying spouse and minor children, but your children cannot work here.
- Your spouse will be permitted to accept employment in the U.S.

A. Do You Qualify for an E-2 Visa?

There are six requirements for getting an E-2 visa:

- You must be a citizen of a country that has an investor treaty with the United States.
- You must be coming to work in the U.S. for a company you own or one that is at least 50% owned by other nationals of your home country.
- You must be either the owner or a key employee of the U.S. business.
- You or the company must have made a substantial investment in the U.S. business.
- The U.S. business must be actively engaged in trade or the rendering of services.
- You must intend to leave the U.S. when your business there is completed.

1. Countries That Have Treaties With the U.S.

E-2 visas are available to citizens of only selected countries that have investor treaties with the United States. Legal residence is not enough. With the exception of E-2 applicants from the U.K., you need not be presently residing in your country of citizenship in order to qualify for an E-2 visa. When you are a citizen of more than one nation, you may qualify for an E-2 visa if at least one of them has an investor treaty with the United States.

Those countries with investor treaties currently in effect are:

Albania
Argentina
Armenia
Australia
Austria
Azerbaijan
Bahrain
Bangladesh
Belgium
Bolivia
Bosnia
Bulgaria
Cameroon
Canada
Chile
Colombia
Congo (Brazzaville)
Congo (Democratic Republic
    of Kinshasa)
Costa Rica
Croatia
Czech Republic
Ecuador
Egypt
Estonia
Ethiopia
Finland
France
Georgia
Germany
Grenada
Herzegovina
Honduras
Iran
Ireland
Italy
Jamaica

Japan
Jordan
Kazakhstan
Korea (South)
Kyrgyzstan
Latvia
Liberia
Lithuania
Luxembourg
Macedonia
Mexico
Moldova
Mongolia
Morocco
Netherlands, The
Norway
Oman
Pakistan
Panama
Paraguay
Philippines
Poland
Romania
Serbia and Montenegro
Senegal
Singapore
Slovak Republic
Slovenia
Spain
Sri Lanka
Suriname
Sweden
Switzerland
Taiwan
Thailand
Togo
Trinidad and Tobago
Tunisia

Turkey
Ukraine
United Kingdom

Additional treaties are pending and will go into effect within the next several years. Check with the appropriate consulate to make sure a treaty is in force before you apply. The list is kept at Volume 9 of the *Foreign Affairs Manual* (FAM), § 41.51, Exhibit 1. (You can find the *Foreign Affairs Manual* on the U.S. State Department website at http://foia. state.gov/regs/search.asp.)

2. Whether Your Company Is Owned by Citizens of a Qualifying Country

To get an E-2 visa, you must be coming to the U.S. to work for a business that is at least 50% owned by citizens of your treaty country. The company may be owned by you or others. If the company is owned in part or in whole by others, and some or all of them already live in the U.S., those people may need to have E-2 visas themselves before the company can act as an E-2 sponsor for you. Specifically:

- at least 50% of the company must be owned by citizens of a single investor treaty country, and
- the owners from the single investor treaty country must either live outside the U.S. and be able to be classified as treaty investors or live inside the U.S. with E-2 visas.

This second condition can be a little confusing. Some examples may help to make it clearer.

EXAMPLE 1: The company is owned 100% by one person. The owner is a citizen of an investor treaty country and lives outside the U.S. in his or her home country.

In this case the owner does not need an E-2 visa for the company to support your E-2 visa application, but must be able to satisfy the criteria for an E-2 visa if he or she were to apply.

EXAMPLE 2: The company is owned in equal shares by two people. Each owner is a citizen of the same investor treaty country. One owner lives in the U.S. on a green card. The other still lives in his home country.

In this case, the owner living abroad must be classifiable for E-2 status. If, however, we changed this example so that both owners lived in the U.S., the owner who is a green card holder would be prohibited by regulations from being a qualifying employer, so the other owner would have to be in E status.

EXAMPLE 3: The company is owned in equal shares by 100 people. Thirty owners are citizens of a particular investor treaty country but live in the United States. Thirty other owners are citizens of the same investor treaty country and they are living in their home country. The remaining 40 owners are U.S. citizens.

In this situation, if the company is to act as an E-2 visa sponsor for others, 20 of the 30 owners who are citizens of the investor treaty country but live in the U.S. must hold E-2 visas. Remember that only 50 of the owners need to be citizens of the treaty country. Of those 50, each must either live outside the U.S. and be classifiable for E-2 status or live in the U.S. on an E-2 visa. In our example, 30 live outside the United States. Therefore, only 20 of the investor treaty country citizens living inside the U.S. need to have E-2 visas to make up the necessary 50% total of qualifying owners.

USCIS allows a different test in the case of large multinational corporations in which it is difficult to determine ownership by stock ownership. If a corporation's stock is sold exclusively in the country of incorporation, it may be presumed to have the nationality of the country where the stocks are exchanged.

3. You Must Be a 50% Owner, or Supervisor, Executive, or Key Employee

E-2 visas may be issued only to the principal owners or key employees of the qualifying business, provided all have the same treaty nationality. To qualify as a principal owner, you must either:

- own at least 50% of the company
- possess operational control through a managerial position or similar corporate device, or
- be in a position to control the enterprise by other means.

To qualify as a key employee you must be considered either an:

- executive or supervisor, or
- a person whose skills are essential to the enterprise.

a. Definition of Executives and Supervisors

For E-2 classification purposes, your position must be executive or supervisory, and give you ultimate control and responsibility for the operation of at least a major part of the enterprise. (See 22 C.F.R. § 41.51(q).) The immigration authorities will apply the following standards to determine whether a given position fits the bill:

- an "executive" position normally gives the employee great authority in determining policy and direction of the enterprise
- a "supervisory" position normally entails responsibility for supervising a major portion of an enterprise's operations and does not usually involve direct supervision of low-level employees, and
- your skills, experience, salary, and title should be on a par with executive or supervisory positions, and the position should carry

overall authority and responsibility in the context of the enterprise, such as discretionary decision making, policy setting, direction and management of business operations, and supervision of other professional and supervisory personnel.

b. Essential Employees

By requiring that employees be essential, the immigration authorities intend to favor specialists over ordinary skilled workers. The employee's skills do not have to be unique or one of a kind but they should be indispensable to the success of the investment. USCIS evaluates employees' skills on a case-by-case basis. However, if the skills possessed by the employee are commonplace or readily available in the U.S. labor market, USCIS might not believe that the employee is essential.

Specifically, the immigration authorities will consider the following to determine whether an individual who is a non-executive, nonsupervisor and who is not at least a 50% owner, should be classified as an E-2 employee because of the essentiality of his or her skills:

- the degree of expertise in the area of operations involved
- the degree of experience and training with the enterprise
- whether U.S. workers possess the individual's skills or aptitude
- the length of the applicant's specific experience or training

- the length of time required to train someone else to perform the job duties of the position
- the relationship of the individual's skills and talents to the overall operations of the entity, and
- the salary the special qualifications can command.

(See 22 C.F.R. § 41.51(r).)

Knowledge of a foreign language and/or culture will not by itself constitute the degree of essentiality required.

4. The Investment Must Be Substantial

You or your company must be in the process of investing a substantial amount in the U.S. business in order to successfully support an E-2 visa application. To "invest" means putting capital or assets at risk with the goal of generating a profit (you can't invest in a nonprofit enterprise). (See 22 C.F.R. § 41.51(l).) It's okay if the money was gifted or loaned to you.

The term "substantial" is not defined in the law by any strict numerical measure. What is considered substantial depends on the type of business. For example, an automobile manufacturer will have to show a greater dollar amount of investment than a retail toy store in order to meet the requirement of substantial investment. The lower the cost of the business, the higher the percentage of funds you'll need to invest in order to qualify.

The State Department advises its consular officers to consider the following in regards to whether the investment is substantial:

- its substantiality in a proportional sense, that is, compared with the amount it would take to buy or create the same sort of business
- whether the investment is enough to ensure your commitment to the successful operation of the enterprise, and
- whether the investment is of a magnitude to support the likelihood that you will successfully develop and direct the enterprise.

(See 9 FAM § 41.51 Note 10.2.)

5. The Enterprise Must Not Produce Marginal Profits

The immigration authorities want to make sure you're not just establishing a minor operation to generate a living for the owners and therefore get you an E-2 visa, so they require that the enterprise not be "marginal." (See 9 § FAM 41.51, Note 11.) Here's the test for a greater-than-marginal enterprise put forth in the FAM:

(1) First, look to the alien's income from the investment. If the income derived from the business exceeds what is necessary to support self and family, then this, too, meets the test.

(2) If the first test is not met, and it becomes necessary to consider other factors, one can look to the economic

impact of the business. The business must have the capacity, present or future, to make a significant economic contribution. The projected future capacity should generally be realizable within five years from the date the alien commences normal business activities. It is recommended that applicants submit a reliable business plan to verify the capacity to realize a profit within a maximum five years.

6. It Must Be a Bona Fide, Active Business

The investment must be in a for-profit business that is actively engaged in trade or the rendering of services, and one that meets the applicable legal requirements for doing business in the state or region. (See 22 C.F.R. § 41.51(m).) Investment in holding companies, stocks, bonds, and land speculation will not support an E-2 visa application, since they are not considered "active." (See 9 FAM § 41.51, Note 9.)

The test is whether or not the business requires active supervisory or executive oversight on a day-to-day basis. Clearly, retail, wholesale, and manufacturing operations require such supervision, while stock purchases and land speculation do not. There are some types of investments, especially in real estate, where the line between a qualifying and nonqualifying business investment is difficult to draw. For example, if you purchase and rent out a single home or duplex, this is not the type of investment that will support an E-2 visa application, even if the dollar amount is adequate. If you purchase and rent out an eight- or ten-unit apartment building, that is probably a marginal case. As the number of rental units becomes greater, the need for daily management increases, and the case for an E-2 visa becomes stronger.

7. Your Intent to Leave the U.S.

E-2 visas are meant to be temporary. At the time of your application, you must intend to depart the U.S. when your business there is completed. As previously mentioned, you are not required to maintain a foreign residence abroad.

The U.S. government knows it is difficult to read minds. Expect to be asked for evidence showing that when you go to the U.S. on an E-2 visa, you eventually plan to leave. In many nonimmigrant categories, you are asked to show proof that you will keep a house or apartment outside the U.S., indicating that you eventually intend to go back to your home country. You do not need to keep a home outside the U.S. to qualify for an E-2 visa—but it would help. You will certainly be asked to show that you have some family members, possessions, or property elsewhere in the world as an incentive for your eventual departure from the United States.

8. Bringing Your Spouse and Children

When you qualify for an E-2 visa, your spouse and unmarried children under age 21 can also get E-2 visas by providing proof of their family relationship to you. Your spouse, but not your children, will be permitted to accept employment in the United States.

To take advantage of the right to work, your spouse should, after arriving in the United States, apply for a work permit. (Although the Social Security Administration says a work permit is unnecessary, USCIS maintains it is, so it's safest to apply.) This is done on USCIS Form I-765. In filling out the form, your spouse should write "spouse of E nonimmigrant" in Question 15, and "A-17" in Question 16.

Your spouse will need to mail this form, together with proof of your visa status, a copy of his or her I-94 card, the filing fee and two photos, to the appropriate USCIS service center for your geographic region. For the address and other information, call USCIS Information at 800-375-5283 or see the USCIS website (www.uscis.gov).

Possibilities for a Green Card From E-2 Status

If you have an E-2 visa, you can file to get a green card, but being in the U.S. on an E-2 visa gives you no advantage in doing so, and in fact may prove to be a drawback. That is because E-2 visas, like all nonimmigrant visas, are intended only for people who plan on leaving the U.S. once their jobs or other activities there are completed. If you apply for a green card, you are in effect making a statement that you never intend to leave the United States. Therefore, the U.S. government will allow you to keep E-2 status while pursuing a green card, but only if you can convince the government that you did not intend to seek a green card when you originally applied for the E-2 visa, and that you will leave the U.S. if you are unable to secure a green card before your E-2 visa expires.

Proving those things can be difficult. If you do not succeed, your E-2 visa may be taken away. Should this happen, it may affect your green card application, since being out of status or working without authorization may be a bar to getting a green card in the U.S., or may create a waiting period if you depart the U.S. and apply for a visa. (See Chapter 3.)

B. Quick View of the E-2 Visa Application Process

Getting an E-2 visa is a one- or two-step process—although the nature of the step depends on where you are now:

- If you're outside the U.S., you file an application at a U.S. consulate there. (The vast majority of nonimmigrant visa applications are filed at consulates, because most cases don't qualify for U.S. filing.)
- If you are already in the U.S. legally on some other type of nonimmigrant visa, you can, if you prefer, apply for a change to E-2 status at a USCIS office inside the United States. (However, if you were admitted without a visa, such as under the Visa Waiver Program, you may not carry out the application step in the United States.)
- If you're outside the U.S., step two is for you to use your visa to enter the U.S. and claim your E-2 status.

 Nothing stops you from helping with your U.S. employer's tasks during this application process. For example, you can fill out forms intended to be completed by your employer and simply ask the employer to check them over and sign them. The less your U.S. employer is inconvenienced, the more it may be willing to act as sponsor for your visa.

C. How to Apply From Outside the U.S.

Applicants outside the U.S. must apply for an E-2 visa at a U.S. consulate in their home country. Check with your local U.S. consulate regarding its application procedures. Many insist on advance appointments. Just getting an appointment can take several weeks, so plan ahead.

Have you been, or are you now, working or living illegally in the United States? If so, see Chapter 3 regarding whether you can still get a visa from a U.S. consulate. You may have become inadmissible or subject to a three-year or ten-year bar on reentry.

Applying at a Consulate Outside of Your Home Country

The law allows most people to apply for an E-2 visa at any U.S. consulate they choose—with one exception. If you have ever been present in the U.S. unlawfully, your visa will be automatically cancelled and you cannot apply as a third-country national (at a consulate outside your home country). Even if you overstayed your status in the U.S. by just one day, you must return to your home country and apply for the visa from that consulate. There is an exception. If you were admitted to the U.S. for the duration of your status (indicated by a "D/S" on your I-94 form and most common with student visas) and you remained in the U.S. beyond the time for which your status was conferred, you will be barred from third-country national processing only if an immigration judge or USCIS (or formerly INS) officer has determined that you were unlawfully present. You may find that your success in applying as a third-country national will depend on your country, the consulate, and the relative seriousness of your offense. Being unlawfully present is also a ground of inadmissibility if the period of unlawful presence is 180 days or more. (See Chapter 3.)

Even if you are eligible for third-country national processing, your case will be given the greatest consideration at the consulate in your home country. Applying in some other country creates suspicion in the minds of the consular officers there about your motives for choosing their consulate. Often, when an applicant expects trouble at a home consulate, he or she will seek a more lenient consular office in some other country. This practice of consulate shopping is frowned upon by officials in the system. Unless you have a very good reason for being elsewhere (such as a temporary job assignment in some other nation), it is often smarter to file your visa application in your home country.

1. Preparing Your Application Paperwork

When you file at a U.S. consulate abroad, the consulate officials will provide you with certain forms, designated by a "DS" preceding a number. Most consulates use Form DS-156 together with a supplemental form especially for E visa applicants called a DS-156E. Instructions for completing these forms, including what to do with them once they are filled out, will come with the forms. You can also get copies of the forms at www.state.gov.

The following checklist will help you prepare your consular application.

E-2 Visa Application Checklist

- ❑ Form DS-156, Nonimmigrant Visa Application.
- ❑ Form DS-156E, Nonimmigrant Treaty Trader/Investor Application.
- ❑ Form DS-157, Supplemental Nonimmigrant Visa Application (needs to be filled out only by male nonimmigrant visa applicants between the ages of 16 and 45).
- ❑ Valid passport for you and each accompanying relative (this proves both your identity, your right to travel, and that you are a citizen from one of the qualifying treaty countries).
- ❑ One U.S. passport-type photo of you and one of each accompanying relative. (This is best done by a professional photographer; the consulate can give you a list.)
- ❑ If your spouse and children will be accompanying you, documents verifying their family relationship to you, such as marriage and birth certificates.
- ❑ If either you or your spouse have ever been married before, copies of divorce and death certificates showing termination of all previous marriages.
- ❑ Proof of the nationality of the qualifying business owners.
- ❑ Proof that you are a key employee of the company.
- ❑ Proof that your sponsoring company is a bona fide, active business.
- ❑ Proof that the business is intended to generate more than a mere marginal income for you and your family.
- ❑ Proof that a substantial investment is being made in the U.S. business.
- ❑ Documents establishing your intent to leave the U.S. when your status expires, such as deeds verifying ownership of a house or other real property, written statements from you explaining that close relatives are staying behind, or letters from a company showing that you have a job waiting when you return from the United States.
- ❑ Visa application fee (currently $100).
- ❑ Visa issuance fee. (The amount of the fee depends on what country you're from. If the country of your nationality charges fees for visas to U.S. citizens who wish to work there, then the U.S. will charge people of your country a similar fee.)

a. Proof of the Nationality of the Qualifying Business Owners

You must show that the qualifying business is owned by citizens of one of the investment treaty countries. If you are not the owner yourself, you will need to show that both you and those who do own the company are citizens of the same treaty country, usually by showing copies of their passports.

Although you will be doing work for the qualifying company in the U.S., the company and its owners may or may not be located there. Therefore, documents must be presented showing where each of the owners is living currently. Affidavits from each of these owners stating their places of residence will serve this purpose. If any are living in the U.S., also submit copies of their passports and I-94 cards, to demonstrate that they hold valid E-2 visas. Remember, if the owners of the company live in the U.S., at least 50% must also hold E-2 visas for the business to support your own E-2 application.

You will need to prove that you or other nationals of your country own not just a small part, but a majority of the qualifying business. If the qualifying business is a corporation, you should submit copies of all stock certificates, together with a notarized affidavit from the secretary of the corporation listing the name of each shareholder and the number of shares each owns. The affidavit must account for all the shares issued to date. Remember, at least 50% must be owned by nationals of your treaty country.

If the qualifying business is not incorporated, instead of copies of stock certificates, you will need to present legal papers proving the existence and ownership of the company. These may be partnership agreements, business registration certificates, or business licenses, together with a notarized affidavit from an official of the company certifying who owns the business and in what percentages.

b. Proof That You Are a Key Employee

If you are not the majority owner of the company, you must submit evidence that your job in the U.S. will fit the USCIS definition of supervisor, executive, essential employee, or person with predominantly supervisory job duties. To prove this, detailed statements from the sponsoring business explaining your specific duties, as well as the number and kind of employees you will supervise, must be presented. If the application is based on your essentiality as an employee, the statements should also describe the nature of the essential knowledge or experience, how it will be used, and why it is essential in your U.S. job. These required statements may be in your employer's own words and do not have to be in any special form.

c. Proof of the Existence of an Active Business

You'll need to submit documents to show that your E-2 visa application is based on a real, ongoing business. Such evidence should include:

- articles of incorporation or other business charter of the qualifying company
- bank statements for the qualifying company
- credit agreements with suppliers
- letters of credit issued
- leases or deeds for business premises and warehouse space

- tax returns filed in the past two years, if any, including payroll tax returns, and
- promotional literature or advertising.

If the business is newly formed, there will be no tax returns yet. You should then submit a detailed business plan including financial projections for the next five years.

d. Documents Showing That the Business Is Not a Marginal Income Producer

You'll need to prove that the business already generates, or will eventually generate, high enough revenues to support you and your family above a marginal income level. If the U.S. business is already operating, payroll records showing that you will employ U.S. workers will help serve the purpose, as will bank statements and the last two years' tax returns. Also include accountants' financial statements for the business, including balance sheets.

If the business is a start-up, include a copy of your business plan, including financial analyses of projected revenues. If you don't have a business plan, use documents such as market surveys, written summaries of trade association statistics, or written reports from qualified business consultants. Be sure that the documents indicate how many U.S. workers will be employed by the business, and highlight any other ways in which the business will make an economic contribution to the community.

e. Documents Showing That the Investment Is Substantial

The business investment made in the U.S. qualifying company must be a genuine investment, and it must be substantial. To show that you truly have invested, or are actively in the process of investing, include:

- Proof that you have irrevocably committed the funds, for example that you've already paid them for purchase of the business, or that you've placed them in escrow pending issuance of the visa. (Simply showing that you have money in a bank account will not be enough.)
- Proof that the assets or funds invested are in your name and you have control over them. You'll need to name the source of these funds (for example, a loan, sale of assets, or bank account), then provide documents tracing the flow of funds from their source to the business (for example, canceled checks deposited in the business checking account) and from the business to the actual investment (for example, canceled checks showing purchase of buildings, land, or equipment). Include any loan and mortgage documents and note whether the loan is secured by the business.
- Proof that the investment is at-risk, that is, subject to personal loss if the business fails. The documents showing the source of and your

control and commitment of the funds should ordinarily serve this purpose.

Documents to prove that the investment is substantial may include:

- documents indicating the purchase price of the business or, for a new business, the expenses necessary to make the business operational
- bank wire transfer memos showing money sent to the U.S. from abroad.
- contracts and bills of sale for purchase of capital goods and inventory
- leases, deeds, or contracts for purchase of business premises
- construction contracts and blueprints for building business premises, and
- comprehensive business plans with cash flow projections for the next five years, showing how the enterprise will support more than you (and your family) by then.

2. Attending Your Consular Interview

As part of your application, the consulate will require you and your family members to attend an interview. During the interview, a consular officer will examine the data in your application for accuracy, especially regarding facts about the substantiality of the business and the nationality of the owners. Evidence of ties to your home country will also be checked. During the interview, you will surely be asked how long you intend

to remain in the United States. Any answer indicating that you are unsure about plans to return or have an interest in applying for a green card is likely to result in a denial of your visa. See Chapter 4 for what else to expect during consular interviews, and what to do if your application is denied.

Once your E-2 visa is approved, you will probably be asked to return later to pick it up. However, your visa may be approved only provisionally, awaiting security checks, which can add weeks or months to the process.

D. How to Apply If You're in the U.S.

If you are physically present in the U.S., you may apply for E-2 status without leaving the country on the following conditions:

- you entered the U.S. legally and not on a visa waiver
- you have never worked illegally
- the date on your I-94 card has not passed, and
- you are admissible and none of the bars to changing status apply to you (see Chapter 3).

If you were admitted as a visitor without a visa under the Visa Waiver Program, you may not apply from within the United States. Similarly, you can't take advantage of this option if you entered the U.S. using a C (alien in transit), TWOV (alien in transit without a visa), D (crewman), K-1 (fiancé), K-2 (dependent of a fiancé), J-1 (exchange visitor), or M-1 (vocational student) visa.

Your eligibility to apply in the U.S. has nothing to do with your overall eligibility for an E-2 visa. Many applicants who are barred from filing in the U.S. but otherwise qualify for E-2 status may still apply successfully for an E-2 visa at a U.S. consulate in another country.

There is another problem that comes up only in U.S. filings. It is the issue of what is called preconceived intent. To approve a change of status, USCIS must believe that at the time you originally entered the U.S. as a visitor or with some other nonimmigrant visa, you did not intend to apply for a different status. If USCIS thinks you had a preconceived plan to use one visa to enter the U.S. with an eye to applying for a different status after getting there, it may deny your application. (You can get around the preconceived intent issue by leaving the U.S. and applying for your E-2 visa at a U.S. consulate in another country.)

In technical terms, what you will be applying for in the U.S. is a change of status. To do so, you'll need to file an application with USCIS on Form I-129 (Petition for a Nonimmigrant Worker), with accompanying documents to prove your eligibility. If your spouse and

children will be accompanying you, they must file for their change of status on a different form, called Form I-539.

If you decide to apply for a change of status within the U.S., realize that you still don't have the E-2 visa that you'll need if you ever leave the U.S.—a change of status gives you only E-2 status. Visas are never given inside the United States. They are issued exclusively by U.S. consulates in other countries. If you file in the U.S. and you are successful, you will get to remain in the U.S. with E-2 privileges until the status expires. But should you leave the country for any reason before that time, you will have to apply for the visa itself at a U.S. consulate before returning to the United States. Moreover, the fact that your E-2 status has been approved in the U.S. does not guarantee that the consulate will also approve your visa. You'll have to present a whole new application, and they will evaluate it with little or no consideration for the previous USCIS decision. For this reason, many people find it easier to leave the U.S. and apply at a U.S. consulate from the start.

1. Preparing the Change of Status Application

The checklist below will help you prepare the documents and forms for your change of status application.

E-2 Change of Status Checklist

- ❏ Form I-129, with E Supplement.
- ❏ Filing fee: $320.
- ❏ If your family members are with you and need a change of status, Form I-539 with accompanying fee (currently $300) and copies of your family members' I-94s or other proof of lawful immigration status and of their relationship to you (such as marriage and birth certificates). One Form I-539 and fee will cover your spouse and all your children.
- ❏ If either you or your spouse have ever been married before, copies of divorce and death certificates showing termination of all previous marriages.
- ❏ A copy of your I-94 or other proof of your current lawful, unexpired immigration status (except that Canadians who are just visiting are not expected to have I-94 cards).
- ❏ Proof of the nationality of the qualifying business owners.
- ❏ Proof that you are a key employee.
- ❏ Proof that the investment is or will be substantial.
- ❏ Proof that the business will produce greater-than-marginal profits.
- ❏ Proof of the existence of a bona fide, active business.
- ❏ Documents establishing your intent to leave the U.S. when your status expires, such as deeds verifying ownership of a house or other real property, written statements from you explaining that close relatives are staying behind, or letters from a company showing that you have a job waiting when you return from the United States.
- ❏ Cover letter (optional).

If requesting quick (premium) processing:

- ❏ Form I-907, with $1,000 filing fee.

For further explanation of some of the key items on this checklist, see Section C1, above.

Although it is not a requirement, one additional item that you may wish to add to the paperwork package is a cover letter. Cover letters act as a summary and index to the forms and documents, and are often used by immigration attorneys or U.S. companies that process many visas for their employees. Cover letters begin with a statement summarizing the facts of the case and explaining why the particular applicant is eligible for the visa. This statement is followed by a list of the forms and documents being submitted. If it is carefully written, a cover letter can make the case clearer and easier to process for the USCIS officer evaluating it. This is particularly important in an E-2 visa case, where the documentation by itself may require explanation, and you probably won't get a chance to meet personally with a USCIS officer. Cover letters must be individually tailored to each case, so if you don't think you can write a good one, just leave it out and submit only your forms and documents; or hire an attorney to help.

2. Mailing the Change of Status Petition

After assembling the I-129 petition, mail it to the USCIS regional service center listed in the instructions to Form I-129. USCIS regional service centers are not the same as USCIS local offices—for one thing, you cannot visit regional service centers in person.

3. Awaiting a Decision on the Visa Petition

Within a few weeks after mailing in the petition, you or your employer should get back a written confirmation that the papers are being processed, together with a receipt for the fee. This notice will also contain your immigration file number. If USCIS wants further information before acting on your case, all petition papers, forms, and documents will be returned with a form known as a Request for Evidence. Supply the extra data requested and mail the whole package back to the service center.

E-2 petitions are normally approved within two to three months. When this happens, USCIS will send you a Form I-797 Notice of Action, showing the change of status has been approved. A

Watch Out for Summary Exclusion

The law empowers a Customs and Border Protection (CBP) inspector at the U.S. airport or border to summarily (without allowing judicial review) bar entry to someone requesting admission to the U.S. if either of the following is true:

- The inspector thinks you are lying about practically anything connected with entering the U.S., including your purpose in coming, intent to return, and prior immigration history. This includes the use or suspected use of false documents.
- You do not have the proper documentation to support your entry to the U.S. in the category you are requesting.

If the inspector excludes you, you cannot be readmitted to the U.S. for five years, unless USCIS grants a special waiver. For this reason it is extremely important to understand the terms of your requested status, and to not make any misrepresentations. If you are found to be inadmissible, you may ask the CBP inspector to withdraw your application to enter the U.S. in order to prevent having the five-year deportation order on your record. The CBP may allow this in some exceptional cases.

new I-94 card will be attached to the bottom of the form.

💡 **Faster processing—at a price.** For $1,000 over and above the regular filing fees, USCIS promises "premium processing" of the visa petition, including a decision within 15 days. To use this service, you must fill out an additional application (Form I-907) and submit the application to a special USCIS service center address. For complete instructions, see the USCIS website at www.uscis.gov.

E. Using Your E-2 Visa to Enter the U.S.

If you applied for your E-2 visa at a U.S. consulate abroad, you have until the expiration date on your E-2 visa to enter the United States. The border officer will examine your paperwork, ask you some questions, and if all is in order, approve you for entry. He or she will stamp your passport and give you a small white card called an I-94 card. It will be stamped with a date showing how long you can stay. Normally you are permitted to remain for two years at a time, without regard to when your visa actually expires (a visa is just an entry document—the I-94 shows the length of your E-2 status). Keep track of the whereabouts of this card, and make spare copies to keep in a safe place. You'll need it to prove your entry and to apply for extensions.

Each time you exit and reenter the U.S., you will get a new I-94 card authorizing your stay for an additional one- or two-year period. If you do not wish to leave the U.S. after that time, you can apply for extensions of stay, which are issued in two-year increments for as long as you maintain your E-2 status qualifications.

F. Extending Your U.S. Stay

E-2 visas can be extended for up to five years at a time and E-2 status stays can be extended for two years at a time. When you enter the U.S. with an E-2 visa, your authorized stay as indicated on your I-94 card, which is limited to two years, may elapse before the expiration date of your visa. Therefore, depending on your situation, you may need to extend your I-94 card, your visa, or both.

Although an extension is usually easier to get than the E-2 visa itself, it is not automatic. USCIS or the consulate has the right to reconsider your qualifications based on any changes in the facts or law. When the original application for an E-2 visa or status was weak, it is not unusual for an extension request to be turned down. As always, however, good cases that are well prepared will usually be successful.

If you have received E-2 status in the U.S. but never applied for a visa, it's best to stay in the U.S. to apply for an extension of your status (in case the consulate disagrees with USCIS's original decision approving your E-2 status). However, if you have an E-2 visa that is still valid but your I-94 card is about to expire, it is generally better to leave the U.S. and return again instead of trying to extend your status in the United States. When you return to the U.S. on your valid E-2 visa, you will automatically receive a new I-94 card and a new one- or two-year period of authorized stay. By leaving and reentering, no extension application will be needed and there will be no reevaluation of your qualifications.

The general procedures for an E-2 extension from within the U.S. are the same as those described in Section D, above. The forms, documents, and fees are identical.

G. Revalidating Your Visa

If you leave the U.S. with an expired E-2 visa stamp, you must have a new visa issued at a consulate before returning (even if you've extended your E-2 status with USCIS). Reread procedures for the application, consular filing, in Section C, above. The procedures for consular visa extensions are identical. If you are outside the U.S. with a valid visa, you need only reenter and a new I-94 card authorizing your stay for one year will be given to you.

Working While Your Extension Application Is Pending

If you file your application for an extension of E-2 status before your authorized stay expires, you are automatically permitted to continue working for up to 240 days while you are waiting for a decision. If, however, your authorized stay expires after you have filed for an extension but before you receive an approval, and more than 240 days go by without getting a decision on your extension application, your work authorization ends and you must stop working.

Chapter 22

Getting a Student (F-1 or M-1) Visa

Whether you want to enter a short cooking course or get a Ph.D. in philosophy, a student visa may allow you to do so. In any given year, approximately 500,000 people will come to the U.S. to study. There is no limit on the number of people who can receive student visas. We'll actually cover two types of student visas in this chapter, the M-1 visa for vocational students, and the F-1 visa for academic students. (See I.N.A § 101(a)(15)(F), 8 C.F.R. § 214(f); I.N.A § 101(a)(15)(M), 8 C.F.R. § 214(m).)

Not everyone planning to study in the U.S. needs a student visa. Tourists who are taking a class or two for recreational purposes can do so without violating their tourist visa status. Similarly, people who have a spouse or parent in the U.S. with an A, E, G, H, J, L, or NATO visa or status, or workers in H status, can attend school so long as it does not interfere with the other terms of their visa or nonimmigrant status.

Key Features of the M-1 Student Visa

Here are some of the advantages and disadvantages of the M-1, vocational student, visa:

- The application process is reasonably quick and straightforward.
- You may come to the U.S. as a full-time vocational or nonacademic student enrolled in a program leading to a degree or certificate.
- You can transfer from one school to another, but only if you apply for and receive permission from USCIS to do so. Once you are six months into the program of studies, you are prohibited from transferring except under truly exceptional circumstances.
- You are never permitted to change your course of study.

- You may not work during your studies.
- You may get permission to work for up to six months after your studies are done. The job must be considered practical training for your field of study.
- You may travel in and out of the U.S. or remain there until the completion of your studies, up to a maximum of one year. If you have not completed your program in a year or by the time your school projected, whichever is less, you must apply for an extension.
- Visas are available for accompanying relatives, although relatives may not accept employment in the United States.

Key Features of the F-1 Student Visa

Here are some of the advantages and disadvantages of the F-1, academic student, visa:

- Once you've been accepted by a U.S. school, the application process is reasonably quick and straightforward.
- You may come to the U.S. as a full-time academic or language student enrolled in a program leading to a degree or certificate.
- You may not obtain an F visa to study at a public elementary school or a publicly funded adult education program. Nor may you obtain an F visa to study at a public secondary school unless you prepay the full cost of such program, for a maximum of one year.

- You can transfer from one school to another or switch academic programs by going through a simple procedure to notify USCIS.
- You may work legally in a part-time job on campus. Also, you may get special permission to work off campus if it is economically urgent or if the job provides practical training for your field of study.
- You may travel in and out of the U.S. or remain there until the completion of your studies.
- Visas are available for accompanying relatives, but relatives may not accept employment in the United States.

Do you need a lawyer? Applying for a student visa is fairly simple, and doesn't usually require a lawyer's help. Most schools provide you a great deal of help and advice with the application process, often through the services of a foreign student adviser or designated school official (DSO). If, however, you've had trouble getting visas in the past, have ever overstayed a visa, or are from a country thought to sponsor terrorism, a lawyer's help can be well worth the investment.

A. Do You Qualify for a Student Visa (M-1 or F-1)?

To qualify for an M-1 or F-1 student visa, you first must have been accepted at a school approved by the U.S. government. You must be also coming to the U.S. as a bona fide student pursuing a full course of study. Your intended school program must lead to an objective such as a degree, diploma, or certificate.

You must also already be accepted by the school of your choice and have enough money to study full-time without working. You must be able to speak, read, and write English well enough to understand the course work or, alternatively, the school can offer special tutoring or instruction in your native tongue to help overcome any language barriers. In addition to your academic and financial qualifications, you must prove that you intend to return to your home country when your program of studies is over.

At every government-approved school there is a person on the staff known as the designated school official. The DSO is recognized by USCIS and the consulates as having primary responsibility for dealing with foreign students.

 An interest in certain subjects may bar you from entry. If you're planning to study a subject with international security implications such as biochemistry, nuclear physics, or missile telemetry, and you're from a country on the U.S. government's list of supporters of terrorism, you may not be allowed a student visa.

1. Acceptance at a Government-Approved School

Student visas are issued only to students who will attend U.S. schools that have received prior approval from USCIS for enrollment of foreign students. Virtually all public and accredited private colleges, universities, and vocational schools have been approved. To become approved, the school must take the initiative and file a formal application with USCIS. If you do not plan to attend a public school or a fully accredited college or university, before you apply for either an F-1 or M-1 visa you should check to be sure that the school you have selected has been approved by USCIS to accept foreign students.

Once the school has accepted you, it will issue you a certificate that you can use to continue with your immigration application.

Coming to the U.S. to Look for a School

As a prospective student, you can come to the U.S. as a tourist for the purpose of locating a school you want to attend. If you do this, however, be sure to tell the consul at your B-2 visa interview that this is your intent so that he or she can make the appropriate annotation in your passport (usually "Prospective Student—school not yet selected"). Otherwise USCIS will presume that you committed fraud by applying for a visitor visa when you intended to come to the U.S. to study. USCIS will then refuse your application to convert to student status.

You Can't Use a Student Visa to Attend a Public School for Free

In the 1990s, Congress decided that the U.S. should not pay to educate people from other countries. It amended the immigration laws to provide that no student visa will be issued to a person wishing to attend a public elementary school (kindergarten through eighth grade) or a publicly funded adult education program. The rules are slightly different for high schools. You can attend a maximum of one year of public high school (ninth through 12th grade), but you will have to pay the local school district for the entire cost of your education for the year.

The cost of the year in a U.S. high school depends on the local school district—you'll have to contact the district directly. The average cost is between $3,400 and $10,000. Some school districts are not able to calculate their costs. If you plan to attend school in one of these districts, you won't be allowed a visa.

There's nothing to stop you from attending a private elementary or high school—except maybe the tuition, which can be as high as U.S. college tuition. You should also know that some immigrants are allowed to attend public schools, such as those accompanying their parents on another visa, as well as undocumented children (whose rights are protected by the Supreme Court's decision in *Plyler v. Doe*, 457 U.S. 202 (1982)). The reasoning is that they have no option to attend school in their home country.

2. Bona Fide Student

Although it should go without saying, your intentions in coming to the U.S. must truly be to study. The U.S. government is on the lookout for people who use a student visa as a means to gain entry to the U.S. for other purposes. This visa has come under particular scrutiny since the terrorist attacks of September 11, 2001, because some of the terrorists were on student visas. In addition, the U.S. immigration authorities are always concerned with preventing people from entering the U.S. who have no intention of leaving. (Many students either overstay their visa illegally, or apply for a green card when their studies are over, for example through marriage or a job offer.) See Section 7, below, for more on proving your intentions to leave on time.

3. Full Course of Study

What is a full course of study? The good news is, you don't have to stay in school during normal school vacations. Also, on-campus employment under the terms of a scholarship, fellowship, or assistantship can be considered part of your full course of study. Other than the general rules, however, the time requirements of full-time enrollment vary depending on the type of program you're enrolled in.

Undergraduate college or university programs. If you are an undergraduate at a U.S. college or university, you must be enrolled in at least 12 semester or quarter hours of instruction per term. An exception to this is if you are in your last term and need fewer than 12 semester hours to graduate.

Postgraduate college or university programs. If you are a graduate student, full-time studies are whatever the designated school official says they are. For example, a graduate student may be working on a dissertation and taking no classes at all, but still be considered a full-time student, if the designated school official approves.

Programs of specialized college-level schools. When your course of studies is at a specialized school offering recognized college-level degrees or certificates in language, liberal arts, fine arts, or other nonvocational programs, you must be attending at least 12 hours of class per week. This means 12 hours by the clock, not 12 semester hours.

Any other language, liberal arts, fine arts, or other nonvocational training program. At least 18 clock hours of attendance a week if the dominant part of the course of study consists of classroom instruction, or at least 22 clock hours a week if the dominant part of the course of study consists of laboratory work.

High school, middle school, and primary school programs. These students must attend the minimum number of class hours per week that the school requires for normal progress toward graduation. However, the school may recommend a lesser load for a foreign student with a limited understanding of English.

Technical, vocational, or other nonacademic programs. To be classified as a full-time student in a technical, vocational, or other type of nonacademic program, you must attend at least 18 clock hours per week, if the courses consist mostly of classroom study. If the courses are made up primarily of laboratory work, 22 clock hours per week is the minimum.

 F-1 students: Watch out for online or other nonclassroom credits. You're limited to taking one online class or three credits per session, term, semester, trimester, or quarter. This also includes closed circuit, cable, microwave, or audio conferencing and other long-distance classes that don't require your physical attendance. What's more, if you're in a language study program, you can't count any online or distance education classes toward your full course of study requirement.

4. Program Leading to the Attainment of a Specific Educational or Vocational Objective

In order to qualify for a student visa, you must be enrolled in a program that leads to the attainment of a specific educational or vocational objective. For example, a diploma or certificate would be an obvious goal. Nevertheless, you could come to the U.S. to take a semester of college courses as your "objective," so long as your study is full-time during that one semester. You must also maintain a full-time course load, as described above.

5. Knowledge of English

To qualify for a student visa, you must know the English language well enough to pursue your studies effectively. Most U.S. colleges and universities will not admit students whose native language is not English until they first pass an English proficiency test such as the TOEFL. Tests can be arranged in your home country. Your chosen school in the U.S. will tell you if such a test is required and how to go about taking it.

Permission to Take a Reduced Load

When you are unable to carry a full-time course load due to health problems or academic issues, you may be permitted to keep your student status even though you are not going to school full-time. However, your course load cannot be reduced to fewer than six semester or quarter hours, or half the clock hours required for a full course of study. A reduced course load to less than half-time is acceptable only for defined medical reasons or for your final school term if the school determines that fewer courses are needed to complete your course of study.

No special USCIS application is necessary to take a reduced load. However, USCIS has the right to challenge your status at a later date. Therefore, get a written statement from your DSO explaining that he or she believes it is medically or academically necessary for you to reduce your course load, and giving the reasons why.

Usually, consular officials let each school decide for itself who is and is not qualified to study there. Still, during the consular interview at which your visa is approved or denied, the official will be listening closely to your ability to understand and communicate in English. Occasionally, even when a school is willing to admit you without a strong knowledge of English, the U.S. consulate may refuse to issue a student visa because it thinks your English is not good enough. You may still be able to satisfy the consulate if the school you plan to attend is willing to supply English language tutoring or, alternatively, offers a course of studies in your native tongue.

6. Adequate Financial Resources

You must show that you have enough money to complete your entire course of studies without working. At the time you apply for a student visa, you must have enough cash on hand to cover all first-year expenses. In addition, you must be able to show a reliable source of money available to pay for subsequent years. This is normally accomplished by having your parents or other close relatives promise in writing to finance your education, and submit proof of their ability to do so.

7. Intent to Return to Your Home Country

Student visas are meant to be temporary. At the time of applying, you must intend to return home when your studies are completed. If you have it in mind to take

up permanent residence in the U.S., you are legally ineligible for a student visa. The U.S. government knows it is difficult to read minds. Therefore, you may be asked for evidence that you will be leaving behind possessions, property, or family members as an incentive for your eventual return. It is also helpful if you can show that you have a job waiting at home after graduation. Of course, if you're young and just starting college, you may not have many such ties—the important thing to emphasize is that it's also too early in your life to have formed a firm intent to leave your home country and settle in the United States.

If you are studying to prepare yourself for an occupation in which no jobs are available in your home country, the immigration authorities would, in the past, have had a tough time believing that you were planning to return home. This should change, however, due to a 2005 State Department cable advising the consulates that:

The fact that the alien plans on studying a subject for which there is no or little employment opportunity in his country of residence is not a basis for denying the visa; because circumstances may change, this fact should not be deemed a negative factor in adjudicating the case. Nor, on the other hand, is the fact that the country of residence can provide the equivalent quality courses in the same subject matter. The student has the right to choose where s/he will obtain an education if accepted by the school.

(This cable's reference number is R 281839Z SEP 05; attorneys who are AILA members can access it at AILA Doc. No. 05110115.)

8. Bringing Your Spouse and Children

When you qualify for an F-1 or M-1 visa, your spouse and unmarried children under age 21 can get F-2 or M-2 visas. Your school will have to issue separate SEVIS Forms I-20 for them. They'll also need to provide proof of their family relationship to you (such as marriage and birth certificates) and show that you have sufficient financial resources to support them in the U.S. so that they will have no need to work. F-2 and M-2 visas authorize your accompanying relatives to stay with you in the U.S., but not to accept employment.

Family members may also enroll in elementary or secondary school (kindergarten through 12th grade), or in any avocational or recreational studies. They may not, however, enroll full-time in a degree-granting course of postsecondary study without obtaining their own visa.

B. How Long the Student Visa Will Last

Most visas come with a fairly automatic length of time you're allowed to stay in the United States. With a student visa, however, it's a bit more complicated. The first thing to understand is that the expiration date on any nonimmigrant visa, including a student visa, merely indicates how long you have the right to request entry to the United States. It doesn't tell how long you may stay in the U.S. once you arrive.

Both F-1 and M-1 entry visas are typically issued for the estimated length of time it will take to complete your proposed program of studies. Consulates will use their judgment in deciding the expiration date of the visa.

More importantly, however, when you enter the U.S. using a valid student visa, you will be given a small white card called an I-94 card. With all other types of nonimmigrant visas, a border officer would normally stamp the I-94 card with an expiration date as you enter the country, to tell you how long you can stay. But with a student I-94 card, particularly for an F-1 student, it's more likely that the border officer will stamp the I-94 card with a "D/S," for duration of status. This means that you may remain in the U.S. in student status for as long as it takes to complete your educational objectives, provided you finish within what USCIS and your school consider a reasonable period of time. The following specific rules control the time you may spend in the U.S. as a student:

- F-1 and M-1 students, and their accompanying family members, can arrive in the United States up to 30 days before the start of classes.
- Once you arrive in the U.S., you may remain in student status without requesting an extension, for up to your projected completion date as indicated on the paperwork from your school (Form SEVIS I-20AB for F students; Form SEVIS I-20MN for M students), plus a 60-day (F-1) or 30-day (M-1) grace period. (This is conditioned on your remaining enrolled in an approved program of studies, maintaining your full-time student status, and not becoming inadmissible or deportable.) If you receive the school's permission to withdraw from your studies, your grace period will be 15 days.
- If your student status expires because your maximum stay (as indicated on your I-20AB or I-20MN) is up, you can apply to your designated school official for an extension of stay. To receive an extension, you will have to show that you are still enrolled in an approved program, that you are still eligible for nonimmigrant student status, and that there is a good reason why it is taking you extra time to complete your studies. You must do so within 30 days of the I-20 expiration date. If that date passes, you are out of status and will have to return home and get a new visa.

C. Quick View of the Student Visa Application Process

Getting either an F-1 or M-1 visa is a two- to three-step process:

- First, you apply to schools, and once you're accepted, your school fills out and sends you a form known as a Certificate of Eligibility (SEVIS I-20). You will use this certificate in preparing your application for a student visa.
- Second, you apply for either a student visa (if you're currently in another country) or for a change to student status (if you're in the U.S., eligible to change status from another visa, and would prefer this to leaving and applying at a consulate).

Possibilities for a Green Card From Student Status

If you have an F-1 or M-1 visa, you are not barred from filing for a green card, but being in the U.S. on a student visa gives you no direct advantage in doing so. Earning a degree may, however, help you indirectly, especially if you happen to be studying in a field where there is a shortage of qualified U.S. workers. (A key element in getting a green card through employment is proving that there are not enough U.S. workers available to fill a position for which you are qualified.) College graduates also have a number of other advantages in applying for a green card through employment. (See Chapter 9 for details.)

Keep in mind, however, that student visas, like all nonimmigrant visas, are meant to be temporary. They are intended only for people who plan on returning home once their studies in the U.S. are completed. Therefore, if you decide to apply for a green card before your studies are finished, the U.S. government will allow you to maintain student status while pursuing a green card, but only if you are able to convince it of two things: first, that you did not intend to get a green card when you originally applied for the F-1 or M-1 visa, and second, that you will return home if you are unable to secure a green card before your student status expires. Proving these things can be

difficult. If you do not succeed, your student visa may be taken away. If this happens, it will not directly affect your green card application. You will simply risk being without a nonimmigrant visa until you get your green card—meaning you'll have to return home in the interim.

If you instead choose to stay out of status for even six or 12 months and then depart the U.S., it may result in a three-year or ten-year bar to returning to the United States. However, current USCIS interpretations state that a student who goes out of status does not begin to accumulate time toward these six- or 12-month unlawful-stay periods until a USCIS official or an immigration judge makes a ruling that the person is out of status. This means that if you stop attending school for some reason, you will not begin to accrue time toward the overstay bars unless you come to the government's attention. This could happen, for example, if you request reinstatement of student status and the USCIS denies it. Then you would begin to accrue unlawful time as of the date of the USCIS's decision, and could face a three-year or ten-year bar to returning to the United States. (See Chapter 3 for a discussion of how being out of status can affect your ability to get a green card.)

- Third, if you're outside the U.S., you use your student visa to enter and claim your student status.

(If you are Canadian, your application procedures will be different from those of other applicants. See Chapter 5.)

D. Step One: Your School Issues a SEVIS I-20

You can't start the visa application process until you have been admitted to a USCIS-approved school. This book does not discuss how to find the right U.S. school or program, nor how to get accepted to it. You'll need to get started well in advance. If you're applying to academic programs, start contacting schools at least a year before you plan to start your studies. Most students submit between five and ten applications to a mix of schools, including some that they know they have a good chance of being admitted to.

Some good resources to consult about schools and admissions processes include www.studyusa.com (publisher of *Study in the USA* magazine), www.princetonreview.com (the Princeton Review, a test preparation company with an admissions services division), and www.ies-ed.com (the International Education Service, which specializes in worldwide student placement).

Also, most U.S. consulates have a library where you can look at materials about schools in the United States. Some U.S. colleges actually recruit in other countries. If you're in high school but your school can't tell you about local college fairs or recruiting activities, contact the nearest American School (a school that caters to American students in other countries or those learning English), which is usually a popular destination for recruiters.

Once a school has accepted you and you've indicated that you will attend (usually by paying a deposit), the school will send you a Certificate of Eligibility form, more commonly called a SEVIS I-20. At the same time, the school will be required to notify the U.S. consulate in your home country.

F-1 students will get what's called a SEVIS I-20AB and M-1 students will get a SEVIS I-20MN. The school should not charge you any money for issuing the I-20. It's a fairly simple document, simply stating to the U.S. government that you have submitted all the right paperwork and financial documents, the school has evaluated your application and it meets its standards, and you have been accepted for enrollment in a full course of study. When you receive the form, review it carefully, and advise the school

Applying at a Consulate That's Not in Your Home Country

The law allows most people to apply for an F-1 visa at any U.S. consulate they choose—with one exception. If you have ever been present in the U.S. unlawfully, your visa will be automatically cancelled and you cannot apply as a third-country national (at a consulate outside your home country). Even if you overstayed your status in the U.S. by just one day, you must return to your home country and apply for the visa from that consulate. There is an exception. If you were admitted to the U.S. for the duration of your status (indicated by "D/S" on your I-94 form) and you remained in the U.S. beyond the time for which your status was conferred, you will be barred from third-country national processing only if an immigration judge or USCIS (or INS, if it was called that then) officer has determined that you were unlawfully present. You may find that your success in applying as a third-country national will depend on your country, the consulate,

and the relative seriousness of your offense. Being unlawfully present is also a ground of inadmissibility if the period of unlawful presence is 180 days or more. (See Chapter 3.)

Even if you are eligible for third-country national processing, your case will be given the greatest consideration at the consulate in your home country. Applying in some other country creates suspicion in the minds of the consular officers there about your motives for choosing their consulate. Often, when an applicant expects trouble at a home consulate, he or she will seek a more lenient consular office in some other country. This practice of consulate shopping is frowned upon by officials in the system. Unless you have a very good reason for being elsewhere (such as a temporary job assignment in some other nation), it is often smarter to file your visa application in your home country.

if it contains any errors. Then you will need to sign the form.

E. Step Two for Applicants Outside the U.S.: Applying at a U.S. Consulate

Anyone with a Certificate of Eligibility (SEVIS I-20) from a U.S. school indicating acceptance by the school into a full-time program can apply for an F-1 or M-1 visa at a U.S. consulate in his or her home country. You must be physically present in order to apply there.

Your application will consist of government forms as well as documents that you collect yourself. You can either get the forms in advance (download them from the State Department website or pick them up from a U.S. consulate), or get your documents together, go to the consulate, pick up and fill out the forms and submit your application on the same day.

You can normally apply 120 days or less before registration will begin at your school. Because of processing delays, it's best to apply as soon as you can within that 120-day window.

Check with your local U.S. consulate regarding its application procedures. Many insist on advance appointments. Just getting an appointment can take several weeks, so plan ahead.

Before your appointment, you'll need to pay a fee to support the U.S. student tracking database called SEVIS. Your school may take care of processing this fee payment for you. If not, you'll need to do it yourself, either online or by mail. To submit the form online, go to www.FMJfee.com, complete the online Form I-901, and pay with a credit card. To submit the form by mail, download it from the Immigration and Customs Enforcement (ICE) website at www.ice.gov/sevis/i901/index.htm, and mail it, together with your check or money order drawn on a U.S. bank and payable in U.S. currency, to the address indicated on the form. Once you get a receipt for having made this payment, you'll need to use it for your consular interview.

⚠️ **Have you been, or are you now, working or living illegally in the United States?** If so, see Chapter 3 regarding whether you can still get an F or M visa from a U.S. consulate. You may have become inadmissible or subject to a three-year or ten-year bar on reentry.

1. Preparing Your Visa Application

Your application should consist of the items on the checklist below.

Checklist for Student Visa Application

❑ SEVIS I-20, filled out by your school and signed by you.

❑ Receipt for having paid the SEVIS fee, (currently $100).

❑ Form DS-156, Nonimmigrant Visa Application.

❑ Form DS-158, Contact Information and Work History for Nonimmigrant Visa Applicant.

❑ Form DS-157, Supplemental Nonimmigrant Visa Application, if you're either a male applicant between 16 and 45 years of age or you come from a state that the U.S. believes sponsors terrorism and you are age 16 or older, whether male or female.

❑ Visa application fee (currently $100).

❑ Visa issuance reciprocity fee (the amount varies by country).

❑ Your passport, valid for at least six months.

❑ One passport-type photo of you and one of each of your spouse and children, 2 inches x 2 inches.

❑ Long-form birth certificate for you and each accompanying relative.

❑ Marriage certificate if you are married and bringing your spouse.

❑ If either you or your spouse has ever been married before, copies of divorce and death certificates showing termination of all previous marriages.

❑ Transcripts, diplomas, and results of any standardized tests required by the school you'll be attending, showing your previous education and your qualifications to pursue your chosen course of study.

❑ Documents showing reasons that you'll return to your home country, such as ownership of real estate, relationships with close family members staying behind, or proof that a job will be waiting for you on your return.

❑ If you're entering a flight training program, additional required documents, as discussed below.

❑ Proof of sufficient funds, such as:

    ❑ USCIS Form I-134, Affidavit of Support from a U.S. friend or relative, or letter from a friend or relative promising support.

    ❑ Bank statements.

    ❑ Personal financial statements.

    ❑ Evidence of your current sources of income.

A few of the items on this checklist require additional explanation.

Evidence of academic qualifications. If you will be attending a U.S. college or university, some consular officers will require you to prove that you are academically qualified to pursue the program, even though the school itself has already accepted you. Therefore, you should present evidence of all of your previous education, in the form of official transcripts and diplomas from schools you attended. Also, submit standardized test results, if your school required such tests. If these documents are not available, submit detailed letters by officials of the schools you previously attended, describing the extent and nature of your education.

Evidence of intent to return. You will need documents establishing your intent to leave the U.S. when your studies are completed. The consulate will want to see evidence of ties to some other country so strong that you will be highly motivated to return there. Proof of such ties can include deeds verifying ownership of a house or other real property, written statements from you explaining that close relatives live there, or letters from a company showing that you have a job waiting when you return from the United States.

Evidence of sufficient funds. Most important, you must submit documents showing that you presently have sufficient funds available to cover all tuition and living costs for your first year of study. The Certificate of Eligibility, Form SEVIS I-20, gives the school's estimate of what your total annual expenses will be. Specifically, you must show you have that much money presently available. You must also document that you have a source of funds to cover your expenses in future years without having to work.

The best evidence of your ability to pay educational expenses is a letter from a bank, or a bank statement, either in the U.S. or abroad, showing an account in your name with a balance of at least the amount of money it will take to pay for your first year of education.

Alternatively, you can submit a written guarantee of support signed by an immediate relative, preferably a parent, together with your relative's bank statements. Unless your relative can show enough assets to prove he or she can support you without additional income, you should also show that your relative is presently employed. You can document this by submitting a letter from the employer verifying your relative's work situation.

Although the guarantee of support may be in the form of a simple written statement in your relative's own words, we suggest you use Form I-134, called an Affidavit of Support. A copy of this form is on the USCIS website at www.uscis.gov. The questions on Form I-134 are self-explanatory. Be aware that the form was designed to be filled out by someone living in the United States. Since it is quite likely that the person who will support you is living outside the U.S., any questions that apply to U.S. residents should be answered "N/A."

Additional documents for flight trainees. If you're applying for an F or M visa for U.S. flight training, you will be required to submit written information and documents specifying the following:

- your reason for the training (be specific)
- current employer and your position
- who is paying for the training (name and relationship)
- your most recent flight certifications and ratings
- information on what kind of aircraft the training is for (document must be signed by a school official in the United States)
- certified take-off weight of the aircraft type (document must be signed by a school official in the U.S.), and
- current rank or title if you are presently working as an active pilot.

2. Attending Your Consular Interview

Most consulates will require an interview before issuing a student visa. During the interview, a consular officer will examine the forms and documents for accuracy. The consular officer will verify your I-20 record electronically through the SEVIS

system. Your documents proving your ability to finance your education will be carefully checked, as will evidence of ties to your home country. During the interview you will surely be asked how long you intend to remain in the United States. Any answer indicating uncertainty about plans to return home or an interest in applying for a green card is likely to result in a denial of your student visa.

Because of new security requirements, you are unlikely to be approved for your visa on the same day as your interview. The consular officer will need to compare your name against various databases of people with a history of criminal activity, violations of U.S. immigration laws, or terrorist affiliations. This can add weeks or months to the processing of your visa, particularly if you come from a country that the U.S. suspects of supporting terrorism.

F. Step Two for Some Applicants Inside the U.S.: Applying to USCIS for a Change of Status

If you are physically present in the U.S., you may apply for a change to F-1 or M-1 status without leaving the country on the following conditions:

- you have been accepted as a student by a U.S. government-approved school and the school has given you a Certificate of Eligibility, Form SEVIS I-20

- you entered the U.S. legally and not under the Visa Waiver Program, or using a C (alien in transit), TWOV (alien in transit without a visa), D (crewman), K-1 (fiancé), K-2 (dependent of a fiancé), J-1 (exchange visitor), or M-1 (vocational student) visa
- you have never worked in the U.S. illegally
- the date on your I-94 card has not passed, and
- you are not inadmissible.

 Eligibility to apply while you're in the U.S. has nothing to do with your overall eligibility for an F-1 or M-1 visa. Applicants who are barred from filing in the U.S. but otherwise qualify for student status can sometimes apply successfully for an F-1 or M-1 visa at a U.S. consulate in their home country.

Overall, USCIS offices do not favor change of status applications. To approve a change of status, USCIS must believe that at the time you originally entered the U.S. as a visitor or with some other nonimmigrant visa, you did not intend to apply for a different status after getting there. If USCIS thinks you had a preconceived plan to use one visa to enter the U.S. with an eye to applying for a different status later, it may deny your application. You can get around the preconceived intent issue by leaving the U.S. and applying for your visa at a U.S. consulate in another country. In fact, your student application will stand a better chance of approval at most consulates than it will if filed in the United States. But understand the pitfalls involved in departing the U.S. (discussed in Chapter 3, especially if you have lived here unlawfully) before making your decision.

If you decide to apply for a change of status within the U.S., realize that you still don't have the F-1 or M-1 visa that you'll need if you ever leave the U.S. and want to return—a change of status gives you only F-1 or M-1 status. Visas are never given inside the United States. They are issued exclusively by U.S. consulates in other countries. If you file in the U.S. and you are successful, you will get to remain in the U.S. with F-1 or M-1 student privileges until the status expires. But should you leave the country for any reason before that time, you will have to apply for the visa itself at a U.S. consulate before returning to the United States. Moreover, the fact that your student status has been approved in the U.S. does not guarantee that the consulate will also approve your visa. For these reasons, many applicants choose to leave the U.S. and apply for their student visa through a consulate.

1. Preparing Your Change of Status Application

Before submitting your application, you'll need to pay a fee (currently $100) to support the U.S. student-tracking database called SEVIS. Your school may take care of processing this fee payment for you. If not, you'll need to do it yourself, either online or by mail. To submit the form online, go to www.FMJfee.com, complete the online Form I-901, and pay with a credit card. To submit the form by mail, download it from the Immigration and Customs Enforcement (ICE) website at www.ice.gov/sevis/i901/index.htm, and mail it, together with your check or money order drawn on a U.S. bank and payable in U.S. currency, to the address indicated on the form. After you get a receipt for your fee, you can proceed with your change of status application.

The checklist below will help you assemble the necessary items for the change of status application.

Checklist for Student Change of Status Application

❑ Form I-539, Application To Extend/Change Nonimmigrant Status, with accompanying fee (currently $300; send a check or money order, not cash). One Form I-539 and fee will cover you, your spouse, and all your children, if they are in the U.S. with you and in the same visa status or accompanying beneficiaries of your current visa status. But be sure to complete the I-539 Supplement for your spouse and children.

❑ SEVIS I-20, filled out by your school and signed by you.

❑ Receipt for having paid your SEVIS fee (currently $100).

❑ Copies of proof of your family members' relationship to you, such as marriage and birth certificates.

❑ Your original Form I-94 (and those of your spouse and children, if they're applying with you) or other proof of your current lawful, unexpired immigration status (except Canadians just visiting the U.S., who are not expected to have I-94 cards).

❑ If either you or your spouse has ever been married before, copies of divorce and death certificates showing termination of all previous marriages.

❑ Transcripts, diplomas, and results of any standardized tests required by the school you'll be attending, showing your previous education and your qualifications to pursue your chosen course of study.

❑ Documents showing reasons that you'll return to your home country, such as ownership of real estate, relationships with close family members staying behind, and proof that a job will be waiting for you on your return.

❑ Proof of sufficient funds, such as:

    ❑ Form I-134, Affidavit of Support from a U.S. friend or relative, or letter from a friend or relative promising support.

    ❑ Bank statements.

    ❑ Personal financial statements.

    ❑ Evidence of your current sources of income.

For additional explanation of some of the items on this checklist, see Section E1, above.

2. Mailing the Change of Status Application

After assembling the change of status application, you must mail it to the USCIS regional service center having jurisdiction over the area where you're currently living. USCIS regional service centers are not the same as USCIS local offices—for one thing, you cannot visit regional service centers in person. See the USCIS website at www.uscis.gov for the regional service centers' addresses and P.O. box numbers.

3. Awaiting a Decision on the Change of Status Application

Within a few weeks after mailing in the petition, you should get back a written confirmation that the papers are being processed, together with a receipt for the fee. This notice will also contain your immigration file number. If USCIS wants further information before acting on your case, all petition papers, forms, and documents will be returned to you with a form known as a Request for Evidence. You should supply the extra data requested and mail the whole package back to the service center.

Until recently, foreign students could submit applications for student status but begin school before receiving the USCIS's okay. Under the new rule,

USCIS promises to issue its approvals (or denials) within approximately 30 days— in return for which it requires applicants to wait for its decision before starting school.

When your application has been approved, the USCIS service center will notify you using a Form I-797 Notice of Action. A new I-94 card will be attached to the bottom of the form. You will also be issued an I-20 Student ID.

G. Step Three: You Enter the U.S With Your Student Visa

Don't try to enter the U.S. more than 45 days before your studies will begin! When you arrive in the U.S. with your new F-1 or M-1 visa, the border officer will examine your paperwork, ask you some questions, and if all is in order, approve you for entry. You will be given a small I-94 card. This will be stamped showing you have been admitted either until a specific date or for the duration of your student status (D/S). Also shown will be the name of the school you have been authorized to attend.

Each time you exit and reenter the U.S., you will get a new I-94 card authorizing your stay and indicating the time limit. When you have stayed in the U.S. on an M-1 visa for a year (or whatever time you were given) and you wish to remain longer, you may apply for one two-year extension of your I-20

Watch Out for Summary Exclusion

The law empowers a Customs and Border Protection (CBP) inspector at the U.S. airport or border to summarily (without allowing judicial review) bar entry to someone requesting admission to the U.S. if either of the following is true:

- The inspector thinks you are lying about practically anything connected with entering the U.S., including your purpose in coming, intent to return, and prior immigration history. This includes the use or suspected use of false documents.
- You do not have the proper documentation to support your entry to the U.S. in the category you are requesting.

If the inspector excludes you, you cannot be readmitted to the U.S. for five years, unless USCIS grants a special waiver. For this reason it is extremely important to understand the terms of your requested status, and to not say anything that could be taken as a lie. If you are found to be inadmissible, you may ask the CBP inspector to withdraw your application to enter the U.S. in order to prevent having the five-year deportation order on your record. The CBP may allow this in some exceptional cases.

to your designated school official. F-1 students may apply for extensions of stay indefinitely, as long as they continue to maintain their eligibility for the status and their DSO grants an extension to complete studies.

H. Extending Your Student Stay

Student visas and student statuses can be extended to allow necessary continuation of your studies. F-1 students can extend their permitted stay up to the revised estimated completion date of their academic program. M-1 students can, after one year, extend their permitted stay for a maximum of two more years.

Your authorized stay as indicated on your Form I-20 may last longer than the expiration date of the entry visa stamped in your passport, or it may expire before your visa expires. Therefore, depending on your situation, you may need to extend your I-20 date, your visa, or both. Statuses as written on the Forms I-20 can be extended only by your DSO in the United States. Student visas can be extended only at consulates (but you can wait until your next trip outside the U.S.).

Extensions are not automatic. Your DSO or the consular officers have the right to reconsider your qualifications based on any changes in the facts or law. If you seem not to be making progress toward your academic or vocational objectives, your extension request may

Schools' Responsibilities to Track International Students

As of 2002, schools must make various reports to USCIS concerning international students. When a school issues an I-20 to a student, it will be required to notify the U.S. consulate in the student's home country. When that consulate approves the student's visa, it will be required to notify USCIS.

During the student's time at school, the school will have to keep USCIS up to date on the student's status and whereabouts through a database called SEVIS. To finance this database, international students have to pay a fee (currently $100) in addition to the usual visa fees.

The information and documents that schools must routinely make available to USCIS for each international student include:

- name, date, and place of birth and country of citizenship
- current address
- visa classification, date of visa issuance or classification granted
- in-school status (full-time or part-time)
- date when studies began
- degree program and field of study
- whether the student has been certified for practical training and the dates of such certification
- date that studies were terminated, and the reason, if known

- written application for admission, transcripts or other course records, proof of financial responsibility, and other documents that the school evaluated in admitting the student
- number of credits completed per semester
- photocopy of Form I-20 ID, and
- record of any academic disciplinary actions due to criminal convictions.

On top of maintaining this database, the school must actually report news of each international student to USCIS each semester, no later than 30 days after the deadline for class registration. The information the schools must report includes: whether each student has enrolled, identification of any student who has dropped below a full course of study without authorization, and the student's current address.

In addition, the school has 21 days in which to report various changes in your situation. This means that you must report all of these to the school as soon as possible—you have only ten days in the case of address changes. These changes include: your failure to maintain student status or complete your educational program, a change in your address or name, your early graduation prior to the program end date on your form SEVIS I-20, or any disciplinary action the school has taken against you.

be turned down. As always, however, good cases that are well prepared will ordinarily be successful.

If you need to extend the duration of your status as shown on the I-20 ID student copy, contact your DSO, who is responsible for making the extension and forwarding the information and paperwork to USCIS. Be sure, however, to request your extension before the end date on your I-20. If you are unable to complete your educational program before that date, and you don't request an extension by then, you are out of status and must apply for reinstatment, or leave the United States.

It is possible for your visa to expire before your duration of status period (as indicated on your I-20) is up. If you should leave the U.S. for any reason after your visa has expired, you must have a new visa issued at a consulate in order to return. If you do not leave the U.S., you do not need to have a valid visa; your I-20 and I-94 control your permission to stay in the United States.

I. Getting Permission to Work

When you have F-1 student status, you can work only under limited circumstances. M-1 students have almost no rights to work. In many cases these work privileges do not come automatically with the visa. You are often expected to file a separate application. There are a number of different types of work situations recognized as permissible for those with F-1 student status, and different rules apply to each one. Each situation is described in this section.

1. On-Campus Employment

An F-1 visa (or status) permits students to work in an on-campus job for up to 20 hours per week when school is in session. During vacation periods, you can work on campus full-time. No special permission or application is required, as long as the job does not displace U.S. residents. Students working on campus can be employed by the school itself or any independent companies serving the school's needs, such as at the school bookstore, or cafeteria suppliers providing food on campus premises.

2. Employment as Part of a Scholarship

F-1 students may also be employed as part of the terms of a scholarship, fellowship, or assistantship. The job duties must be related to your field of study. No special work permission or application is required. This is true even when the actual location of the job is off campus.

3. Practical Training

Both F-1 and M-1 visas allow students to apply for permission to work on the basis of practical training. Practical training for F-1 students can be either curricular or postcompletion ("optional" or "OPT"). Curricular practical training occurs before graduation as part of your study program, while postcompletion training takes place afterward.

Curricular practical training is available only to F-1 students who have been enrolled in school for at least nine months. The nine-month enrollment requirement can be waived for graduate students requiring immediate participation in curricular practical training. All requests for curricular practical training are approved by the designated school official (DSO), who notifies USCIS.

Only the following types of work situations qualify as curricular practical training:

- alternate work/study programs
- internships, whether required or not required by the curriculum
- cooperative education programs, and
- required practicums offered though cooperative agreements with the school.

Both F-1 and M-1 students can get permission to work in postcompletion (optional) practical training (OPT) after graduating. If F-1 students, however, have already worked for more than one year in curricular practical training, they are not eligible for postcompletion practical training.

Postcompletion practical training can be approved for up to one year for F-1 students and six months for M-1 students. Part-time practical training is deducted from the total period available at one-half the full-time rate. F-1 students are eligible for a new one-year period of post-completion optional practical training after every level of higher education they complete. For example, a student could do one year of OPT upon completing a bachelor's degree, an additional year after a Master's, and then, if the student newly enrolls in a doctoral program, a third year once the Ph.D. is completed. Both the designated school official and USCIS must approve all applications for postcompletion practical training. (Instructions are given in Section 6, below.)

4. How to Apply for OPT Work Permission Based on Optional Practical Training

Both F-1 and M-1 foreign students must apply to USCIS for work permission to accept optional practical training (OPT) employment. Practical training employment is any position where the work is directly related to your course of studies.

a. OPT Work Permit Application Procedures for F-1 Students

As an F-1 student, you must apply for permission to take optional practical training before completion of your study program. You may not apply until you have been enrolled as a student for at least nine months. If you apply before your full course of study is completed, you may be granted permission to take practical training only if it is necessary to fulfill a specific requirement of your particular academic program or if the work will be scheduled exclusively during regular school vacations. If the practical training will begin after you graduate, you may work simply because you wish to do so.

When practical training is to start after your studies are completed, you must not file your application for work permission more than 60 days before your graduation. You can be granted permission to work in a practical training position for a total of no more than 12 months. You must have an offer of employment.

To apply, assemble the items on checklist below. Then ask your designated school official to review the paperwork to decide whether you meet all the requirements for work permission. If you appear to qualify, the DSO will give you a recommendation for employment, endorsed on Form I-20 ID, which you must include with your application. He or she will also enter the recommendation into the SEVIS database.

⚠ **When filling out the work permit application, use your home address.** USCIS says that a lot of students just put their college address on the form, and then USCIS doesn't know where to send the card—so it does nothing.

Checklist for F-1 OPT Work Permit Application

- ❑ Form I-765, with filing fee (currently $340). Answer Question 16 "(c)(3)(i)."
- ❑ I-20 ID student copy.
- ❑ I-94 card.
- ❑ Job offer letter from prospective U.S. employer (for post-completion training only). The letter should explain the details of the work you will perform and show clearly that the work is in the same field as your course of studies.

Submit the application to the USCIS service center designated for the region where you are attending school. (The addresses are available on the USCIS website or on the instructions to the form itself.) Keep the fee receipt USCIS will give you so you can prove that the I-765 was filed in case USCIS loses it.

Most USCIS offices will make a decision on your application within several weeks. The law requires USCIS to make a decision on your employment authorization application within 90 days.

Special Rules for F-1 Students Who Take Practical Training as a Required Part of Their Studies

If, prior to graduation, you accept practical training employment that is a required part of your studies, as is frequently done by students on fellowships, only 50% of your employment time will be deducted from the allotted 12-month total. Practical training in this special situation is called curricular practical training, and has the effect of allowing you to work for a total of 24 months prior to graduation instead of only 12. If you work for six months in curricular practical training, you are required to deduct only three months from your allotment, meaning you may still accept nine months of additional practical training employment prior to graduation and the full 12 months after graduation. If, however, you work more than 20 hours per week, you lose the benefit of this special rule. Under these circumstances, once again you must deduct the whole amount of time you worked, meaning you are limited to a maximum of 12 months of practical training prior to graduation.

If the decision is in your favor, you will receive a work authorization card.

b. OPT Work Permit Application Procedures for M-1 Students

As an M-1 student, you can apply for permission to take practical training only after you have completed your entire program of studies. Applications for work permission must be filed not more than 60 days before your graduation. M-1 students can be granted permission to work in a practical training position only for a period of one month for each four months of study, with a total overall maximum of six months.

While the time periods for getting practical training work permission for F-1 students differ from those for M-1 students, the procedures, forms, and documents are almost exactly the same. See Subsection a, immediately above. The one difference is that on Question 16, M-1 students will answer "(c)(6)."

5. Economic Necessity

Only F-1 students are eligible for work permission based on economic necessity. You will remember that in order to obtain a student visa, you were required to show that you had enough money on hand to cover all of your first-year costs. Therefore, work permission on the basis of economic necessity will never be granted during your first year of studies.

As an F-1 student, you can request work permission after the first year if an unforeseen change in your financial situation has occurred, and if you meet the following conditions:

- you have maintained F-1 student status for at least one academic year
- you are in good standing at your school
- you are a full-time student
- you will continue to be a full-time student while working
- you will not work for more than 20 hours per week while school is in session, and
- you have tried but failed to find on-campus employment.

USCIS recognizes as unforeseen circumstances such things as losing a scholarship, unusually large devaluation of your home country's currency, unexpected new restrictions enacted by your government that prevent your family from sending money out of the country, large increases in your tuition or living expenses, unexpected changes in the ability of your family to support you, or other unanticipated expenses, such as medical bills, that are beyond your control. Work permission can be granted for one year at a time, and must be renewed each year.

⚠ Request employment authorization based on economic necessity only if you have no other choice. If USCIS denies the application, USCIS may also decide that you are not eligible to continue in your student status, since you are basically telling USCIS that you don't have sufficient funds to support yourself.

6. How to Apply for Work Permission Based on Economic Need

You'll start by filling out USCIS Form I-765 and assembling supporting paperwork. Then your DSO must review your paperwork to decide whether or not you meet all the requirements for work permission. If you appear to qualify, the DSO will certify a recommendation for employment, by endorsing it on Form I-20 ID and entering it into the SEVIS database.

Next, you submit the application and endorsed form to the USCIS regional service center serving the the geographic area where you live. (The addresses are on the USCIS website and on the form itself.) The fee is currently $340.

It is very important to keep the fee receipt USCIS will give you so you can prove that the I-765 was filed.

USCIS is required to make a decision on your employment authorization application within 90 days. If the decision is in your favor, you will receive a work authorization identification card. Most USCIS offices will attempt to decide your application within a few weeks.

The checklist below will help you prepare and assemble your work permit application.

Checklist for Economic-Necessity-Based Work Permit Application

❑ Form I-765, with filing fee (currently $340). Answer Question 16 of the form "(c)(3)(iii)."

❑ I-20 ID (student copy).

❑ Documents to support your claim that an unexpected change in circumstances is creating your economic need, such as:

  ❑ Letters from government officials of your home country stating that there has been an unusual devaluation of the national currency or that your country's laws have changed and prevent your family from sending money out of the country to help support you as they once did

  ❑ Documents from your school showing a substantial tuition increase

  ❑ Bills from hospitals and doctors evidencing a costly family illness or birth of a child, or

  ❑ If someone who has been supporting you is no longer able to do so, a statement from a doctor or a death certificate showing that the person has become ill or died, or documents demonstrating that the person is having financial problems and so is unable to continue with your support.

J. Transferring to a Different School

If you decide that your school is not right for you and you wish to transfer to another, you may be able to do so. Requirements for transfers are different for F-1 students and M-1 students.

1. Applications for Transfers of F-1 Students

As an F-1 student, you may transfer from one school to another by following a specific procedure. You must be a full-time student at the time—otherwise you will have to request reinstatement to student status.

First, you must notify your current school DSO of your transfer plans. The DSO will update your record in SEVIS as a "transfer out" and indicate the school to which you intend to transfer, and a release date. The release date will be the current semester or session completion date, or the date of expected transfer if earlier than the established academic cycle. The current school will retain control over your record in SEVIS until you complete the current term or reach the release date. If you request it, your current DSO may cancel the transfer request at any time prior to the release date.

Once you reach the release date, the transfer school will be granted full access to your SEVIS record and then becomes responsible for you. (Your old school will no longer have access to your SEVIS records.) Your new DSO must complete the transfer of your record in SEVIS and may issue a SEVIS Form I-20. You are then required to contact the DSO at the transfer school within 15 days of the program start date listed on the SEVIS Form I-20. Upon notification that you are enrolled in classes, the DSO of the transfer school must update SEVIS to reflect your registration and current address, thereby acknowledging that you have completed the transfer process. In the remarks section of the student's SEVIS Form I-20, the DSO must note that the transfer has been completed, including the date, and return the form

to you. The transfer is complete when the transfer school notifies SEVIS that you have enrolled in classes. (See 8 C.F.R. § 214.2(f)(8)(ii).)

2. Applications for Transfers of M-1 Students

As an M-1 student, you can transfer from one school to another, but only during your first six months of study, unless the transfer is required by circumstances beyond your control (such as your school closing down). If you transfer schools without following these procedures, you are considered out of status.

You would apply to transfer by notifying your current school of your plans. Your school must then update the SEVIS database to show you are a "transfer out" and input the release date for transfer. Then your transfer school is permitted to generate a SEVIS Form I-20 (but will not gain access to your SEVIS record until the release date is reached).

Upon receipt of the SEVIS Form I-20 from the transfer school, you must submit USCIS Form I-539 (in accordance with 8 C.F.R. § 214.2(m)(11)) to the USCIS service center with jurisdiction over your current school. You may enroll in the transfer school at the next available term or session. You must get in touch with the DSO of the transfer school as soon as you begin attending. The DSO must then update your registration record in

SEVIS. (See 8 C.F.R. § 214.3(g)(3).) Upon approval of the transfer application, the USCIS officer will endorse the name of your new school on your SEVIS Form I-20 and return it to you.

If your request to transfer is denied, you will receive a written decision by mail explaining the reason. USCIS has discretion to deny your application to transfer for any legitimate reason. There is no way of making a formal appeal to USCIS if your request is turned down.

K. Changing Your Course of Studies

F-1 students can change their courses of studies within the same school as long as they remain in qualifying programs. No formal permission from USCIS is required to change major areas of studies.

M-1 students are never permitted to change their courses of studies. If an M-1 student wishes to make such a change, he or she will have to return to a consulate and apply for a completely new student visa. ■

Getting a J-1 Exchange Visitor Visa

The exchange visitor visa (J-1) was created to promote educational and cultural exchanges between the U.S. and other countries. It is mostly available to people who have signed up with an approved program focused on teaching, receiving training, or conducting research. (See I.N.A. § 101(a)(15)(J), 8 C.F.R. § 214.2(j).) There is no limit on the number of people who can receive J-1 visas.

Do you need a lawyer? Applying for a J-1 visa is fairly simple, and doesn't usually require a lawyer's help. Most schools or exchange visitor organizations provide you a great deal of help and advice with the application process. If, however, you've had trouble getting visas in the past, have ever overstayed a visa, or are from a country thought to sponsor terrorism, a lawyer's help can be well worth the investment. Also, if you later decide to apply for a different nonimmigrant status or green card, but think you're subject to the two-year home residence requirement, you'll definitely need a lawyer's help.

A. Do You Qualify for a J-1 Exchange Visitor Visa?

You qualify for a J-1 exchange visitor visa if you are coming to the U.S. as a student, scholar, trainee, teacher, professor, research assistant, medical graduate, or international visitor and if

Key Features of the J-1 Exchange Visitor Visa

Here are some of the advantages and disadvantages of the J-1 exchange visitor visa:

- Once you've been accepted as a participant in an approved exchange visitor program, the application process is reasonably quick and straightforward.
- Your spouse and children may receive visas to accompany you.
- You may work legally in the U.S. if work is part of your approved program or if you receive permission to work from the official program sponsor.
- Your spouse and children may apply to USCIS for permission to work, so long as they prove that the money is not needed to support you.
- You may travel in and out of the U.S. or remain there until the completion of your exchange visitor program.
- Participants in certain types of programs may be required to return to their home countries for at least two years before applying for a green card, before a change to another nonimmigrant status, or before an L or H visa petition is approved on their behalf.

you are participating in a program of studies, training, research, or cultural enrichment specifically designed for such individuals by the U.S. Department of State (DOS), through its Bureau of Educational and Cultural Affairs (ECA). You must already be accepted into the program before you can apply for the visa.

Some common programs for which J-1 visas are issued include the Fulbright Scholarship program, specialized training programs for foreign medical graduates, and programs for foreign university professors teaching or doing research in the United States.

You must have enough money to cover your expenses while you are in the U.S. as an exchange visitor. Those funds may come from personal resources. If your J-1 visa is based on work activities, the salary may be your means of support. If you are a J-1 student, the money may also come from a scholarship.

You must be able to speak, read, and write English well enough to participate effectively in the exchange program of your choice. In addition to all other qualifications, you are eligible for a J-1 visa only if you intend to return to your home country when the program is over.

To summarize, there are five requirements for getting a J-1 visa:

- you must be coming to the U.S. to work, study, teach, train, consult, or observe U.S. culture in a specific exchange visitor program approved by the DOS

- you must already have been accepted into the program
- you must have enough money to cover your expenses while in the United States
- you must have sufficient knowledge of English to be able to participate effectively in the exchange visitor program you have chosen, and
- you must intend to return home when your status expires.

1. An Exchange Visitor Program Approved by the DOS

J-1 visas allow you to study, teach, do research, or participate in cultural activities in the U.S. as part of any program specifically approved by the DOS. Sponsors of acceptable programs may be foreign or U.S. government agencies, private foreign and U.S. organizations, or U.S. educational institutions. Such groups wanting program approval must apply to the DOS. Those making successful applications will be authorized to issue what are known as Certificates of Eligibility to J-1 visa applicants. They indicate that the applicant has been accepted into an approved program. Each approved program appoints an administrator known as the responsible officer (RO). The responsible officer plays a formal role in dealing with the immigration process for program applicants.

There are over 1,500 DOS-approved programs in existence. Current information about exchange visitor programs is available from DOS at http://exchanges.state.gov.

2. Acceptance Into a Program

Before applying for a J-1 visa, you must first apply for acceptance into the DOS-approved program of your choice. Application is made directly to the program sponsor. Until you have been accepted, you do not qualify for a J-1 visa.

3. Financial Support

You must establish that you have enough money to cover all expenses while you are in the United States. The money may come from you, your family, or scholarships and salaries that are part of the program itself. Since most exchange visitor programs involve either employment or scholarships, this particular requirement is usually easy to meet.

4. Knowledge of English

To qualify for an exchange visitor visa, you must know English well enough to participate effectively in the exchange visitor program. If your program is for students, you should know that most U.S. colleges and universities will not admit people whose native language is not English unless they first pass an English proficiency test, such as the TOEFL. Tests can sometimes be arranged in your home country. The school will tell you if such a test is required and how to go about taking it.

Consular officials usually let each school decide for itself who is and is not qualified to study there. Still, the consulate may refuse to issue an exchange visitor visa based on its own judgment that you do not know enough English to function as a U.S. student.

5. Intent to Return to Your Home Country

Exchange visitor visas are meant to be temporary. At the time of applying, you must intend to return home when your program in the U.S. is completed. If you have it in mind to take up permanent residence in the U.S., you are legally ineligible for an exchange visitor visa.

The U.S. government knows it is difficult to read minds. Expect to be asked for evidence showing that when you go to the U.S. on a J-1 visa, you are leaving behind possessions, property, or family members that will serve as incentives for your eventual return. It is also helpful to show that you have a job waiting at home when your program is completed.

If you are studying or training to prepare yourself for an occupation in which no jobs are available in your home country, the immigration authorities may have trouble believing that you are planning to return there. To avoid trouble, it's best to choose a field of study that will give you career opportunities at home when you are finished.

6. Foreign Medical Graduates: Additional Qualifications

If you are coming to the U.S. as a foreign medical graduate for the purpose of continuing your medical training or education, there are some added requirements. First, you must have passed Parts I and II of the U.S. National Board of Medical Examiners examination or its equivalent. Information on taking the exam is available from the Educational Commission for Foreign Medical Graduates in Philadelphia, at 215-386-5900, www.ecfmg.org.

Like all J-1 visa applicants, foreign medical graduates must prove they will return home when their status expires. However, your evidence must include a written guarantee from the government in your home country verifying that employment will be available to you when your U.S. medical training is completed.

Foreign medical graduates applying for J-1 visas should understand that they are legally required to return home for at least two years before becoming eligible to apply for green cards. However, they are exempt from this requirement if they agree to work for three years in an underserved area—that is, an area

recognized by the Secretary of Health and Human Services (HHS) as having a shortage of health care professionals.

7. Bringing Your Spouse and Children

When you qualify for a J-1 visa, your spouse and unmarried children under age 21 can get J-2 visas to accompany you. They will need to provide proof of their family relationship to you, such as marriage and birth certificates. Your exchange program will also need to provide each of them a SEVIS Form DS-2019 issued in their own name. J-2 visas authorize your accompanying relatives to stay with you in the U.S., but they may not accept employment unless they first obtain special permission from USCIS.

B. How Long the J-1 Visa Will Last

How long you'll be allowed to stay in the U.S. on your J-1 visa depends on the type of program you'll be participating in (Sections 1 through 14, below) and the dates of your participation.

In seeking a J-1 visa, you will be asked to present a Certificate of Eligibility, formerly known as Form IAP-66, now reworked and renumbered as SEVIS DS-2019. This form is provided to you by the sponsor of the exchange visitor program in which you will take part.

The form will list the specific dates you are expected to be participating in the program. Upon entering the U.S. with a J-1 visa, you will be authorized to remain only up to the final date indicated on the Certificate of Eligibility.

The Certificate of Eligibility is usually issued for the period of time needed to complete the particular exchange visitor program for which your J-1 visa is approved. USCIS regulations, however, place some maximum time limits on J-1 visas according to the type of program.

1. Students

Most students may remain in the U.S. for the duration of their programs plus an additional 18 months of practical training employment. Practical training is any employment directly related to the subject matter of the student's major field of study. Remaining in the U.S. for the additional 18 months of practical training is at the student's discretion. Post-doctoral training is limited to 36 months minus any previously used practical training time.

However, students between the ages of 15 and 18½ who are participating in a high school exchange program (living with a U.S. host family or residing at an accredited U.S. boarding school) are limited to one year's stay. They cannot work, except at odd jobs such as babysitting or yard work.

2. Teachers, Professors, Research Scholars, and People With Specialized Skills

Exchange visitors who are teachers, professors, research scholars, or people with specialized skills may be issued J-1 visas for no more than five years, plus 30 days in which to prepare to depart the United States.

3. International Visitors

International visitors whose purpose it is to promote cultural exchange, such as those working in the cultural/ethnic pavilions of Disney's Epcot Center, may be issued J-1 visas for no more than one year, plus 30 days in which to prepare to depart the United States. Persons qualifying under this category may also be eligible for Q visas.

4. Foreign Medical Graduate Students

Foreign medical graduates may be issued J-1 visas for the length of time necessary to complete their training programs, up to a usual maximum of seven years (with limited exceptions), plus 30 days in which to prepare to depart the United States.

5. Other Medically Related Programs

Participants in any medically related programs other than those for foreign medical graduates may be issued J-1 visas for the duration of their educational programs plus 18 months of practical training. However, the total time of both program participation and practical training may not be more than three years.

6. Business and Industrial Trainees

Business and industrial trainees may be issued J-1 visas for a maximum of 18 months, except interns, who are limited to 12 months. Trainees in flight programs may be issued J-1 visas for a maximum of 24 months. However, flight students must provide extra documentation about their plans, for security reasons.

7. Employees of the International Communications Agency

Participants in this particular exchange visitor program may be issued J-1 visas for up to ten years or even longer if the director of the International Communications Agency makes a special request to USCIS.

8. Research Assistants Sponsored by the National Institutes of Health

Participants in the NIH research assistants exchange visitor program may be issued J-1 visas for a period of up to five years.

9. Au Pairs

Au pairs who are between ages 18 and 26 may come to the U.S. on J-1 visas to live in and perform child care (but not do other housework) for U.S. families. Au pairs may work no more than ten hours per day, 45 hours per week, be paid at least the minimum wage, and must attend an institution of higher education to earn at least six hours of academic credit. As of this writing, only a few agencies have been approved to issue Certificates of Eligibility for bringing au pairs to the United States. Stays are limited to only one year and cannot be extended. If this program interests you, check the State Department website at http://exchanges.state.gov.

10. Government Visitors

Visitors may be invited by the U.S. government to participate in exchanges that strengthen professional and personal ties between key foreign nationals and the United States and U.S. institutions. They may be issued J-1 visas for the length of time necessary to complete the program, but no more than 18 months.

11. Camp Counselors

Youth workers over the age of 18 coming to serve as counselors in U.S. summer camps may be issued J-1 visas for no more than four months.

12. Summer Work Travel

Postsecondary students may use a J-1 visa to work and travel in the United States for a four-month period during their summer vacations, through programs conducted by Department of State-designated sponsors.

13. Short-Term Scholars

Professors and other academics participating in short-term activities such as seminars, workshops, conferences, study tours, or professional meetings may be granted up to six months on a J-1 visa.

14. Exceptions to the General Rules

Any exchange visitor may be allowed to remain in the U.S. beyond the limitations stated above if exceptional circumstances arise that are beyond the exchange visitor's control, such as illness.

C. Students: Comparing J-1 Visas to F-1 and M-1 Visas

Students coming to the U.S. often have a choice between J-1 exchange visitor visas and M-1 or F-1 student visas. Student visas are discussed in Chapter 22. J-1 programs for students are very limited as to the level of education and types of subjects that can be studied. By contrast, F-1 and M-1 visas can be issued for almost any type of education program imaginable, including vocational, secondary, and high school programs as well as all courses of study at colleges and universities.

Assuming there is an exchange visitor program that will fit your needs as a student, there are certain advantages to holding a J-1 visa. It is much easier to get work permission as an exchange visitor than it is on a student visa. With a J-1 visa you may remain in the U.S. for up to 18 months after you graduate for the purpose of working in a practical training position. F-1 student visa holders are limited to 12 months of practical training employment and M-1 students are limited to only six months.

F-1 and M-1 student visas, however, are more flexible than exchange visitor visas in several ways. With an F-1 student visa, you may transfer from one school to another or change courses of study quite freely. After graduation, you may enroll in a new educational program without having to obtain a new visa. On a J-1 visa, you must remain in the exact program for which your visa was issued. Most important, certain J-1 visa programs automatically make you subject to a two-year home residency requirement, which will cause problems should you later want to apply for a green card, change to another nonimmigrant status, or have a nonimmigrant worker L or H visa petition approved.

D. Can You Apply for a Green Card From J-1 Status?

J-1 visas, like all nonimmigrant visas, are meant to be temporary. They are intended only for people who plan on returning home once the exchange program in the U.S. is completed. Should you decide to apply for a green card before your program is finished, the U.S. government will allow you to keep J-1 status while pursuing a green card, but only if you are able to convince it that you did not intend to get a green card when you originally applied for the J-1 visa and that you will return home if you are unable to secure a green card before your exchange visitor status expires. Proving these things can be difficult. If you do not succeed, your J-1 visa may be taken away. Some program sponsors have been known to withdraw J-1

privileges after an exchange visitor has applied for a green card.

The most serious drawback to applying for a green card from J-1 status is that many J-1 visas are granted subject to a two-year home residency requirement. If you choose an exchange visitor program that carries this requirement, it means that you must return to your home country and remain there for at least two years before you are eligible to either apply for a green card, be approved for a change of status, or have an L or H visa petition approved for yourself—even if you marry a U.S. citizen or have some other compelling reason to want a green card.

It is possible to apply for a waiver of the home residency requirement. Although the procedures for filing waiver applications are simple, getting approval can be extremely difficult, especially for foreign medical graduates. Most exchange visitors can get waivers if the governments of their home countries consent to it. Even if the home government does consent, USCIS approves waiver applications only under compelling circumstances. Most, it simply denies.

The reason the U.S. prefers not to grant waivers of the home residency requirement is that many J-1 visa programs are set up and financed by foreign governments for the specific purpose of getting U.S. training for their citizens. The foreign governments hope that those who are trained will eventually return and use their new skills to benefit their homeland. Were the U.S. government to interfere with these goals by allowing J-1 visa holders to remain in the U.S., there would be political discord between the U.S. and the other nations involved. Therefore, the U.S. makes every effort to see that J-1 exchange visitors keep their bargains and fulfill the home residency requirements.

Not all J-1 visa holders are subject to a home residency requirement. It applies only to participants in the following types of exchange visitor programs:

- programs for foreign medical graduates coming to the U.S. to receive additional medical training
- programs where the expenses of the participants are paid by the U.S., a foreign government, or international organization, and
- programs for teaching individuals certain skills that are in short supply in their home countries. The DOS maintains a list of such skills and the countries where they are especially needed. The skills list can be accessed at http://exchanges. state.gov/education/jexchanges.

The Certificate of Eligibility, Form DS-2019, which you will receive when you are accepted into an approved J-1 program, has a space on it showing whether or not your J-1 visa is subject to a home residency requirement. If it is, the U.S. consulate issuing the visa will have you sign a declaration stating that you understand your obligation to return to your home country for at least two years before being allowed to apply for a green card or other U.S. visa. The consulate will also make a notation of the home residency requirement in your passport.

Be aware that the consulate does not have the power to decide who will or won't be subject to a home residency requirement. The facts of your situation, not the consulate's notation on your visa or DS-2019, determine whether you must meet this requirement. Some consulates routinely mark all J-1 visas subject to the home residency requirement, no matter what the facts. The consulate's notation is a strong indication that you are probably subject to the home residency requirement, but it is not the final word. If you have doubts about the correctness of the consulate's notation, it is worth checking into the matter.

E. Quick View of the J-1 Visa Application Process

Getting a J-1 visa is a two- to three-step process:

- First, your program sponsor sends you a Certificate of Eligibility.
- Second, you apply for either a visa (from a U.S. consulate in another country) or, if you're already living legally in the U.S. and prefer not to travel, for a change of nonimmigrant status (from USCIS).

Applying at a Consulate That's Not in Your Home Country

The law allows most people to apply for a J-1 visa at any U.S. consulate they choose—with one exception. If you have ever been present in the U.S. unlawfully, your visa will be automatically cancelled and you cannot apply as a third-country national (at a consulate outside your home country). Even if you overstayed your permitted stay in the U.S. by just one day, you must return to your home country and apply for the visa from that consulate. There is an exception. If you were admitted to the U.S. for the duration of your status (indicated by a "D/S" on your I-94 form) and you remained in the U.S. beyond the time for which your status was conferred, you will be barred from third-country national processing only if an immigration judge or USCIS (or INS, if it was called that then) officer has determined that you were unlawfully present. You may find that your success in applying as a third-country national

will depend on your country, the consulate, and the relative seriousness of your offense. Being unlawfully present is also a ground of inadmissibility if the period of unlawful presence is 180 days or more. (See Chapter 3.)

Even if you are eligible for third-country national processing, your case will be given the greatest consideration at the consulate in your home country. Applying in some other country creates suspicion in the minds of the consular officers there about your motives for choosing their consulate. Often, when an applicant expects trouble at a home consulate, he or she will seek a more lenient consular office in some other country. This practice of consulate shopping is frowned upon by officials in the system. Unless you have a very good reason for being elsewhere (such as a temporary job assignment in some other nation), it is often smarter to file your visa application in your home country.

- Third, if you are outside the U.S. and receive a visa, you enter the U.S. and claim your J-1 status.

(If you are Canadian, your application procedures will be different from those of other applicants. See Chapter 5.)

F. Step One: Your Sponsoring Organization Issues a Certificate of Eligibility

You can't start the visa application process until you have been admitted to an exchange program approved by the

U.S. Department of State (DOS), through its Bureau of Educational and Cultural Affairs (ECA). This book does not discuss how to find the right U.S. school or program, or how to get accepted to it. However, the State Department provides a list of approved organizations, at http://exchanges.state.gov/education/jexchanges. (Click the link for "Search Designated Sponsors.") You'll probably need to get started well in advance.

Once a program has accepted you, it will issue you a document called a Certificate of Eligibility, or SEVIS Form DS-2019. You do not fill out or sign any part of it. But be sure to carefully check the form for accuracy, then ask your sponsoring organization to correct any errors. You'll use the DS-2019 in the next steps of your application process.

G. Step Two for Applicants Outside the U.S.: Applying at a U.S. Consulate

Anyone with a Certificate of Eligibility (SEVIS Form DS-2019) from an exchange visitor program sponsor can apply for a J-1 visa at a U.S. consulate in his or her home country. You must be physically present in order to apply there.

You can normally apply 120 days or less before your program begins. Because of processing delays, it's best to apply as soon as you can within that 120-day window.

Check with your local U.S. consulate regarding its application procedures. Many insist on advance appointments. Just getting an appointment can take several weeks, so plan ahead.

Your application will consist of government forms as well as documents that you collect yourself. You can either get the forms in advance (download them from the State Department website or pick them up from a U.S. consulate), or you can get your documents together, then go to the consulate, pick up and fill out the forms and submit your application on the same day.

Before your appointment, you'll need to pay a fee to support the U.S. student-tracking database called SEVIS. Your school or sponsoring organization may take care of processing this fee payment for you. If not, you'll need to do it yourself, either online or by mail. To submit the form online, go to www.FMJfee.com, complete the online Form I-901, and pay with a credit card. To submit the form by mail, download it from the Immigration and Customs Enforcement (ICE) website at www.ice.gov/doclib/sevis/pdf/I-901.pdf, and mail it, together with your check or money order drawn on a U.S. bank and payable in U.S. currency, to the address indicated on the form. For more information on these requirements, see www.ice.gov/sevis/i901/index.htm. Once you get a receipt for having made this payment, you'll need to use it for your consular interview.

⚠ **Have you been, or are you now, working or living illegally in the United States?** If so, see Chapter 3 regarding whether you can still get a J-1 visa from a U.S. consulate. You may have become inadmissible or subject to a three-year or ten-year bar on reentry.

1. Preparing Your Visa Application

Your application should consist of the items on the checklist below.

Checklist for Exchange Visitor Visa Application

❑ Form SEVIS DS-2019, filled out by your sponsoring organization.

❑ Receipt for having paid the SEVIS fee (currently $100).

❑ Form DS-156, Nonimmigrant Visa Application.

❑ Form DS-158, Contact Information and Work History for Nonimmigrant Visa Applicant.

❑ Form DS-157, Supplemental Nonimmigrant Visa Application, if you're either a male applicant between 16 and 45 years of age or you come from a state that the U.S. believes sponsors terrorism and you are age 16 or older, whether male or female.

❑ Visa application fee (currently $100).

❑ Visa issuance reciprocity fee (the amount depends on your country.)

❑ Your passport, valid for at least six months.

❑ One passport-type photo of you and one of each of your spouse and children, 2 inches x 2 inches.

❑ Long-form birth certificate for you and each accompanying relative.

❑ Marriage certificate if you are married and bringing your spouse.

❑ If either you or your spouse has ever been married before, copies of divorce and death certificates showing termination of all previous marriages.

❑ If your program involves studying at a school, transcripts, diplomas, and results of any standardized tests required by the school you'll be attending, showing your previous education and your qualifications to pursue your chosen course of study.

❑ Documents showing reasons that you'll return to your home country, such as ownership of real estate, relationships with close family members staying behind, or proof that a job will be waiting for you on your return.

❑ If you're entering a flight training program, additional required documents, as discussed below.

❑ If your program doesn't include salaried employment, proof of sufficient funds, such as:

  ❑ USCIS Form I-134, Affidavit of Support from a U.S. friend or relative, or a letter from a friend or relative promising support.

  ❑ Bank statements.

  ❑ Personal financial statements.

  ❑ Evidence of your current sources of income.

A few of the items on this checklist require additional explanation.

Evidence of intent to return. You will need documents establishing your intent to leave the U.S. when your visa expires. The consulate will want to see evidence that your ties to your home country are so strong that you will be highly motivated to return. Proof of such ties can include deeds verifying ownership of a house or other real property, written statements from you explaining that close relatives are staying behind, or letters from a company outside the U.S. showing that you have a job waiting when you return from the United States.

Evidence of sufficient funds. If you will be attending school in the U.S., and neither employment nor a scholarship is part of your exchange visitor program, you must present evidence that you have sufficient funds available to cover all of your costs for the first year of study. You must also show that you also have a source of funds to cover your expenses in future years, so that you will be able to study full-time without working. If your particular exchange visitor program provides you with a scholarship or employment, evidence of such support in the form of a letter from the program sponsor will satisfy this requirement.

If the exchange visitor program sponsor will not be furnishing you with financial support, you will have to show either that you can meet your own expenses without working, or that a close relative is willing to guarantee your support. The best evidence of your ability to pay educational expenses is a bank statement or letter from a bank, either in the U.S. or abroad, showing an account in your name with a balance of at least one year's worth of expenses in it. Alternatively, you can submit a written guarantee of support signed by an immediate relative, preferably a parent, together with your relative's bank statements. Unless your relative can show enough assets to prove he or she is able to support you without additional income, you should also show that your relative is presently employed. You can document this by submitting a letter from the employer verifying your relative's work situation.

Although the guarantee of support may be in the form of a simple written statement in your relative's own words, we suggest you use USCIS Form I-134, called an Affidavit of Support, available on the USCIS website (www.USCIS. gov). The questions on Form I-134 are self-explanatory. However, the form was designed to be filled out by someone living in the United States. Since it is quite likely that the person who will support you is living outside the U.S., any questions that apply to U.S. residents should be answered "N/A" (for "not applicable").

Additional documents for flight trainees. If you're applying for a J-1 visa for U.S. flight training, you will be required to submit written information and documents specifying the following:

- your reason for the training (be specific)
- current employer and your position
- who is paying for the training (name and relationship)
- your most recent flight certifications and ratings
- information on what kind of aircraft the training is for (document must be signed by a school official in the United States)
- certified take-off weight of the aircraft type (document must be signed by a school official in the United States), and
- current rank or title if you are presently working as an active pilot.

2. Attending Your Consular Interview

Most consulates will require an interview before issuing a J-1 exchange visitor visa. During the interview, a consular officer will examine the forms and documents for accuracy. The consular officer will verify your DS-2019 record electronically through the SEVIS system. Documents proving your ability to finance your study will be carefully checked, as will evidence of ties to your home country. During the interview you will surely be asked how long you intend to remain in the United States. Any answer indicating uncertainty about plans to return home or an interest in applying for a green card is likely to result in a denial of your student visa.

Because of new security requirements, you are unlikely to be approved for your visa on the same day as your interview. The consular officer will need to compare your name against various databases of people with a history of criminal activity, violations of U.S. immigration laws, or terrorist affiliations. This can add weeks or months to the processing of your visa, particularly if you come from a country that the U.S. suspects of supporting terrorism.

H. Step Two for Some Applicants Inside the U.S.: You Apply to USCIS for a Change of Status

If you are physically present in the U.S., you may apply for a change to J-1 status without leaving the country on the following conditions:

- you have been accepted into an approved program, and the program has given you a Certificate of Eligibility, Form DS-2019
- you entered the U.S. legally and not under the Visa Waiver Program, nor using a C (alien in transit), TWOV (alien in transit without a visa), D (crewman), K-1 (fiancé), K-2 (dependent of a fiancé), J-1 (exchange visitor), or M-1 (vocational student) visa.
- you have never worked in the U.S. illegally

- the date on your I-94 card has not passed, and
- you are not inadmissible.

 Eligibility to apply while you're in the U.S. has nothing to do with overall eligibility for a J-1 visa. Applicants who are barred from filing in the U.S. but otherwise qualify for student status can sometimes apply successfully for a J-1 visa at U.S. consulates abroad.

Overall, USCIS offices do not favor change of status applications. To approve a change of status, USCIS must believe that at the time you originally entered the U.S. as a visitor or with some other nonimmigrant visa, you did not intend to apply for a different status. If USCIS thinks you had a preconceived plan to use one visa to enter the U.S. with an eye to applying to change to a different status, it may deny your application. You can get around the preconceived intent issue by leaving the U.S. and applying for your visa at a U.S. consulate in another country. In fact, your student application will stand a better chance of approval at most consulates than it will if filed in the United States. But understand the pitfalls involved in departing the U.S. (especially if you have lived here unlawfully) before making your decision. (See Chapter 3.)

If you decide to apply for a change of status within the U.S., realize that you still don't have the physical visa that you'll need if you ever leave the U.S.—a change of status gives you only

J-1 status. Visas are never given inside the United States. They are issued exclusively by U.S. consulates in other countries. If you file in the U.S. and you are successful, you will get to remain in the U.S. with J-1 privileges until the status expires. But should you leave the country for any reason before that time, you will have to apply for the visa itself at a U.S. consulate before returning to the United States. Moreover, the fact that your J-1 status has been approved in the U.S. does not guarantee that the consulate will also approve your visa. For these reasons, many people choose to leave the U.S. and apply through a consulate.

1. Preparing Your U.S. Change of Status Application

Before submitting your application, you'll need to pay a fee (currently $100) to support the U.S. student tracking database called SEVIS. Your school may take care of processing this fee payment for you. If not, you'll need to do it yourself, either online or by mail. To submit the form online, go to www. FMJfee.com (using a credit card and completing the online Form I-901). To submit the form by mail, download it from the Immigration and Customs Enforcement (ICE) website at www.ice. gov/doclib/sevis/pdf/I-901.pdf, and mail it, together with your check or money order drawn on a U.S. bank and payable in U.S. currency, to the address indicated on the form. For more information on these requirements, see www.ice. gov/sevis/i901index.htm. After you get a receipt for your fee, you can proceed with your change of status application.

The checklist below will help you assemble the necessary items for the change of status application.

Checklist for J-1 Change of Status Application

❑ Form I-539, Application To Extend/Change Nonimmigrant Status, with accompanying fee (currently $300; send a check or money order, not cash). One Form I-539 and fee will cover you, your spouse, and all your children, if they are in the U.S. with you and in the same visa status or accompanying beneficiaries of your current visa status. But be sure to complete the I-539 Supplement for your spouse and children.

❑ SEVIS DS-2019, filled out by your school and signed by you.

❑ Receipts for having paid your SEVIS fee (currently $100).

❑ Copies of proof of your family members' relationship to you, such as marriage and birth certificates.

❑ Your original Form I-94 (and those of your spouse and children, if they're applying with you) or other proof of your current lawful, unexpired immigration status (except Canadians just visiting the U.S., who are not expected to have I-94 cards).

❑ If either you or your spouse has ever been married before, copies of divorce and death certificates showing termination of all previous marriages.

❑ If your program involves studying at a school, transcripts, diplomas, and results of any standardized tests required by the school you'll be attending, showing your previous education and your qualifications to pursue your chosen course of study.

❑ Documents showing reasons that you'll return to your home country, such as ownership of real estate, relationships with close family members staying behind, or proof that a job will be waiting for you on your return.

❑ If your program doesn't include salaried employment, proof of sufficient funds, such as:

    ❑ Form I-134, Affidavit of Support from a U.S. friend or relative, or a letter from a friend or relative promising support.

    ❑ Bank statements.

    ❑ Personal financial statements.

    ❑ Evidence of your current sources of income.

For additional explanation of some of the items on this checklist, see Subsection G1, above.

2. Mailing the Change of Status Application

After assembling the change of status application, you must mail it to the USCIS regional service center having jurisdiction over the area where you're currently living. USCIS regional service centers are not the same as USCIS local offices—for one thing, you cannot visit regional service centers in person. There are four USCIS regional service centers spread across the United States. See the USCIS website at www.uscis.gov for the regional service centers' addresses and P.O. box numbers.

3. Awaiting a Decision on the Change of Status Application

Within a few weeks after mailing in the petition, you should get back a written confirmation that the papers are being processed, together with a receipt for the fee. This notice will also contain your immigration file number. If USCIS wants further information before acting on your case, all petition papers, forms, and documents will be returned to you with a form known as a Request for Evidence. You should supply the extra data requested and mail the whole package back to the service center.

Change of status applications are normally approved (or denied) within one to three months. When this happens, the USCIS service center will notify you using a Form I-797 Notice of Action. A new I-94 card will be attached to the bottom of the form.

I. Step Three: Entering the U.S. Using Your J-1 Visa

You'll be allowed to enter the U.S. up to 30 days before the start of your classes or program, but no earlier. When you arrive in the U.S. with your new J-1 visa, the border officer will examine your paperwork, ask you some questions, and if all is in order, approve you for entry. Then the officer will give you an I-94 card. It will be stamped "D/S" indicating that you can stay until the completion of your program. As a practical matter, however, you are permitted to remain up to the expiration date on your SEVIS Form DS-2019 Certificate of Eligibility. Each time you exit and reenter the U.S., you will get a new I-94 card.

Watch Out for Summary Exclusion

The law empowers a Customs and Border Protection (CBP) inspector at the U.S. airport or border to summarily (without allowing judicial review) bar entry to someone requesting admission to the U.S. if either of the following is true:

- The inspector thinks you are lying about practically anything connected with entering the U.S., including your purpose in coming, intent to return, and prior immigration history. This includes the use or suspected use of false documents.
- You do not have the proper documentation to support your entry to the U.S. in the category you are requesting.

If the inspector excludes you, you cannot be readmitted to the U.S. for five years, unless USCIS grants a special waiver. For this reason it is extremely important to understand the terms of your requested status, and to not make any misrepresentations. If you are found to be inadmissible, you may ask the CBP inspector to withdraw your application to enter the U.S. in order to prevent having the five-year deportation order on your record. The CBP may allow this in some exceptional cases.

Schools' Responsibilities to Track International Scholars

Schools must report to USCIS concerning scholars on J visas. When a program issues you a Certificate of Eligibility, it must tell the U.S. consulate in your home country. When that consulate approves your J visa, it must notify USCIS. During your time in the U.S., the school must keep USCIS up to date on your status and whereabouts, through a database called SEVIS. To finance this database, you must pay a $100 SEVIS fee.

Schools must update SEVIS on your:

- name, date, and place of birth and country of citizenship
- current address
- visa classification, date of visa issuance, or classification granted
- academic or program status (full-time or part-time)
- certification for work authorization, and
- date that program was terminated, and the reason, if known.

On top of maintaining this database, the school must actually report news of changes in your status or activities to USCIS. Most importantly, the school has 21 days in which to advise USCIS that your address has changed—and you have only ten days after moving to tell your school.

J. Extending Your J-1 Stay in the U.S.

J-1 visas and statuses can be extended in the U.S. to enable you to complete your particular exchange visitor program. However, since J-1 statuses are usually granted for the period of time considered reasonable for the type of exchange visitor program in which you are participating, extensions are not easy to get. USCIS has the right to reconsider your qualifications based on any changes in the facts or law, and will want to hear a compelling reason why you have been unable to complete your exchange visitor program within normal time limits. As always, however, good cases that are well prepared will ordinarily be successful.

When you enter the U.S. on a J-1 visa, your I-94 card will be stamped to indicate that you can stay in the U.S. for the duration of your status (D/S), limited by the time period on your Certificate of Eligibility. However, if you come from a country where J-1 visa time privileges are especially limited, your visa may expire before your I-94 card does. In such a situation, if you wish to leave the U.S. and then reenter to complete your exchange visitor program, you will have to extend your visa. To extend the visa that is stamped in your passport, you must apply at a U.S. consulate abroad.

Whether and how you can extend your J-1 stay depends on whether you were admitted for the duration of your status (with a "D/S" mark on your I-94) or until a specific date. It's easier with a D/S mark—in that case you can simply explain the situation to the Responsible Officer (RO) at your school or program (most of them like you to give them at least 30 days notice) and ask the RO to prepare a new Form DS-2019 showing the new expected completion date. The RO then notifies the State Department, and your extension becomes official.

If, however, you were admitted until a specific date, you must not only get a new Form DS-2019, but also seek actual approval from USCIS (if you don't want to leave the U.S.) or the State Department (if you're willing to leave and either reenter or reapply through a U.S. consulate).

To apply within the U.S., you would use Form I-539 (the form used for changing status, which you may have used once already—it's on the USCIS website). You'll also need to enclose the appropriate fee, your new Form DS-2019, copies of your old DS-2019 and your I-94 (and those of your family members, if any), and a letter from your program sponsor stating how long the extension is needed for, and explaining in as much detail as possible why you are unable to complete your program within the expected amount of time. Mail your package to the USCIS regional service center indicated on its website at www.uscis.gov. It may take several months to get an answer from USCIS, so plan ahead so that your permitted stay doesn't expire while the application is pending.

To apply from outside the U.S., your procedure depends on whether not only your I-94, but also your J-1 visa has run out. If only the I-94 has run out, but your visa is still good, you can simply arrive at the airport with your existing J-1 visa, your new DS-2019, your old DS-2019, and, to be safe, all the supporting materials you used to get your J-1 visa in the first place. You will be given a new I-94 showing your new departure date.

If not only your I-94 but also your J-1 visa has run out, you'll need to reapply for everything through a U.S. consulate. In addition to your new DS-2019, you'll need to gather all the materials you used to apply for your original visa, as described in Section G, above.

Working While Your Extension Application Is Pending

If you file your application for extension of J-1 status before your authorized stay expires, you are automatically authorized to continue working for up to 240 days while waiting for a decision. If, however, your authorized stay expires after you have filed for an extension but before you receive an approval, and more than 240 days go by without getting a decision on your extension application, you must stop working.

Waivers of Two-Year Home Residency Requirements

You may be participating in the type of exchange visitor program that makes it mandatory for you to spend two years residing in your home country after completing your program before you are eligible to apply for a green card or other U.S. visa. If you wish to escape this obligation and apply for a green card immediately, you will first have to apply for a waiver of the home residency requirement. You cannot get around the requirement by spending two years in a third country or by switching to a different visa status within the United States.

To apply for a waiver, you'll have to show that you deserve it under one of the following five grounds:

- **No objection from your home government.** Unless you are a foreign medical graduate, the easiest way to obtain a waiver is by having your home government consent to it through a "no objection letter." In this letter, your government would assert that it doesn't mind your staying in the U.S. to apply for a green card—despite the fact that it may have helped finance your exchange

Waivers of Two-Year Home Residency Requirements, (cont'd)

program participation. Contact your home country's embassy in Washington, DC, to request such a letter.

- **Request by an interested U.S government agency.** If you're working on a project of interest to an agency of the U.S. government, and that agency decides that your continued stay is vital to one of its programs, it may support your request for a waiver.

- **Fear of persecution in your home country.** If you can show that you would be persecuted upon return to your home country based on your race, religion, or political opinion, you can apply for a waiver. Note that, unlike applicants for political asylum, you cannot qualify if you fear persecution based only on your nationality or membership in a particular social group. Also, the standard is higher than in ordinary asylum cases, in which applicants need only prove a "reasonable fear" of persecution—you, by contrast, must show that you "would be" persecuted upon return. If you meet this standard, you'd probably be better off skipping the waiver process and submitting a separate application for political asylum.

- **Exceptional hardship to your U.S. citizen or permanent resident spouse or child.** If your spouse or any of your children are U.S. citizens

or permanent residents, and you can show that your departure from the U.S. would cause them exceptional hardship, you may be granted a waiver. However, USCIS will demand a greater showing of hardship than the "mere" emotional pain of separation, or economic or language difficulties. The classic exceptional hardship case is one in which your family member has a medical problem that would be worsened by your departure or by traveling with you to your home country; or where the family member would be persecuted if he or she departed with you.

- **Request by a state department of health.** If you're a foreign medical graduate with an offer of full-time employment at a health care facility in an area that's been designated as having a shortage of doctors, and you agree to begin working there within 90 days of receiving the waiver and to continue working there full-time for at least three years, you may be granted a waiver.

As you might guess, the waiver application process is complex and often depends on persuading reluctant government officials that you fit into a category whose boundaries are not clearly defined. We do not cover the waiver application process in this book, but strongly advise you to get help from an experienced immigration lawyer.

K. Working as an Exchange Visitor

Special rules apply for you to be able to work while you're in the United States.

1. When You Can Work Without Special Permission

Exchange visitors are permitted to work in the U.S. if the job is part of the particular exchange program in which they are participating. Many J-1 programs, such as those for college and university professors or graduate medical students, are specifically created to engage the exchange visitor in employment. Others, like those for graduate students, often involve part-time employment in the form of teaching or research assistantships. The job may be located on or off the school premises. As long as the employment is part of the program, no special work permission is required.

2. When You Need Special Permission to Work

Working outside the bounds of your program often requires special permission, as described in the following subsections.

a. Practical Training

If your J-1 visa was issued for a study program, you may accept work that is not specifically part of the program but is related to the subject matter of your studies. This can include work that begins after your program is completed (but no more than 30 days after) with an 18-month aggregate limit. Such employment is called practical training. You must have written permission from the responsible officer of your exchange visitor program to accept a practical training position. USCIS plays no role in granting permission for practical training.

b. Economic Necessity

Remember that in order to get a J-1 visa, you must show that you have sufficient financial resources to support yourself while participating in an exchange visitor program. As we discussed earlier, such resources may be in the form of scholarships or salary earned for work that is part of or related to the program. However, if unforeseen financial problems arise after you arrive in the U.S., you may get work permission for employment that is unrelated to your exchange visitor program if the employment will not adversely affect your ability to be a full-time participant in the program. There is no special application, but you must have written approval from the responsible officer of your exchange visitor program.

3. Employment for Accompanying Relatives

Your accompanying spouse or minor children may apply to USCIS for permission to work. However, they cannot get work permission if the money earned helps to support you, or is needed to support you. They are expected to use the money for such things as recreational and cultural activities and related travel.

If your accompanying spouse or children want to work, they must file separate applications for employment authorization. This can be done by completing the items on the checklist below and filing them with the USCIS service center nearest to where your program in the U.S. is being carried out (the address is on the USCIS website and the instructions to the form).

It is very important to keep the fee receipt USCIS will send so your family members can prove that the I-765 was filed (in case USCIS loses it).

USCIS is required to make a decision on employment authorization applications within 90 days. If the decision is in your accompanying relative's favor, he or she will receive a work authorization card.

If the decision is not made within 90 days, your relative will, at his or her request, be granted an interim employment authorization which will last for 240 days. To receive an interim card, your relative must visit a local USCIS district office and show the fee receipt. Then an interim work authorization card will be issued.

Once approved, the work permit will be valid for the duration of your (the J-1 principal's), authorized stay as indicated on your Form I-94 or a period of four years, whichever is shorter.

Family Member Work Permit Application Checklist

- ❑ Form I-765 (Answer Question 16 "(c)(5)").
- ❑ Copies of I-94 cards.
- ❑ Two photos.
- ❑ Filing fee (currently $340).
- ❑ Written statement explaining why the employment is for purposes other than supporting the J-1 visa holder, plus any supporting evidence regarding what's said in the statement.
- ❑ A monthly budget, detailing your sources of income and your expenses.

L. Annual Reports for Foreign Medical Graduates

All foreign medical graduates training in the U.S. on J-1 visas are required to file annual reports with the USCIS local office having jurisdiction over their places of training. The reports are filed on Form I-644, which is self-explanatory. A copy of this form can be obtained from your program sponsor. Failure to file this report each year will result in the cancellation of your visa. ■

Chapter 24

Getting a Visa as a Temporary Worker in a Selected Occupation (O, P, or R Visa)

A few types of short-term work visas are available to people doing specialized work. These include O and P visas for certain outstanding workers in the sciences, arts, education, business, entertainment, and athletics, and R visas for religious workers. (See I.N.A. § 101(a)(15)(O), 8 U.S.C. § 1101(a)(15)(O), 8 C.F.R. § 214.2(o)(1)(ii)(A)(1); I.N.A. § 101(a)(15)(P), 8 U.S.C. § 1101(a)(15)(P), 8 C.F.R. § 214.2(o)(1)(i); and I.N.A. § 101(a)(15)(R), 8 U.S.C. § 1101(a)(15)(R); 22 C.F.R. § 41.58; 8 C.F.R. § 214.2(r).)

A job offer from a U.S. employer is a basic requirement for all these visas. There is no annual limit on the number of people who can receive O, P, or R visas.

Do you need a lawyer? You can't apply for an O, P, or R visa without having an employer first—and it's in your employer's interest to hire a lawyer to help. A lawyer can help make sure that your application gets done right the first time.

Key Features of the O, P, and R Visas

Here are some of the advantages and disadvantages of these specialized work visas:

- You can work legally in the U.S. for your O, P, or R sponsor. If, however, you want to change jobs, you must get a new visa.
- O, P, and R visas can be issued quickly.
- O visas will be granted for the length of time necessary for a particular event, up to a maximum of three years, with unlimited extensions in one-year increments.
- P visas will be granted for the length of time needed to complete a particular event, tour, or season, up to a maximum of one year. However, P-1 athletes may be admitted for a period of up to five years with one extension of up to five years.
- R visas will be granted initially for up to three years, with extensions up to a maximum total of five years.
- You may travel in and out of the U.S. or stay there continuously for as long as your visa stamp and status are valid.
- Your spouse and unmarried children under age 21 may accompany you, but they may not not accept employment in the United States.

A. Do You Qualify for an O, P, or R Visa?

Pay close attention to the eligibility criteria for these visas: The O, P, and R visa categories are quite narrow in scope.

1. O-1 Visas: Persons of Extraordinary Ability in the Arts, Athletics, Science, Business, and Education

O-1 visas are available to persons of proven extraordinary ability in the sciences, arts, education, business, or athletics. To be considered a person of extraordinary ability, you must have sustained national or international acclaim, or, if you work in motion pictures or television productions, you must have a demonstrated record of extraordinary achievement. O-1 visas can be given only on the basis of individual qualifications. Membership in a group or team is not by itself enough to get you the visa. In addition, you must be coming to work or perform at an event or a series of events in the area of your extraordinary ability.

a. Extraordinary Ability in Science, Education, Business, or Athletics

To meet O-1 standards, you must be able to show that you have extraordinary ability and that you have received sustained national or international acclaim. This can be demonstrated if you have gotten a major internationally recognized award such as a Nobel Prize, or if you have accomplished at least three of the following:

- received a *nationally* recognized prize or award for excellence
- membership in associations that require outstanding achievements of their members in your field of expertise, as judged by recognized national or international experts
- published material in professional or major trade publications or major media about you and your work
- participated, on a panel or individually, as a judge of the work of others in your field
- made an original scientific, scholarly, or business-related contribution that is of major significance in the field
- authored scholarly articles in professional journals or major media
- been previously employed in a critical or essential capacity for an organization with a distinguished reputation, or
- command or have commanded a high salary or other outstanding remuneration for your services.

If the above criteria do not readily apply to your occupation, the company petitioning for you may submit comparable evidence in order to show that you are "extraordinary." Be sure to explain why the above criteria do not apply.

b. Extraordinary Ability in the Arts

If you are applying as an O-1 alien of extraordinary ability in the arts, you should first make sure your work fits the definition of art. The category of arts is defined broadly in the USCIS regulations, to include:

. . . any field of creative activity or endeavor such as, but not limited to, fine arts, visual arts, culinary arts, and performing arts. Aliens engaged in the field of arts include not only the principal creators and performers but other essential persons such as, but not limited to, directors, set designers, lighting designers, sound designers, choreographers, choreologists, conductors, orchestrators, coaches, arrangers, musical supervisors, costume designers, makeup artists, flight masters, stage technicians, and animal trainers.

(See 8 C.F.R. § 214.2(o)(3)(ii).)

You must also be coming to the U.S. to perform in the area of extraordinary ability and must be recognized as prominent in your field of endeavor. You can demonstrate your recognition with documents showing that you have been nominated for or have received significant national or international awards or prizes in your particular field, such as an Oscar, Emmy, Grammy, or Director's Guild Award. Alternately, you can supply (to your employer, for submission on your behalf) at least three of the following forms of documentation:

- evidence that you have performed, and will perform, services as a lead or starring participant in productions or events that have a distinguished reputation as evidenced by critical reviews, advertisements, publicity releases, publication contracts, or endorsements

- evidence that you have achieved national or international recognition for achievements evidenced by critical reviews or other published materials by or about you in major newspapers, trade journals, magazines, or other publications

- evidence that you have performed, and will perform, in a lead, starring, or critical role for organizations and establishments that have a distinguished reputation, as evidenced by articles in news-papers, trade journals, publications, or testimonials

- evidence that you have a record of major commercial or critically acclaimed successes (as evidenced by title, rating, standing in the field, box office receipts, motion pictures, or television ratings) and other occupational achievements reported in trade journals, major newspapers, or other publications

- evidence that you have received significant recognition for achievements from organizations, critics, government agencies or other recognized experts in the field. Such testimonials must be in a form that clearly indicates the author's authority, expertise, and knowledge of your achievements or,

- evidence that you have either commanded a high salary or will command a high salary or other substantial remuneration for services in relation to others in the field, as evidenced by contracts or other reliable evidence.

If the above criteria do not lend themselves to your situation, your petitioning employer may submit alternative but comparable evidence in order to establish your eligibility.

2. O-2 Visas: Support Staff for People With O-1 Visas

O-2 visas are available to people who work as essential support personnel of O-1 athletes and entertainers. O-2 visas are not available in the fields of science, business, or education. O-2 workers must be accompanying O-1 artists or athletes and be an integral part of the actual performance. The O-2 worker must also have critical skills, as well as experience with the particular O-1 worker, that are not general in nature and cannot be performed by a U.S. worker.

In the case of motion picture or television productions, there must be a preexisting, long-standing working relationship between the O-2 applicant and the O-1 worker. If significant

Special Rules for Workers on Television and Movie Productions

If you're an artist, entertainer, director, technical, or creative staffperson seeking a visa to work on a television or motion picture production, certain special rules apply to you. First, you must prove not merely a "high level of achievement," but a "very high level of accomplishment" in the motion picture and television industry. You'll need to show evidence that your skill and recognition is significantly higher than that ordinarily encountered. You'll need to show the same sorts of evidence as other artists, but you won't have the option of showing comparable evidence if you can't come up with anything on the USCIS's list.

portions of the production will take place both in and out of the U.S., O-2 support personnel must be deemed necessary for the achievement of continuity and a smooth, successful production.

3. O-3 Visas: Accompanying Relatives of Those With O-1 and O-2 Visas

O-3 visas are available to accompanying spouses and unmarried children under age 21 of O-1 or O-2 visa holders. O-3 visas allow relatives to remain in the U.S., but they may not work. They may seek permanent residence while in O-3 status.

⚠ **Although people on O-1 visas and their spouses and children on O-3 visas are permitted to apply for permanent residence (a green card) while in nonimmigrant O status, this is not true of O-2s (support staff).** They must have the intent to depart the U.S. and they must maintain a residence abroad during their U.S. stay.

4. P-1 Visas: Outstanding Athletes, Athletic Teams, and Entertainment Companies

P-1 visas are available to athletes or athletic teams that have been internationally recognized as outstanding for a long and continuous period of time. Entertainment companies that have been nationally recognized as outstanding for a long time also qualify. Unlike O visas, which always rest on the capabilities of individuals, P-1 visas can be issued based on the expertise of a group. However, don't be surprised to find a lot of overlap between uses and qualifications for O and P visas.

In the case of entertainment companies, each performer who wishes to qualify for a P-1 visa must have been an integral part of the group for at least one year, although up to 25% of them can be excused from the one-year requirement, if necessary. This requirement may also be waived in exceptional situations, where due to illness or other unanticipated circumstances, a critical performer is unable to travel. The one-year requirement is for performers only. It does not apply to support personnel. It also does not apply to anyone at all who works for a circus, including performers.

Like O-1 visas, P-1 visas are issued only for the time needed to complete a particular event, tour, or season. You may also be allowed some extra time for vacation, as well as promotional appearances and stopovers incidental and/or related to the event. Individual athletes, however, may remain in the U.S. for up to ten years.

a. Athletes

To qualify as a P-1 athlete, you or your team must have an internationally recognized reputation in the sport. Evidence of this must include a contract with a major U.S. sports league, team, or international sporting event, and at least two of the following:

- proof of your, or your team's, previous significant participation with a major U.S. sports league
- proof of your participation in an international competition with a national team
- proof of your previous significant participation with a U.S. college in intercollegiate competition
- written statement from an official of a major U.S. sports league or the governing body of the sport,

detailing how you or your team is internationally recognized

- written statement from the sports media or a recognized expert regarding your international recognition
- evidence that you or your team is internationally ranked, or
- proof that you or your team has received a significant honor or award in the sport.

b. Entertainers

P-1 visas are not available to individual entertainers, but only to members of groups with international reputations. Your group must have been performing regularly for at least one year, and 75% of the members of your group must have been performing with that group for at least a year. When your employer files a petition on your behalf, the employer will have to supply proof of your group's sustained international recognition, as shown by either its nomination for, or receipt of, significant international awards or prizes, or at least three of the following:

- proof that your group has or will star or take a leading role in productions or events with distinguished reputations
- reviews or other published material showing that your group has achieved international recognition and acclaim for outstanding achievement in the field

- proof that your group has and will star or take a leading role in productions or events for organizations with distinguished reputations
- proof of large box office receipts or ratings showing your group has a record of major commercial or critically acclaimed successes
- proof that your group has received significant recognition for achievements from organizations, critics, government agencies, or other recognized experts, or
- proof that your group commands a high salary or other substantial remuneration.

c. Circuses

Circus performers and essential personnel do not need to have been part of the organization for one year to get a P-1 visa, provided the particular circus itself has a nationally recognized reputation as outstanding.

d. Waiver for Nationally Known Entertainment Groups

USCIS may waive the international recognition requirement for groups that have only outstanding national reputations, if special circumstances would make it difficult for your group to prove its international reputation. Such circumstances could include your group having only limited access to news media, or problems based on your group's geographical location.

e. Waiver of One-Year Group Membership

USCIS may waive the one-year group membership requirement for you if you are replacing an ill or otherwise unexpectedly absent but essential member of a P-1 entertainment group. This requirement may also be waived if you will be performing in any critical role of the group's operation.

5. P-2 Visas: Participants in Reciprocal Exchange Programs

P-2 visas are available to artists or entertainers, either individually or as part of a group, who come to the U.S. to perform under a reciprocal exchange program between the U.S. and one or more other countries. All essential support personnel are included. The legitimacy of the program must be evidenced by a formal, written exchange agreement. In addition, a labor union in the U.S. must have either been involved in the negotiation of the exchange or have agreed to it. The U.S. individual or group being exchanged must have skills and terms of employment comparable to the person or group coming to the U.S.

6. P-3 Visas: Culturally Unique Groups

P-3 visas are available to artists or entertainers who come to the U.S., either individually or as part of a group, to develop, interpret, represent, teach, or coach in a program that is considered culturally unique. The program may be of either a commercial or noncommercial nature.

You must be coming to the U.S. to participate in a cultural event or events that will further the understanding or development of your art form. In addition, your employer will have to submit on your behalf:

- statements from recognized experts showing the authenticity of your or your group's skills in performing, presenting, coaching, or teaching the unique or traditional art form and showing the basis of your knowledge of your or your group's skill, or
- evidence that your or your group's art form is culturally unique, as shown by reviews in newspapers, journals, or other published materials, and that the performance will be culturally unique.

Essential support personnel of P-3 aliens should also request classification under the P-3 category. The documentation for P-3 support personnel should include:

- a consultation from a labor organization with expertise in the area of the alien's skill
- a statement describing why the support person has been essential in the past, critical skills, and experience with the principal alien, and

• a copy of the written contract or a summary of the terms of the oral agreement between the alien and the employer.

7. Support Personnel for P-1, P-2, and P-3 Visa Holders

Highly skilled, essential persons who are an integral part of the performance of a P-1, P-2, or P-3 visa holder may also be granted P visas. These persons must perform support services that cannot be readily performed by a U.S. worker and that are essential to the successful performance of services by the P-1, P-2, or P-3 visa holder. The support person must have appropriate qualifications to perform the services, critical knowledge of the specific services to be performed, and experience in providing such support to the P-1, P-2, or P-3 visa holder. (See 8 C.F.R. § 214.2 (p)(3).)

8. P-4 Visas: Accompanying Relatives of People With P-1, P-2, and P-3 Visas

P-4 visas are issued to the spouses and unmarried children under age 21 of any P visa workers. The accompanying relatives are permitted to remain in the U.S., but they cannot work.

9. R-1 Visas: Religious Workers

An R-1 visa is available to a person who has been a member of a legitimate religious denomination for at least two years and has a job offer in the U.S. to work for an affiliate of that same religious organization. R-1 visas may be issued both to members of the clergy and to lay religious workers. The initial stay can be up to three years, and the maximum stay is five years.

The criteria for qualifying are the same as those for religious workers applying for special immigrant green cards discussed in Chapter 12 (see that chapter for the details), with one big difference. Unlike the green card category, it is not necessary that R-1 visa workers were employed by the religious organization before getting the visa. They need only have been members for two years.

Usually, people qualifying for R-1 visas also qualify for green cards as special immigrants and may prefer to apply directly for a green card.

10. R-2 Visas: Accompanying Relatives of Those With R-1 Visas

Spouses and unmarried children under age 21 of R-1 visa holders can get R-2 visas. This allows them to stay in the U.S., but not to accept employment.

Possibilities for a Green Card From O, P, or R Status

Having an O, P, or R visa gives you no legal advantage in applying for a green card. Realistically, however, it is probably easier to get an employer to sponsor you for an O, P, or R visa than for a green card. Also, coming to the U.S. first with a temporary work visa gives you the opportunity to decide whether you really want to live in the U.S. permanently. Once you are in the U.S. with a work permit, it is also usually easier to find an employer willing to sponsor you for a green card.

O and P visa holders are not required to have the intention of returning to their home countries. Accordingly, applying for a green card while in the U.S. on an O or P visa will not jeopardize your status.

R visa holders *are* required to have the intention of returning home once the visa or status expires. Therefore, if you apply for a green card, it may be difficult to obtain or renew an R visa. Many religious workers qualify for green cards as special immigrants. If you are a religious worker and want to remain in the U.S. permanently, you should read Chapter 12 before applying for an R visa.

B. Quick View of the O, P, and R Visa Application Process

Once you have been offered a job, getting an O, P, or R visa is a two- or three-step process:

- First, your U.S. employer files what's called a "visa petition" on USCIS Form I-129. If you're already in the U.S. in lawful status, this petition can simultaneously ask that your status be changed to O, P, or R, in which case the process will successfully end here.
- If you're outside the U.S., then after the visa petition is approved, you submit your own application for an O, P, or R visa to a U.S. consulate.
- Finally, you use either your visa or the notice of your approved visa petition to enter the U.S. and claim your O, P, or R status.

 Nothing stops you from helping with the employer's tasks during this application process. For example, you can fill out forms intended to be completed by your employer and simply ask the employer to check them over and sign them. The less your U.S. employer is inconvenienced, the more it may be willing to act as sponsor for your visa.

C. Step One: Your Employer Submits a Visa Petition

Your employer starts the process off, by filing a visa petition with USCIS, on Form I-129. For O and P visas, that petition can be filed up to one year before a scheduled event, competition, or performance. (If you're self-employed, you will need to hire an agent in the U.S. to file the petition for you; see 8 C.F.R. § 214.2(o)(2)(i).) The object of the petition is to prove four things:

- that you qualify for O, P, or R status
- that your future job is of a high enough level or appropriate nature to warrant someone with your advanced or specialized skills
- that you have the correct background and skills to match the job requirements, and
- in the case of O and P visas, that appropriate labor unions or similar organizations have been consulted concerning your eligibility.

1. Simultaneous Change of Status If You're Already in the U.S.

If you're already in the U.S. in lawful status, such as on a student or other temporary visa, the petition can be used to ask that your status be immediately changed to O, P, or R worker. (Part 2, Question 5, of Form I-129 offers choices addressing this issue.) You can't, however, take advantage of this option if you entered the U.S. on a visa waiver, nor if you entered using a C (alien in transit), TWOV (alien in transit without a visa), D (crewman), K-1 (fiancé), K-2 (dependent of a fiancé), J-1 (exchange visitor), or M-1 (vocational student) visa. You must have:

- entered the U.S. legally
- never worked in the U.S. illegally, and
- not passed the expiration date on your I-94 card.

There is another problem that comes up only in U.S. filings. It is the issue of what is called preconceived intent. To approve a change of status, USCIS must believe that at the time you originally entered the U.S. as a visitor or with some other nonimmigrant visa, you did not intend to apply for a different status. If USCIS thinks you had a preconceived plan to use one visa to enter the U.S. with an eye toward applying for a different status after getting there, it may deny your application. (You can get around the preconceived intent issue by leaving the U.S. and applying for your O, P, or R visa at a U.S. consulate in another country.)

Your spouse and children, if they are also in the U.S. with you, can't change their status by being mentioned on your Form I-129. They must submit separate Forms I-539. They can submit these either at the same time as your employer submits Form I-129, or afterward. (If they submit them afterward, however, they will need to include either a copy of the

USCIS receipt notice indicating that your petition is pending, or a copy of the petition approval notice.)

 Your eligibility to apply in the U.S. has nothing to do your overall eligibility for an O, P, or R visa. Many applicants who are barred from filing in the U.S. but otherwise qualify for O, P, or R status may still apply successfully for an O, P, or R visa at a U.S. consulate in another country.

If you decide to apply for a change of status within the U.S., you will receive only O, P, or R status, not the O, P, or R visa. The visa is a physical stamp in your passport that you will need if you ever want to reenter the United States. Visas are never given inside the United States. They are issued exclusively by U.S. consulates in other countries. If you file in the U.S. and you are successful, you will get to remain in the U.S. with O, P, or R privileges until the status expires. But should you leave the country for any reason before that time, you will have to apply for the visa itself at a U.S. consulate before returning to the United States. Moreover, the fact that your O, P, or R status has been approved in the U.S. does not guarantee that the consulate will also approve your visa. For these reasons, many people prefer to leave the U.S. and apply through a consulate.

2. Assembling the Visa Petition

The checklist below will help you and your employer assemble the necessary items for the visa petition.

Checklist for O, P, or R Visa Petition

- ❏ Form I-129, with O, P, or R Supplement.
- ❏ Filing fee (currently $320).
- ❏ If you will be applying in the United States and your family members are with you and need a change of status, Form I-539 with accompanying fee (currently $300) and copies of your family members' I-94s or other proof of lawful immigration status and of their relationship to you (such as marriage and birth certificates). One Form I-539 and fee will cover your spouse and all your children. This form is meant to be filled out and signed by your family members, not by your employer.
- ❏ If you're in the U.S., a copy of your I-94 or other proof of your current lawful, unexpired immigration status (except that Canadians who are just visiting are not expected to have I-94 cards).
- ❏ If you're outside the U.S., a copy of your passport.

Additional documents for principal applicants (not support personnel):

❑ College and university diplomas, if needed to prove your qualifications.

Additional documents for O-1 visas:

❑ Consultation report from a peer group or labor management organization with expertise in your field.

❑ Written employment contract or written summary of an oral contract.

❑ Employer's written statement explaining the nature of the employment, the specific events or activities you will be participating in, the beginning and end dates of your participation, and why your participation is needed.

❑ Either:

  ❑ Proof of your extraordinary ability in science, education, business, or athletics, as described in Section A1a, above, or

  ❑ Proof of your extraordinary ability in the arts, as described in Section A1b.

Additional documents for O-2 visas:

❑ Employer's written statement explaining the nature of the employment, the specific events or activities you will be participating in, the beginning and end dates of your participation, and why your participation is essential to the successful performance of an O-1 visa holder.

❑ Consultation report from a labor and management organization with expertise in your field.

Additional documents for P-1 visas:

❑ Consultation report from a peer group or labor management organization with expertise in your field.

❑ For athletes, your employment contract with a U.S. league or team, or an individual contract.

❑ Proof of your or your group's international reputation, as described in Section A4, above.

Additional documents for P-2 visas:

❑ Consultation report from a peer group or labor management organization with expertise in your field.

❑ A copy of the formal reciprocal exchange agreement.

❑ A statement from the sponsoring organization explaining how the particular exchange relates to the underlying agreement.

❏ Evidence that your skills are comparable to those of the U.S. artist on the other side of the exchange.

❏ Evidence that an appropriate labor organization in the U.S. was involved in negotiating or approves of the exchange.

Additional documents for P-3 visas:

❏ Statements from recognized experts showing the authenticity of your or your group's skills in performing, presenting, coaching, or teaching the unique or traditional art form and showing the basis of your knowledge of your or your group's skill, or

❏ Reviews in newspapers, journals, or other published materials, showing that your or your group's performance is culturally unique.

Additional documents for support personnel of P-1, P-2, and P-3 visas:

❏ A consultation from a labor organization with expertise in the area of your skill.

❏ A statement describing why the support person has been essential in the past, and his or her critical skills and experience with the principal P visa holder.

❏ Statements or affidavits from people with firsthand knowledge of your experience in performing the critical skills and essential support services needed by the principal P-1, P-2, or P-3 visa holder.

❏ A copy of the written contract or a summary of the terms of the oral agreement between you and your employer.

Additional documents for R visas:

❏ Diplomas and certificates showing your academic and professional qualifications.

❏ Detailed letter from the U.S. religious organization, fully describing the operation of the organization both in and out of the U.S., and explaining that the foreign organization belongs to the same denomination as the U.S. organization.

❏ Letter from the U.S. organization giving details of your U.S. job offer, including how you will be paid, and the name and location of where you'll be providing services.

❏ Written verification that you have been a member of that same organization outside the U.S. for at least two years.

❏ Evidence that the religious organization in the U.S. qualifies as a tax-exempt organization under § 501(c) of the Internal Revenue Code, or is affiliated with an organization that qualifies.

If requesting quick (premium) processing:

❏ Form I-907, with $1,000 filing fee.

A few items on this checklist require some extra explanation, provided in the subsections below.

a. Form I-129 and O, P, or R Supplement

The basic form for the visa petition is immigration Form I-129 and its appropriate Supplement. The I-129 form is used for many different nonimmigrant visas. In addition to the basic part of the form that applies to all types of visas, it comes with several supplements for each specific nonimmigrant category. Simply use the supplement that applies to you.

The employer can choose to list more than one foreign employee on a single I-129 petition. This is done if the employer has more than one opening to be filled for the same type of job or if it is a group petition. Supplement 1, which is also part of Form I-129, should be completed for each additional employee.

b. Job Verification

Your employer must show that the job you have been offered really exists. To do this, the employer must produce either a written employment contract with you or a written summary of an oral contract. The terms of your employment, including job duties, hours, salary, and other benefits, must be mentioned in the document. If you will be going on tour, a tour schedule should be included. For O and P visas, the employer should also submit a detailed written statement explaining the nature of your employment, the specific events or activities in which you will be participating, and why your participation is needed. P-2 petitions must also include a copy of the formal reciprocal exchange agreement, as well as a statement from the sponsoring organization that explains how the particular exchange relates to the underlying agreement.

c. Consultation Report for O and P Visas

All O and P visa petitions must be accompanied by a consultation report or written advisory opinion from an appropriate peer group, labor union, and/or management organization, concerning the nature of the work to be done and your qualifications. Alternatively, you may request USCIS to obtain an advisory opinion for you, but this will significantly delay your case.

For O-1 petitions, the opinion can simply be a letter stating that the organization has no objection to your getting an O-1 visa. In P-1 petitions, the opinion must explain the reputation of either you or your team and the nature of the event in the United States. The opinion in all O-2 cases and for P-1 visa support personnel must contain an explanation of why you are essential to the performance and the nature of your working relationship with the principal performer. It must also state whether or not U.S. workers are available or assert that significant production activities will take place both in and out of the U.S.

and, therefore, that your presence is required for continuity.

P-2 advisory opinions must verify the existence of a viable exchange program. P-3 opinions must evaluate the cultural uniqueness of the performances, state that the events are mostly cultural in nature, and give the reason why the event or activity is appropriate for P-3 classification.

3. Mailing the Visa Petition

After assembling the Form I-129 visa petition, your U.S. employer must mail it to either the California Service Center or the Vermont Service Center, whichever has jurisdiction over the area where you'll be working. If you'll be working in various locations across the U.S., your employer must choose the service center with jurisdiction over the employer's place of business. If you'll be coming from outside the U.S., your employer must send duplicate versions of the form (two signed originals; copies are not acceptable).

USCIS regional service centers are not the same as USCIS local offices—for one thing, you cannot visit regional service centers in person. See the USCIS website at www.uscis.gov for the regional service centers' addresses and P.O. boxes.

4. Awaiting a Decision on the Visa Petition

Within a few weeks after mailing in the petition, your employer should get back a written confirmation that the papers are being processed, together with a receipt for the fee. This notice will also contain your immigration file number. If USCIS wants further information before acting on your case, all petition papers, forms, and documents will be returned to your employer with a form known as a Request for Evidence. Your employer should supply the extra data requested and mail the whole package back to the service center.

O, P, and R petitions are normally approved within two to four months. When the petition has been approved, USCIS will send your employer a Form I-797 Notice of Action. If you plan to submit your visa application at a U.S. consulate abroad, USCIS will also notify the consulate of your choice, sending a complete copy of your file. Only the employer receives communications from USCIS about the petition, because technically it is the employer who is seeking the visa on your behalf.

 Faster processing—at a price. For $1,000 over and above the regular filing fees, USCIS promises premium processing of the visa petition, including a decision within 15 days. To use this service, the employer must fill out an additional application (Form I-907) and submit the application to a special USCIS service center address. For complete instructions, see the USCIS website at www.uscis.gov.

An approved petition does not by itself give you any immigration privileges. It is only a prerequisite to the next step, submitting your application.

D. Step Two: Applicants Outside the U.S. Apply to a U.S. Consulate

After the petition filed by your employer has been approved, USCIS will send a Form I-797 Notice of Action, with which you can apply for a visa at a U.S. consulate—normally in your home country. (Some consulates will insist upon waiting for formal notification directly from USCIS, but most will accept an original Form I-797 from you.) Check with your local U.S. consulate regarding its application procedures. Many insist on advance appointments. Just getting an appointment can take several weeks, so plan ahead.

If you're visa exempt, you can skip this step. Citizens of Canada and certain others need not apply to a U.S. consulate. Instead, they can proceed directly to the U.S. with their Form I-797 and supporting documents to request entry. (See 8 C.F.R. § 212.1.) If you're risk-averse, however, applying at a consulate first might be the safer route.

Have you been, or are you now, working or living illegally in the United States? If so, see Chapter 3 regarding whether you can still get an O, P, or R visa from a U.S. consulate. You may have become inadmissible or subject to a three-year or ten-year bar on reentry.

The following checklist will help you prepare your consular application.

O, P, and R Visa Application Checklist

❑ Form DS-156, Nonimmigrant Visa Application (available at U.S. consulate).

❑ Form DS-157, Supplemental Nonimmigrant Visa Application (also available at U.S. consulate; but it only needs to be filled out by male nonimmigrant visa applicants between the ages of 16 and 45, as well as all applicants over age 16 who come from countries that the U.S. believes sponsor terrorism).

❑ Notice showing approval of the visa petition submitted by your employer or agent.

❑ Valid passport for you and each accompanying relative.

❑ One U.S. passport-type photo of you and one of each accompanying relative. (This is best done by a professional photographer; the consulate can give you a list.)

❑ If your spouse and children will be accompanying you, documents verifying their family relationship to you, such as marriage and birth certificates.

❑ Documents establishing your intent to leave the U.S. when your status expires, such as deeds verifying ownership of a house or other real property, written statements from you explaining that close relatives are staying behind, or letters from a company showing that you have a job waiting when you return from the United States.

❑ Visa application fee (currently $100).

❑ Visa issuance fee (depending on what country you're from; if the country of your nationality charges fees for visas to U.S. citizens who wish to work there, then the U.S. will charge people of your country a similar fee as well).

As part of your application, the consulate will require you and your family members to attend an interview. During the interview, a consular officer will examine the data in your application for accuracy. Evidence of ties to your home country will also be checked. During the interview, you will surely be asked how long you intend to remain in the United States. Any answer indicating uncertainty about plans to return or an interest in applying for a green card may result in a denial of your R-1 visa. Note that O-1/O-3 and P-1 visas do not require that you have no interest in applying for green card.

See Chapter 4 for what else to expect during consular interviews, and what to do if your application is denied.

E. Step Three: You Enter the U.S. With Your O, P, or R Visa

You have until the expiration date on your visa to enter the United States. The border officer will examine your paperwork, ask you some questions, and if all is in order, approve you for entry. He or she will stamp your passport and give you a small white card called an I-94 card. It will be stamped with a date showing how long you can stay. Normally, you are permitted to remain up to the expiration date on your visa petition. Each time you exit and reenter the U.S., you will get a new I-94 card authorizing your stay up to the final date indicated on the petition.

F. Extending Your U.S. Stay

Although an extension is usually easier to get than the O, P, or R visa itself, it is not automatic. USCIS has the right to reconsider your qualifications based on any changes in the facts or law. As always, however, good cases that are well prepared will be successful.

To start the extension process, your employer will have to file a new visa petition. If you don't wish to leave the U.S., extending your status by means of this petition will be sufficient. However, if you leave the U.S. before the end of your overall stay, you will also need to visit a U.S. consulate outside the U.S., in order to get an O, P, or R visa stamp in your passport (to allow your reentry).

1. Extension Petition

Extension procedures are identical to the procedures followed in getting the initial visa, except that less documentation is generally required. However, the best practice is to fully document the extension request with all of the documents submitted with the initial petition, as USCIS will probably not have the file on site.

Working While Your Extension Petition Is Pending

If you file your petition for an extension of O, P, or R status before your authorized stay expires, you are automatically permitted to continue working for up to 240 days while you are waiting for a decision. If, however, your authorized stay expires after you have filed for an extension but before you receive an approval, and more than 240 days go by without getting a decision on your extension petition, continued employment is not authorized and you must stop working.

2. Visa Revalidation

If you leave the U.S. after your extension has been approved, but the underlying visa has expired, you must get a new visa stamp issued at a consulate. Read Section D, above. The procedures for consular extensions are identical. ■

Words Commonly Used in Immigration Law

Immigration law is full of words and terms whose meanings are not obvious. We've used many of these words in this book and you may encounter others as you use additional resources. For help in unpacking their meanings, see the plain-English definitions below.

Accompanying relative. In most cases, a person who is eligible to receive some type of visa or green card can also obtain green cards or similar visas for immediate members of his or her family. These family members are called accompanying relatives, and may include only your spouse and unmarried children under the age of 21.

Advance Parole. See Parole, below.

Alien Registration Receipt Card. The official name used in immigration law for a green card. The USCIS calls this document the I-551.

Asylum status. See Refugee and political asylee, below. People seeking political asylum status are in a different situation from refugees, even though the basis for eligibility is very similar. Those applying for refugee status apply from outside the U.S., while potential asylees apply for asylum after having arrived in the United States (for example, on a tourist visa or after illegally crossing the U.S. border).

Attestation. Sworn statements that employers must make to the U.S. Department of Labor before they may petition to bring foreign workers to the United States. Attestations may include statements that the employer is trying to hire more U.S. workers, or that foreign workers will be paid the same as U.S. workers. Attestations are required only for certain types of employment-based visas.

Beneficiary. If your relative or employer files a petition to start off your immigration process, you are a beneficiary. Almost all green cards as well as certain types of nonimmigrant visas require petitioners, and whenever there is a petitioner there is also a beneficiary. The word "beneficiary" comes from the fact that you benefit from the petition by becoming qualified to apply for a green card or visa.

Border Patrol. The informal name for an agency called Customs and Border Protection (CBP), which, like USCIS, is part of the Department of Homeland Security (DHS). Its primary functions include keeping the borders secure from illegal crossers and meeting legal entrants at airports and border posts to check their visas and to decide whether they should be allowed into the United States.

Citizen (U.S.). A person who owes allegiance to the U.S. government, is entitled to its protection, and enjoys the highest level of rights due to members of U.S. society. People become U.S. citizens through birth in the United States or its territories, through their parents, or through naturalization (after applying for citizenship and passing the citizenship exam). Citizens cannot have their status taken away except for certain extraordinary reasons.

Consular processing. The green card application process for immigrants whose final interview and visa decision will happen at a U.S. embassy or consulate in another country (outside the U.S.).

Consulate. An office of the U. S. Department of State located in a country other than the United States and affiliated with a U.S. embassy in that country's capital city. The consulate's responsibilities usually include processing visa applications.

Customs and Border Protection (CBP). See Border Patrol, above.

Department of Homeland Security (DHS). A huge government agency created in 2003 to handle immigration and other security-related issues. Nearly all immigration-related departments and functions (including USCIS, CBP, and ICE) are under DHS control.

Department of Labor (DOL). A U.S. government agency involved with many types of job-related visas. It is the DOL that receives applications for labor certifications and decides whether or not there is a shortage of U.S. workers available to fill a particular position in a U.S. company.

Department of State. U.S. embassies and consulates are operated by the branch of the U.S. government called the Department of State (DOS). Generally, the DOS determines who is entitled to a visa or green card when the application is filed outside the U.S. at a U.S. embassy or consulate, while USCIS, under the Department of Homeland Security, regulates immigration processing inside the United States.

Deportable. An immigrant who falls into one of the grounds listed at I.N.A. § 237, 8 U.S.C. § 1227, is said to be removable, or in the older legal lingo, deportable. Such a person can be removed from the U.S. after a hearing in immigration court. Even a permanent resident can be removed or deported.

District office. A USCIS office in the U.S. that serves the public in a specific geographical area. District offices are where most USCIS field staff are located. They usually have an information desk, provide USCIS forms, and accept and make decisions on a few—but not all—types of applications for immigration benefits.

Diversity visa (the Lottery). A green card lottery program is held for persons born in certain countries. Every year (more or less), the Department of State determines which countries have sent the fewest number of immigrants to the U.S., relative to the size of the country's population. A certain number of persons from those countries are then permitted to apply for green cards. Lottery winners are selected at random from qualifying persons who register for that year's lottery. To enter, you must meet certain minimum educational and other requirements.

EAD. See Employment Authorization Document, below.

Embassy. The chief U.S. consulate within a given country, usually located in a capital city. The embassy is where the ambassador stays. Most embassies handle applications for visas to the United States.

Employment Authorization Document. More commonly called a work permit, this is a card with a person's photo on that indicates that he or she has the right to work in the United States. Green card holders no longer need to have an EAD.

Executive Office of Immigration Review (EOIR). See Immigration Court, below.

Expedited removal. The procedures by which officers at U.S. borders and ports of entry may decide that a person cannot enter the United States. (See I.N.A. § 235(b), 8 U.S.C. § 1225 (b).) The officer can refuse entry when he or she believes the person has used fraud or is carrying improper documents. People removed this way are barred from reentering the U.S. for five years.

Fraud interview. A specialized USCIS interview in which one or both members of an engaged or married couple are examined to see whether their marriage is real, or just a sham to get the foreign-born person a green card.

Green card. Actually a slang name for an Alien Registration Receipt Card or I-551. We use the term green card throughout this book because it is familiar to most people. At one time, the card was actually green in color. Currently, the card is pink. Nevertheless, people all over the world continue to refer to it as a green card.

This plastic photo identification card is given to individuals who successfully become legal permanent residents of the United States. It serves as a U.S. entry document in place of a visa, enabling permanent residents to return to the U.S. after temporary absences. The key characteristic of a green card is its permanence. Unless you abandon your U.S. residence or commit certain types of crimes or immigration violations, your green card can never be taken away. Possession of a green card also allows you to work in the U.S. legally.

You can apply for a green card while you are in the U.S. or while you are elsewhere, but you can actually receive the green card only inside U.S. borders. If you apply for your green card outside the U.S., you will first be issued an immigrant visa. Only after you use the immigrant visa to enter the U.S. can you get a green card.

Those who hold green cards for a certain length of time may apply to become U.S. citizens. Green cards have an expiration date of ten years from issuance. This does not mean that the permanent resident status itself expires, only that the resident must apply for a new card.

I-94 card. A small green or white card given to all nonimmigrants when they enter the United States. (The green ones are given to people who enter on a visa waiver.) The I-94 card serves as evidence that a nonimmigrant has entered the country legally. Before the I-94 card is handed out, it is stamped with a date indicating how long the nonimmigrant may stay for that particular trip. It is this date and not the expiration date of the visa that controls how long a nonimmigrant can remain in the United States. A nonimmigrant receives a new I-94 card with a new date each time he or she legally enters the United States. Canadian visitors are not normally issued I-94 cards.

Immediate relative. If you are an immediate relative of a U.S. citizen, you are eligible to receive a green card. The government does not limit the number of immediate relatives who may receive green cards. The list of those who are considered immediate relatives is as follows:

- spouses of U.S. citizens. This also includes widows and widowers who apply for green cards within two years of the U.S. citizen spouse's death.

- unmarried people under the age of 21 who have at least one U.S. citizen parent.

- parents of U.S. citizens, if the U.S. citizen child is over the age of 21.

Immigrant. Though the general public usually calls any foreign-born newcomer to the United States an immigrant, the U.S. government prefers to think of immigrants as only including those people who have attained permanent residence or a green card. Nearly everyone else is called a nonimmigrant, even if they are in the United States.

Immigrant visa. If you are approved for a green card at a U.S. consulate or U.S. embassy, you will not receive your green card until after you enter the United States. In order to enter the U.S., you must have a visa. Therefore, when you are granted the right to a green card, you will receive an immigrant visa. An immigrant visa enables you to enter the U.S., take up permanent residence, and receive a green card.

Immigration and Customs Enforcement (ICE). This agency of the Department of Homeland Security handles enforcement of the immigration laws within the U.S. borders.

Immigration and Naturalization Service (INS). The name of the former U.S. government agency that had primary responsibility for most immigration matters. However, in 2003, the INS was absorbed into the Department of Homeland Security, and its functions divided between U.S. Citizenship and Immigration Services (USCIS), Customs and Border Protection (CBP), and Immigration and Customs Enforcement (ICE).

Immigration Court. More formally known as the Executive Office for Immigration Review or EOIR, this is the first court that will hear your case if you're placed in immigration proceedings. Cases are heard by an immigration judge, who doesn't hear any other type of case. USCIS has its own crew of trial attorneys who represent the agency in court.

Inadmissible. Potential immigrants who are disqualified from obtaining visas or green cards because they are judged by the U.S. government to be in some way undesirable are called inadmissible (formerly, excludable). The grounds of inadmissibility are found at I.N.A. § 212, 8 U.S.C. § 1182. Green card holders who leave the United States for six months or more can also be found inadmissible upon attempting to return. In general, most people are found inadmissible because they have criminal records, have certain health problems, commit certain criminal acts, are thought to be subversives or terrorists, or are unable to support themselves financially. In some cases, there are legal ways to overcome inadmissibility.

Labor certification. To get a green card through a job offer from a U.S. employer, you must first prove that there are no qualified U.S. workers available and willing to take the job. The U.S. agency to which you must prove this is the U.S. Department of Labor and the procedure for proving it is called labor certification.

Lawful permanent resident. See Permanent resident, below.

Lottery. See Diversity visa, above.

National Visa Center (NVC). Located in Portsmouth, New Hampshire, and run by a private company under contract with the DOS for the purpose of carrying out certain immigration functions. The NVC receives approved green card petitions directly from USCIS or the DOS. In some cases, the NVC may hold onto these files for years, while the immigrant is on the waiting list for a visa. The NVC initiates the final green card application process by sending forms and instructions to the applicant and forwarding the file to the appropriate U.S. consulate abroad.

Naturalization. When a foreign person takes legal action to become a U.S. citizen. Almost everyone who goes through naturalization must first have held a green card for several years before becoming eligible for U.S. citizenship. They must then submit an application and pass an exam. A naturalized U.S. citizen has virtually the same rights as a native-born U.S. citizen.

Nonimmigrant. People who come to the U.S. temporarily for some particular purpose but do not remain permanently. The main difference between a permanent resident who holds a green card and a nonimmigrant is that all nonimmigrants must intend to be in the U.S. only on a temporary basis. There are many types of nonimmigrants. Students, temporary workers, and visitors are some of the most common.

Nonimmigrant visa. Nonimmigrants enter the U.S. by obtaining nonimmigrant visas. Each nonimmigrant visa comes with a different set of privileges, such as the right to work or study. In addition to a descriptive name, each type of nonimmigrant visa is identified by a letter of the alphabet and a number. Student visas, for example, are F-1, and treaty investors are E-2. Nonimmigrant visas also vary according to how long they enable you to stay in the United States. For example, on an investor visa, you can remain for many years, but on a visitor's visa, you can stay for only up to six months at a time.

Parole. This term has a special meaning in immigration law. It allows a person to enter the U.S. for humanitarian purposes, even when he or she does not meet the technical visa requirements. Those who are allowed to come to the U.S. without a visa in this manner are known as parolees. Advance Parole may be granted to a person who is already in the U.S., but needs to leave temporarily and return without a visa. This is most common when someone has a green card application in process and wants to leave the U.S. for a trip.

Permanent resident. A non-U.S. citizen who has been given permission to live permanently in the United States. If you acquire permanent residence, you will be issued a green card to prove it. The terms "permanent resident" and "green card holder" refer to exactly the same thing. Both words in the phrase "permanent resident" are important. As a permanent resident, you may travel as much as you like, but your place of residence must be the U.S., and you must keep that residence on a permanent basis.

Petition. A petition is a formal request to USCIS that you be legally recognized as qualified for a green card or for some type of nonimmigrant visa. It is usually filed by an employer or family member (the petitioner) on behalf of an intending immigrant or visa applicant, to start off the application process. Paper proof that you do indeed qualify must always be submitted with the petition.

Petitioner. A U.S. person or business who makes the formal request that you be legally recognized as qualified for a green card or nonimmigrant visa. The petitioner must be your U.S. citizen relative, green card holder relative, or U.S. employer. No one else may act as your petitioner, though some categories of people may self-petition. Almost all green card categories and some types of nonimmigrant visa categories require you to have a petitioner.

Preference categories. Certain groups of people who fall into categories known as "preferences" are eligible for green cards only as they become available year by year, subject to annual numerical limits. The preferences are broken into two broad groups: family preferences and employment preferences. The number of green cards available each year to the family preferences is around 480,000 and the number available in the employment preferences is 140,000. The categories are:

- **Family first preference.** Unmarried children (including divorced), any age, of U.S. citizens.
- **Family second preference. 2A:** Spouses and unmarried children under 21 years, of green card holders; and **2B:** unmarried sons and daughters (over 21 years) of green-card holders.
- **Family third preference.** Married children, any age, of U.S. citizens.
- **Family fourth preference.** Brothers and sisters of U.S. citizens where the U.S. citizen is at least 21 years old.
- **Employment first preference.** Priority workers, including persons of extraordinary ability, outstanding professors and researchers, and multinational executives and managers.

- **Employment second preference.**
  Persons with advanced degrees and persons of exceptional ability, coming to the U.S. to accept jobs with U.S. employers for which U.S. workers are in short supply or where it would serve the national interest.

- **Employment third preference.**
  Skilled and unskilled workers coming to the U.S. to accept jobs with U.S. employers for which U.S. workers are in short supply.

- **Employment fourth preference.**
  Religious workers and various miscellaneous categories of workers and other individuals.

- **Employment fifth preference.**
  Individual investors willing to invest $1,000,000 in a U.S. business (or $500,000 if the business is in an economically depressed area).

Preference relatives. A general term for a foreign relative of a U.S. citizen or green card holder as defined in the preference categories listed above. Preference relatives and immediate relatives are the only foreign family members of U.S. citizens or green card holders who are eligible for green cards on the basis of their family relationships.

Priority Date. If you are applying for a green card in a preference category, your application is controlled by a quota. Since only a limited number of green cards are issued each year, you must wait your turn behind the others who have filed before you. The date on which you first entered the immigration application process is called the Priority Date. Your Priority Date marks your place in the waiting line. Each month, the U.S. Department of State makes green cards available to all those who applied on or before a certain Priority Date. You can get a green card only when your date comes up on the DOS list.

Public charge. This term is used in immigration law to refer to an immigrant who has insufficient financial resources and goes on welfare or other government assistance. Immigrants who are likely to become a public charge are inadmissible.

Qualifying relative. A general term for either an immediate relative or a preference relative. A qualifying relative is any person whose familial relationship to a U.S. citizen or green card holder is legally close enough to qualify that person for a green card or other immigrant benefit, such as a waiver.

Refugee and political asylee. Persons who have been allowed to live in the U.S. indefinitely to protect them from persecution in their home countries. The difference between these two terms is that refugees receive their status before coming to the U.S., while political asylees apply for their status after arriving in the United States by some other means. Both may eventually apply for green cards.

Removal proceeding. Formerly deportation, carried on before an immigration judge to decide whether or not an immigrant will be allowed to enter or remain in the country. While, generally speaking, a person cannot be expelled without first going through a removal hearing, someone arriving at the border or a port of entry can be forced to leave without a hearing or ever seeing a judge. If an immigrant is found removable, he or she can be deported, or forced to leave the United States.

Service center. A USCIS office responsible for accepting and making decisions on particular applications from people in specified geographic areas. Unlike USCIS district offices, the service centers are not open to the public; all communication must be by letter, with limited telephone or email access.

Special immigrant. Laws are occasionally passed directing that green cards be given to special groups of people. When it comes to visa allocation, special immigrants are considered a subcategory of employment-based visas, and receive 7.1% of the yearly allotment of 140,000 such visas. Common categories of special immigrants are workers for recognized religions, former U.S. government workers, and children dependent on a juvenile court.

Sponsor. For immigration purposes, usually means a petitioner. See Petitioner above.

Status. The name of the group of privileges you are given when you receive immigration benefits, either as a permanent resident or a nonimmigrant. Nonimmigrant statuses have exactly the same names and privileges as the corresponding nonimmigrant visas. A green card holder has the status of permanent resident. Visas and green cards are things you can see. A status is not.

While you must be given a status with each visa, the reverse is not true. You can get a nonimmigrant status by applying in the U.S., and you can keep that status for as long as you remain on U.S. soil. You will not, however, get a physical visa at the same time because visas can be issued only outside the United States. The theory is that since a visa is an entry document, persons already in the U.S. do not need them. This is important for nonimmigrants, because they can travel in and out of the U.S. on visas, but not with a status. Those with permanent resident status do not have the same problem, of course, because they have green cards.

If you have nonimmigrant status, but not a corresponding visa, you will lose your status as soon as you leave the United States. You can regain your privileges only by getting a proper nonimmigrant visa from a U.S. consulate before returning.

Temporary Protected Status (TPS). A temporary status for persons already in the U.S. who came from certain countries experiencing conditions of war or natural disaster. TPS allows someone to live and work in the U.S. for a specific time period, but it does not lead to a green card.

U.S. consulates. See "Consulate," above.

U.S. embassies. See "Embassy," above.

Visa. A stamp placed in your passport by a U.S. consulate outside of the United States. All visas serve as U.S. entry documents. Visas can be designated as either immigrant or nonimmigrant. Immigrant visas are issued to those who will live in the U.S. permanently and get green cards. Everyone else gets nonimmigrant visas. Except for a few types of visa renewals, visas cannot be issued inside U.S. borders, and so you must be outside the U.S. to get a visa.

Visa Waiver Program. Nationals from certain countries may come to the U.S. without a visa as tourists for 90 days under what is known as the Visa Waiver Program. These countries currently include Andorra, Australia, Austria, Belgium, Brunei, Denmark, Finland, France, Germany, Iceland, Ireland, Italy, Japan, Liechtenstein, Luxembourg, Monaco, the Netherlands, New Zealand, Norway, Portugal, San Marino, Singapore, Slovenia, Spain, Sweden, Switzerland, and the United Kingdom. Persons coming to the U.S. on this program receive green-colored I-94 cards. They are not permitted to extend their stay or change their statuses, with very limited exceptions.

Work permit. See Employment Authorization Document, above. ■

Index

R

S

Get the Latest in the Law

(1) Nolo's Legal Updater
We'll send you an email whenever a new edition of your book is published!
Sign up at **www.nolo.com/legalupdater**.

(2) Updates at Nolo.com
Check **www.nolo.com/update** to find recent changes in the law that
affect the current edition of your book.

(3) Nolo Customer Service
To make sure that this edition of the book is the most recent one, call us at
800-728-3555 and ask one of our friendly customer service representatives
(7:00 am to 6:00 pm PST, weekdays only). Or find out at **www.nolo.com**.

(4) Complete the Registration & Comment Card ...
... and we'll do the work for you! Just indicate your preferences below:

Registration & Comment Card

NAME   DATE

ADDRESS

CITY   STATE   ZIP

PHONE   EMAIL

COMMENTS

WAS THIS BOOK EASY TO USE?   (VERY EASY)   5   4   3   2   1   (VERY DIFFICULT)

☐ Yes, you can quote me in future Nolo promotional materials. *Please include phone number above.*

☐ Yes, send me **Nolo's Legal Updater** via email when a new edition of this book is available.

Yes, I want to sign up for the following email newsletters:

   ☐ **NoloBriefs** (monthly)
   ☐ **Nolo's Special Offer** (monthly)
   ☐ **Nolo's BizBriefs** (monthly)
   ☐ **Every Landlord's Quarterly** (four times a year)

☐ Yes, you can give my contact info to carefully selected
partners whose products may be of interest to me.

NOLO

IMEZ 13.0

Nolo
950 Parker Street
Berkeley, CA 94710-9867
www.nolo.com

YOUR LEGAL COMPANION